THE APO$TATE

**Whistleblower Exposes Deep State
Better Business Bureau's Awards Racket**

CARYN SUZANN CAIN

MOVING TARGET PUBLICATIONS

THE APO$TATE
Whistleblower Exposes Deep State Better Business Bureau's Awards Racket
All Rights Reserved.
Copyright © 2020 Caryn Suzann Cain
v13.0

The opinions expressed in this manuscript are solely the opinions of the author and do not represent the opinions or thoughts of the publisher. The author has represented and warranted full ownership and/or legal right to publish all the materials in this book.

This book may not be reproduced, transmitted, or stored in whole or in part by any means, including graphic, electronic, or mechanical without the express written consent of the publisher except in the case of brief quotations embodied in critical articles and reviews.

MOVING TARGET PUBLICATIONS

ISBN: 978-0-578-21690-4

Library of Congress Control Number: 2019901284

Cover Photo © 2020 Caryn Cain. All rights reserved - used with permission.

PRINTED IN THE UNITED STATES OF AMERICA

*DEDICATED TO
THE REPUBLIC OF AMERICA,
VETERANS, AND CONSUMERS*

*DEEPEST GRATITUDE TO
SEAN*

ACKNOWLEDGMENTS

Gracious stewards hosted enlightening yesteryear. I thank Michael Shrimpton, author of the revelatory *Spyhunter* (2014), for his informative correspondence. I felt special camaraderie with Michael because we were both attacked, humiliated, and discredited for reporting the truth. His incredible British Intelligence background, expertise, and insight exposed contentious world history, which, in turn, underscored my allegations questioning Barack Obama's fifth-column presidency and connections with current revolutionary insurrection. Furthermore, I offer sincere appreciation to the following dedicated librarians, researchers, and volunteers for their assistance: Kelley Hunt, interlibrary loan librarian, Montgomery County Library, Conroe, Texas; Pat Nichols, Genealogy Department, Montgomery County Library, Conroe, Texas; Jamie Matthews, visitor services coordinator, Huntsville, Texas; Lesley Martin, Chicago History Museum, Chicago, Illinois; Patricia Barrett, Archives Department, LaGrange College, LaGrange, Georgia; David DeShong, director, Anadarko Community Library, Anadarko, Oklahoma; Lena Billy, volunteer, National Hall of Fame for Famous American Indians, Anadarko, Oklahoma; Scott Biegen, librarian, Palm Springs Public Library, Palm Springs, California; Miranda Rectenwald, University Archives Department, Washington University, St. Louis, Missouri; Salma, librarian, Olin Library, Washington University, St. Louis, Missouri; New York Public Library, Reference Department, New York, New York; Houston Public Library, Reference Department, Houston, Texas.

And thankfulness seems trite when expressing my profound gratefulness to Sean who rode the dark and desperate times with me always offering intuitive assistance, encouragement, and thought, which calmed and inspired my writer's soul.

I also extend special recognition to Donald E. Napp, Co-Class Agent for "The Class of '51 Newsletter" sponsored by the Association of Former Students at Texas A&M University. Mr. Napp orchestrated my emotional meeting with Master Sergeant Joseph Elias Ramirez Sr., an American hero who was a Scout Ranger (sniper) with the Philippine Army unit and a Korean War POW. Sniper

Joe (my nickname) was holding my wounded uncle, 1st Lieutenant Mabry Elder Cain, 8th Cavalry Regiment, 1st Cavalry Division, when he was fatally Burp Gunned across the chest during an enemy attack. Mabry was the Korean War's first recipient of the Silver Star. Thereafter, Sniper Joe was shot, captured, and tortured for three years in the same North Korean camp that imprisoned, tortured, and killed renowned Catholic priest Father Emil Kapaun.

TABLE OF CONTENTS

Preface i
Introduction vi

Part One
Chapter 1: Whistleblower 3
Chapter 2: Awards For Excellence 23
Chapter 3: Rating Score 57

Part Two
Chapter 4: BBB History 75
Chapter 5: George Presbury Rowell 164
Chapter 6: John Irving Romer 170
Chapter 7: The Associated Press 175
Chapter 8: Scientific Discoveries and Inventions 177
Chapter 9: Spanish-American War 1898 190
Chapter 10: John Wanamaker 192
Chapter 11: Joseph Herbert Appel 198
Chapter 12: Dr. Harvey Washington Wiley 204
Chapter 13: Upton Sinclair and *The Jungle* 211
Chapter 14: Dr. Herbert Sherman Houston 216
Chapter 15: Samuel Candler Dobbs 219
Chapter 16: Vigilance Committee 236
Chapter 17: National Vigilance Committee 238
Chapter 18: Merle Sidener 245
Chapter 19: Arthur Frederick Sheldon 251
Chapter 20: Federal Trade Commission 255
Chapter 21: World War I 269
Chapter 22: Prohibition 274
Chapter 23: Before You Invest, Investigate! 282
Chapter 24: Stock Market Crash 287

Chapter 25: Logan Billingsley 298
Chapter 26: Edwin Clarence Riegel 311
Chapter 27: Senator Duncan Fletcher 316
Chapter 28: Frank Dalton O'Sullivan... 326
Chapter 29: Hurnard Jay Kenner 341
Chapter 30: John James Bennett Jr. 367
Chapter 31: Thomas Edmund Dewey 373
Chapter 32: Eunice Roberta Hunton Carter... 377
Chapter 33: Dutch Schultz... 381

Part Three
Chapter 34: World War II 387
Chapter 35: Bureau Lawsuits.. 392
Chapter 36: Unforgivable Omissions.. 407
Chapter 37: Trial 427
Chapter 38: Post-Trial 452
Chapter 39: Epilogue 458
Chapter 40: Emails and Evidence... 469
References 488

PREFACE

The mystical Sphinx was coronated the advertising industry's mascot and represents the divine power of the Order of Illuminati, founded by Adam Weishaupt on May 1, 1776, in Bavaria. Advertising Freemasons battled false advertising by creating the Vigilance Committee, which became the Better Business Bureau. But the Christian BBB morphed into a globalist overlord whose racketeering and securities fraud contributed to the Stock Market Crash of 1929. Subsequent attempts to regulate the Bureau were buried by the Democratic Party, and FDR inducted the nonprofit into the Deep State after Pearl Harbor. Accordingly, the front book cover features my conceptual opinion and art rendering of the Bureau as a whorish parasitic hypocritical sanctimonious superficial seductive serpentine Sphinx pandering profit over truth.

As I wrote closing pages, all hell was breaking loose. The COVID-19 coronavirus pandemic surpassed 800,000 worldwide deaths, the Democratic Party's Black Lives Matter and Antifa stoked global rioting and a cancel-culture of American heritage, the 2020 presidential election apocalyptically raged, and my manuscript was cyberstalked and sabotaged at every turn. Surreal globalist-fueled insurrection and digital censorship underscored reasons for writing *The Apostate*. I reported the Council of Better Business Bureaus and Houston Better Business Bureau to state and federal authorities for awards fraud. Consequently, the Houston Bureau hijacked my private trial and attempted to imprison me for exposing its specious monopolizing *Awards for Excellence*. I threatened the icon's pristine scam-busting image that camouflaged phony awards and rating scores. Merit programs financed B-men's transatlantic participation with the Obama administration and the European Union (EU), which advanced New World Order (NWO) initiatives. Growing globalist legions threatened the destruction of the United States Republic and its laws, liberties, culture, and values. I alleged that the Bureau aligned with the Democratic Party and the Obama administration to covertly merge the United States with the EU to establish a United States of the European Union. The EU's despotic Islamic-based blasphemy laws evidenced a precursor and blueprint for today's oligarchic political censorship of American social media, which targets, persecutes, and oppresses conservative voices. I fell somewhere in-between and was caught in their deviant dark web. But the EU was only as strong as its weakest link, and the Bureau's phony awards program was the chink in its armor.

The Bureau controls America's business industry and courts through its draconian digital dynasty. Memberships are coerced through oppressive self-serving awards and rating scores that disparage free trade and reincarnate the Bureau's scandalous yesteryear proclivities. In 1932, the U.S. Senate indicted the Better Business Bureau system for racketeering and "unfair trade practices, promoting gambling on the Stock Exchange, using the mails to defraud, and encouraging unfair trade practices and attempting to restrain radio communication." Today, I am alleging similar and worse; that the BBB is a Deep State provocateur peddling bogus merit programs for "FFIRS": FINANCE gainful participation in a globalist revolution; FACILITATE America's annexation by the EU; INFILTRATE digital airways as a fifth-column globalist acolyte; RULE global commerce; and SEAT a despotic sovereign NWO.

Scrubbed history was reintroduced that safeguarded the Bureau's shocking past and Deep State operations. Historical revelations described the Bureau's Illuminati trajectory and how the Bureau morphed into an unlicensed autocratic nation state protected by crony state and federal regulatory agencies. I presented extensive insider's knowledge, experience, and research to substantiate my herein opinions and allegations. Accordingly, I expose the Bureau's racketeering operations under the same veil of free speech and right of opinion that B-men convoluted and exploited to exalt above reproach the icon's bogus awards and rating scores.

The Houston Bureau turned my private civil employment trial against a former employer, also its member, into a criminal trial in an attempt to feloniously incriminate me in a Gestapo kangaroo court for reporting its awards racket to the Texas Attorney General and Federal Trade Commission (FTC), who proved to be compromised crony cohorts of the Bureau. Requital through publication was pursued by my fuming angst, gale wind initiative, Sherlock Holmes' inquisitiveness, and punitive pen to expose the Bureau's perilous tricky-lipped retaliation that derailed my railroaded trial. I will reveal the Bureau's militarized evolution into today's unfettered autocracy; that predecessors assisted Hoover's fledgling intelligence community and were inducted into FDR's Deep State; and that successors partnered with the Obama administration's Department of Commerce (DOC) and FTC as well as the EU in a NWO conspiracy to establish a cyber-controlled empire evidenced by current tyrannical European gambits.

Researching the Bureau nuanced investigating a centurial crime scene. Golden-coattailed thugs have controlled the U.S. court system since the *Roaring Twenties* in addition to manipulating commerce and perpetrating handcuffable securities and electoral fraud. Profiteering successors assumed that predecessors' sleight of hand buried gilded dirt, but an extensive scavenger hunt unearthed several deep-sixed scandals. Recovered data was too extensive to include in this book's exposé. I incorporated only the most pertinent information relative to my defense and allegations against the Houston Bureau for perpetrating fraud and money laundering through an awards racket. Author's disclaimer advises that personal experience only pertained to the *Awards for Excellence,* promoted by the Houston Bureau and sponsored by the Houston Foundation.

The Apostate was almost published prior to my 2015 trial to level the playing field by educating a potential jury pool of the Bureau's varnished history and hypocritical operations. Earlier publication was nixed, though, because of my back-stabbing obstructionist attorney and unfolding corroborating developments. Consequently, the renowned Bureau and celebrity employer "poisoned the jury pool" by their strategized vainglory.

I visited the apostate's barren Houston office several times and was always mystified by its blank pallet disregarding a phenomenal advertising birthright. My whistleblower's persuasion realized that history was omitted to hide an incriminating paper trail. Fortunately, the Bureau's random online braggadocio unlocked a treasure trove of festooned telltales. I hit the mother lode when discovering *History and Traditions,* a Washington State University address written in 1971 by B. Charles Wansley, former president of the Better Business Bureau of Metropolitan Oakland, Inc. Serendipitous karma earmarked Wansley's proselytizing pages to accentuate Frank Dalton O'Sullivan, a criminologist and publisher, whose guiding light bestowed treasure-hunter's euphoria when discovering his jaw-dropping 1933 book, *Rackets*. Another Wansley-wielded golden nugget bestowed H. J. Kenner, general manager of the New York Better Business Bureau, and his whitewashing 1936 book, *The Fight for Truth in Advertising*. Miraculous fate captured O'Sullivan and Kenner as dueling literary enemies and their epée de combat documented the Bureau's controversial past. And fortuitous fin de siècle bestowed the 2000 neo-fiction, *The Better Business Bureau Murders*, written by Frank W. Dressler, former president of the Better Business Bureau of Eastern Pennsylvania. Dressler inadvertently detailed the franchise's sink-or-swim juncture in the 1990s as the reason for unleashing the ambrosial online awards program in 2000 to challenge encroaching twenty-first-century competition in the field of consumer advocacy.

Uncanny kismet drew me to *Rackets*, which underscored O'Sullivan's criminalist investigative training, newspaper reporter's background, and prolific publishing career to expose the Bureau's duplicity. It was no coincidence that O'Sullivan appeared in my life as a former Bureau critic and victim. He remained by my side as I continued our battle against the Bureau. His spirit encouraged me and provided strength during a vicious trial whereby successors retaliated against me for reporting their globalized multimillion-dollar awards program same as predecessors attacked him for exposing their globalized securities racket that fueled the 1929 Crash, 10-year Great Depression, and watershed Wall Street reform.

While writing my book's first pages, happenstance gifted me with several of O'Sullivan's first-edition Prohibition-era publications that revealed the Bureau's checkered vigilante heritage. We both suffered at the hands of the Bureau and plied our power of empirical pens to express convictions and expose apostasy. I marveled at our similar paths. We became soulmates separated by eternity. His pervasive words spoke to me warning dire consequences from the Bureau's illicit proclivities, impregnable control, and unfettered expansion. The Bureau's current marketplace monopoly and globalist outreach proved him right, and the awards program supercharged the Bureau's omnipresence by transforming a sacred cow into a cash cow. Accordingly, O'Sullivan summoned me from perpetuity's observant pale mist with his timeless foreboding warning: "We have other information, besides that given in this book, regarding the operations of the Better Business Bureau." Premature death silenced O'Sullivan's coup de grâce encore. Instead, I offer *The Apostate* to bookend *Rackets*.

History questions the Bureau's modern consumer eminence garnered through Internet wizardry. The advertising industry spawned the horse-and-buggy vigilante that mutated into today's cyber leviathan. Historical records were gleaned from genealogical articles, twentieth-century and twenty-first-century publications, and archived newspaper clippings. Digital references encompassed past and present controversy. "Wikipedia" was intentionally included to highlight deceitful trial histrionics by the Bureau's attorney who misquoted the encyclopedia and lied to jurors to discredit my factual testimony. I reported the attorney to the Houston Bar Association, but their iron-clad buddy system prevailed. Filing a charge of malfeasance against the judge would have proven similarly pointless.

I lost two verdicts fighting the globalist cabal. My unique experience exposed a three-tiered court system that I pigeonholed as poor, wealthy, and filthy rich. I wallowed among the disadvantaged and witnessed deep-pocketed bribery that adjudicated my sucker-punched misfortune. Silver linings from my employment trial's miscarriage of justice produced IRS charges against the employer, but Bureau investment, globalist cronyism, double standards, and collective constitutional abuse wielded the tax court to tie the district court's collateral loose strings and dismiss charges. The employer's IRS conviction was sabotaged to prevent connection to my awards-fraud complaints because the Bureau's online business-reporting system listed government actions. *The Apostate* is my rebuttal.

Consumers must beware! It is my opinion that the Bureau is a bewitching lying conniving cheating thieving entrapping greedy ruthless sleazy slippery venomous snake charmer hiding poisonous ulterior motive. Knights Templar imposters are pursuing world dominance by oppressing free trade through privileged closed-market capitalism. Consumer-financed and Bureau-endorsed members comprise an unwitting globalist militia of businesses coalescing across the planet theatrically lionizing the BBB's iconic brand and specious merit programs under local, state, and federal authoritarian smoke screens.

Nazi Joseph Goebbels' infamous quote, "Accuse the other side of that which you are guilty," summarized the Better Business Bureau's deviant modus operandi that denied my constitutional rights to a fair trial, bribed a district court judge, and reinstated caveat emptor.

INTRODUCTION

I won the Houston Bureau's coveted Pinnacle award for the employer by writing an award-winning application, which proved fraudulent when he refused to implement operations that I wrote were in place. The Bureau did not perform field audits to screen application misstatements despite its awards program churning millions of dollars each year. The employer embedded consumer fraud when silencing my objections, threatening to fire me, and blacklisting my future employment. After leaving the employer's company, I reported his awards fraud to local and national Bureau leadership, but B-men sided with the employer, vilified and stalked me, hijacked my private lawsuit, and fabricated felonious fiduciary and theft charges. The Houston Bureau tried to imprison me in order to protect the organization's pristine reputation as a scam buster and hide its awards racket that controlled U.S. commerce, facilitated EU initiatives, and baited trusting consumers through regal pageantry, gilded perception, and sugarcoated euphemisms.

My Co-Plaintiff and I sued the employer, but the Bureau commandeered our employment discrimination lawsuits as a venue to discredit me and bury my damning awards' testimony and evidence. Successors replicated predecessors' nefarious Prohibition-era proclivities that gamed players from Wall Street to Court Street. The Bureau played our lawsuits like Nero's fiddle on steroids. B-men conspired a diabolical premeditated plan that delayed our trial while completing another relative trial to solicit a go-to verdict, in order to inoculate the Houston Bureau against liability for participating in our trial and perpetrating defamation and deceptive trade. Thereafter, our civil trial was greenlit to criminalize me. The Bureau segued its attorney into our lawsuit and fabricated counterclaims of slander, breach of fiduciary duties, and conversion/theft.

The Houston Bureau and employer maliciously targeted me for exposing their awards fraud to state and federal authorities. Their "Plan A" sought felonious breach of fiduciary duties and theft charges; and "Plan B" leveraged dismissal of judgment in exchange for the employer's release from liability.

The crux of my complaint alleged that the Houston Bureau's charity foundation operated the *Awards for Excellence* as an online awards racket that profited from exaggeration, implication, and illusion by misconstruing ethics, evaluation, and excellence. The Bureau tricked consumers into purchasing members' products and services under pretense of award-winning merit when awards were akin to an arbitrary Digger arcade game. Onsite audits were not performed to verify application statements, guarantee merit, and/or validate awards' highest quality of excellence being advertised. Instead, a sketchy honor code selected awards from best-written applications with tacit compliance disregarding inevitable cheaters' noncompliance conjured by the stroke of an illicit pen underwriting wealth and power. And the Bureau rotated annual awards' allocation like musical chairs to assure brand advertising, consistent revenue, and marketplace monopoly. Sanctimonious awards were promoted by fantastical name, exaggerated propaganda, and pomp and pageantry, which enabled members to siphon ill-gotten millions from consumers and turnstile revenue back to the Bureau through advertising and membership fees; the Bureau then filtered revenue to the national Council of Better Business Bureaus (CBBB or Council) through laundered "Bureau dues."

While investigating the BBB's history, I described my traumatic experience with the Houston Bureau, Houston Foundation, and CBBB. The franchise included over 100 branch offices micromanaged by CBBB, with many sponsoring an integrity awards program. I tried to right wrongs by reporting the employer's awards fraud and requesting award revocation, but eternal damnation unleashed when I broke the secret society's protocol of silence to become the first person to expose CBBB's awards' racket. In my opinion, substantiated by research and experience, the hallowed Better Business Bureau is a fake, imposter, and apostate.

My narrative related personal experience through the First Amendment's rights of free speech and opinion while the U.S. Constitution still exists. The American Republic is under siege. The Bureau participates in the EU's NWO movement that seeks to enslave humanity; a despotic agenda imitates comic book surrealism hiding unworldly powers bestowed by titans of the universe staging world chaos to forge a twenty-first-century Orwellian "Oceania."

A wizard could not compete with the unbridled sorcery and humbuggery of the Better Business Bureau. Consumers are the Bureau's unwitting victims and source of power. Otherwise, the Bureau would implode from lack of revenue currently produced by the bogus awards program and bias rating scores that dangle business products and services from sanctimonious digital scrolls comprised of dues-paying members.

After participating in the Houston Bureau's *Awards for Excellence* and winning several awards, my eyes were opened when acquiring the almighty Pinnacle. The awards are carnival trinkets peddled by the Bureau to finance expanding global assets protected by a de facto code of silence wielded by an insidious bully stick, which explained why no one snitched before me. Thereafter, whistleblowing repercussions involved the Bureau's hypocritical crony cabal of Big Business, Big Government, Big Court, and Big IRS ludicrously flouting laws of the land with impunity.

My younger days were apolitical and filled with small town values and compliant closed minds. Politics were forced upon me when my good name and country were threatened. I was raised by a proud southern military family dating to the American Revolutionary War and knew the despairing sorrow of blood sacrifice and milites requiescentes (soldiers at rest). Accordingly, I detest those who mistreat America, citizens, and military veterans like spoils of enterprise. Hitman Jackie Cogan's quote, "America is not a country, it's a business," succinctly exemplifies the plutocratic mindset of the Bureau's modern capitalist successors whose Puritan predecessors succumbed to the Prohibition era's organized crime, when the saint became a sinner.

The Apostate recaptured the Bureau's sinister history, which spawned contemporary fiendish stratagems underscored by irrefutable evidence to counter skeptics, sycophants, and naysayers. My whistleblower's journey intensified after determining the sacrosanct BBB was a pernicious double agent exploiting consumerism to participate in underground insurrection to seed EU governance. Research uncovered decades of corruption that rigged the court system, manipulated the media, fixed elections, and perpetrated cataclysmic stock fraud, which predated the Bureau's indoctrinations into Hoover's Mexican Repatriation and FDR's Deep State; the same slithering infestation that rigged my private trial to incriminate and silence me from exposing its Unholy Grail.

I also explored the Bureau's previous partnership with the Obama administration and EU, including the former Safe Harbor program that was ruled unconstitutional and reopened, on "August 1, 2016," as the current EU-US Privacy Shield Framework program, which purportedly asserts business standards to protect participating European and American data. Since 2019, the "BBB EU Privacy Shield" program has operated in accordance with EU-US Privacy Shield. My conspiracy theory, supported by research, experience, and chronological events, alleged that Safe Harbor manifested a plot by the Obama administration and EU to replace the U.S. Republic with the NWO's Islamic theocracy by seeding censorship of transatlantic airways proven by current Sharia Blasphemy laws ruling European social media; that Obama was supposed to hand control of the United States to the EU through Hillary Clinton's Democratic presidential victory; and that the Bureau's digital business-reporting services are complicit components. In fact, the Safe Harbor program was deemed unconstitutional because the U.S. Intelligence Community (IC) was hacking transatlantic data courtesy of the Patriot Act. The IC has continued applying the act pursuant to EU-US Privacy Shield. Consequently, previous

EU-Islamist initiatives detoured to Big Business, Big Hollywood, Big Media, and Big Government evidenced by a growing number of Muslim politicians and pro-Islamic social media and entertainment platforms that harass, intimidate, and persecute conservative voices on the wings of racism, Islamophobia, and xenophobia.

My book's comments and opinions on Radical Islamic Terrorism are based on experience; I was the informant who advised the FBI of a financial connection between U.S. Islamic charities and worldwide terrorist funding that financed the attacks on September 11, 2001. At the time, I worked for a temporary employment agency that placed me at a management group in the Houston Galleria financed by a wealthy UK-based Muslim philanthropist. The Houston office bought land and built mosques. Among other duties, I managed property near residential airparks in Florida, which, after 9/11, begat alarming conversations with a retired U.S. Air Force colonel. Consequently, I advised the FBI of my employer's suspicious activities relative to 9/11 that included his mysterious whirlwind British/European trip in August, his jubilant celebration during the fall of the Twin Towers, his questionable construction of masjids (mosques) in Florida, and his Lichtenstein bank accounts, which I alleged funneled charitable contributions to finance U.S. and international terrorist sleeper cells.

Terrorism's gravity and repercussions underscored NWO advancement derided by FDR and heralded by the late 41st POTUS George H. W. Bush in his 1991 State of the Union address: "The world can, therefore, seize this opportunity to fulfill the long-held promise of a new world order, where brutality will go unrewarded and aggression will meet collective resistance." To the contrary, on February 26, 1993, the first bomb blasted New York City's World Trade Center. In 2000, CBBB launched the awards program. A year later, on September 11, 2001, terrorist-piloted commercial airplanes aimed at several targets including the World Trade Center's Twin Towers and the Pentagon that resulted in 2,997 casualties with over 6,000 injured in addition to at least "1,000" subsequent deaths and "20,874" people sickened by toxic exposure (as of August 31, 2018), per the 9/11 Victim's Compensation Fund. A week later, on September 17, 2001, 43rd POTUS George W. Bush attended the Islamic Center of Washington, D.C., and praised Christianity's mortal enemy declaring, "Islam is peace." To be fair, "W" was responding to Muslim Americans' complaints of retribution after the attack; he was attempting to diffuse animus by defending them as taxpaying citizens and victims. But W's approach and response was ill-timed, insensitive, and marginalized America's gaping wound caused by Islam's collective adherence to Sharia law whose fringe barbarity had just attacked America. In fact, Turkish Muslim President Recep Tayyip Erdoğan sternly warned, "There is no moderate Islam; Islam is Islam!" Implication reiterated that Islam does not assimilate, it conquers!

The Apostate alleged that the CBBB, Houston Bureau, and Houston Foundation vicariously connected to terrorism via clandestine anti-American NWO initiatives, and the nonprofit respectively operated independent of law through globalist courts and crony government agencies. Accordingly, if justice prevailed, charges should include deceptive trade practice, theft, larceny, racketeering, money laundering, IRS fraud, malicious prosecution, collusion, bribery, tampering with evidence and jury, and perjury, in addition to other constitutional violations that include treason. I am not an attorney but argue that respective charges would be feasible if federal agencies judiciously performed mandated duties. Henceforth, I have bared my soul to pursue justice and accountability and expose the Bureau's metastasizing malign masquerade.

I cannot emphasize enough that HISTORY MATTERS! The Better Business Bureau became the antithesis of its birth mission, but nobody knew it. Buried history enabled its Holy Mantle to shroud its autocratic rise to power. I hope to educate consumers regarding the Bureau's actual history that betrayed the advertising industry's Truth in Advertising Movement, which begat the *Printers' Ink* Model Statute in 1911, and established the Bureau's progenitor "Vigilance Committee of the Advertising Club of New York" in 1912.

By 2000, CBBB and its Bureau franchise evolved into a collective corporate machine peddling lucrative awards to buy a seat at the globalist Round Table. Successors hypocritically preached predecessors' truth-in-advertising mantra bragging, "From advertising review to cybersecurity, research shows that consumers depend upon us to help them make choices and to promote trust in the marketplace." Consequently, I warn that altruistic Bureau programs are pillared by specious awards that have saturated and compromised the marketplace. Furthermore, consumers should be advised that only members can participate in awards; that businesses are forced to join or be ruinously disparaged; that the Bureau currently rubberstamps unproven awards to every participating member to market brand image; and that the Bureau heat-seeks celebrity members. For example, CBBB advertised, "HomeAdvisor uses BBB Accreditation data to help consumers find trustworthy home service providers in its directory of more than 100,000 pre-screened service professionals." I admire HomeAdvisor and took offense to the Bureau's time-honored tradition, which I coined as "stolen thunder," whereby the Bureau exploits a respected business name and/or photo opportunity to advance its specious programs under expressed or implied coalition. The Bureau used the same aggrandizing advertising ploy in the 1920s by posting the names of venerable landmark newspapers on its letterhead and/or bulletins to subliminally lionize operations.

The Apostate particularly highlighted the Bureau's deceptive propaganda machine that invoked regulatory overkill to hide fraudulent services. Kenner managed the original New York Bureau and embedded the practice of smoke-and-mirrors' sanctimony in 1936 when responding to O'Sullivan's racketeering charges verified by New York's governing body and the U.S. Senate. In fact, Kenner's *The Fight for Truth in Advertising* was the quintessence of cover-up and was published only after FDR salvaged Kenner's damaged reputation by hypocritically placing him as an anti-fraud dignitary in the new Securities and Exchange Commission. Thereafter, Bureau fraud evolved into hallowed humbuggery.

I reviewed over 100 years of the Bureau's mesmerizing sleight of hand, smoke-and-mirrors' virtue, government brownnosing, and manic growth that forged its iconic name. Skeptical pushback is expected to dismiss any notion that the hallowed Bureau harbors an evil twin. But I reiterate that the centurial Bureau is an advertising mastermind and knows every trick in the book; that I participated in its bogus operations; that my complaints are documented and date-stamped; that I have proof of Bureau fraud and employer collusion; and that my trial proceedings are on court record.

Furthermore, I detailed the burgeoning atrocity of a corrupt court system and double standards from whence the Bureau built an empire. Recent globalist court decisions empowered the Bureau and its specious services to exploit consumers. My civil rights were denied by a crony judge who ramrodded illicit charges at the Bureau's behest. Consumers must understand that globalism has overtaken the judicial system to control the courts, judges, attorneys, and verdicts with operations evidencing despotic one-government censorship whereby only wealthy acolytes prevail. My shanghaied trial demanded judicial review to investigate the collaboration of the presiding district court judge, Houston Bureau, employer, and opposing counsel, but I had no regulatory recourse having been dismissed by state and federal watchdog agencies.

The IRS is also discussed as an autocratic despotic globalist that enabled the growth of subversive 501(c) foundations including the various Bureau organizations. Unfettered IRS tyranny repeats heritage history that fueled the American Revolutionary War; patriots are still fighting taxation without representation, except that King George III was replaced by the IRS as a vicious suppressive draconian tax manipulator micromanaging struggling Americans into insurmountable debt and lingering poverty. The IRS should be downsized and centralized into one division; too many hands in the pot create unwarranted waste, confusion, threats, and liens.

As a former multi-awards' winner, whistleblower, and trial plaintiff, I am uniquely qualified to speak on behalf of myself and consumers. Obama's FTC dismissed my individual complaint on the basis that national guidelines required multiple plaintiffs. My deceptive trade complaints were submitted to the FTC preceding and during the course of CBBB's launch of a pay-for-play rating score and specious accountability program, which were hypocritically approved by backslapping federales aggrandizing ethereal ethics. The FTC's illicit cronyism with the Bureau dates to 1920's organized crime. Then, FDR and Truman secretly converted the Bureau into an immunized WWII Deep State mole that metastasized into a free-wheeling plutocratic despotic oligarch operating like a nation state and controlling the U.S. court system.

The Apostate detailed how the Bureau built a modern digital empire by scrubbing a sketchy Progressive Era legacy and weaponizing legerdemain to expand its saintly apostasy and Deep State agenda. The Bureau worked with a centurial list of American presidents, but none more worrisome than Democratic former President and "Muslim, Socialist Puppet" Barack Hussein Obama Soetoro whom I allege to be a NWO minion and harbinger of Islam in America.

Laborious research unmasked the Bureau's eye-opening and jaw-dropping yesteryear that mocks its modern beatification. And chronological events emphasized the Bureau's scams and scandals, which reinforced my claims. In fact, dusty literary feuds validated that B-men succumbed to crony capitalism to transcend pauper's plight. Original 1930's first-edition books proved contemporary data was riddled with inaccuracies and prejudicial innuendos to distort history and dumb-down consumers. H. J. Kenner's book walked a fuzzy line by cherry-picking authentic history while diffusing the Bureau's dark past to preserve Elysian successors' pristine image of truth. As a result, revisionist tweaking spawned illusionist marketing. Enterprising spin masters ditched their truth-in-advertising moral compass and invented profiteering puffery that sanctimoniously hitch-hiked the new "information superhighway." The Bureau's integrity awards epitomize the adage "too good to be true" and seduce consumers with entertaining Barnum-and-Bailey showmanship and caveat-emptor humbuggery. Additionally, the Bureau's consumer-ingratiating philanthropy, arbitration procedures, and business-reporting services provide pomp, pageantry, and purpose, but programs are pillared by awards fraud that defiles its pulpit-pounding birthright and undermines consumer advocacy.

My allegations rose from empirical experience, hardcore suspicion, research, history, and unfolding politics that precluded any accusation of tin-foil conspiracy theories. I spent seven years in legal proceedings and refused numerous high-dollar settlements after exposing the Bureau's fake awards program. After my 2015 trial's folie à deux failed to feloniously charge me, I worried about being whacked because only a Deep State minion could pull district court's malfeasant shadow strings. Additionally, my smoking gun threatened CBBB's "global assets" presented in its 2015 annual report.

The Bureau's hidden history compromised my trial's jury. Throwback scams and scandals were replaced by revisionist laurels and charismatic regalia. Accordingly, *The Apostate* turned every stone retrieving the BBB's dark history that lurked in obscure details. Like the EU, the globalist Bureau was born from

Christianity whose ecclesiastic flock are now persecuted and martyred by globalism's blood-drenched killing fields. Puritan predecessors preached moral doctrine through church pulpits, but crony-capitalist successors proselytize through the stroke of a weaponized keyboard; consequently, advocate transcended to fiend. History will reflect the Bureau's national and international autocratic exploitation pertaining to WWI, Prohibition, the New York Stock Exchange (NYSE), organized crime, FTC, Hoover, the Crash of 1929, FDR, the Securities and Exchange Commission (SEC), Truman, WWII, and the Internet.

I alleged that the Bureau hoodwinked and betrayed consumers with theatrical demagoguery and specious merit. Enterprising B-men suckled crony Big Business protected by malfeasant Big Court and empowered by corrupt Big Government that conspired with ruthless Big Globalism! Centurial history reflected the Bureau's art of stolen thunder whereby the organization exploited a business, person, and/or event to siphon respective success and/or celebrity. Consequently, an impregnable leviathan emerged from gilded propaganda, ignorant word of mouth, and strategized bona fides garnered from a century of rubbing elitist elbows with the NYSE, advertising glitterati, New York "swells," Democratic Party, DOC/FTC, SEC, World Wars, and POTUS's, which exemplified the truism "judged by the company you keep."

Globalist roots were explored to explain why the Better Business Bureau of Greater Houston and South Texas (Houston Bureau), Better Business Bureau of Metropolitan Houston Educational Foundation (Foundation), and CBBB have not been charged with awards fraud, money laundering, and racketeering for operating an illegal enterprise through a charity foundation. (Author's non-attorney disclaimer further advises that herein use of "Bureau" includes all aforementioned entities unless specified otherwise; that the entire organization is complicit due to gainful brand association.) CBBB washes "poison fruit" received from independent Bureaus/foundations, which peddle specious award programs, exploit consumers, eliminate competition, and monopolize the marketplace. In 1932, Florida Senator Duncan Fletcher charged the "Better Business Bureau" with Blue-Sky securities fraud and racketeering respective to the Stock Market Crash of 1929. Consequently, Senator Fletcher documented historical Wall Street reformation in his "Stock Exchange Practices Report of the Committee on Banking and Currency," published on June 16, 1934.

I previously warned the Houston Bureau's president that I would report him to CBBB for awards fraud and he condescendingly invited me to do so while predicting national leadership would agree with him. He dismissed me with the arrogance of a Roman emperor forcing embarrassing revelation that I had been among millions of naive idealistic "sheeple" who believed the Bureau's gilded bunkum. Twelve years and several excruciating lawsuits later, I am exposing the Bureau. I know their hypocritical sins; I played their exaggerated games;

I sparred with their Legion's foot soldiers in court; I deflected their judicial malfeasance; I uncovered their Deep State heritage; and I weathered their cyberhacking. Nobody but me can carry this splintered cross. Years of exhaustive research and traumatic litigation revealed the Bureau's buried dirt that underpinned its questionable proclivities and conquistadores' endgame seeking to enshrine "BBB" with the other despotic acronyms ruling the world.

Circumstances suggested the Houston Bureau established its foundation as a money-raising storefront to take advantage of the IRS's nose-blind 501 nonprofit rules. Big IRS is Big Business and established 501(c)(3) charity foundations as a legitimate venue to pimp globalism's Big Money evidenced by recent IRS firewalls preventing public scrutiny of mutually beneficial tax returns, e.g., the Houston Bureau and Houston Foundation. I believe the Houston Foundation epitomized a racketeering monopoly, which sponsored a fundraising awards scam that enabled the Houston Bureau to solicit expensive membership fees, eliminate competition, and control commerce. Snake-charming B-men invented a cost-effective money mill that banked on the icon's bellwether kudos. But consumers are misled by the Bureau's FTC-immunized digitized magic, sanctimonious Hollywood regalia, and serpentine enhancements. Accordingly, enterprising bushmasters created an autonomous nation state by rattling digital keys.

As a former chief financial officer, I reported awards fraud to state and federal authorities upon discovering the Bureau's ultimate culpability. The awards drum millions of dollars in business and attract consumers like bees to honey. I worked company trenches and wrote the application as an idealized concept to correct spiraling service and operational issues and to protect our customers, but I submitted the application based on the employer's promise to implement. We won. He lied. Consequently, he criminalized my application and entrapped me in consumer fraud by exploiting the Pinnacle that I provided him. It was part of his depraved predatory profile as an abusive misogynistic psychopath who shackled me to his tortuous bondage after he tricked me into heavy debt during the second Great Depression of 2008.

The Apostate detailed how I ratted out duopolized rats and spilled globalist beans to unresponsive state and federal authorities. Thereafter, the Houston Bureau commandeered my private employment lawsuit against the employer to silence me. The Bureau's covert retaliation laid a juristic mouse trap that crossed Swiss-cheese wires between my separate employer/employee lawsuit complaints and my awards-themed employer/employee fraud allegations. Cutthroat accomplices fixed court proceedings and despotically altered trial evidence and testimony in a failed attempt to criminally indict me to prevent my exposure of their prestigious *Awards for Excellence* cash cow. Furthermore, my attorney empowered adversaries by alienating the jury and unforgivably ignoring my background, employment trauma, and Bureau research.

Accordingly, I described opposing counsel's promotion of the Bureau's rating score to exalt the employer while tag-teaming with the malfeasant judge to suppress mention of the awards program. The Bureau's tricky-lipped attorney accused me of an employer shake down while conveniently omitting my employment complaints that described the employer's abuse, discrimination, career blacklisting, and consumer fraud. I brought the elephant into the courtroom when forcing an awards' soliloquy that ended with my coup fatal accusing the employer of being "a liar and a thief" for stealing the Pinnacle. The Bureau blinked and abandoned pending witness sabotage by its duplicitous awards director masquerading as a lowly records clerk. Unfortunately, my incriminating awards exposé was stopped before revealing the Bureau's dark past; that the Bureau's bogus awards program linked to history's most corrupt era, which entangled organized crime with New York City's banking and securities elite; and that successors continue predecessors' collaboration with America's Deep State in an attempt to expand their brand image and ground brick-and-mortar storefronts to tender lucrative pay-for-play memberships on the wings of specious merit programs.

As a result, I was baptized a committed whistleblower to right ensnaring wrongs. In my qualified squealer's opinion, the scam buster is scamming consumers. Extravagant awards operate on false implication of merit, and award-winning members are lionized paper-tiger recipients. I believe that the "fruit of the tree doctrine" applies making the Bureau and members equally liable for awards-related deceptive trade practice. The Bureau knowingly and willingly promotes bogus awards to the public while disingenuously shrouding profiteering award-recipient members under an irrefutable canopy of ethics. Furthermore, I am not blaming innocent rank-and-file employees subjected to employers' gainful skullduggery.

I confronted the Bureau's secret society and was cast into the treacherous bowels of spy-novel conspiracy. All the while, the Bureau's celestial histrionics bedazzled fiendish puffery; exemplar merit programs paraded flea-bitten dog and pony shows; my lawsuit turned into a seven-year itch; trial culminated in an Illuminati gangland massacre; wise guys flexed Deep State muscles; and crony cyber snoops continued to hack my computer in collective effort to guard the Bureau's awards program that financed NWO initiatives.

My book worked life's raw edges, spoke from the heart, and offered earned opinion as soulful accoutrements from the School of Hard Knocks supported by a wide berth of research. Euphemism, metaphors, and wordsmithry were generously indulged to emphasize my adversary's lucrative fantasy world of venomous humbuggery, and its slithering seamy dystopian autocratic plutocratic oligarchic racketeering serpentine underbelly coiled like the Rod of Asclepius around parasitic globalism that exploits humanity from cradle to grave. Robber-baron history is repeating itself with laureled monopolies sprouting on every crooked street corner and controlling consumers through anarchist media, politics, and courts.

The Bureau's scandalous history was exemplified by the Houston Bureau's *Awards for Excellence*. The present cannot be understood without knowing the past. I am alleging that the Bureau rigged our trial's verdict and tricked jurors due to dearth of information. Jurists did not know the Bureau's true history to deflect opposing counsel's fork-tongued sanctimony and the judge's greased-palm malfeasance. Research revealed critics' dusty perpetuity that debunked the Bureau's virtual beatification consequently questioning commercial propaganda and online hype as limited, laundered, and/or legerdemain; some links were later removed, but initial references will still be published with many supported by printed copies. The Bureau's quixotic modus operandi hoodwinks consumers through misrepresentation, exaggeration, and/or omission of facts. Tricky merit implies stringent testing when on-site auditing is impossible due to limited resources.

I reported my former employer's awards fraud to the barista of business whom I discovered was the architect of avarice. During the interim I faced catastrophic whistleblower consequences that banished me from the workforce and branded me a villain after reporting the Bureau's colossal pay-for-play awards scam to state and federal authorities. Awards were trafficked under the aegis of a venerable philanthropic foundation. And double standards witnessed the unfettered hallowed icon hypocritically bird-dog scammers while scamming the public. Consumers were sold disingenuously endorsed members' products and services covertly based on unevaluated quid pro quo merit underwriting a master plan to eliminate competition and monopolize the marketplace. As a result, Wizard of Oz "accreditation" built a gilded Emerald City immunized by a globalist phantasmagoric court system gaming social justice.

The Bureau's sanctimonious molting uncloaked a blasphemous apostate; a fake, quack, gypster, con artist, and imposter pimping a centurial legacy. I consider the Bureau to be a slithering fanged foe; history's peerless master of humbuggery; the anaconda of snake oil salesmen; and Medusa of consumers masquerading as an iconic beacon of truth.

The Apostate compiled an intricate puzzle of moving parts with the smallest piece equally important. Accordingly, history does matter, and why Part Two chronicled globalism's evolution from 1800's Puritan reform with an emphasis on the advertising industry. Distinguished trailblazers, inventions, and events built America through advertising that created my reptilian nemesis as the industry's saber-rattling badge to defang false advertising. One hundred years later, I alleged this sarpá succumbed to deception's lucrative poison. Like an entrancing King Cobra, the Bureau charmed consumers from a mystical basket while hypnotically peddling ethical overtures and wriggling into dictatorial plutocracy through fraud's iridescent scales of confusion, exaggeration, misrepresentation, distortion, disparagement, trickery, corruption, collusion, and evil. I also exhumed slithering slime that successors buried, including predecessors' sinister involvement in one of the worst financial disasters in history that drove the greatest reforms on Wall Street. Part One and Part Three described how I got myself into and out of a Deep State snake pit while warning that we should all continue to look over our shoulders because no one is safe; that we live in glass houses trip-wired for cybersabotage; and that reality is manipulated perception ... a fata morgana ... an illusion. Yesteryear called it humbuggery: "To be humbugged one must be deceived."

My allegations emphasized that the Bureau's massive consumer fraud is nurtured by Illuminati who control planetary strings; that the NWO's Mephistophelian forces are more powerful than ever; and that until a cancerous Deep State is excised, an embedded enemy remains a metastasizing threat to the U.S. Republic with bipartisan traitorous globalist crosshairs laser-focused on the White House. Accordingly, Illuminati exploit every aspect of our lives, including the air we breathe. And freedom and constitutional rights are pacifying delusions proffered by a merciless cult that rides the burdened backs of the world's hardworking people from skyscrapers to mud huts. We exist to serve, support, and enrich Illuminati leeches.

I blamed the FTC for enabling the Bureau's spectacular metamorphosis into a globalist aristocratic iconoclastic monocratic plutocratic autocratic oligarch allowed to operate with impunity above the laws of the land. Empowerment began in 1928 when the Periodical Publishers Association deemed the National BBB their "agency of assistance" during an FTC conference, which resulted in the Bureau's crony relationship with the federal watchdog. FDR's 1941 Deep State coronation of the Bureau built on his understated relationship with the prestigious New York Bureau and General Manager H. J. Kenner, when first advancing within the powerful New York Democratic Party. As governor of New York, FDR maintained a cordial and wary relationship with the Bureau evidenced by his telling reprimand: "No honestly intentional membership corporation should hide its roster; no group of men should be permitted to operate in the dark." The Bureau maintained reverent loyalty by strong-armed disparagement and religious connotation that nuanced the Christian military order of the Knights Templar (1119-1314).

The Apostate especially called out the FTC for facilitating the Bureau's monopolizing awards racket. In 1902, *Dietrich Loewe et al. v. Martin Lawlor et al.*, aka *Danbury Hatters' Case*, highlighted violation of the Sherman Antitrust Act. Consequently, in 1930, the *Hatters' Case* represented power of authority in 58 defamation lawsuits against 24 Bureaus charging an aggregate loss of $15,000,000; a judgment of $240,000 per Bureau was divided among each member. Seventy years later, in 2000, CBBB implemented the thimble-rigging awards shell game to fund twenty-first-century expansion by sucker-punching consumers with weasel words and smoke-and-mirrors' pageantry. Then, in 2009, CBBB systemically introduced phony rating scores to legitimize fake awards and coerce memberships. I was watching television and a local business featured an advertisement that emphasized the Bureau's "A" rating score marked out and corrected with an "A+"; theatrics represented humbuggery at its finest by advertising the Bureau, legitimizing its rating score, and exalting the member in one fell swoop.

Also discussed was the FTC's failure to abide by the Federal Trade Act of 1914 by which it was established. As a result, recent globalist court renderings recognized CBBB as a separate nation-state entity, and the organization was immunized above reproach. The rating score program was shielded as an opinion, and convoluted Texas law protected the Houston Bureau against claims of deceptive trade practice. As a result, B-men snookered consumers under the hallowed veil of a crime fighter and scam buster.

Furthermore, the Bureau connected to fake news exposed in the unparalleled 2016 presidential election, which tainted distinguished predecessors who built trailblazing newspaper and advertising industries. Mint Press News described modern media as an "Illusion of Choice" because its "1,500 Newspapers; 1,100 Magazines; 9,000 Radio Stations; 1,500 TV Stations; and 2,400 Publishers are owned by 6 Corporations and 272 Executives that control 90% of what 277 million Americans see, hear and read." The term "media" (Latin for "medius" and the plural form of "medium") became the embedded reference for newspapers during the *Roaring Twenties*. History taught that newspapers provided underground communications during the American Revolution and proliferated after the Civil War. Thereafter, an influential Christian-based temperance movement melded with an emerging advertising industry to establish ethical business standards, prosecutorial advertising legislation, and the first Vigilance Committee that became the Better Business Bureau.

The Apostate credited Logan Billingsley and his Manhattan Board of Commerce for historic Wall Street reform and exposing the Bureau's bogus "Before You Invest, Investigate" securities program, which contributed to the Crash of 1929. The Manhattan Board created the Stock Exchange Reform Committee to investigate the New York Bureau for securities fraud and collusion with the New York Stock Exchange (NYSE). Billingsley garnered the support of New York State Attorney General Hamilton Ward Jr.; New York Secretary of State Edward Flynn; E. C. Riegel, president of the Consumers Guild of America; U.S. President Herbert Hoover, New York Representative (later Mayor) Fiorello LaGuardia, and Senator Fletcher. The Bureau vindictively retaliated by exposing Billingsley's bootlegging background complete with slanted inaccuracies replicated by modern Bureau brown-nosing novelists, but my research reinstated truth and filled in the blanks created by scrubbed history. Senator Fletcher declared, "The hook-up between the New York Stock Exchange, the Investment

Bankers' Association, and their puppet, which is known as the Better Business Bureau" to be "the greatest racket ever known in its history."

I reviewed politics over the past century that fueled the Bureau's incredible rise to power through its most prestigious New York City Bureau that influenced presidential elections and national events. The New York Bureau promoted the re-election of Democratic President-elect Thomas Woodrow Wilson in 1916 and denigrated GOP presidential frontrunner Donald Trump in 2016. The New York Bureau weaponized its rating score to discredit one of Trump's New York businesses during a critical primary debate. Since announcing his candidacy and taking oath of office, Trump confronted a relentless barrage of globalist attacks, including the House of Representative's unsuccessful impeachment trial perceived as a backdoor attempt to cancel his 2016 Republican presidential victory.

Additionally, I would be remiss if not mentioning a striking similarity between Billingsley and Trump. Both men were wealthy flamboyant New York real estate developers who fought the same New York Bureau, experienced intense lives, were ridiculed as flawed characters, and stonewalled globalism.

The 2016 presidential election was supposed to complete the Bureau's NWO induction coordinated with a U.S.-EU merger through Hillary Clinton's expected presidency. Trump interrupted the NWO's insidious plans; he respectively warned, "These WikiLeaks emails confirm what those of us here today have known all along: Hillary Clinton is the vessel for a corrupt global establishment that is raiding our country and surrendering our sovereignty ... This criminal government cartel doesn't recognize borders, but believes in global governance, unlimited immigration, and rule by corporations."

Later publication of *The Apostate* proved to be a wise decision because relative information continued to pour in during and after the presidential election on November 8, 2016, complementing my narrative. Compounding issues and controversies fueled an ongoing proverbial train wreck that I could not ignore. The Bureau exposed globalist ties during the election when its New York office antagonistically badgered candidate Trump in early primaries whereby promising President Trump unprecedented globalist revenge.

Consumers must question why CBBB and the Better Business Bureau franchise wield nation-state powers, control the U.S. court system, perpetrate deceptive trade with immunity, participate in transatlantic federal programs, and reign as Illuminati. My answer is because the BBB is a servant of NOVUS ORDO SECLORUM, "The New World Order."

Before his death, on April 12, 1945, FDR realized the IC's growing tyrannical power that underscored NWO initiatives and prophetically warned, "They (who) seek to establish systems of government based on the regimentation of all human beings by a handful of individual rulers call this a new order. It is not new and it is not order."

PART ONE

CHAPTER 1

WHISTLEBLOWER

My blood curled when I first met the employer. The way he sat in his chair reminded me of a coiled cobra with venom-dripping fangs poised to strike. My internal radar triggered like an off-the-chart Geiger counter warning deadly radiation. Red flags morphed into landmines. But I needed the job and started work the next day, March 19, 2003.

The employer became a member of the Houston Bureau in 1986 and never won an award. He felt like an outsider and demanded wealth's recognition. His fifth-grade street-urchin's acumen lacked prerequisite scholastic skills, and he compensated by lying, cheating, and stealing. He was a master of osmosis and vicariously learned through others' success. Accordingly, I taught him innovative business, sales, and marketing techniques, which provided him award-winning Bureau application templates, timeless intellectual property, and magical advertorials. My genie's pen granted, "My master, the Great Caruso," his enduring wish to "rub elbows" with the Bureau's brass same as he hobnobbed with highflying jetsetters on the golf course. Hell's Kitchen spawned both the Bureau and Italian employer amidst New York's gangsters, rackets, speakeasies, prostitutes, and Mafia kingpins busted by Thomas Dewey's 1930's organized-crime trials and padlocked by Rudy Giuliani's 1980's slam dunk. I won him three consecutive annual awards. The third award clenched the Pinnacle and advanced his company to first place in the window and door industry with revenue dramatically increasing from an average of $3,000,000 dollars per year to over $12,000,000 dollars per year during America's second Great Depression of 2008. Thereafter, my whistleblowing tenacity joined him at the hip with Bureau Illuminati.

In May 2006, I introduced the employer to the Houston Bureau's glitterati awards' circle as a runner-up recipient. Two awards were distributed: the coveted first-place Pinnacle and second-place Winner of Distinction (Distinction). The

THE APO$TATE

awards transformed lackluster businesses into demigods for the price of a membership. At the time, the Distinction award carried acclaim as an exemplary rite of passage and pathway to the business industry's priceless Pinnacle; status also embedded hotly contested competition because the recipient unseated a previous award winner. Before 2010, the Bureau maintained tacit honor-among-thieves decorum, which marshalled sanctimonious restrictions to build value into its *Awards for Excellence* program. When I participated only one Pinnacle and two Distinction winners were chosen per business category, and both awards required exceptional application entries. Competition was brutal and excluded perennial underdog members forcing picaroons' mutiny. Rebels creatively compensated by advertising commercial accolades including the Good Housekeeping Seal, the Chamber of Commerce, and respective vendor commendations. The Bureau realized competitive breach and euthanized consumer-advocate outliers to maintain allegiance and marketplace monopoly. After 2010, Distinction awards were rubberstamped to every participating member while rotating the Pinnacle among the top 30 or so contenders to maintain regal gravitas. In the interim, the Bureau brainwashed consumers to trade only with members, which implied nonmembers were inferior.

Extreme duress surrounded my first awards' victory. In February 2006, the employer threw an application on my desk while snarling, "Win it!" A week earlier, he and his psychopathy tried to kill me. I was treated like a captive after accepting his quid pro quo deal six months beforehand that required purchase of a home near the office and a new car in exchange for a long-overdue raise and 24/7 availability. Consequently, I was shackled by up-to-your-eyeballs debt in a spiraling economy. I learned too late that he was a serial predator protected by a sealed history. His modus operandi blindsided vulnerable female employees with prohibitive own-your-soul encumbrance to enable victimization. Male employees received larger salaries, a handshake, and unconditional raises, but I was underpaid, tortured, and oppressed.

His wife was a former special education teacher who taught him to redirect his misogynistic vitriol towards me through "transferal of aggression" to protect her multimillion-dollar marriage. He obliged her and tortured me in his sick and twisted cuckoo's nest while randomly flipping ogre personalities and seesawing between sanity and insanity. Every day was a "kink scene" that battled his orgasmic release of demons. He suffered reoccurring psychotic breaks in four-to-five monthly cycles, which always ended with explosive irrational altercations whereby I was victimized, fired, and rehired only if I humiliated myself, acquiesced to his bondage, and begged for my job; behavior characterized depraved foreplay including mental whipping, emotional abuse, and condescension. He would randomly seek me out and violently scream at me while brandishing angry fists that threatened to pound me senseless. Ultimately, the pervert abused employer's stranglehold to physically assault me. I blamed his complicit wife for encouraging him to harass me as a helpless employee; she used to work for him, knew what he was doing to me, and did nothing. She once told me that he was her "last marriage no matter what," which reiterated that she had sold her soul to the devil.

He hated women, particularly mature women. I learned that extra dollars were only dangled in return for self-indulgent leverage that guaranteed enslavement. In his myopic dystopian world, men ruled, and women served. Salaries proved gender discrimination; men started at $45,000 per year and women started at $30,000; it did not matter that I offered a college degree and years of advanced advertising/marketing/business/financial acumen, which made his company millions. I was forced to beg for minimum raises as an office manager supporting five positions including backup for my future Co-Plaintiff, Wayne, vice president of operations, who had no college degree. By 2008, I was making $65,000 a year as CFO when male executives, including Wayne, made around $200,000 per year, including a $160,000 salary, sales-related commissions, and benefits that were denied to me despite my executive position, financial and marketing contributions, and award accomplishments that paid my peers' corporate salaries and bonuses. My net salary was also marginalized by overwhelming financial debt forced upon me by the employer. Accordingly, unequal pay is ruinously far-reaching and especially hurts women by adversely affecting domestic, housing, legal, and financial sectors as well as crucial retirement benefits.

Whereas employers normally appreciate employee initiative, the employer repaid me with vile animus. I loved my job because it offered a rare opportunity to apply my varied skill set, but the employer unmercifully humiliated and demeaned me in front of employees, vendors, and customers. The employer trip-wired my employment; incriminated, discriminated, and dehumanized me; never called me by my name and otherwise referred to me as "her"; and threatened me to "never smile, laugh, or talk to anyone" (despite my interactive duties). Additionally, I was his personal secretary and my office moonlighted as his "Lucy's psychiatry booth." He forced his guilt, filth, and prejudice on me that denigrated women, Blacks, the elderly, and the disabled. His hourly incursions caused me excessive unpaid overtime required to complete my mainstay financial duties involving mounds of time-sensitive paperwork. Despite the employer's daily abuse, I managed widespread operational, administrative, and financial duties while working seven days a week and cultivating industry excellence and repeat business.

His braggadocio evidenced criminally laced sexual perversions that included spying on employees showcased by his library of porno tapes gathered over decades. He told me that his favorite tape was "his marketing manager shtupping his secretary" in the telemarketing room of his first office building.

THE APO$TATE

Unfortunately, he turned his Peeping-Tom antics on me and monitored my every move and conversation in the office using the company's telephone intercoms and embedded cameras. He held me responsible for derogatory remarks made by others about him, which resulted in a vicious tirade of acrimonious verbal abuse that insinuated I was the wrongdoer.

The Bureau attracted sidewinders like the employer by invoking a frivolous honor system to regulate its multimillion-dollar awards program. The employer was damaged goods and never unpacked his crocodile baggage consequently dragging the gutter, an orphaned childhood, homelessness, and festering mommy issues into his every move. He resented the civility of his Horatio Alger success and preferred the marauding barbarity of Genghis Khan.

The employer once apologetically confessed to me that he could not help himself and that he had "to let the poison out." His off-the-cuff recherché admission confirmed that he was aware of his predatory psychopathic flaws. Otherwise, he showed no remorse or reform as a perverted thieving conniving incorrigible misogynistic cutthroat liar. Luciferian nirvana drove him, and a Jekyll and Hyde persona insured his success. He paid lip service to integrity for image sake while closet-hustling truth as a negotiable commodity.

Unfortunately, I hired on during the perfect storm of his mid-life crisis. He desperately wanted to reclaim his youth and preferred the company of 20-year-olds. After a few Christmas party cocktails, while oblivious to his insulted wife sitting beside me, he confided missing his hot-stud days walking the streets of New York with "babes on each arm." Their subsequent exchange of verbal barbs included her response that she would "look the other way if he ever fell overboard" during a cruise trip. Then, he updated his website with a picture of his cheerleader stepdaughter as a call-in operator. He also instructed no hires past the age of 45. Consequently, young inexperienced bar hops became mandatory sales recruits despite their incorrigible irresponsibility that missed company meetings and ignored scheduled customer appointments; they could not sell his over-priced wares even if their misguided lives depended upon it. As a result, he was forced to rely on his tenured staff adept at professionally handling high-profile customers.

My duties included customer relations with the Houston Bureau and awards team. I dealt with the franchise's website advertising, logo, Reliability Business Reports, customer complaints, mediations and arbitrations, awards program, and rating score. B-men knew me after years of interaction that undeniably substantiated my exemplary reputation and ethical background. I appreciated their staff nicknamed the "Dream Team" and was amusingly entertained by their mysterious judges, coined "Silver Foxes," whom I would have considered whimsical flair if not for the profundity of awards. I respected the Bureau's cadence of virtuous morality when vice and scandals were commonplace and was proud to walk in the icon's hallowed footsteps. I believed in truth, acted with integrity, and enforced honesty. I also swore an allegiance to truth in advertising and committed to the same ethical business standards when accepting my equivalent degrees in advertising and journalism. The difference was that I kept my promise.

Flash forwarding to February 15, 2008, the gates of Hell opened around me as I faced a frantic 4-p.m. deadline to enter the Houston Bureau's "16th Awards for Excellence." Victory depended upon my creative answers to five wide-ranging comprehensive application questions pertaining to ethical business operation and customer service excellence. During final hours, company sales and services went berserk and my administrative assistant, Tasha, decided to have a meltdown, then quit, and instigated company-wide drama by blaming me; she later admitted falsely accusing me as an excuse to claim unemployment benefits. Her misconduct was collateral damage from the employer's abuse that demeaned me, marginalized my office, and subjected me to others' unfettered fraud and abuse. In the interim, I was expected to win the almighty Pinnacle.

Unlike before, I drafted an outside-the-box multi-purposed application concept to correct company issues that guaranteed a Pinnacle. The downside was the plan assumed procedures were already in operation forcing me to depend upon the employer's dicey promise. First and foremost, I emphasized integrity and the need to implement outlined procedures. Second, procedures would correct mounting problems within his company; I worked the daily trenches, dealt with customers, and knew the weak links. Third, new dynamics would allow him to easily accommodate and service a flood of Pinnacle business. And, fourth, I suggested building his celebrity as a television spokesman by self-promoting his company and products under the Pinnacle's aegis of excellence.

The fourth nudge floated his stardom by catering to his unbridled narcissism while downplaying his fear of aging and low self-esteem. He considered himself an unpresentable spokesman and paid for celebrity radio endorsements. In fact, the employer looked like a Mafia hitman with twitchy eyes, awkward etiquette, and shifty civility with the collective warning hair-trigger rage. A star was born when I convinced him to make his first commercial by comparing him to a local television personality who self-promoted his popular furniture store; they were the same age and mega-wealth; and, both owned lake-front mansions near Austin. I continued to remind him of his company's spiraling shortcomings while verifying that he would implement application procedures. He promised to bring his video recorder the following week to produce training tapes per application statements. Hands-on triad management participation included the employer, Wayne, and me. Innovative logistics would incorporate a special method of training and education in all departments.

My final application tallied 25 pages including attachments. Flourishing

THE APO$TATE

touches added subtle overkill such as turning a substantial tax deduction into a charitable donation and an employee volunteer project into a Good Samaritan; anything with a commendable flipside was virtuously touted. I contacted customers and dredged files soliciting the most convincing testimonials from installation reviews that were labeled, "Happy Notes." The employer was mesmerized by the final draft and quickly approved submittal. Before sending, I reminded myself that he was certifiably insane, and his volatile history promised turncoat trouble. A month earlier, I was scheduled to start an MBA in accounting to develop my position as CFO, but he found out and violently threatened me into cancelling school the same night classes began. Then, he left me worrying for a week if I had a job just because I wanted to further my education same as other employees. In the meantime, I had only minutes remaining until final deadline while the employer nervously crisscrossed my office asking, "What's my percentage of winning the Pinnacle?" To shut him up, I emphatically offered, "95%!" I knew we had won and withheld the other five to make him sweat. It was 3:58 p.m., pressing "send" turned me into a whistleblower.

Afterwards the employer abruptly shut down all application implementation with no explanation. He threatened to fire me if I mentioned the application again. I was played and not surprised. Treachery was an integral part of his depraved modus operandi that I had repeatedly suffered. Awards would be allocated in four months and we both knew a Pinnacle was waiting with his name etched in perpetuity. In the meantime, and as I forewarned, slipshod service compounded, employment issues magnified, customers complained, and sales dropped. I was left at the mercy of a criminal whom I beatified as a saint with the touch of a button.

During the four-month nomination interlude prior to the awards banquet, the Silver Foxes never visited our business and application statements were not field-audited. Otherwise, onsite verification would have exposed existing fraud and immediately disqualified the employer. Additionally, there was no compliance disclaimer and/or warning against misstatements posted on the application that encouraged high-stakes' fraud. We had previously won Distinction awards, but the Pinnacle offered different dynamics, qualifications, wizardry, acclaim, and consequences.

The employer inexplicably sabotaged all the security procedures described in the awards application, which I was personally responsible to safeguard as CFO. Customers' security, privacy, and confidentiality were central selling points and assured repeat business. We dealt with elite high-profilers and stored extremely delicate financial data. My duties also processed loan documents and maintained job jackets making me responsible for security breaches; consequently, customers trusted me. To the contrary, the employer violated customers' security; he stopped all background checks, hired questionable personnel, and falsely advertised that employees and installers were respectively screened and factory trained. In fact, I had no idea with whom I was working and/or sending to customers' homes. The employer made no sense and was unconcerned about destroying his company's reputation and endangering customers' safety.

Two days before the awards ceremony, the employer hired a 1st degree felon, convicted of stealing over $200,000 from a former employer. He personally selected her, approved her employment, and specifically assigned her to my accounting department despite her felonious presence violating every security measure that I presented in the awards application. Over my stringent objections, she was given carte-blanche admittance to my office, desk, checks, and customer files. She had access to customers' birth dates, Social Security numbers, driver's licenses, bank and savings account numbers, and financial and employment information. It was part of his diabolical plan to incriminate me to counter his vicious assault that loomed over him like "the Sword of Damocles." I emphasize that he was fully aware of her criminal conviction because he later denied such. Her background report was the last employee investigation performed and the employer discussed the report with me and her parole officer.

Thereafter, the employer commenced an interrogation of my job duties and his line of questioning was absurd, suspicious, and alarming. He asked about accounting procedures, check processing, customer file maintenance, and loan processing. Questioning was relative to my personal responsibility and function as CFO; and violation of any aspect could incriminate me for breach of fiduciary duties. Customer security measures had been outlined in the awards application that the employer was aware. I had been employed for over five years and met with him on a regular basis to review accounting procedures and financial reports, and processed checks were personally delivered to him at the end of every day. Additionally, the employer knew my desk better than me, used my files on a daily basis, sifted through drawers for various stowed items, and was even caught stealing my stash of sugar packets that I offered employees since he was too cheap to provide coffee condiments. My office was accessible and transparent to him.

His actions became overtly foreboding when, out of the blue, he warned me that "it's easy to set up someone." Pieces to a shifty puzzle began to fall into place. He had physically assaulted me two years earlier and the statute of limitations had just expired two years to the date when I submitted the 2008 awards' application. Interim employment had been tantamount to a land-mined obstacle course. He was obviously posturing to incriminate me to mask years of his skullduggery, and the felon offered a get-out-of-jail-free card. She was also a perfect victim being 10 years younger, abjectly desperate, and dragging her conviction like a ball and chain. I took his threat as an omen of pending treachery and began looking over my shoulders.

THE APO$TATE

The employer and Wayne attended the Houston Bureau's *Awards for Excellence* ceremony. Of course, I was not invited, but I would have conjured an excuse not to go. We both knew that he had won, and I wanted no further part. Quitting was not an option due to financial and legal repercussions. Furthermore, I would lose everything that I worked so hard to achieve and be left responsible for consumer fraud. The employer was already blackmailing a salesman and I did not want my name added to his Darth Vader list.

During the first quarter of the Great Depression of 2008, the economy tanked placing emphasis on the awards to attract a shrinking customer base devastated by a torrent of home foreclosures. The awards program impersonated King Arthur and his trusty Excalibur to guarantee product-and-service excellence and give Bureau members an edge over nonmember competition. Skeptical consumers sought extra assurance through the Bureau's prestigious Pinnacle that transcended fame to become legendary.

The Houston Bureau's star-studded glitz and glamour awards luncheon was held on Wednesday, May 7, 2008. Glitterati emanated Hollywood mystique. Attendees received a congratulatory letter as a Winner of Distinction finalist while knowing that precious few would receive the Bureau's metamorphic Pinnacle. Houston's business elite crowded into the InterContinental Hotel's largest ballroom while the elusive Silver Foxes secretly skulked behind enchanted curtains. The awards banquet generated prestigious pomp and pageantry to create an ambiance of serene majesty and quintessential power. New Pinnacle recipients would be celebrated as celestial deities of the marketplace and seated on exalted pedestals above reproach.

Opening ceremonies royally hailed an imperial Silver Fox scampering his way to the podium. All eyes zoomed front and center as a collective hush fell over the crowd. Salvation was at hand. Hearts raced and ears strained. Blinding jealousy overflowed as winning company names were solemnly announced. Camera lights flashed as awestruck laureates of excellence strutted their red-carpet walk to gilded glory and receipt of the Bureau's most-coveted crystal magic.

Then the heavens opened. Trumpets blared. A silent roll of the drums grew deafening as our business category took its consecrated bow while competitors exchanged icy side stares. The employer was primed to hear only his name and edged to the front of his anxious seat ready to spring; his pirate's gaze fixed on glistening treasure. Then destiny bellowed: "The Pinnacle winner is ..." Our company's name majestically reverberated like a thundering echo throughout the banquet hall dramatizing first-timer's euphoria. Audible grunts of disgust escaped the crowd muted by reluctant polite applause; the employer was hated in the industry. Jumping to his feet, he double-timed it to the podium. The employer stood before 1000 members and accepted the Pinnacle - on behalf of sacred truth!

Banqueters had no idea that the employer had just stolen the Pinnacle. His rap sheet already included swindling customers, tax evasion, money laundering, and cheating installers and sales staff. He squirreled millions into overseas shell accounts, and the Pinnacle camouflaged all sins.

Distraught losers watched in anguished defeat realizing newly beatified Pinnacle winners would sap their business. Flunkies had to wait a year for another chance. There could only be one Pinnacle awarded to each category with no guarantee of distribution to every section, representing a touch of advertising genius to infuse subliminal credibility.

At the time, the Bureau promoted its winners as "crème de la crème." The objective of the Pinnacle was to promote superiority of members' products and services above those of nonmembers; to exalt the Bureau in the marketplace; and, to indoctrinate consumers to trade only with Bureau members.

Publicity photos were part of the Pinnacle's phenomenon that commemorated stellar business achievement. The employer triumphantly waded through celebratory photos holding his Pinnacle. He and his twitchy eyes looked like the cat that ate the canary. Pinnacle winners were allotted special advertising rights on the Houston Bureau's popular web page; the employer's picture and company name would rotate next to the phrase, "Start Your Search With Trust." Accordingly, the Detroit Better Business Bureau advised, "BBB is in the top 350 most visited websites in the US with 100 million unique visitors each year."

About two weeks after the banquet, the Bureau forwarded the Pinnacle's awards' insignia. I added the sacred seal to business letterhead, envelopes, contracts, magazine advertising, radio spots, television commercials, and the company's website. The employer also awards-wrapped his company truck after I informed him that the Houston Bureau's chief executive officer and Pinnacle winner completely shrouded his fleet of vehicles with awards insignia and the BBB's logo; roving advertising allowed companies to street-hustle consumers wherever their vehicles traveled while parading the Bureau's brand image.

I still had to contend with the felon. It was bad enough that the employer stole the Pinnacle, but I could not accept the possibility of a mole. Furthermore, my concern was not about the felon as a person; her employer probably framed her to cover his cooked books, and I did not want the same apocalyptic fate. Accordingly, I tried to protect myself and prepared for internal sabotage. The employer's continued refusal to move the felon to another innocuous department confirmed my suspicions. I worried incessantly about being set up for a criminal fiduciary offense respective to the employer's proffered subliminal threat and constantly cross-checked my every step. Checks, credit cards, cash, and financials were processed daily and turned into the employer; submitted backup confirmations went into my personal file. And I was in my office the same hours as the felon. But, ultimately, the employer controlled all roads leading to accounts receivable.

Services were deteriorating. Infrastructure was crumbling. And ethics ranged from slippery to nonexistent. The employer never thanked me for the Pinnacle. His warped mindset believed my application's ethereal bunkum. Thereafter, I suffered venomous repercussions when requesting implementation of award-application procedures. His psychopath's burst bubble threatened me with a series of expletive deletes: "Shut the f--k up!"; "You're fired if you mention the application again!"; and, "Stop bothering me about the f-----g Better Business Bureau because I already won the God D--- Pinnacle and it doesn't matter anymore!" The employer's blasphemous description of the Pinnacle captured the irony of his perpetrating consumer fraud to win the trophy's virtuous fortune. Consequently, he unleashed a cascading domino effect of service issues resulting in completion delays that postponed collections and revenue that he would hold me accountable.

It was heartbreaking to watch the employer ruin his company. I hated him but loved his company. Customers were appreciative because I ethically managed their accounts and worked late hours to complete threads of correspondence. They would be shocked when I emailed them at 1:00 a.m. in the morning and/or answered their late-night phone calls. I invested years of sweat equity towards the company's success working up to 80 hours a week with no sick days, holidays, or weekends; vacation days were rare, and work infused. The Pinnacle drew an elite customer base and repeat business sought Wayne and me because they trusted us.

The Pinnacle victory should have guaranteed the company's forerunner status in the industry. To the contrary, the Pinnacle's crystal commitment to excellence empowered the company's deceptive trade. The employer ignored my warnings that uncorrected issues would compound as happened. Customers claimed fraud and accusatorily questioned me, "Why wasn't I doing something?" One particular customer was in tears having invested precious savings to buy our company's overpriced windows and denounced our "awful disappointing service" that she could have contracted elsewhere for half the cost; that we "were supposed to be the best because we were a Pinnacle winner." Her disappointment was painfully palpable and indicative of things to come; and, the nightmare that I tried to avoid.

While his company fell apart, the employer blissfully boasted his prestigious Pinnacle throughout industry circles. He waved his award in the faces of competitors at every opportunity as retaliation for their previous victories. All the while, I deflected acrid repercussions of hypocrisy, betrayal, and fraud.

The felon was fired on May 30, 2008, three weeks after being hired and three weeks after the employer stole the Pinnacle. I submitted a verbal complaint regarding her access to my office and storeroom customer files fearing that I was being set up for a similar fate of embezzlement. Unfortunately, my complaint red-flagged the felon's employment and caused her dismissal. It was not my intent to have her fired. In fact, I requested that she be resituated outside of financing. She was probably more nervous than me being placed back in accounting and would have accepted a job in any department.

The way that he fired the felon was cruel. He toyed with her enjoying every second of her agony as she desperately begged for her job. After firing her the first time, he demanded that I call her back for rehire, which meant he was messing with both of us. Negotiations went back and forth. The employer intentionally encouraged her false hope and then he abruptly fired her a second time landing a doubly crushing blow.

When I approached the employer regarding the felon's unemployment benefits, he instructed me to refute her claim by stating that she withheld her criminal background. He created a fraud scenario knowing she had no credibility to defend herself. As a result, she lost direly needed benefits. She emailed me for help, but job restraints and lingering paranoia prevented assistance. My hope was that she utilized an extensive paper trail maintained by her parole officer that proved the employer lied. Unfortunately, the state of Texas catered to employers and her claim was likely denied.

Meeting the felon and experiencing her criminal consequences was eye-opening. I began to wonder if she had been set up as a patsy. Fraudulent employers embed accounting chicanery to hide cooked books same as lawyers embed civil-process impediments to prevent lawsuits. Accordingly, if job scope includes fiduciary responsibilities, retention of exonerating evidence may become imperative for self-defense. Fair warning, though, repercussions can create a Catch-22 because copying company documents is considered "conversion" and may include felonious theft charges particularly when bound by a nondisclosure agreement.

Wayne's employment was compromised and mine was capsizing. The employer had been interviewing business consultants for Wayne's position for several months and he already hired an office manager being groomed for mine. He shamelessly requested job descriptions for both our titles. Wayne was told to screen candidates according to their ethnicity and age. The employer instructed him to write "B" for Black; "H" for Hispanic; and "O for older. He removed female applicants and chose resumes with no indicators that signaled young-male Caucasians. One prospect stood out. He spent a week shadowing our footsteps and questioning accounts. It was obvious that he was going to be Wayne's replacement. In latter July, the employer hired David H. and placed him in the new office where Wayne was previously scheduled to move as vice president. David was all bluster with no window experience and an opportunistic fraud like the employer.

On the morning of August 7, 2008, I unexpectedly received a FedEx package containing a check in the amount of $7,500; an accompanying note claimed one-half advance of my upcoming Christmas bonus. I learned to be a super sleuth working for the employer; the check was a "tell" that Wayne was a goner and payment was a bribe to keep me working in his absence. At that point, I could do nothing until dust settled.

Wayne had been out of the office all day. The employer's newly married stepdaughter was building an enormous $40,000,000-dollar mansion and Wayne was managing the installation of windows and doors. He returned around 5:00 p.m. and walked into a trap. I did not have the opportunity to forewarn him because I never left the building and my office and phone were bugged. The employer immediately engaged him in cordial conversation that moved them into the warehouse; it was a reconnaissance mission to clarify warehouse' status and ask questions regarding products, inventory, and orders. Wayne misunderstood the employer's congeniality as implication that everything was okay, including his job. Thirty minutes later, they returned to the employer's office and the chameleon employer turned into The Terminator. He accused Wayne of theft, failing to train Marcos as the new service manager, and allowing an over-purchase of caulking inventory costing $5,000. Of course, none of it was true.

Wayne became defensive and the employer went psycho. The employer had obviously spoken to an attorney and was following instructed procedure. Wayne's jig was up, and it was time to clam up! The employer tape-recorded Wayne's employment termination and captured his use of the word "insubordinate," further confirming that his fifth-grader's legalese was coached by an employment attorney. After establishing what the employer thought was justified termination, he yelled, "You're fired! Get the f—k out of my building right now." It was the employer's classic signature to invoke all-encompassing obscenity-laced indignation and probably why the recording remained incognito. Wayne's employment termination was relatively anticlimactic unlike the employer's violent demonic assault against me whereby he physically transformed, attacked me, debased my gender, called me names, insulted my family, and left my job dangling.

The employer followed Wayne in lockstep as he tried to enter his office immediately across the hall. He redirected Wayne sneering, "No, keep going," while demanding, "Give me your office keys!" Wayne was perp-walked through the back warehouse. The employer slammed the door behind him in humiliating disgrace comparable to a commander ripping stripes from an officer's uniform.

The employer yelled at me, "Get Wayne's warehouse keys!" When I reached the parking lot, Wayne was sitting in his car embarrassed, angry, and shell-shocked. He had worked over 20 years for the employer as a salesman prior to becoming vice president; he devoted his life to the company and facilitated millions in revenue despite the historic 2008 Great Depression. Nevertheless, the delusional employer scapegoated Wayne for his fraud and failures that caused deteriorating sales and service.

Wayne's departure left me dodging explosive employer trip wires, chaotic service issues, and angry customers. David was a pathetic arrogant devious clock-watching carpetbagger whom the employer appointed chief operations officer (COO). The employer told me to speak to him through David despite my duties as the employer's personal secretary. Then he appointed David as my supervisor and instructed me to train him; but David reincarnated the misogynistic employer and refused my female expertise. Consequently, I continued handling service to avoid David's whiny hissy fits, including throwing his pencil on the desk because I interrupted his daydreaming.

Statisticians claimed that "the recession of 2007-2009 was the harshest downturn since the 1930's Great Depression." I was able to keep my job as long as I did because Wayne protected me. With him gone, the ghostwriting was on the wall; my job was over. Accordingly, I considered the employer's $7,500 bribe as a down payment on the $15,000 Christmas bonus that he owed me in four months, payment towards training our replacements, and payment for added operations and service duties. I had just won him the Pinnacle that spiked sales by several million dollars and I did not receive a comparable salary or quarterly bonuses like my two male corporate counterparts, yet the employer wanted to wipe the slate clean with a younger crew even if it meant destroying his company. Wayne and I "rode the wave" as far as we could.

By the end of August 2008, circumstances went from horrific to maniacal. I submitted my "conditional" resignation, which the employer refused twice. He told me that we would discuss matters in a few days. It was a stall tactic for him to visit his attorney. Otherwise, we never met. In the interim, the employer received legal notice from Wayne's first attorney advising breach of contract. The employer demanded that I write a derogatory affidavit against Wayne for "ammunition," but I refused knowing that such a rat report would ruinously contradict my prospective employment lawsuit. Unfortunately, Wayne went radio silent during that time and I had no idea where he stood. Wayne later advised that he monitored the office via remote camera for two weeks until he was removed as an authorized user. He saw the employer constantly standing in my doorway.

The employer's litigious overtones inspired me to self-defensively copy specific documents relative to accounts receivable, his tax evasion, and awards fraud. Additional innocuous documents were at my home from years of carry-over to offset the employer's discriminatory warning that I was not allowed to speak to employees. I did not copy company trade secrets, only circumstantial documents, to offset the employer's apparent intent to set me up for breach of fiduciary duties.

The first week of September found Thursday ending ominously. Curtis, the normally meek-and-mild office manager, usually left at 5:00 p.m., but he stayed late that afternoon. My interest peaked when he passed my office oozing treachery. Moments later, I heard muffled voices emanating from the employer's front office. The occasion begged victim's reconnaissance, so I gathered my daily reports as an excuse to approach his door. Looking in, I witnessed a scene reminiscent of the *Godfather*. Curtis was bowing and thanking the Italian employer as if he had just kissed his Da Capo ring. A deal was cut, money traded hands, and a dead fish had my name on it.

The following day, Friday, September 5, 2008, was my last. I walked in the door and David was lurking in the shadows. In a guarded gumshoe voice, he tipped-off the employer, "She's here." The cloak and dagger routine was obnoxious, but speaking loud enough for me to hear him was insulting. He thought that I didn't know what was going on? I finished the morning's incoming business, left for lunch, and returned at 2:00 p.m. Thereafter, I waited for doomsday to unfold. As expected, conniving Curtis made the first move. He stormed into my office, grabbed my finance paperwork, and demanded that I train him per the employer. It was the final straw that I warned the employer not to draw. My resignation letter stated that I would consider myself "fired" if the employer terminated my employment without allowing me to properly clear my desk. My job was different from Wayne's in that I absorbed fiduciary liability while managing company revenue. Open collections and pending accounts-receivable payments turned matters prosecutorial. I also had awards fraud hanging over my head, but the jig was up and there was no going back. Liberation was at hand. I grabbed my purse, told Curtis that checks were in the top drawer, and left.

As I turned the corner, the employer stood in the hallway outside Wayne's former office that had been converted into a service department. He saw me approaching, but I caught him in mid-conversation. I channeled Joan of Arc bravado as I passed him while pervasive after-thought found me running to my car like a scared rabbit in case he followed. I felt that he regretted his actions. After all, even an insane person finds sanity once in a while. Furthermore, David and Curtis were incapable of operating the company like Wayne and me. The employer drove away the two people who made him millions and genuinely cared about his company. Impact was priceless; the horrified look on his face when I left was a "gotcha" moment that I treasure. Thirty minutes later, Curtis called me at home asking my whereabouts. My brush-off response advised that I would email the employer. For the record, though, any employer contact after employment termination should be avoided without legal representation. If a lawsuit follows, any communication can and will be diabolically twisted for counterclaims.

Hurricane Ike blew through Houston a week later, on September 13, 2008, and delayed my scheduled whistleblower's meeting with the Houston Bureau. In early October, I met with the senior investigator and coordinator of the

Awards for Excellence program at the Bureau's Galleria office. I had to do something with consumer fraud and employer retaliation hanging over my head.

I followed private protocol and requested that the Houston Bureau investigate the employer and revoke his Pinnacle. As long as the employer kept the award, he would continue baiting innocent consumers. I warned the investigator not to confuse my complaints of awards fraud against the employer with "employer/employee" dispute dynamics that the Bureau supposedly did not handle. The topic of my awards application was business ethics and content described respective training and customer service excellence. I provided evidence and a list of witnesses. Primary proof was the application to confirm misstatements; that procedures had not been implemented; and that security measures were grossly violated. I emphasized that my testimony could be verified by an onsite audit while questioning the lack thereof especially since awards influenced millions of dollars in consumer commerce every year. The Bureau's outrageous answer touted an honor code.

The investigator was provided numerous examples of the employer's deceptive trade practice contrary to ethical customer service excellence that I described in the application. I had to prove "true lies." One example evidenced the employer staging his wife to use her professional name to visit a customer masquerading as an objective third party to quote a lowball estimate for damage repair caused by his installers. I explained that they both stood outside my office debating how to best cheat the customer. Fortunately, the customer discovered their scam and contracted an attorney to successfully demand the employer pay the actual cost amounting to several thousand dollars. Another example was the employer hiring the felon and jeopardizing customer confidentiality opposed to strict security measures outlined in the application. There were many other examples including money laundering and cheating customers, installers, and salespeople out of hard-earned income. Furthermore, the employer committed all offenses prior to accepting the Pinnacle!

Dan Parsons, president of the Houston Bureau, stepped into the investigative loop. After several days of email correspondence with the investigator and receipt of my evidence, Parsons forwarded me a condescending email that warned, "Enough!" Parsons curtly advised me that he met with the employer and his wife; that the Houston Bureau would not pursue the investigation any further; and, that he determined an "employer/employee" dispute. He never mentioned the Pinnacle and/or awards fraud, which were the reasons for my complaint. Additionally, he dismissed my threat to report the Houston Bureau to the national CBBB as pointless because CBBB would affirm the Houston Bureau's decision. Parsons never met with me, and I was not allowed a rebuttal. His actions suggested that his meeting with the employer was collaboration to silence my awards complaints and hide their joint consumer fraud. He implied that I was a disgruntled employee and spun my awards-fraud complaint into an employee grievance that the Houston Bureau later parlayed into slander during trial.

The employer followed his meeting with Parsons by sending me a certified letter, dated November 8, 2008, demanding that I return all copies of company documents. As a result, he inadvertently incriminated the Houston Bureau for breach of investigator/client privilege and his certified demand letter marked formal commencement date for conversion's statute of limitations. According to Texas Civil Practices & Remedies Code (TCPR) Ann. § 16.003(a), "The limitations period for a claim of conversion is two years." Accordingly, statute should have expired November 8, 2010, but the Bureau's attorney brought a counterclaim of conversion in 2013, which the district court approved for a jury charge with the addition of felonious theft in 2015.

After being sucker-punched by the Houston Bureau, I pursued my complaints with CBBB, the Texas Attorney General, and FTC. Of course, CBBB misconstrued my allegations as an "employer/employee" issue, did not mention awards fraud, affirmed the Houston Bureau's decision, and closed the investigation. The Texas Attorney General had some apathetic flunky dismiss me. Then, the FTC generically blew me off.

The Houston Bureau refused to revoke the employer's Pinnacle whereby incentivizing consumer fraud. The employer maintained his "A+" rating score and special advertising rights on the Houston Bureau's website. His picture and company services rotated next to the revered headliners of "Honesty, Integrity, and Truth" and "Search for Truth." In fact, the Bureau's various websites connected with hundreds of thousands of consumers on a monthly basis; bbb.org reported Alexa.com's tracking data that the "number of people that visited this site during May, 2014" as "1,048,614."

Wayne and I filed employment lawsuits against the employer. Our complaints did not mention and did not include CBBB, the Houston Bureau, and/or their affiliates. The employer fired Wayne and breached his sales contract triggering punitive damages listed at $126,000 dollars. I considered myself also fired by the employer and pursued unemployment benefits that were refused by the employer. Wayne's breach of contract lawsuit was approached first and was fully paid after a bitter two-year battle; our attorney was going to settle for much less until I insisted that he pursue the full amount. During the interim, Wayne assisted me with my unemployment benefits that were approved a year after I was fired. The vindictive employer fought me tooth and nail and hired one of Houston's best-known employment law firms whose lead attorney contributed to the judge's election campaign. We filed our employment lawsuits in November 2008. But matters quickly landed in appellate court consequent to the employer's submittal of a summary judgment for dismissal. We won our appeal a year later. Thereafter, we contended with the employer's revolving door of attorneys and continuances until the Bureau commandeered proceedings in 2013.

The state of Texas ruled several times against the employer during several unemployment hearings that reached the highest appellate level. The rulings were profoundly significant because the Texas Workforce Commission (TWC) notoriously ruled against employees unless there was overwhelming supportive evidence. My employment attorney did not assist me with unemployment benefits, nor did he heed the appellate hearing officer's expert decision that perfectly outlined my employment complaint and confirmed the employer's discrimination.

I lost my house, car, career, and credit after the miscreant employer stalked and blacklisted me from employment. He destroyed my reputation and ability to make a decent living. My life became the antithesis of my wealthy Memorial upbringing.

In 2009, my home was foreclosed. GMAC was not going to ignore my home's $17,000-positive equity when so many houses were under water. In fact, I forfeited my hard-won unemployment benefits from the employer to procure a job with TWC in order to accommodate loan modification requirements. Additionally, my youngest son moved in with me to contribute his employment salary as well. On May 4, 2009, I called GMAC to confirm final loan modification only to be advised of home foreclosure. There were other options that I could and would have pursued, but GMAC deceptively strung me along for several weeks to give them time to complete foreclosure. I learned that GMAC was among several prominent mortgage companies successfully sued by the federal government for defrauding homeowners with bogus loan modifications, yet homeowners were ruined and lost their homes.

Then Wells Fargo repossessed my Envoy SUV. Bankers delayed settlement for several months until humiliating repossession. Thereafter, my son bought me a 1990 Volvo with a $1250 down payment; the driver's window was stuck halfway, and I drove with the opening covered in taped plastic.

After parting company with the employer, he blacklisted me. My employment referrals crossed his desk and he torpedoed all of them. Otherwise, procuring financial employment, commiserate with my six years' worth of respective work history and salary, was impossible. Consequently, I was relegated to employers who did not seek a referral, which limited opportunity and income. The Texas Workforce Commission operated the Workforce Solutions employment offices and did not require employment references. I procured a position as an employment counselor at the Tidwell Workforce Solutions' office located in the roughest outlying area of downtown Houston. I was the only Caucasian employee. The job paid $2,000 a month less a mandatory teacher's union fee and tax deductions. Our office was a guinea pig for a new self-service computer concept (now widespread) and provided computers for personal job searches managed by a downsized staff. Job applicants were mostly African American, newly released from prison, unskilled, and computer challenged. I spent most of my time teaching appreciative applicants how to operate the computer; they wanted to work and were desperate for a job, but their incarceration stigmatized them. An older Black man approached me with tears in his eyes, grabbed my arm, fell on his knees, and begged me for a job.

President Trump attempted to remedy post-prison hardship through the First Step Act (FSA), which he signed into law on December 31, 2018. FSA was launched to curb prison recidivism and provided rehabilitative vocational training. But FSA's downside authorized undeserving convicts' mandatory release that posed endangerment to citizens, e.g., Joel Francisco, the 41-year-old gang leader of the "Almighty Latin Kings," was released from a life sentence under FSA and murdered a man "less than a year after being freed from federal prison."

The employer discovered my TWC job from his first deposition held on September 29, 2009, and afterwards he stalked me, bribed my supervisor, and had me fired. I was on friendly terms with everyone at the Workforce office prior to the deposition, but I was terrorized immediately after copies of the deposition were distributed. I was covering the front desk's incoming calls and a caller cryptically asked me, "Who called 911?" He repeated my deposition statement verbatim whereby I described how the employer prank-called 911 resulting in a Black policeman appearing at the employer's business and asking me the same exact question. The employer previously snooped my conversation with an employee suffering a dire medical emergency and our private conversation included my comment that I would call 911 if the employer ever attacked me again. Accordingly, the employer read my respective deposition statement and then proceeded to stalk and harass me. He dispatched a stooge to the Tidwell office to call me at the front desk and question a nonexistent 911 call. I grew alarmed when realizing his call originated from our back-office telephone center. The employer was capable of anything and bribing the supervisor and/or stalking me was right up his alley. I instinctively glanced behind me scrutinizing every face for future security. There was no one to turn to and reporting the problem to TWC was pointless. I did not know how deep into the state cesspool that the employer slithered, but his venomous fangs bared when the friendly supervisor turned fiend! No matter the situation, she criticized and humiliated me in front of coworkers and clients, just like the employer. Things got so bad that a 70-something-year-old Black woman came to my rescue and scolded the Black supervisor for mistreating me. Then sneaky tweaky Rosy planted a notebook full of clients' Social Security numbers in my desk in an attempt to incriminate me for identity fraud. I defended myself, but TWC fired me; I was not allowed a hearing to clear false accusations. Consequences were sweeping, far-reaching, and ruinous. TWC also segued into federal positions, and repercussions destroyed my last opportunity for respectable indiscriminate salaried employment that bypassed the employer.

Workforce Solutions was operated by various contractors and their leadership hired TWC employees. My experience with the Tidwell contractor indicated penny-pinched client services, outstanding client complaints, and rogue moonlighting management. Cameras were not allowed inside Workforce Solutions' offices and TWC did not monitor contractors aside from sketchy counterproductive time-consuming reports that impeded job-search assistance.

After I reported the employer for contest fraud, his Houston Bureau rating was lowered from an "A+" to "A-" although his "Reliability Report" listed excessive service complaints. I believe at one point that the employer's rating briefly fell to a "B", but his rating score quickly returned to an "A+". I had no doubt that the employer complained about his lowered rating score and the Bureau accommodated him. A nonmember would have received a much lower rating and the Bureau would have ignored their complaint.

Opposing counsel staged the employer's first deposition to lay groundwork for his counterclaim of slander that I considered malicious prosecution for reporting his awards fraud to state and federal regulatory agencies. He focused on an expression that I used in one of my complaint letters, which alleged the employer's "services had sunk into the toilet." In fact, those were the employer's words that I referenced regarding his company's deteriorating operations. I responded by suggesting the attorney check the Houston Bureau's Reliability Report that listed the employer holding 16 unresolved service complaints in a matter of months. During my employment, we never exceeded more than three complaints per year and issues were immediately settled.

The attorney's face turned ashen when he realized absence of slander. He was visibly panic-stricken and desperately leafed through his notes searching for anything that he could remotely spin as a substitute. He ended the deposition by posing frivolous hypotheticals. I previously dealt with him during a justice court hearing when retrieving my personal planner from the employer. Background research revealed that he had been previously disbarred by the state of Texas relative to a controversial trial involving a female plaintiff. He was obviously trying to recuperate when the employer contracted him for our lawsuit.

The attorney committed suicide a few months after the deposition. I questioned if he was also victimized by the employer. He fit the employer's predatory profile that exploited desperate people. I believed that his death was connected to our case because his law firm could not find his respective notes, suggesting that he deliberately destroyed evidence. Additionally, the female founding partner of the law firm refused to continue representing the employer. During trial, the employer exploited the attorney's death and nauseatingly moped about his dead attorney in front of the jury. I believed that the psychopathic employer threatened the attorney to fatal extent after his failure to prove slander against me. The decedent's online memorial indicated that he was not a tortured soul. He was apparently popular. Shocked mourners questioned, "WHY?"

We filed our employment lawsuits in November 2008, but trial was repeatedly delayed. Research indicated that our delays were consistent with another member's defamation lawsuit against the Houston Bureau, which was filed in 2012; consequent judgment was rendered in the Bureau's favor in 2013, and the same year when the Houston Bureau commandeered the employer's defense and infused its fifth-column attorney to hijack our trial and introduce new counterclaims through a second forced Bureau-oriented deposition.

The employer's empowered behavior at his second deposition, on September 18, 2013, was tellingly reprehensible. He acted like a spoiled brat with deep pockets. The deposition imitated the Spanish Inquisition and was recorded via video camera. The employer and his wife sat across from me; he made outrageous faces, and she stared darts. Opposing counsel set a belligerent tone by histrionically waving copies of my award complaints, which I sent to the Texas Attorney General and FTC. The employer manipulated opposing counsel's words like pulling strings on a puppet; he frantically tugged the attorney's sleeve and shoved handwritten notes under his nose to point of distraction that caused erratic questioning. The employer was imploding. He was not allowed to talk to me and could not control me. It was therapeutic watching him squirm like a worm. Theatrics turned into frustration when they failed to fluster me or foil my answers resulting in opposing counsel's asinine question, "Did I realize that my documents were now public?" My polite answer was, "Yes." My stifled answer was, "Of course, jerk, why do you think I did it?" The employer and Bureau wanted to incriminate me for reporting their awards fraud to regulatory agencies. Whereas the deposition was liberating, consequences were binding. The fix was in and trial was scheduled, kept, and conned.

My complaints followed protocol established by the Bureau's founders to promote ethics and integrity, but successors vilified me for reporting the truth. The New York Bureau's General Manager H. J. Kenner (from 1926 to 1947) and author of *The Fight for Truth in Advertising* warned, "If through error a bureau deals unjustly with any business or with any man, all that is required is an appeal to its board of directors and the wrong is acknowledged and righted. It is fundamental to such work that fairness shall rule in its acts and that it must not let a sense of power, existing through the powerful principles of truth and honesty it serves, misdirect its good intentions."

CHAPTER 2

AWARDS FOR EXCELLENCE

The Houston Bureau's illusory *Awards for Excellence* program is an example of predecessors' lucrative formula for humbuggery. CBBB restructured the twenty-first-century Deep State Better Business Bureau into an impregnable autocratic nation state riding the financial wings of a specious awards program that cloaks the organization's hallucinatory genetics of exaggeration and implication bulwarked by crony-courtroom power plays. Members have attempted to adjudicate mounting operational complaints, but laws and verdicts seemingly adapted to decimate any lawsuit brought against the franchise. Steely legal impediments have secured the organization's gilded pedestal.

CBBB is the Bureau franchise's national headquarters and is registered as a foreign entity even though it micromanages the organization's rules, regulations, and programs; annual reports evidence a paper trail, connecting CBBB's financial dots with the Bureaus. Accordingly, the Houston Bureau posted a "tell" on its 2018 "BBB Awards for Excellence" web page advising, "© 2018, Council of Better Business Bureaus, Inc., separately incorporated Better Business Bureau organizations in the US, Canada and Mexico, and BBB Institute for Marketplace Trust. All Rights Reserved." In other words, the franchise won a lawsuit that acknowledged CBBB was a separate entity from the Bureaus and the organization issued a braggart's disclaimer to deflect future complainants.

The Bureau is a master at manipulating laws of the land under the guise of pristine ethics and market trust; a weaponized digital reporting system and unmerited programs control Big Cloud and Big Commerce. Businesses are coerced to become members or face the Bureau's disparaging wrath whereby nonmembers are labeled with implication of subpar products and services. Members are acutely aware that the Bureau lords over an imposing influential online presence visited by millions of viewers. Accordingly, blind allegiance is demanded. Otherwise, challenge is met with contempt, vilification, membership revocation, and/or ruinous rating score. Yesteryear coined such practice as defamation that today's globalist courts have twisted into free speech. In fact, several states, including Texas, have adopted First-Amendment legislation that the Bureau has exploited to legitimize and expand its questionable operations.

The Texas Citizens Participation Act (TCPA), located at TCPR, Section 27.005, has become a "go-to" law invoked by scheming movant parties to spin the First Amendment's rights as means to legally disparage adversaries, insulate rackets, whitewash deceptive trade, and eliminate competition. Civil claims that allege defamation are called "Strategic Lawsuits against Public Participation" or "SLAPP," and face penalties for infringement of free speech, petition, and/or association. The state of Texas incorporated TCPA as anti-SLAPP legislation. Plaintiffs who fail to prove defamation's high bar face harsh TCPA-inflicted penalties under Section 27.009, including sanctions, court costs, attorney's fees, and other expenses. As a result, TCPA has convoluted into the antithesis of its purpose to silence complaints and empower defamation. The TCPA's punitive repercussions deter legitimate claims, create double standards, and impede free speech enabling tricksters and serial predators like the Bureau to operate specious services through bias case law.

Several significant member lawsuits attempted to pierce the Bureau's Teflon shield and are described in a later chapter, but upfront mention highlights two recent landmark lawsuits brought by "a former Chairman of the Houston BBB Board of Directors" from "2007 to 2008" and owner of "John Moore Services, Inc. and John Moore Renovation, LLC, (collectively, John Moore)" against the Better Business Bureau of Metropolitan Houston, Inc. Defendants also included the Better Business Bureau of Metropolitan Houston Education Foundation and Dan Parsons, as the "Chief Executive Officer of the Houston BBB."

I discussed awards fraud with John Moore's owner around October 2008, and disclosure may have been the reason why he ended his chairmanship with the Houston Bureau at the end of that year. I interviewed for an accounting job, but nothing gelled, and I moved on.

John Moore's lawsuits exposed the Houston Bureau's insidious unfettered power, clout, and cronyism with the state of Texas. Case text expounded upon the Houston Bureau's secret society and listed names of its elusive board of directors. Lawsuit claims alleged rating score bias, deceptive trade, monopoly violations, and hypocritical standards applicable to use of awards insignia (no mention of awards fraud). Ultimately, the appellate court enforced TCPA, which consequently enabled the Houston Bureau's bias rating scores, consumer fraud, and defamation, which alternately threatened to shield its specious awards program. Hindsight evidences that John Moore's chronological court proceedings aligned with our lawsuits' repeated delays, and that the Houston Bureau exploited John Moore's verdict to rig our trial.

November 2010 was a pivotal timeframe resulting in John Moore's membership cancellation with the Houston Better Business Bureau. John Moore's owner complained about the Houston Bureau's rating score methodology with contention possibly inspired by ABC *20/20*'s article, "Terror Group Gets An "A" Rating From Better Business Bureau?," published on November 12, 2010, which exposed the rating score as a scam. John Moore resigned its membership with the Houston Bureau and moved its headquarters from the Houston Bureau's jurisdiction to Bryan-College Station. The Houston Bureau changed John Moore's ratings from an "A+" to "NR" for "not rated."

In April 2012, the Houston Bureau downgraded John Moore's rating score to an "F". Thereafter, John Moore brought "two state court lawsuits" against the Houston Bureau "over a business quality rating and the right to display past awards [*Awards for Excellence*]." In short, the Houston Bureau filed a TCPA-based motion to dismiss John Moore's first lawsuit, but dismissal was denied by the trial court. The Houston Bureau appealed, and John Moore filed a second lawsuit to add to the first lawsuit while waiting for appellate decision. The appellate court ultimately reversed both trial court denials and remanded cases back to trial court to assess damages pursuant to TCPA. During the first lawsuit, the Texas Legislature amended TCPR, Chapter 51, to allow stay of trial proceedings during an interlocutory appeal, and the Supreme Court of Texas denied John Moore's request for petition to review.

John Moore's first lawsuit focused on the rating score and alleged, "[C]laims for fraud, tortious interference with existing and prospective business relationships, business disparagement and defamation." The Houston Bureau's conviction for defamation would have also enabled deceptive trade claims including the *Awards for Excellence*, but the Bureau deflected fraud liability by invoking the TCPA's right of free speech. The second lawsuit expounded upon the first lawsuit and added awards insignia alleging, "[C]laims for fraud, state law antitrust violations, breach of contract, civil conspiracy, and violations of the DTPA [Deceptive Trade Practices Act]." The Houston Bureau again deflected liability under TCPA. Both lawsuits forged landmark decisions that inadvertently legitimized the Bureau's specious ratings program and threatened to also shroud the awards program under similarly twisted TCPA legalese.

I knew the owner of John Moore and witnessed his operations firsthand; he and his company were exemplary in the home improvement industry. John Moore's court proceedings reminded me of the Bureau's alleged scandalous court proclivities during the *Roaring Twenties* and empowerment during the *Somber Thirties*. Chronology of events and repercussions emphasized that members were controlled by the Bureau's plenary power; that the mighty John Moore could not overcome the Houston Bureau; and that the Deep State Bureau exploited John Moore's lawsuits to seat itself as an autocratic nation state.

THE APO$TATE

John Moore's two lawsuits and respective appeals uncannily connected to our lawsuits. I believe the Houston Bureau intertwined the John Moore case with ours to enable unfettered defamation against us. In fact, trial proved that the Bureau's witness was scheduled to defame me, and the employer bragged about his "A+" rating score. John Moore's first lawsuit appeared to have commenced in 2012. The Houston Bureau filed a TCPA-based motion to dismiss, which the trial court denied. The Houston Bureau appealed, and the appellate court reversed the trial court on July 16, 2013 (No. 01-12-00990-CV). Effective June 13, 2013, the Texas Legislature amended TCPR, Section 51.014(a)(12), to particularly grant an automatic stay of trial proceedings during an interlocutory appeal rising from denial of a TCPA motion to dismiss (as sought by the Houston Bureau). On February 14, 2014, case law stated, "The Supreme Court of Texas denied petition to review" the appellate court's reversal which favored the Houston Bureau. On August 11, 2014, the appellate court remanded John Moore's first lawsuit to trial court whereby the Houston Bureau's motion to dismiss was granted and TCPA judgment commenced. In the interim, when the first appeal was still pending, John Moore filed a second parallel lawsuit whereby the Houston Bureau again filed a TCPA-based motion to dismiss that was also denied by trial court; the appellate court reversed trial court on June 2, 2016; (Court of Appeals of Texas, Houston (1st Dist.), 500 S.W. 3d 26 (Texas. App. 2016)). The second case was also remanded back to trial court for motion to dismiss and TCPA punitive judgment. The first lawsuit's TCPA judgment was assessed around $250,000 (No. 01-14-00906-CV); the Houston Bureau asked for $375,000.

The same year that John Moore filed its first lawsuit, the employer abruptly changed to a seventh and final set of attorneys wherein schematics changed, and counterclaims were introduced. I am alleging that the Houston Bureau commandeered the employer's floundering defense proceedings in 2012 and infused its high-profile court-friendly attorney to synchronize counterclaims against us in accordance with John Moore's expected appellate decisions. In fact, the Houston Bureau applied dynamics of defamation and braggadocio of its rating score during our private trial. Additionally, our trial delays closely coincided with significant dates associated with John Moore's first lawsuit. The employer's attorney inexplicably delayed our May 2013 trial, which I allege was due to the Houston Bureau's waiting period for the appellate court's reversal of John Moore's trial court ruling. Two months later, on July 16, 2013, the appellate court granted the Houston Bureau's first appeal. Consequently, the employer's attorney forced a second Bureau-oriented deposition in September 2013 even though our lawsuits did not mention the Better Business Bureau. Then, in August 2014, the Texas Supreme Court refused to review John Moore's first lawsuit and our trial was subsequently scheduled for January 2015.

The John Moore trials emphasized the profundity of the *Awards for Excellence* and rating score, and explained why the Bureau hijacked our trial, delayed our trial, and advanced our trial only after its questionable operations were immunized by appellate court's ruling. Three months after John Moore's appellate verdict, the newly TCPA-emboldened Houston Bureau seized the employer's lawsuit and forced us into a Bureau-oriented deposition, on September 18, 2013, that focused on defamation accompanied by the employer's counterclaims of slander, breach of fiduciary duties, conversion, and theft. The employer sought a conversion indictment because I acknowledged copying company documents, not trade secrets, for defensive purposes and to report his consumer fraud, but I believe that felonious charges of theft and breach of fiduciary duties were suggested by the Houston Bureau with intent to silence and imprison me to protect the *Awards for Excellence*.

I allege that the Houston Bureau prearranged our trial proceedings with the Court and that its racketeering operations are protected by the state of Texas. Accordingly, in 1933, O'Sullivan defined a "racket" as "any enterprise which operates for profit and gains its ends by force or threats, by harassment of opponents or competitors, or by illicit methods of any kind, especially where the operations are veiled in secrecy because they will not stand the test of genuine or official investigation."

The Council introduced awards in 2000. I began winning awards in 2006 when the fledgling program was growing avaricious fangs. Consequently, I witnessed a boilerplate awards program digitally transform into an over-the-top crème-de-la-crème phenomenon that lionized winners as "the BBBest" in the industry. The awards epitomized the proverbial lie that grew grander with every recital while the Bureau advanced unchecked, above reproach, and reigned supreme as a profit-gauging globalist masquerading as a pulpit-pounding Puritan. No one suspected that the iconic watchdog was award-doping the public to support its conspiratorial NWO aspirations. As a result, the popularity and prestige of awards skyrocketed with every *Who's Who* in business scrambling to capture the Bureau's pot of gold.

In 2008, I reported the Houston Bureau for consumer fraud after winning its most coveted Pinnacle award for the employer and after learning the Bureau's "Barnum and Bunk" and "hokum and make-believe" corruption. I previously won two second place Winner of Distinction awards that turned consumer heads, but unlike the sacred Pinnacle that raised the elitist bar to beatification. Offenders could not call me a liar because I broke bread among them. Their lies and deceit consecrated me a whistleblowing consumer activist who exposed their Wizard of Oz humbuggery. The Bureau's hostile response to my acknowledged application misstatements underscored the basis of my complaint that the flame of truth was doused; that awards were bogus; that evaluation was nonexistent; that merit was exaggerated; and that consumers were victims. When I approached the Bureau to correct its scam awards program, cover-up grew worse than the crime.

On January 25, 2018, NBC-Montana published the article, "Better Business Bureau warns that award scams are going around," whereby a B-man described awards as "vanity awards" and "money grabs." He sternly advised, "Most legitimate awards do not come with costs to the recipient. Make sure you know the nomination process." As such, I am alleging that said wink-wink warning was shameless hypocritical bunkum that actually described the Better Business Bureau's integrity awards as the mother lode of awards nirvana and wellhead of modern award scams; that CBBB designed the awards program for the Bureau franchise as a cost-effective superficial vanity award to increase memberships and grab money from wide-ranging expensive membership fees while hiding a bogus awards nomination process that excludes nonmembers.

Accordingly, I am alleging larceny, money laundering, and racketeering respective to awards fraud perpetrated by the Better Business Bureau of Greater Houston and South Texas, Better Business Bureau of South Texas Consumer Education Foundation Inc., Better Business Bureau of Metropolitan Houston Educational Foundation (replaced the South Texas Foundation after 2008), and the Council of Better Business Bureaus, Inc. in Arlington, Virginia. I worked directly with all afore listed entities.

The 501(c)(6) Better Business Bureau of Greater Houston and South Texas (Houston Bureau) business league and 501(c)(3) Better Business Bureau of Metropolitan Houston Educational Foundation (Houston Foundation) operate in consortium. In keeping with IRS mandates, the Houston Bureau flexes muscle and the Houston Foundation finagles money. Fraud arose when CBBB designed and launched the money-grabbing awards racket through participating franchise foundations, shielded by Big IRS and Big FTC, to subsidize and expand operations by incentivizing lucrative memberships, choking competition, and monopolizing the marketplace. I am alleging that cooked books obfuscate 501(c) interaction and trickle ill-gotten revenue throughout the franchise.

Henceforth, both 501(c) organizations need each other to successfully operate emphasizing the fallacy and pretense of separate classifications micromanaged by the Bureau-brownnosing IRS. The 501(c) organizations separated business from charity same as the Glass-Steagall Act of 1933 separated banking from investments, but I believe the system has been financially and politically compromised with mutually beneficial business-as-usual riding muddied undercurrents; that 501(c) separation is an enabling poker-face; that the Bureau and Foundation engage a racket that topically complies while subversively connives; and, that 501(c) encourages corruption by restricting public purview of an incriminating paper trail. The Bureau exploits accreditations (memberships) channeled by the Foundation's award program while the Foundation serves as a window-dressed money changer converting digitized merit into cash. Additionally, the Bureau receives backdoor revenue from the Foundation's multiplicitous fundraising, which includes large government grants (Foundation's 2015 Form 990 listed "$353,033") that vicariously force taxpayers to finance the Foundation's awards fraud. The IRS permits telescopic consumer scrutiny via Form 990s, but not microscopic side-by-side comparisons of Form 990s, annual reports, and tax returns that bury violations, like racketeering and money laundering, between federal firewalls.

I allege that the IRS protects C-6 and C-3 sleight of hand by impeding investigative process. The public is supposed to have access to nonprofit information, but the IRS blocks retrieval by requiring confidential gatekeeper information like an Employment Identification Number (EIN). The IRS refused to give me the Houston Bureau's EIN required to order its Form 990. The agent suggested contacting the Bureau or an employee, but both ideas were impractical. After my state and federal complaints, the Houston Bureau scrubbed and safeguarded its EIN under lock and key further underscoring impropriety. (I was fortunate to find both Foundation EINs from out-of-date and current IRS master files.) The IRS also refused to give me copies of the Houston Foundation's annual reports. According to the director from the IRS's Compliance Planning and Classification department: "IRC Section 6103 requires that tax returns and return information must be confidential, and disclosure cannot be made except as authorized by the IRC. Therefore, we can't disclose whether we have initiated an investigation based on the information you submitted, and we can't disclose the status of any investigation." Difficulty in retrieving Bureau data was a particularly sore subject for me. Trial discovery would have provided EIN and tax records, but the serpentine Bureau slithered behind the employer's company to prevent retrieval.

Whereas I was unable to retrieve complete sets of the Houston Bureau's annual reports and Form 990s along with the Houston Foundation's respective records, discovery remains ongoing. Nevertheless, the Houston Foundation cannot deny that it sponsors specious awards, and the Houston Bureau cannot deny its respective conjoined working relationship. Furthermore, the Houston Bureau and Houston Foundation cannot deny that they work in tandem to sponsor an awards program that dominates the marketplace and disparages nonmember competition. Henceforth, any litigious Bureau pushback against *The Apostate* will beget an *Apostate II* that will trigger my discovery tsunami that will subpoena all Houston Bureau/Houston Foundation-related financials starting from day one that will match-up annual combinations of Form 990s, annual reports, and tax returns with no stones left unturned, including identification of all contributors and contributions.

The Foundation Group eloquently surmised that foundations were formed "to organize financial resources toward a cause." But my question is, what cause? I believe that the Bureau and IRS are crony globalists accommodating NWO initiatives and promoting anti-American subversion evidenced by the latest privacy laws that promote safeguards to protect business/charity hookups under the inviolability of 501(c) organizations. A review of IRS master files highlighted many foundations known to be linked to anti-American subversion. I suggest that illicit organizations sire foundations as money laundering schemes to siphon taxpayers' treasure, hide contributors, and promote anti-American political ideologies.

IRS 501(c) organizations overlook controversial and complicated franchise relationships like the Houston Bureau/Houston Foundation mishmash that exploits IRS confidentiality loopholes to protect deceptive trade practice. I reported the Houston Bureau's bogus awards program to the FTC pertaining to the Federal Trade Act of 1914 and to the Texas Attorney General pertaining to fraud, but both regulators gave me the bum's rush.

My awards fraud complaints filed with the state were in accordance with Texas Penal Code, Chapter 32, as follows: Section 32.42, Deceptive Business Practices; subsection (a)(4) states, ""Contest" includes sweepstakes, puzzles, and game of chance"; and, subsection (a)(5)(A) states, ""Deceptive sales contest" that misrepresents the participant's chance of winning a prize"; each aforementioned subsection also offers applicable subparts that are too expansive to add herein. Additionally, Section 32.44, Rigging Publicly Exhibited Contest, subsection (a), states, "A person commits an offense if, with intent to affect the outcome (including the score) of a publicly exhibited contest"; subparts also apply.

Texas laws are contrived in a manner to protect Big Special Interest and Big Illuminati like the Bureau. The John Moore lawsuits highlighted the fact that pursuit of justice against a state-protected actor is virtually impossible. Accordingly, if the mighty John Moore was trounced, how in the hell could a peon like me win a no-winner? Ignoring state laws and/or cherry-picking offenders defeats the purpose of having laws, which emphasizes globalism's alarming consequences that grease the avaricious palms of crony politicians and adjudicators.

I believe that the Bureau franchise magnified its organization to stratospheric size largely due to Big Court and Big IRS. History reminds of the Bureau's 1920's diabolical tactic "to clog up the courts all over the United States ...." Today, the Bureau need not worry about clogging the courts because Big Court and Big IRS are part of the Deep State whose network wraps the Bureau in a protective cocoon of double standards and red tape.

The Better Business Bureau franchise is comprised of approximately 116 independent offices and growing. Franchising equates to licensing that solicits fees. According to the International Franchise Association, "In franchising, franchisors (a person or company that grants the license to a third party for the conducting of a business under their marks) not only specify the products and services that will be offered by the franchisees (a person or company who is granted the license to do business under the trademark and trade name by the franchisor), but also provide them with an operating system, brand and support." As such, CBBB is the franchisor and the Bureaus are the franchisees. Therefore, my extrapolation determined that CBBB-siphoned "Bureau dues" included tainted awards-begotten revenue. IRS privacy firewalls protect the Bureau's netherworld conglomerate to confuse and complicate scrutiny. Henceforth, the awards program has flourished unencumbered.

The Revenue Act of 1943 required 501(c)(3) nonprofits to file a Form 990 (Return of Organization Exempt From Income Tax) and "report sources of income and all assets and liabilities," according to Bizfluent.com. As of "August 17, 2006," a Form 990 is "open to public inspection." Accordingly, CBBB's 2009 Form 990 listed "Members Dues" at "$4,884,226." Subsequent annual reports evidenced a steady increase of franchise money flow: 2010 ("$2,117,000"), 2011 ("$4,349,530"), 2012 ("$4,951,068"), 2013 ("$5,225,003"), 2014 ("$9,662,715"), and 2015 ("$13,735,934"). (I retained hard copies of afore listed Form 990 and annual reports in case reference links were removed.) Furthermore, be it noted that CBBB's 2010 annual report reflected considerable loss of revenue as a result of fallout from ABC *20/20's* scandalous documentary exposing CBBB's bogus rating score, but the 2015 annual report reflected considerable gain from friendly court decisions that immunized bogus programs and from dearth of information that hid Bureau indiscretions from the public.

Business leagues derived from the Tariff Act of 1913. The IRS described provenance of the act and advised that "passage was the result of a U.S. Chamber of Commerce request for an exemption for nonprofit "civic" and "commercial" organizations - a request that resulted in the enactment of what is now ... IRC 501(c)(6) (for nonprofit "commercially oriented" organizations)." On November 8, 1966, a tax amendment was added "to permit ... National and American Football Leagues to go forward without fear of an antitrust challenge under either the Clayton Antitrust Act or the Federal Trade Commission Act." According to The Nest, "Section 501c6 recognizes business leagues as tax exempt. Like all tax-exempt organizations recognized by the Internal Revenue Service, a business league 501c6 cannot inure benefit to any individual or single shareholder, and all net earnings must go back into the organization."

IRS 501(c)(6) regulations render wink-wink legalese exploited by the Bureau. Whereas "common business interest" is obvious, I question the Bureau's operations relative to "profit," "regular business," and "individual" performance. Accordingly, "Reg. 1.501(c)(6)-1 defines a business league as an association of persons having a common business interest, whose purpose is to promote the common business interest and not to engage in a regular business of a kind ordinarily carried on for profit. Its activities are directed to the improvement of business conditions of one or more lines of business rather than the performance of particular services for individual persons." As such, I believe that CBBB and the Houston Bureau violated spirit of law when establishing a profiteering individual-oriented foundation pimping pay-for-play specious awards for memberships; and, that Reg. 1.501(c)(6)-1 should have incriminated the franchise for exploiting its IRS classification because CBBB designed the awards to benefit individual members and to eliminate non-member competition. Furthermore, the IRS considers members same as individuals: "Reg. 1.501(c)(6)-1 speaks in terms of services to "persons," which refers not only to members, but also to individuals and entities who are not members."

In 1954, the 501(c)(3) charity was introduced by Texas Democratic Senator Lyndon Baines Johnson. The Jesus-Is-Savior.com website advised that "all donations, contributions, gifts, etc. given to churches were automatically tax-deductible under the old English common law, known as the "Law of Charities"." The Tax Reform Act of 1969 was signed by Republican President Richard Nixon and, for the first time, included an Alternative Minimum Tax ("supplemental income tax") and defined "private foundation." According to IRS.gov, "Organizations described in section 501(c)(3) are commonly referred to as charitable organizations" described as "a private operating foundation is a private foundation that devotes most of its resources to the active conduct of its exempt activities."

On October 26, 2018, the Council on Foundations (COF) reported, "Each year, private foundations are required to pay an annual excise tax equal to 2 percent of their net investment income (known as the private foundation excise tax)" with algorithms enforcing "charitable expenditures" to prevent five-fingered tax savings. Disclaimed legalese means well, but IRS impediments prevent scrutiny of all tax records to verify charitable expenditures' compliance. Additionally, current lobby efforts will enrich and empower foundations by simplifying "the private foundation excise tax to a flat rate of 1 percent." Reasoning sides with foundation convenience; that "calculating the tax rate requires foundation staff to constantly monitor and adjust their investments and spending – time and money that would be better spent serving their communities."

According to the IRS, "To be tax-exempt under section 501(c)(3) of the Internal Revenue Code, an organization must be organized and operated exclusively for exempt purposes set forth in section 501(c)(3), and none of its earnings may inure to any private shareholder or individual. In addition, it may not be an *action organization*, i.e., it may not attempt to influence legislation as a substantial part of its activities and it may not participate in any campaign activity for or against political candidates." To the contrary, and based on the operations of the 501(c)(6) Houston Bureau and 501(c)(3) Houston Foundation that act on CBBB's systemic synchronized directives for the entire franchise, I allege that the Bureau franchise and respective foundations are conspiratorial "action organizations"; that the Bureaus and foundations operate a coordinated profiteering militarized agenda orchestrated by CBBB; that the Bureaus and foundations hide illicit activities and IRS violations behind a façade of philanthropy; that the Bureaus and foundations insidiously influence politics and operate as secret societies protected by crony local, state, and federal government agencies (including the IRS); that the Bureaus and foundations violated inurement that is a legal term defined as "to be of use, benefit, or advantage to an individual"; that the foundations were illicitly "organized or operated for the benefit of private interests" because only members can participate in its awards program and members are individuals running independent businesses who benefit from the unlawful exclusion of nonmembers; that if the foundations operated their awards programs according to IRS mandates, all businesses could participate regardless of membership status; that CBBB schemed to expand the organization's monopolistic operations under the protective canopy of its foundations to blur special interests and private gain; that the foundations abuse 501(c)(3) authority to solicit taxpayers' money in the form of grants that force taxpayers to unwittingly support awards fraud; that the foundations engage racketeering and money laundering by peddling specious awards whose unclean revenue is then sanitized under "gifts, grants, contributions and membership fees" and returned to CBBB as hygienic Bureau dues and/or dues; that the foundations' IRS-protected accounting legitimizes laundered revenue generated by a closed-circuit money-laundering racket akin to an underground sprinkler system filtering revenue to CBBB, Bureaus, and members; that the foundations are becoming increasingly opaque and not cross-checked by tax returns; and, that the foundations may hide illicit gains from racketeering activities involving untold millions of dollars.

I also believe that the NWO hybridized a horde of foundations to intercede, infiltrate, and infect social standards. Not surprising, 501(c)(3) organizations are the largest growing nonprofits: "In 2010, public charities, the largest component of the nonprofit sector, reported $1.51 trillion in revenue, $1.45 trillion in expenses, and $2.71 trillion in assets," according to Urban Institute. Gilded façade hides anti-American financial and political agendas under creative accounting's sacrosanct shroud. Left-leaning hybrid foundations insidiously influence commerce and politics despite conflicting regulatory mandates that prohibit political involvement. When researching IRS Form 990 master files, nonprofit cronyism appeared rampant wherein foundations "mobilized resources" questioning subversive motive and insider-funding. I particularly call attention to Media Matters of America, Washington, D.C., that was established in May 2004 and is affiliated with globalist billionaire financier George Soros. Discover the Networks described Media Matters as a "web-based, not-for-profit ... progressive research and information center dedicated to comprehensively monitoring, analyzing, and correcting conservative misinformation"; that Media Matters held "notable friendly ties to Al Jazeera, the anti-American, Qatar-based Arabic television station and satellite network" and "had "regular contact with political operatives" inside the Obama White House." Conservatives consider Media Matters to be a Soros attack dog that controls mainstream media (MSM). On October 20, 2010, according to Politico, "George Soros announced that he has given $1 million to Media Matters." Three weeks later, on November 12, 2010, ABC *20/20* exposed the "Better Business Bureau" for pay-for-play rating score fraud with national revelation akin to a bombshell scandal. Unfortunately, investigative journalism discreetly dropped the subject and withered into left-wing silence, which questioned Media Matters' intervention.

I am alleging that the Houston Bureau's 501(c)(3) charity foundation is a money laundering NWO-affiliated enterprise. My allegation was inadvertently supported by a former Bureau president whose narrative prognosticated CBBB's twenty-first-century globalist blueprint exploiting the Bureau's twentieth-century upstart footprints. I believe that the CBBB, Bureaus, and foundations are globalist lapdogs evidenced by the organization's cavalier awards fraud, frenetic growth, and immunized political activism supporting the Left's radicalized Democratic initiatives. *Roaring-Twenties*' skullduggery re-emerged when the primordial New York Bureau collaborated with ancestral newspaper brethren to disparage an anti-globalist member and Grand Old Party candidate who became 45th POTUS.

The 2018 subheader for the Houston Bureau's awards' application touted, "Benefiting the Better Business Bureau Educational Foundation"; an innocuous description to seemingly mask a loaded conundrum involving fake awards, money laundering, and racketeering. Until I started complaining, the Houston Bureau hid the official name of its foundation, "Better Business Bureau of Metropolitan Houston Educational Foundation." Furthermore, the term "benefiting" is an exaggerated gilded perception to legitimize a bogus awards program whose ill-gotten benefits pillar the entire organization. In fact, the cloak-and-dagger subheader linked to a fine-printed disclaimer advising, "The Better Business Bureau Education Foundation is a charitable non-profit organization that informs, educates and advocates on behalf of consumer and helps combat unethical business practices and provides protection from fraudulent schemes." Accordingly, I am alleging that said disclaimer attempts to subliminally legitimize a specious awards program; that the disclaimer is as bogus as the awards that it protects; and that the disclaimer spins awards' credibility by seamlessly blending fact with fiction through implication, perception, confusion, tricky wordsmithry, double standards, and sacrilegious hypocrisy. Weasel-worded phrases like "provides protection from fraudulent schemes" subliminally hide awards fraud behind gilded philanthropy. Yesteryear referred to such humbuggery as "throwing the scent off the trail."

It is my opinion that the Bureau's revered foundation is a fake storefront window-dressing a globalist money laundering racket much like the 1920's pharmacies masked backdoor bootlegging. The Houston Foundation is supposed to be a humble compliant nonprofit educational philanthropic charity. Instead, the Bureau's 501(c)(3) charity morphed into a commercial overlord wielding nation-state powers funded by a promotional profit scheme's covert despotic autocratic plutocratic oligarchic supremacist operations that collaborate with EU-driven transatlantic death-star initiatives; and, its awards director attempted to incriminate me for reporting the Houston Foundation's awards fraud.

As of April 9, 2018, the "Exempt Organizations Business Master File Extracts" listed a "record count" of "1,669,731." I had to check line-by-line not knowing the Foundation's real name and finally located the "Better Business Bureau of Metropolitan Houston Educational Foundation" on sentence line number 55137, including the EIN number. The Houston Bureau had no excuse to omit "Metropolitan" on its award application other than to confuse records, impede retrieval, blur evidence, and obstruct justice. IRS records are not user-friendly and require an exact name and/or EIN number. Be it further advised that only after I contacted the IRS in 2018, ordered a copy of its 2016 Form 990, and complained to the IRS that the Metropolitan Houston Educational Foundation hid its EIN number, did the Foundation start listing its "Federal ID Tax #741662104" on an ancillary page inviting ticket purchase to the *Awards for Excellence* luncheon. Otherwise, the Houston Bureau still shrouds its EIN number in secrecy.

The South Texas Foundation's (EIN 74-2518772) original Form 990 financials were purged, but basic contact information remained in an archived master file. The "Principal Officer's Name and Address" stated, "Dan Parsons, 1333 West Loop South Suite 1200, Houston, TX 77027," with "Tax Period" noted as "2007 (01/01/2007 – 12/31/2007)"; the organization was terminated after 2008. The current Metropolitan Foundation (EIN 74-1662104) listed Elena Christensen as principal officer also located at "1333 West Loop South Suite 1200, Houston, TX 77027." I believe that switch-out of foundations and "Principal Officers" was damage control because occurrence corresponded with my respective local, state, and federal awards-fraud complaints in latter 2008, and that the chameleon Bureau invoked musical-chair legalese to scrub historical culpability and confuse public records.

My whistleblower's experience determined that the Bureau franchise is a business league dependent upon its charity foundations as tax-exempt money-grabbing storefronts, which snare contributions, grants, and gifts while moonlighting specious awards. The Better Business Bureau of Metropolitan Houston Educational Foundation's 2016 Form 990 referred to the *Awards for Excellence* and shamelessly declared: "**Form 990, Part III, Line 4c:** THE BBB AWARDS FOR EXCELLENCE RECOGNIZES BUSINESSES AND NON-PROFITS FOR THEIR ACHIEVEMENTS AND COMMITMENT TO OVERALL EXCELLENCE AND QUALITY IN THE WORKPLACE PROCEEDS FROM THE EVENT HELP FUND THE BBB EDUCATION FOUNDATION WHICH EDUCATES CONSUMERS ABOUT SCAMS AND FRAUDULENT BUSINESS PRACTICES IN THE GREATER HOUSTON AREA FUNDRAISING EXPENSES OF $70,419 WERE INCURRED IN CONNECTION WITH THE EVENT, OF WHICH $14,430 WERE IN KIND DONATIONS." (Quote typed as published.) Accordingly, the Bureau's height of hypocrisy boasted that its foundation educated consumers about scams while the Houston Foundation allegedly and underhandedly operated a bogus awards program that scammed consumers. Additionally, the Houston Foundation listed phantom expenses to legitimize awards-related fundraising for the Houston Bureau while knowing that consumers had no reason to question and/or had no means to respectively review and compare accounting due to IRS privacy laws restricting access to tax returns. Furthermore, CBBB's annual reports confirm receipt of Bureau/foundation revenue as Bureau fees and/or dues that are tainted by ill-gotten awards proceeds. Henceforth, the Houston Foundation cannot deny sponsoring the *Awards for Excellence*, cannot deny specious nature of awards, cannot deny that awards-related funding tracks to CBBB, cannot deny my award fraud complaints, and cannot deny that questionable operations have continued. In fact, the Houston Foundation's Form 990 evidences how the Bureau deceives consumers through humble bragging and spurious innuendos. Therefore, I propose that CBBB's awards program is one of the greatest twenty-first-century consumer scams magnified by the organization's notoriety as a scam buster.

Larceny is theft defined as "the wrongful taking and carrying away of the personal goods of another from his or her possession with intent to convert them to the taker's own use," according to Dictionary.com. As a reminder, I filed awards-fraud complaints against the Houston Bureau with the Texas Attorney General and was ignored. Texas Penal Code, Title 7, Chapter 31, Section 31.01, addresses theft as "deception" defined as "creating or confirming by words or conduct a false impression of law or fact that is likely to affect the judgment of another in the transaction, and that the actor does not believe to be true." Section 31.01 listed additional terms that I believe also apply to awards fraud: "Appropriate" was defined as "to acquire or otherwise exercise control over property other than real property"; "Property" was defined as "a document, including money, that represents or embodies anything of value"; "Service" was defined as "labor and professional service"; and, "Steal" was defined as "to acquire property or service by theft." Accordingly, I allege that the *Awards for Excellence* program violates Section 31.01 as a professional service that operates under a veil of deception; embodies intangible value; allocates property in the form of a trophy, seal, and/or advertising paraphernalia; and, acquires public revenue by misrepresentation with intent to steal.

Money laundering was defined as "the process by which criminals disguise the original ownership and control of the proceeds of criminal conduct by making such proceeds appear to have derived from a legitimate source," according to International Compliance Association. There are three stages of money laundering including "placement," "layering," and "integration."

Racketeering was defined as "crimes committed through extortion or coercion," and a protection racket was defined as "a criminal entity [that] may threaten to cause harm to a business or an individual's private property if the owner does not pay a fee for protection," according to Investopedia. Additionally, Wikipedia expounded upon racketeering as "committing multiple violations of certain varieties within a ten-year period." The Racketeer Influenced and Corrupt Organizations Act (18 U.S.C. §§ 1961–1968), or "RICO Act" was signed into law on October 15, 1970. Furthermore, RICO's official mandate pursues "the elimination of the infiltration of organized crime and racketeering into legitimate organizations operating in interstate commerce," according to Justice.gov, which specified three respective criminal violations: (1) "Section 1962(a) makes it a crime to invest the proceeds of a pattern of racketeering activity or from collection of an unlawful debt in an enterprise affecting interstate or foreign commerce." (2) "Section 1962(b) makes it a crime to acquire or maintain an interest in an enterprise affecting interstate or foreign commerce through a pattern of racketeering activity or collection of an unlawful debt." (3) "Section 1962(c) makes it a crime to conduct the affairs of an enterprise affecting interstate or foreign commerce "through" a pattern of racketeering activity or through the alternative theory of collection of an unlawful debt." (4) "Section 1962(d) makes it a crime to conspire to commit any of the three substantive RICO offenses."

Accordingly, I allege that revenue received in any manner from the awards program is ill-gotten because the program is specious, monopolistic, and fleeces consumers. Awards revenue is hygienically steam-cleaned when laundered through CBBB in the form of fees or dues. All Bureaus are culpable and benefit from the organization's iconic brand image and collective receipt of tainted revenue. Huge sums of money are involved, yet the Bureau lacks consumer candor failing to advise a "Shermanesque" statement that the awards program is exclusive to members, is not transparent, relies on a flimsy honor code, is judged on unsubstantiated application paperwork, invokes an in-house pecking order, does not perform onsite vetting, and lacks qualification by unaffiliated certified experts. The program's praiseworthy name engages aggrandized exaggeration that implies irrefutable merit, and respective utopian promotion suggests criminal intent. Dressler's crossroads' account described CBBB's brick-and-mortar about-face that unleashed online "integrity" awards. CBBB pandered quixotic merit-fused names including *Awards for Excellence, Pinnacle,* and *Distinction Awards* that mislead consumers through trickery, implication, and deception to offset lack of a verifiable evaluation process. Furthermore, there is no qualified regulatory process to manage members' misstatements, which suggests deceptive trade practice. Until I complained, the Houston Bureau did not have an expulsion or revocation policy for misstatements. A ludicrous honor code concealed massive consumer fraud promoting Russian-roulette high stakes. Consequently, I allege that the Houston Bureau is operating a state-approved and enabled criminal enterprise underpinned by the fact that the Texas Attorney General and FTC refused to investigate and/or hold the Houston Bureau/Houston Foundation accountable. As a result, the Bureau's trickster modus operandi has tyrannically saturated the marketplace and enforced the weight and effect of a monopoly that exploits consumers by gilded propaganda, lack of information, revisionist history, and fraud.

The Better Business Bureau spent over 100 years brainwashing mainstream society into blind allegiance. Unwitting consumers were trained to tug the Bureau's bias complaint venues, accept ever-changing dictums, and patronize specious programs pillaring globalism. Typical online vigilance triage directs victims towards the Bureau, Texas Attorney General, and/or the FTC. Other options suggest the FBI, CFPB, or some obscure ".org" where complaints congregate and compost. Either way, an abundance of regulatory agencies and the IRS have progressively flouted commerce laws to empower special interests and insulate hydra organizations, including the Bureau, from consumer scrutiny.

Shameless blind-eyed FTC cronyism particularly built the Bureau's disingenuous digital dynasty. The CBBB and Bureau franchise have grown nation-state powers advanced by federally immunized deceptive trade practice. FTC personnel interact in CBBB's national programs and empower the apostate's fake mantle of government authority that proffers shell-game ethics; CBBB knocks on FTC doors and receives open-sesame wishes. As a result, FTC's aggrandizing affiliation anointed the BBB's secret society as an unregulated sovereign entity befitting its Deep State heritage. Henceforth, the Bureau's history was restricted, truth was exaggerated, and a veneer of ethics was imposed to bilk a trusting public. The FTC and Bureau shared *Roaring-Twenties'* mayhem, but nowhere was it found that the FTC supported and/or participated in the U.S.

Senate's indictment of the Bureau for Blue Sky securities fraud and racketeering. Accordingly, history should indict the FTC for complicit cronyism and for empowering the Bureau's current 1920's racketeering remix that sponsored an online business-reporting service complemented by an annual multimillion-dollar awards scam exalted by monopolistic pay-for-play rating scores. I believe that the FTC, CBBB, and Bureaus are equally culpable as scamming consumer kingpins hypocritically birddogging lower-caste scammers to maintain their sanctimonious masquerade.

Awards fraud left an irrefutable paper trail. I authored an employer-induced bogus awards application submitted in February 2008; the Bureau nominated my application for the Pinnacle award in May 2008; I reported awards fraud to and was dismissed by the Houston Bureau in October 2008, the CBBB in November 2008, the Texas Attorney General in December 2008, and, the FTC on February 10, 2009. During the same time period, in January 2009, CBBB systemically launched its unevaluated pay-for-play ratings score program that extorted expensive memberships from nonmember businesses upon threat of disparagement. The ratings program was married to the bogus online awards program unleashed in 2000 to promote members and eliminate competition. Two months later, April 19, 2009, CBBB nudged the FTC to rubberstamp its new "accountability program" under the premise that "the BBB system seeks to promote ethical business and advertising practices." Five months later, August 15, 2009, the genie FTC magically granted CBBB's omnipotent wish based on esoteric interests, ethereal ethics, and bellwether affiliations.

After leaving my thug employer, on September 5, 2008, awards fraud was hanging in the wind. I was subject to the employer's blackmail and left liable for consumer fraud as the author of the bogus application that won the coveted Pinnacle award worth millions of dollars in commercial trade. Winning both the Pinnacle and Winner of Distinction awards made me realize that the only difference between first and second place awards was pomp and circumstance. Both awards were unevaluated, and applications were not verified by field audits to prove tangible merit. My good-faith intentions approached the Houston Bureau, as the awards patron, to right wrongs consequent to the employer's refusal to implement application procedures as he promised me. I expected the Bureau's welcoming cooperation, investigation, and resolution through revocation of the employer's Pinnacle. The staff knew me from years of handling complaints and participating in the *Awards for Excellence* in addition to having just completed a successful arbitration proceeding a few days earlier. Like most consumers, I knew vintage Better Business Bureau propaganda and accepted the organization at venerable face value underscored by my advertising degree and oath to ethical business practice.

I spoke with Monica, "Investigations & Trade Practices Coordinator," and scheduled an in-office meeting under the promise of confidentiality and judicious veil of arbitration, but plans were delayed by category-2 Hurricane Ike's Galveston landfall on Saturday, September 13, 2008 (the Houston Bureau would later hijack my private employment trial and exploit the storm to attempt felonious breach of fiduciary counterclaims to silence my complaints of awards fraud). I met Monica, on October 3, 2008, at the Houston Galleria office and explained the employer's awards fraud in detail; that application procedures were never implemented; that services did not deserve the Pinnacle; and that operations had deteriorated to the extent that customers were calling and complaining due to shoddy workmanship and dangerous aftereffects. I repeatedly emphasized that the Bureau's investigation should focus on my application theme about employer/employee training and not my employer/employee issues that the Bureau did not handle. Correspondence continued for the next two weeks and Monica's last email, dated October 15, 2008, advised, "I wanted to let you know that Dan did receive your email. We are still looking into this matter."

The next day, I received Parsons' rude email advising that he deep-sixed my awards complaint after his team huddle with my former employer and his wife: "Ms. Cain ... OK ... enough. I have been in the loop through all of this. Monica, the head of our education foundation (who hosts the BBB awards) and I met with (redacted) this morning to hear what they had to say. From my standpoint, suffice to say that the BBB is taking no further role. This is an employer-employee issue out of the purview of any action we could or would take. If you wish to seek out other "BBB authorities," do so. They will tell you the same thing. That said, the Foundation is still seeking some information and they will contact you, in writing, with their findings."

My first impression surfaced as utter shock followed by blistering anger. In eight succinct sentences Parsons arrogantly discredited and vilified me while guilefully dodging the subject of awards fraud. He also misstated Monica's business title as "head of our education foundation" when her actual title was "Investigations & Trade Practices Coordinator," which had nothing to do with awards. In fact, the Better Business Bureau of Metropolitan Houston Educational Foundation's 2016 Form 990, "Part VII Section A. Officers, Directors, Trustees, Key Employees, and Highest Compensated Employees," listed Candace Twyman as "Executive Director" of the foundation with compensation of "$110,172" in addition to "other compensation" for "$3,527." There is a huge disparity between an investigator and a foundation officer particularly when the same shell game resurfaced in my 2015 trial, and the Houston Bureau attempted to present Twyman as a perjured witness masquerading as a lowly records clerk; respective court documents evidence Twyman's "execution of a document using deception" with respective felony holding a seven-year statute of limitations;

trial ended January 2015. Furthermore, Parsons neglected to mention that he was also a principal officer at the Houston Foundation. Accordingly, the Bureau was a master of obfuscation, exaggeration, misrepresentation, and deflection while reminding that each of the preceding options represent deception.

The Houston Bureau hijacked my private employment trial, inserted the awards director as a key witness for the employer, presented cover copies of my awards fraud complaints as examples of slander, staged felony charges of breach of fiduciary duties and theft, and then attempted to avoid any mention of the *Awards for Excellence*. The Witness List named "Better Business Bureau" followed by "Corporate Representative, Custodian of Records and Candace Twyman" with the collective claiming, "*Knowledge of the false statements made by Caryn Cain about [Employer Redacted] and [Company Redacted] to the Better Business Bureau.*" The Bureau strategically placed Twyman's name in a deceptively contrived manner at the end of low-ranking job titles to confuse and omit her real conflictive corporate title as "Executive Director, The Better Business Bureau Education Foundation" (evidenced by the Houston Foundation's 2016 Form 990 and Twyman's email verification forwarded to my attention, dated February 15, 2008, which accepted my application that won the Pinnacle). Implication suggested opposing counsel meant to weaponize Twyman's awards' expertise against me under the obscure guise of a records clerk. To the contrary, I made no false statements and supported my allegations with evidence. Additionally, I wrote the awards' application as chief financial officer and operations backup and insisted that my fraud claims be verified by field audits, which the Bureau refused. Furthermore, I never spoke with Twyman regarding awards fraud and only corresponded with Monica and Parsons. Additionally, the Houston Bureau violated confidentiality and business practice; Parsons' email stated that my complaint was "out of the purview of any action we could or would take," yet he attempted to imprison me through the Houston Bureau's manipulation of my private lawsuit evidenced by the employer's respective depositions, counterclaims, witnesses, and trial proceedings.

In fact, I never heard from the Houston Foundation. On October 29, 2008, I submitted fraud complaints to CBBB. And, on November 13, 2008, I received a response from Shirley Wuest, signed as "Consultant, BBB Resource Center." In part, she replied, "There was no marketplace issue in this instance. BBBs do not process complaints regarding employee/employer issues. We are therefore unable to respond to your questions. Please contact your local, county or state board of labor or your office of employment services regarding this matter. You should find the telephone number in your local telephone directory." Her message seemed coordinated with Parsons' "Enough" dismissal of my complaints and Wuest listed him as a copied recipient of her letter. Once again, deflection persisted with no mention of my fundamental complaint of awards fraud. I believed that Parsons pre-qualified his response to me with CBBB as the sovereign regulator of the franchise and that the national headquarters determined ultimate legal strategy to convolute my whistleblower's complaints into a disgruntled employee.

At the time, I wasn't aware that Parsons held concurrent leadership positions with both the Houston Bureau and Houston Foundation, which was a throwback to the 1920s when advertising luminaries like James C. Auchincloss multitasked several prestigious positions as governor of the NYSE, president of the National Better Business Bureau, Inc., and president of the New York Bureau. Apparently, my complaints spooked Parsons' double accountability that threatened dual incrimination because he ditched his position with the Better Business Bureau of South Texas Consumer Education Foundation Inc.

My award complaints submitted in October 2008 preceded national rollout of CBBB's new rating score. At the time, I did not know that CBBB was in the process of launching a new rating score program in January 2009. My awards fraud complaints threatened systemic launch that explained CBBB's abrupt dismissal of my complaint. Pie-in-the-sky awards and rating programs were designed to complement each other by engaging subconscious "good cop bad cop" sleight of hand. The awards seduced consumers with enticing illusion of irrefutable excellence while the rating score extorted businesses for memberships under threat of disparagement. Ironically, in 2010, a conservative ABC *20/20* documentary shockingly exposed the globalist Bureau's rating score as a pay-for-play scam to coerce memberships. But, by 2016, ABC was considered a globalist news organization espousing "fake news" and would never drop a dime on the globalist Bureau. As a result, the ABC *20/20* rating score exposé is recherché history. Further irony involved the exposé's interview with former Connecticut Attorney General Richard Blumenthal who previously chastised CBBB's national Torch awards. But today's Senator Blumenthal supports the Democratic Party's globalist radical policies, which suggests cronyism with CBBB.

The Bureau's business reporting methodology reports status of any unaccredited business that is akin to disparagement and ruination emphasizing respective ability to control the marketplace. Accordingly, B-men have no excuse for failing to clearly advise consumers of awards' shortcomings that threaten consumer welfare and fleece millions of dollars. The Bureau operates moment-to-moment at the helm of a keyboard; is unregulated and freewheeling; and is immunized against criminal implication by a simpatico FTC that ignores victimization of innocent shoppers pickled by a trolling Pied Piper piping digital enchantment.

I was involved only in local awards and did not participate in national or international programs; not every Bureau offered awards due to location and business capacity. My former employer operated in Houston and was a member of the Houston Bureau whose foundation sponsored the *Awards for Excellence*. Award names were customized, but programs followed a CBBB-approved generic format.

CBBB created the integrity awards program as a cost-effective online cash cow whose website operation dramatically marginalized expenses. In fact, Dressler inadvertently exposed the awards as the organization's profit-based blueprint for twenty-first-century digital evolution. He described the watershed juncture in May 1994 when CBBB was considering the Internet as a financial savior; the turning point when the Bureau chose profit over truth. Six years later, CBBB launched the online awards program indicating that Dressler's murder mystery interwove real-time chronology similar to Upton Sinclair's resonating classic, *The Jungle*. Awards were tied to accreditation (membership) that connected to the Bureau's endorsement of members and disparagement of nonmembers. Consequently, the organization transformed into a kingpin validating CBBB's capitalist strategy that promoted revenue, monopolization, and globalism.

In 1936, H. J. Kenner invented incriminating tag words that I allege describe the Bureau's modern awards program including "misleading," "insinuations," "not founded," "imply," "violate," "not honest," "implication," "exaggerated," "predatory," "baits," "not capable of proof," "untrue," "impressions," "unfair attacks," and "implied." Additionally, Kenner listed nine "misuses of advertising" as follows:

1. Misleading statements, insinuations, and illustrations that give impressions of value or service not inherent in the product.
2. Suggestions of cures and palliatives, and lures of beauty and health building, not founded on scientific fact.
3. Part of truths of scientific information that imply a benefit not supported by science.
4. Indecent copy and pictures that violate the privacy of life.
5. Testimonials that are not honest or honorable in their implication.
6. Comparative prices that are exaggerated or misleading.
7. Predatory price-cutting and the use of "baits" to mislead the public.
8. Claims of general underselling not capable of proof and untrue in their insinuations and impressions.
9. Unfair attacks, actual or implied, on competitors or competing products.

The awards program undermines founders' respective achievements and contributions. In 1888, George Presbury Rowell, the father of advertising, introduced *Printers' Ink* Advertising Journal that he endearingly called "The Little Schoolmaster." Additionally, Rowell created the first awards and rating system for his renowned *American Newspaper Directory's* 5,778 newspapers that he intertwined with *Printers' Ink*. He orchestrated an advertising merit system that was personally regulated and graded based on actual business practice. Rowell encouraged ethical standards in the publishing and advertising industries by issuing "The Little Schoolmaster In The Art of Advertising" silver trophy, and *Printers' Ink* provided a monthly listing that marked upstanding publications with a star; those without a star lost business. The Bureau "borrowed" Rowell's award-incentive reporting process to format an online business-reporting service denoting accredited versus unaccredited businesses with stars replaced by rating scores; unaccredited businesses with low rating scores lost business.

The newspaper industry followed Rowell's example and established the "Truth Trophy" in the form of a silver globe set on an ebony base with the word "Truth" inscribed in gold across its western continents. In 1913, the newspapers in Baltimore presented their city's Vigilance Committee the trophy to begin an annual tradition of awarding adherence to truth in advertising.

The Bureau introduced the pyramid-shaped Pinnacle as its collective adaptation of the Little Schoolmaster and Truth Trophy. Symbolic connection to Freemasonry remains questionable. "Time For Change" stated, "The pyramid is a symbol of human development." Otherwise, Scottisrite.org argued, "While the all-seeing eye of providence is a common symbol used by Masons and others to represent the omniscience of God, when combined with a pyramid it has no official Masonic meaning."

The Truth Seal was introduced in Fort Worth, Texas, two years after the first New York Vigilance Committee was launched in 1912 and represented the forerunner of the modern "Accreditation Seal" and awards emblem as an endorsement of business and guarantee of excellence. Kenner described the Truth Seal's use of an honor code as an early attempt by founders to cost-effectively barter the Vigilance Committee's reputation for profit: "Whether or not the new Truth Seal should be licensed to advertisers for a fee, if and when they signed a pledge to stand behind their advertised statements, was a question which gave rise to discussion at the time. In 1914, the executive committee of the association authorized the advertising club at Fort Worth to experiment with the idea, under the guidance of the club's president, James Montgomery Brown." Kenner referred to the powerful Associated Advertising Clubs of America as "the association" that nurtured and influenced the early advertising clubs to convert into Vigilance Committees after 1912 and to adopt the name "Better Business Bureau" after 1916. Accordingly, the Truth Seal proved that endorsement existed and carried a price tag since the Bureau's conception. Furthermore, the fact that Kenner publicly exposed controversial licensing "for a fee" was phenomenal and emphasized the Old Guard Bureau's relative transparency compared to the New Guard Bureau's tight-lipped secrecy invoking disclaimers to dodge founders' morally binding legacy.

There were critics and advocates of the Truth Seal. Critics were Puritans born during the austere era of the Civil War and Christian temperance movements; they were preachers, editors, publishers, agents, retailers, and idealists whose moral convictions felt pimping an ungovernable endorsement encouraged dishonest business. Kenner wrote, "The opponents of the plan contended that it was undesirable to farm out the Truth Seal endorsement for a price; they maintained that, though it might be feasible to investigate products and to approve them on the basis of scientific, physical tests, blanket endorsement for the claims of individual advertisers was impracticable and open to serious objection." To the contrary, supporters were capitalists who worshipped revenue over dishonesty; that implementation of an honor code underscored by threat of revocation assured best business. Accordingly, Kenner stated, "Advocates thought that, if the seal were granted and then withdrawn from those who violated truth standards, such penalty would be more effective than statutory law in curbing misstatements and that advertisers who paid for use of the emblem would take special pains with the accuracy of their claims, so as not to lose it."

Kenner agreed with critics that endorsement was "controversial" and warned, "Experience through the years has borne out that judgment." His following comment, "Today, the certification of advertisers' products to the public by emblems of associations and others, besides the makers, is by some considered an easy way to win public confidence," bridged time and substantiated my claim that the Bureau proffers its prestigious endorsement to peddle fake awards. In fact, the Fort Worth advertising club unsuccessfully launched the Truth Seal. Kenner conceded, "The experiment went on in that city for about a year, and the plan was then abandoned." Henceforth, a precarious endorsement based on a sketchy honor code will never sustain truth as I proved with the *Awards for Excellence*.

It seems that globalist successors used Kenner's documentation as a capitalist's blueprint to fabricate modern operations and programs. As a result, a stark contrast in policies and ethics is evident between two Bureau managers who published books from two different timelines. In-between Kenner's book published in 1936 and Dressler's book published in 2000, the Bureau adopted a disingenuous endorsement disclaimer that it "does not endorse any product, service or company." I suggest that a substantial lawsuit encouraged the Old Guard's endorsement disclaimer and why the Seal was buried until 2000 when deteriorated moral compass and dire financial straits opened Kenner's book and renamed the Truth Trophy and Truth Seal as the Pinnacle and Integrity Awards. Consumers will never know the entire truth because the Bureau has hidden most of its early history including ruinous lawsuits. Additionally, successors control the modern court system to make sure dirt stays swept under the gilded judicial rug.

THE APO$TATE

Former AG Blumenthal filed a complaint with CBBB regarding the national "2008 BBB Torch Award Program (TAP)." The TAP complaint questioned qualification process and validity of award applications, "Specifically, my investigation questioned the reliability of the self-nominating process in which the TAP judges ... used only the documents and information provided by the nominees to make their decisions. Furthermore, the judges did not contact third parties, such as customers or other businesses or government agencies, to verify the accuracy of any of the information contained in applications." My complaint added the fact that judges did not perform onsite application verifications.

The court system empowered bogus Bureau programs evidenced by a ground swell of liberal globalism driven by radical news. The U.S. Supreme Court first proved invasive Democratic bias on July 5, 2012, when upholding the Obamacare mandate and ruling its draconian penalty to be a reasonable tax. Thereafter, a Florida district court invoked the First Amendment to validate the Bureau's bias rating score under the rights of an opinion despite blatant defamation and consumer fraud involving the annual theft of millions of dollars reaped under false pretense.

As of this publication, I am not aware of any awards fraud-related lawsuits aside from awards-related insignia, but I fear that lawsuits alleging awards fraud will skate on TCPA-induced free speech same as rating score litigation. Hope for regulatory reform appeared in 2017 with a False Claims Act-related lawsuit, *United States ex rel. Gohil v. Aventis, Inc.*, No. 02-2964, 2017 U.S. Dist. LEXIS 3236 (E.D. Pa. Jan. 9, 2017), filed in Pennsylvania, that denied the defendant's invocation of free speech and ruled actions "were false and/or misleading." According to Whistleblowers Blog, "The Relator alleges that Aventis trained and directed its sales force to misrepresent the safety and effectiveness of the chemotherapy agent in order to expand the market share for Taxotere beyond its FDA approval as a "second line treatment"" and "that Aventis had engaged in a kickback scheme that included sham grants, exorbitant speaking fees, and excessive preceptorship fees paid to physicians in order to incentivize them to prescribe Taxotere."

The *Awards for Excellence* program promotes local members as a cost-effective online shell game bandying misrepresentation, theatrics, and trickery to produce profit at the expense of members and consumers. Businesses pay expensive memberships to participate. Contestants pay pricey meal tickets to fund the lavish awards banquet and prestigious trophies. Pinnacle and Distinction recipients generate revenue for businesses by advertising Bureau-branded awards. Ultimately, consumers bear the brunt of bunkum when patronizing overvalued award winners who return wealth to the Bureau through memberships and advertising. Such activity was called a racket during the Prohibition era.

Award recipients are selected under shade of melodramatic secrecy.

Application entries embrace laureled services. Strict deadline protocol requires application submittal on a specified day in mid-February, by 4:00 p.m. In March, about a month after the deadline, generic congratulatory letters notify award winners; letters serve as laudatory teasers and invite contestants to purchase tickets ($85 dollars for individuals or $500 for tables) in order to attend awards distribution where they "might" win the coveted Pinnacle. In the interim, between February and May, judges finalize nominations. Hollywood suspense builds until the first two weeks of every May when the Bureau hosts a glitzy tour-de-force banquet to announce revered Pinnacle winners while acknowledging residual participants as Distinction runners-up. Competition, curiosity, and cronyism guarantee turnout attendance. Afterwards, the Houston Bureau's website triumphantly heralds the latest gilded award-winning superstars.

A review of the Houston Bureau's annual awards' statistics for Pinnacle and Distinction recipients indicated mushrooming success. Retrieved data was as follows: the year 2007 allocated 64 Distinction awards on May 2, 2007; 2008 issued a total of 105 winners with 21 Pinnacles and 84 Distinctions awarded on May 7, 2008; no data between 2009 and 2011; 2012 issued a total of 245 winners with 30 Pinnacles and 215 Distinctions awarded May 2, 2012; 2013 issued a total of 252 winners with 32 Pinnacles and 220 Distinctions awarded May 8, 2013; 2014 issued a total of 262 winners with 32 Pinnacles and 230 Distinctions awarded May 7, 2014; 2015 issued a total of 292 winners with 32 Pinnacles and 260 Distinctions awarded May 13, 2015; 2016 issued a total of 272 winners with 32 Pinnacles and 240 Distinctions awarded May 11, 2016; 2017 issued a total of 308 winners with 32 Pinnacles and 276 Distinctions awarded May 10, 2017; 2018 issued a total of 283 winners with 31 Pinnacles and 252 Distinctions awarded May 9, 2018; 2019 issued a total of 264 winners with 28 Pinnacles and 264 Distinctions awarded May 15, 2019; and 2020 was delayed due to the COVID-19 pandemic.

I believe that after 2010 the Bureau threw open hallowed doors and issued Distinction awards to all participants as suggested by subsequent contests that evidenced an unlimited number of recipients per business class. Previous limited-award protocol was revised when empty-handed members complained that omission inherently red-flagged their products and services and demoted them to nonmember status without an award to boast superiority. The Bureau stemmed the tide of ship-jumpers by engaging a free-for-all awards allocation further emphasizing deceptive trade practice. As a result, a slew of fake awards was dumped on the streets. More awards equated to increased revenue, brand image advertising, and market share for the Bureau and minions.

It should also be noted that the ratings statistics for 2015 winners' business files posted a majority of "A+" rating scores. I personally verified each winner's online status as of May 24, 2015, and realized two glaring incongruities contrary to the Houston Bureau's strict awards guideline policies. One Distinction recipient featured an "F" rating and was listed as unaccredited. Another unaccredited Distinction recipient held an "A+" rating and was a former 2013 Pinnacle winner. Both issues involved nonpayment of expensive membership fees that can vary from several hundred to several thousand dollars a year depending upon size of the business.

Above all, the membership fee must be paid because everything involving the Bureau boils down to money. The euphemism for a membership fee is "eligibility" defined as, "All applicants must be in good standing as an accredited business with the BBB of Metropolitan Houston." Only members can participate in awards and nonpayment of membership should be an automatic disqualifier, yet a prejudicial disingenuous accreditation process, fake awards program, and flawed logic allowed both aforementioned Distinction winners to remain unaccredited for several months while being promoted online as accredited award recipients to untold thousands of consumers. The awards were issued on May 13, 2015, but three months later, on August 13, 2015, both still wore unaccredited halos. Both members also continued advertising awards' insignia even though stipulated guidelines required discontinuation of advertising and return of respective insignia due to nonpayment of membership. Bureau policy disclaimed: "You can use the Logo ONLY as long as you maintain accredited status with the Houston BBB. Once you no longer have accredited status with the Houston BBB, you must immediately cease all use of the Logo including but not limited to, removal from your website, advertisements, commercials, billboards, social media, signage, and vehicles." Additionally, an "F" rating combined with an unaccredited status questioned adherence to supposedly strict accreditation qualifications. Circumstances proved that a bogus ratings program and flexible leniency favored members. Eight months later, on January 5, 2016, a follow-up review of both winners' business profiles indicated "A+" rating scores and approved accreditation. I am intentionally elaborating membership accreditation to pre-empt the Bureau from slithering out of respective accountability.

When initially reviewing award winners' business files in August 2015, I called one of the unaccredited businesses rated "A+" to question their award allocation because only paying members can participate. A professional businesswoman expertly responded that "the awards system is a process to recognize and reward members." She spoke eloquently but dodged my question regarding the Bureau's accreditation policy that should have disqualified her company's award for nonpayment of fees. Our brief conversation was abruptly ended by her assurance that "the business was in the process of renewing its accreditation." I obviously struck a nerve. She offered the same shifty clandestine cavalier invincible empowered immune elitism that was projected by the president of the Houston Bureau while he allegedly collaborated with my former employer to ruin me and hide their crony awards fraud. Her brochure-glossed answer suggested that she was one of the Bureau's Silver Foxes who judged the *Awards for Excellence* and were owners or officers representing prestigious businesses in Houston and surrounding areas.

About 31 Pinnacle winners were routinely cut from the herd and honored to promote regalia, mystery, and drama akin to Hollywood's prestigious Oscar nominations. Members essentially waited their turn for Pinnacle rotation. If any business repeatedly hogged 1st place, upper echelon members complained to the Silver Foxes and complainants coincidentally won the following year. Wealthy and/or influential participants enjoyed yearly pinnacle status.

No one stops to query how the Bureau's small brick-and-mortar office, with limited personnel, expertise, and financial means, can accurately evaluate a short-fused crowded precarious widespread competitive multi-business merit program. An ethical awards process based on "excellence" should require the Bureau to physically qualify each awards application; meaning that judges must physically visit and personally evaluate hundreds of businesses within four months' timeframe. To the contrary, the Bureau operates a profit-based awards program that retrieves, launders, and exploits members' respective revenue. In fact, the Bureau has no legitimate onsite certification process to qualify contest applications despite turnstile of millions of dollars every year, yet the Bureau advertises implication of unquestionable qualified excellence, which infers deceptive trade practice. Furthermore, the Bureau is peddling a fake bill of goods that hoodwink consumers into contracting potentially hazardous services. In fact, I became a whistleblower because of such compounding fraud. My employer operated a home-improvement business and he stole the lucrative Pinnacle to attract business in a downturned economy; he aggressively advertised himself as a Pinnacle winner while promoting deteriorating operations and untrained installers whose deviant morals and shoddy workmanship endangered consumers.

In comparison, maritime regulator American Bureau of Shipping (ABS) implements a stringent onsite qualification process that supports world-renowned certification. Services can cost several thousand dollars because of multiple cross-checks that verify workplace and public safety. The ABS evaluation unit employs a cadre of highly educated professionals including geologists, oceanographers, and petroleum engineers. Businesses submit to lengthy evaluation testing and complete intense assessment packets before earning tight-fisted approval. To the contrary, the Bureau's awards program is specious and exaggerates stringent member certification and evaluation by advertising merited innuendos such as *Awards for Excellence*, "BBBest," and "crème de la crème."

Encroaching twenty-first-century consumer-advocacy competition forced the Bureau to ditch piety and corporatize. The Bureau's renowned dependency upon memberships and donations was supplemented by commercializing business services and expanding evaluation of marketplace commerce. According to Clevelandbbb100.org, "The first BBB site on the Internet (not even yet called World Wide Web) was from the BBB of Massachusetts, Main, Rhode Island & Vermont in 1991, providing a searchable reliability report database. It was one of the earliest sites on the Internet to do so." At the time, though, CBBB was still deliberating how to coordinate advertising memberships with gainful commercialism.

As of May 2, 1994, Dressler wrote that "no decision had been made by the nearly 150 local Better Business Bureaus about permitting members of local Bureaus to advertise that they are BBB members. The concern here was protecting the integrity of the Better Business Bureau trademark." Additionally, the Bureau's 1994 disclaimer touted, "As a matter of policy, the Better Business Bureau does not endorse any product, service or company." Six years later, though, CBBB introduced the integrity awards that promoted the Bureau's subliminal endorsement with intent to build a brainwashed fan base. Scheming B-men profitized the Bureau's iconic image to introduce a scam awards program underwritten by a wily de facto endorsement disclaimer that abused consumers' trust and the Bureau's revered reputation.

In fact, the Bureau's vintage history revolved around endorsement, so it is deceitful for the modern Bureau to deny such policy. Confusion and lack of information are advertising decoys disguising quackery. Successors have gone to great lengths to hide predecessors' incriminating past and why I have also gone to great lengths to expose it! The Bureau's early-nineteen-hundred proclivities set the stage for present-day deceptive trade practice. Consequently, the Bureau should be held accountable for nondisclosure and misrepresentation in the marketplace that has reverted commerce to horse-and-buggy days of caveat emptor and buyer beware!

The awards program was designed to financially revitalize the Bureau, enable twenty-first-century expansion, and dominate encroaching consumer advocacy groups. CBBB hid monopolistic operations under a non-profit business league and charity foundation. The organization profited from suppression of free trade by expressing and/or implying that members were superior to nonmembers. Generations of bias propaganda conditioned consumers to only shop members endorsed by the Bureau. As a result, nonmembers were alienated and victimized by quixotic programs like the *Awards for Excellence*.

I take credit for forcing the Houston Bureau to introduce its first "Compliance Statement" to address members' misstatements on award applications. After my complaints in 2008, the Houston Foundation added a disclaimer to its 2009 application in addition to four ethics-related "Entry Form Questions" that stated, "I understand that by signing this application I certify our compliance with

AWARDS FOR EXCELLENCE

federal, state and local laws and regulations governing our business or industry. Any misstatement of material fact may justify recession of the award. We agree to abide by the BBB guidelines for referencing the BBB Awards for Excellence in any advertisement or public announcement. All submitted entries become property of the BBB and cannot be returned." Accordingly, I allege that previous omission of the Compliance Statement emphasized the Bureau's disregard for truth and emphasis on profitable memberships. Furthermore, I choked on the phrase "compliance with federal, state and local laws." It is my opinion that the Deep State Better Business Bureau controls such entities and laws, e.g., the Texas Attorney General ignored my awards-fraud complaints against the Houston Bureau; and, John Moore Services' two lawsuits against the Houston Bureau were overturned by the Deep State Better Business Bureau's control of the courts and Texas legislature that amended TCPR Chapter 51 pertaining to the Houston Bureau's request to stay trial proceedings during an interlocutory appeal.

After my incriminating awards-fraud allegations and IRS-related fraud implications against the employer during trial in 2015, the Houston Bureau produced an extended Compliance Statement on its awards' application. Disclaimer warned, "I understand that by signing this application I certify my compliance with federal, state, and local laws and regulations governing my business, charity or industry. Any misstatement of material fact may justify recession of the award. I understand that the BBB will provide guidelines for using and/or referencing the BBB Awards for Excellence and any trademark or logos associated with the Awards for Excellence. I agree to abide by and follow the BBB guidelines, as well as all future versions of the BBB guidelines, as they may be amended from time to time at the sole discretion of the Houston Bureau and/or the Better Business Bureau of Metropolitan Houston Educational Foundation. I understand and agree that, should I no longer be accredited with or a member in good standing of the Houston BBB, I shall cease all use of the trademarks and logos associated with the Awards for Excellence. All submitted entries become property of the BBB and cannot be returned."

Accordingly, the Houston Bureau/Houston Foundation resorted to righteous sanctimonious quasi-governmental overkill to mask their ultimate culpability for sponsoring a specious awards program. The Compliance Statement was updated with prosecutorial legalese *after* the Houston Bureau hijacked my private employment trial in 2015 when I exposed the employer's awards fraud. The updated statement vindicated me and incriminated the Houston Bureau for collaborating with a criminal member, knowingly promoting a criminal's business services to consumers, and perpetrating unlawful actions against me before, during, and after a private trial with intent to harm me and silence my damning awards-fraud testimony. Furthermore, I found it reprehensibly sickening that

THE APO$TATE

the updated compliance statement exploited the U.S. Constitution to justify and legitimize a bias specious online game with no merit to its name.

A compliance statement is only as good as its whistleblower. I was a rare commodity for speaking up. To date, I have been the only one who has dared to report the Bureau's phony *Awards for Excellence* contest. Furthermore, it seems absurd that the Bureau thinks adding more questions to their application would whitewash an unethical contest, but Bureau overkill is a time-honored practice exemplified by Kenner's *The Fight for Truth in Advertising* that smothered critics' accusations with an avalanche of Bureau reform achievements and high-profile playdates. Similarly, the Bureau added more ethics questions to the award application to invoke perception of a rigorous interrogation intended to superficially embed merit.

A contemporary generation respects the Bureau and its programs as evidenced by the *Rip-off Report*, a consumer advocate website that monitors Bureau fraud. One of its recent surveys quoted upsetting statistics emphasizing the extent that the Bureau's bogus programs and services have snookered the public; that "70% of consumers say they are more likely to buy from a BBB accredited business and 84% believe this BBB accreditation means a business meets high standards of trustworthiness." Data supported my reason for writing *The Apostate* to educate innocent consumers who are being blind-sided and egregiously exploited by the Bureau. I unveiled the Bureau's shocking secrets that proved the legendary icon's proclivity for deceptive trade; that the *Awards for Excellence* program was a byproduct of bygone hypocritical practice and mindset; and that the saint is a sinner!

The "Fruit of the Tree" doctrine could theoretically be abstracted to embrace members profiting from an ill-conceived awards program; the tree being the Bureau and fruit representing awards. During trial opposing counsel projected blurred cover pages of my awards-related complaint letters on courtroom walls as evidence of "slander" against the employer without advising subject matter, regulatory recipients, and that my letters also incriminated the Houston Bureau for awards fraud. I undermined the Bureau's deception by emphatically accusing the employer of awards fraud and called him "a liar and a thief." As a result, awards fraud and the Bureau's involvement were inadvertently entered into court record, so every participating member, with exception of rank-and-file employees, is now equally liable. Furthermore, the Bureau and members should not rely on disingenuous disclaimers to continue cheating consumers with fake awards because disclaimers are improvised loopholes contrived to camouflage consumer fraud emphasizing that "cover-up is worse than the crime!"

The employer maniacally advertised his Pinnacle victory to the public placing enormous billboards throughout Houston freeways emblazoning his picture next to "TRUST." He ran radio and television advertising promoting his

Pinnacle; one crony endorser exaggerated that he won the Pinnacle three years in a row. Furthermore, the Bureau's celebrated Hall of Fame website rotated the employer's picture, name, and business next to the words, "Trust, Honesty, Integrity." Additionally, on May 21, 2015, five months after trial and eight days after the Houston Bureau's "23rd Awards for Excellence" banquet, the employer's website advertised, "Our company prides itself in offering trustworthy and reliable service to the great city of Houston and its surrounding areas. We've been the recipient of the prestigious Pinnacle Award from the Better Business Bureau (BBB); the Pinnacle Award is the highest award presented by the BBB within their business category. In addition, the BBB has also given us the Award for Excellence from 2006 through 2015." Whereas the employer's write-up sounds impressive, it is misleading. Above all, we are talking about fake awards with every mention and advertisement thereof representing consumer fraud. The employer was issued a runner-up award, but implied that he continued to win the Pinnacle. Additionally, and most pathetically, the employer kept flouting his one and only ill-gotten Pinnacle. He learned from the best; in typical Bureau style he employed weasel wordsmithry, exaggeration, and implication. His Distinction award was referred to as "the Award for Excellence" because description obfuscated and aggrandized type of award reiterating why the Bureau adopted the name.

I continued to monitor the employer's company and service issues with results corroborating my initial complaints submitted to the Houston Bureau. My Pinnacle-winning award application promoted customer safety as well as financial and installation security that the employer diabolically violated. My whistleblower's warnings proved true and his company spiraled into deteriorating operations while annually rubberstamped with an "A+" rating score. He falsely advertised vetted certified installers yet omitted background verifications and hired felons who perpetrated home theft and problematic construction.

The Bureau's time-honored code of silence has embedded, empowered, and spread awards fraud over the years. A *Who's Who* of prominent hometown members participates in the awards program that generates millions of dollars in kickbacks to the Bureau and CBBB every year. Accordingly, B-men stalked me reiterating that snitches get stitches for threatening their cash cow

Only Pinnacle winners can advertise on the Houston Bureau's popular website. In 2008, I contracted for the employer a slot of Pinnacle-endorsed advertising for $2,500 (I do not remember the length of contract). According to BBB. org's 2012 annual report, "BBBs' websites are among the most visited in North America, with more than ten million visitors a month in 2012 (nearly a third of them returning)." The 2013 annual report listed "132,385,251 BBB Business Review Inquiries" as a total yearly statistic for "Better Business Bureaus in the U.S. and Canada."

THE APO$TATE

The Houston Bureau continues to imply through parsed words and gilded legalese that its awards are stringently evaluated. On May 11, 2014, the Houston Bureau's "2014 BBB Awards for Excellence" webpage boasted, "This coveted award recognizes your commitment to excellence in the marketplace and gives consumers greater confidence in choosing your company. Your organization should be proud of your success." Be it noted that afore sprinkled weasel words "coveted," "excellence," "confidence," and "proud" were incorporated to legitimize a bogus program. The Bureau knows that skeptical consumers seek meritorious figures of speech when choosing contractors and why consumers pay more money for award winners. As a result, an impregnable twenty-first-century global empire arose from the scattershot of confusing bits and pieces of rules, regulations, and disclaimers that dodge connecting incriminating dots. It is unconscionable that the Bureau unleashed a multimillion-dollar merit scam despite forefathers' warning in 1914 of respective controversy and failure.

The franchise's member accreditation disclaimer engages trickery by working the shadows of fine print to spout generic denial of evaluation and endorsement of members' products and services. Disclaimed misleading confusing vague shifty legalese does not mention awards, but ethereally projects an all-inclusive protective canopy over all of the Bureau's programs and services. Furthermore, double standards question if the nonprofit practices what it preaches pertaining to "Standards for Charity Accountability" that require "truthfulness of their representations."

The public has no idea of the colossal power emanating from CBBB and the Houston Bureau! In July 2012, the *Houston Business Journal* article, "Houston has more than 100,000 small businesses," reported, "Out of the 122,517 businesses in the Houston-Sugar Land-Baytown metropolitan area, 119,005 are small businesses ... That ranks the Houston area No. 9 nationwide and No. 2 statewide for total number of small businesses .... Additionally, nearly 73 percent of Houston's small businesses - 86,854 - are microbusinesses ..." The article also described a small business as "having fewer than 100 employees" and microbusiness as "having fewer than 10 employees." In April 2014, the *Texas Monthly* article, "As If You Needed It, Further Proof That Houston Is So Much Bigger Than Most Cities," stated, "[Houston] is roughly the same size as the entire island of Oahu." And the website Reactionsearch.com advised, "In 2010 the Houston-Sugar Land-Baytown metropolitan statistical area's gross domestic product was $385 billion. By GDP, the Houston MSA would be the world's 22nd largest economy if it were its own country" and that "Houston is second only to New York City for cities with the highest number of Fortune 500 Companies" with 25 of such companies located within 50 miles of Houston and 23 located in Houston.

Around 2010, the Houston Bureau published a revised awards usage disclaimer: "**NEW** guidelines for the use of the Awards for Excellence logo," which have remained basically the same as of 2017. Seven guidelines were listed: "1) Anytime you advertise or otherwise state in writing that you won the award, you must indicate the year (2014) the award was received .... 2) You can only advertise the receipt of this award in our 18 county BBB service area. The only exception is on your company website. 3) You are not allowed to say you are the "best" in customer service ethics, or any **category** of business. 4) You are not allowed to use the word "endorse." You CAN use the word "congratulations." 5) You must indicate on the award if the corporate office received the award or if it was the franchisee .... 6) You can no longer use the Logo with the wreath/branches even when you indicate the year. It is not an approved Logo .... 7) You can use the Logo ONLY as long as you maintain accredited status with the Houston BBB. Once you no longer have accredited status with the Houston BBB, you must immediately cease all use of the Logo including but not limited to, removal from your website, advertisements, commercials, billboards, social media, signage, and vehicles. Your membership or accreditation with another BBB branch does not entitle you to use the Logo."

CBBB regulates the Bureau-franchise policy that includes the awards program within the description of "national initiatives and ongoing programs." Consequently, the national dashboard condones awards fraud because the program claims adherence to CBBB's "BBB Code of Business Practices" and/or "Standards of Trust"; additionally, "CBBB is the network hub for BBBs in the US and Canada." Be it also reminded that I was rebuffed by CBBB after advising awards fraud by the Houston Bureau.

Every awards program should require irrefutable proof of merit. Outstanding exemplars are the Academy Awards (Oscars) that "recognizes excellence in cinematic achievement" and the American Advertising Awards, formerly known as ADDY Awards, that honor "the creative spirit of excellence in the art of advertising." Both programs provide tangible proof of quality underscoring merit unlike the Better Business Bureau's integrity awards that flaunt sanctimonious ethics supported by blathering puffery.

Fake merit is a danger to the public. I worked in the home improvement industry and constantly worried about our customers suffering harmful backlash from shoddy workmanship peddled on the wings of a fake award. A recent calamity served deadly example of repercussions from failure to qualify merit. On March 15, 2018, a 179-foot, 950-ton pedestrian bridge collapsed at Florida International University (FIU) the same day it opened and killed six people. Investigation revealed that a required "secondary design check" was cost-effectively omitted; actions were particularly reckless since the "first of its kind" bridge used new "Accelerated Bridge Construction (ABC) methods." An FIU press release, dated March 10, 2018, reported, "Funding for the

$14.2 million bridge … is part of a $19.4 million Transportation Investment Generating Economic Recovery (TIGER) grant from the U.S. Department of Transportation." According to Ricochet.com, "The TIGER program has come under repeated fire for awarding money based on politics rather than merit."

I allege that humbuggery, misrepresentation, exaggeration, bait and switch, hypocrisy, betrayal, and carnival ethics describe the awards program that was invented to generate consistent marketplace revenue to finance a marauding globalist masquerading as a nonprofit foundation. Consumers were misled to believe that the *Awards for Excellence* guaranteed irrefutable merit when reality dictated a sham promotional profit scheme; consumers were unwittingly forced to roll the dice on unverified business practice peddled as endorsed unequivocal excellence. The awards represent the ultimate pay-for-play that sells memberships for merit; a self-serving figment of the Bureau's centurial imagination driven by an iconic name, prestigious reputation, staggering power, and global aspirations underpinned by a thimble-rigging shell game that fleeces millions of dollars from consumers every year. Members are anointed consecrated deities in a virtual world of artificial superiority that transcends reality by engaging monopolizing overtones to disparage nonmember competition. I consider the "good-business awards" to be the shape-shifting scam of the century and antithesis to the Bureau's oath to truth in advertising sworn by forefathers in 1911.

In 1936, Ken R. Dyke, chairman of the board for the Association of National Advertisers, prophetically summarized my fraud complaints against the *Awards for Excellence* in his Boston convention speech outlined in *Truth in Advertising*: "In our mad scramble for immediate profits, we American business men, as individuals and as a group, are too prone to look for the sale in front of our noses and close our eyes completely as to what may happen, not only to our advertising results, but to the success of business itself ten years hence, because of the tactics we're employing today. *The boomerang turns slowly, but it does come back with a real sock!*"

CHAPTER 3

RATING SCORE

The Bureau's bogus school-style rating score was fittingly born in superficial Hollywood and became as contentious as the creation of tinsel town.

As only fate could dictate, the name "Hollywood" originated from mispronunciation. In 1886, Scottishman H. J. Whitley, the "Father of Hollywood," was standing on a hill in the Cahuega Valley of the Santa Monica Mountains when he met a Chinese man and asked him what he was doing. The man replied, ""I holly-wood", meaning 'hauling wood'." Whitley thought it was a great name considering he had "already started over 100 towns across the western United States." Unfortunately, while orchestrating a land deal to buy 500 acres for "Hollywood," Whitley's concept was shanghaied from word of mouth. Long story short, in August 1887, land investor Harvey Henderson Wilcox (1832-1891) recorded first use of the name when he "filed with the Los Angeles County Recorder's office a deed and parcel map of property he had sold named "Hollywood, California"." Over a century later, William Glenn Mitchell, CEO of Hollywood's Los Angeles Bureau, invented the equally fanciful alpha rating score in 2005 at the behest of CBBB. In January 2009, CBBB launched the alpha rating score nationwide commencing takeover of U.S. commerce.

Once again, history repeated itself. The media and Hollywood turned into radical left-wing extremists engaging anarchy and "political terrorism"; deviant double-standards intermingled socialism and communism exemplified by the radical wing of the Democratic Party and globalist Republicans during and after the 2016 presidential election. Terminology is often confused. Socialism is an economic system that preserves the classes while promoting the welfare of all at the expense of others, and communism is an intense version of socialism that eliminates private ownership and enslaves citizenry; accordingly, both ideologies depend upon capitalism to exploit wealth. Movie legend actor John Wayne respectively exclaimed, "We were just good Americans, and we demanded the right to speak our minds. After all, the communists in Hollywood were speaking theirs." He was likely referring to a surge of American grassroots communism that rose in 1947 after WWII (1939-1945) and included "McCarthyism" (Senator Joseph McCarthy, (R., Wisc.)), the Second Red Scare (1947-1960), "The Hollywood Ten" (prominent film industry personnel were accused of promoting communism in 159 films between 1929 and 1949, but were exonerated by U.S. Office of War Information Chief Analyst Dorothy B. Jones in 1972), and the Ethel and Julius Rosenberg trial in 1951 (execution by electric chair in 1953 at Sing Sing Correctional Facility in New York) whereby presiding Judge Irving Kaufman held that consequences of their espionage involving nuclear weapons empowered "Communist Aggression in Korea" causing deaths of American soldiers during the Korean War.

Consumers are not aware of the Bureau's globalist initiatives and priorities, Eurocratic corporate connections, political and judicial underpinning, and sketchy past that support its bias rating score misconstrued as ironclad evaluation. I believe the Bureau's rating score is a pay-for-play scam immunized by the globalist court system as an "opinion" under the First Amendment despite blatant sanctimonious hypocritical egregious far-reaching consumer fraud. The rating score nuances a safety net to incentivize skeptical consumers to contract Bureau members, and why members heavily advertise their rating scores. In turn, the rating scores were married to the awards program to assure the proliferation, dominance, and expansion of the Bureau; annual award ceremonies routinely rubberstamp high rating scores. As a result, rating scores wield an inviolable bully stick to guarantee consistent membership revenue, marketplace control, and elimination of competition.

The rating score was specifically introduced to enhance and legitimize a disingenuous awards program suggesting deceptive advertising and deceptive trade practice. In order to qualify and embed the perception of member excellence, the Bureau invented magical rating scores to endorse virtual awards otherwise analogous to digital party favors. The mix of a fuzzy right with a profound wrong does not eliminate consumer fraud and reminds of the Bureau's recipe for righteous confusion to mask illicit activity. All the while, the Bureau's opinion continues to reign supreme as a minion of Illuminati.

Twenty-first-century corporatization, made possible by the lucrative awards program, witnessed the Bureau's metamorphosis into an autocratic world power. Twentieth-century expansion was previously impeded due to stair-stepping wars, encroaching consumer advocacy competition, lack of financial substructure and motivational venue (Internet), and a binding moral compass. In the late 1900s, a cash strapped CBBB reached an ethical crossroads and chose profit over truth consequently capitalizing from its sanctimonious veneer memorialized by yesteryear laurels. As a result, a do-or-die capitalist epiphany corrupted an incredible Christian-based advertising-born legacy and transformed a centurial birth mission built on ethical standards into a corporate machine manufacturing bang-for-the-buck false pretense. The Bureau evolved into a wealthy sacrilegious hypocrite raking in millions from crocodile piety as the irrefutable bellwether of truth. Federal cronyism and a popular get-rich-quick scheme greased the juggernaut's path to consummate power enabled by Eurocratic politics whereby globalism evolved into a despotic plutocratic regime.

CBBB launched a sequence of profiteering Internet-based programs that intrinsically fused the organization with the revolutionary "information superhighway." The first searchable Internet database appeared in 1991; the awards program was created in 2000; an experimental school-style alpha rating program was tested in 2005; and CBBB systemically switched its satisfactory/unsatisfactory rating system to alpha rating scores in 2009. The Bureau's online reporting system interwove rating scores with the awards program to fabricate a venerable façade of member excellence. Consequently, consumers were brainwashed into patronizing only Bureau members, which created an entrenched over-rated awards cash cow.

In 2016, the U.S. transferred sovereign control of the World Wide Web (www) to the Internet Corporation for Assigned Names and Numbers (ICANN), an EU affiliate, while CBBB simultaneously synchronized the Bureau's participation in the EU-U.S. Privacy Shield transatlantic digital program regulated by the DOC and FTC. As a result, CBBB and the Bureau franchise assumed global governance in lockstep with the EU's U.S.-assisted aspirations under the Obama administration to establish a United States of Europe, including a military headquarters and "defense force" as was announced in November 2016. The NWO was battening the hatches and completing its methodical overthrow of individual nations while the Bureau rode shotgun to guarantee its 30 pieces of silver. In the interim, consumers remained blissfully ignorant of the Bureau's globalist involvement connected to tectonic shifts in world affairs and why the Bureau's bogus awards and rating programs inexplicably received a free pass. After 100 years, the Bureau successfully infiltrated the power grid of the U.S. government, solidified geoeconomical partnerships, and transformed into Illuminati.

Memberships linked to chic 1800's advertising clubs and hosted the advertising, publishing, and printing titans of New York City. *Who's Who* biographies boasted prestigious affiliations like the exclusive Sphinx Club, Poor Richard's Club, and the Associated Advertising Clubs of America. Clandestine memberships preserved Puritan Old Guard morals contrary to an opportunist New-Guard extravaganza that publicized memberships to feed promotional profit schemes like the ethereal *Awards for Excellence*.

The Bureau's current rating score gauges evaluation using an alpha-numeric letter grading system ranging from the highest score of "A+" to the lowest of an "F". CBBB's official website, BBB.org, elaborated: "BBB grades are based on information in BBB files with respect to the following factors" that are described as "grading elements": (1) Business's complaint history with BBB. (2) Type of business. (3) Time in business. (4) Background information on business in BBB files. (5) Failure to honor commitments to BBB. (6) Licensing and government actions known to BBB. And (7) Advertising issues known to BBB.

There are also a "maximum number of points that can be earned or deducted in each element of the BBB rating system": (1) Complaint volume, 15-0 points. (2) Unanswered complaints, 40-0 points. (3) Unresolved complaints, 30-0 points. (4) Complaint resolution delayed, 5-0 points. (5) Failure to address complaint pattern, 0 to -31 points. (6) Type of business, 0 to -41 points. (7) Time in business, 10-0 points. (8) Transparent business practices, 0 to -5 points. (9) Failure to honor mediation/arbitration, 0 to -41 points. (10) Competency licensing, 0 to -41 points. (11) Government action (per action), 0 to -25 points. (12) Advertising review (per incident), 0 to -41 points. And (13) BBB trademark infringement, 0 to -41 points. Additionally, the Bureau's "100 point scale" assigned rating scores: 97-100 (A+), 94-96.99 (A), 90-93.99 (A-), 87-89.99 (B+), 84-86.99 (B), 80-83.99 (B-), 77-79.99 (C+), 74-76.99 (C), 70-73.99 (C-), 67-69.99 (D+), 64-66.99 (D), 60-63.99 (D-), and 0-59.99 (F).

Accordingly, the Bureau's complicated and strict rating score system represents the quintessence of humbuggery and exaggeration, which promote the perception of omnipotent authority through smoke-and-mirrors' merit and weasel-worded evaluation. In reality, the rating score is nothing more than aggrandized "opinion" attempting to legitimize conjecture and promote members; the ruse was exposed in 2010 by ABC *20/20*'s documentary that busted the LA Bureau and CBBB for peddling a pay-for-play profit scheme that sold expensive membership fees in return for high rating scores.

As it turned out, I filed awards fraud complaints in October 2008 and January 2009 when CBBB was systemically launching the draconian rating score introduced in 2005 by the LA Bureau to replace the innocuous satisfactory/unsatisfactory rating system. Timing, schematics, and financial objectives explained why the Houston Bureau president forewarned me that CBBB would agree with his decision to dismiss my complaint of awards fraud. My complaints threatened to upset the organization's globalist apple cart as evidenced by CBBB's burgeoning affiliation with the newly elected Obama administration and DOC that linked to the EU's NWO aspirations. A review of CBBB's annual reports proved an uptick in revenue after adopting the LA Bureau's experimental rating system. Following an expected slump during rollout in 2009, a progressive increase in organizational profit prevailed; "Total revenue" was listed as "$16,015,721" for 2008, "$15,154,047" for 2009, "$18,336,000" for 2010,

RATING SCORE

"$18,742,702" for 2011, "$21,243,431" for 2012, "$21,765,742" for 2013, "$23,725,023" for 2014, and "$28,020,198" for 2015.

On January 21, 2009, *Los Angeles Times* writer David Lazarus penned the article, "Better Business Bureau grades companies on a peculiar curve," which represented the first contentious query since the new ratings program was introduced at the beginning of the month. Lazarus exposed the Bureau's fledgling ratings program as pay-for-play and the same accusation that I also alleged four months earlier in my awards-fraud complaints. Nonmember businesses were issued failing or low grades by the Bureau and received high scores after purchasing a membership. He stated facts and tacitly implied ratings bias that awarded higher rates for members and lower rates for nonmembers. The Bureau wrapped its response packaged in standards to diffuse any connection between low rates and disparagement of competition.

Lazarus determined grading bias in favor of members. He highlighted "Chef-to-the-stars" Wolfgang Puck's famous *Spago* restaurant in Beverly Hills that was a nonmember and issued a "B-" rating. He compared *Spago* to the inconspicuous *Café Santorini* that was a dues-paying member boasting an "A+" rating. He also researched Bureau records and determined that members received higher grades. Conclusion asserted that "a random search of the organization's database of about 4 million North American companies seems to show that the roughly 400,000 accredited businesses, even those that get numerous complaints, very often receive higher grades than unaccredited companies with spotless complaint records." Lazarus asked CBBB President and CEO Steve Cox, "Why do so many unaccredited businesses get significantly lower grades?" Cox answered, "I can't explain that. Clearly we need to do a better job in articulating what the differences are." In essence, Cox lobbed a smoke bomb to hide a connection between memberships and high rating scores by insinuating the root issue was accreditation miscommunication.

On November 12, 2010, ABC *20/20* presented the scathing article, "Terror Group Gets 'A' Rating From Better Business Bureau?," which was followed that evening by the shocking documentary, "Better Business Bureau: The Best Ratings Money Can Buy." ABC *20/20's* correspondents Joseph Rhee and Brian Ross exposed the Bureau's rating scam that breached its iconic Wizard of Oz mystique hiding a cloistered hierarchy and internalized operations. Interviews from several Los Angeles business owners confirmed bias pay-for-play dynamics and detailed how their ratings changed from low or failing to high rating scores after payment of membership dues. Accordingly, "Two small-business owners" were filmed speaking to "Better Business Bureau telemarketers" who confided "that their grades of C could be raised to A plus if they paid $395 membership fees." Thereafter, both businesses made credit card payments to purchase memberships and their grades immediately changed to an "A+".

61

THE APO$TATE

Transactions were also reported regarding the accreditation of fake companies. A blogger and critic of the Bureau "teamed up with some buddies to pay $425.00 to register Hamas," a Middle Eastern terrorist group, and were issued an "A-" rating score. A sushi restaurant in Anaheim, California was also issued an "A-" rating score. Additionally, *Stormfront*, the alleged "white supremacist" website, was accredited under the name "Aryan Whitney" and issued an "A+" rating score.

Ross also reported that the Disneyland Resort in Anaheim, California, and the Ritz Carlton Hotel in Boston were both nonmembers and were issued "F" ratings. He re-emphasized that Chef Wolfgang Puck's *Spago* was issued a "B-" and "an F for some of his other restaurants" even though all organizations were known for impeccable taste, operational standards, and qualifications. Interestingly, CBBB raised all respective substandard grades a week after ABC *20/20's* documentary and article were broadcast and a week after CBBB's receipt of Connecticut Attorney General Ralph Blumenthal's disciplinary letter, dated November 10, 2010, that questioned the rating program's misleading and inaccurate criteria. The Ritz-Carlton and *Spago's* were both upgraded to an "A-". CBBB touted an unwritten rule that only members receive the highest grade of an "A+" while the highest grade that nonmembers can receive is an "A-", which proved rating score disparity between members and nonmembers.

ABC *20/20* included an interview of Blumenthal in their broadcast to complement his published complaint letter to CBBB and "called on the Bureau to stop using its grading system." Blumenthal questioned dynamics, integrity, and fairness of the Bureau's Torch Awards Program ("TAP") and rating scores; he especially called attention to ethics and warned, "I am deeply concerned that certain BBB practices threaten its reputation and effectiveness as a reliable resource for consumers. In particular, the BBB's current rating system is based, in part, on the payment of inadequately disclosed accreditation fees. This financial influence is potentially harmful and misleading to consumers"; he highlighted TAP as unevaluated and unmerited and advised, "I am also concerned that the BBB has granted good-business awards based on inadequate research and judging criteria"; he underscored rating bias and cautioned, "I am concerned that the new alpha rating system skews ratings results in favor of BBB dues-paying businesses"; and, he deemed the rating system inherently defective and prejudicial and concluded, "There are clear, practical and logistical limits to the BBB's ability to accurately and fairly implement a full ratings system for businesses."

Blumenthal chastised the "Better Business Bureau Serving Connecticut" for nominating a fraudulent company as a recipient of TAP. The Connecticut Department of Consumer Protection criminally prosecuted the two owners of Custom Basements of Connecticut, LLC ("CBC") and ordered "Restitution to Former Customers" in the amount of $94,000. The company ultimately invoked bankruptcy and shuttered doors.

Whereas the Houston Bureau's *Awards for Excellence* is a local domestic awards program, TAP allocated awards to larger globally oriented businesses. The Cincinnati Area, Southern Ohio, Northern Kentucky, Southeast Indiana Better Business Bureau's website advised, "The Torch Awards have been presented annually at the national and international level since 1996. In 2001, the Cincinnati Better Business Bureau instituted the Torch Award program at our local level," but TAP was denounced when Blumenthal determined TAP "skews ratings results in favor of BBB dues-paying businesses." Accordingly, I believe the attorney general's allegations against TAP also enjoin local awards programs because fundamental dynamics are similar, misleading, and profiteering with intent to build memberships and funnel revenue to CBBB.

After vigorously denying earlier allegations of illicit activity and dismissively claiming sales errors, CBBB responded to Blumenthal's complaints. On November 16, 2010, CBBB held a "special meeting" that resulted in amending rating score guidelines by simply dropping one of its most disparaging factors, but otherwise the program continued the same pro-monopoly initiatives. CBBB's disclaimed weasel-worded press release entitled, "A Message from the President of CBBB," was distributed on November 18, 2010, and reported, "By next week, the BBB ratings system will no longer give additional points to accredited businesses because of their accredited status. While we believe that businesses that have been approved for accreditation and commit to abide by these standards warrant additional points, we have acknowledged that others view this as creating an appearance of unfairness. What matters most now is to make changes to address those concerns – which is exactly the steps we have taken. BBB will continue to issue ratings based on the other 16 ratings factors currently used."

ABC *20/20* also published a follow-up article, "Better Business Bureau To Investigate Its Own Los Angeles Chapter," written by Joseph Rhee, dated November 22, 2010, and reflected the aftermath of the initial ABC News *20/20* documentary. CBBB was shame-faced into an investigation that ultimately scapegoated the Better Business Bureau of the Southland (Los Angeles); hypocrisy was reprehensible considering CBBB micromanaged the BBB franchise and programs. The LA Bureau's Mitchell confirmed that he was following CBBB's internal edict; that he was incriminated to protect national leadership; and that only CBBB could systemically approve and launch the new rating score program. He was further supported by Kiry Peng, also a former corporate officer at the LA Bureau, who confirmed Mitchell's allegations. Peng stated, "It is ironic that the BBB accuses us of failing to follow organizational policy on the one hand, and then labels us a 'bad apple' when we do. The reality is very simple: the pay-for-play policy was the BBB's, not ours."

THE APO$TATE

Cox vigorously defended the rating score that was introduced in January 2009 and was almost immediately red-flagged by the *Los Angeles Times*. He dogmatically responded with exonerating propaganda that "BBB accreditation and the BBB ratings system is not about generating money," but acknowledged that "plain and simple, we made a mistake." He continued equivocation stating, "While we want to recognize our shortcomings, any attempt to question the integrity of the entire BBB organization is completely and totally without merit," yet neither he nor CBBB made any efforts to correct such "shortcomings" until its dirty laundry was splashed across national television and denounced by Connecticut's Attorney General. Consequently, CBBB double downed on the ratings program evidenced by the John Moore lawsuits.

It was ludicrous for CBBB to claim meritorious behavior when it knowingly, willingly, and gainfully continued to perpetrate awards fraud against consumers. The organization has no excuse and cannot claim that it was not forewarned. My experience with the Bureau taught reverse logic that whatever it denied was true, and Cox denied profiting from the rating system despite the LA Bureau being caught red-handed on film pimping rating scores.

A June 2016 review of the Connecticut Bureau's website did not mention TAP, which suggested the program was closed after Blumenthal's respective complaints. A new local program appeared in TAP's place and advertised the *Website Marketing Message Award* featuring similar honor-code dynamics as the *Awards for Excellence*. The entry application declared, "Businesses must submit a Word document, not to exceed 1,000 words, addressing why your business merits winning the award." Thereafter, Hollywood-style regalia hosted a 'BBB Awards Banquet & Annual Meeting' where "the winning company will receive a plaque to showcase their hard work and dedication to ethical marketing." But presentation suggested the same thimble-rigging shell game that I confronted.

Damage control sent the LA Bureau's former management bus-diving. They were publicly humiliated and replaced by compliant puppets. Fortunately, disgraced scapegoats gallantly rebounded to defend themselves whereby exposing CBBB's sovereign internal directives, profiteering initiatives, and disingenuous broad-brushed public optics. The LA Bureau was the first fatality with Mitchell ramrodded into resignation when at his most vulnerable during recuperation from open-heart surgery. CBBB's investigative results from the LA Bureau rating score scandal were published in the 2013 annual report. Accordingly, CBBB's "Chair," Board of Directors, Sharon Abrams reported, "In March, we expelled the former BBB of the Southland (Los Angeles) for recurrent failure to meet standards. This decision came after every reasonable option was exhausted ... The board explored a number of options and, in the end, reassigned the territory to a coalition of three California BBBs with experienced CEOs committed to standards."

CBBB charged the LA Bureau with failure to adhere to standards. Fired operatives went on record after leaving the organization to defend their actions and exposed CBBB's ultimate control. Mitchell denounced CBBB as the ringleader that implemented all programs; and that he invented the rating score as a solution to the national headquarters' internal edict to increase revenue and memberships. In fact, he followed footprints of another manager who designed the awards program based on the same CBBB directive.

True to form, CBBB covered up the Southland rating score scandal by issuing a business award to the Bureau's reopened digital doppelganger; temporary staff received a *Summit Award* from the American Society of Association Executives. Back-patting is a notorious practice of the Bureau and offers a veneer of respect when there is none and/or is desperately needed. The "virtual BBB" was operated by 100 volunteers and 40 Bureaus and absorbed all previous businesses. Then, on December 4, 2013, CBBB held a grand opening for the former Southland Bureau's new full-service Bureau located "in an historic building at 448 South Hill Street in the Pershing Square neighborhood" and "the first in downtown Los Angeles in decades."

Recent political developments compel further "Blumenthal" disclosure. MSM, Hollywood, and Democratic leadership swerved hard left and Senator Blumenthal seems to have followed. As a result, I doubt that his current liberal persona would impugn CBBB today as he did in 2010. On February 9, 2017, Senator Blumenthal stepped back into contentious limelight when allegedly misrepresenting comments made by just-announced Supreme Court nominee Neil Gorsuch in what was considered another veiled globalist attempt to undermine the Trump administration. President Trump responded by publicizing the Senator's previous violation of the Stolen Valor Act of 2005 when he was attorney general. In March 2008, Blumenthal fraudulently claimed that he served in Vietnam, which outraged veterans. He was consequently charged with violating the Stolen Valor Act. Four years later, in June 2012, the case reached the Supreme Court whose progressive globalism dismissed charges by repealing the act; justices "struck down" the law "branding the false claim "contemptible" but nonetheless protected by the First Amendment." Critics blamed the decision on "Blumenthal's firewall of editorial writers," which implied media intervention.

CBBB oversees the Bureau franchise and orchestrated the implementation of the awards program and rating score; the Bureaus have limited rights and are not authorized to create rules, regulations, or programs on their own even though they are independent franchise operations. Globalist courts allowed CBBB sovereign serpentine wiggle room contrived to separate the fiefdom of Bureaus from its worldwide snakes' nest to impede liability. Both the rating score and awards merit programs operate on humbuggery and garner millions of dollars every year for the CBBB, Bureaus, foundations, and members. Consequently, there is no amount of disclaimed legal obfuscation that can hide the fact that consumer fraud is being perpetrated; that plausible deniability cannot be claimed; and that culpability cannot be passed to some hapless scapegoat. Henceforth, the Bureau's criminal accountability is demanded especially considering a centurial truth-in-advertising heritage.

Bureau founders fought tooth and nail to establish a prosecutable false advertising law while launching the Vigilance Committee to enforce respective mandates; golden coattails would turn in their graves if they saw their star child today, perpetrating the same fraud that it was created to regulate. Astonishingly, modern operations repurposed wayward predecessors' scams, e.g., "Before You Invest, Investigate," which continue the same globalist agenda. In fact, CBBB introduced the alpha ratings score as a marketing tool for Bureau members to create superficial superiority and to embellish its awards program. It was truly ironic that MSM, the Bureau's ancestral cousin, was the first to expose rating score fraud in 2010 and the first to digress into globalism in 2016.

As only destiny could foresee, the year 2016 celebrated a centurial milestone commemorating the year 1916 when the Vigilance Committee changed its name to "Better Business Bureau." And the New York Bureau was the first Vigilance Committee. In the early 1900s, the New York Bureau promoted the Democratic Party including President Thomas Woodrow Wilson and President Franklin Delano Roosevelt (FDR). Consequently, I believe FDR pulled golden strings on behalf of the New York Bureau after it was excoriated for racketeering and securities fraud by the U.S. Senate Banking and Currency Commission.

The year 1916 also introduced the first political advertising in newspapers by presidential candidates. Incumbent President Wilson won the election, on November 7, 1916, over his Republican rival U.S. Supreme Court Chief Justice Charles Evans Hughes (1862-1948). Seven months earlier, on May 22, 1916, Chief Justice Hughes ruled against the Coca-Cola Company in the historic *Barrels and Kegs Case* that determined a violation of the Pure Food and Drug Act of 1906; it was his last ruling before leaving the U.S. Supreme Court to run for POTUS. During the onset of litigation, Coca-Cola Sales Manager Samuel Dobbs planted himself as president of the venerable Associated Advertising Clubs of America (AACA) to overcome nose-diving beverage sales and negative publicity from federal charges. After Dobbs left the AACA, the association initiated progenitors of the modern CBBB and Better Business Bureaus to regulate false advertising. In fact, Coca-Cola remains a national sponsor of CBBB to this day.

A century later, déjà vu revisited the New York Bureau when its leadership colluded with MSM brethren supporting the frontrunner Democratic presidential nominee in order to discredit the Republican opponent in history's most controversial, corrupt, high-stakes, and globally ensconced election. The New York Bureau once again took control because the GOP presidential frontrunner was its member and henchmen targeted his company's rating score. The

Republican candidate's strict immigration and anti-globalist campaign threatened the Illuminati's pending takeover of America.

The election of 2016 proved to be a life-altering game changer unlike no other in history and unleashed worldwide political firestorms and terrorism. It was the year that Americans were introduced to unparalleled election anomalies, such as corrupt media, voter fraud, frivolous recounts, rebuke of the Electoral College, and emergence of faithless electors resulting in an astronomical battle between grassroots Americans and the NWO's "useful idiots." Political advertising largely moved from the impersonal formalities of television to the cohesive citizen journalism of social media and polarized voters through non-partisan patriotism to American principles. Socialism sought control of the U.S. Federal Government and globalists staged the election process to legally dismantle the Republic of America. Voters quickly rallied after discovering they had been disfranchised by crony Democrat and Republican establishment elites who were manipulating elections and self-servingly choosing candidates. Elitist forces of communism, domestic anarchy, deranged political correctness, illegal immigration, and global terrorism threatened to annihilate American civilization and culture.

GOP presidential candidate Donald John Trump rose against unparalleled NWO domination. Twitter hashtag 'Women for Donald Trump!' shared the most outstanding objective explanative insightful sweeping perceptive profound summary: "Trump is raising a MEGA-Movement, a counter-revolution, by standing against the Globalist Elite that own both the Republican and Democrat Parties, and own the Media that own all the Spin Doctors like NeoCon Review's gang of 22, Charles Krauthammer, and Megyn Kelly. He is standing against the establishment that controls the six corporations that own the T.V. and radio media, all of the major newspapers, most of the small so-called independent papers, and the 99 percent of the publishing houses. These are the people that also own and control the Federal Reserve and all the Western Central Banks that have held our economy hostage to their New World Order Agenda, robbed us of Constitutional Governance, and relegated our children and Grand Children to debt slavery in a quasi-Marxist Poverty State. This ELECTION is between Donald Trump and the Globalist Criminals that control every aspect of our Government, every NGO that is pushing a Globalist agenda – from the Rockefeller Foundation, George Soros, UNESCO, USAID, and the Clinton Foundation. Simply put, this is the most important election in our lifetime."

Uber-magnate Trump confronted a massive counterattack from the Illuminati who orchestrated relentless waves of insurgent globalist forces to stop him. He entered the 2016 presidential race and quickly became the GOP's frontrunner and presumptive nominee. His right-wing populist campaign messages resonated with an angry public fed up with government tyranny, fake news, illegal immigration, and voter fraud. Trump vowed to protect America first, build a barrier wall to stop illegal invasion, and halt Muslim immigration to pre-empt Radical Islamic Terrorism. He miraculously united a "silent majority" of diverse patriots while exposing elections as being rigged; that voters were disfranchised by the NWO whose embedded delegates determined national elections.

From the onset of the first presidential primary, Trump developed a manic tabloid relationship with New York attorney Megyn Kelly, the edgy prime-time anchor of the *Kelly File* on the Fox News Channel. Kelly was among three moderators who hosted the first GOP presidential primary debate on August 6, 2015, at the Quicken Loans Arena in Cleveland, Ohio. Trump supporters accused her of hijacking the debate's limelight and bushwhacking Trump for network ratings. The debate digressed into a two-year food fight that ended with Trump becoming POTUS and Kelly retreating to "Megan Kelley Today" morning show on NBC. Three years later, on October 24, 2018, NBC "fired" Kelley. A year later, Kelly returned to national headlines when honorably supporting abused women in the workforce who were "muzzled by NDA's [non-disclosure agreements]."

The Republican 11th Primary debate, on March 3, 2016, was held at the Fox Theatre in Detroit, Michigan. Trump's participation inspired another record-breaking television audience. The rematch featured a more cordial veneer, but subdued sparring continued. Vicious barbs, insults, and innuendos flew between Trump and Kelly during the fiery interlude of the August 2015 and March 2016 debates, but a "part deaux" ambush laid in wait to discredit Trump who had since surged in the polls. This was the juncture when the New York Bureau stepped into the fray. A few days earlier, on February 28, 2016, Trump appeared on NBC's *Meet the Press* and was asked about Trump University, founded on May 23, 2005; the name changed to "Trump Entrepreneur Initiative" in June 2010 and the organization was a member of the New York Bureau. NBC's questioning focused on "multiple lawsuits alleging false marketing for what was essentially an entrepreneurship seminar, not a college." Trump responded that the school received ""98 percent approval rating and high marks" from participants," and twice commented, "We have an A from the Better Business Bureau." That same day, NBC News published a review, "Better Business Bureau: Trump Right on 'A' Rating – Mostly"; the operative disparaging word was "mostly" because the school's rating scores varied from an "A+" to a "D-". The New York Bureau's involvement as a contributor to the article was highly suspicious, and publicly denigrating a member was against policy. As a result, the Bureau made Trump Entrepreneur Initiative's rating score a scandalous issue in the debate. Kelly focused attention on the school's "D-" score that Trump deflected by emphasizing his earlier press comments, "We have a 98 percent approval rating, we have an A from the Better Business Bureau (BBB) and people like it."

Trump asked the New York Bureau to fax confirmation of his school's rating score during the debate's intermission. When the debate continued, Trump acknowledged receipt of a business profile (he was probably handed the document and assumed provenance from the New York Bureau), but moderators disregarded the information and the viewing audience was told nothing. After the debate, the Bureau implied receiving numerous "questions regarding Trump University" and responded by throwing Trump under the bus when advising that they did not respond to Trump and/or issue him a business profile during the debate. Accordingly, Foxbusiness.com reported, "The document presented to debate moderators did not come from the Better Business Bureau that night." As a reminder, the rating score is a bias opinion, but gravitas has grown to such extent that the rating score has become inviolable divine providence.

On March 14, 2016, Newsmax.com published the article, "Megyn Kelly: Claim of 'A' Rating for Trump University Just a 'Head Fake'." She legitimatized the Bureau's bogus rating score system by belaboring disparity between its highest and lowest scores. Trump responded by requesting that his seven-million-plus Twitter followers boycott her show. As a result, Kelly suffered a damaging exodus of viewers. On April 15, 2016, the article, "Megyn's Secret: Star Anchor Kept Trump Meeting From Fox Boss Ailes, NY Mag Reports," disclosed, "Ever since she tangled with Trump in front of the 24 million viewers watching the debut GOP debate last summer – a performance that transformed her in the eyes of many into a fearless interviewer and feminist symbol – Kelly has become Ailes biggest star, and biggest management headache … (A February poll reported that Fox's standing with Republicans had plummeted by 50 percent since the beginning of the year.)"

I am claiming that the February 28th NBC article was a Bureau hit piece planted by media henchmen to sabotage Trump prior to "Super Tuesday" voting on March 1, 2016, and four days prior to the debate (including an extra leap year day). Criticism focused on student lawsuits. And the New York Bureau provoked fraud innuendos by issuing a precarious statement that Trump University and/or Trump Entrepreneur Initiative "had an 'A-plus' rating but had 'fallen as far as D-minus'." In fact, several students did lodge lawsuits against Trump University, consequently lowering its rating score. Trump eventually settled lawsuits for $25,000,000 million, but political adversaries continued controversy. Ironically, the state of New York accused Trump of operating without a business license same as Republican Attorney General Hamilton Ward accused the New York Bureau in 1930. Unlike Trump, the New York Bureau invoked underground politics to bury Ward's licensing indictment and rigged state elections to replace Ward with Democratic Attorney General John Bennett, serving from 1931 to 1942. Thereafter, the New York Bureau and franchise escaped licensing requirements and have remained unlicensed ever since.

Coincidentally, the NBC article referenced "BBB Serving Metro New York," which was the successor to the original Vigilance Committee that begat

THE APO$TATE

the Better Business Bureau. Lost history reminds that the Old Guard New York Bureau was charged with securities fraud and collusion with the NYSE among a litany of criminal allegations involving General Manager Kenner who was arrested for defamation.

Unlike my former employer whom the Houston Bureau embraced to protect its awards program, the New York Bureau undermined Trump because he was anti-globalist. The New York Bureau trip-wired the March debate by bookending the event with weasel-worded opening and closing propaganda. Published hints and subtle nuances chipped at Trump's credibility the same as character assassination. After seeding political backlash for Trump, the New York Bureau turned "tight-lipped" leaving public opinion to wallow in false implication.

A firestorm erupted after Trump's innocent declaration of an "A" rating score. He spoke as a proud member and obviously did not know he had been betrayed by the Bureau. Even more importantly, he did not know about the Bureau's shocking rating score scandal exposed by ABC *20/20* that tainted the Bureau's reputation and stigmatized the rating program.

When Trump mentioned the Bureau's rating score, a decisive photo opportunity also presented itself. Not only did the Bureau betray Trump, it used him for publicity to legitimize its bias rating program. Advertising founders built the Bureau's name and brand services through the dynamics of public relations and power of association involving some of the most incredible events in history. But the Bureau shamed its legacy for allowing an exaggerated, self-serving program to infect a critical presidential election and compromise a candidate's electability.

Kelly was supported by a powerhouse team of investigative producers who should have been aware and notified her of the Los Angeles Bureau's pay-for-play ratings scandal six years earlier. The Bureau was left wearing a scorching scarlet letter ("B" for Bogus). But Kelly never mentioned the rating score scandal and Trump was unaware. Consequently, Trump was victimized by rating score humbuggery.

Trump's historical revolutionary movement was referred to as a "phenomenon" and drew comparisons to the spectacular Progressive revolution that sculpted America and created the Better Business Bureau. Many patriots believed the election of 2016 was the last opportunity to save America's founding ideals from an irreversible socialist spiral into the dark ages.

The 2016 election was the year that voters learned elections were rigged. The Republican Party admitted, "Political parties choose their nominee, not the general public." Out-of-control voter fraud and rogue state delegates attempted to ignore voters' choice, but Trump prevailed as the presidential GOP nominee. Eerie similarities reminded of the American Revolution except King George

III was replaced by collaborating Republican and Democratic elitists. And although the Second Coming engaged a relatively bloodless revolution, the same battle erupted against tyranny, oppression, and nonrepresentation.

Trump's former campaign manager, Paul Manafort, likened outrageous electoral fraud to Prohibition-era antics. He explained, "We're trying to let voters decide, members of the Republican Party, Independents decide who the nominee should be, not the party bosses. That's the system of the 1920s … not 2016." It was the same "system" that the Old Guard Bureau employed to evade criminal prosecution respective to the state of New York's licensing demands.

It was historically appropriate that the New York Bureau and advertising industry mixed with the 2016 election. Trump's flamboyant lifestyle, showmanship, and exceptional business acumen highlighted the magic of advertising that built America. The 1900s was all about advertising that enabled the birth of the Bureau, and Trump brought both full circle.

Like the awards, the Bureau's rating score is a shiny trinket representing an advertising gimmick designed to attract consumer trade. The rating score has continued the Bureau's centurial practice of intimidation satisfied by payment of an expensive membership fee. There is no science to substantiate the Bureau's rating score, but respective worth is attached to accreditation that promotes the Bureau's gilded endorsement of products and services in the marketplace.

To the defense of Trump and thousands of other well-meaning and exceptional businessmen promoting their Bureau endorsement and rating scores, most members honor respective standards. But evidence will support my claims that the Bureau's landmark awards and rating score programs are unscrupulous and outweigh other beneficial programs. CBBB counters criticism through sanctimonious hypocrisy showcased in its article, "Investigations into Substandard Marketplace Behavior," that advised, "In 2015, local BBBs conducted more than 11,000 investigations that proactively identified "marketplace practices that are deceptive, misleading, unethical, or questionable"."

In 2005, CBBB launched the alpha ratings score as a publicity ploy to upgrade, reinvigorate, and legitimize its Y2K online awards extravaganza launched five years earlier. The rating score began as an internal code and member evaluation was added to the Bureau's commercialized business files after the introduction of the Internet in the latter 1900s. Beforehand, the Bureau was a hardcore secret society that hid operations and did not allow members to advertise. According to Slate.com, "Member businesses' names were made public only in local BBBs' annual reports, but this information was not widely disseminated." The first rating scores, "satisfactory" or "unsatisfactory," were implemented around 1950. Forty-four years later, as of May 1994, CBBB was still deliberating whether to allow members to advertise memberships. CBBB worried about "protecting the integrity of the Better Business Bureau trademark," but CBBB cast worries to the wind when it launched the surreal awards program in 2000.

Recent accreditation and rating disclaimers deny endorsement despite the Bureau's incredible history based on endorsement. CBBB's website, BBB.org, stated, "BBB accreditation does not mean that the business's products or services have been evaluated or endorsed by BBB, or that BBB has made a determination as to the business' product quality or competency in performing services." Furthermore, BBB.org's rating score disclaimer declared, "BBB grades are not a guarantee of a business' reliability or performance, and BBB recommends that consumers consider a business' grade in addition to all other available information about the business." The Bureau spent a century brainwashing society to implicitly trust its operations, so the rating disclaimer was especially disingenuous when advising consumers to seek secondary business information.

Accordingly, there is no one better than the Better Business Bureau to quote when exposing its rating program as another pay-for-play street corner scam: "Tell the Truth; honestly represent products and services, including clear and adequate disclosures of all material terms."

PART TWO

CHAPTER **4**

BBB HISTORY

I am humbled that fate included me within the unprecedented history of the Better Business Bureau, but disappointed that my name will bookmark the condemnation of an iconic consumer advocate for specious awards, deceptive trade practice, and subversion against the United States Republic. My lawsuit wrote a new Bureau chapter emphasizing that history matters. Destiny intervened when predecessors' truth-enforcing employment attorney wrote a false advertising law to prosecute abusers, but irony prevailed when successors' fraud-facilitating attorney breached my private employment trial to protect its false advertising.

The Bureau should be celebrating and sharing its incredible advertising history, yet the franchise's generic websites have remained strangely silent. Since writing *The Apostate* over the past 12 years, historical information has been largely scrubbed especially after the Internet handover to ICANN on October 1, 2016. Research data was gleaned from various historical sources including the *Printers' Ink* Advertising Journal and *Printers' Ink 50 Years* commemorative publication, which reviewed the advertising industry during the Progressive Reformation Era between 1888 and 1938; *Printers' Ink 50 Years*, was published four years after the U.S. Senate's Pecora Commission investigation ended in 1934. The Bureau was indicted for securities fraud, but the advertising industry's PR machine restored its disgraced reputation; *Printers' Ink* wrote, "Today fifty-six local Bureaus guard the public against fraudulent advertising and selling methods, and promote integrity and confidence in all phases of business." Thereafter, FDR completed the Bureau's redemption and transformation through the SEC and Deep State. In 2000, CBBB launched the integrity awards blasting the Bureau's digital empire into stratospheric success by shamelessly exploiting and betraying American consumers. To understand the gravity of treachery, the Bureau's advertising birthright must be reviewed.

The "Great White Way" debuted "over Madison Square in 1892" and sparked "illuminated" advertising in between the *Gay Nineties* and *Somber Thirties*. The mesmerizing lights of Broadway danced with entertaining magical flair shining on America's turbulent evolution driven by Henry Ford's *Tin Lizzie*, WWI, Depression of 1920-1921, Spanish Flu pandemic, Prohibition, *Roaring Twenties*, organized crime, Stock Market Crash and Great Depression, Pecora Commission, SEC, Dewey's mob trials, Pearl Harbor, WWII, Korean War, and Giuliani's kingpin smack down. In 1912, the advertising industry launched the Bureau's prototype as a regulatory division to enforce the newly drafted *Printers' Ink* Model Statute advertising law. Unfortunately, by 1922, the New York Bureau's moral compass deteriorated, and operations simulated organized crime when partnering with the NYSE and Investment Bankers Association to manipulate state-level Blue Sky laws for unfettered sale of worthless securities.

Two and a half years after the Black-Tuesday blowout on October 29, 1929, the New York Bureau was caught in a national backlash. On March 4, 1932, Republican President Herbert Clark Hoover launched the U.S. Banking and Currency Commission to initiate investigative hearings on stock practices. Republican New York House Representative Fiorello Enrico La Guardia was among the first plaintiffs to introduce criminal evidence against the New York Bureau and General Manager H. J. Kenner in addition to allegations from E. C. Riegel and Logan Billingsley. Complaints landed with Florida Democratic Senator Duncan Upshaw Fletcher who indicted the Better Business Bureau system for Blue Sky fraud and racketeering.

The advertising industry was alarmed at the Bureau's fall from grace and worried about collateral damage. The Bureau exploited landmark newspapers and the forthright *Printers' Ink* Advertising Journal as prestigious propaganda venues. Accordingly, *Printers' Ink* was among the first to respond: "The friends of the Better Business Bureaus view with some apprehension the charges which are being brought against some of these bureaus as to unwise management and improper activities. If such charges were brought only by crooks or racketeers, they could be ignored. But they seem to be coming in increasing numbers from business men of high standing. In fact, the criticisms are being multiplied to such an extent as to become almost a definite trend." Unfortunately, a presidential election interrupted the Bureau's rehabilitative comeuppance. Democratic New York Governor Franklin Delano Roosevelt took the White House on November 8, 1932, and saved booze and the Bureau. FDR laundered cover-up of the disgraced Bureau through presidential endorsement and redeeming optics when hypocritically appointing securities fraud-beleaguered New York Bureau General Manager H. J. Kenner as a high-profile SEC anti-fraud dignitary. Thereafter, FDR's WWII Deep State reconnaissance integrated Bureau reporting services to create a military-oriented business intelligence agency.

In July 1896, the advertising elite of New York established the ultra-exclusive

Sphinx Club. It reorganized as the Advertising Men's League and changed its name to the Advertising Club of New York in 1910, which became the "Vigilance Committee of the Advertising Club of New York" on March 12, 1912. Then, in 1916, the National Vigilance Committee accepted acclaimed sales entrepreneur Arthur Sheldon's suggested name "Better Business Bureau"; the Minneapolis Vigilance Committee was the "first" chapter to adopt the new name later that year.

Organized advertising began when local advertising clubs coalesced in 1904 as the "International Advertising Association" that became the "Associated Advertising Clubs of America" (AACA) in 1905. Six years later, on August 1-4, 1911, the AACA's revolutionary Boston Convention launched the Truth in Advertising Movement. Eight months later, the AACA launched the Vigilance Committee of the Advertising Club of New York as the first vigilance committee with legal power to prosecute false advertising. In 1914, assassin's bullets sparked WWI and America's advertising industry commenced first globalist outreach with a VIP-studded international convention held in Toronto, Canada, which changed the AACA's name to Associated Advertising Clubs of the World (AACW), and influenced the Vigilance Committee's name change two years later. A name can make or break a product or service in the world of advertising, so leadership frequently changed the association's name in keeping with current trends.

The year 1916 proved historical. The advertising industry leapfrogged during the Progressive Reformation Era's astounding technological and communicative advances that built America. In particular, four events occurred: (1) Incumbent 28th Democratic President Wilson defeated Republican presidential nominee Supreme Court Chief Justice Charles Evans Hughes. (2) Wilson aligned with the AACA. (3) Wilson made newspapers a popular venue for political advertising. (4) The Vigilance Committee changed its name.

Wilson set the stage for the Bureau's globalist trajectory. He was first inaugurated 28th POTUS on March 4, 1913. President Wilson secured re-election by strategically endorsing the megawatt AACA and its influential bloc of Democratic votes in a rousing speech at Philadelphia's Independence Hall in June 1916. Advertising history swung full circle when Chief Justice Hughes left the Supreme Court to run against incumbent President Wilson. Beforehand, on May 22, 1916, Hughes rendered his last opinion that reversed lower-court decisions in *The United States vs. Forty Barrels and Twenty Kegs of Coca-Cola ("Barrels and Kegs Case")* and ruled in favor of the U.S. Federal Government in its second case to enforce the landmark Pure Food and Drug Act of 1906. Hughes supported Dr. Harvey Washington Wiley as head of the FDA who brought charges against The Coca-Cola Company ("Coca-Cola"). The company's up-and-coming Sales Manager Samuel Dobbs countered Coca-Cola's federal indictment by procuring the AACA's prestigious presidency. Wiley aligned with Republican President Theodore Roosevelt's trust-busting regulatory initiatives. The *Barrels and Kegs Case* forged a bond between Coca-Cola and the National Vigilance Committee (CBBB). In fact, CBBB's 2015 annual report listed Coca-Cola as a "National Partner" with its "2015 Board of Directors and Officers" acknowledging Coca-Cola's chief marketing counsel as its "Chair."

The presidential election of 1916 marked the first year when newspapers were heavily utilized for advertising by political candidates. The ANPA published an article in *Printers' Ink*, Vol. XCIX, April 26, 2017, No. 4, entitled, "Help Afforded Advertisers," that stated, "It is evident that the 1916 Presidential campaign marked the big beginning of the employment of newspaper advertising as a strong factor in elections."

The year 1916 also emphasized that NOMENCLATURE MATTERS! After President Wilson's Philadelphia speech, Bureau leader Merle Sidener recognized the Vigilance Committee's foreboding tar-and-feather connotation and sought a prestigious facelift from sales guru Arthur Sheldon. Consequently, the lionizing "Better Business Bureau" moniker beamed irrefutable ethics and sparked a global empire built on subliminal self-righteousness.

In retrospect, President George Washington enacted the Postal Service Act on February 20, 1792, which created the "U.S. Post Office Department." The first revolutionary battles were fought on April 19, 1775, in Massachusetts at Lexington and Concord. On July 26, 1775, the Continental Congress launched the "Continental Post" whereby Benjamin Franklin was appointed "the first postmaster general." For the next century, the advertising industry was inextricably linked with and dependent upon archaic American Revolutionary laws controlling the U.S. mail service.

A second earth-shattering Massachusetts' revolution exploded in August 1911 and launched the advertising industry's Truth in Advertising Movement during the AACA's Boston convention. The attending catalyst was Editor John Irving Romer who was the visionary overseer of Publisher George Presbury Rowell's 1888 *Printers' Ink* Advertising Journal, considered the regulatory bible of the advertising industry. *Printers' Ink* steered early advertising and published word was considered written in stone. After the rabble-rousing Boston convention, Romer contracted Harry Dwight Nims, a New York employment attorney, to write the groundbreaking *Printers' Ink* Model Statute. Nims completed the statute's final draft on October 25, 1911, which *Printers' Ink* published on November 16, 1911. In turn, Romer approached the AACA for organizational support and establishment of a network of vigilance committees to promote the statute's enactment. At the time, Kenner clarified that New York and Massachusetts had consumer fraud laws, but legislation was toothless compared to the statute's misdemeanor penalty. Thereafter, the AACA convinced the NYSE to subsidize the Advertising Club of New York as the first experimental vigilance committee.

The Bureau's centurial journey embraced a phenomenal series of events and vibrant array of incredible characters, which projected an iconic golden mirage. To the contrary, research located obscure history and photographs that collectively questioned the Bureau's contemporary revisionist propaganda and emphasized dearth of information. The Bureau's dark discrepancies were seemingly buried to enable profiteering programs, which hid creeping far-reaching Orwellian tentacles. As a result, expert advertising and public relations promote a quintessential "ethics" brand image while despotic operations insidiously infiltrate society to dispense judge-and-jury injustice leaving countless lives sullied and silenced by its disparagement and incursion.

The public instantly recognizes "BBB," but not "AAF." The "American Advertising Federation (AAF)" is the current successor of the AACA, which launched the Bureau's archetypal Vigilance Committee. The AAF remained true to ethical industry standards and issues an award only after evaluating advertising projects (not applications) in keeping with George Rowell's stringent practices. Additionally, AAF leadership does not persecute citizens, monopolize the marketplace, and/or tamper with the court system. To the contrary, in 1922, red flags started waving when the New York Bureau launched "Before You Invest, Investigate," and, in 1927, when the National Better Business Bureau (CBBB) separated from the AACW and incorporated as the "National Association of Better Business Bureaus, Inc." The national headquarters' need for a corporate shield was telling and signaled a decisive turning point emphasized by the Crash two years later. Consequently, I allege that the Bureau deviated from regulator to lawbreaker and that modern B-men wield nation-state powers, persecute individual citizens, and proffer bogus awards and rating scores that control global commerce.

Current history includes the Bureau's affiliation with the Deep State, Obama administration, and the EU super state to emphasize tacit immunity, resistance to government regulation, and burgeoning global strength. Consumers must not be fooled by the Bureau's philanthropic educational façade, venerable reputation, and/or consumer advocacy. The Bureau is Illuminati and connects to local, state, federal, and international tyranny. B-men speed dial lawyers, judges, and politicians while stationing branch offices as globalist outposts to command a marketplace militia. The Bureau's WWII community-surveillance reporting services served as a prototype for modern intelligence communities and operated under the guise of monitoring wartime bond fraud similar to WWI's regulation of Liberty Bonds. According to the United States History website, the U.S. WWII certificates "were first called Defense Bonds. The name was changed to War Bonds after the Japanese attack on Pearl Harbor, December 7, 1941."

THE APO$TATE

Many ask who and what are Illuminati? The Socio-Economics History Blog website reviewed, "Dr. John Coleman: Know Your Enemy – The Illuminati "Committee of 300"," and identified Illuminati within the Committee of 300 headed by the Queen of England whose "inner circle" is the "Order of the Garter." Three respective comments particularly underscored my book's basic theme of awards fraud by the BBB as the world's most famous secret society and undercover-globalist: (1) "The Committee of 300 with its 'aristocracy,' its ownership of the U.S. Federal Reserve banking system, insurance companies, giant corporations, foundations, communications networks, presided over by a hierarchy of conspirators." (2) "Each is a hierarchy with an inner circle at the top, who deceives those below with lies, such as claiming a noble agenda; thus duping them into following a web of compartmentalized complicity." (3) "Secret societies exist by deception." Accordingly, I believe the Illuminati exploit every aspect of our lives including the air we breathe. Moreover, our civilian rights and choices are pacifying delusions proffered by Illuminati as a merciless cult that rides the burdened backs of the world's hardworking people from skyscrapers to mud huts. We exist to serve, support, and enrich Illuminati leeches.

The history of the Committee of 300 explained how wealth was created, embedded, and distributed around the planet with ultimate objective "to gain world-wide control." The Committee of 300 was "a product of the British East India Company's Council of 300" and the British East India Company was "chartered by the British royal family in 1600." It was a watershed juncture in world history when the British Monarchy flourished, and unimaginable wealth forged an "untouchable ruling class." The British East India Company established opium drug trade with China making it "the largest company on earth in its time" that globally entrenched "powerful alliances" promoting the NWO. In the mid-1800s, Chinese began immigrating to America when building Lincoln's transcontinental railroad and brought opium that infiltrated all levels of society. American Illuminati were "wallowing in tainted opium money" and covertly financed other industries within the burgeoning Progressive Reformation Era. Humbuggery followed and repercussions insidiously embraced narcotics that ensnared mainstream America. False advertising threatened the circulation and readership of publishing and printing empires. As a result, a guardian ecclesiastic advertising industry produced schizophrenic consumer advocacy whose sanctimonious regulatory façade masked exploitive capitalism. Today's U.S. Illuminati are called the Eastern Liberal Establishment whose members partner with the "British Crown" and run "the United States from top to bottom through their secret upper-level, parallel government, which is tightly meshed with the Committee of 300, the ultimate secret society."

Britain's modern House of Windsor is considered linchpin Illuminati and holds direct lineage to the Ernestine line of the Germanic Wettin Dynasty or

Haus Wettin" from the Holy Roman Empire and "became the rulers of several medieval states" including the Saxon Eastern March in the year 1030, Meissen in 1089, Thuringia in 1263, and Saxony in 1423. Haus Wettin was one of the oldest dynasties in Europe whose agnates "ascended the thrones of Great Britain, Portugal, Bulgaria, Poland, Saxony, and Belgium." The "Duchy of Saxe-Coburg-Saalfeld" was established in 1699 and was a state of the Holy Roman Empire, Confederation of the Rhine, and state of the German Confederation. Thereafter, the Duchy of Saxe-Coburg and Gotha ruled from 1826 to 1918 with families holding sovereignty of "the United Kingdom, Belgium, Portugal, Bulgaria, and Saxe-Coburg-Gotha." Coburg is located in "upper Bavaria, Germany" and Gotha "was a rich trading town on the trade route *Via Regia*" in central Germany. Due to WWI "anti-German" sentiment, King George V (George Frederick Ernest Albert, (1865-1936)), second son of Albert Edward, Prince of Wales, who became King Edward VII, "changed the name of his branch from Saxe-Coburg and Gotha to Windsor in 1917." King George V chose the name "Windsor" because it was "the Royal Family's place of residence." For the same reason, in 1920, the Belgian Royal House also changed its name "to *van België, de Belgique* or *von Belgien* ("of Belgium") in the country's three official languages (Dutch, French and German)."

The Committee of 300 is a successor of the British East India 300 and "the driving force behind the criminal agenda to create a "New World Order", under a "Totalitarian Global Government"." Ancestral British East India Illuminati countries Germany, Bulgaria, Belgium, and the UK (voted Brexit in 2016) are now members of the EU, the hornet's nest fueling the NWO. The bulk of what Dr. Coleman outlined as Illuminati agenda has already happened or is in process of happening further validating his claims. Their most apocalyptic machination contrived to instill ruinous desperation consequently depopulating the world through starvation, diseases, alcoholism, drugs, genocide, and wars. If there are any doubts, look at what is currently happening across the globe.

As of September 2010, the "Western Illuminati Organization Chart" at (http://www.stevequayle.com) breaks down the "Elite Network" into eleven basic levels that also branch into additional subcategories: (1) Prison Warder Consciousness (Fourth Dimension). (2) Global Elite (Black Nobility, Illuminati, Committee of 300). (3) Illuminised Freemasonary, Knights of Malta and other 'Knights' Societies, Skull and Bones Society, **other Secret Societies.** (4) Mind Manipulation (Drug Companies, National Health Organizations), Elite Military, Intelligence Agencies, Drugs/Arms Trade, Religion (Vatican, Christianity, Islam, Judaism, New Age), Banking/Business (Bank of England, Oil Cartels, World Trade Organization, International Monetary Fund (IMF)/World Bank, North Atlantic Treaty Organization (NATO), Politics (Capitalism, Fascism, Communism, Zionism, Liberalism, Socialism, Green Politics). (5)

Round Table/Royal Institute of International Affairs. (6) Bilderberg Group ("an annual private conference of 120 to 150 people of the European and North American political elite, experts from industry, finance, academia, and the media, established in 1954"; the group's first meeting was held at "the Hotel de Bilderberg in Oosterbeek, Netherlands"; policies promoted "one-world government"). (7) Nation States. (8) EU, other "trading" blocs. (9) United Nations (UN). (10) Media. (11) Human Race.

Every conceivable aspect of global religion, politics, and governance was included within the Chart except the Chinese whom modern Illuminati have deemed an enemy and target. I found it interesting that the media was placed at the lowest level of the Illuminati totem pole and only outranked the human race. Bottom-dweller placement suggested that news outlets were being exploited almost as badly as the general public whom I will dignify as consumers relative to my collective theme of awards fraud, deceptive advertising, and deceptive trade. The Chart confirmed that Joe Blow and Jane Doe International, representing various peoples and languages, are being unwittingly fleeced by Illuminati to support globalist wealth and initiatives.

Dr. Coleman's "300 List" included several recognizable names throughout the world: Her Royal Highness Queen Elizabeth II, Charles - Prince of Wales, William - Prince of Wales, Tony Blair, David William Donald Cameron, George H. W. Bush, Bill Clinton, Al Gore, John Forbes Kerry, Timothy Geithner, Susan Rice, Ben Bernake, Colin Powell, Warren Buffet, Bill Gates, Henry Kissinger, General Wesley Kanne Clark Sr., Shimon Peres, Mikhail Gorbachev, George Soros, Jean-Claude Juncker, Nicolas Sarkozy, and Francois Fillon. I question if the latest Illuminati scrolls include former President Barack Obama and Chancellor Angela Merkel considering their mutual "untouchable" status that left escalating carnage in their wake.

I believe that the 1920's "Before You Invest, Investigate" securities program evidenced the Bureau's first globalist venture with the NYSE. Robber baron profiteering superseded ecclesiastic consumer advocacy. The Bureau exploited the church's bully pulpit and Christian ethics to join the early NWO movement emphasizing Dr. John Coleman's belief that "the One World Government began setting up its "church" in the 1920's/1930's, for they realized the need for a religious belief inherent in mankind to have an outlet, and, therefore, set up a "church" body to channel that belief in the direction they desired."

Consumers only know what they are told, and the Bureau's gilded propaganda notoriously coddles its authoritarian white knight image. In keeping with Wansley's auroral *History and Traditions* and Kenner's defensive *The Fight for Truth in Advertising*, the Daniels Fund Ethics Initiative presented a festooned historical recap entitled, "Better Business Bureau: Protecting Consumers and Dealing with Organizational Ethics Challenges." First of all, my empirical experience and irrefutable research question the BBB's assumed symbiosis with ethics; second, the article's rendition of Bureau-related history is essentially a puff piece pitted with incomplete one-sided innuendos; and, third, the article's impressive regulatory nuance hides reality's counterfeit means.

The Bureau is an American landmark and product of the advertising industry; a relic from the spectacular Progressive Reformation Era that built America. Several of the advertising industry's founding fathers evolved from the Civil War whose bloodshed was officially ended by President Andrew Johnson on May 9, 1865. Thereafter, the Reconstruction period, from 1865 to 1877, spawned Christian temperance movements, which influenced the enactment of the Pure Food and Drug Act of 1906 that encouraged the introduction of the prosecutorial *Printers' Ink* Model Statute in 1911. In the midst of technological advances, America's "Golden Age" of railroads, from 1880s to 1920s, connected East and West coastlines spreading business across the country. Advertising organized as clubs in major cities under a national association. In turn, trains acquiesced to cars and planes while two World Wars embedded international advertising.

At the time, Puritan agents, agencies, publishers, printers, newspapers, and merchants represented the moral fiber of society from whence honorable western journalism emerged, but while America prospered, so did false advertising. Stewards suffered debilitating repercussions, which threatened circulation, readership, and profits. As a countermeasure, advertising affiliates organized under the AACA that created the Vigilance Committee as its regulatory arm and wielded the statute as its punitive sword. The end of WWI flooded the job market with returning soldiers converting to vigilance men. Military acumen strategically expanded Vigilance Committees in most every major city, but the rebranded Better Business Bureau developed crony-capitalist initiatives that surrendered twentieth-century commitment and led to twenty-first-century betrayal.

It is impossible to recap the Bureau's complete history that was secreted away by the fabled Sphinx. An extensive timeline was beleaguered by lost, buried, and/or distorted information while reminding that today's digital data is controlled by ever-changing covert Big Cloud. Fortunately, a scavenger hunt through time pieced together an incredible treasure trove of notable nuggets recovering yesteryear's events, motivators, and provocateurs. A mindboggling compilation described America's tumultuous coming of age in tandem with the equally chaotic evolution of the BBB that rode advertising's golden coattails.

"Advertising vigilantes" contributed far-reaching advertising reform and profoundly impacted contemporary business standards and consumer protection laws. Luminaries included George Rowell, John Romer, John Wanamaker, Joseph Appel, Harry Nims, Merle Sidener, Arthur Sheldon, Dr. Herbert Houston, Samuel Dobbs, and H. J. Kenner. They were teachers, retailers, lawyers, bankers, salesmen, advertising agents, publishers, editors, newspapermen, and writers. Their mission was voluntary, and sometimes self-serving, but pursued a regulatory crusade that established Vigilance Committees throughout the countryside to combat false advertising when feckless state and federal laws were still evolving. Founding predecessors presented the torch as a symbol of eternal truth in advertising that underscored honesty, integrity, and trust.

After the Civil War ended, railroads began pioneering America's western frontiers empowered by the Morrill Tariff and the Pacific Railroad Act. According to the Library of Congress, "Prior to 1871, approximately 45,000 miles of track had been laid. Between 1871 and 1900, another 170,000 miles were added …." The Morrill Tariff (sponsored by "Republican Congressman and steel manufacturer" Justin Smith Morrill from Vermont) was signed into law, on March 2, 1861, by Democrat President James Buchanan, two days before Republican Abraham Lincoln's inauguration. Lincoln supported the Morrill Tariff and campaigned for a high protective tariff. Wikipedia noted, "On February 14, 1861, President-elect Lincoln told an audience in Pittsburgh that he would make a new tariff his priority in the next session if the bill did not pass by inauguration day on March 4."

President Buchanan hailed from Pennsylvania as did steel magnate Andrew Carnegie, and their respective special interests influenced passage of a tariff to increase direly needed revenue. In fact, during the "first year," the Morrill Tariff "increased the effective rate collected on dutiable imports by approximately 70%" and enabled the U.S. steel industry to build America's railroads. Beforehand, "American tariff rates were among the lowest in the world … the average rate for 1857 through 1860 being around 17% overall (*ad valorem*), or 21% on dutiable items only," according to Wikipedia. When Lincoln entered the presidency, the U.S. Treasury had "less than $500,000 on hand and millions in unpaid bills."

Lincoln signed the Pacific Railroad Act into law, on July 1, 1862, which had been previously delayed by Southern opposition and later facilitated by Southern secession. According to the Library of Congress, "This act provided Federal government support for the building of the first transcontinental railroad, which was completed on May 10, 1869." On that date, historical records indicated that California Governor Leland Stanford drove the "Last Spike" (gold-plated) in the "Golden Spike Ceremony" at Promontory Summit, Utah. To the contrary, Transcontinental Railroad advised, "Despite the publicity for the "last spike", the American rail network did not yet actually run to either coast. In August 1870, the final connection was made." Furthermore, "[O]n June 4, 1876 a train named the Transcontinental Express arrived in San Francisco 83 hours and 39 minutes after it left New York City." Lincoln's transcontinental railroad was a "Civil War effort" that "would support communities and military outposts on the frontier," "give settlers safe and dependable passage west," and "tie new states California and Oregon to the rest of the country." The Pacific Railroad Act was amended in 1863, 1864, 1865, and 1866. The original Pacific Railroad was "a 1,907-mile contiguous railroad line" built by three companies: Western Pacific Railroad Company, Central Pacific Railroad Company of California, and Union Pacific Railroad Company. The Library of Congress confirmed, "By 1900, four additional transcontinental railroads connected the eastern states with the Pacific Coast."

Andrew Carnegie (1835-1919) immigrated from Dunfermline, Scotland, and settled in Braddock, Pennsylvania, where he built "his first steel mill, the Edgar Thomson Steel Works in 1872." The Morrill Tariff empowered America's steel industry by taxing steel imports that were mainly drawn from Britain at the time. British imports were sold at reduced prices and abetted American business moguls like Carnegie. He later sold Carnegie Steel to banking magnate J.P. Morgan "for $480 million in 1901" that became United States Steel Company. Carnegie was an avid reader and spread his wealth to education funding "over 2,500 libraries" in addition to numerous "colleges, schools, nonprofit organizations and associations" that consequently enabled technical and medical research and established scholastic Pell grants. His extraordinary educational legacy blended with the Bureau's Truth in Advertising Movement.

Carnegie contributed to many educational organizations and the Bureau was likely among his recipients because it depended upon charitable donations and evidenced a corresponding interest in education. In 1911, Carnegie established "Carnegie Corporation of New York" as an educational foundation. Accordingly, AACA records for the August 1911 Boston convention indicated a focus on education. Dr. Herbert Houston, vice president of Doubleday, Page & Company (publishers of *The Jungle*), was quoted as saying, "In short, this convention is itself the proof that the Associated Advertising Clubs believe in Education." Additionally, outgoing AACA President Samuel Dobbs acknowledged that he oversaw the appointment of Dr. Houston as chairman of the "Educational Course Committee" at the previous year's AACA convention held in Omaha, Nebraska. No doubt that the businessmen of the great and powerful AACA had insider's knowledge of Carnegie's pending plans to establish a cash-cow educational foundation and pursued his generosity.

Thereafter, on March 12, 1912, the AACA launched the first Vigilance Committee in New York whose founding membership included Dr. Houston. He was later appointed president of the Associated Advertising Clubs of the World in 1914. Dr. Houston played an integral part in the development of the early advertising industry including the Better Business Bureau; his involvement would have attracted Carnegie's benevolent attention. Carnegie's foundation also set a philanthropic example to others including Asa Candler, owner of Coca-Cola and benefactor of Emory University, whose respective philanthropy was originally inspired by tax repercussions from President Thomas Woodrow Wilson's Revenue Act of 1913 that represented "the first federal income tax of the 20th century." The modern Bureau's philanthropic foundations continue Carnegie-esque educational programs.

The Progressive Reformation Era's technological revolution popularized advertising whose antiquarian roots bridged time with the Roman Empire's Marcus Titulus Cicero who promoted ethical disclosure and warned of deceptive trade. Cicero, (born 1/3/106 BCE in modern Arpino, Italy; died 12/7/43 BCE in modern Formia, Italy), introduced fair advertising and consumer advocacy as ancient wisdom. Although born into wealth, Cicero identified with the common man and was dubbed "father of his country." As an eternal legend, Cicero was one of Rome's most celebrated gifts to perpetuity as an esteemed lawyer, tactician, politician, scholar, orator, philosopher, author, and showman. He was also a consumer activist promoting social ethics during the travails of a crumbling Roman Republic that wielded the brutal death of Julius Caesar. The Bureau's proclivity for stolen thunder aligned with Cicero's celestial aura as a crusading educator for truth in advertising and rode Cicero's golden toga into the hearts and pockets of trusting consumers by quoting him as the ultimate consumer advocate: "*All things should be laid bare so that the buyer may not be in any way ignorant of anything the seller knows.*" Appel, author of the *Ten Commandments of Advertising*, reminded that the Bible also warned of false advertising: "As a nail sticketh fast beneath the joinings of the stones, so doth sin stick close between buying and selling" (Apocrypha: Ecclesiasticus, XXVII, 2)."

The Bureau's ancestry dates to luminary George Rowell who opened Rowell Advertising Agency in 1865. Rowell introduced trailblazing advertising methods and publications such as the *American Newspaper Directory* in 1869 and *Printers' Ink* Advertising Journal in 1888. As a result, he introduced the first collective newspaper index, advertising journal, awards system, and rating scores. The Better Business Bureau adopted Rowell's merit concepts.

The Association of General Newspaper Agents was formed in New York in 1888 and considered "the first organized advertising group" instigated at the behest of the American Newspaper Publishers Association (ANPA). Purpose was to arbitrate business between publisher, sales agent, and advertiser.

Due to travel limitations in the latter 19th century, the U.S. advertising industry organized under two different regional associations located in the East and West. Reconstructing a chronological timeline of national advertising history proved challenging, confusing, scattershot, and deficient because historical data was dusty, date dodging, and disregarded name changes. Accordingly, the New York-centered eastern group was the most prominent and assembled as the International Advertising Association (IAA) in 1904; IAA became the

Associated Advertising Clubs of America (AACA) in 1905; AACA was renamed Associated Advertising Clubs of the World (AACW) in 1914; and, AACW became Advertising Federation of America (AFA) in 1929. In the western region, the Advertising Association of the West (AAW) emerged after President Lincoln opened the Wild West through the Homestead Act, on May 20, 1862, and the Transcontinental Pacific Railway Act on July 1, 1862. West Coast advertising embedded through Hollywood's christening in 1887 and the invention of television in 1927 but mushroomed during the atomic age.

Twentieth-century upstart technology, e.g., Ford Model "N" was invented in 1906 and first passenger airplane (airboat) was invented in 1914, opened communications between advertising clubs on the East and West Coasts bringing marketplace comradery, advertising, and sales. As a result, in February 1967, the eastern AFA merged with the western AAW to form today's American Advertising Federation (AAF).

In 1900, *Printer's Ink* interacted with turn-of-the-century advertising clubs to self-regulate total advertising revenue in the amount of "$95,000,000." By 1905, the AACA boasted total advertising revenue of "$145,000,000." After the 1911 Boston convention, the AACA approached the NYSE for funds to establish the first New York Vigilance Committee that opened March 12, 1912. The Vigilance Committee was created as an enforcement arm of the AACA to regulate the *Printers' Ink* Model Statute, introduced by *Printers' Ink* five months earlier. The statute represented a profound turning point that blended advertising regulation with consumer advocacy.

The concept for a national advertising association, tentatively named "International Federation of Advertising Interests," was first presented by S. De Witt Clough, president of Abbott Laboratories. In July 1903, Clough contacted *Printers' Ink* "suggesting that a national group would be a valuable supplement to the local clubs in the dissemination of correct advertising ideas." C. F. Olmsted, advertising manager of the Natural Food Company (now known as Shredded Wheat), "was active in the preliminary spadework" and H. D. Perky, president/owner of H. D. Perky, was "at the helm." The name eventually chosen was "International Advertising Association" and the organization was formed and introduced at the group's first convention held in Chicago, Illinois, in 1904. The name changed the following year to Associated Advertising Clubs of America at their convention in St. Louis. According to Archive.com, the AACA was known for its annual conventions that served as "milestones of advertising progress."

Publishers and printers became respected community leaders and represented the most prominent newspapers and farm journals in America. Like heads of state, they managed advertising clubs to combat growing advertising fraud that threatened Big Business. The clubs assembled a national advertising association that splintered into special-interest associations to accommodate the burgeoning

THE APO$TATE

industries of advertising agencies and agents. Wars, politics, and economic depressions forged an impregnable bond between the U.S. Federal Government and advertising industry.

In 1894, the Agate Club emerged as the first truth-based advertising assembly. *Printers' Ink* stated, "The Agate Club was formed at Chicago by a group of leading magazine advertising representatives" and "lays undisputed claim to being the oldest club of advertising men in point of continuous service."

Around the same timeframe, in the late 1800s, the Mallet Club gathered in New York City to represent the printing and periodical industries. In 1902, the Mallet Club was renamed the Quoin Club. The names "Mallet" and "Quoin" were tools of yesteryear's printing trade during the "imposition" process of assembling a page of type. The wooden mallet was used "to ensure that furniture is fixed in case and that print was level to guarantee an even printing"; and, the quoin was "a locking tool used to hold type or bases snug on the press bed ... two are needed to lock up a form, one for vertical hold, one for horizontal."

In 1896, the prestigious Sphinx Club assembled as a galvanized effort by New York City's advertising elite. The Sphinx Club incorporated as the "Advertising Men's League" in 1906; was renamed "The Advertising Club of New York" in 1910; formed the first "Vigilance Committee of the Advertising Club of New York" in 1912; and was renamed the "Better Business Bureau" in 1916. The ultra-exclusive Sphinx Club originally consisted of "sixteen members" with an office located at 443 Fourth Avenue, New York City; members were listed as either a "resident" or "non-resident" according to in-state or out-of-state domicile. Today the Sphinx Club is known as the Ad Club.

The Sphinx Club
Photo of original cover of 1906 publication of
The Sphinx Club New York; photo source: Caryn Cain.

Membership in the Sphinx Club evoked the enchantment of King Arthur's Knights of the Round Table. Distinguished titans of organized advertising reincarnated the secret society of the Knights Templar. Sphinxsters began filtering out of the general assembly of the Associated Advertising Clubs of America when it became the internationally enhanced Associated Advertising Clubs of the World in 1914. The advertising industry began dividing into large-scale specialized advertising associations, such as publishing, printing, advertisers, and agencies. The fissure was facilitated by the gradual demise of old school masters like George Rowell, but founders' distinguished legacies assured dedicated allegiance to respective divisions within the advertising industry.

The Ad Club and the Better Business Bureau each developed foundations whose modern disparities accentuate the Bureau's Deep State militarization. The Ad Club Foundation is a non-regulatory organization that "develops and administers educational outreach programs including scholarships and summer internship positions"; there are no tricky gimmicks or bogus merit programs, no elimination of competition, no Deep State history and/or plenary powers, and no persecution of private citizens. To the contrary, I allege that the Houston Bureau's Foundation links to CBBB's Deep State network and global politics enabling infinite outreach, infiltration of federal regulatory agencies, and unfettered deceptive trade; that the Houston Foundation sponsors a specious profiteering awards program, impedes fair trade, controls the marketplace, enforces Deep State powers, controls the courts, and persecutes private citizens. Furthermore, the Houston Foundation acts contrary to IRS exemption mandates that require its programs to include and treat equally all marketplace business evidenced by the *Awards for Excellence* that excludes nonmembers.

Joseph Appel was an attorney, author, and celebrity sales manager of John Wanamaker stores. Appel was among the founders of the Truth in Advertising Movement. He joined the advertising industry in 1906 and was a member of the spectacular Sphinx Club that he considered "the first *organized* stand against dishonest advertising." During the same timeframe, Appel assisted with the organization of the Poor Richard Club and bestowed its name "in a bedroom at the Bellevue-Stratford hotel on February 16, 1906." Appel laid sacred ground with his *Ten Commandments of Advertising* that was later repackaged by the Bureau as their standards for ethical business practice. If not for Appel's written contributions expounding upon the Sphinx Club, there would be respective dearth of historical information today. His book *Growing Up with Advertising*, published in 1940, stated, "The voice of the famous and influential Sphinx Club, composed as it was of both advertising men and publishers, and many retailers, was powerful and significant." He added that it "was famous during two or three decades for its full dress, five dollar dinners with wine, served under the watchful eye of Oscar of the Waldorf. It was organized in 1896 with the motto, "Honesty in Advertising" and it served as the first rostrum for organized opposition to misleading advertising."

The Sphinx Club celebrated a promising 20th century by authoring, *The Sphinx Club, New York (1904)*. The book's front cover emblazoned the mystical sphinx positioned between two Roman columns. Members were described as "general advertisers, advertising agents, advertising writers, advertising illustrators, teachers of advertising, publishers of advertising and their representatives, and, in fact, for everyone directly interested in the buying, selling, preparation, and placing of advertising space." Appel described the event that introduced the Sphinx Club to its legacy of truth in advertising: "The first thundering, unequivocal, documented denunciation of fraudulent advertising was made in 1903 by John Adams Thayer, then advertising manager of the *Delineator* (and later publisher of *Everybody's*). He showed the Sphinx Club stereopticon slides of specific objectionable advertising, and roundly attacked deceit and fraud as fatal destroyers of advertising confidence on the part of the public."

Kenner also offered a similar tribute to the same occasion in *The Fight for Truth in Advertising*, but added more details: "Advertising men, in 1903, heard one of their own rise up and denounce fraudulent and confidence-destroying advertising. At a meeting of the Sphinx Club, New York, John Adams Thayer, then advertising manager of the *Delineator*, attacked objectionable advertising, scoring roundly certain instances of fraud and deceit. To visualize the subject, he illustrated his talk with stereopticon views of current examples, among them: the Parker "Lucky Box," Francis Truth – the "Divine Healer," and "520%" Miller. This address from one of the advertising leaders of his day attracted widespread attention among publishers and advertisers .... The club was a proving ground for much of the impetus given to activities for protecting the integrity of advertising as the new century opened."

Appel wrote that he became indoctrinated into the Truth in Advertising Movement after accepting an invitation to speak for the Sphinx Club in New York. He reflected on the occasion writing, "It was just about at this juncture (1906) in the history of the advertising "clean-up" movement that I was able to add my voice for the first time in New York ... James O'Flaherty, brought me into New York advertising circles ... by luring me into making a speech before the Sphinx Club."

Author Stephen Fox explained the concept of the Sphinx Club: "The men in the business did not know one another ... It was thought that if they were to sit around the same table once a month there would be a little less throat-cutting and general misbehavior." Fox also clarified how the Club earned its name: "In New York this group was called the Sphinx Club because nothing discussed internally was to be repeated to outsiders." (I suggest that a respective modern Sphinx spin is "What happens in Vegas stays in Vegas" that was derived from "What happens here, stays here" that was coined in 2003 by "R&R Partners" ad agency in Las Vegas.) As a result, the Sphinx Club started a tradition of secrecy that was adopted by the Better Business Bureau to hide skullduggery, maintain empowering image of truth, and protect golden coattails from liability. According to Adage.com, the Sphinx Club met "monthly at the Fifth Avenue Hotel and in the old Waldorf-Astoria Hotel, on the site now occupied by the Empire State Building."

Advertising agents in the Sphinx Club gathered to self-regulate and contain a growing problem that threatened to ruin their livelihood and force publishing houses out of business. The Progressive Era brought an influx of fraudulent advertising that adversely affected distribution of publications and advertising sales, which provided the lifeblood of the advertising industry. Advertising became unreliable and created skittish readership afraid to buy featured products. Appel appropriately summed up the closeout of the century by predicting a protracted battle against fraudulent advertising: "Thus it will be seen that the "Gay Nineties" were giving unmistakable notice here and there of the grave problems which would have to be solved sooner or later by the advertising and publishing professions; problems that, as we now see, were not solved even by fairly vigorous group action until almost half a century later, when (1939) the government took an active hand."

Also, in 1906, "The Poor Richard Club" was formed in Philadelphia, Pennsylvania. Appel named the club after Benjamin Franklin's *Poor Richard's Almanack* that was published between 1732 and 1758 and "contained a calendar, weather, poems, sayings, and astronomical and astrological information." The *Poor Richard's Almanack* was a "best seller" (over 10,000 pamphlets printed annually) in the colonies, and was renowned for *Poor Richard's Proverbs* composed of "witty phrases" and "wordplay." In fact, Franklin's quotes still reverberate today: "A penny saved is a penny earned"; "When the wine enters, out goes the truth"; "Honesty is the best policy"; "It takes many good deeds to build a good reputation, and only one bad one to lose it"; "Either write something worth reading or do something worth writing"; "In this world nothing can be said to be certain, except death and taxes"; and, "Fish and visitors stink after three days."

The Poor Richard Club was a blue-collar version of the Sphinx Club comprised of agents and managers. Appel wrote, "Poor Richard Club was born in a bedroom of the Bellevue-Stratford hotel on February 16, 1906, when a gathering of advertising and newspaper men formed an organization. Those present were: Clarence K. Arnold, advertising agent; Stephen C. Berger, of the *Public Ledger*; A. A. Christian, advertising manager of Gimbels; Percival K. Frowert, advertising agent; M. F. Hanson, of the *Record*; W. Percy Mills and William Simpson of the *Bulletin*; George L. Mitchell, advertising agent; Walter Ostrander, real estate; J. W. Morton, Jr., advertising manager of Strawbridge & Clothier; Milton Rubincam, of the *Evening Telegraph*; Edward I. Bacon, of the

Inquirer, and Joseph H. Appel, advertising manager of John Wanamaker's."

Appel's every word represented rare advertising history. He wrote, "When I again faced the Sphinx Club, in 1910, I was reinforced by a large contingent of Poor Richardites, for in our honor the club was holding a "Philadelphia Night"." Additionally, he educated perpetuity by noting, "Unlike the postman I knocked *thrice* at the Sphinx door. It was in 1914, after I had been transferred to the New York Wanamaker store ... And I again startled the Sphinx Club by proposing that they undertake the erection of a big *advertising building* that would become headquarters for such organizations as the Chamber of Commerce, the Merchants' Association, the Aldine Club, the Advertising Men's League, the Quoin Club, the Associated Press, the United Press, the various publishers' Associations, the typographical and engraving organizations, and all bodies interested in business and advertising." Appel was a mentor whose achievements were admirable, noble, and innovative with intention to consolidate the power of the advertising industry under one roof. Unfortunately, over the next few years, the advertising industry fractured due to mounting tensions between competitive factions, such as publishers and engravers, which made cohesive ventures impossible. In 1915, The Poor Richard Club moved operations to the Dr. Joseph Leidy House located at 1319 Locust Street until membership declined and the building was sold in 1979. The club disbanded several years later.

From 1902 until 1917, the Quoin Club included the National Periodical Association (NPA) within its membership roster. The NPA advertised its office location as, Fifth Avenue Building, New York City. In 1915, the Quoin Club included 29 publications as members with a combined circulation of "over 7,000,000 copies each issue" that would "likely reach 25,000,000 people throughout America every month." Professional biographies listed membership in the Quoin Club as a prestigious advertising credential in the "*Who's Who of Advertising*." After 1917, the Quoin Club merged with the "Periodical Publishers' Association," and continued business under that name.

In April 1917, *Printers' Ink* referred to the Quoin Club in the article, "Help Afforded Advertisers by A.N.P.A. Bureau of Advertising," and reported, "The Bureau has been asked by the Quoin Club, representing the magazine interests, to join with it in opposing any further exhibits at the A. A. C. of W. convention on the ground that it is impossible to get sufficient attention to pay for the money invested." The article was significant and reflected fractured relationships within the AACW while highlighting a pivotal juncture in the advertising industry's evolution. The Quoin Club and NPA were among several publishers who filed suit in 1916 against the New York Photo-Engravers' Union claiming violation of the Donnelly antitrust law. Circumstances were awkward considering many in the Photo-Engravers Union were also members of the AACW.

The Quoin Club incorporated advertising ethics within operational guidelines and dealt with "postal rates, service and legislation; labor and manufacturing problems; magazine paper prices; group cooperation with respect to advertising standards," and merchandising of magazines. *Simmons' Spice Mill* magazine highlighted the club's mission in its article, "Explaining Advertising to the Public," which stated, "The purpose of national advertising is to make widely known the names and trade-marks of goods upon which the manufacturer places the stamp of responsibility – this sign of willingness to be judged by the quality of his goods. The trade-mark identifies the goods – advertising makes them known. The two things work together automatically for higher standards of quality."

The NPA brought to the Quoin Club a *Who's Who* membership that produced the most popular publications of the day. Members were loyal supporters and patrons of the renowned *Printers' Ink*. The NPA's logo was an outline of the United States with "NATIONAL PERIODICAL ASSOCIATION" printed inside. The association proudly highlighted its co-existence with the Quoin Club stating in parenthesis above its advertised membership list, "FOR FIFTEEN YEARS THE QUOIN CLUB." Members included "Ainslee's, American Magazine, Century, Christian Herald, Collier's Weekly, Continent, Cosmopolitan, Country Life, Countryside Magazine, Every Week, Farm and Fireside, Garden Magazine, Good Housekeeping, Harper's Magazine, Hearst's, House and Garden, Independent, Judge, Leslie's Weekly, Literary Digest, McCall's, Metropolitan, Mother's Magazine, National Geographic, Outlook, Popular, Red Cross Magazine, Review of Reviews, St. Nicholas, Scribner's, Short Stories, Smith's, Something-To-Do, Sunset, To-day's Housewife, Vanity Fair, Vogue, Woman's Home Companion, and World's Work."

In 1916, the Quoin Club joined publishers in charging photo-engravers with price fixing that violated antitrust laws. Initial trial proceedings favored the photo-engravers because antitrust laws at that time did not encompass intangible commodities.

In 1921, an appeal to the New York Supreme Court amended the Sherman and Donnelly antitrust laws with the enactment of the Meyer-Martin Bill, which held the photo-engraving industry accountable by changing antitrust laws to include both tangible and intangible commodities. WWI depleted European publishing suppliers' stock of ink and paper forcing U.S. publishers to buy respective supplies in the states at twice the cost. As a result, the price doubled for books and magazines, but lowered "retail sales."

The Donnelly Act of 1899, described as "New York's antitrust law, sections 340-347 of New York's General Business Law," protected "interstate activities" within New York, and closely resembled the Sherman Act with some variations. The Donnelly Act "prohibits price fixing, bid rigging, territorial and customer allocations, monopolization, boycotts, and tying arrangements, among other practices." Criminal penalty was stated as, "Private parties may also bring lawsuits to enjoin these practices and obtain treble damages. Violation of the Donnelly Act is also a felony, punishable by a criminal fine of up to $1,000,000 for corporations and up to $100,000 and 4 years imprisonment for individuals."

Trial quickly determined that the Donnelly antitrust law did not apply because photo-engravings were not considered "commodities." *Editor & Publisher* described the failed legal battle: "Suit was brought during 1917 against the New York Photo-Engravers' Board of Trade under the Donnelly antitrust law. Early in the proceedings it was ruled that the action taken by the Photo-Engravers' Union was not contrary to law, and after deliberating for months the court decided that the *employers violated no law because photo-engravings are not commodities under the law.*"

On April 16, 1921, the Meyer-Martin Bill ("Section 340 of the New York State general business law") was passed to amend the Donnelly Act succinctly ending price-fixing across the nation and included all forms of commodities. Whereas the bill focused on photo-engravers because of the situation being contested by publishers, it was drafted to include all trades. The bill brought the photo-engravers into the "scope" of the Donnelly Act removing "the restriction concerning commodities in common use" and prohibited "anything in the nature of a combination or association to fix prices." The American Federation of Labor attempted to block passage of the bill, but it was pushed through both houses of the New York State Legislature under "emergency message" from Nathan Lewis Miller (1868-1953), 43rd governor of New York between January 1, 1921 and December 31, 1922. The *Editor & Publisher* magazine, on April 23, 1921, reported that the Meyer-Martin Bill was the result of joint efforts by the Publishers Association of New York City and the New York Publishers Association.

The year 1904 introduced the International Advertising Association and the St. Louis World's Fair in Missouri. Beforehand, *Printers' Ink* wrote that "thirty-five advertisers, media men and agency men met at New York, with George H. Hazen as chairman." Consequently, *Printers' Ink* reported that "one hundred and thirty-five" advertising delegates met in St. Louis to establish the International Advertising Association; occasion coincided with the opening of the World Trade Fair, i.e., "The Louisiana Purchase Exposition," on April 30, 1904. President Theodore Roosevelt participated in opening ceremonies whereby paying homage to his murdered predecessor's founding patronage of the World's Fair.

Three years earlier, President William McKinley promoted the World's Fair and broadcasted "a proclamation inviting the international community to participate." Then, on September 6, 1901, McKinley was shot twice in the abdomen by 28-year-old anarchist Leon Czolgosz while greeting visitors at the Temple of Music during the Buffalo Pan-American Exposition. McKinley died eight agonizing days later from "gangrene." Vice President Roosevelt became 26th POTUS on September 14, 1901. Czolgosz was tried on September 23rd, sentenced to death on September 26th, and "executed by electric chair on October 29, 1901."

A decade earlier, on July 2, 1890, the Sherman Anti-Trust Act was introduced to combat uber-wealthy robber barons' monopolistic control of business. McKinley, the last president to serve in the Civil War, was a puppet of the Republican Party establishment and was elected to protect respective special interests. His presidency was financed by Andrew Carnegie, John Pierpont Morgan Sr. (1837-1913), and John Davison Rockefeller Sr. (1839-1937), as respective steel, banking, and oil magnates. Roosevelt was placed as an impotent vice president to impede his progressive reformation efforts until Czolgosz threw a wrench in deep-pocketed plans. Consequently, President Roosevelt attacked monopolies with a vengeance. Forty companies were sued for antitrust violations including the Northern Securities Company railroad trust (SCOTUS rendered decision in 1904 in favor of the federal government) and Standard Oil Company of New Jersey (SCOTUS rendered decision in 1911 in favor of the federal government).

The Spanish-American War of 1898 exposed outrageous corruption in the food industry that was buried by the U.S. War Department. President McKinley presided over the Cuban War and catered to special manufacturing interests that processed contaminated canned meat shipped to American troops. President Roosevelt participated in the Cuban War as a Lieutenant Colonel in charge of the "Rough Riders." In 1906, Roosevelt supported Dr. Harvey Wiley's Pure Food and Drug Act that "banned food and drugs that were impure or falsely labeled from being made, sold, and shipped." Also, in 1906, author Upton Sinclair published *The Jungle*, which exposed meat packing atrocities and guaranteed passage of the act.

The Department of Agriculture's esteemed Dr. Wiley was a longtime proponent of food legislation. He censured adulterated foods and sought remedial assistance from the powerful Women's Christian Temperance Union. Their joint pleas to President Roosevelt, combined with incendiary public fallout from *The Jungle*, resulted in the Pure Food and Drug Act. Thereafter, the Truth in Advertising Movement was inadvertently sparked when Dr. Wiley sued Coca-Cola for violation of the act. With a bitter trial pending, Coca-Cola dispatched handsome Sales Manager Samuel Dobbs to solicit the presidency of the prestigious AACA. Two years later, after the *Barrels and Kegs Case* trial started in March 1911, Dobbs relinquished his presidency of the AACA at the August 1911 convention.

Food and drug violations during the late 1800s underscored epic monopolies controlling the business industry. Whereas the Pure Food Act did not pertain to false advertising, it created the groundswell that rallied the AACA's truth crusade. In October 1909, the U.S. Attorney General filed charges against The Coca-Cola Company of Atlanta for violation of the Pure Food and Drug Act. The federal lawsuit was officially titled, *The United States vs. Forty Barrels and Twenty Kegs of Coca-Cola*. Consequently, Coca-Cola suffered condemnation and dramatic loss of sales. Dobbs pursued the AACA's presidency as a redemptive countermeasure and served from 1909 to 1911; timeframe represented interval between initial indictment and trial commencement. Timing and circumstances suggested Dobbs sought leadership in the prestigious AACA as a publicity maneuver to improve sales, stabilize company credibility, and prime the public for a favorable trial verdict. A protracted roller coaster trial proved intense and highlighted the combative wits of Dr. Wiley and Coca-Cola's owner, Asa Candler. Trial began "March 13, 1911," and was initially won by Coca-Cola, but landed in the Supreme Court and settled "out of court" on "November 12, 1917," in the FDA's favor.

Advertising as a science was never taken seriously by American universities until Dr. Walter Dill Scott (1869-1955) legitimized the industry. According to AdAge, Dr. Scott was "[b]orn in 1869 near Cooksville, Ill.," and "earned a Ph.D. in psychology from the University of Leipzig in Germany in 1900 and, on his return to the U.S., became an instructor in psychology at Northwestern University." His first book, *The Theory of Advertising*, appeared in 1903 and captured the advertising industry's widespread attention. Dr. Scott applied psychology to advertising and determined that "consumer suggestibility was based on three factors: emotion, sympathy, and sentimentality." *Printers' Ink* credited Dr. Scott with formulating "the precursors of what was later to be taken up by the advertiser as a normal part of marketing procedure – research." Kenner also quoted Dr. Scott, "'There is no force in America that can suppress fraudulent advertising and thus win the confidence of the public in advertisements, except the advertisers themselves,'" wrote Professor Walter Dill Scott, at that time."

In 1908, John Romer assumed command of *Printers' Ink* as editor. He made advertising history after attending the AACA's Boston convention in 1911 by introducing a law to resolve the industry's debilitating toothless false advertising enforcement quagmire. Whereas Appel inspired the truth movement with his *Ten Commandments of Advertising*, Romer provided the vehicle and greenlit punitive law analogous to loading a bullet in an empty gun. Romer hired New York employment attorney Harry Nims to draft the *Printers' Ink* Model Statute and introduced the law in *Printers' Ink*. Thereafter, he approached the AACA to establish vigilance committees to enforce the statute. The AACA acted on Romer's advice that their "advertising clubs should organize vigilance committees for the purpose of investigating misrepresentations alleged to exist in the advertising originating in their cities, and for the purpose of cooperating with local prosecuting officers under the law." In 1912, Romer was listed as a founding member of the first Vigilance Committee and first National Vigilance Committee.

The NYSE financially supported the AACA and Vigilance Committees with symbiotic cronyism contributing to the Crash of 1929. The U.S. Senate charged the New York Bureau with racketeering and securities fraud regarding its NYSE-affiliated "Before You Invest, Investigate" program that implied the

Bureau's ability to screen and pre-qualify safe investments; scandalous impact and backlash was muted by the Bureau's crony network that included landmark newspapers and Romer's righteous *Printers' Ink*. Additionally, years later, the *Printers' Ink "50 Years"* bi-centennial edition made no hindsight mention of the New York Bureau's trouncing by the U.S. Senate or Coca-Cola's indictment for violation of the Pure Food Act. To the contrary, *Printers' Ink* promoted respective parties' exemplary integrity and/or consumer advocacy.

The state of New York's world-class New York City and its five boroughs of Manhattan, the Bronx, Queens, Brooklyn, and Staten Island remain synonymous with the birth of America, the NYSE, and the advertising industry. In fact, most everything that we take for granted today originated there. The City of York, Pennsylvania, was named in honor of York, England, and served as a temporary U.S. capital from September 1777 until June 27, 1778. During such time, the Continental Congress was on the run from the British during the American Revolution (1764 to 1789) and adopted the Articles of Confederation in the City of York on November 15, 1777. The Articles represented America's first Constitution and remained in effect from March 1, 1781, to 1789. According to City of York, "[I]t was here that the words "The United States of America" were first spoken."

The classic City of York introduced a litany of "firsts" including, but certainly not limited to, America's first church in 1733, first stone homes in 1734, first roads in 1739, first city in 1741, first public hall around 1812, first coal in 1818, first telegraph in 1844, first police department in 1845 ("dark blue uniforms" copied London's police), first motor in 1853, first telephone in 1881, first electricity in 1882, and first electric neon advertising in 1891. The city became a renowned center of trade underpinned by crony politics and bias voting. Furthermore, the name "New York" was coined in the late 19th century; according to History.com, "In 1895, residents of Queens, the Bronx, Staten Island and Brooklyn–all independent cities at that time–voted to "consolidate" with Manhattan to form a five-borough "Greater New York"."

In 1789, there was no "organized stock exchange" when General George Washington was victoriously inaugurated president of the United States after a long-and-bloody revolution that was almost lost had it not been for France's tide-turning military assistance and funding. The NYSE formally organized in 1817 as a byproduct of the Buttonwood Agreement that was signed on May 17, 1792, by 24 stock traders; signers represented the first members of the NYSE. According to "Wall Street Walks," a division of the New York Visitor and Convention Bureau, "In the agreement they agreed to trade securities only amongst themselves, to maintain fixed commission rates, and to avoid other auctions." Only members could participate with business performed under a Buttonwood tree located "at about 68 Wall Street today." The historic

Buttonwood tree marked America's first financial district, and national mourning occurred when a storm tragically blew it over "on June 14, 1865."

The Tontine Coffee House opened in 1793 as the NYSE's first official building that was "located at the northwest corner of Wall and William Streets." The current NYSE building was completed on "April 22, 1903," and was located at "8-18 Broad Street" with the main trading floor located at "11 Wall Street." The NYSE adopted an "exclusive members-only" policy.

New York City was also first to animate advertising through the miracle of electricity that inspired the magic of neon lights. During the late 1800s, the "Great White Way" empowered the advertising industry with newfound respect by lighting Broadway's enticing streets to exotically entertain a mesmerized public. According to author Robert Rusie, "In 1891, the first electric marquis was lit on Broadway. The theater was on Madison Square at the intersection of Broadway and Fifth Avenue at W. 23rd Street. The Flatiron Building now occupies the site. By midway through the following decade, the street blazed with electric signs as each theater announced its shows and stars in white lights." Furthermore, safe brilliant lighting ended the anxiety and destruction caused by flammable oil lamps.

False advertising has always been an insidious enemy of the advertising industry and relentlessly threatened business mainstays of integrity and patronage. The first postal laws after the American Revolution were insufficient because they only applied to the mail service that primarily distributed to an outlying agricultural society. As the urban environment progressed and cities multiplied, deceptive advertising followed and became the bane of existence for the advertising and publishing industries. Fraudsters jeopardized reader confidence, publication credibility, and circulation of magazines, periodicals and newspapers. Then pharmaceutical fraud arose to present a new challenge that egregiously addicted a trusting public.

Census indices "in 1920" reflected movement of a rural populace into urban areas. For the first time, most of society had shifted to the cities with statistics showing the total United States population at 106,021,537 with an urban population of 54,253,282 or 51.2% and a rural population of 51,768,255 or 48.8%. False advertising adapted to burgeoning communications, technology, and industrial advancement, and migrated into the cities as an insidious companion of opportunity that infiltrated every aspect of society. New York City became particularly vulnerable due to Prohibition and rise of organized crime. The city seduced advertising, banking, and investment power brokers; ultimately, collusion forged interdependency and a code of silence because allies were all members of the Bureau. As a result, Wall Street and the New York Bureau forged an impregnable relationship that survived the catastrophic 1920s and 1930s due to gilded connections within a high-profile membership base.

In retrospect, the post office was established by President George Washington (1732-1799) and provided the first false advertising laws. On April 30, 1789,

Washington was inaugurated president of the United States, "on the balcony of Federal Hall on Wall Street in New York." Among the first laws of a new nation, Washington introduced the Postal Act of 1792, which created the U.S. Post Office Department. The Postal Act also produced the first regulatory advertising law to monitor the mail system. Publishing and advertising agents used the mails to distribute advertising whose sales supported respective industries. Kenner reflected on the early history of advertising fraud stating, "As newspapers and periodicals multiplied and enlarged their circulations, the quack and the charlatan were attracted to this medium." Consequently, the advertising industry was limited to insufficient postal laws that failed to regulate domestic fraud, misrepresented products, and fly-by-night gimmicks.

Industrialized society became increasingly reliant upon the printed word with caveat emptor ("let the buyer beware") highlighting vulnerability due to dishonest sales tactics. Wansley wrote, "Activities of those who used the mails to perpetrate their frauds upon the public were so numerous and so blatant that in 1872 Congress empowered the Post Office Department to take action against them." Unfortunately, the postal system proved insufficient and offered basic laws limited to its legal purview. Society had no consumer protection until the Progressive Era forced new legislation through the truth movement.

It was stated that the "The Post Office Act (17 Stat. 283, enacted June 8, 1872) formally incorporated the United States Post Office Department into the United States Cabinet"; Section 148 (§148) made it illegal to distribute "any obscene or disloyal materials through the mail." The Postal Act was also known as the obscenity law and indirectly prohibited abortion whereby initiating the birth control movement. It regulated mail distribution of "obscene, lewd, or lascivious" materials used for contraceptive purposes. The Comstock Act of 1873 amended the Postal Act of 1872 and was defined as an "Act of the Suppression of Trade in, and Circulation of, Obscene Literature and Articles of Immoral Use." It also regulated abortion and contraception as pertained to "immoral use." The Comstock Act was amended in 1971 when Congress omitted "language concerning contraception," and in 1973 when "Roe v. Wade" prohibited only unlawful abortion leaving grounds for states' rights to determine what was deemed lawful.

Between the 1890s and 1920s, the Progressive Era ushered a life-altering industrial revolution that particularly tested the advertising industry. Advertising clubs and associations united to regulate deceptive trade practice consequent to the incredible advances in manufacturing, technology, travel, telecommunications, and pharmaceuticals that became the galvanizing bête noir ("bitter enemy") of the early Vigilance Committees. In particular, medicinal advertising fraud prevailed as a debilitating nightmare that threatened the core of the family unit. Commonly used drugs were addictive narcotics, and food and beverages contained harmful adulterated ingredients such as alcohol, caffeine, cocaine, and preservatives.

THE APO$TATE

Opiates invaded American culture in the latter half of the 19th century due to the railroads, the Civil War, and immigration. Sixteenth POTUS Abraham Lincoln signed into law the Homestead Act and the Transcontinental Pacific Railway Act with both laws jointly opening access and encouraging travel to western territories. An influx of immigrant Chinese laborers laid train tracks and introduced opium to American culture. Author Diana L. Ahmad wrote, "The first opium dens in the United States appeared in San Francisco's Chinatown."

Narcotics, "commonly morphine and heroin," were included in early patent medicines and widely prescribed by the medical profession resulting in an addicted society. Laudanum was a very potent narcotic combination of opium, morphine, and codeine. Women were particularly affected because the opiate was dispensed as a "cure-all" for female ailments. Laudanum had "wide-range uses" including melancholy, nervous disorders, insomnia, menstrual cramps, menopause, colds, meningitis, cardiac diseases, coughing, tuberculosis, dysentery, rheumatism, and general aches and pains. In fact, Lincoln's wife, Mary Todd Lincoln, "was a laudanum addict" and after his assassination used the drug to attempt suicide. Wikipedia.org stated, "Between 150,000 and 200,000 opiate addicts lived in the United States in the late 19th century and between two-thirds and three-quarters of these addicts were women." The pharmaceutical industry wasn't regulated until the Pure Food and Drug Act of 1906.

Bayer Heroin Bottle
Title: "Originally containing 5 grams of Heroin substance. The label on the back references the 1924 US ban, and has a batch number stamp starting with 27, so it probably dates from the 1920's."
Photo source: Author Mpv_51 granted public domain; Wikipedia Commons; [https://en.wikipedia.org/wiki/Narcotic#/media/File:Bayer_Heroin_bottle.jpg].

In 1866, Confederate Lt. Col. Dr. John Stith Pemberton (1831-1888), a chemist and pharmacist, invented the original recipe for Coca-Cola while developing a painkiller to overcome morphine addiction that he contracted after "being slashed across the chest by a saber" in the Battle of Columbus, Georgia. During the American Civil War, the wounded were usually treated with morphine resulting in "soldier's disease" that threatened lifetime addiction. Injuries were compounded by lack of doctors and catchall field-dressing procedures that prohibited individualized laborious surgeries. When chloroform wasn't available, whiskey or biting a bullet offered wretched anesthetic alternatives. "Amputation was the most common treatment for broken or severely wounded limbs ... More than half of leg amputations at the thigh or knee ended up being fatal. 83% of amputations were fatal if the amputation was done at the hip joint," according to Factinate.

Dr. John Stith Pemberton
Inventor of Coca-Cola recipe.
Photo taken prior to 1888; photographer unknown.
Source: Wikipedia Commons; [http://www.cocaine.org/coca-cola/index.html]; public domain.

Dr. Pemberton called his first experimental drink "Dr. Tuggle's Compound Syrup of Globe Flower." His second mix was named "Pemberton's French Wine Coca," later renamed "Coca-Cola," which was intended as a medicine and contained alcohol, coca leaves, kola nuts, and caffeine. Most of the recipe's ingredients violated the Pure Food and Drug Act and were considered ""habit-forming" and "deleterious" substances." In fact, Coca-Cola contained several stimulants including cocaine that was later classified a narcotic by the "Controlled Substances Act of 1970." Dr. Pemberton performed "about 12,000 chemical tests" perfecting the recipe and used Peruvian coca leaves, which the Incas called "Divine Plant." Druglibrary.org stated, "In 1844, the alkaloid cocaine was first isolated in pure form from coca leaves." Then, in 1886, destiny turned the drink into a fountain soda "when the syrup was inadvertently mixed with carbonated rather than plain water." Thereafter, an Atlanta temperance movement forced Dr. Pemberton to remove the alcohol content while unaware at the time that the beverage also contained cocaine.

In 1888, Atlanta businessman Asa Griggs Candler "gained complete legal control" of the Coca-Cola formula and preserved Dr. Pemberton's original ingredients. Candler began removing cocaine after an IRS trial that "ended in July of 1901 with a hung jury." In 1907, prior to Coca-Cola's indictment in 1909, Dr. Wiley "found old testimony from the 1901 IRS mistrial which showed the recipe contained a small amount of cocaine and 2 percent alcohol." In fact, Candler stated in the IRS trial "that there was a "very small proportion" of cocaine in Coca-Cola." His testimony was validated when "a chemist found four-hundredths of a grain of cocaine per ounce of syrup in 1902." Then, in 1903, Candler contracted "Schaefer Alkaloid Works of Maywood, New Jersey," to "decocainize the coca leaves." On May 22, 1916, U.S. Supreme Court Chief Justice Charles Evans Hughes rendered final ruling in favor of the FDA in the *Barrels and Kegs Case* trial. Coca-Cola pled "no contest" and "the case was settled out of court on November 12, 1917." The Pure Food and Drug Act was amended to include caffeine as a harmful substance, and Coca-Cola "agreed to reduce the caffeine content by half, to no more than 0.61 grains per ounce of syrup, while doubling the amount of decocainized coca leaf and kola nut," to resolve the government's initial misbranding charge.

Bookkeeper and marketer Frank Mason Robinson (1845-1923) worked with Dr. Pemberton and coined the name "Coca-Cola" for its attractive alliterative sound. Robinson placed the first Coca-Cola newspaper ads "in 1887." He designed the logo using a commercial and hand drawn "Spencerian script" for bottle labels and ads. Shortly before Dr. Pemberton's death on August 16, 1888, the doctor and his son, Charles Pemberton, also an "opium user," sold the remaining Coca-Cola patent rights to Candler "for a total investment of $2,300."

The FDA indictment caused Coca-Cola's sales to plummet across the world and exposed the formula's questionable ingredients. According to author Mark Pendergrast, "The two main charges were that Coca-Cola was adulterated and misbranded ... a product was adulterated if it had a deleterious added ingredient ... that caffeine was both harmful and an "added" ingredient ... Coca-Cola was misbranded ... because it did not in fact have the whole coca leaf in it (i.e., cocaine was removed), and it had only an infinitesimal amount of kola nut." Dobbs' glamorous leadership of the AACA redeemed Coca-Cola's sales and reputation. He emerged an iconic world-renowned celebrity whom high society (including the advertising industry and Bureau) name-dropped for clout, credibility, and fortune.

It is my belief that the enterprising, manipulative, and shrewd Dobbs spearheaded the plan to recoup Coca-Cola's reputation by exploiting the more-than-willing AACA and its gilded name. The AACA offered impeccable integrity and clout as the perfect national ally to offset a globally publicized trial that butted heads against social icon Dr. Harvey Wiley. A public relations guru could not have marketed proceedings any better and why Coca-Cola won the first two trials until the U.S. Supreme Court stepped in and reversed the lower courts' native-son decisions.

After accomplishing his mission, Dobbs departed AACA's leadership. Documented history confirms that the U.S. Attorney General filed charges against Coca-Cola in October 1909, and that Dobbs pre-empted pending charges by pursuing and solidifying leadership of the AACA at its late summer convention about two months earlier. The *Barrels and Kegs Case* trial began March 13, 1911. Thereafter, Dobbs forfeited his AACA presidency at the next earliest opportunity, during the historic Boston convention on August 1-4, 1911.

Dobbs passed the AACA's presidential reins to George W. Coleman, "then advertising manager of the *Christian Endeavor World*, and in later years its publisher." A parting gift was given to Dobbs from "Henry B. Humphrey of the H. B. Humphrey Advertising Company of Boston who [was] president of the Eastern Division and one of the best known members of the Pilgrim Publicity Association." It was written, "President Dobbs got the surprise of his life and, incidentally, received a touching tribute from his fellow members, when he was presented with a cabinet containing three hundred pieces of finest Gorham silver."

THE APO$TATE

Samuel Candler Dobbs
Coca-Cola sales manager and president,
AACA president, investment banker; Dobbs (left, beige suit)
passed AACA presidency to George W. Coleman (right)
at 1911 Boston convention. Photo source: "Seventh Annual
Convention of the Associated Advertising Clubs of America";
commemorative convention yearbook published by
Pilgrim Publicity Association, 1912; archive courtesy of HathiTrust; [https://babel.
hathitrust.org/cgi/pt?id=umn.31951002210587j;
view=1up;seq=6]; public domain.

Turning-point advertising history documented Dobbs' "LAST WORDS OF THE OUTGOING PRESIDENT." Dobbs' exit statement read, "I am now laying down the responsibilities of office of two years and turning it over to more worthy hands. If I have done anything in the past two years, or the past four days, that has offended any man, I have done it out of sincerity of purpose and an honest heart. I lay down my duties with pleasure, hoping that you will grant me the privilege of working in your ranks and loving me as I love you. I now present to you your new President, but before I do so, may I again acknowledge Chicago's beautiful gift that they handed me in Omaha – this splendid gavel that I shall ever treasure with the sweetest memories. This morning I was called to this room, without any knowledge of the purpose, and this [pointing to a chest of silver] was handed to me, which I now, with permission of this organization, hand to my wife. And now Mr. Coleman will assume charge."

Advertising agencies, clubs and relative trades that had anything to do with space advertising began to surface around the country after the American Civil War. The countryside was in repair and advertising sold its wares. Confederate General Robert E. Lee surrendered to the Union's General Ulysses S. Grant at Appomattox Courthouse on April 9, 1865. Five days later, actor and "Confederate sympathizer" John Wilkes Booth assassinated Lincoln.

The Civil War erupted over principles of secession and slavery. Lincoln used the bloody Battle of Antietam to introduce his Emancipation Proclamation that codified the Civil War's banner issue as slavery. (Future President William McKinley was a sergeant for Union forces and participated in the Battle of Antietam.) Ironically, the North fought against slavery, but established the South's slave nation. After the American Revolutionary War, slavery had subsided due to farmers switching to less "labor-intensive cash crops" like wheat. In 1793, northerner Eli Whitney invented the cotton gin that profoundly changed history. Cotton only grew in the South and embedded southern slavery.

The Progressive Reformation Era began in the latter 1800s and demanded advertising to promote an influx of newly invented products. Lincoln's Pacific Railroad Act and Homestead Act solidified the North's sovereignty, attracted immigrants, and settled western territory. Civilization of the Wild West developed commerce, transportation, and advertising.

Post-Civil War business dynamics contended with limited communications and time-consuming cross-country travel, which resulted in a bifurcated advertising industry on the East and West Coasts. American advertising emerged from the original 13 colonies and concentrated "almost exclusively in the two cities of New York and Chicago" from where it "expanded into many other centers." *Printers' Ink* wrote, "By 1906 there was at least one advertising club in each of fifteen cities. National or regional groups included ... the Pacific Coast Advertising Men's Association, Periodical Publishers' Association, Advertising Club of Western New York, Banking Publicity Association and American Golf Association of Advertising Interests." The Progressive Reformation Era launched an advanced wave of interconnecting technology, communications, and transportation.

George Rowell was largely responsible for organizing and standardizing the advertising industry that created the Better Business Bureau as its regulatory division against false advertising. He opened Rowell Advertising Agency in 1865 and proceeded to introduce trailblazing publications such as the *American Newspaper Directory* in 1869 and *Printers' Ink* Advertising Journal in 1888, which begat the first newspaper directory, advertising journal, awards system, and rating scores. His innovative concepts changed retail marketing. The AACA's 1911 convention yearbook stated, "George P. Rowell, the Grand Old Man of Advertising, began his work years ago, and the Association of American Advertisers has greatly improved upon the methods of this great man who first led the way. The work we are doing is a work that has had more to do with elevating honesty in advertising circles and eliminating falsehood than the efforts of any other body of men in the profession." The Bureau franchise later adopted (and perverted) Rowell's awards and rating score criteria.

The advertising industry and the Bureau evolved through annual conventions held in various cities to maintain connections with outlying advertising clubs comprising its membership. To maintain relevance and enthusiasm, the national advertising association continued to periodically change its name with aggrandizing reorganization announced at respective conventions. The first 15 years of conventions were especially innovative and moved the advertising industry and Bureau to an international platform.

From 1904 to 1910, conventions were essentially "toothless" because there were no advertising laws to enforce anti-fraud mandates. In sequential order, respective conventions were as follows: 1904 was hosted by the International Advertising Association in St. Louis, Missouri; 1905 was hosted by the AACA also in St. Louis; 1906 did not list a convention underscored by Kenner's comment that "in 1906 the advertising clubs numbered hardly more than a score, in middle western cities" (FYI: "score" = 20; "threescore" = 60; "threescore and ten" = 70); 1907 was hosted by the AACA in Cincinnati, Ohio; 1908 was hosted by AACA in Kansas City, Missouri; 1909 was hosted by AACA in Louisville, Kentucky; and 1910 was hosted by AACA in Omaha, Nebraska.

The epochal AACA convention on August 1-4, 1911, held at Faneuil Hall in Boston, Massachusetts, broke hallowed ground adding grit and gusto to a new era of advertising. A wide array of politicians, publishers, agents, and advertising glitterati attended and forged the Truth in Advertising Movement. The "retiring national president" of the AACA, Samuel Dobbs, opened ceremonies. The AACA wrote, "President Dobbs read a letter to the convention from ex-president Theodore Roosevelt. He sent his best wishes and greetings to the men present. At the mention of Roosevelt's name there was shouting and cheering. The demonstration lasted for several minutes. It was voted to send a telegram to the ex-President expressing the appreciation of the convention for his good wishes." Esteemed author Joseph Appel was a guest speaker and introduced his *Ten Commandments of Advertising*. Thereafter, Dobbs returned to Coca-Cola's *Barrels and Kegs Case* trial in Atlanta, Georgia, which began six months earlier. Then *Printers' Ink* Editor John Romer, who attended the convention as a member of the AACA's "educational committee," hired attorney Harry Nims to draft the *Printers' Ink* Model Statute that resulted in the creation of the vigilance committees as the statute's enforcers.

The Houston Adcraft Club formed in 1911 in order to attend the AACA's Boston convention. The convention yearbook listed "Houston Adcraft Club, Houston, Texas," under "Southwestern Division." The Houston Adcraft Club became the "Houston Advertising Federation" that incorporated in Texas as "Houston-Advertising Club, Inc." and currently operates as "American Advertising Federation-Houston." AAF-Houston's slogan is "Truth."

Club members returned to Houston and set precedence by clamping down on suspicious advertising. *Printers' Ink*, Vol. LXXVII, November 2, 1911, No. 5, printed the article, "How Ad Club Protects The Advertising Public," that advised, "An illustration of the manner in which advertising clubs claim to protect the advertising public was given recently when the Houston (Texas) Adcraft Club flatly turned down two advertising propositions which ordinarily would have been generally patronized … On both petitions the Adcraft committee recommended adversely, saying that such advertising as proposed was of but little or no benefit to the business interests of Houston, and was of the sort the club was supposed to protect against."

In May 1913, the Houston Adcraft Club united with the Beaumont Club to enable all Texas members to attend the AACA convention that was scheduled in Baltimore two months later. The *Associated Advertising* magazine, Vol. IV, August 1913, No. 8, published the article, "Baltimore Meeting of Associated Ad Clubs," that reported, "When that live organization, the Houston Adcraft Club, started its individual text-book course in educational work it inaugurated at the same time a membership campaign, with buyers and sellers lined up as individual teams. The buyers brought in a few more members than the sellers out of the sixty men enrolled, and the latter paid the forfeit by a banquet given to the club early in May. This club united with Beaumont to send a large delegation to Baltimore."

The Houston Adcraft Club played a major part in both World Wars. The club organized America's "first War Advertising Committee" to handle government war-related publicity during WWI. Similar advertising service was continued during WWII, and the Adcraft Club was awarded "three national awards for "Club Achievement"" by the United States Treasury, which managed national advertising during the First and Second World Wars.

In May 1912, the AACA convention was held in Dallas, Texas. The convention introduced a new slogan: "The world stamped with truth"; its emblem featured a "circular seal with "Truth" inscribed on a globe." Earlier that year, March 12th, the AACA established the "Vigilance Committee of the Advertising Club of New York." Thereafter, on May 20, 1912, "[a] Dallas newspaper" published an article describing the revivalist event: "Sixteen noted advertising men occupied the pulpits in sixteen Dallas churches yesterday morning and delivered lay sermons – strong, forceful addresses, all burdened with the thought: 'Advertising must tell the truth, It must be honest'." Kenner presented the unidentified quote, but research identified the incognito Dallas newspaper as *The Dallas Morning News*, established on October 1, 1885, and a subsidiary of *The Daily News*. Prior to Texas' statehood in 1845, the advertising industry participated in the "Gone to Texas" pilgrimage in 1842, which launched *The Daily News* in Galveston as the Republic's original newspaper; Wikipedia.org noted, "It was first published April 11, 1842, making it the oldest newspaper in the U.S. state of Texas." *Printers' Ink* also weighed in on *The Daily News* and advised, "Its ads, dealing mainly with shipping items, pointed to the want ads of today. There were no merchant princes. "Store shopping" was truly "trading" and the spirit of *caveat emptor* was tacitly understood."

The July 1913 AACA convention was held in Baltimore, Maryland. The assembly was remarkable on several fronts: (1) A "Declaration of Principles" was adopted. (2) The *Printers' Ink* Model Statute was first enacted in Ohio. (3) It was the first time that surplus funds were available in the AACA treasury, which highlighted the voluntary nature and expense of participation underscoring why only wealthy executives held leadership positions. (4) The exclusive Quoin Club was still active and involved in the AACA.

Otherwise, the 1913 convention's attendance was relatively small and totaled about 100 members. Acclaimed "leadership" included "President George W. Coleman, William H. Ingersoll, John Irving Romer, H. D. Nims, Richard H. Waldo, and H. D. Robbins." A respective article was published in *Printers' Ink*, Vol. LXXXIII, May 22, 1913, No. 8, entitled, "New York Delegates Meet," and announced that Quoin Club leaders would meet prior to the Baltimore Convention of 1913 and discuss the AACA's prospective agenda. The meeting was a luncheon that took place on May 15, 1913, at the "Fifth Avenue Building." The Quoin Club officers at the time were listed as "President: Richard Waldo; Chairman of Program Committee: W. J. McIndoe; President of "AACofA" (Associated Advertising Clubs of America): Coleman." The AACA's Coleman reported that, for the first time, the AACA accrued "five to ten thousand dollars in the treasury to defray the travelling expenses of the next president." He said the previous administration had no money for travel and had to elect "an "executive man" who could pay his own way."

The year 1914 made advertising history. The Associated Advertising Clubs of America changed its name to Associated Advertising Clubs of the World (AACW) during its first international convention held in Toronto, Canada, which marked the advertising industry's formal globalist initiative. The Vigilance Committee also received its first request to assist with advertising copy to comply with the ethical standards set forth three years earlier by the Truth in Advertising Movement: "The Minneapolis BBB was consulted by a hardware merchant who had a fire and wanted to advertise a sale of damaged merchandise. Thus began a practice, continued to this day, of consultations between advertisers and Better Business Bureaus to work out accurate claims *before* advertising appears."

On June 21, 1915, the AACW opened its annual convention with evangelical flair in Chicago, Illinois. Dr. Herbert Houston was appointed the AACW's new president. Thereafter, Dr. Houston procured $15,000 from AACW to set up offices for the National Vigilance Committee at the association's headquarters then located in Indianapolis, Indiana. And H. J. Kenner, the Minneapolis Bureau's manager, was appointed the National Vigilance Committee's first manager.

The 1915 convention reiterated religion's fundamental involvement in the advertising industry's early truth crusade. Henry D. Estabrook, New York attorney and famed orator, charismatically rallied the crowd comprised of "thousands of advertising men and women." He spoke like a Bible-thumping preacher with evangelical flare: "Truth is the holiest name of God – holier even than love." He rhetorically queried, "Do you mean it? ... Is it your pledge – your consecration?" A man caught up in the rapture quickly jumped to his feet and shouted, "Yes! Yes!" The crowd responded in "resounding affirmation" and "cheer followed cheer."

One of the convention's celebrated guest speakers was "Bishop Warren [Akin] Candler of Atlanta" from the Methodist Episcopal Church, South. The bishop's presence at the convention was reverently shrouded by his nephew Samuel Dobbs' glittering presidential leadership of the AACA. Bishop Candler (1857-1941) was the brother of Asa Griggs Candler, founder of The Coca-Cola Company, and 41st mayor of Atlanta from 1917-1919. The bishop was also "Emory College president from 1888 to 1898" and was appointed chancellor of Emory University in 1914 after Asa donated "$1 million" to fund its chartering in Atlanta.

The convention's 155 newspaper delegates "adopted a resolution to reject fraudulent advertising." Louis Wiley, business manager of The *New York Times*, was a guest speaker at the convention and described deceptive advertising that the newspaper would ban: "Fraudulent or doubtful financial offerings; Bucket shops; Attacks of a personal character; Large guaranteed dividends; Offers of something for nothing; Guaranteed cures; Massage; Matrimonial offers; Fortune tellers, palmists, etc.; Suggestive books; Objectionable medical advertising; Offers of large salaries; Want advertisements which request money for samples of articles."

The year 1915 also witnessed the formation of two major associations, which splintered from the AACW. "Big advertisers" felt the AACW was an ineffective reformer and left in droves to form the Association of National

Advertisers (ANA). Two years later, the agencies also left AACW and formed the American Association of Advertising Agencies (AAAA). The *Advertising Age* magazine described the AACW's implosion: "On June 4, 1917, the New York, Chicago, Philadelphia and Boston advertising associations and the new Southern Association of Advertising Agents formally announced the formation of the American Association of Advertising Agencies at a meeting in St. Louis"; the magazine further reported, "Pressure to form an association had come from the media, particularly newspapers." Accordingly, the ANA and AAAA worked together in the following years with advertising critics accusing them of performing "feckless reform gestures" and rendering "weak leadership," which reiterated advertising mutineers' reasons for leaving the AACW.

In June 1916, the annual AACW convention was held at Independence Hall in Philadelphia, Pennsylvania. The stature of the prestigious AAWC had grown multifold and commanded the presence of 28th President Thomas Woodrow Wilson. The incumbent president was also running for re-election in 1916 and his idealistic Democratic-Party platform supported the Bureau's special-business interests: "I wish very much that truth and candor might always be the standard of politics as well as the standard of business." Wilson's pro-business first term enacted the Federal Reserve Act, on December 13, 1913, to establish the Federal Reserve System and Federal Reserve Notes as "legal tender." Favorable newspaper headlines included "PRESIDENT'S SIGNATURE ENACTS CURRENCY LAW"; "Wilson Declares It the First of Series of Constructive Acts to Aid Business"; "Banks All Over The Country Hasten to Enter Federal Reserve System"; and, "Wilson Sees Dawn of New Era in Business." President Wilson's distinguished endorsement at the convention encouraged the AACA to upgrade its sinister sounding "Vigilance Committee." Thus, Arthur Sheldon's aggrandizing illusionary name, "Better Business Bureau," was adopted in 1916.

On September 21-25, 1919, the AACW held a historic assembly, known as "The Great-After-The-War Convention" in New Orleans, Louisiana. Opening ceremonies were held at Tulane University and convention headquarters were located at the Grunewald Hotel, now known as "The Roosevelt" (President Theodore Roosevelt). Attention was drawn to improving advertising campaigns. Above all, and for the first time, women were welcomed to committee ranks, which paid homage to the newly minted Nineteenth Amendment (women's right to vote) passed by the U.S. Senate "on June 4, 1919," and ratified on "August 18, 1920."

Long-standing rules were changed to promote women in advertising. The *Associated Advertising* magazine reported that the AACW "adopted a resolution for an amendment to the association constitution providing a place on the committee for an advertising woman." The first female member of the AACW's

Executive Committee was Jane J. "JJ" Martin, a "copywriter" and "advertising manager for Sperry & Hutchinson Co.," that produced S&H Green Stamps and was the "largest and oldest trading stamp company" established "in 1896." Martin was also a "founding member" and the "president of the New York League of Advertising Women" otherwise known as "Advertising Women of New York (AWNY)." The *Associated Advertising* magazine stated, "Miss Martin did much of the missionary work that has made the Women's Conference of the Associated Clubs of the World a regular institution."

Jane J. Martin
ACW's first female executive committee member; founder and president of Advertising Women of New York (AWNY).
Photo: Unknown photographer at "The Great-after-the-war Convention" or "Victory Convention" in 1919. Photo source: AACW's *Associated Advertising* magazine, November 1919;
[https://babel.hathitrust.org/cgi/pt?id=iau.31858034256317; view=1up;seq=535]; public domain.

The convention celebrated the end of WWI while the Bureau exploited the military and wartime strategy. After the war, previously closed Bureaus began to slowly reopen, and infiltration mimicked German Sturmtruppen (Stormtroopers). According to Wikipedia, "The Germans developed a "doctrine of autonomy", the forerunner of both blitzkrieg and modern infantry tactics, using groups of stormtroopers, who would advance in small mutually covering groups from cover to cover with "autonomy" to exploit any weakness they discovered in enemy defenses." Vigilance Committees followed the 1920 population shift from rural to urban areas and expanded like a military operation that strategically positioned offices for maximum civilian reconnaissance. Kenner reflected, "Some of these bureaus became dormant after the United States entered the European conflict. But, with the war over, most of them were revived, and many more were organized in principal cities."

Servicemen returning from WWI joined the ranks of the Truth in Advertising Movement and contributed invaluable military skills. After Armistice Day, now called Veterans Day, on November 11, 1918, soldiers eagerly accepted employment at various Bureaus during the looming 1920-1921 Depression and deadly flu pandemic that was crisscrossing the United States. Between 20 and 40 million people throughout the world died of the "Spanish Flu" ("La Grippe") including an estimated 43,000 U.S. troops, representing one-half of mobilized forces in Europe, due to trench warfare's squalid conditions.

In June 1922, Seymour L. Cromwell, president of the NYSE, "pledged, on behalf of the Exchange, the funds necessary to underwrite the formation of a Better Business Bureau." Consequently, the Exchange enabled "the Associated Advertising Clubs and the Advertising Club of New York to establish the Better Business Bureau of New York City" that incorporated in "June 1922" and launched on "July 1, 1922." Thereafter, the New York Bureau launched the "Before You Invest, Investigate" program created by the Cleveland Bureau in 1920. The corporate shield protected individual members from incrimination, which questioned ulterior motive for the New York Bureau's incorporation prior to engaging the bogus investigative program. The Bureau's collaboration with the NYSE and Investment Bankers Association was denounced as a racket by the U.S. Senate's Committee on Banking and Currency after the Stock Market Crash of 1929.

The New York Bureau advertised impressive regulatory actions and affiliations in a manner that implied quasi-governmental authority in order to embed public trust, legitimize illicit programs, and cloak NYSE-affiliated criminality. Despite General Manager Kenner's nefarious sponsorship of the racketeering "Before You Invest, Investigate" securities program, his self-righteous braggadocio described two securities fraud cases pursued by his office. The first case commenced in August 1922: "Charles Beadon ... planned to unload several million dollars of shares of ... the International Radio Corporation ... The Bureau issued a bulletin of facts about the false representations ... and the corporation was forced into bankruptcy ...." The second case occurred the following month, in September, whereby "Post Office inspectors at New York caused the arrest of the principals of Winthrop Smith & Company, operated as a "blind pool"" that resulted in indictments and imprisonment for mail fraud. Kenner's mention of the Winthrop case was particularly hypocritical because the case involved abuse of Blue Sky state laws same as his New York Bureau was accused of violating by the U.S. Senate. The "Before You Invest, Investigate" program implied qualification of worthless Blue Sky-protected NYSE securities as safe investments. In fact, the AACW and National BBB linked to crony federal prosecutors in the "Post Office Inspection Service," and whose collaboration guaranteed the Bureau franchise's respective regulatory indictments and acclaim. Kenner wrote, "Especially in cooperation with Federal authorities, truth in advertising activities were advanced through the leadership work of Lou E. Holland of Kansas City, who was president of the national advertising association for three years, from 1922 to 1925. He was president also of the National Better Business Bureau for two years, from 1925 to 1927."

In June 1924, the AACW convention was held in London, England. The London convention was hosted by "The Thirty Club" that was founded "in 1905 or 1906" as a "dining club for "the betterment of advertising"." Thereafter, The Thirty Club forged a transatlantic relationship with the AACW when six members from the Advertising Club of New York visited London in January 1910. The Thirty Club later attended the AACA/AACW's convention held in Toronto in 1914, and then lobbied to host the AACW's London convention in 1924.

On May 11, 1925, the AACW convention was held in Houston, Texas. That same year, the National Vigilance Committee changed its name and incorporated as "National Better Business Bureau of the Associated Advertising Clubs of the World." Guest speaker Secretary of Commerce Herbert Hoover (elected 31st POTUS on March 4, 1929) delivered the convention's opening address entitled, "The public relations of advertising," that lauded the Bureau franchise: "The first step in progress was when the medium, recognizing its responsibility to the readers, exercised censorship over extravagant, distasteful and misleading copy. The next great step was the organized action of advertising managers, advertisers and advertising mediums through moral session of the National and local Better Business Bureaus ... Such associations as yours in the erection of ideals of a profession, in the determination of methods and definitions of standards for the elimination of abuse, is selfgovernment and it is selfgovernment in the greatest form of which democracy has yet given conception - that is, selfgovernment outside of government."

All the while, the National BBB and Bureaus were abusing Blue Sky laws, perpetrating interstate mail fraud, operating a massive securities racket with the NYSE and bankers, and restraining radio communications. Hoover's secretary-of-commerce speech complimented the Bureau as an exemplar of morality in 1925 while the Bureau was fleecing millions from speculators. One can only imagine the egg plastered on President Hoover's face when Senator Duncan

THE APO$TATE

Fletcher advised him of criminal indictments against the Bureau involving historic Wall Street fraud that begat the Crash and forced Hoover's hand to commence U.S. Senate investigative hearings.

Hoover's presence at the Houston convention emphasized the Lone Star state's dynamic business growth fueled by conversion from cattle, cotton, and lumber to oil and shipping. The Texas "Business Rush" began in 1842 with the slogan "Gone to Texas" and predated the "California Gold Rush" that began on January 24, 1848. In fact, "Gone to Texas" re-emerged in 2018 evidenced by an influx of out-of-state license plates from every state in the Union that have saturated Texas roadways.

The city of Houston, a.k.a. "Babylon on the Bayou," was established by brothers Augustus Chapman Allen and John Kirby Allen on August 30, 1836. The Allen brothers traveled to Texas "shortly after the battle of San Jacinto in search of the state's most interior point with year-round water transportation to the gulf. They selected the headwaters of Buffalo Bayou as the site for the new city, which they named for Sam Houston, hero of San Jacinto," according to the Federal Reserve Bank of Dallas. A chamber of commerce was established and advertised Houston as the capital of commerce "where 17 railroads meet the sea." In 1844, the Port of Houston was established after a steamboat traveled "up the Buffalo Bayou" (Houston's "36-foot-deep Houston Ship Channel was completed" in 1914). A year later, December 29, 1845, Texas became the Union's 28th state under the administration of James Knox Polk, 11th POTUS from 1845 to 1849.

As a native Texan, I especially honor General Samuel Houston (1793-1863); a lawyer, statesman, soldier, and hero. The Virginia-born Tennessee-raised Texas-strong Sam Houston honed diplomatic skills after running away from home at the age of 16 and was adopted by Cherokee Chief Oolooteka who named him "Colonneh or the "Raven"."

Huntsville, "founded in 1835 by Pleasant Gray," is a short drive from my home and nestles General Houston's historic gravesite at Oakwood Cemetery where I wrote *The Apostate's* "Texas" segment. His monument was erected on April 21, 1911. Five months later, the AACA's historic Boston convention began on August 1, 1911, and launched the Truth in Advertising Movement that begat the Better Business Bureau's prototype, the "Vigilance Committee of the Advertising Club of New York."

The nuance of General Houston and his Texas Army, Confederate veterans of the Civil War, inspired me as I wrote my thoughts amidst the solitude, tranquility, and magnificence of the Texas hill country. Walking through Oakwood Cemetery was like speed traveling momentous yesteryear. Every thoughtful step and timeless tombstone brought reminder of unparalleled history untouched by contentious contemporaneous opinion, revision, and/or politics. I walked among freed spirits touched by the American Revolutionary War, Civil War, and World War I. Soldiers, fathers, mothers, children, and extended families begged my visitor's attention and respect. Confederate souls solemnly reminded me that they, too, were honorable U.S. veterans. On May 23, 1958, Congress approved "U.S. Public Law 85-425, Section 410"; military or naval service of the Confederate States of America was deemed the same as military or naval service of the United States.

General Houston represented watershed Texas and American history. I could hear a young "3rd Lieutenant" Houston fighting in General Andrew Jackson's army at the Battle of Horseshoe Bend on March 26, 1814. He would later contend with several momentous Texas battles including "the first battle for Texas Independence" Battle of Gonzales (October 2, 1835), Battle of Goliad (October 10, 1835), Battle of the Alamo (February 23 – March 6, 1836), Battle of Coleto in Goliad (March 19 and 20, 1836), the massacre of over 300 Texian prisoners at Presidio La Bahia Fort in Goliad (March 27, 1836), and the Texas Revolution's decisive Battle of San Jacinto (April 21, 1836).

His monument's inscription featured a quote authored by Andrew "Old Hickory" Jackson (1767-1845), 7th POTUS from March 4, 1829 to March 3, 1837, and proclaimed, "The World Will Take Care of Houston's Fame." General Houston enabled President Jackson's dream to make Texas a state of the Union. Prior to Texas' statehood in 1845, Houston was the "first and third" president of the Republic of Texas from October 22, 1836 to December 10, 1838, and from December 21, 1841 to December 9, 1844. Thereafter, General Houston served as seventh governor of Texas from December 21, 1859 to March 16, 1861, when the Texas Convention removed him from office because "he refused to take the oath of loyalty to the newly formed Confederate States of America." Houston was a "passionate Unionist," railed against Texas' secession from the Union, and "warned Texans that civil war would result in a Northern victory and destruction of the South."

Once and a while, my pen and I nodded at a drifter paying respect to the Raven. His dignified manner and respectful approach suggested a veteran. We first met when I found him standing at General Houston's grave lost in thought. It was a "Polaroid" moment that stuck with me. He presented like a soldier melding with history that honored the granite monument's inherent sanctity, patriotism, bloodshed, and sacrifice; his emotion was palpable; his appreciation immeasurable; and his loyalty unspoken.

I worried about calling attention to Oakwood Cemetery because of twisted radicals hell-bent on destroying southern historical markers and monuments to support their despotic race-baiting globalist narrative that undermines the fact that HISTORY HAPPENED. Every time I approached the cemetery, my protective attention immediately scanned the perimeter of decorative antique wrought-iron fencing and entry gate while fervently praying that all historical treasure remained intact and undamaged. My grandmother, Ginny, had a similar fence and gate in nearby Palestine, and such memories sustain me more than I care to admit. Henceforth, it is imperative that the state of Texas and historical societies protect and preserve such priceless mementos and prosecute vile defilers by any and all means possible. Keep in mind that once gone forever gone and irreplaceable loss cheats future generations. As such, on or about September 13, 2019, I was pleased and relieved to see that Charlottesville Circuit Court Judge Richard E. Moore honored Confederate statues as state-protected war memorials in a lawsuit brought by residents against the City Council. Judge Moore set respective historical safeguarding precedent by ruling that the statues of General Robert E. Lee and General Stonewall Jackson inferred "historical preservation," not "racial discrimination," and imposed an injunction preventing their removal, according to the *Richmond Times-Dispatch*.

The year 1927 dramatically altered Bureau history. The National Better Business Bureau separated from the AACW and incorporated as the "National Association of Better Business Bureaus, Inc." Hindsight's hyped reason was "to provide for greater specialization and legal safety in its work," according to Kenner. To the contrary, reality hid a more onerous reason called a corporate shield. The AACW perfectly timed its separation from the Bureau franchise; the Crash occurred in 1929 and the New York Bureau was indicted by the U.S. Senate for securities fraud and racketeering in 1932. As a reminder, Kenner wrote such remark in 1936 after FDR waved his magic redemptive SEC wand over Kenner as general manager of the disgraced New York Bureau. Consequently, Kenner wrote revisionist history with rose-colored glasses and exalted the Bureau above reproach. Research proved that he exaggerated truth and that wrong became right with the flourish of his gilded pen. Business as usual continued and new loopholes were threaded. On November 2, 1927, NYSE-titan James C. Auchincloss was appointed president of the newly incorporated National Better Business Bureau, Inc. At the time, Auchincloss was also "a governor of the New York Stock Exchange, was then also president of the New York Bureau, and served it in that capacity for six years."

In September 1928, the AACW convention was held in Chicago, Illinois. The "Solicitor of the Post Office Department" Horace J. Donnelly gave the opening address. The Cleveland Bureau advised, "The first Canadian BBB was founded in 1928. It was located in Montreal." Also, that year, Wansley noted that "the periodical publishers, in a trade practice conference with the Federal Trade Commission, designated the National Better Business Bureau as their agency of assistance in determining the acceptability of advertising copy." And the rest is history! Critics, such as O'Sullivan, complained the Bureau exaggerated its celebratory title and embedded its name through affiliation with and implication of a governmental footprint.

In 1929, the Associated Advertising Clubs of the World changed names to "Advertising Federation of America" (AFA) at its annual convention held in Berlin, Germany. The name change highlighted advertising unity and global outreach. Accordingly, the Bureau promoted international relations with "advertising organizations in Canada, Great Britain and Continental Europe." Impact surpassed previous overseas conventions held in Toronto, Canada, in 1914 and London, England, in 1924.

In 1930, the AFA held its annual convention in Washington, D.C., under an aegis of business ethics and consumer awareness. Appel advised in *Growing Up With Advertising* that he was present at the convention and that "advertising was in the strategic position to assume the leadership in consumer education." He also gave strict instructions against profit-fleecing consumers when warning, "Such leadership carries with it tremendous responsibility. Everything that touches public thought and public welfare transcends the mere rights of the individual or organization that seeks personal profit through public co-operation." Appel influenced the Bureau's evolution as an educational foundation, but the Bureau ignored his warning against specious promotional profiteering programs, e.g., *Awards for Excellence*.

On December 26, 1930, the first and only attempt was made to regulate the Better Business Bureau. Republican New York Attorney General Hamilton Ward agreed with the Bronx Chamber of Commerce's submitted complaint that the "Better Business Bureau was a camouflaged detective agency, and should be compelled to take out a detective agency license." On December 26, 1930, Ward ruled that the "Better Business Bureau of New York" must procure such license under "section 70 of the general business law." He was supported by Secretary of State of New York Edward Flynn, the former sheriff of Bronx County and "[c]hairman of the Executive Committee of the Bronx County Democratic Committee (1922-1953)." Ward lost to Bureau-friendly Democrat John Bennett in the 1930 state election. After Bennett assumed office, Flynn issued a second licensing demand to the New York Bureau on January 2, 1931. General Manager Kenner ignored both Ward and Flynn, and Bennett buried the subject of the Bureau's licensing during his five terms of office, from 1931 to 1942.

Kenner's *The Fight for Truth in Advertising* deceptively implied the New York Bureau's amicable relations with the late Attorney General Ward. Kenner's gloss-over reflected, "Attorney General Hamilton Ward of New York State, through his assistant, Watson Washburn, also waged war on large and small operators in the underworld of finance during 1929." In fact, the New York Bureau was one of those "operators." Such revisionist writing was typical Bureauese that embellished legalese to whitewash any occasion that incriminated the Bureau; otherwise, the public was unaware because evidence had been destroyed or hidden.

THE APO$TATE

Ward left office on December 31, 1930, and died less than two years later, on October 8, 1932. His death was a stroke of luck for the New York Bureau and allowed the entire organization to avoid licensing and regulation. Thereafter, Flynn was silenced by his crony affiliation with the New York Democratic Party and New York Governor Franklin Delano Roosevelt who was elected POTUS on November 8, 1932, exactly one month after Ward died.

In August 1932, the AFA convention was held in Columbus, Ohio. A Bureau-brown-nosing letter from Paul J. McCauley, assistant attorney general for the office of Democratic New York Attorney General Bennett, was read at the convention: "On occasions which are far too numerous to detail, I have had occasion to look to the Better Business Bureau for cooperation, and I have never been disappointed." Accordingly, McCauley inadvertently confirmed a covert connection between Bennett and the New York Bureau. O'Sullivan alleged Bennett was planted as the new attorney general in 1930 to derail former Attorney General Ward's decree that required the Bureau's licensing.

In 1934, the AFA convention was held in Milwaukee, Wisconsin. The convention heralded FDR's Securities and Exchange Act of 1934 that formed the Securities and Exchange Commission (SEC) on June 6, 1934. The year before, FDR enacted the Securities Act of 1933 to overcome abuse of Blue Sky laws, which contributed to the Crash of 1929. The 1933 Act was enforced by the FTC, and the 1934 Act established the SEC to take control of securities regulation from the FTC.

In August 1934, the National Association of Better Business Bureaus also held its conference in Milwaukee; the guest speaker was newly ensconced SEC Commissioner George C. Mathews (1886-1946), in office from 1934 to 1940. New York Bureau General Manager Kenner's consequent SEC appointment suggested that the National Association of BBBs exploited the conference and Mathews. The year before, on October 27, 1933, FDR appointed Mathews to the FTC when its duties included securities regulation under the Securities Act of 1933. The following year, after the SEC assumed the FTC's duties involving securities regulation, FDR moved Mathews, a Republican, from the FTC to the SEC. Then FDR appointed Mathews as one of five commissioners (other four commissioners were Chairman Joseph P. Kennedy (D), James M. Landis (D) who replaced Kennedy as chairman on September 23, 1935, Robert E. Healey (R), and Ferdinand Pecora (D) who was replaced by J. D. Ross (D) on October 5, 1935). The National BBB first established crony rapport with the FTC in 1928 that inherently forged a covert alliance with Mathews underscored by his respective bosom-buddy comment at the conference: "The Chief Examiner of the Federal Trade Commission has furnished me with a tabulation showing that over a period of years 389 matters dealing with competitive methods have been referred to the Trade Commission by Better Business Bureaus in leading cities of the country." Furthermore, Mathews was a pro-business anti-regulation economist, which benefited the Bureau.

In April 1935, B-men attended the National Fraud Conference in Washington, D.C., and, also met with the SEC. Thereafter, Kenner was appointed chairman of an SEC committee to "outline a plan for the actual organization and operation of the new department" known as the "Securities Violations Section of the Securities and Exchange Commission." Kenner described the department's regulatory methods similar to a vigilante group: "The files of the Securities Violations Section, in July, 1936, contained more than 22,000 names of individuals who, within the past decade, had been engaged in the sale of securities by allegedly fraudulent methods. These names and information were sent in to the government by the official and voluntary agencies of the country." It was the height of hypocrisy that Kenner, above all people, was chairing a fraud-prevention committee while sanctimoniously denouncing others for the same securities fraud that he and the New York Bureau committed less than three years earlier and that were publicly denounced by the U.S. Senate's Committee on Banking and Currency.

From June 28 to July 2, 1936, the AFA's Silver Jubilee convention was again held in Boston to celebrate the 1911 convention that begat the truth movement. One last time, history gathered original glitterati participants Samuel Dobbs, George Coleman, and Merle Sidener as guest speakers. David Sarnoff, then president of Radio Corporation of America, was also a guest speaker and emphasized truth in advertising: "Probably more than in any other medium, the success of radio advertising depends on its command of the subtle but decisive elements of public confidence and good-will, and the direct moral responsibility of the advertiser for his claims." Sarnoff's participation was telling particularly since the Bureau was charged with restraining radio communications in 1931. It was standard procedure for the advertising industry to mask indiscretions through photo-op illusions crafted to subliminally gild respective indiscretions. The AFA published the convention's guest speeches in *Truth in Advertising: Twenty-Fifth Anniversary*, as a supplement that also included a special message from FDR.

The AFA also sponsored Kenner's book about four months after the convention. Forthcoming notice was published in *Truth in Advertising*: "The Federation is now publishing a book entitled, "The Fight for Truth in Advertising" written for us by H. J. Kenner, manager of the New York Better Business Bureau and one of the leaders in the truth movement. This book is an authentic presentation of the developments which have taken place in the past twenty-five years in connection with the struggle to purge advertising of undesirable elements. The publisher will have the book ready for general distribution shortly after this convention."

As the newly appointed chairman to oversee the design of the "Securities

Violations Section of the Securities and Exchange Commission," Kenner traded the Bureau's inglorious Klan connotation for pietistic grandeur of the Knights Templar. Kenner's exploitation of the SEC to redeem the Bureau's tarnished name after the U.S. Senate hearings mimicked Dobbs seeking the prestigious AACA's presidency to clear Coca-Cola's besmirched reputation after federal indictment for violation of the Pure Food & Drug Act. On May 28, 1936, Jim M. Landis, chairman of the SEC, sent a message to Bureau/NYSE magnate James C. Auchincloss confirming their respective organizations' crony affiliation: "The Securities and Exchange Commission appreciates the assistance rendered by the Better Business Bureau of New York City in the Commission's efforts to suppress fraudulent dealings in securities. We sincerely hope that there will be no curtailment of your activities in this respect and we look forward to the continuance of our effective cooperation." Five months later, in October 1936, Kenner triumphantly published *The Fight for Truth in Advertising* to revise scandalous history, boast the Bureau's involvement with the SEC, and denounce critics (including Billingsley and O'Sullivan).

But there was one loose string left to tie. Following O'Sullivan's death in 1939, the Bureau vindictively sued his protégé, Kate Whelan, for defamation. It was not enough that the Chicago Bureau drove O'Sullivan to an early grave; the franchise collaborated to annihilate his loyal secretary to once and for all bury its criminal past that she reminded. O'Sullivan previously deflected Bureau lawsuits due to his exemplary credibility as a publisher, author, and internationally renowned C.S.I. detective. Unfortunately, Whelan only offered forlorn memories. The lawsuit was retaliatory payback for O'Sullivan's publication of *Rackets* and ongoing criticism of Bureau operations that exposed racketeering and fraud. Whelan continued his crusade posthumously publishing "reprints of previous articles of *The Lance*" that was a newspaper produced by The O'Sullivan Publishing House. Thirty years later, former California Bureau President Wansley paint-brushed Bureau culpability with weasel-worded braggadocio that "Miss Whelan, however, failed to reckon with the fury of a righteous man maligned when she called H. L. McEldowney, then manager of the Detroit BBB, a racketeer!"

In typical Bureau style, Wansley glossed-over incriminating details. His excoriation of Whelan omitted the Bureau's collateral damage from the Pecora Commission less than a decade earlier that left the Bureau's image in shambles. In 1932, the Better Business Bureau was investigated by the U.S. Senate Committee on Banking and Currency and labeled a "racket" by Senator (later Chairman) Duncan Fletcher, for perpetrating securities fraud with the NYSE and Investment Bankers Association. Several authorities from the state of New York also levied a litany of criminal allegations including conviction for operating without a license. Whelan reminded readers of the Bureau's nefarious proclivities that B-men desperately tried to bury, and why Democrat John Bennett was elected to replace Republican Attorney General

Hamilton Ward, who rendered the Bureau's licensing mandate. Circumstances suggested the Bureau twisted Whelan's legitimate racketeering accusations against McEldowney into slander while mustering a national war chest to slam-dunk her demise through McEldowney's lawsuit empowered by a Bureau-friendly court.

While the Pecora Commission was gearing up in 1933, O'Sullivan published incriminating evidence in *Rackets* that seeded Whelan's complaint and corroborated her future accusation against the Detroit Bureau's McEldowney. Apparently, there was a substantial lawsuit filed in Detroit in the early 1930s because O'Sullivan specifically quoted two Detroit court officials whose comments vicariously implicated the Detroit Bureau: "Judge Edward J. Jeffries, Recorder's Court, Detroit, Mich.," stated, "I do not think that anybody takes the Better Business Bureau very seriously. Such institutions usually exercise their functions on the little fellows, leaving the big fellows entirely unmolested. The great menace confronting our free institutions for democratic government is the usurping and exercising and directing of government functions by those outside the administration of the law, for either ambitious, pecuniary, or other purposes, all of which are equally dangerous to our free institutions." And, "Corporate Counsel John H. Witherspoon, Detroit, Michigan," advised, "I am in accord with the sentiment that those who establish private detective agencies of prosecution and punishment usurp the natural functions of the State and are its insidious enemies; and if not checked, would ultimately displace the State and substitute the rule of the racket for the system of jurisprudence that is the product of man's slow but sure development over the centuries." Attorney Witherspoon inadvertently predicted the Bureau's globalist trajectory.

The lead up to WWII found the Bureau struggling with the Great Depression that it facilitated, but FDR's Deep State brought salvation. Former Bureau President Wansley reflected: "During the war, business income was "frozen" – and so was Bureau income." Wansley's glossy History and Traditions revised and omitted the Bureau's Deep State involvement in American history and enabled its modern globalist coronation as an untouchable autocrat above reproach. Research suggested that immediately after Pearl Harbor, Senator Truman convinced FDR to induct the Bureau into the intelligence community under the First War Powers Act. Consequently, the Bureau's reporting services were covertly weaponized to monitor Japanese American movement within the United States. The Bureau probably coordinated with the "Office of the Coordinator of Information (COI)" that later morphed into the CIA on September 18, 1947. FDR was inclined to contract the Bureau because the organization previously assisted President Hoover as a civilian agency with the Mexican Repatriation program (euphemism was "Neighborhood Enforcement Policy") from 1928 to 1936. To the contrary, Wansley wrote a propaganda piece that revised events based on wartime advertising as a cover to hide FDR's Deep State induction of the Bureau after the Japanese attack on Pearl Harbor: "[I]n 1941 ... a Senate committee headed by the then Senator Harry S. Truman investigated the question of whether advertising should be controlled and regulated as part of the mobilization of the U.S. wartime economy. After hearing testimony on the effective self-regulatory work being done by the advertising industry and the Bureaus, the committee recommended that no emergency regulation of advertising be undertaken. That recommendation was followed by Congress."

The public was told the Bureau was pursuing stock swindles involving Liberty Bonds when, in reality, its nationwide offices were covertly monitoring Japanese American movement within the United States; research uncovered clear and present danger of internal sabotage. Kenner wrote, "In wartime and early post-war days, literally hundreds of millions of dollars were being taken from financially illiterate citizens. The general public had little or no investment education. Liberty Bond sales campaigns during the war had been so effective that nearly every family had some. Blue-sky promoters were after them, like buzzards flocking to a feast."

After Japan's attack on Pearl Harbor, on December 7, 1941, FDR organized the "Declaration by United Nations," on January 1, 1942, which was approved by 26 Allied countries pledging support against Axis aggression. Allied forces included the U.S., UK, France, USSR, Australia, Belgium, Brazil, Canada, China, Denmark, Greece, Netherlands, New Zealand, Norway, Poland, South Africa, and Yugoslavia. Axis powers included Germany, Italy, Japan, Hungary, Romania, and Bulgaria. On October 24, 1945, the "United Nations" became official when 50 countries met in San Francisco, California, and drafted the "United Nations Charter," signed by members on June 26, 1945. Poland later signed as the 51st member.

The Office of the United Nations High Commissioner for Human Rights (OHCHR) defined its mission as "to work for the protection of all human rights for all people; to help empower people to realize their rights; and to assist those responsible for upholding such rights in ensuring that they are implemented ...." Unfortunately, the UN's modern mission has fallen short and caused more harm than good. UN operations align with current EU dictates that support open borders and forced placement of "refugees" from terrorist-ridden countries. Additionally, UN peacekeepers have acted irresponsibly and charged with exploitation and sexual abuse made even more egregious when victims were the poorest of the poor. Blue Helmets recklessly introduced cholera "that has killed at least 9,500 people in Haiti since 2010" while preying on its women and children. On June 11, 2015, the Associated Press (AP) reported that "the U.N.'s Office of Internal Oversight Services — a U.N. watchdog within the U.N. — said members of a peacekeeping mission had "transactional sex" with more than 225 Haitian women. The women traded sex for basic needs, including food and medication." Then, on April 13, 2017, U.S. Ambassador Nikki Haley urged accountability for UN-peacekeeper abuse and called attention to AP's "investigation detailing how at least 134 Sri Lankan peacekeepers sexually abused and exploited nine Haitian children between 2004 and 2007."

Most recently, as of December 16, 2017, Obama-loyalists and rogue globalist governances attempted to energize the former president's NWO game plan by requesting UN forces be deployed in Chicago to address gun violence. According to Americasfreedomfighters.com, "The city of Chicago known as a city with some of the strictest gun control laws in the nation, yet home to the area with some of the highest homicide rates stemming from firearms, is now asking for United Nations armed soldiers to patrol city streets." Chicago's globalist overreach and disregard for citizen welfare reiterates the city's long-standing Democratic pitfalls, which exploit the Black community, and ignore impoverished trench warfare that fuels a vicious cycle of death and violence. President Trump tried to intervene by deploying the National Guard, but Chicago's Democratic hierarchy pushed back. But some things never change. O'Sullivan was from Chicago, and he railed against the city's organized crime during the 1920s and 1930s.

On April 4, 1949, the North Atlantic Treaty Organization (NATO) was signed and enacted by Truman. Its predecessor was the Treaty of Brussels, signed on March 17, 1948, and included "Belgium, the Netherlands, Luxembourg, France, and the United Kingdom." NATO was formed as a military alliance to protect Europe against the encroaching dual threat of communist USSR and China; consequences begat the Korean War on June 25, 1950. Esteemed British Indian Army officer and Churchill's "chief military assistant" General Hastings Lionel ('Pug') Ismay (1887-1965) was NATO's first secretary general from 1952 to 1957; he was also referred to as 1st Baron Ismay, a diplomat and member of the House of Lords from 1947 to his death on December 17, 1965. General Ismay famously stated that NATO's primary objective was "to keep the Russians out, the Americans in, and the Germans down." NATO's homepage advised that "the Alliance's creation was part of a broader effort to serve three purposes: deterring Soviet expansionism, forbidding the revival of nationalist militarism in Europe through a strong North American presence on the continent, and encouraging European political integration." The Charter of the United Nations' Article 5 held Allies in agreement that "an armed attack against one or more of them … shall be considered an attack against them all" and stipulated "use of force." Headquarters were "initially based in London, the Headquarters were moved to Paris in 1952 before being transferred to Brussels, Belgium in 1967." Wikipedia.org described the current location in Haren, Brussels: "A new €750 million headquarters building began construction in 2010, was completed in summer 2016, and was dedicated on 25 May 2017."

THE APO$TATE

The 12 founding NATO members were "Belgium, Canada, Denmark, France, Iceland, Italy, Luxembourg, the Netherlands, Norway, Portugal, the United Kingdom and the United States." Current membership totals 28 countries: Albania, Belgium, Bulgaria, Canada, Croatia, Czech Republic, Denmark, Estonia, France, Germany, Greece, Hungary, Iceland, Italy, Latvia, Lithuania, Luxembourg, Netherlands, Norway, Poland, Portugal, Romania, Slovakia, Slovenia, Spain, Turkey, UK, and U.S.A.

The European Union originated from the Maastricht Treaty, signed in Maastricht, Netherlands, on February 7, 1992, and became effective November 1, 1993. Its birth mission was to promote "political-economic" opportunity for an insular "single market." On June 14, 1985, the Schengen Agreement was signed "near the town of Schengen, Luxembourg," and established Europe's open-bordered Schengen Area comprising 26 nations (excluding the UK and Ireland) that eliminated "internal border checks" or passports, "with other Schengen members and strengthened border controls with non-Schengen countries." As of June 21, 2007, Germany's Chancellor Angela Merkel represented the "Presidency of the Council of the European Union." On December 13, 2007, the Treaty of Lisbon was drafted and became effective December 1, 2009, which established the European Union. Earlier treaties were amended to implement a legally binding "Charter of Fundamental Rights of the European Union" that proclaimed the EU sovereign ruler while also providing a process for separation. Twenty-eight countries currently comprise the EU: Austria (1995); Belgium (founder); Bulgaria (2007); Croatia (2013); Cyprus (2004); Czech Republic (2004); Denmark (1973); Estonia (2004); Finland (1995); France (founder); Germany (founder); Greece (1981); Hungary (2004); Ireland (1973); Italy (founder); Latvia (2004); Lithuania (2004); Luxemburg (founder); Malta (2004); Netherlands (founder); Poland (2004); Portugal (1986); Romania (2007); Slovakia (2004); Slovenia (2004); Spain (1986); Sweden (1995); and United Kingdom (1973). On January 31, 2020, the UK left the EU.

The European Atomic Energy Community (EAEC) was created to provide nuclear power for Europe by "developing nuclear energy and distributing it to its member states while selling the surplus to non-member states"; the agency operates as a "separate legal treaty" from the EU. On October 24, 2007, the International Thermonuclear Experimental Reactor (ITER) project was launched "to produce full-scale electricity-producing fusion power stations" and is "funded and run by seven member entities—the European Union, India, Japan, China, Russia, South Korea, and the United States." In 2013, the EAEC commenced construction of the ITER Tokamak complex located in Saint-Paul-lès-Durance, in southern France: "The facility is expected to finish its construction phase in 2021 and will start commissioning the reactor that same year and initiate plasma experiments in 2025 with full deuterium–tritium fusion experiments starting in 2035."

Nuclear development initiatives by the EAEC should rally global concern because experiments insinuate potential armament. Wikipedia.org respectively advised, "Initially, fusion research in the USA and USSR was linked to atomic weapons development, and it remained classified until the 1958 Atoms for Peace conference in Geneva." Accordingly, I believe that the EU was covertly weaponizing its political-economic birth mission to enforce a NWO stranglehold on Europe. Global Research reported, "On November 13, 2017, 23 out of 28 European Union (EU) states *signed a declaration to create what is expected to form the nucleus of a joint European army.*" As of December 10, 2018, the EU openly flaunted its army when assisting pro-EU French President Emmanuel Macron to quell right-wing protests with "armored vehicles" that featured the EU's symbol.

Establishment of a formal EU army in 2017 was preceded a year earlier by the EU's State of the Union address, dated September 14, 2016, which advised a border militia. A working defense program called "Frontex" included a "European Border and Coast Guard" comprised of "600 agents on the ground at the borders with Turkey in Greece and over 100 in Bulgaria" that will add "at least 200 extra border guards and 50 extra vehicles deployed at the Bulgarian external borders as of October." The EU reflected a deteriorating situation particularly after the eye-opening passage of Brexit three months earlier, on June 23, 2016; a respective press release gloomily advised that "there is not enough Europe in this Union. And that there is not enough Union in this Union … Our European Union is, at least in part, in an existential crisis." Personal data protection was also emphasized, "This is why Parliament, Council and Commission agreed in May this year a common European Data Protection Regulation. This is a strong European law that applies to companies wherever they are based and whenever they are processing your data." In fact, data regulation referred to the 2016 EU-US Privacy Shield Framework program, but also threw a red flag as an adjunct euphemism for censorship proven by the EU's subsequent implementation of the first blasphemy law in 2018.

Thereafter, the EU battened hatches and determined to win the following year's French presidential election. The French location of ITER demanded keeping France in the EU particularly since right-wing presidential candidate Marine Le Pen threatened a "Frexit." France's final presidential election, held on May 7, 2017, became paramount to the EU's survival and why globalist kingpin Obama traveled to France to assist pro-EU candidate Macron. It was no coincidence that Democratic voter-fraud tactics implemented during the U.S. presidential election also erupted in France. Upon victory, Macron immediately reiterated French support for the EU. Then, in December 2018, French protestors (called "Yellow Vests") rebelled against Macron's rising fuel taxes. A French law came into effect on July 1, 2008, that required drivers and passengers to have reflective safety vests and warning triangles in case their vehicle was immobilized and occupants were stranded on the roadside. On January 1, 2016, motorcyclists and scooter riders were added to the 2008 law and "drivers found without safety vests and warning triangles can be fined up to €750," according to *French Entrée*. Consequently, political controversy evolved into a populist yellow vest movement (*"Mouvement des gilets jaunes"*) that demanded "lower fuel taxes, reintroduction of the solidarity tax on wealth, a minimum wage increase, and Emmanuel Macron's resignation as President of France." Hopefully, by the next 2022 presidential election(s), Macron is gone, and Le Pen is in!

The EU built a government, bank, military, and pending nuclear capability under the guise of power plants and holds alliance with the UN and NATO Illuminati. There are seven EU intergovernmental institutions: European Council, European Commission, Council of the European Union, European Parliament, Court of Justice of the European Union, European Central Bank, and the European Court of Auditors. In particular, the European Commission is the "Guardian of the Treaties" and includes "an executive cabinet of public officials, led by an indirectly elected President," which means the EU selects its leaders. Additionally, like the United States, the EU operates a bicameral legislature or "two-house legislature" composed of the Council of the European Union (upper house) and the European Parliament (lower house). Bicameralism dates back to colonial days when the legislature was designed to represent "the mother country" and colonists.

In 1955, the Council of Europe introduced the EU's blue flag, known as the Flag of Europe. The final design was a revised Crown of Thorns featuring 12 gold stars, which represented the people of Europe and ethereally floated around a wreath to emphasize unity. A postman for the Council, Arsène Heitz (1908-1989), was the first of the flag's two designers. His concept was based on a statue of the Virgin Mary, named "Woman of the Apocalypse," displayed at the Roman Catholic Cathedral of Our Lady of Strasbourg located in Strasbourg, Alsace, France; she wore a shining halo of 12 stars and stood on a blue globe emblazoned with a snake and gold stars. The second designer was Paul M. G. Lévy (1910-2002), the Council's director of information, who "drew the exact design of the new flag as it is today."

BBB HISTORY

"Woman of the Apocalypse"
Roman Catholic Cathedral of Our Lady of Strasbourg
located in Strasbourg, Alsace, France (1859); artist: Caryn Cain.

It is morally unconscionable and insanely ironical that a flag rooted in the Catholic religion now spreads Radical Islam that burns Catholic churches and heinously murders clergy and flock. One of countless horrific attacks against Christians occurred on July 26, 2016, at the Catholic Church of the Gambetta in the quaint town of Saint-Etienne du Rouvray, about seven miles south of Rouen, Normandy, in northern France. Islamic terrorists Abdel Malik Petitjean and Adel Kermiche, both 19 years old, attacked the church during morning Mass. Father Jacques Hamel, 86 years old, was forced to his knees. He identified his attacker declaring, "Begone Satan," before being savagely beheaded. Another male parishioner, also 86 years old, was critically wounded by the murderous demons wielding knives and "fake guns and imitation explosives." Christians must heed Father Hamel's martyred message and eradicate Radical Islam's Mephistophelian manifestations while realizing the tribulations we face under the progressive globalist veil of multiculturalism. The EU's bloodstained response offered no remorse and reiterated underlying NWO initiatives that support a European caliphate: "The powerful European Commission President,

Jean-Claude Juncker, has vowed that "no matter how bad terrorism or the migrant crisis gets, the European Union will never give up on open borders"," according to Jihadwatch.org. Then, the following year, in May 2017, the EU's German minion, Chancellor Angela Merkel, defiantly decreed, "Germany will become an Islamic State."

The EU transformed into a dystopian dictatorship forcing upon the world its vision of a one-government United States of Europe. The European Commission determined that the Internet was the key to the EU's global conquest and Islamic fiefdom empowered by Obama's treachery that seeded a Muslim-controlled U.S. Federal Government to enable North America's seamless annexation. A string of interconnected cyber-politico activity revolved around Obama's expected POTUS handoff to Hillary Clinton on November 8, 2016, to cement an EU super state. In May 2016, the EU unleashed a "Code of conduct on countering illegal hate speech online." In July 2016, the Bureau activated its longstanding EU-U.S. transatlantic online partnership. Then, on October 1, 2016, the Obama administration conceded American Internet sovereignty to ICANN. I believe that Obama's conspiratorial plans were interrupted when Trump won the 2016 presidential election. The EU's subsequent contingency plan strategized online iron-fist initiatives. On January 19, 2018, the European Commission issued a press release that essentially implemented blasphemy laws that censored derogatory transmissions against Radical Islam, and respectively acknowledged that media giants Facebook, Instagram, Twitter, YouTube, Google +, and Microsoft "have committed to combatting the spread of such content in Europe through the Code of Conduct." The Code of Conduct was described as "complements legislation fighting racism and xenophobia which requires authors of illegal hate speech offences - whether online or offline - to be effectively prosecuted." Accordingly, draconian EU tyranny censored free speech and levied consequent penalties to facilitate Islamic advancement through media, entertainment, business, law, politics, and consumerism, same as globalists began replicating in the United States.

Europeans mounted a counterattack against EU tyranny through a populist "La Résistance" movement that covertly spread across Europe. Fed-up fringes rose in France, Hungary, Poland, Italy, Austria, Germany, Sweden, and the Netherlands to save European civilization and culture. The EU desperately retaliated against mutiny with punitive force. In May 2018, the EU fined popular French journalist and author Eric Zemmour "5,000 euros for inciting hatred against Muslims" and for warning an "Islamic invasion" and "religious civil war in France." Then, on May 10, 2018, the Sentencing Council for England and Wales addressed hate speech against Muslims by imposing a respective 10-year prison sentence coined as "targeting online a "protected characteristics" including "race; sex; disability; age; sexual orientation; religion or belief; pregnancy and maternity; and gender reassignment"," according to Breitbart London.

All the while, American politics ignored the EU's open-immigration initiatives diabolically spreading terrorist repercussions to western shores supported by strong-armed radical Democrats violating long-standing U.S. immigration laws. Be it reminded that a litany of immigration rules are listed under the 2006 publication edition of the United States Code, Supplement 5, Title 8 – Aliens and Nationality; Chapter 12 – Immigration and Nationality; Subchapter II Immigration; Part II – Admission Qualifications for Aliens; Travel Control of Citizens and Aliens Section 1182 – Inadmissible aliens. Furthermore, POTUS has a right to defend national security: "Whenever the President finds that the entry of any aliens or of any class of aliens into the United States would be detrimental to the interests of the United States, he may by proclamation, and for such period as he shall deem necessary, suspend the entry of all aliens or any class of aliens as immigrants or nonimmigrants, or impose on the entry of aliens any restrictions he may deem to be appropriate."

Immigration law stems from the McCarran Walters Act of 1952, co-sponsored by Nevada Democrat Senator Patrick Anthony McCarran (1876-1954) and Pennsylvania Democrat Representative Francis Eugene Walter (1894-1963); the act governed immigration to and within the United States. According to Chapter 2, Section 212, law prohibited "entry to the U.S. if the alien belongs to an organization seeking to overthrow the Government of the United States by force, violence, or other unconstitutional means. Any immigration without assimilation is an invasion by enemy forces." It is interesting to note that Democrat President Truman vetoed the McCarran Walters Act (overridden by a vote of 278 to 113 in the House and 57 to 26 in the Senate) because it was ""un-American" and discriminatory"; so said the man who entrenched the Bureau to spy on Americans in 1941, unleashed atomic bombs "Little Boy" (70,000 instantly killed in Hiroshima) and "Fat Man" (20,000 instantly killed in Nagasaki) in 1945, and two years later created the CIA.

In 1947, the New York Bureau's General Manager Kenner retired and spirited a dark past into obscurity. History forgot him as the dedicated Templar who redeemed the Bureau. O'Sullivan described the Bureau's fall from grace: "The consensus of opinion of the Better Business Bureau System, after investigation, seems to be that the Bureaus are not designed to project ideals or elevate standards. The characteristic policy of the Bureau managers seems to be to strike its victims, not in the open with the methods of the crusader, but with the underhanded methods of the secret Klan." Kenner repackaged the Bureau through stolen thunder, trickery, revision, and pageantry; he manipulated FDR's friendship to garner exonerating prestigious participation in the president's SEC and Deep State. Gilded optics absolved the Bureau's sins despite fleecing an untold number of speculators through its phony "Before You Invest, Investigate"

THE APO$TATE

securities program. The magnitude of Blue Sky securities and mail fraud engaged by the Bureau, NYSE, and Investment Bankers Association triad was one of the final straws that influenced the creation of the U.S. Senate Committee on Banking and Currency.

In 1949, the Advertising Club of New York (Ad Club) established the Advertising Hall of Fame requested by Advertising Federation of America (AFA) President Andrew Haire. In 1973, according to Adage.com, "The Advertising Hall of Fame move[d] to the American Advertising Federation headquarters in Washington, D.C."

In 1950, Truman addressed the "Annual Conference for the Association of Better Business Bureaus in Washington." His sugar-coated speech aggrandized the Bureau: "Your Bureaus have not relied on propaganda extolling the virtues of business. They have gone to work to clean out the shady areas in the commercial world. They have set out to give real meaning to their slogan: Private enterprise in the public interest." Accordingly, Truman extolled the Bureau's ethics while hiding its scandalous Wall Street indictment and Deep State induction.

In 1953, Texan-born 5-star U.S. Army General Dwight David Eisenhower (1890-1969), former supreme commander of the Allied Expeditionary Forces in Europe during WWII, became 34th POTUS (1953-1961), and followed President Truman's IC footprints. Accordingly, Eisenhower applauded the Deep State Bureau franchise when stating in part, "I am aware that thousands of business firms and millions of our people benefit from the diligent efforts of your association ... That they have prospered and grown is very meaningful." His Republican presidential slogan, "I like Ike," and litany of accolades, commendations, tributes, accomplishments, and contributions indiscriminately gilded groupies including the Bureau as the ringmaster of stolen thunder.

In 1958, British author and sociologist Michael Dunlop Young (1915-2002) published *The Rise of the Meritocracy* as a satirical account of a draconian dystopian society acting as a collective judge and jury empowered by contrived merit resulting in "the haves and the have nots." The timeframe, description, and methodology brought to mind the Better Business Bureau. Young gave an interview with *The Guardian* at the age of 85, six months before his death, and clarified his book's message: "It is good sense to appoint individual people to jobs on their merit. It is the opposite when those who are judged to have merit of a particular kind harden into a new social class without room in it for others." Young acknowledged that his term "meritocracy" had a global ripple effect and had "gone into general circulation, especially in the United States," which questioned the Bureau's respective twentieth-century adaptation resulting in its twenty-first-century elitist empire. His comment, "The business meritocracy is in vogue. If meritocrats believe, as more and more of them are encouraged to, that their advancement comes from their own merits, they can feel they deserve whatever they can get," was nonexclusive, but remarkably characterized the Bureau's current bastardized meritocracy vetted by heavy-handed globalism.

In February 1967, the eastern AFA merged with the Advertising Association of the West (AAW) to form today's American Advertising Federation (AAF). Chronological history reminds that AACA formed in 1905, became AACW in 1914, and was renamed AFA in 1929. Then, in 1967, the AFA-AAW merger established AAF.

In 1970, the Council of Better Business Bureaus was named as the Bureaus' sixth and current national headquarters located in Arlington, Virginia. CBBB's progenitor was the National Vigilance Committee formed in 1912. To avoid monopoly and racketeering liabilities, CBBB filed as a foreign entity separate from the Better Business Bureaus that are independently owned and operated franchises governed by a "board of directors."

On December 4, 1981, President Ronald Reagan signed Executive Order 12333, a.k.a. "Twelve Triple-Three," that amended the National Security Act of 1947. Its preamble described reason and purpose: "Timely, accurate, and insightful Information about the activities, capabilities, plans, and intentions of foreign powers, organizations, and person, and their agents, is essential to the nation security to the United States." As a result, Reagan vastly expanded IC's data collection powers. The Office of the Director of National Intelligence reported, "The U.S. intelligence budget has two major components: the National Intelligence Program and the Military Intelligence Program." The "total budget in 2015 was $66.8 billion," according to *Los Angeles Times*. There are officially 17 IC agencies, but I allege there are 18, including the Better Business Bureau:

1. Coast Guard Intelligence, Homeland Security, est. 1915.
2. Marine Corps Intelligence, Defense, est. 1939.
3. Better Business Bureau, inducted 1941.
4. Bureau of Intelligence and Research, State, est. 1945.
5. Central Intelligence Agency, Independent, est. 1947.
6. Twenty-Fifth Air Force, Defense, est. 1948.
7. National Security Agency, Defense, est. 1952.
8. National Reconnaissance Office, Defense, est. 1961.
9. Defense Intelligence Agency, Defense, est. 1961.
10. Intelligence and Security Command, Defense, est. 1977.
11. Office of Intelligence and Counterintelligence, Energy, est. 1977.
12. Office of Naval Intelligence, Defense, est. 1982.
13. National Geospatial Intelligence Agency, Defense, est. 1996.
14. Office of Terrorism and Financial Intelligence, Treasury, est. 2004.

15. Office of the Director of National Intelligence (DNI), Presidential Cabinet, est. 2004.
16. Intelligence Branch, Justice, est. 2005 [Bureau of Investigations (BOI), est. 1908; Federal Bureau of Investigation (FBI), est. 1935].
17. Office of National Security Intelligence, Justice, est. 2006.
18. Office of Intelligence and Analysis, Homeland Security, est. 2007.

Reagan's EO 12333 placed ultimate responsibility on the National Security Agency (NSA) and its director to securely process and distribute intercepted intelligence. According to Title 10 U.S. Code § 201, "Certain Intelligence Officials: consultation and concurrence regarding appointments; evaluation of performance," law mandates that "the Director of the NSA is recommended by the Secretary of Defense and nominated for appointment by the President."

After the terrorist attacks, on September 11, 2001, EO 12333 was amended several times, but former President Obama's latest change under Section 2.3 essentially approved IC's unlimited worldwide surveillance powers on the if-come of breach of national security while acknowledging possible harm to targeted persons. In fact, Section 2.3(C)(1)(f) pre-emptively warned adverse repercussions from surveillance: "The potential for substantial harm, embarrassment, inconvenience, or unfairness to U.S. person if the USPI is improperly used or disclosed." As a result, American's civil rights were infringed with no regard to individual privacy or violation of constitutional or statutory laws. In fact, each American was generically dubbed a ""USPI" for "U.S. person information".".

Twelve Triple-Three was enacted to gather strategic military Intel but did not consider a radical shadow government offshoot operated by rogue IC successors persecuting civilians and pursuing NWO dominance. Surveillance was weaponized and transfigured into digital artillery. Consequently, insurgent sub-rosa vassals now operate with impunity and exploit dictatorial discretion. The nation's classified resources have been subjected to IC "shorthanded" programs including "LOVEINT" (2013) that enable agents' childish whims to "spy on the emails or phone calls of their current or former spouses and lovers." Accordingly, a spy's pipe dream sprung footloose and fancy-free dragon masters and their high-tech wizards armed with unlimited powers that infiltrated every phase of life through tactical malware further tweaked by human vice. Bottom line, the Obama administration reduced cyberhacking to fetish fondling. Think of all that you do in a day, private and public, and then imagine some pervert monitoring your every action within range of your Obama-smartened phone, TV, computer, laptop, or anything with GPS including vehicles and baby monitors; whether turned on or off.

Obama was spying on the masses for at least two years prior to his amendment of E.O. 12333, Section 2.3. The former president used the NSA as his personal game station deploying several surveillance programs. U.S. Air Force Lieutenant General Thomas McInerney (Ret.) produced a letter from Admiral James "Ace" Lyons Jr. (Ret.), "the former commander in chief of the U.S. Pacific Fleet," that exposed a "secret supercomputer system called "The Hammer"" that the NSA used for "illegal and unconstitutional data harvesting and wiretapping," which questioned "violation of the espionage act."

As a victimized American citizen, I can vouch that the IC is a loose cannon and abusing Section 2.3. My life changed the day an IC spook stared back at me from my cell phone. I was in the middle of checking emails. My screen suddenly cleared, and I found myself looking into a dimly lit computer room with a twenty-something groomed business-casual clean-shaven dark-haired stylish-cut slightly built Caucasian man ethereally staring back at me. He was sitting in front of a spread-out system of double-banked monitors and working a central keyboard; his face looked upwards at me as though camera surveillance was feeding from a top-tiered screen. His reaction was spontaneous and scrutinizing while I was shell-shocked and seething; I do not remember who cut-off who first. Within days, the FBI issued what was probably a cover-up advisory that smart phones were being hacked and recommended lens covers for privacy but did not address adjunct remote-controlled hijacking. During the same timeframe, I noticed my cell phone's microphone icon was lit and turned on despite the settings option being turned off; remote operations continued for several days until the application abruptly ended. Additionally, my computer systemically crashed for no apparent reason and had never done such before. I called my local Internet carrier and had great difficulty reestablishing a link; tech support advised that I had been locked out of my network as though a shadow download was in progress. Afterwards, my trusty laptop acted suspiciously; among several issues, my computer fluttered and flashed as though uploading screen grabs and Internet speed dramatically slowed as though implanted spyware was reading my material. Apparently, a worm (tracking cookie, trojan-something?) was attached to my manuscript; every time I opened my file I was forced to link with an offsite sponsor. As I neared completion of my manuscript, monitoring changed to obstruction and destructive cybersabotage.

I used Microsoft Word and began scrutinizing every feature and glitch, which became overwhelmingly distracting considering the concentrative nature of writing. The FBI had previously used Microsoft's "Saving AutoRecovery" feature to recoup deleted unsecured classified emails involving former Secretary of State Hillary Clinton, but IC Internet snooping was far more advanced and landmined. *Zdnet. com's* article, "PRISM: Here's how the NSA wiretapped the Internet," dated June 8, 2013, cautiously advised material was "to be treated as strictly hypothetical" while advising, "The NSA started to capture data from Microsoft in 2007 ... Yahoo was next in 2008 and Google, Facebook and PalTalk in 2009."

THE APO$TATE

Thereafter, WikiLeaks shocked the world when exposing the Deep State's dirty laundry. WikiLeaks confirmed that the public had long been subject to government surveillance and released intercepted documents in four parts: (1) "Year Zero" on March 7, 2017, that "showed the CIA's iOS and Android [mobile phone] exploits." (2) "Dark Matter" on March 23, 2017, that "is said to include details of the CIA's global hacking program, and these documents describe hacking methods allegedly used by the agency to access Apple devices and upload data." (3) "Marble Framework" on March 31, 2017, that "is used to hamper forensic investigators and anti-virus companies from attributing viruses, trojans and hacking attacks to the CIA." (4) "Grasshopper" on April 7, 2017, that detailed how the CIA built "customised malware payloads for Microsoft Windows operating systems." In fact, on October 25, 2019, the Pentagon "awarded its $10 billion "war cloud" computing contract to Microsoft over rival Amazon," according to The Hill.

The extent of unbridled surveillance by the Deep State was underscored by recent U.S. efforts to extradite WikiLeaks' founder Julian Assange for "soliciting and publishing classified information and conspiring to hack into a government computer," per *The Guardian*. Additionally, *The Guardian* reported, "Assange faces an 18-count indictment, issued by the U.S. Department of Justice that includes charges under the Espionage Act." Yet it's okay for the Deep State to violate my personal privacy and hack my cell phone and computer; my manuscript used Microsoft and was daily tagged, tracked, and trashed from 2017 until publication in 2020; I had no choice but to use Microsoft documents for publication. Furthermore, Assange's explosive revelations exposed former Secretary of State and 2016 Democratic presidential candidate Hillary Clinton's massive violations for compromising classified information; he was imprisoned, but she is still walking free. What happened to "Lock' her up!"?

My personal experience confirmed that the CIA's Mobile Devices Branch (MDB) was actively operating weaponized malware in addition to other offsite IC incursion. WikiLeaks' Vault 7 warned that MDB "developed numerous attacks to remotely hack and control popular smart phones … Infected phones can be instructed to send the CIA the user's geolocation, audio and text communications as well as covertly activate the phone's camera and microphone." Accordingly, I believe that MDB hacked both my cell phone and laptop respective to Obama's last-minute Executive Order that suspiciously coincided with President-elect Donald Trump's inauguration on January 20, 2017, and that amended Reagan's EO 12333 with Section 2.3 referred to by the National Security Agency (NSA) as, "PROCEDURES FOR THE AVAILABILJI.TY OR DESSEMINATION OF RAW SIGNALS INTELLIGENCE INFORMATION BY THE NATIONAL SECURITY AGENCY UNDER SECTION 2.3 OF EXECUTIVE ORDER 12333 (RAW SIGINT AVAILABILITY PROCEDURES)."

There is no doubt that the CIA abused IC powers to spy on private citizens. WikiLeaks' "Year Zero" exposed "several hundred million lines of [hacking] code" that "appears to have been circulated among former U.S. government hackers and contractors in an unauthorized manner." Vault 7 advised that "the CIA has gained political and budgetary preeminence over the U.S. National Security Agency (NSA)." Furthermore, by the beginning of 2017 (which introduced Obama's expansive Section 2.3), the CIA's Center for Cyber Intelligence (CCI) and "hacking division," had developed an unfettered version of NSA with "over 5000 registered users and had produced more than a thousand hacking systems, trojans, viruses, and other "weaponized" malware." Vault 7 identified the Engineering Development Group (EDG) as a "software development group within CCI" that "is responsible for the development, testing and operational support of all backdoors, exploits, malicious payloads, trojans, viruses and any other kind of malware used by the CIA in its covert operations world-wide."

Considering my face-to-face remote-controlled cell phone encounter of the weird kind, I was thankful for keeping my decades-old analogue television whereby preserving whatever household privacy remained. Circumstances explained why analogue cell phones were forcibly switched to android smart phones, as my carrier did in 2014; government spooks were seeding covert surveillance initiatives.

Laws of the land and rights of privacy are being egregiously flouted creating an infinite array of legal and safety repercussions. Stealth robotics and artificial intelligence have insidiously infiltrated mainstream society to exploit and micromanage the public, politics, and commerce. Intellectual property, including publishing, can take years to develop and/or write, but sabotaging cybercrime is instantaneous reminding of horse-and-buggy days when whoever reached the patent office first received credit and reward with no consideration of originator, effort, and/or investment. As an anti-globalist writer and former trial plaintiff who fended off the Deep State Bureau, I am particularly vulnerable and disturbed that my privacy and keyboard are subject to IC's arbitrary rape; that Big Cloud is allowed to harass me while weighing on my paranoia, compromising my intellectual property rights, hacking my manuscript, framing me, and/or jeopardizing my life particularly since I dropped a dime on an Illuminati's cash cow.

In the past, dirt was creatively swept under the rug, but nowadays whistleblowers and journalists are routinely murdered and laid to questionable rest under the nefarious subtitle, "died under suspicious circumstances." Posthumous investigations were quickly cold-cased, and the media dropped coverage like a hot rock. In fact, election year 2016 highlighted an alarming number of fatalities (still ongoing) that were linked to Democratic presidential candidate Hillary Clinton's family and foundation; an endless "death list" whose victims committed unforeseen suicide and/or haphazardly died from a street shooting, accident, plane crash, or fell off a building.

Recent events underscore the emergence of an autocratic rogue cyber nation that is controlling the airways and inner sanctums of every city, state, and country. Henceforth, cybercrime will be the final frontier; a virtual Wild West; the OK Corral of Big Cloud shrouding a shootout between maverick marshals, digital guns, and malware bullets. Whoever controls celestial circuitry controls respective inhabitants forcing socialism and slavery that equates to suppression and submission. We are on the fringes of apocalyptic insanity and overriding artificial intelligence.

Additionally, WikiLeaks recovered information relative to the CIA's capability of hacking vehicle computer systems that questioned the "car-crash" death of journalist Michael Mahon Hastings before publishing his CIA exposé. News.com respectively reported, "As of October 2014 the CIA was also looking at infecting the vehicle control systems used by modern cars and trucks ... The purpose of such control is not specified, but it would permit the CIA to engage in nearly undetectable assassinations." Circumstances and available technology pointed to Hastings' car being remotely hijacked while he was driving and was turned into a hotwired microwave; street cameras photographed his car in flames before crashing into a palm tree; assassination was plausible considering an embedded GPS tracking device can remotely "disable or enable" vehicle "computer-controlled steering."

Hastings was a war correspondent in Afghanistan and Iraq as well as "a contributing editor to Rolling Stone and reporter for BuzzFeed"; he was also a renowned "critic of the Obama administration, Democratic Party, and surveillance state." In addition to several significant investigations, Hastings was responsible for the resignation of U.S. Army General Stanley Allen McChrystal, commander of NATO's International Security Assistance Force in Afghanistan. Hastings spent a month with McChrystal and published a respective article, "The Runaway General," in the June 2010 issue of *Rolling Stone*. As a result, on June 23, 2010, President Obama fired McChrystal for disparaging insubordination and replaced him with General David Howell Petraeus, commander of United States Central Command. On June 20, 2011, Petraeus was unanimously nominated as director of the CIA, but resigned on November 9, 2012, amid scandal of an extramarital affair and leaked classified information. In May 2013, Petraeus became chairman of New York-based Kohlberg Kravis Roberts & Co. L.P. (KKR Global Institute) and was named partner in December 2014. Consequently, from 2013 until present date (2019), Petraeus has been a regular attendee at Bilderberg meetings held around the globe. The Bilderberg Group is considered a conspiratorial NWO secret society composed of "140 royals, corporate kings, technology brainiacs, international bankers, politicians and military experts" and listed sixth on the Western Illuminati Organization Chart.

On June 7, 2013, Hastings published his last article for *BuzzFeed* entitled, "Why Democrats Love to Spy On Americans." Five days later, he posted a tweet from "Michael Hastings (@mmhastings)" that stated, "At dirty Wars Q&A: @jeremyscahill jokes google is "NSA's secret database" playing all next week at landmark theater in LA." Another six days, he was dead. According to Wikipedia (referencing *Associated Press* and *Los Angeles Times*' articles), "On June 18, 2013, Hastings died in a single vehicle automobile crash in his Mercedes C250 Coupé at approximately 4:25 a.m. in the Hancock Park neighborhood of Los Angeles ... video from a nearby security camera purportedly shows Hastings' vehicle speeding and bursting into flames." Description of events suggested foul play involving remote-controlled handling of the car particularly considering an explosion and fire occurred prior to collision; he was burned beyond recognition and his death was conveniently ruled "an accident"; small traces of medical marijuana and amphetamine were found during autopsy. At the time of his death, Hastings was working on an article about "CIA Director John O. Brennan." Accordingly, nothing silences critics faster than a heinous death among the ranks, which may explain why *BuzzFeed* became an ardent liberal Democratic media outlet.

In fact, the CIA is operating the Internet under intelligence and reconnaissance programs scouted by In-Q-Tel venture capital firm. In-Q-Tel (derived from inventor "Q" in James Bond movies) was chartered by the CIA to acquire intelligence-gathering programs, such as Google; similar to Big Government ransacking prisons to extract expert state-of-the-art hackers to gun Big Cloud as a derivative concept of FDR's "set a thief to catch a thief."

Google essentially kick-started the modern IC as a web-browser research project that In-Q-Tel referred to the CIA. In January 1996, Stanford University PhD research students "Larry Page and Sergey Brin" introduced their search-engine project coined "BackRub" that was renamed "Google." On September 4, 1998, Google incorporated as a privately held company. On August 19, 2004, Google held an initial public offering (IPO) with "19,605,052 shares at a price of $85 per share ... The sale of $1.67 billion gave Google a market capitalization of more than $23 billion," according to Wikipedia.org. Also, in August 2004, Google bought the notorious Keyhole Inc. for $35 million whose satellite-mapping database was called "Keyhole EarthViewer" that became Google Earth "in 2005." On November 13, 2006, Google finalized its acquisition of YouTube "for $1.65 billion in Google Stock." On September 2, 2008, Google introduced Google Chrome as a data-collecting web browser for Microsoft Windows. On August 15, 2011, Google acquired Motorola Mobility "for $12.5 billion." On January 26, 2014, Google acquired the London-based DeepMind Technologies (artificial intelligence and robotics) for a reported $400 million dollars. Then, on August 10, 2015, Google reorganized as a subsidiary of Alphabet. By October 2016, Google was considered "the most visited website in the world."

THE APO$TATE

The CIA "chartered" In-Q-Tel to provide the U.S. government surveillance and reconnaissance technology. On September 29, 1999, Peleus (In-Q-Tel (IQT)) was founded by Norm Augustine and Gilman Louie as a "government (taxpayer) funded Venture capital firm," headquartered in Arlington, Virginia. Mission statement was "to identify and invest in companies developing cutting-edge technologies that serve the United States national security interests." Accordingly, In-Q-Tel is a separate "Virginia-registered corporation ... bound by its charter agreement and annual contract with the CIA."

Keyhole, Inc. was created by Intrinsic Graphics in 1999. Purpose was "to stream large databases of mapping data over the internet to client software ...." Thereafter, Keyhole, Inc. launched Google Earth that sprung a motherlode of mapping and satellite programs. *Guardian*.com reported, "As it turns out, the same platforms and services that Google deploys to monitor people's lives and grab their data could be put to use running huge swaths of the US government, including the military, spy agencies, police departments and schools. The key to this transformation was a small startup now known as Google Earth." CNN popularized Keyhole while covering the "2003 invasion of Iraq." Keyhole was "contacted by the CIA's venture capital firm, In-Q-Tel, and the National Geospatial-Intelligence Agency, for use with defense mapping databases," according to Wikipedia. Then, in 2003, Vicarious Visions acquired Intrinsic Graphics. In 2004, Google bought Keyhole, Inc. and produced numerous mapping, reconnaissance, and space programs; acquisition of Keyhole included former In-Q-Tel executive Rob Painter. According to *Guardian*.com, "[Painter] came with deep connections to the world of intelligence and military contracting, including US Special Operations, the CIA and major defence firms, among them Raytheon, Northrop Grumman and Lockheed Martin. At Google, Painter was planted in a new dedicated sales and lobbying division called Google Federal, located In Reston, Virginia ...." Keyhole brought many global complaints of invasion of privacy and threat to national security. Wikipedia.org respectively advised, "The typical argument is that the software provides information about military or other critical installations that could be used by terrorists."

In keeping with Hastings' inference days before his death that Google was part of the NSA's database, I confirmed on several occasions that my obscure words and unusual catch-phrases researched on Google's browser were rehashed hours later by mooching media commentators privy to shoplifted data and adept at intellectual hijacking. Additionally, my face-to-face virtual encounter of the weird kind emphasized the illicit extent that private American citizens are being covertly micromanaged, digitally censored, and browser marketed. How many advertising commercials duplicate real-life scenarios from stolen privacy? Modern surveillance threatens déjà-vu rack and ruin with history repeating disaster and persecution. Prohibition birthed organized crime, and, 100 years later, spyware spawned cybercrime.

In 1987, Reagan forwarded a video-taped message to the convention of the Council of Better Business Bureaus. In part, he stated, "Few organizations have the rich heritage of service that distinguishes the history of the Better Business Bureaus. Fewer still can point with pride to years of selfless sacrifice, yet that is the hallmark of the Bureaus activities ... Down through the years the Better Business Bureaus have resolutely stayed the course, showing themselves to be the best friend American consumers have ever had ...." Two points came to mind: (1) CBBB and the Bureaus screwed millions of people around the globe leading up to the Crash of 1929. (2) At the time of Reagan's speech, CBBB was scheming a twenty-first-century blueprint to dominate U.S. commerce as evidenced by its launch of a phony integrity awards program in 2000 with underlying intent to increase memberships, raise revenue, eliminate competition, and monopolize the marketplace per NWO globalist plans.

In 1990, 41st POTUS George Herbert Walker "HW" Bush (1924-2018) addressed CBBB's annual convention, which nuanced a quintessential Deep State reunion. Dr. John Coleman named "George H.W. Bush" as "Illuminati," and as a former director of Truman's CIA, HW would have been privy to the Bureau's Truman-facilitated Deep State induction. Accordingly, HW's speech gushed sweet IC nothings: "One of the greatest strengths of our free enterprise system lies in the willingness of American business men and women to respect the rights of consumers while advancing their companies' interest. Over the years, Better Business Bureaus have effectively promoted truth and fairness in the marketplace and, in so doing, have earned the confidence and gratitude of the American public ... On behalf of a grateful Nation, I salute you."

On November 30, 2018, HW entered eternity leaving behind distinguished accolades and accomplishments as "a decorated naval pilot, Texas Congressman, National Chairman of the Republican National Committee, Ambassador to the UN, and Special Envoy to China." HW was also the 11th director of central intelligence (DCI) from 1976 to 1977, which indoctrinated him into the Deep State during the period that "came to be known as "time of troubles" for the CIA"; he was the only DCI to become POTUS and served one term from 1989 to 1993. Additionally, HW was considered bi-partisan establishment and respectively delivered a globalist-infused State of the Union Address on January 29, 1991: "What is at stake is more than one small country; it is a big idea: a new world order, where diverse nations are drawn together in common cause to achieve the universal aspirations of mankind -- peace and security, freedom, and the rule of law ... The world can, therefore, seize this opportunity to fulfill the long-held promise of a new world order, where brutality will go unrewarded and aggression will meet collective resistance." Most telling was HW's historic 2016 GOP defection whereby he voted for Democrat Hillary Clinton instead of Republican Donald Trump. HW's death brought national mourning, particularly in Texas, but parting sorrow should not revise history and/or relinquish globalist accountability. His utopian rose-colored glasses proved despotically short-sighted in light of globalism's current NWO oligarchic directives that have forced draconian censorship, barbarity, and genocide to replace Western culture, civilization, and values with a compliant third-world Islamic demographic.

The Bush family represented a father-and-son presidential dynasty. As a Texan, I particularly blame both former presidents and minions, including former Governor Rick Perry, for turning Texas into a swing state with imminent Democratic takeover hovering on the next electoral horizon due to globalist politics, broken immigration laws, porous borders, and backdoor amnesties. In fact, incumbent Texas Republican Senator Ted Cruz barely won re-election on November 6, 2018, over Democrat Robert Francis "Beto" O'Rourke, 50.89% to 48.32%; future elections guarantee a full-blown Democratic Texas. Former President Obama accomplished his mission to "Brown" America while throwing Black and White Americans under the bus.

Jesse Lee Peterson, conservative founder and president of the Brotherhood Organization of a New Destiny (BOND), promoted the deportation of illegals citing adversity against the Black community: "They're taking the jobs .... They're also affecting when it comes to the health care, because black women ... they're not able to get in with the long lines and the long wait. Many of them have been forced out of their own communities. It's really bad."

Actually, Peterson understated harsh reality. The border crisis built a thriving cartel community where I live north of Houston along the I-45 corridor. Thug municipal leaders exploited underground initiatives to empower the city and themselves. Apartment communities serve as backdoor halfway houses to a relentless Hispanic invasion facilitated by large diversity-driven corporations that provide jobs and homes otherwise refused to non-Latinos.

On October 25, 2019, Numbers USA reported, "On Thursday [10/24/2019], the Center for Immigration Studies held a panel discussion at the National Press Club in coordination with the release of a new report "examining real-world case studies in which the Equal Employment Opportunity Commission (EEOC) has sued employers for systemically favoring low-skill immigrants over native workers"." In fact, non-Latinos are having trouble getting any job because noncitizens pilfer and pass jobs to friends and family. Furthermore, employment ads from government, housing, grocery, businesses, and box stores advertise preference for "bilingual" applicants, which is code for Blacks and Whites need not apply. Accordingly, it is an egregious fallacy that illegals do not take good jobs. A Brown tidal wave has risen to supervisory stature that only hires Hispanics, which sparks a chain reaction that siphons good jobs from indigenous jobseekers resulting in violence, homelessness, and despair.

Native-son Black and White homelessness has become a growing problem due to illegal immigration and COVID-19 evictions. Well-paying warehouse, retail, restaurant, government, and school jobs were previously americana havens but are now predominately staffed by noncitizens. Where I live, outside of Houston, Fortune 500 companies built a burgeoning industrial park whose hiring staff is usually Hispanic, and scorched-earth dynamics are spreading. Additionally, the Cartel clandestinely owns and operates businesses and warehouses originating from Mexico that solicit Hispanic labor. Accordingly, my comments are not meant to be racist, nor directed towards patriotic Mexican Americans; I am simply stating observation of employment disparity that is creating an employment bubble. Many Mexican Americans worked hard to earn citizenship and success, but statistics prove that illegal immigrants largely vote Democratic, which undermines capitalism and enables globalism. Consequently, ethnic discrimination threatens indigenous livelihood and/or ability to pursue higher learning, competitive employment, and quality lifestyle. A man complained on an Internet job board that he thought he had a job but was "passed over and pissed!"

An ignored 2016 clarion call warned of the Democratic Party's insidious rise in Texas. Accordingly, Democratic servants are now replacing Republican masters who, for decades, abused immigration laws in return for cheap labor; many were BBB members. The 2020 election forebodingly cautioned an imminent attack against the U.S. Republic. Ironically, Governor Greg Abbott distributed urgent get-out-the-vote email alerts while realizing his dubious re-election; he ignored my awards-fraud complaints against the Houston Bureau when he was attorney general. All the while, the NWO schemed to recoup what they lost ... POTUS. Additionally, let me be clear, I believe in legal immigration that will enrich America, but not the current insanity that violates U.S. law, encourages horde invasions and terrorism, steals federal treasure, impoverishes citizens, rigs elections, and neuters national defense.

When Texas falls, so will the American Republic. The U.S. Constitution was a noble experiment bound to fail because idealistic principles were unrealistic, proffered unenforceable laws, catered to subversive special interests' overriding clout and coup, and recklessly immunized Trojan horse incursions under a sacrilegious canopy of huddled masses. I always warned, "Give an invader an inch and they will take the country!"

HW penned the Immigration Act of 1990 that was introduced in 1989 by Democratic Senator Ted Kennedy and enacted on November 29, 1990. According to Wikipedia, "It increased total, overall immigration to allow 700,000 immigrants to come to the U.S. per year for the fiscal years 1992–94, and 675,000 per year after that ... It provided family-based immigration visa,

THE APO$TATE

created five distinct employment based visas, categorized by occupation, and a diversity visa program that created a lottery to admit immigrants from "low admittance" countries … or countries where their citizenry was underrepresented in the U.S."

George Walker "W" Bush, 43rd POTUS from 2001 to 2009, and 46th governor of Texas from 1995 to 2000, continued amnesty measures pursued by his father. Accordingly, a respective "op-ed" referenced W and highlighted destructive consequences of America's broken immigration policies. On the Issues.org told the story of Flavius Julius Valens Augustus, a.k.a. Valens, Eastern Roman Emperor from 364 to 378 A.D., who in 376 A.D. benevolently granted asylum to "a large band of Gothic refugees" despite respective violation of Roman law. Two years later, they killed him. The website compared "W" to Valens and warned, "Valens has his modern counterpart in George W. Bush. For in May 2006, Republican senators at Bush's urging joined Democrats to offer a blanket amnesty to 12 million illegal aliens and permit US businesses to go abroad and bring in foreign workers. Senators had been shocked by the millions of Hispanics marching in America's cities under Mexican flags. And as was the emperor Valens, President Bush was hailed for his compassion and vision."

In 1994, Dressler highlighted CBBB's pivotal juncture when the organization first joined the Internet. In the process, he inadvertently verified CBBB's sovereign control of the organization through various deliberations awaiting resolution that included whether or not to allow members to advertise their memberships. In fact, CBBB approved membership advertisement with the introduction of the awards program in 2000. Like Upton Sinclair's *The Jungle*, Dressler's book mixed insider knowledge with fiction and detailed CBBB's tailspinning predicament prior to its digital remake. As a result, he defined when and why the Bureau's birth mission of truth was abandoned.

While solving the thickening plot of a murder mystery, Dressler sprinkled exceptional Bureau revelation. His date-stamped storyline, from May 2, 1994 to May 23, 1994, detailed far-reaching Bureau schematics. His narrative addressed previously unknown circumstances involving CBBB's micromanagement and operations including advertising, memberships, endorsement, business reports, rating system, encroaching consumer-advocacy competition, and the Internet. It was a critical time period that determined the fate of the Bureau. He also inadvertently answered the overriding question of why the Bureau breached moral compass to create a phony awards program. Basically, the organization was broke. Revenue was direly needed to compete in the twenty-first century. Accordingly, in 2000, CBBB launched the cost-effective awards program on newly created websites that bank shot the franchise to phenomenal success.

In 2000, Dressler poignantly summed up the Bureau's twentieth-century fin de siècle affairs when asking, "How do you get out of this financial bind?"

Unfortunately, no other Bureau personnel wrote a historical book like Kenner that highlighted specific events, vigilance activities, and operations. Kenner proved that the technological revolution was the Bureau's greatest asset. As the inventions of radio and television progressed and refined, the Bureau adapted and/or fabricated its code of standards to respective industries to embed its brand image and business services. Stair-stepping global catastrophes, particularly WWI, WWII, and the Korean War, cemented relations between the federal government, advertising industry, and Bureau.

Dressler's narrative unwittingly depicted the plight of a declining legend at the close of the twentieth century whose unbridled success was impeded by virtuous birthright. Founders established the Vigilance Committee to enforce the *Printers' Ink* Model Statute. Additionally, Rowell's impeccable standards loomed like a celestial halo reminding the advertising industry's ethical commitment, but, just like an amoral litigator loyal only to his bank account, the Bureau resolved obstructive moral dilemma by embracing deceit. Thereafter, gilded humbuggery peddled a virtuous storefront lucratively thimble-rigging Wizard of Oz trickery.

Considering the renowned secrecy of the Bureau, Dressler remarkably clarified otherwise undocumented history regarding organizational posturing and backstories that illuminated modern cornerstone programs. His 1990's narrative reflected significant changes that aligned with CBBB's purported twenty-first-century rollout; that the organization's endorsement policy was quietly reversed by disclaimers warning the Bureau "did not endorse its members' products, service or company"; that the organization's reporting system was renamed "reliability reports" that were "provided solely to assist in exercising … best judgment and are subject to change at any time"; and that the first rating system was launched to grade businesses as being either "satisfactory" or "unsatisfactory."

By the 1990s, the Internet broke ground and the Bureau franchise was struggling to overcome competition from several consumer-reporting organizations. Dressler queried, "Virtually all of the Bureau's core activities were subject to intense competition. Government agencies, church groups, other non-profit groups, law firms and many others were in the business of mediating and arbitrating disputes … How can the system monitor all this given such limited resources? And what will it do as the "information superhighway" becomes available in more and more homes. What was needed was a strategy for the 21st Century. What roles should the BBB play in the 21st Century?" Accordingly, CBBB questioned how to successfully phase operations into the new millennia as euphemism for how to control the marketplace?

Dressler emphasized the importance of procuring memberships as the life blood of the organization aside from low-income consumer programs. He wrote, "One way or another our work must go on, and it is especially important that our Membership Service Center be staffed at all times. Lest we forget, our members pay our salaries." Additionally, Dressler clarified, "Unlike most other associations, however, Bureaus rely almost completely on membership dues to fund these activities. Better Business Bureaus do have some consumer complaint settlement programs (mediation and arbitration) that generate modest income. Still, most Bureau budgets are 90 to 98% dues funded while most other associations rely on dues for 50% or less of their budgets." Dressler's book paved the way for the organization's awards program and alpha-numeric rating score that were introduced to increase memberships.

Bureau founders initially worried about implications of fraud and extortion resulting from membership advertisement as occurred in the twenty-first century. Slate.com concluded, "The BBB recognized that such publicity might corrupt businesses into using their membership fees to bribe local BBBs. Worse still, it might corrupt local BBBs into using membership fees to shake down businesses, effectively turning the BBB into a protection racket."

The 1990s witnessed CBBB's ascension into the Internet age. CBBB forwarded an internal SOS signal to the BBB franchise to develop profit-motivated programs. As a result, an Internet accessible business database was introduced in 1991; the Torch Award Program (TAP) for national and international companies was established in 1996; local integrity awards were created in 2000; and the alpha-numeric rating system was designed in 2005 and systemically integrated with the awards and online business files in 2009. The awards and rating programs drastically increased memberships and franchise revenue. Businesses faced a choice of either nonmember digital disparagement or endorsed member participation. It was the same *Roaring Twenties*' song and dance, but a century apart. Yesteryear's Mafioso tactics were reorganized as today's cyber bully of the "Wild Net"; a new frontier where weasel words roam free. As a result, general consensus decided that membership was the most lucrative and least painful. Thereafter, CBBB's annual reports reflected staggering expansion in keeping with Dressler's 1994 storyline foretelling twenty-first-century digital operations. CBBB operates the bbb.org website and works with national sponsors including regulatory agencies such as the DOC and FTC. Additionally, the franchise's brick-and-mortar assets control local businesses via websites.

In early 2009, CBBB and its National Advertising Review Council (NARC) established the "Online Interest-Based Advertising Accountability Program" (Accountability Program) that developed "Online Behavioral Advertising" (OBA) "Principles" described as "the collection and use of data from a particular computer or device regarding web viewing behaviors over time." The basic concept was to provide accountability and protect online consumer privacy and data security. BBB.org advised that the Accountability Program "refers cases of non-participation or uncorrected non-compliance to the Federal Trade Commission." In February 2009, I submitted complaints to the FTC and was abruptly dismissed despite offering irrefutable evidence to prove massive awards fraud by CBBB and the Houston Bureau. On August 15, 2009, the FTC rubberstamped CBBB's Accountability Program under bona fides of "ethics."

In 2011, Sharon Abrams, CBBB's former "Chair, Board of Directors," described national operations as "the umbrella organization for 116 local, independent, non-profit BBBs across the U.S. and Canada. The system as a whole (Council and local BBBs) has a combined budget of approximately $181 million, with approximately 2,000 employees serving consumers and the business community in every state and province. CBBB is also home to our globally recognized national programs on dispute resolution, industry self-regulation, and online privacy." That same year, CBBB formed its "first government affairs program" that expanded relations with "Congress, the Administration and other key influencers." Additionally, the collective organization chronicled over 103 million informational requests, 927,000 consumer complaints and "more than six million hits a month" on their website.

The 2011 annual report followed a scandal-ridden 2010 that revealed a bias corrupt unbridled impenitent conniving thieving Better Business Bureau. ABC *20/20's* documentary exposed a pay-for-play scheme by the Los Angeles Bureau that sold premium rating scores to enhance online business files for the price of a membership while emphasizing that CBBB approved and implemented the program. CBBB spent the year 2011 dispensing damage control by amplifying new developments and programs. Similar scandal laundering occurred after the U.S. Senate's 1932 indictment of the New York Bureau that was whitewashed by FDR's pristine SEC.

CBBB's damage control included proselytizing contrived achievements during 2011 that advised commencement of "regular "Scam Alerts" to warn consumers about fraudulent businesses and practices"; integration of CBBB's U.S. and Canadian operations; introduction of "BBB Search" as an iPhone App; contact with PROFECO, Mexico's consumer affairs agency to open the country's first Better Business Bureau; and, expansion of "Children's Food and Beverage Advertising Initiative" (CFBAI). Additionally, the "BBB Reliability Reports" were renamed "BBB Business Reviews." Early AACA convention history taught successors to engage name changes and optics to divert attention when status quo became toxic or boring.

The 2012 annual report listed completed projects and international expansion while celebrating a centurial milestone marking watershed advertising history when the first Vigilance Committee and first National Vigilance Committee were introduced a century earlier. Data was presented in a ticker-tape format along the bottom of each page in keeping with the Bureau's NYSE heritage. The report listed government, international, and private sector Bureau programs that collectively emphasized an entrenched federal relationship and included "White House Privacy summit; U.S. House of Representative's Energy and Commerce Committee, Federal Trade Commission, U.S. Department of Defense, Centers for Disease Control and Prevention, National Association of State Attorneys General, and Canadian Competition Bureau."

Erroneous facts were published in the 2012 annual report. Closer scrutiny of CBBB's historical recollection revealed several glaring errors that underscored successors' shocking ignorance, reckless disregard, and/or intentional distortion of Bureau history. The same mistakes were duplicated in a later press release published online by the New York Bureau and entitled, "New BBB advertising standards reflect 21st century advertising in traditional and new media," dated February 12, 2015, which introduced "comprehensive changes" made to its *BBB Code of Advertising* standards regulating "websites, social media, texting and other channels." CBBB advertised skewed material confident that consumers had no knowledge to realize misstatements. Troubled truth encompassed bogus programs making a mockery of the organization's sacred brand image of the eternal torch chosen by founders to be "lighted in a vigilant fight against this modern foe of truthful advertising." Nevertheless, the presser warned, "The key proviso of the Code is that 'the primary responsibility for truthful and non-deceptive advertising rests with the advertiser'."

In a stunning insult to "those gallant crusaders in 1911," CBBB wrongly credited Dobbs as the author of the revolutionary *Ten Commandments of Advertising*. CBBB stated in its 2012 centennial annual report, "National Vigilance Committee is formed in Dallas based on "Ten Commandments of Advertising: by Samuel Candler Dobbs of Coca-Cola"." In fact, Joseph Appel authored the *Ten Commandments of Advertising* and introduced his work at the famous 1911 Boston Convention that sparked the Truth in Advertising Movement. Additionally, the largess of cornerstone advertising history happened *after* Dobbs relinquished his presidency to George Coleman at the 1911 convention. Then, Dobbs became immersed in the *Barrels and Kegs Case* trial and maintained a low profile as a distinguished rank-and-file Bureau member. Appel and several other esteemed trailblazers, described in further chapters, actively promoted, propagated, and popularized the truth movement that begat the Bureau. There is no doubt, though, that Dobbs contributed to advertising history. His final curtain call presented a memorable speech entitled, "A Quarter Century of Progress," at the Advertising Federation of America's 25th Anniversary celebration of the 1911 convention "held in Boston June 28 to July 1, 1936."

Another inaccurate presser boasted that the "Better Business Bureau of Minnesota and North Dakota is proud to be known as "the first BBB!" We're a non-profit organization founded by ethical business owners in the Twin Cities in 1912." In fact, the Vigilance Committee of Minneapolis did open in 1912 and was the first to adopt "Better Business Bureau," but not until 1916 when

Arthur Sheldon suggested the name. Accordingly, the Minneapolis Bureau's garbled propaganda illustrates a typical example of reckless reporting that confuses and misinforms the public.

Appel was legendary in the advertising and retail industries. He was the longtime sales manager for acclaimed retail merchant John Wannamaker, founder of the renowned Wannamaker Stores in New York, Philadelphia, and Europe. Additionally, Appel was a member of the exclusive Sphinx Club and formed a spin-off organization named, The Poor Richard's Club. He was a respected guest speaker, Bureau consultant, and authored numerous books on sales techniques throughout the early 1900s. It was his revered advertising reputation and rabble-rousing sales flair that underpinned the truth movement. Additionally, advertising celebrities like Merle Sidener, president of Sidener, Van Riper & Keeling advertising agency and chairman of the National Better Business Bureau, and Dr. Herbert Sherman Houston, vice president of Doubleday, Page & Company, president of the AACW, and the Bureau's international education ambassador, represented authentic trailblazing pioneers. Most of all, *Printers' Ink* Editor John Irving Romer deserves ultimate credit for introducing the *Printers' Ink* Model Statute, which provided the AACA impetus to establish the first Vigilance Committee that became the Better Business Bureau.

CBBB's 2012 annual report also misconstrued the Bureau's criminal involvement in one of the most notorious NYSE racketeering scams in history while seemingly confident that lapsed time, ignorant constituency, and buried evidence offered fresh opportunity by milking the namesake of a previous cash cow. CBBB advised, "1945 New Ad Slogan: "Before You Invest, Investigate," BBB's warned of swindlers. National BBB dedicates a division to protect service members from con artists." At the end of WWII, the Bureau reintroduced its "Before You Invest, Investigate" slogan like a phoenix soaring from the ashes of Prohibition and disregarded its genesis as a bogus investigative securities program that fleeced millions of speculators and irrefutably contributed to the Crash. In fact, the slogan was first introduced by the Cleveland Bureau in 1920 and was implemented by the New York Bureau on July 1, 1922. It was mindboggling that CBBB shamelessly peddled the same tarnished slogan 11 years after the U.S. Senate Banking Committee's Pecora Commission published its 394-page "Stock Exchange Practices" report in June 1934 that was written by Chairman Fletcher who previously denounced the Bureau's phony investigative program as a "racket."

Bureau managers Kenner and Wansley remarkably detailed both dateline spectrums of the "Before You Invest, Investigate" slogan. Kenner detailed the history of the original slogan introduced by the "Better Business Bureau of the Cleveland Advertising Club" and Wansley described its WWII knock-off. Both instances advertised protecting a certain class of workers from "getrichquick" schemes by soliciting them to first invest in Bureau programs. Kenner highlighted the slogan's initial focus on the "individual worker" in "industrial plants" as a "service to protect wage-earning investors especially – before they parted with their money ...." Thereafter, Wansley glorified the Bureau's "War Savings Protection Program" that "aimed at keeping the millions of dollars earned by servicemen and war industry workers out of the hands of waiting shysters." Both advertising campaigns proved lucrative for the Bureau.

CBBB also omitted acknowledgment of two particular advertising pioneers who directly influenced the development of the modern Bureau. George Rowell developed the programs and ethical standards adopted by the Bureau. And H. J. Kenner was the first-hired vigilance man, the National Bureau's first executive secretary, and the resourceful general manager of the controversial New York Bureau who obfuscated the Bureau's dirty footprints in *The Fight for Truth in Advertising*.

Additionally, CBBB's 2012 annual report introduced the Bureau's participation in the DOC's U.S.-EU Safe Harbor digital protection program that was launched in 2000, the same year that CBBB coincidentally unleashed an integrity awards program. Dressler inferred that CBBB was broke in the latter 1900s and needed a lucrative venue to compete in the upcoming twenty-first century. Circumstances suggested that the integrity awards financed the Bureau's transatlantic partnership with the DOC/FTC and EU. Safe Harbor's stated objective was to regulate "the way that U.S. companies could export and handle the personal data of European citizens," and the Bureau's digital dynasty and business-reporting services complemented such program. Henceforth, circumstances and chronological events support my allegation that Safe Harbor was designed to ultimately enable the EU to control universal airways; that the EU was counting on the Democrats maintaining control of the White House in 2016; and that CBBB wanted a piece of the action and wiggled its way into Safe Harbor in hopes of building brick and mortar in Europe.

CBBB participated in the Safe Harbor program beginning in 2011 until it was cancelled in 2015, evidenced by the Council's "Procedure Report" listing respective years' statistics. The timeframe aligned with my allegation that the Obama administration planned to meld the U.S. with the EU; and that Obama channeled Truman by seeding the Bureau's reporting services with the EU through the Safe Harbor program. The Safe Harbor Privacy Principles were essentially business practice standards similar to Rowell's ethical standards and were introduced by the EU and U.S. "between 1998 and 2000"; the respective project name was called "Safe Harbor Framework," which closed on October 6, 2015, after "the European Court of Justice invalidated Safe Harbor" due to concern "of US government agencies' access to European citizens' data for surveillance purposes." Closure of Safe Harbor confirmed the program's digital censorship capabilities that could be expanded and weaponized by the EU to control planetary airways. Accordingly, everything should be questioned regarding the EU and NWO.

On August 1, 2016, Obama's DOC/FTC launched the EU-U.S. Privacy Shield Framework program to replace Safe Harbor. The FTC's recent update stated, "On July 16, 2020, the European Court of Justice issued a judgment declaring invalid the European Commission's Decision 2016/1250/EC of July 12, 2016 on the adequacy of the EU-U.S. Privacy Shield Framework." Previous complaint was not entirely remedied because the program "includes exceptions to allow for some US mass surveillance of EU citizens data," which implied the U.S. Patriot Act. The program partnered with the Bureau's online reporting system to monitor private transatlantic online communications under the auspice of "helping grow the digital economy." On October 24, 2019, the DOC released a presser on the "Third Annual Review" of the EU-U.S. Privacy Shield whereby U.S. Secretary of Commerce Wilbur Ross declared the program a success; statistics indicated that "more than 5,000 companies have made public and legally enforceable pledges to protect data transferred from the EU in accordance with the Privacy Shield principles."

The Obama administration surrendered U.S. sovereignty of the World Wide Web at midnight, "September 30, 2016," to the Internet Corporation for Assigned Names and Numbers (ICANN). Accordingly, control of the Internet was transferred two months after the EU-U.S. Privacy Shield Framework program was launched on August 1, 2016. Mary E. Power, CBBB president and CEO, victoriously touted, ""BBB has played a critical role in developing and supporting the EU Safe Harbor Framework since its inception and we're pleased to support the EU-U.S. Privacy Shield. We applaud the work of the Department of Commerce, the European Commission, and other U.S. and EU officials in establishing this new arrangement to promote transatlantic data flows. We look forward to building on our 16 years as an independent privacy dispute resolution provider, continuing our legacy of trust with the business community."

Otherwise, the Privacy Shield program seemed to coordinate with lame-duck President Obama's nefarious EO 12333, Section 2.3, and expansion of the IC's surveillance powers. In fact, the Privacy Shield program is regulated by the FTC, whose crony cohorts are the CBBB and Bureau. My concern is that private data is not private and is subject to government skullduggery, which in this case includes the threat of a New World Order takeover that begins with an innocent program to protect citizen data flow. The Obama administration initially approved release of U.S. sovereignty to ICANN in March 2014 with subsequent transfer seemly aligned with the initial Safe Harbor Framework program, which regrouped as the EU-US Privacy Shield program in August 2016, and was supposed to be followed by former Secretary of State Hillary Clinton's projected presidential victory on November 8, 2016.

During the interim, the EU was considering an Islamic blasphemy law that would include social media. In November 2009, a Christian woman, Elisabeth Sabditsch Woff, was teaching an Islamic seminar and commented that Mohammad was a pedophile for marrying nine-year-old Aisha. Consequently, she was convicted of violating Austria's Criminal Code, Section 188, for "denigration of religious beliefs of a legally recognized religion." As a result, on October 25, 2018, the European Court of Human Rights introduced the first Islamic blasphemy law prohibiting anti-Islamic speech. In 2020, American social-media oligarchs began censoring their websites and integrating a form of the EU's blasphemy laws.

ICANN is an autonomous international nonprofit currently based in Los Angeles, California, and subject to the EU's influence and operations. ICANN was created in 1998 by Jon Postel, "a computer scientist at the University of California," to coordinate "the Domain Name System" with "actual computer addresses." Since that time, *USA Today* reported, "The 18-year-old contract for ICANN has been held by the U.S. Commerce Department's National Telecommunications and Information Administration but is not scheduled to be renewed on Sept. 30 when it comes to an end." Accordingly, America's Internet handover was forewarned and looming, which questions the Obama administration's respective schematics that evidenced a historic shift of power involving the triad of the U.S., EU, and CBBB. Dynamics reminded of the tectonic shift of power after the Crash of 1929 whereby the NYSE, Investment Bankers Association, and Better Business Bureau were indicted for securities fraud.

On November 8, 2016, the U.S. presidential election projected a Democratic victory for Obama-successor Hillary Rodham Clinton, but produced a Republican landslide. Pieces to a planetary puzzle were ready to fall into place until Donald Trump threw a wrench in globalist plans with a Truman-Dewey upset!

Then, on March 6, 2017, the EU advised that it was considering "a nuclear weapons program." Circumstances suggested a vindictive backlash from the U.S. election that interrupted NWO plans to annex America. The EU's pursuit of nuclear empowerment further validated my theory that globalists and their minions were plotting world domination.

The 2013 annual report highlighted CBBB's investigative results from ABC *20/20*'s rating score scandal three years earlier. CBBB offset scam-fringed implications with a flurry of international activities reinforced by virtuous propaganda. As expected, CBBB singled out William Mitchell, CEO of the "BBB of the Southland" in Los Angeles, as its scapegoat and officially expelled the office from the organization for "recurrent failure to meet standards." CBBB denied initiating internal directives that resulted in Mitchell creating the program, but never answered why it approved systemic implementation. In the interim, the globalist-owned courts granted the pay-for-play ratings score immunity as an opinion (John Moore cases among others) and why CBBB waited to announce Mitchell's terminus fate. Nevertheless, my private lawsuit was tangled in the middle. With contrived absolution in hand, CBBB continued its global march and reiterated its vision: "An ethical marketplace where buyers and sellers can trust each other." Furthermore, CBBB confirmed its ultimate mission, "To be the leader in advancing marketplace trust." Several respective objectives included "Creating a community of trustworthy businesses," "Encouraging and supporting best practices," "Setting standards for marketplace trust," "Celebrating marketplace role models," and, "Denouncing substandard marketplace behavior."

CBBB engaged typical PR overkill after being exposed for pay-for-play rating score fraud. A whirlwind of plans and activities promoted burgeoning relations with the EU, Mexico, China, Japan, and Canada. As a reminder, the Bureau's first international convention was held in 1914 in Toronto, Canada, and then spread to Europe with conventions held in London, England, and Berlin, Germany; the same countries that the second Obama administration was aggressively developing NWO globalist initiatives. Accordingly, when closing the Los Angeles Bureau, CBBB also replaced rebelling Canadian offices with compliant staff, which questioned a greater undertaking involving its doctrine of autonomy strategy to posture offices within the coming EU super state. I believe the EU was building a NWO with intentions to add the U.S. and Canada as western cornerstones, and just like WWI, the Bureau had offices positioned in both nations to take advantage of globalist progression.

The 2014 annual report outlined burgeoning expansion into all phases of business. As a result, the Bureau emerged as a virtually impregnable leviathan operating under the protection of free speech with discretionary power to eliminate competition and control the marketplace. Consequently, critics consider the Bureau to be a masked monopoly. Unfortunately, there is no Teddy Roosevelt to enforce antitrust laws. Most local, state, and federal authorities are affiliated with the Bureau. Furthermore, I believe that Obama's FTC has been compromised by coordinating government reporting services with the Bureau as though accepting the organization as a federal agency even though it is not. Lawsuits dating back to 1930 alleged court influence and judicial impropriety, which inadvertently honed the Bureau's invincible shield. The FTC was created as an impartial consumer watchdog but has since embraced conflict of interest by intermingling with CBBB to forge an impregnable alliance whereby FTC exploits CBBB's unlicensed autonomy and CBBB exploits FTC's federal status.

On May 27, 2014, PROFECO, the Mexican Federal Consumer Protection Agency, united with CBBB and launched "Buró de Mejores Practicas Comerciales" as a new Better Business Bureau in México City. Other international expansion included a Japanese Consumer Affairs Agency pilot program and discussions with the Israeli "Consumer Protection and Fair Trade Authority" to open a Better Business Bureau office.

On June 24, 2014, CBBB sponsored the BBB Self-Regulation Conference in affiliation with the University of Virginia's Darden School of Business' Institute for Business in Society at the Ronald Reagan Building in Washington. The conference's stated purpose was "to articulate best practices and uses for self-regulation" and highlighted fraud schemes. To the contrary, there was no mention of CBBB's self-regulated "Before You Invest, Investigate" securities scam that contributed to the Crash of 1929 or its modern day self-regulated bogus integrity awards program that fleeces millions from trusting consumers. Of course, one of the conference's guest speakers was "Maureen Ohlhausen, commissioner of the Federal Trade Commission." Ohlhausen's gilded government presence added a theatrical touch of ethereal ethics, but also questioned why the FTC refused to investigate my complaint against the Bureau involving massive awards fraud? The answer dates to 1928 when the FTC broke strict rules of engagement and congressional mandates to crony-up with CBBB's predecessor, the National Association of Better Business Bureaus, Inc.

In 2018, Peter Woolfork was appointed to a three-year term as chairman for CBBB's Board of Directors. I particularly mentioned the chairman because his impressive resume connected to 43rd POTUS William Jefferson Clinton, in office from 1993 to 2001. Chairman Woolfork was former "special assistant/communications to the Assistant Secretary, U.S. Department of Education, during Bill Clinton's administration." His distinguished chairmanship vicariously connected CBBB and the Bureau franchise to former President Clinton whereby evidencing the organization's historic proclivity of stolen thunder that exploits presidential gravitas.

It is my opinion that Barack Hussein Obama Soetoro was a Manchurian candidate and placed by Illuminati to control and hobble the world's largest superpower and merge treasure with the rising NWO. Two authors, Dr. Jerome Corsi and Michael Shrimpton, provided opposing Obama "birther" information. Dr. Corsi reiterated standard propaganda that Obama was born on August 4, 1961, in Hawaii; that his mother was Caucasian activist and anthropologist Stanley Ann Dunham; that his birth father was Barack Hussein Obama Sr. whom Dunham married in 1961 and divorced in 1963; that Dunham subsequently married African Muslim Lolo (Hawaiian for "Crazy") Soetoro in 1965; and that Soetoro took Obama Jr. to Jakarta and raised him as a Muslim from 1968 to 1971. According to Dr. Corsi, "The *Times* also interviewed Israella Darmawan, Obama's first-grade teacher at the Catholic school. "At that time, Barry was also praying in a Catholic way, but Barry was a Muslim," she told the newspaper. "He was registered as a Muslim because his father, Lolo Soetoro, was a Muslim"." To the contrary, British Intelligence adviser and barrister Shrimpton revealed a much different nefarious account that legally nullified Obama's presidency in his sensational 2014 book, *Spyhunter*, as well as his YouTube video (https://www.youtube.com/watch?v=3oIoecEGIJw). Shrimpton asserted that British MI5 held Obama's true personal files with provenance being Nairobi (capital of Kenya); that Obama was born in 1960 in Mombasa, Kenya; that Dunham was not pregnant in July 1961, which disavowed Obama's supposed birth on August 4, 1961; and that DNA tests questioned Dunham's maternal affiliation with Obama. In fact, Obama offhandedly confirmed Shrimpton's version when stating in *Dreams of My Father* that he was born in Kenya. In later years, Obama pursued hard-left politics and "black-liberation theology" that led him to Trinity United Church of Christ's former Pastor Jeremiah Wright Jr. and Alinsky's *Rules for Radicals*. Obama inferred an arbitrary decision to become a Christian that Dr. Corsi relegated to Alinsky's school of thought promoting "a calculated decision to position yourself favorably in the eyes of those you want to lead, whether you believe in the decision or not." Alinsky predicated such viewpoint on the teachings of his mentor Machiavelli who stated, "For the majority of mankind are satisfied with appearance, as though they were realities and are often more influenced by the things that seem than by those that are." Machiavelli was essentially referring to humbuggery that further underscored a crony parallel between Obama and the Bureau whose organization built a lucrative empire based upon mystical illusion.

Research insinuated the Obama administration stretched Islamic tentacles to ensnare Sancta Sedes, The Holy See or Vatican City, and secretly orchestrated the shocking and historic resignation of German Pope Benedict XVI on February 28, 2013. Cardinal Joseph Aloisius Ratzinger was ordained Pope Benedict XVI on April 19, 2005, and became the first pope to resign since Pope Gregory XII in 1415. I believe the pope emeritus (retired designation) was given a bum rap because he aligned with the conservative theological principles of his predecessor, Pope John Paul II. In September 2006, ABC News reported that Benedict (Latin for "the Blessed") delivered an address "at the University of Regensburg, in which he quoted a remark about Islam by Byzantine Emperor Manuel II Palaiologos that some of the teachings of the Prophet Muhammad are "evil and inhuman"." Additionally, Benedict disagreed with the Obama administration on "abortion, contraceptive services, and stem cell research." Timing and circumstances spoke volumes. On March 13, 2013, liberal Argentinian Jesuit Cardinal Jorge Mario Bergoglio became the 266th Pope and was ordained Obama-friendly Pope Francis I. As a Catholic, I believe that Francis is a delusional enigmatic radical NWO minion; he has stated support for Islam, worldwide open migration, socialism, and America's Democratic Party while remaining reprehensibly indifferent to citizens' rights, national defense, and the persecution, displacement, torture, and murder of Christians. On January 3, 2019, Pope Francis, according to M2 Voice, "told the Italian newspaper La Repubblica that the United States of America has "*a distorted vision of the world*" and Americans must be ruled by a world government, as soon as possible, "*for their own good*"."

According to Breitbart article, "Unholy Alliance: Christian Charities Profit from $1 Billion Fed Program to Resettle Refugees, 40 Percent Muslim," Catholic charities profited from refugee resettlement in the United States orchestrated by the United Nations High Commission on International Refugees that dispersed internationals "in all 50 states and the District of Columbia." The U.S. government funded refugees "hundreds of millions of dollars" in addition to "a number of entitlements" from the Department of Health and Human Services when millions of Americans, including myself, have gone years without medical or dental treatment. Recent statistics showed that "the Obama administration increased the number of refugees the United States accepts annually, from 85,000 in fiscal year (FY) 2016 to 110,000 in FY 2017."

I believe that the Obama administration was not vetting refugees, but secretly promoting the spread of Radical Islam through borderless censored destructive tyrannical socialist counter-cultured anti-national White-genocidal globalist EU initiatives. Pope Francis supported Obama and zealously embraced Muslim progressivism while ignoring its inhumane demonic psychopathic barbaric extremist agonizing gruesome murder of Christians including Catholic priests, nuns, and parishioners who were savagely tortured, raped, stoned, shot, hung, crucified, beheaded, burned to death, or dissolved in nitric acid. Anguished souls surviving the first round of horrendous atrocities still met the grim reaper when hurled into the hell of sex slavery forcing freedom by suicide.

Hindsight emphasizes globalism's blossom under former President Obama's "Hope and Change" regime that fueled socialism and communism in America. Dr. Corsi explained that he "pursued Obama's extensive connections with Islam and with radical racial politics, including those articulated by such extremists as Malcolm X and Louis Farrakhan, in order to bring these issues from the shadows where Obama has tried to keep them hidden." Furthermore, Dr. Corsi believed that Obama's 2008 presidential campaign was profoundly influenced by Alinsky who "used the battle cry of "Change" as a code word for a socialist redistribution of wealth."

America was hobbled by Obama's two-term administration. Big Business, Big Cloud, Big Auto, Big Oil, Big Insurance, and Big Pharma robber barons ruled the land. The middle class digressed into chattel labor and was strangled by America's dowry of taxation without representation. Additionally, senior citizens were robbed by the Obama administration's misappropriations that subsidized a socialist healthcare plan and illegal immigration to entrench Democratic voters; baby boomers received little or no cost of living (COLA) increases despite rising living expenses and Medicare costs at the most vulnerable time in their lives when obtaining supplemental income to offset shortcomings is limited or nonexistent; try getting a decent job after the age of 65, considered as "elderly" by Texas law. According to *Fox News*, a report "produced by Republicans on the Senate Homeland Security and Governmental Affairs Committee" advised that "as of June 2015, "the [Obama] Administration awarded approximately $750 million in tax credits on behalf of individuals who were later determined to be ineligible because they failed to verify their citizenship, status as a national or legal presence"." Furthermore, on March 25, 2016, in conjunction with *The Wall Street Journal's* survey of 25 counties across the U.S., *The Daily Caller News* reported that "despite a provision in the Affordable Care Act explicitly prohibiting government-subsidized care for illegal immigrants ... at least 750,000 illegal immigrants are receiving care in those counties, costing taxpayers more than $1 billion."

Obama's presidential tenure seemingly invoked the Marxist principles of writer, rebel, and community organizer Saul David Alinsky (1909-1972) who schemed to subjugate America's citizens, laws, power, prestige, and treasure. Obama's administration underwrote a series of insidious scandals including Fast & Furious, Benghazi, IRS, the Iran deal, the Muslim Brotherhood, immigration fraud, IC surveillance, DACA, Uranium One, Obamacare, Clinton Foundation, $500 Billion HUD misappropriation, Social Security/Medicare misappropriation, Fusion GPS, and a multitude of scandals still unfolding.

In fact, Obama's personal records still remain sealed begging the question, why? According to Twitter handle *SouthernBelle4Trump*, hidden documents are many and questionable: "Occidental College records; Columbia College records; Columbia Thesis paper; Harvard College records; Selective Service Registration; Medical records; Illinois State Senate Schedule; Illinois State Senate records; law practice client list; certified copy of original birth certificate; signed embossed paper certification of live birth; baptism record; "Foreign Student Aid" as a college student; and, customs documentation stating "Used____??____country's "passport" when you visited Pakistan in 1981"."

I allege that the NWO implemented a covert coup d'état and seated the Muslim Brotherhood through the Obama administration to control the U.S. Federal Government resulting in current widespread corruption, porous borders, and deluge of illegals and unvetted refugees. Unfortunately, the U.S. Constitution's diversity and freedoms have enabled an unfettered unaccountable invasion emboldened by a radical Democratic Party and feckless Republican Party.

On January 3, 2013, Investigative Project published the article, "Egyptian Magazine: Muslim Brotherhood Infiltrates Obama Administration," that alarmingly advised, "Six American Islamist activists who work with the Obama administration are Muslim Brotherhood operatives who enjoy strong influence over U.S. policy." The operatives were listed as: " Arif Alikhan, assistant secretary of Homeland Security for policy development; Mohammed Elibiary, a member of the Homeland Security Advisory Council; Rashad Hussain, the U.S. special envoy to the Organization of the Islamic Conference; Salam al-Marayati, co-founder of the Muslim Public Affairs Council (MPAC); Imam Mohamed Magid, president of the Islamic Society of North America (ISNA); and Eboo Patel, a member of President Obama's Advisory Council on Faith-Based Neighborhood Partnerships." Then, on June 30, 2016, Breitbart published the article, "Capt. Joseph John: Muslim Brotherhood 'Fifth Column' Has Infiltrated U.S. Government." Captain Joseph R. John, USN (Ret), the chairman of Combat Veterans for Congress PAC, wrote that "members of the Muslim Brotherhood and its Islamist front groups have become "a very dangerous 'Fifth Column' in the United States, appointed by Obama to very high and sensitive positions in the US Government agencies"."

The *Egyptian Magazine* and Captain John issued two of several legitimate warnings that advised the NWO's enemy invasion of America by Muslim extremists. Subversive actions fit like a crossword puzzle with the EU's open border initiatives piecing together a one-government super state that blended the northern continent with Europe. With America in its pocket, the EU would become invincible and control the world.

The Obama administration promoted and encouraged Islam to the point of endangering American culture and citizens evidenced by increased government infusion of Muslim officials, accelerated refugee immigration, and entrenched Radical Islamic Terrorism in the U.S.A. On June 28, 2016, Freedom Outpost published the article, "Obama's Muslim Homeland Security Advisor Demands National Registry Be Created," and alarmingly revealed that the U.S. Government "is riddled with Muslims who are anti-American." Gamal Abdel-Hafiz was named and described as "Cairo-born," "worked at the FBI for 22 years," and chosen by President Obama as an adviser on terrorism. He was accused by "FBI veteran investigators" of interfering with "ongoing terror investigations." Abdel-Hafiz wanted to create a gun registry that would effectively compromise the Second Amendment and label anyone owning a gun as a criminal; such action is one of The Path to Islam's final steps that take control of a defenseless country. His demand to register law-abiding American gun owners made little headline contrary to globalist uproar against Trump's suggestion to register Muslims amidst burgeoning terrorism.

America's apocalyptic annihilation is being threatened by a triad of political, germ, and cyberwarfare. On March 7, 2012, NATO forces took control of the U.S. military; that ""international permission," rather than Congressional approval, provided a 'legal basis' for military action by the United States." Coincidentally, the Obama administration compromised America's strategic defenses by inexplicably forcing sequestration that dangerously depleted military armament and defense capabilities. Porous borders continue to invite an amalgamation of terrorist warfare. The electrical grid and operational infrastructure remain dilapidated and archaic. Furthermore, cyberwarfare relentlessly and insidiously threatens catastrophic death tolls through electronic magnetic-pulse shutdown or electrical grid blackouts forcing a modern dark age.

Obama positioned an army of Islamic refugees mixed with terrorists throughout the United States, filtered U.S. treasure to overseas terrorist-affiliated organizations, and endorsed building/spreading mosques throughout America. In fact, an investigation by Channel 2 Action News discovered Obama's State Department was sending millions of U.S. taxpayer dollars to "refurbish mosques" in Muslim countries. Mosques have been repeatedly exposed for arming, enabling, and promoting Radical Islam.

The Muslim Brotherhood ran the U.S. Federal Government while Obama's Deep State engaged regime tampering in the Middle East and colluded with the globalist money rackets of the IMF, EU, NATO, and UN. Obama melded U.S. politics with the open-border initiatives of the EU resulting in the worldwide spread of radical terrorism by ISIS that he underhandedly dismissed as a "JV Team." By the end of 2015, ISIS engaged horrific genocide that carved a metastasizing Islamic caliphate "in western Iraq and eastern Syria." Horrific beheadings included American journalist James Wright Foley in August 2014. And Royal Jordanian Air Force Captain Muath Safi Yousef al-Kasasbeh was captured, caged, and burned alive on December 24, 2014, while ISIS broadcasted his barbaric death and inadvertently forged a world martyr instead of terrorist conquest; Captain Al-Kasasbeh showed divine strength, courage, and gallantry as flames rushed his fuel-drenched body while maintaining extraordinary heroism amidst the taunting chants of ISIS deviants cheering his agonizing death and the obliteration of his charred body into pieces by the pounding of a bulldozer. To the contrary, cowardly ISIS leader Abu Bakr al-Baghdadi cried, whined, and whimpered after being cornered in a tunnel by President Trump's U.S. troops, on October 26, 2019, and then detonated his suicide vest that killed him, surrounding jihadists, and three accompanying children. President Trump destroyed ISIS' 45,000 marching army, which strengthened under the Obama administration, and removed outstanding ISIS remnants as of March 2019 with Al-Baghdadi's death officially ending another savage chapter of global atrocities. But fringe procreative ISIS elements remain and threaten revival.

I believe the Obama administration deliberately maintained porous U.S. borders that attracted a flood of illegal aliens, refugees, drug runners, human traffickers, gangs, and terrorists who were financed, legitimized, and elevated above citizens by globalist nonprofits in order to build a socialist United States in unison with the EU's conversion of Europe. Thereafter, defiant grassroots patriots would be incrementally replaced by an immigrant caste reminiscent of pre-Civil War servitude ruled by Illuminati's one-government party.

On April 2, 2016, President Obama joined Turkey's President Recep Tayyip Erdoğan at the inauguration of the United States' largest mosque, "the Diyanet Center of America," located at 9704 Good Luck Road, Lanham, Maryland; a state named after the Virgin Mary. The $110-million-dollar mosque used materials, craftsmen, and laborers shipped from Turkey. Construction reeked of secrecy and conspiracy, which questioned the design of infrastructure considering mosques are renowned terrorist training centers and ammo dumps. Along with the introduction of the "16-acre" Diyanet Center, Turkish officials exposed Obama's intent to embed Islam in America. *FreedomPost.com* wrote, "This is Erdoğan's dream, a symbolic link with all mosques (minarets) across the globe, especially in the Caucasus in order to unite all Muslim lands to himself. Such a connection is why Erdoğan is building a grand mosque in the U.S. (with many more to come with the help from President Barack Hussein Obama) as claimed by Turkey's Minister of Foreign Affairs, Mevlüt Çavuşoğlu." Accordingly, circumstances suggested that Obama was developing a caliphate in the western hemisphere.

On June 23, 2016, Great Britain voted to leave the EU. Brexit (Britain + exit) victoriously returned Britannia and the Union Jack to Queen and country. Brexit votes totaled 17,410,742; Remain votes tallied 16,141,241. Those opposed to the EU were coined "Eurosceptics." As expected, Brexit temporarily impacted global finances, but rebounded. On June 30, 2016, the FTSE 100 "had completely rebounded from Brexit," per Breitbart London.

I particularly mentioned Brexit because the referendum offered hope to break up the EU by encouraging other members to leave. Brexit aligned with conservative American initiatives and highlighted the deteriorating security of both the UK and USA as a result of uncontrolled Middle East immigration and accompanying terrorism, and why I vehemently joined British patriots promoting its passage. Other EU countries hoped to pursue similar exits to salvage eroding indigenous civilizations and cultures destroyed by EU immigration mandates. Brexit floundered under British Prime Minister Theresa May; I believe that May was planted by the EU to dismantle Brexit and stop potential hemorrhaging of other disgruntled EU member nations. The former mayor of London, Boris Johnson, replaced May as Prime Minister, on July 24, 2019, and promised to "form "a cabinet for modern Britain" with the primary task of finally delivering Brexit." Prime Minister Johnson kept his promise and Brexit became effective on February 1, 2020.

London has since turned into a caliphate disdainfully referred to as

"Londonistan." The Qatar Investment Authority (QIA) "has already invested E10 billion in Britain, with more planned." Investments include The Shard, Olympic Village, "swathes of the Canary Wharf financial district," Harrods, No 1 Hyde Park, "20 per cent of the London Stock Exchange," and "20 per cent of the Camden market, the biggest grunge emporium in the country." According to the Migration Observatory, "In 2014 about 1.3 million foreign-born people were living in Inner London and nearly 1.7 million were living in Outer London." As a result, Muslim Mayor Sadiq Khan rose to power and engaged alarming tyrannical undertones that censor free speech and promote Islam and Sharia law in both the UK and USA; Americans must not ignore such warlord aggression that is adversely influencing U.S. politics and literally threatening to destroy our Judeo-Christian civilization and culture.

It is my opinion that Obama melded UN and NATO powers to overrule American sovereignty including the U.S. military. The UN provided military force while NATO allegiance allowed intervention despite threats of human rights violations and global terrorism. Even though he was replaced by President Trump, Obama and his loyal Deep State have continued shadow operations to regain the White House.

Since 2011, I believe the Obama administration was plotting a coup d'état by intentionally depleting U.S. military forces in order to introduce replacement UN globalist forces in preparation for annexation by the EU's NWO. In fact, Obama dangerously hobbled U.S. defense forces. The Heritage Foundation stated, "For example, Army Chief of Staff Gen. Raymond T. Odierno declared, "[The] Army cannot fulfill its role in the defense strategy" if all cuts required under the Budget Control Act of 2011 are fully implemented." Additionally, flatoutunconstitutional.com reported, "Thanks to Pamela Geller at D.C. Clothesline, as well as other sources, we learned that the Obama administration is allowing the Sharia Law compliant United Nations to start establishing a presence in American cities with a Global Police Force, ostensibly to fight extremism, called the Strong Cities Network." Nine months later, on June 26, 2016, dcclothesline.com advised occurrence of "mysterious troop movement"; that "U.N. vehicles were spotted near I-81 near Lexington, VA and were being carried by flatbed, two to a trailer"; that military convoys with helmeted soldiers were transporting "Humvees, troop transport trucks, and tankers" carrying construction equipment; and that "there have been numerous reports of an increase in military movement in the NC, VA, West VA, and Ohio region."

The Muslim Brotherhood's Trojan horse attack surfaced with Obama's election on November 4, 2008, and mutated on March 23, 2010, when he signed into law the Affordable Care Act (ACA), i.e., Obamacare, that was facilitated by traitorous bipartisan Republican and Democratic globalists and Muslim conquistadores. As a result, the ACA singlehandedly and historically destroyed the backbone of the 40-hour work week when employers deleteriously cut hours to avoid respective ACA repercussions. Today, there is no standard "full time" work week for hourly employees resulting in a Catch-22 demand for increased minimum wage laws that threaten to downsize jobs. One of the hardest hit sectors was college students who cannot find sustainable wage jobs to pay their student loans, yet government-created quagmire ignores their bursting bubble, employment discrimination, and impoverished lives to continue assisting illegals and Dreamers. Additionally, the ACA created a subordinate Muslim system of dhimmitude that forced a tax penalty if Americans did not join an expensive welfare-based universal health insurance meant to service an open-border invasion under Obama's U.S./EU NWO. (President Trump removed the tax mandate, but the next Democratic takeover will reinstate it.) "Dhimmitude" is an Arabic term loosely translated as Islamic servitude forced upon Christians and was first introduced by former Lebanese Maronite (Eastern-rite Roman Catholic) President Bachir Gemayal (1947-1982) in a speech that he delivered on September 14, 1982, the same day and hours before he was assassinated by Habib Shartouni via bomb explosion; Gemayal's words live on: "Lebanon is our homeland and will remain a homeland for Christians … we refuse to live in any dhimmitude!"

The article, "BREAKING: Egypt Charges Obama and Hillary with Conspiring with Terrorist Muslim Brotherhood," reminded of Obama's relationship with the Muslim Brotherhood whom he planted as covert enemy agents throughout the U.S. Federal Government. Obama's Muslim Homeland Security Adviser Gamal Abdel-Hafiz demanded a "national registry" of Americans under the thin veil of gun control, yet denigrated GOP presidential nominee Trump when he promoted a registry of Muslims similar to counterterrorist measures implemented by Hoover's "Neighborhood Enforcement Policy" and FDR's Japanese American internment.

In fact, Obama did initiate an American registry. In 2012, the Obama administration's U.S. Attorney General Eric Holder "gave the National Counterterrorism Center sweeping new powers to store dossiers on U.S. citizens, even if they are not suspected of a crime." By May 2013, Democratic California Representative Maxine Waters bragged that Obama had compiled a massive databank of private citizen's records: "The President has put in place an organization with the kind of database that no one has ever seen before in life." Furthermore, the "database will have information about everything on every individual." Obama's database suggested interaction with the Deep State Better Business Bureau's business database because intermingled databases would control the nation. As a result, dystopian banana-republic corruption, blackmail, and extortion now trade skeletons for a soul.

CBBB and the Better Business Bureau were spawned by Wall Street, and successors continue respective association today through the Financial Industry Regulatory Authority (FINRA). FINRA "is a non-governmental organization that regulates member brokerage firms and exchange markets" and is regulated by the SEC. Mention of CBBB and the Bureau's association with FINRA may seem ho-hum because consumers are unaware of CBBB and the Bureau's scandalous history that undeniably contributed to the Crash and Great Depression. FINRA currently serves as CBBB's securities intermediary, which provides the Bureau franchise an industrial strength disclaimer to avoid a rerun of its securities-fraud indictment in 1932. CBBB and FINRA are both non-governmental self-regulatory agencies, but both act in a superior authoritarian capacity. Furthermore, CBBB buries itself in-between the "U.S. Commodity Futures Trading Commission" (CFTC) and FINRA under a banner of "Institute for Marketplace Trust," so that consumers are overwhelmed by implication of irrefutable ethics.

For the third time, CBBB refurbished its bogus Prohibition-era securities slogan, "Before You Invest, Investigate." CBBB's gilded wizardry affixed "Ask and Check" to CFTC's "Before You Invest" disclaimer; such nostalgic repurposing of the same root slogan underpinned O'Sullivan's complaint that the first "Before You Invest, Investigate" program proved extremely lucrative for the early CBBB and NYSE at the expense of trusting speculators. The slogan fueled the Bureau's first cash cow, and the same bootlegging humbuggery continues today by mixing confusion with weasel words to revive a delectable Wall Street meal ticket; a glowing example whereby dearth of information enabled unfettered recycling of scandalous throwback history.

FINRA is the successor to the National Association of Securities Dealers, Inc. (NASD) that operated and regulated "the Nasdaq stock market and over-the-counter markets." NASD was formed in 1939 as a result of the Maloney Act of 1938 that was an amendment to the Securities Exchange Act of 1934. Testopedia.com explained, "The Maloney Act of 1938 created the NASD as the Self Regulatory Organization for the OTC market" whose dealers previously handled business over-the-phone. NASD is now an "electronic exchange known as NASDAQ."

Retrospectively, "In 1971, NASD launched a new computerized stock trading system called the National Association of Securities Dealers Automated Quotations (NASDAQ) stock market," according to Wikipedia.org. Two years later, NASDAQ separated from NASD. In July 2007, NASD "consolidated" with FINRA that "regulates trading in equities, corporate bonds, securities futures, and options." FINRA serves as a catch-all agency: "All firms dealing in securities that are not regulated by another SRO [self-regulatory agency] … are required to be member firms of the FINRA." Total revenues for 2012 were "US$878.6 million" and "funded primarily by assessments of member firms' registered representatives and applicants, annual fees paid by members, and by fines that it levies."

On October 23, 1938, George C. Mathews, SEC Commissioner, discussed the implementation of the Securities Exchange Act of 1934 with the Investment Bankers Association of America at their annual convention held at the Greenbrier Hotel in White Sulphur Springs, West Virginia. His speech encouraged the formation of NASD (FINRA). Mathews advised that the act represented a "professional edifice commensurate with the importance of the investment banking and over-the-counter securities businesses in our national economy."

Mathews' ethereal hindsight overlooked criminal banking history. In 1915, the Investment Bankers Association instructed members to ignore state legislated Blue Sky laws and commit mail fraud by selling interstate securities. The following year, Kenner date-stamped his New York Bureau's link-up with the banking industry and the Vigilance Committees adopted the virtuous name "Better Business Bureau." By 1922, the collective was shilling a fake investment screening program. Bankers were symbiotic to business and advertising; members of the Investment Bankers Association were also members of the AACW and its regulatory National Vigilance Committee.

On July 30, 2007, NASD merged with the NYSE's "regulation committee" to establish FINRA as a private self-regulatory corporation regulated by the SEC. FINRA's fundamental purpose was to safeguard investors and guarantee an ethical market. It is considered the "largest independent regulator" for all U.S. operating securities firms. According to FINRA.org, "FINRA is not part of the government. We're an independent, not-for-profit organization authorized by Congress to protect America's investors by making sure the securities industry operates fairly and honestly." Website statistics reported 3,500 employees, 17 U.S. offices, an average of 30 billion daily transactions, and supervision of over 638,322 brokers.

The Bureau's "Before You Invest, Investigate" program ended before Florida Democratic Senator Duncan Upshaw Fletcher published his summary findings in the "Stock Exchange Practices Report," in June 1934. Beforehand, on January 25, 1932, Senator Fletcher described the crony relationship of the NYSE, the Investment Bankers Association, and the Better Business Bureau as "the greatest racket ever known in history." The Senator explained how the racket schemed to manipulate and sanitize illicit Blue Sky stock transactions through "Before You Invest, Investigate." In March 1932, the Manhattan Board of Commerce's Logan Billingsley joined Senator Fletcher to request widening Senate investigations past its focus on "short selling" to include "all ramifications of the Exchange." Then, on January 15, 1933, Ferdinand Pecora took over Senate hearings. Furthermore, James Cahill, secretary of the Stock Exchange

Reform Committee of New York City (established by the Manhattan Board of Commerce), requested an investigation by the Department of Justice. Cahill was quoted as saying, "The voluminous evidence alleging conspiracy, which was recently filed with the Banking Committee of the Senate against the New York Stock Exchange and the Better Business Bureau system, be referred to the Federal grand jury for consideration." He also warned that those patronizing the NYSE "are the very same interests who maintain and secretly control the activities of this so-called Better Business Bureau system," which explained why the organization escaped the wrath of the Pecora Commission.

The history of the Better Business Bureau is a chronicle of unparalleled events driven by drama, scandal, exploitation, illusion, exaggeration, and cover-up. Research and evidence proved that successors' phenomenal success relied on dubious business practice. Modern successors never expected the Bureau's centurial sins to be exposed by silent voices, dusty archives, and crumbling pages.

In the midst of the Bureau's pivotal planetary expansion ... was me. CBBB and the Bureau obviously realized compounding liabilities connected to a scam awards program and con-artist member. Operatives tried to silence me to preserve the organization's cash cow funding a NWO agenda and seat at the globalist Round Table.

I am a proud whistleblower and respective trial plaintiff and warn consumers that the Deep State Better Business Bureau is a vile imposter participating in a NWO conversion and why the organization inexplicably receives freewheeling immunity. The franchise has morphed into a nation state akin to NATO, the UN, and the EU, which have nefariously convoluted their birthright duties into unholy powers. Consequently, the Bureau's Templar-nuanced membership insignia forces stigmata on commerce and consumers. Accordingly, consumers must realize that their purse strings ultimately control the Bureau. Henceforth, the Bureau must be downsized; specious awards program must end; conflict of interest with the FTC must be investigated, severed, and regulated; and a business license must be procured and adhered to same as other consumer reporting agencies. The Bureau should be morally bound to laws and highest accountability for any measure of misrepresentation, deception, and/or exaggeration.

Aldous Huxley (1894 to 1963) was a British writer and the modern world's Nostradamus who introduced the twenty-sixth-century *Brave New World* to twentieth-century mankind. His mystical predictions of a technological future came true. Huxley's death on November 22, 1963, was overshadowed by the assassination of John F. Kennedy on the same day. His remarkable quote inadvertently and profoundly paraphrased the Bureau's mythical success, "The trouble with fiction ... is that it makes too much sense. Reality never makes sense."

CHAPTER 5

GEORGE PRESBURY ROWELL

George Presbury Rowell
Founder of *American Newspaper Directory*
and *Printers' Ink* advertising journal.
Photo date: Before July 15, 1908.
Photo source: *Printers' Ink*, "LOOKING BACKWARD AND FORWARD,"
Vol. LXIV, July 15, 1908, No. 3, P. 37; [https://babel.hathitrust.org/cgi/pt?id=
njp.32101066805795;view=1up;seq=145]; public domain.

He was the father of advertising, publisher extraordinaire, and a founder and president of the ultra-exclusive Sphinx Club; a secret society that regulated false advertising before the truth movement began in 1911. His 1800's advertising methodology, regulatory programs, and ethical standards provided a role model for the modern Better Business Bureau.

As a former schoolmaster, he used his publishing skills to teach advertising ethics. In 1869, his *American Newspaper Directory* represented the first compiled list of 5,778 newspapers that audited business practice and "included estimates of their circulation, a first step toward a standard of value of space." He also implemented a cash discount, agent's commission that served as a guarantee of advertising payment, and "list system" to sell ad space. In 1888, he published the regulatory trailblazing *Printers' Ink* Advertising Journal. Over a century later, the Better Business Bureau spun Rowell's Tiffany's inscribed silver "Little Schoolmaster" trophy into an inscribed crystal Pinnacle trophy, his cryptographs into rating scores, and his *Printers' Ink* into online BBB Reliability Reports.

George Presbury Rowell was born in Concord, Vermont, on July 4, 1838. His parents were Samuel Rowell and Caroline E. Page. He grew up in New Hampshire and attended school at Lancaster Academy. Two marriages were listed to Sarah Burnside Eastman and Jennette Rigney; he fathered two children with Sarah. In 1858, at the age of 20, he worked as a schoolteacher in Stratford, New Hampshire. Consequently, teaching led him to advertising when he was "promoted ... to the position of bill collector for the Boston *Post*." In 1864, "he sold ads for a theater program and netted $600 for a few weeks' worth of work." A year later, Rowell became an advertising agent in Boston. He introduced the list system when "he contracted with a number of papers to buy a large amount of space for the entire year, then turned around and sold the space in smaller units to advertisers. Since he was able to get a lower price by his quantity purchases, he could undersell other agents." Accordingly, he established the concept of "wholesale" advertising. On March 5, 1865, he opened "Rowell Advertising Agency" in New York. The exact date of his agency's establishment was previously elusive, but was confirmed by *Printers' Ink*, Vol. LXXVI, July 20, 1911, No. 3, in the article, "THE GRAND OLD MAN OF ADVERTISING," whereby Bert Moses, president of the Association of American Advertisers, paid tribute to Rowell and his life's achievements.

After opening his agency, Rowell commenced publishing newspapers. In 1867, he produced the *Advertisers' Gazette* newspaper, the predecessor of *Printers' Ink*. In 1871, he changed the *Gazette's* name to the *American Newspaper Reporter* described as "primarily a house organ of the Rowell advertising agency." In 1869, Rowell produced the first newspaper directory appropriately named the *American Newspaper Directory* that offered the "first complete list" of a total of 5,778 American newspapers.

In the latter 1800s circulation accuracy grew paramount and Rowell guaranteed information rendered in the directory. In 1878, Rowell asked publishers to submit "signed statements of their circulations" and offered "a standing reward of $100 for disproof of such figures." There were five occurrences during a single year whereby Rowell paid the reward, but most publishers refused to commit to circulation numbers forcing him to estimate data to the best of his knowledge. The directory was also discussed in *Printers' Ink*, Vol. LXIV, July 15, 1908, No. 3, in the article, "Looking Backward and Forward," written on July 4, 1908; Rowell noted, "The American Newspaper Directory puts forth its 40th annual volume." Thereafter, *Printers' Ink*, Vol. LXIV, September 2, 1908, No. 10, described the directory's manner of certifying compliant newspapers and notified change of qualification in the article, "The Harrisburg, Pa., *Telegraph*," that partly advised, "The *Telegraph* is the latest paper to secure the Star Guarantee of Rowell's American Newspaper Directory"; the "Guaranteed Star" required an "affidavit" that insured circulation figures for 12 months.

Rowell established the famous and innovative *Printers' Ink* on "July 20, 1888." The journal was the first advertising magazine to promote honest advertising while also managing business, politics, and finance. *Printers' Ink* was a weekly publication that was issued every Wednesday. Rowell endearingly referred to his journal as "little Printers' Ink" calling it "the Little Schoolmaster" respective to his early teaching career. He encouraged advertising excellence by issuing a prestigious inscribed silver trophy every year to deserving organizations whose proven merited performance was awarded "the Little Schoolmaster In The Art of Advertising." Merit was not negotiable.

Printers' Ink, Vol. XXVII, February 15, 1899, No. 1, made reference to George P. Rowell issuing the silver trophy, "The Little Schoolmaster In The Art of Advertising," to the *Kansas City Star* newspaper. Rowell stated, "That paper after four months' careful weighing of evidence having been pronounced the one published West of Chicago which gives an advertiser the best service in proportion to the price charged." The Little Schoolmaster trophy was inscribed by "Tiffany & Co. Makers" and represented the first commercial award effort within the advertising industry to acknowledge ethical business practice. Rowell's award system applied stringent onsite evaluation whereby he allocated an excellence award only after spending months assessing a recipient's conduct.

Rowell used various markings to rate newspapers in the *American Newspaper Directory* that he called "his life-long pet." He treated publishers like school children posting gold stars by their names in *Printers' Ink* for good behavior and represented his personal endorsement of their newspaper. Additionally, he devised graphics for personal auditing. According to author Stephen Fox, "By an arcane system of codes and symbols Rowell conveyed other vital data for a given entry: a circulation figure printed in plain Arabic numerals was deemed trustworthy; "Z" meant the paper gave a statement considered dubious; "Y" meant the paper gave no statement at all; "!!" implied something suspicious about the paper; a white pyramid meant the paper might have expired; and so on." Additionally, *Printers' Ink* published the article, "Bull's Eye Gold Marks (OO) in Rowell's Newspaper Directory," written by Editor John Romer, and explained significance as "the paper bearing them has a peculiarly high standing with advertisers, and that the latter value the paper more for the class and quality of its circulation than for the mere number of copies printed." Romer further explained, "The requirements are reasonable, and when a figure rating is desired there is no difficulty in securing it. Furthermore, when a letter rating is accorded it is because the publisher has shown indifference or antagonism to the correct rating of his circulation."

As a result, Rowell unwittingly introduced a pay-for-play stratagem that the modern Bureau convoluted into an alpha-numeric rating score. Fox reflected, "The *Directory* made Rowell well esteemed by agents and advertisers, not so well by publishers, who charged that a paper had to place an ad in the annual volume to get a good circulation rating." Similar claims arose against the Bureau for requiring a business to purchase a membership to receive a respectable rating score and/or participate in the awards program.

Romer acknowledged that Rowell's honesty and demand for truth in advertising "made him untold enemies and cost him untold dollars"; that "no higher tribute can be paid a man than to say he fought for a principle to his last days at tremendous cost, when by giving up the struggle he could have gathered in the gold in streams." Rowell created a chain reaction of remarkable events that encouraged Romer to spark enforcement of the Truth in Advertising Movement.

Printers' Ink traversed business, advertising, and legal platforms while promoting ethical guidelines, interaction, updates, and trade employment. As a result, the advertising industry developed into a force majeure enabling a pulpit for complaint, advertising, and business. Tacit advertising standards and consumer guidelines emerged to combat false advertising that threatened readership, circulation, and profit margins.

There are 60 volumes of *Printers' Ink*, dating from 1888 to 1967, which feature generations of exceptional advertising history on every page and can be found at "Hathi Trust Digital Library" (https://catalog.hathitrust.org/Record/000531744). Famous names and occasions mesmerize readers and share memories. Advertising, wording, and content of articles detail what history has left out. Many of the articles align with the various authors featured in this book sharing insight and/or correcting dubious statements.

In 1905, Rowell authored *Forty Years an Advertising Agent 1865-1905*, which was also presented as a series of articles in *Printers' Ink* whereby he railed against false advertising that he called "false promises." The same year, Rowell's efforts galvanized as the AACA; it was a pivotal time period when "organized fighting for truth in advertising began" and local advertising clubs "united as the Associated Advertising Clubs of America," according to Appel.

Printers' Ink, Vol. LXIV, July 15, 1908, No. 3, showcased Rowell's final adieu 20 years after founding *Printers' Ink*. He wrote the article, "Looking Backward and Forward," on his birthday, July 4, 1908, while visiting Camp Percy on Christine Lake. Rowell reflected, "In your issue of July 1st I read that you will celebrate the 20th anniversary of the birth of the Little Schoolmaster. That day was an occasion of interest to me. It was I that caused it to come about ... I expect little PRINTERS' INK to make reputation and fortune for its managers. No one interested in advertising can afford to miss the weekly lessons it is now so competent to teach. With congratulations and good wishes, I am. GEORGE P. ROWELL."

Historical Rowell trivia surrounded Camp Percy, now referred to as the Percy Summer Club. The New Hampshire Public Radio explained Camp Percy's origin: "So, Rowell finds this fish-filled lake and this underdeveloped forest land all around it, and he invited those fellow wealthy sportsmen to join him in purchasing over 350 acres in Stark, New Hampshire. Including, of course, the lovely North Lake (soon to become Christine Lake, named for the first lady visitor to the camp)."

Romer reminisced that Rowell traveled the last year of his life and visited "old world scenes." In keeping with Rowell's chosen professions as a teacher and publisher, he reveled in history, art, and literature. Furthermore, Rowell appreciated wisdom with age; Romer reflected that "nothing amused him more ... than to be spoken of as an old man."

On the night of August 28, 1908, at the age of 70, Rowell passed away at his family home in Poland Spring, Maine; his wife and friends were by his bedside. Out of respect for Rowell's love of history, I researched iconic trivia that revealed Poland Spring's origin dated to 1794 as was determined by the Poland Spring Preservation Society. Furthermore, the town's landmark Main State Building "was originally built in 1893 for the Chicago Worlds Fair also known as the Colombian Exposition. The Fair was to celebrate the 400th anniversary of the arrival of Christopher Columbus."

The advertising legend traveled one last time to destiny's final rest in Lancaster, New Hampshire. Rowell's trailblazing achievements and contributions were exemplary and his distinguished affiliations were impressive and included "a life member of the New England Society of New York, a member of the American Geographical Society of New York, Historical Society, American Forestry Association, New York Chamber of Commerce, Society of Mechanics and Tradesmen, and New York Charity Organization Society." Additionally, he was "a member of the Sphinx, Union League, and Merchants Clubs of New York City." Rowell was a proud Freemason and belonged to an elite "Masonic Fraternity," which, at the time, included George Washington, Benjamin Franklin, Paul Revere, John Hancock, and U.S. Chief Justice John Marshall.

The *New York Times* announced his death in the article, "GEORGE P. ROWELL DEAD; New York Publisher Dies at Poland Springs, Me." Rowell was sick for the last two months of his life and explained his earlier comment in "Looking Backward and Forward" when he lamented, "I complete my three score and ten, and from now on, as the expression is, I live on borrowed time." Romer also similarly noted, "Perhaps with a premonition that the end was not far away, he had only two months before his death, disposed of a controlling interest in these properties to a group of the younger generation of advertising men, believing that in this way the success of his favorite enterprises would best be assured."

Printers' Ink, Vol. LXIV, September 9, 1908, No. 11, formally announced Rowell's passing in the article, "Mr. Rowell's Death." A full-page picture featured Rowell sitting for his portrait as an elegant and elderly schoolteacher holding what looked to be a copy of *Printers' Ink*. It was more than appropriate for Romer, another distinguished trailblazing advertising legend, to memorialize Rowell's contributions and achievements that promoted ethics and standards within the advertising industry: "What Geo. P. Rowell has done for advertising can hardly be appreciated by the younger generation of advertising men .... He introduced order and system and, more than any other man, caused advertising to rank as it does, to-day."

The elite secret society of the advertising industry left a touching message for the grand schoolmaster who forged advertising standards and protocol: "At a meeting of the Executive Committee of the Sphinx Club, of which organization George P. Rowell was president during 1899-1900, a resolution of regret was passed and an expression of deep and sincere sympathy extended to the surviving members of his family .... WILLIAM LORUENSER, Secretary, Sphinx Club of New York, Aug. 29, 1908."

CHAPTER 6

JOHN IRVING ROMER

John Irving Romer
Editor *Printers' Ink* Advertising Journal; founder of
Printers' Ink Model Statute; father of the Vigilance Committee
renamed Better Business Bureau; artist: Caryn Cain.

He was the editor of *Printers' Ink* advertising journal from 1890 to 1933 and continued the advertising standards and ethics of founder George Rowell. The Progressive Era and technological revolution brought an onslaught of false advertising worsened by the advertising industry's lack of regulatory authority. After attending the Associated Advertising Clubs of America's Boston convention on August 2, 1911, he resolved the Truth in Advertising Movement's lingering regulation problem that befuddled advertising glitterati since genesis of organized advertising in the 1800s. He hired a lawyer to draft a prosecutable advertising law. Over the following year, he worked with the NYSE and AACA to enact the *Printers' Ink* Model Statute that penalized fraud as a misdemeanor crime.

JOHN IRVING ROMER

John Irving Romer was born at 12 St. Luke's Place, New York, on October 9, 1869. His parents were John and Joanna (Barnum) Romer. He lived in Manhattan, New York, and East Orange, New Jersey. The 1910 U.S. Census stated his father was born in New York and his mother was born in Connecticut; that his wife's name was Katherine W. Romer (31 years old at the time, placing her birth year about 1879) and they had a 2-year-old daughter Arline N. Romer (placing her birth about 1908). His surname is "German and Swiss German (Römer)" and represented an "ethnic name for a Roman."

Rowell legally positioned Romer as editor and publisher of *Printers' Ink* upon his death on August 8, 1908, and issued Romer part ownership to assure the continuation of his legacy. Ten years later, on August 24, 1918, and according to law, Romer published his ownership credentials in *Printers' Ink*: "STATEMENT OF THE OWNERSHIP, MANAGEMENT, CIRCULATION, ETC., REQUIRED BY THE ACT OF CONGRESS OF AUGUST 24, 1912, of PRINTERS' INK, published weekly at New York, N.Y., for April 1, 1918. State of New York, County of New York, as: Before me, a Commissioner of Deeds in and for the State and county aforesaid, personally appeared John Irving Romer, who, having been duly sworn according to law, deposes and says that he is the editor of PRINTERS' INK and that the following is, to the best of his knowledge and belief, a true statement for the ownership, management, etc., of the aforesaid publication for the date shown in the above caption, required by the Act of August 24, 1912, embodied in section 443, Postal Laws and Regulations, printed on the reverse of this form, to wit: 1) That the names and addresses of the publisher, editor, managing editor, and business manager are: Publisher, PRINTERS' INK Publishing Co., 185 Madison Ave., New York, N.Y., Editor, John Irving Romer, 185 Madison Ave., New York, N,Y.; Managing Editor, Lynn G. Wright, 185 Madison Ave., New York, N.Y.; Business Manager, J. M. Hopkins, 185 Madison Ave., New York, N.Y. 2) That the owners are: PRINTERS' INK Publishing Co., 185 Madison Ave., New York, N.Y.; John Irving Romer, 185 Madison Ave., New York, N.Y.; Richard W. Lawrence, 185 Madison Ave., New York, N.Y.; J. M Hopkins, 185 Madison Ave., New York, N.Y. 3) That the known bondholders, mortgagees, and other security holders owning or holding 1 percent or more of total amount of bonds, mortgages, or other securities are: There are none ... John Irving Romer, Editor"

False advertising adversely affected circulation and profits and threatened to force publishers out of business. As editor of the industry's foremost advertising journal, Romer presented the statute to enforce advertising guidelines to reinstate consumer confidence that advertisers' claims were truthful. Kenner wrote, "Such a man of practical mind, was John Irving Romer of the advertising journal, *Printers' Ink*. Covering the Boston 1911 convention for his magazine, he caught up the truth keynote and featured it in the reports which he wrote and *Printers' Ink* published. He called for action."

The historic Boston convention offered saber-rattling and rabble-rousing enthusiasm but lacked teeth without regulatory legislation. Romer, however, did have an answer that would resolve the advertising industry's lingering regulatory plight. He introduced the *Printers' Ink* Model Statute in *Printers' Ink*, Vol. LXXVII, November 16, 1911, No. 7, in the article, "LEGAL REPRESSION OF DISHONEST ADVERTISING," that extended over the breath of several following issues. He reminded the advertising industry of its failure to develop prosecutorial regulation and warned, "The only criticism of the Boston Convention that has been heard anywhere is that it did not present a *definite plan* for the elimination of objectionable forms of advertising ... Honest men will continue to be honest and dishonest men will continue to follow their devious methods, laughing in their sleeves at those who seek to accomplish reforms by mere preachments. The trouble has been to know exactly what form of action to take."

After the convention, Romer followed up with an article in *Printers' Ink*, Vol. LXXVI, August 10, 1911, No. 6, entitled, "Utilizing the Convention Impetus," and called the event "the biggest thing that ever happened in advertising circles." Romer described convention speakers as collectively offering "one general train of thought" and that being, "to put advertising on a higher *ethical* basis, on a basis of higher *efficiency*, and of more *co-operative inter-relations* between allied sections of the industry." He ended the article theatrically predicting "one taper will light a thousand, and yet shine as it has shone." Romer was the taper and he did light the way. He took a very simple pragmatic approach and hired New York employment attorney Harry Dwight Nims (1875-1968), a veteran of World War I, to write a secure law "that could not be shot full of holes the first time it should be put to the test." Romer acknowledged unchartered territory stating, "We call attention to the fact this is pioneer work; that until PRINTERS' INK started this investigation, the problem had never been approached in the thorough way its importance deserves and the ground-work thoroughly laid. To put a law upon the statute books is one thing. To make the law effective is another."

Nims completed the draft on October 25, 1911. The *Printers' Ink* Model Statute introduced misdemeanor criminal consequences for advertising fraud; original text stated, "Any person, firm, corporation or association who, with intent to sell or in any way dispose of merchandise, securities, service, or anything offered by such person, firm, corporation or association, directly or indirectly, to the public for sale or distribution, or with intent to increase the consumption thereof, or to induce the public in any manner to enter into any obligation relating thereto, or to acquire title thereto, or an interest therein, makes, publishes, disseminates, circulates, or places before the public, or causes, directly or indirectly, to be made, published, disseminated, circulated or placed before the public, in this State, in a newspaper or other publication, or in the form of a book, notice, handbill, poster, bill, circular, pamphlet, or letter, or in any other way, an advertisement of any sort regarding merchandise, securities, service, or anything so offered to the public, which advertisement contains any assertion, representation or statement of fact which is untrue, deceptive or misleading, shall be guilty of a misdemeanor."

The statute was the result of Romer's concern that the convention's enthusiasm did not match regulation. His respective line of questioning formatted the statute: "The only criticism of the Boston Convention that has been heard anywhere is that it did not present a *definite plan* for the elimination of objectionable forms of advertising ... Can the power of the law be invoked to eradicate dishonest advertising? If so, can a police force be marshaled which will make the law effective? I believe I can answer yes to both questions ...."

The AACA's prevailing obstacle had been regulation because false advertising enforcement was outside the purview of U.S. Mail laws. Romer described impetus for the statute: "The trouble has been to know exactly what form of action to take. It is evidently a case for expert advice ... We asked this lawyer, H. D. Nims, author of the standard legal work, "Nims on Unfair Business Competition," to make a careful study of this whole subject ... to go back to the fountain-head of common law relating to the sale of goods under false pretenses, and to investigate the statutes of the various states having any bearing upon fraudulent and misleading advertising."

The statute required a sponsor to promote state ratification. Romer brought in the AACA and the NYSE to form the Vigilance Committee of the Advertising Club of New York as the first Vigilance Committee that was launched on March 12, 1912, to enforce the statute. Romer and Nims were listed among the "board of directors" totaling 33 members in the "first local vigilance committee." The number "33" was meaningful; 1800's secret societies like the Sphinx Club were comprised of Freemasons who were descendants of the Knights Templar. Additionally, the Sphinx is considered the most powerful symbol of "Illuminati" from whence all power derived. In fact, the front cover of *The Sphinx Club, New York (1904)* included a Sphinx; the book's cover design was likely influenced by the Sphinx Club's founding member and Freemason, George Rowell. Freemasons formed the AACA as organized advertising that begat the Better Business Bureau; the number 33 was a significant symbol for Freemasonry and also referenced Christianity in that Jesus was crucified at the age of 33. The Houston Bureau continued Freemason synchronicity with its numerical address being "1333."

Three months later, the AACA established the "National Vigilance

THE APO$TATE

Committee of the Associated Advertising Clubs of America" to process national complaints and affairs not handled by the local Bureaus; Romer is listed among its first 18 members. The Vigilance Committees grew in numbers and aggressively pursued enactment of the statute as a legal means to combat false advertising while establishing a national network with offices in every major city. Kenner wrote, "The Printers' Ink model statute was introduced in the legislatures of about fifteen states in 1913, and first became a law in Ohio through the alertness of Jesse H. Neal, chairman of the Vigilance Committee of the Advertising Club of Cleveland, with the help of advertising clubs in other cities." The statute ended the futility of powerless crusading and provided legal deterrent against false advertising that was "backed up by a police power."

Romer was still working for *Printers' Ink* when he passed away in 1933 at the age of 64. His obituary described him as "the millionaire publisher of Printers' Ink." He was inducted into the AAF Hall of Fame in 1949. The *Printers' Ink* Model Statute became law with various modifications in the District of Columbia and 43 states.

CHAPTER 7

THE ASSOCIATED PRESS

Many of the nation's most famous newspapers originated in New York City as the world's renowned hub of advertising, which attracted the most prestigious advertising clubs, agencies, and associations. Between 1725 and 1800, 137 newspapers "appeared" in the colonies. According to the New York State Education Department (NYSED.gov), "By 1828, about 120 newspapers were being published in New York State, 20 of those in New York City." The first published New York newspaper was the *New-York Gazette* issued on November 8, 1725. The second was the *New-York Weekly Journal* "issued by John Peter Zenger beginning November 5, 1733."

Zenger was accused of "seditious libel" and jailed for criticizing "oppressive" British Royal Governor of New York, Sir William Cosby (1690-1736), in office between 1732 and 1736. During Zenger's absence, his wife, Anna, continued business as usual "making her the first woman to write, edit, and publish a newspaper in New York State (and only the third in U.S. history)." Zenger was later brought to trial in a landmark case referred to as "The Zenger Trial." His attorneys, Andrew Hamilton (1676-1741) and William Smith Sr., successfully defended him and established the legal precedence "that truth is a defense against charges of libel." Hamilton also defended the constitutional rights and civil responsibility of free press, and that the press has "a liberty both of exposing and opposing tyrannical power by speaking and writing truth."

On "May 22, 1946," the *Associated Press* (AP) was created by "six New York newspapers" to establish a faster route by horse between the North and the war in Mexico. According to the New York Library, "David Hale, publisher of *The New York Journal of Commerce*, called together James Gordon Bennett of *The New York Herald*, Horace Greeley of the *New-York Tribune*, and representatives of the *Morning Courier and New-York Enquirer*, the *New York Morning Express*, and *The Sun*, who together formed the Associated Press of New York."

THE APO$TATE

The U.S. Post Office delivered news too slow. Consequently, alternative methods of communication were implemented for faster reporting "by pigeon, pony express, railroad, steamship, telegraph, and teletype." Accordingly, the AP improved mainstream contact in tandem with the technological revolution. In 1935, photographs were sent by wire; in 1941, print "expanded to radio broadcast news"; in 1973, a radio network was created; in 1994, APTV was launched as "a global video news gathering agency, headquartered in London"; in 2003, a Corporate Archives was assembled with records that "span the years 1848 to the present and are organized into 40 record groups totaling 2,000 linear feet"; in 2005, a digital database was designed to store all AP information and provide an immediate global response; and, in 2006, AP "joined YouTube." As of 2007, AP "operates AP Network" and links to 1,700 newspapers and "more than 5,000 television and radio broadcasters."

Current headquarters are located in Manhattan, New York. AP is "a not-for-profit cooperative, owned by 1,500 U.S. newspapers" governed by a Board of Directors "comprised of publishers, editors, and broadcast and radio executives." Staff is located in "280 locations in more than 100 countries." Revenue has continued to slide since 2010. As of 2015 AP posted "$183.6 million in net income."

CHAPTER 8

SCIENTIFIC DISCOVERIES AND INVENTIONS

The discovery of electricity and its repurposing enabled inventions of the telegraph, telephone, radio, and television, which created a new dimension of technology, communication, and transportation that melded business with advertising. Consequently, science shifted to a competitive game of credit acknowledgment for lifetime acclaim and financial reward. Inventions were often a collective effort involving several scientists, but final credit of discovery was given to whoever beat the other to the U.S. patent office for first filing.

By 1878, simultaneous electrical discoveries were introduced by American inventor Thomas Alva Edison (1847-1931) and Serbian-American inventor Nicola Tesla (1856-1943). Incandescent light bulbs gave way to neon lights that revolutionized American advertising inviting a new age of industrial and technological advances. Edison was initially financed by banker John Pierpont Morgan (1837-1913) who bought Edison General Electric Company for two million dollars. In September 1882, the first "electric street lamps" were introduced in New York using Edison's low-voltage "direct-current system (DC)."

Tesla, a genius, visionary, electrical engineer, and physicist, designed a "far reaching" high voltage "alternating current system (AC)." He competed against Edison's direct current. Tesla's AC current became popular because it could be adjusted and/or "stepped up" whereas Edison's could not. He was financed by Pittsburg industrialist George Westinghouse (1846-1914), a Civil War veteran and the "inventor of railroad airbrakes." Tesla was a former employee of Thomas Edison, and, in 1887, "filed for seven U.S. patents in the field of polyphase AC motors and power transmission." In 1891, he was granted U.S. patent No. 454,622 for the Tesla Coil used in radios and defined as an "electrical resonant transformer circuit." Tesla's AC current lit up the 1893 Chicago World's Fair and was the first time such an event was "all electric." According to PBS.com,

THE APO$TATE

"The Columbian Exposition opened on May 1, 1893. That evening, President Grover Cleveland pushed a button and a hundred thousand incandescent lamps illuminated the fairground's neoclassical buildings. This "City of Light" was the work of Tesla, Westinghouse and twelve new thousand-horsepower AC generation units located in the Hall of Machinery."

At the same time that the advertising and publishing industries were developing, so were scientific discoveries and inventions that would dramatically improve everyday living to sculpt a nation with innovative changes in communications, travel, commerce, politics, federal and state legislation, entertainment, and architecture. Harnessing electricity produced a wide spectrum of revolutionary communications and technology. Trains would establish the North's control and dominance over the South; add safety brakes to save lives and upgrade travel; and, contribute to an industrial revolution during the intensive Progressive Reformation Era. Electricity would dazzle advertising's fertile imagination producing electrified lights that would subliminally entice a fascinated public and enable astounding building technology creating architectural masterpieces with innovative skyscrapers gracing city horizons. The automobile would bring independence and opportunity. Planes connected continents proving mankind's triumphant mastery of aeronautics. And ships could communicate from sea to land. As a result, independent advertising groups began to merge and network on common ground due to advancements in cross-country travel and communications.

Trains preserved the Union and built a nation. Their inventor traced roots to the American Revolution. Colonel John Stevens III (1749-1838) was an "American lawyer, engineer and inventor" credited with building the first passenger-carrying steam locomotive in 1825 at his home in Hoboken, New Jersey, which launched the railroad industry in America. Additionally, Stevens held honorable heritage and personal distinction with defining achievements as a former captain in General George Washington's army in 1776; his father, John Stevens (1715-1792), "served as a delegate to the Continental Congress" and opposed the Stamp Act of 1765 that sparked the American Revolution; his sister, Mary Stevens (died 1814), married Robert R. Livingston (1746-1813), a "Founding Father" and "a member of the Committee of Five that drafted the Declaration of Independence, along with Thomas Jefferson, Benjamin Franklin, John Adams, and Roger Sherman." Livingston later negotiated the Louisiana Purchase in 1803; "constructed the first steam-powered ferry and first U.S. commercial ferry service"; and was "influential in the creation of U.S. Patent law."

The Baltimore and Ohio Railroad incorporated in 1827 and held a celebrated legacy. The railroad "was the first common carrier and Class I railroad in the U.S. as well as one of the oldest. During its peak years, the railroad extended as far east as Staten Island New York and as far west as Illinois." B&O began ceremoniously laying track on July 4, 1828, with Charles Carroll (1737-1832) of Carrollton, Maryland, laying the "first stone." Carroll was 90 years old as well as the only Catholic signatory of the Declaration of Independence and its "last surviving signer." The B&O Railroad and its president, John W. Garrett (1820-1884), later assisted the Union by reporting on Confederate troop movement during the Civil War. William Henry Harrison (1773-1841), 9th POTUS and inaugurated on March 4, 1841, highlighted railroad's burgeoning potential as "the first President to arrive in Washington, D.C. by train."

Abraham Lincoln was the first Republican president and 16th POTUS, inaugurated on March 4, 1861; and, Millard Fillmore, 13th POTUS from 1850 to 1853, represented the last president of the Whig Party. Seven years earlier, on March 20, 1854, the Republican Party (Grand Old Party (GOP)) formed to prevent expansion of slavery. Lincoln promoted a transcontinental railway and telegraph system that saved the Union during the Civil War and populated the Wild West with immigrants drawn to America's heartland by offer of free land. He signed into law the "Pacific Railway Act of 1862" that enacted "the construction of a railroad and telegraph line from the Missouri River to the Pacific Ocean." Lincoln recognized the far-reaching benefits of a cross-country railway system extending from sea to sea that would populate as well as establish Union control to deter the South's expansion of slavery into the West as southern states were already seceding from the Union when he took office.

The National Park Service website described Lincoln's new legislation: "Pacific Railway Act, July 1, 1862: This law created the great transcontinental railroad, which was completed in 1869 and linked the east and west coasts. Lincoln ensured that the railroad ran along a northern rather than southern route. The southern route had been the one preferred by Southern politicians prior to the Civil War." A month earlier, on May 20, 1862, Lincoln signed into law the Homestead Act that would draw a multitude of immigrants to America, steeped in Union patriotism. According to the National Park Service, "The Homestead Act opened millions of acres of the public domain to settlement and cultivation. This Act was open to anyone who met very basic and progressive requirements, including women, immigrants, and, beginning in 1868, African Americans. Eventually, homesteads were found in 30 states and covered 270 million acres."

Lincoln abolished slavery with a "preliminary Emancipation Proclamation" declared on September 22, 1862, after the bloody Battle of Antietam on September 17, 1862. He offered "free land" to immigrants settling the West that would inherently impede slavery and the Confederacy. In fact, many of the 1800's publishing and advertising pioneers were immigrants who contributed to the intense Progressive Reformation Movement. Furthermore, Upton

THE APO$TATE

Sinclair's *The Jungle* used a fictitious immigrant storyline to expose meatpacking atrocities that started a chain reaction and inspired the passage of the Pure Food and Drug Act, which resulted in the formation of the first Vigilance Committee that became the Better Business Bureau.

Electricity's development involved a collective effort dating back to antiquarian Greek and Roman times. Whereas Benjamin Franklin was credited with discovering electricity, he only confirmed lightning was electrical. Static electricity was actually discovered by the Greeks around 600 BC. In the 1930s, archeologists dug up ancient batteries used by early Romans described as "clay pots with sheets of copper inside." In 1600, English physician William Gilbert (1544-1603) coined the Latin term "electricus" to define what we now call static electricity. About the same time, English scientist Sir Thomas Browne (1605-1882) applied Gilbert's efforts establishing the word "electricity." In 1752, Benjamin Franklin performed his famous experiment using "a kite, a key and a storm" to prove that "lightning and tiny electric sparks were the same." In 1831, British physicist and chemist Michael Faraday (1791-1867) set the stage by developing the "electric dynamo" as the first power generator. Then, in 1836, Joseph Henry (1797-1878) developed "intensity batteries" used a year later by Samuel Morse to procure a U.S. patent for the telegraph. Henry's other achievements included appointment as "President Lincoln's science advisor," the "scientific unit 'Henry' (H) to measure inductance," and "founding father of the National Weather Service."

By 1878 both American scientist Thomas Alva Edison (1847-1931) and British physicist and chemist Sir Joseph Wilson Swan (1828-1914), knighted by King Edward VII, had each invented an "incandescent filament light bulb ... that would light for hours on end." Then, Edison and Swan jointly formed a company to produce the first "filament lamp." In September 1882, the first "electric street lamps" were introduced in New York that used Edison's "direct-current system (DC)." While Edison was credited for lighting New York's Broadway, Swan was renowned for lighting up Parisian streets with his incandescent bulbs during its 1891 international exhibit. Swan revolutionized history as "the person responsible for developing and supplying the first incandescent lights used to illuminate homes and public buildings, including the Savoy Theatre, London, in 1881." In December 1889, Edison formed Edison Manufacturing Company with incorporation in New Jersey on May 5, 1900; one of the main products sold was the "Edison-Lalande primary battery" with a production plant established in Bloomfield, New Jersey.

Edison was nicknamed "The Wizard of Menlo Park" and held over 1,093 U.S. patents including the "stock ticker" (1870-1970), the phonograph (1877), carbon microphone in telephones (1877-78), Kinetographic motion picture camera (1891), and incandescent light bulb with carbon filament (1879). In

1900, he established General Electric Research Laboratory that produced the first industrial research in the United States. In 1890, U.S. electrical engineer Daniel McFarlane Moore (1869-1936) joined "the engineering department of the Edison Manufacturing Company." Moore went on to develop "light-producing tubes of gas" that Edison saw as a threat to his incandescent bulb. In 1894, Moore left Edison's company and established "Moore Electric Company" and "Moore Light Company." By 1896, he had developed "the Moore Lamp" using nitrogen or carbon dioxide gas-filled glass tubes emitting luminous white light. Moore's two companies and patents were later "absorbed" by General Electric in 1912.

Around 1917, Moore went to work for GE and designed neon "glow lamps." In 1898, Scottish chemist Sir William Ramsey (1852-1916) and English chemist Morris W. Travers (1872-1961) discovered "neon" gas that emitted a "brilliant red color." Then, in 1902, Georges Claude (1870-1960), the "Edison of France," partnered with Paul Delorme to formally launch Air Liquide, based in Paris, France, whereafter he developed "the Claude system for liquifying air." Wikipedia.org stated that Air Liquide "supplies industrial gases and services to various industries including medical, chemical and electronic manufacturers." Additionally, Referenceforbusiness.com noted that Claude "had applied for the first patent on neon tubes in 1907" and his invention of neon lighting "appeared on the streets of Paris in 1910." In 1915, Claude was issued a U.S. patent "covering the design of the electrodes for neon tube lights" that "became the basis for the monopoly held in the U.S. by his company, Claude Neon Lights, through the early 1930s." Claude "was imprisoned in 1945" as a German "collaborator" during WWII.

According to Untappedcities.com, ""The Great White Way" became a nickname for Broadway in the 1890s ... when the street was one of the first to be fully illuminated by electric light." Edison's invention of the incandescent bulb replaced dangerous and smelly open-flamed gas lights used in theaters along Broadway enabling its current entertainment notoriety. Additionally, Untappedcities.com quoted author Thomas E. Rinaldi: "The world's first electrically lit large commercial billboard was erected over Madison Square in 1892. (It read, "BUY HOMES ON LONG ISLAND/SWEPT BY OCEAN BREEZES," and was paid for by the Long Island Rail Road)." Artkraft Strauss was the company that produced and designed the magnificent signs that creatively illuminated and transformed Broadway into the Great White Way. Artkraft.com advised the company has been in business "since 1897" and featured clips of the mammoth signs they built in Times Square that were several stories high and as wide as a building.

Printers' Ink kept in sync with technology and reflected the social conscience of the latest notable invention. Each development inspired another and was due to the collective efforts of several scientists with final credit of discovery given to whoever first filed the respective U.S. patent. *Printers' Ink*, Vol. LXIV, August 26, 1908, No. 9, ran the article, "THE GREAT WHITE WAY," discussing "electric illumination" that had revolutionized advertising over "the past two and three years" or since around 1905. The article referred to prototype neon lighting described as "incandescent lamps of lower candle power and new colors" that lined the streets of New York's Broadway and theatre district.

Entertaining light magically lit up the capital of advertising and changed the world. Historic occasion noted, "Thousands upon thousands of electric lamps light up this busy district every night from dusk until the wee small hours. No New Yorker ever walks into it without having his blood stirred and his pride tickled." The article also noted how fast the city became dependent upon "this magnificent illumination" and that without it Broadway would go dark. It warned, "Tear down every sign not directly connected with a business or a theater, and "the Great White Way" would vanish. Of Broadway, there would be left only a commonplace street, indifferently lit up by a few ordinary business signs."

In March 1915, the Ford Motor Company embraced the Great White Way. Ford splashed its famous slogan, "WATCH THE FORDS GO BY," previously introduced in 1907, on an "electric spectacular" atop a building in Detroit, Michigan. The sign featured an open carriage positioned on a street with a driver dressed in a driving coat and beret sitting in the front seat with one hand on the wheel and the other on the stick shift. A passenger was sitting in the back seat, and also dressed in a driving coat and hat. Both their scarves were depicted as being blown behind them to indicate speed. Below the carriage, large capital letters and numbers anchored the sign reflecting the month and ticking count of cars sold, i.e., "MARCH SALES 43,849," whereby subliminally encouraging each passerby to buy a Fordmobile and add their purchase to the emblazoned number.

Prior to the automobile, the advertising industry remained regional due to travel limitations. But, in 1906, Henry Ford (1863-1947) changed the advertising industry and commercial landscape of America with his Model "N" four-cylinder 15-horsepower automobile priced at $600 dollars and built in Detroit, Michigan. In 1908, Ford presented his popular 20-horsepower Model "T", the "Tin Lizzie," for $825. In 1914, he re-introduced a cheaper one-colored Model T under the mantra, "customers could buy a Model T in any color they wanted, "as long as they wanted black"." William C. Durant was Ford's primary competitor and a speculator and entrepreneur who "bought up numerous auto manufacturing companies, including Buick, Ransom Olds's Oldsmobile, Cadillac, and Chevrolet, as well as parts makers such as Fisher body and Charles Kettering's electric starter and battery company."

SCIENTIFIC DISCOVERIES AND INVENTIONS

The telegraph represented a collective breakthrough effort in electrical evolution. According to History.com, "[T]he credit for inventing the telegraph generally falls to two international sets of researchers: Sir William Cooke (1806-79) and Sir Charles Wheatstone (1802-75) in England, and Samuel Morse, Leonard Gale (1800-83) and Alfred Vail (1807-59) in the U.S."

Samuel Finley Breese Morse (1791-1872), an American painter and inventor, designed the telegraph that established far-reaching communicative cornerstones. He incorporated a set of signals named "Morse Code" that featured an electrical sequence that electrified a wire and cut the flow of electricity at certain intervals to form a dot and dash language; the famous Morse code signal "SOS" does not specifically stand for anything, but code was developed as an easily transmitted universal distress signal where ""S" is three dots and "O" is three dashes." In 1837, Morse applied for a U.S. patent on his telegraph device using electricity provided by "Joseph Henry's 1836 "intensity batteries"." Then, in 1843, Morse procured funding from the U.S. Congress to set up the first "telegraph system between Washington, D.C., and Baltimore, Maryland," according to History.com. On May 24, 1844, he telegraphed via Morse Code the first message, "What hath God wrought!"

Morse's invention for the telegraph was the predecessor of the radio. The website "United States Early Radio History" wrote, "The first major use of radio was for navigation, where it greatly reduced the isolation of ships, saving thousands of lives, even though for the first couple of decades radio was generally limited to Morse code transmissions."

In 1888, German professor of physics Heinrich Hertz (1857-1894), proved that "electricity can be transmitted in electromagnetic waves," according to Famousscientists.org. In fact, radio waves influenced the evolution of radio, television, and radar. The "Hertz" measurement was named after him.

Ezra Cornell (1807-1874), future founder of Cornell University in New York, designed the underground cable insulation for the Washington-Baltimore telegraph system. He was contracted by Morse at an annual salary of $1,000 and designed underground lead pipe insulation and an installation plow during the summer of 1843. Cornell applied for a U.S. patent on his plow design described as "a new and useful Machine for cutting trenches and laying pipes" and was awarded patent rights on February 28, 1944. During this timeframe, Cornell's employer, Morse, fought several inventors on behalf of arguing sole rights pertaining to the telegraph and was awarded "telegraph patent rights" in 1847. Thereafter, Cornell became one of the founders of "Western Union Telegraph Company" in 1856. Then, James Buchanan (1791-1868), 15th POTUS from 1857 to 1861, signed the Pacific Telegraph Act of 1860 and Western Union won the bid to build the first transcontinental telegraph completed in October 1861. President Lincoln used the telegraph as state-of-the-art communication with battlefield commanders during the Civil War.

Andrew Johnson was inaugurated 16th vice president of the United States on March 4, 1865, and became 17th POTUS on April 15, 1866, after the assassination of President Lincoln. Johnson remodeled the White House and "installed the first telegraph office in the White House." In 1874, Thomas Edison developed the "Quadruplex System" allowing telegraph wires to transmit up to four messages at the same time. Then, in 1891, electrician Ike Hoover, with the Edison General Company of New York, spent four months installing "electric light wiring" in the White House during the Harrison administration. Hoover remained at the White House as master electrician and served 42 years. Thereafter, Benjamin Harrison (1883-1901), 23rd POTUS and inaugurated on March 4, 1889, was afraid to use the newly installed electrical system and light switches for fear of being electrocuted. And President Hoover would turn the lights on in the White House every evening, leave them on overnight, and turn them off the next day.

Three inventors worked on the telephone. In 1876, Alexander Graham Bell (1847-1922) was issued U.S. patent rights for his telephone design because he filed the respective patent application hours before inventor Elisha Gray (1835-1901). Both inventors, though, exploited the work of inventor Thomas Watson (1854-1934) who worked with Bell and constructed a "crude" working phone. History ultimately memorialized Bell for making the first telephone call on March 10, 1876, to assistant Thomas Watson whereby revolutionizing history with his simple statement, "Mr. Watson--come here--I want to see you."

The invention of radio also involved many scientists. Ultimate credit named Italian inventor Guglielmo Marconi for inventing wireless communication. Author David E. Kyvig stated, "[Marconi] discovered how to transmit telegraphic code through the air in 1896." A series of developments followed. In 1909, the College of Engineering, in San Jose, California, began broadcasting using Morse Code; in 1913, after the sinking of the Titanic in 1912, "advances in vacuum tube technology effectively amplified wireless telegraph and radio signals"; in 1915, a "voice message" was sent from Virginia and heard in Paris and Hawaii; in 1916, ham radio operators networked a message from Iowa to New York; and, in 1917, a message was relayed back and forth between Los Angeles and New York.

Additional scientists also contributed to radio's stair-stepping evolution. In 1891, Serbian-American inventor Nikola Tesla (1856-1943), who worked with Thomas Edison, was granted U.S. patent No. 454,622 for the Tesla Coil used in radios and defined as an "electrical resonant transformer circuit." In 1904, Guglielmo Marconi (1874-1937), "Italian inventor and electrical engineer," was awarded a U.S. patent "for the invention of radio" transmitting "long range radio signals." In 1906, Reginald Fessenden (1866-1932) and Lee DeForest

(1873-1961) invented "amplitude-modulated (AM) radio" that allowed "more than one station" to send signals. On December 24, 1906, Fessenden made the first radio broadcast at Brant Rock, Massachusetts, by playing "O Holy Night" and reading from the Bible, which could be heard by "ships at sea." Almost a year later, October 17, 1907, Marconi set up the first "regular transatlantic radio-telegraph service" between "Clifden, Ireland and Glace Bay, Newfoundland." His patents would control "ship to shore communications." In fact, FCC.gov reported, "His radio apparatus is widely considered to be the reason that over 700 people survived the Titanic disaster in 1912." In 1909, a California electronics instructor, Charles David Herrold (1875-1948), built the world's "second radio station" using "spark-gap" technology meant to prevent electrical surges. In 1911, Tesla worked with German wireless telephone company, Telefunken, founded May 27, 1903, and constructed radio towers in Nauen, Germany, whereby "creating the only wireless communication between North America and Europe." Then, in 1913, maritime safety rules were upgraded when the International Convention for the Safety of Life at Sea required "shipboard radio stations to be manned 24 hours a day."

On April 14-15, 1912, the British Royal Mail Ship (RMS) *Titanic* sunk "into the North Atlantic Ocean about 400 miles south of Newfoundland, Canada." Several famous American and British citizens died including "British journalist William Thomas Stead and heirs to the Straus, Astor, and Guggenheim fortunes." The death of over 1500 people led to public outrage in the United States and Britain, which forced maritime safety reform. After the *Titanic* tragedy, "wireless telegraphy using spark-gap transmitters quickly became universal on large ships." Additionally, History.com noted, "In the disaster's aftermath, the first International Convention for Safety of Life at Sea was held in 1913. Rules were adopted requiring that every ship have lifeboat space for each person on board, and that lifeboat drills be held. An International Ice Patrol was established to monitor icebergs in the North Atlantic shipping lanes. It was also required that ships maintain a 24-hour radio watch."

Prior to the sinking of the *Titanic,* famous retailer John Wanamaker was the first merchant to add "wireless transmission" to his New York and Philadelphia stores. Wanamaker's Sales Manager Joseph Appel reminisced that May 19, 1911, was a historic occasion bringing much fanfare; that "the Mayor of Philadelphia, John E. Rayburn, sent a radio message to the Mayor of New York, William J. Gaynor, reading: "Sincere greetings and congratulations on completion of enterprise which gives the Wanamaker wireless one more tie for service and friendship to unite our cities." To John Wanamaker who was then in Ems, Prussia, a Marconi message was sent across the ocean, reading: "Wanamaker wireless inaugurated, first message Philadelphia Mayor to New York Mayor. Your coworkers send heartiest congratulations"." Furthermore, Appel advised that,

THE APO$TATE

on May 22, 1911, the store stations became "official stations of the Marconi Wireless Telegraph Company," which for receipt of messages charged "$2 for the first ten words, 12c for each additional word; address and signature free of charge." Several months later, in "the winter of 1922," Wanamaker's New York store operated the WOO radio station that was "the first radio broadcasting station on Manhattan Island and operated it for nearly a year, following arrangements made with station WJZ of the Radio Corporation of America." Appel wrote a special footnote referring to David Sarnoff, former president and general manager of the Radio Corporation of America, and "one of the first operators at Wanamaker's." He noted that Sarnoff was the operator at the Philadelphia Wanamaker store, station WOO, who received "the first word of the sinking of the *Titanic*."

Appel described *Titanic's* catastrophe by quoting Sarnoff's first-hand account: "I began to receive the first details of the disaster – the fact that the *Titanic* had sunk, that the *Carpathia* had taken off a number of passengers. I immediately gave the news to the press. Then bedlam broke loose. Reporters and relatives and friends of passengers on the doomed liner hung breathlessly over my shoulder while I copied the names of those who had been saved, scanning every letter as I placed it on paper and hoping that the next word would spell the name of a loved one." As a result, Sarnoff christened radio as a profound communicative asset: "But the very tragedy of the *Titanic* disaster crystallized in the minds of everyone the value of radio, and the art was given a new status. One almost immediate result was the passing of laws of national and international character to safeguard life at sea by making it compulsory for every ship carrying fifty or more persons to be equipped with radio telegraph apparatus, with provision for two operators to be constantly on watch so that distress signals might be received or sent out in time of need."

In 1917, before the First Great War ended in 1918, the U.S. government controlled all radio production and technology on behalf of the war effort. The government lost its monopoly over the radio industry after the war ended but orchestrated the same "effect" by establishing the "Radio Corporation of America" on October 17, 1919. RCA represented the War and Navy Departments' creation of "a national radio system for the United States." The Army and Navy approached General Electric to buy out the "British-owned" Marconi Company and its U.S. subsidiary, Marconi Wireless Telegraphy Company of America, and incorporate them as Radio Corporation of America, a publicly held company with controlling interests owned by GE. According to Wikipedia.org, "The result was federally created monopolies in radio for GE and the Westinghouse Corporation and in telephone systems for the American Telephone & Telegraph Company." In 1930, Federal anti-trust charges forced GE and Westinghouse to separate from RCA. In 1939, RCA introduced its "all-electronic" television at the New York World's Fair. On July 1, 1941, the Federal Communications Commission approved the first "commercial television transmission" that inspired RCA television production. Then, in 1986, GE sold its 50% interest in RCA to Bartelsmann Music Group; two years later, GE sold its remaining RCA rights to produce consumer products, including televisions, to French-owned Thomson Consumer Electronics. By 2013, GE sold all of its controlling interest in the National Broadcasting Company to "Comcast," and GE retained its RCA division in "government services."

Wikipedia also reported, "The first radio news program was broadcast August 31, 1920 by station 8MK in Detroit, Michigan, which survives today as all-news format station WWJ under ownership of the CBS network." Then the first paid radio commercials were dispatched in March 1922 when Remick's Music Store in Seattle "sponsored a one night a week program on station KFC" and promoted sales of the songs played on the program. And, in August 1922, AT&T's New York radio station WEAF offered 10 minutes for $100 dollars and advertising was purchased by a "Long Island real estate firm" to sell apartments.

Regulation of radio originated with the "U.S. Department of Commerce and Labor" that was created on February 14, 1903, under the presidency of Theodore Roosevelt. Investigations were orchestrated under the Bureau of Corporations; its mission was to "create jobs, promote economic growth, encourage sustainable development and improve standards of living for all Americans." After the sinking of the *Titanic* on April 14-15, 1912, the U.S. Congress enacted the Radio Act on August 13, 1912. According to Middle Tennessee State University, "The act provided for the licensing of radio operators, a separate frequency for distress calls, and twenty-four hour radio service for ships at sea. The act also required all amateur radio broadcasters to be licensed, and it prohibited them from broadcasting over the main commercial and military wavelengths." Amateur radio operators created excessive radio chatter that impeded the *Titanic's* distress signals.

On March 4, 1913, the Department of Commerce and Labor was divided into the Department of Commerce and Department of Labor. The DOC maintained regulatory powers over radio communications. The Bureau of Corporations, as the former investigative branch, was spun into the Federal Trade Commission as a result of the Federal Trade Commission Act that was signed into law on September 26, 1914, by Democrat Thomas Woodrow Wilson (1856-1924), 28th POTUS from 1913 to 1921. The FTC was empowered to break up trusts, regulate deceptive trade practice, and protect consumers.

On February 18, 1927, the Radio Act of 1927 replaced the Radio Act of 1912 and was signed into law by Republican John Calvin Coolidge Jr. (1872-1933), 30th POTUS from 1923 to 1929. The Radio Act created the "Federal Radio Commission" with powers to grant and deny licenses and assign frequencies and power levels, but its authority over newly invented public broadcasting was still limited and did not regulate radio networks or advertising.

In 1927, the Bureau was neck-deep in cahoots with the NYSE and Investment Bankers Association with its illicit "Before You Invest, Investigate" securities program. The Bureau seized upon radio's newfound opportunity to reach a greater audience to promote its bogus investigative securities program, advance crony Wall Street interests, maintain fabricated quasi-government façade, and monopolize radio communication. And investors flocked to the Bureau's heralded failsafe investigative programs to buy NYSE securities. Consequently, the Bureau enjoyed regulatory groundswell, Wall Street gravitas, and globalist fortune until the Crash on October 29, 1929. Three years later, the Bureau was indicted by the U.S. Senate for Blue Sky securities fraud, interstate mail fraud, racketeering, and influencing radio communication.

The latter charge stemmed from the Bureau's meeting in October 1931 with seven Boston radio stations. It was yet another case of stolen thunder whereby the Bureau recognized radio broadcasting as a popular trailblazing enterprising frontier to conquer and control. The Bureau established radio broadcasting standards and formed a pact to decline "objectionable advertising" as approved by the Federal Radio Commission. The participating broadcasters were "WDZA, WEEI, WHDH, WLEX, WLOE, WNAC, WSSH." Kenner's rose-colored revisionist braggadocio reflected, "Radio broadcasting stations began to cooperate with Better Business Bureaus in the later 20's, to help stem the tide of stock swindling."

The Communications Act passed by Congress in 1934 replaced the Federal Radio Commission with the Federal Communications Commission and transferred all previous regulation and licensing while adding jurisdiction over communication carriers like "telephone and telegraph companies." In July 1935, Anning S. Prall, chairman of the Federal Communications Commission, endorsed radio advertising self-regulation in an address to the National Association of Broadcasters; the Association adopted a "code of standards" that same year.

The invention of radio affected every aspect of American life and changed the course of communications and advertising. Two American politicians, Herbert Hoover and FDR, played an integral part in the development of radio and embedded its use within mainstream society. Hoover instigated "conference reports," which led to the enactment of the Radio Act of 1927. And Roosevelt used the radio to hold "fireside chats" as a source of encouragement throughout the Great Depression.

Two years prior to being inaugurated 31st POTUS, on March 4, 1929, Secretary of Commerce Hoover initiated measures to expand the commercial use and regulation of radio broadcasting. From 1922 until 1927, Hoover engaged radio conference reports, which framed the Radio Act's cornerstone principles.

SCIENTIFIC DISCOVERIES AND INVENTIONS

Thereafter, Hoover enlisted the participation of Washington Senator Clarence Dill and Maine Representative Wallace White to pass the Dill-White Bill that became known as the Radio Act "that was signed into law by President Calvin Coolidge on February 23, 1927"; beforehand, radio licensing and broadcast frequencies were not regulated. The act created the Federal Radio Commission (FRC) and empowered the DOC to shut down any offensive radio stations. Thus, Hoover was credited with contributing to the development of modern radio despite confronting many obstacles. According to Wikipedia, "[Hoover's] powers were limited by federal court decisions ... he was not allowed to deny broadcasting licenses to anyone who wanted one. The result was that many people perceived the airwaves to suffer from "chaos," with too many stations trying to be heard on too few frequencies."

FDR delivered his first fireside chat via radio on March 21, 1933, which resulted in a total of 30 inspirational radio speeches through June 1944. Topics included "banking, unemployment and European fascism." According to History.com, "During the 1930s, approximately 90 percent of American households owned a radio."

CHAPTER 9

SPANISH-AMERICAN WAR 1898

Theodore Roosevelt participated in the Spanish-American War from April 25, 1898 to August 13, 1898, which ended Spain's control of Cuba and added American territory in the Pacific and Caribbean. From 1895 to 1898, Cuban revolutionaries fought for independence from Spanish government forces. Then, on February 15, 1898, a mysterious explosion sunk the ACR-1 USS *Maine* in Havana Harbor; 261 Americans out of a crew of 355 were killed; the ACR-1 battleship designation represented, "The first armored cruiser of the United States Navy." The media stoked the battle cry, "Remember the *Maine*! To hell with Spain!" As a result, on April 25, 1898, the United States and Spain declared war on each other. Secretary of State John Hay called it a "splendid little war" because the battle lasted less than 4 months, but greatly expanded American borders into the crucial Pacific-Asian realm. Upon close of war, on August 12, 1898, the United States annexed the Hawaiian Islands. And, on December 10, 1898, the Treaty of Paris was signed whereby "Spain renounced all claim to Cuba, ceded Guam and Puerto Rico to the United States, and transferred sovereignty over the Philippines to the United States for $20,000,000."

The Battle of Guantánamo Bay was fought during the Spanish-American War from June 6-10, 1898. In 1901, the Platt Amendment opened the Naval Station Guantanamo Bay or *GTMO* "because of the airfield designation code or *Gitmo* b." Then, in 1903, a lease was drawn to guarantee continued operation of GTMO; no expiration date was stipulated. The naval base sits on 45 square miles of "land and water" on the southeastern tip of Cuba and provided a "detention" facility for the War on Terror.

Fidel Castro's Cuban Revolution in 1959 demanded that the United States evacuate GTMO "alleging that the base was imposed on Cuba by force." Ungrateful irony showcased another Cuban rebel spinning predecessors' exploitation of the United States. Nineteenth-century forensics overlooked or ignored the strong possibility that conniving Cuban rebels sabotaged the USS *Maine* to prod the United States into war against Spain; otherwise, Spain would not have initiated a war it could not win. Then, in 2013, Cuba appealed to the United Nation's Human Rights Council and demanded the United States "return the base and "usurped territory"" that they considered "occupied" land since the Spanish-American War. To date, GTMO is still operating.

On July 1, 1898, Lt. Col. Theodore Roosevelt, led the 1st United States Volunteer Cavalry, a.k.a. the "Rough Riders," in the famous Battle of San Juan Hill. The Rough Riders were specially chosen by Roosevelt and were a mix of frontiersmen and "recruits from Harvard, Yale, Princeton, and many another college; from clubs like Somerset, of Boston, and Knickerbocker, of New York; and from among men who belonged neither to club nor to college …."

There were extraordinary complaints of bad food during the Cuban War. Troops were fed "embalmed" meat and "opened their tins of beef to discover knots of gristle, hunks of rope, and mummified maggots." Accordingly, Pittsburg surgeon William Daily filed a field report stating refrigerated beef "tasted of boric acid and salicylic acid"; meat contained chemical preservatives "injected by unprincipled packers." The United States was unprepared for the Cuban War because "the Union army had largely disbanded after the Civil War and Reconstruction."

The Cuban War highlighted egregious lack of regulation within the U.S. food industry supported by depraved political corruption. William McKinley (1843-1901), 25th POTUS, serving from 1897 until he was assassinated in 1901, mishandled worsening relations between troops and the War Department, which concealed deleterious food and sanitation complaints submitted by field officers and medical staff in Cuba. Unsanitary hygiene spread deadly diseases and "more than 2,500 American Officers and men died of yellow fever, typhoid, malaria, dysentery, and other diseases … This was over ten times the number that died of wounds in battle."

Teddy Roosevelt proceeded to become 26th POTUS, serving from September 14, 1901 to March 4, 1909. During the course of his presidency, it was fitting that he approved and signed into law the Pure Food and Drug Act of 1906. He was also known as a trust buster and broke up the colossal monopolies of Carnegie, Morgan, and Rockefeller. His wisdom and warning of the NWO still resonates today as the globalist Deep State threatens the existence of the Republic of the United States: "Behind the ostensible government sits enthroned an invisible government, owing no allegiance and acknowledging no responsibility to the people."

CHAPTER 10

JOHN WANAMAKER

John Wanamaker
U.S. Postmaster General under President William Henry Harrison;
founder of Wanamaker stores; artist: Caryn Cain.

He was the founder of 15 Wanamaker Department Stores in New York City, Philadelphia, London, and Paris. Wanamaker was an honorable merchant and early pioneer of truth in advertising and subtly mixed product education with innovative sales technique. Advertising space and news columns were used to attract and encourage readers with good faith catch phrases like "full and frank facts about merchandise" and "tell the truth about goods." Kenner reflected, "John Wanamaker of Philadelphia was not only the earliest user of large space in newspapers – he used a full page in 1879 and was the first merchant to do so – but he emphasized truthfulness in advertising. In 1868, he admonished his salesmen: "What we advertise, we must do. Tell the customer the exact quality of the goods, if he does not know it"."

Wanamaker was foremost an American patriot and cherished his position as the 35th United States postmaster general appointed by President Benjamin Harrison (1833-1901), 23rd POTUS, serving from March 4, 1889 to March 4, 1893. According to USPS.com, "Postmaster General John Wanamaker ... was a merchant who became one of the most innovative and energetic people ever to lead the Post Office Department."

During his tenure as postmaster general, Republican Wanamaker made waves with his Democratic associates. Innovation brought much controversy. He streamlined the Post Office firing several thousand Democratic postal workers who retaliated by accusing him of buying his position because he contributed $10,000 to Harrison's presidential campaign; he installed state-of-the-art pneumatic tubes; created commemorative stamps; opened 5,000 rural routes; expanded parcel-post delivery and mail order; and, banned postal sale of lottery tickets that ended U.S. lotteries until 1964. He took an efficient, commonsense approach that increased business by offering convenient free delivery at a time when "in 1890, nearly 41 million people – 65 percent of the American population – lived in rural areas." As a result, he eliminated a rural population's time-consuming travel to the main Post Office. Wanamaker concluded that outreach delivery to farms and outlying small towns, defined as "populations of from 300 to 5,000 people," might keep a younger generation at home and ease unsettling "isolation."

John Wanamaker was born July 11, 1838, in Philadelphia, Pennsylvania, in a rural area later known as the "Grays Ferry neighborhood of South Philadelphia." His parents were brick mason John Nelson Wanamaker and Elizabeth Deshong Kochersperger. His mother's ancestors hailed from "Rittershoffen in Alsace, France, and from Canton Bern in Switzerland." In 1860, Wanamaker married Mary Erringer Brown (1839-1920). Their six children, born during and after the Civil War, included Thomas Brown Wanamaker (1862-1908); Lewis Rodman Wanamaker (1863-1928); Horace Wanamaker (1864-1864); Harriet E. "Nettie" Wanamaker (1865-1870); Mary Brown "Minnie" Wanamaker (1869-1954); and Elizabeth "Lillie" Wanamaker (1876-1927).

Wanamaker's two oldest sons assisted him and expanded the Wanamaker stores. The oldest son, Thomas, was an intellectual and had accounting finesse. Whereas the elder Wanamaker was a conservative Republican, Thomas identified with rising-star socialist author Upton Sinclair at the close of the Victorian era. In 1899, Thomas bought *The North American* newspaper that catered to a socialist agenda and published a Sunday edition much to his father's Puritan chagrin.

His second oldest son, Rodman, a Princeton graduate, was conservative like his father and had "a penchant for merchandise rather than for finances or figures." Rodman capitalized on his French residency and European heritage to popularize Wanamaker stores as stylish importers of Parisian wares and clothing. Appel wrote that he served "an apprenticeship as assistant merchandise buyer, going to Paris in 1888 as resident manager there – "because there was no place for me in the Philadelphia Store," he used to say – remaining in Paris"; and that Rodman was credited with hooking Americans on French goods by "laying the foundation in research and study of European markets and art centers that made him America's outstanding example of the artist-mind in merchandise."

In 1858, at the age of 20, Wanamaker worked as the first full-time secretary for the Young Men's Christian Association (YMCA) and earned $1000 per year. He increased YMCA membership from 57 to over 2000 members. Additionally, he supported the growing temperance movement and garnered promises of abstinence from YMCA members. The following year, he established the contentious Bethany Sunday School that eventually became "the largest Sunday school in the country." In 1861, Wanamaker resigned from the YMCA, but later served as its president from 1870 to 1883.

Wanamaker "went to work with a scant two years of schooling ... opening his own business without fortune, favor or many friends," according to Appel. His first store was "Oak Hall" in partnership with his brother-in-law, Nathan Brown. The store was located at the corner of Sixth and Market Streets in Philadelphia, next to George Washington's presidential home, and after the first decade earned $2,085,528 a year.

Eight years later, Wanamaker opened John Wanamaker & Co. at 818 Chestnut Street in Philadelphia. Nathan had passed away since opening the Oak Hall store and Wanamaker began trading on his own popular namesake. In 1875, he converted an abandoned railroad depot and named it John Wanamaker & Co., a.k.a. "The Grand Depot," located at Thirteenth and Market Streets.

In 1896, Wanamaker expanded into New York City and bought the six-floor "Iron Palace" built in 1862 by mercantile entrepreneur Alexander Turney Stewart. The store was named Wanamaker's and sat on an entire block located at Broadway and Tenth Street featuring a "cast-iron front, glass dome skylight and grand emporium."

The automobile had just begun to enter the market in the early 1900s. On October 1, 1908, Ford Motor Company and owner Henry Ford introduced the "Tin Lizzie" or Model T for $850. His first car was the ethanol-powered Ford Quadricycle, produced in 1896, and dubbed the "horseless carriage." It was chain-driven using four bicycle tires. The first Quadricycle was sold to Charles Ainsley in 1896 for $200. By 1903, Ford began undercutting competition by $600 and created a price war that angered the "Association of Licensed Automobile Manufacturers (LAM)." The Association retaliated by demanding Ford pay royalties to George B. Selden who owned U.S. Patent No. 549,160 for the Selden engine. Ford disputed the patent refusing to pay royalties. LAM sued

Ford for patent infringement and censored him in the marketplace. Wanamaker supported Ford and set up his New York and Philadelphia stores as Ford dealerships despite substantial liability. Appel surmised, "In taking over the Ford agency for New York and Philadelphia he automatically became co-defendant with the Ford Motor company in the suits that had already been brought. This did not deter him. He welcomed the fight."

Henry Ford was not well known at the time, but Wanamaker was. Ford Motor Company was saved by John Wanamaker's integrity, representation, and endorsement by protecting customers against LAM repercussions. One of Wanamaker's clever ads for Ford Motor read, "Remember that John Wanamaker will take care of all his customers in any litigation growing out of the infringement suits over the Ford car, without a cent of cost to any of them. Get a Ford car and enjoy it. We'll take care of the tom-toms. Don't give $600 to the Bogey Man."

Fortunately, consumers responded favorably. Thanks to Wanamaker, by the time Ford won the LAM lawsuit in 1912, "he was entrenched as America's greatest manufacturer of popular-priced motor cars." In *Advertising and Selling* magazine, dated July 13, 1927, Frederick C. Russell wrote that "it is important to note that Wanamaker had put across a vital message to the public – and over ten million people have bought Fords, automatically stimulating sales of twice as many cars produced by competitors."

In 1910, Wanamaker refurbished the Grand Depot into a 12-floor marble palace that was dedicated by President William Howard Taft who declared Wanamaker ""the greatest merchant in America" and his store "a model for all other stores of the same kind throughout the world"," according to Appel. The store was known for its spectacular "Wanamaker Grand Court Organ" and "2,500-pound bronze "Wanamaker Eagle"." He also added to his empire with European Wanamaker stores in London and Paris.

Wanamaker proved successful because he traded honorably under the slogan, "One price and goods returnable." He ended price haggling and assured product satisfaction by offering a money-back guarantee, which was unheard of at the time. Appel wrote, "Wanamaker's money-back offer ... was a slow and painful growth out of the old slavish system of barter and haggle."

He was a business genius who "established mutual confidence between buyer and seller" by pioneering new advertising techniques and store conveniences that modern shoppers take for granted. Wanamaker's contributions were numerous and included first department store; first price tag; first exit polling (customer satisfaction); first one-half page and full-page advertising spaces; first informational-styled copy; first full-time ad copywriter; first restaurant in a store (1876); first electrical lighting (Thomas Edison) in a store (1878); first elevators in a store (1889); first buyers to be trained overseas in foreign markets

THE APO$TATE

(sent 10 buyers to Europe every year); first in-house insurance; and, first "White Sale" (January 1878). Wanamaker also early on promoted civil rights for African Americans and Native Indians.

Appel considered Wanamaker a "crusading pioneer" even though he was called the merchant prince and preferred "to call himself a merchant pioneer." Wanamaker's ethical beliefs aligned with the truth crusade that organized in 1911 evidenced by his demand that "No marks or labels were allowed on merchandise that were not genuinely true." Furthermore, "the advertising of the store revolutionized advertising by its plainness, straightforwardness, and reliability." Appel described Wanamaker as "a merchant who believed (again in his own words) that "the Golden Rule of the New Testament has become the Golden rule of business."

He was opposed to unions and created John Wanamaker Commercial Institute as an alternative to keep his employees content. It was a training school that taught reading, writing, and arithmetic in the form of bookkeeping. Housing was also provided for female employees and a library was built to maintain an educated, social environment.

Wanamaker was a devout Christian and philanthropist. In 1878, he partnered with hatmaker John B. Stetson and seed entrepreneur W. Atlee Burpee to establish the Sunday Breakfast Rescue Mission for the homeless that is still in operation today.

His last day at work was on September 19, 1922, when he engaged a meeting with "three of his chief executives and talked over affairs of the store and of the world in general." Then, he attended a lodge meeting at the Masonic Temple and did not return to his Lindenhurst home until the bone-chill of midnight. Consequently, he became seriously ill with a "deep cold" and moved to his Walnut Street home to be closer to doctors. On December 10, 1922, his butler was traveling to the New York store and Wanamaker told him, "Bracken, don't go empty-handed. Take something to Rodman, give him my love and tell him I will soon be over to see him."

On December 12, 1922, at the age of 84, Wanamaker passed away at his Philadelphia townhome located at 2032 Walnut Street. Wanamaker also owned homes in "Cape May Point, New Jersey, Bay Head, New Jersey, New York, Florida, London, Paris, and Biarritz." Upon his death, his wealth was estimated at "$100 million (USD), ($1,413,717,694 today)." The pages of history welcomed "the last surviving member of Benjamin Harrison's Cabinet." Services were held on December 14th at the Bethany Presbyterian Church and "he was interred in the Wanamaker family tomb in the churchyard of the Church of St. James the Less in Philadelphia." Thomas Edison honored his fallen friend as a pallbearer.

Wanamaker's was continued by his son, Rodman, until his death six years later. The stores were owned by a family trust and Rodman Wanamaker's will provided for the chain to continue operating via a trustee system. In 1978, the Wanamaker stores were sold to Carter Hawley Hale, Inc. who resold the stores to Woodward & Lothrop in 1986. W&L suffered bankruptcy and was declared defunct by 1995. The Wanamaker stores "were sold to the May Department Stores Company on June 21, 1995. In August 2006 the flagship Philadelphia store was converted from a Lord & Taylor to a Macy's."

John Wanamaker was a brilliant businessman and marketing visionary who appreciated the importance of history as a pathway for future generations. He believed in the truth movement and avidly practiced honest advertising in his stores. His final words bestowed personal gratefulness to consumers and reflected hard-earned marketplace integrity: "To be frank, and outspoken, the writer of this, the old leader in this business whom the people have so highly honored, declares plainly that he made a compact with himself that this business should be recognized and stand of itself, for itself, on the highest pinnacle of truth, justice and honor."

CHAPTER 11

JOSEPH HERBERT APPEL

Joseph "Joe" Herbert Appel
Advertising manager for Wanamaker Stores; author of the *Ten Commandments of Advertising*. Photo dated before September 1919.
Source: *Associated Advertising*, September 1919, Vol. 10, No. 9, P. 46;
[https://babel.hathitrust.org/cgi/pt?id=iau.31858034256317;view=1up;seq=416];
public domain.

He was an attorney, author, and advertising manager for retail icon John Wanamaker from 1899 to 1936 and wrote most of the ad copy such as "first in Philadelphia and then in New York," which made the Wanamaker store chain famous. Appel also authored the iconic *Ten Commandments of Advertising* that was introduced at the 1911 Boston Convention and sparked the Truth in Advertising Movement. His ethical standards were adopted by the advertising industry. An esteemed celebrity in his own right, Appel was an original member of the Sphinx Club and one of the founders of The Poor Richard's Club in New York whose name he coined and whose members he endearingly called "Poor Richardites." He participated in advertising industry's truth crusade for 25 years serving "as a director of the Advertising Federation of America from 1930 to 1938, and for two years as its treasurer."

Appel wrote that he became indoctrinated in the early truth movement after accepting an invitation to speak for the Sphinx Club in New York that he credited as "the first *organized* stand against dishonest advertising." The Sphinx Club's motto was "Honesty in Advertising." He reflected on the watershed event: "It was just about at this juncture (1906) in the history of the advertising "clean-up" movement that I was able to add my voice for the first time in New York ... James O'Flaherty, brought me into New York advertising circles ... by luring me into making a speech before the Sphinx Club."

Joseph Herbert Appel was born in Lancaster, Pennsylvania, in 1873. His father Thomas Gilmore Apple (1829-1898) married Emma Matilda Miller (1827-1921) in 1851. He was the youngest of their 11 children. His last name was explained as Saxon (German), and a variation of "Adelbod, Adbold, Appold, Appel, Apel, and Apple," which his father told him "meant "a bold, noble man, who roved – honorably"."

He traced his European ancestry to John Peter Appel who immigrated to America "in 1733 from the Palatinate in the Upper Rhine district of Germany, near Switzerland." His ancestor settled with "his wife and three children" on a "250-acre farm" in eastern Pennsylvania, then called "Bucks county." An Irish lineage was added when Thomas "Tommy" Gilmore immigrated from Belfast in 1770. Tommy fought in the American Revolutionary War and rode in the boat carrying General George Washington during "his famous crossing of the Delaware." The story was told that Tommy fell overboard, and the good General instructed his men: "Fish him out, he is too good a soldier to lose." Thereafter, Tommy married Rachel Young. Their daughter Elizabeth married his grandfather Andrew Appel. They were both "zealous church-folk." Elizabeth was "a strong Lutheran" and his Uncle Theodore described her as having a "florid face, fair complexion, [and] full of Irish sensibilities." To the contrary, Andrew was "a strong Reformed" and "a miller" (an operator of a grain mill). Eventually the family united within the Reformed religion. Andrew had a soft heart and ignored stern neighborly advice "to put his boys out to work – "bind them out"." Instead, he insisted upon educating his children even "if it took the last coat on his back (and my uncle comments "in fact, he did not have many coats")."

Appel's German Reformist heritage explains the ecumenical flair of his *Ten Commandments of Advertising* that underpinned the early Bureau. The early advertising industry was brimming with patriotic Puritan zealots, temperance activists, teachers, and preachers representing generations of European immigrants. Many were German Reformers espousing strict Christian principles in keeping with Appel's code of business ethics that fueled the Truth in Advertising Movement, *Printers' Ink* Model Statute, and Vigilance Committee.

German immigrants played an integral part of American history participating in the American Revolutionary War and the Civil War. European settlers represented a growing grassroots vote in mid-1800; there were 130,000 German Americans in the state of Illinois. After the 1858 Lincoln/Douglas debates, that resulted in Douglas's re-election to the Senate, Lincoln bought the German newspaper *Illinois Staats-Anzeiger* in May 1859. It was an exceptional strategy that cut through language and political barriers. Readership was mostly Democrat, but Lincoln gained their trust and converted many into Republican voters by communicating in their native language.

Theologian, professor, and monk Martin Luther (1483-1546), born in Eisleben, Saxony, (Holy Roman Empire at the time) ignited the Protestant Reformation through his *Ninety-five Theses* that was introduced on October 31, 1517. As a result, the Dutch and German Reformed Churches in Europe separated from the Roman Catholic Church. In the 1700s, the German Reformers began immigrating to America and settled in Philadelphia. Appel reflected, "The age was full of religious fervor." Accordingly, his grandfather Andrew had three sons who became preachers.

His father, Thomas, grew up in Easton, Pennsylvania, and was the youngest of 13 children and "the seventh son in regular order without any break by the intrusion of a daughter – this was considered a good omen." In 1840, at the age of 11, his parents moved west to Saegerstown, PA, but returned to Easton five years later where Thomas attended "the classical school of the Rev. Dr. John Vanderveer." By 1850, he was studying theology at Marshall College located in Mercersburg, PA. His graduation was implied in 1852 when he was ordained a minister of the Reformed Church and "took charge of Dr. Vanderveer's school." Then, in 1865, he was "appointed president of Mercersburg College that had taken over the buildings of Marshall College (founded in 1836), when it moved in 1853 to Lancaster, Pa., to unite with Franklin College (founded by Benjamin Franklin in 1787) under the name Franklin and Marshall." Thomas emerged a scholar and influential Reformer serving as president of Mercersburg College from 1865 to 1871; professor in the Theological Seminary of the Reformed Church in the United States at Lancaster from 1871 to 1898; and, president of Franklin & Marshall College from 1877 to 1889. He was also "a long time editor of the *Reformed Church Review*."

Appel attended Mercersburg College in Lancaster the same time his father was its president; he graduated around 1892. Then, he studied law as an apprentice for three years in his "brother's office" and passed a board review to be "sworn in as a full-fledged lawyer." Appel acknowledged that his "first law-case before a jury was pretty nearly my last case. I wasn't destined to be a lawyer and I soon discovered it. I was appointed by the Court to defend a man charged with theft. He wasn't much of a man and I wasn't much of a lawyer. We made a good team." Consequently, Appel lost the case; word spread resulting in painfully slow business over the following six months. His life drastically changed when a lawyer friend asked him, "[W]ant a newspaper job – on McClure's *Times* in Philadelphia?" It paid $20 a week. He took the job and never practiced law again.

He started as "State Editor" and his duty "was to read all the State newspaper exchanges, make clippings, and prepare a column for each morning's *Times* on "State Politics"." Additionally, he held positions as "city editor, telegraph editor, news editor, foreign editor, editorial writer, night editor." Appel worked for McClure's *Times* for four years. In 1899, at the age of 26, he noticed a store's advertising and wrote the owner offering advice on how to improve the ad copy. He also explained that he was about to marry and was looking for a new job to better his life. His missive ended, "I feel confident that I can give a new impetus to the advertising end of your store and desire a chance to explain my views in person. Kindly reply at your earliest convenience." Appel reflected that "the reply came at once," and commanded, "Come and see me."

The owner was John Wanamaker, after his tenure as postmaster general for President Harrison. Appel accepted Wanamaker's job offer as "a writer of advertising" that led to advertising manager of the copy department. It would be his last job that lasted 35 years. He knew how to write newspaper advertising, but quickly learned that store advertising was different: "In advertising one must first attract an audience – by sheer force of personality pluck them out of the busy world and make them read." He offered his secret to advertising success as "find the vital point in the story to be told; tell it in short sentences; stop."

Appel reflected on the Bureau expanding into "consumer education" that influenced modern programs. He quoted Kenner in December 1939: "Better Business Bureaus have been interested in consumer education for more than twenty-five years .... The first Better Business Bureau was established nearly twenty-six years ago. Consumer-service, to adults particularly, in the sense of protection against misrepresentation of merchandise, securities and service, has been basic to the work of these organizations always. These voluntary agencies of business are now active in the public interest in 63 of the principal cities of the United States and Canada. More are being established."

He appreciated science and inventors for their contribution to creature comfort, national prosperity, and giving him a job: "I am strongly for all new inventions and products of science and research that lighten human burdens and bring more happiness to all the people. I have advertised all my business life to present these new products to the people, urging them to buy for their own good." He also worried, though, that the technological revolution happened too quickly and that regulation of advertising had not caught up with false advertisers: "The misuse of scientific authority in supporting advertised products, or their use, is another evil which it is more difficult to watch, because of the lack of technical knowledge on the part of publishers." As an example, he referred to a Bureau bulletin: "In New York the misuse of advertising became so flagrant that the Better Business Bureau issued a special bulletin on the subject in 1931." The Bureau's sanctimonious bulletins proved ludicrously hypocritical the following year when Kenner and the New York Bureau were charged with securities fraud and racketeering by the U.S. Senate. Of course, Appel glossed-over respective corruption in his book despite the Bureau's direct involvement in history's most notorious and catastrophic chapter that caused untold deaths, immeasurable heartache, and historical Wall Street reform. Furthermore, it is interesting to note that wherein Appel protected the Bureau, he threw the FTC under the bus: "The Federal Trade Commission itself doubts whether it has actual legislative authority to issue rules and regulations in the form of a guide." Appel wrote his comments in 1940 and his blatant disparity indicated the Bureau's growing power over and above federal agencies. In fact, a year later, the Bureau was inducted into FDR's Deep State.

Appel discussed attending the 1929 convention, held in Berlin, Germany, when the Associated Advertising Clubs of the World changed to "Advertising Federation of America." It was another name change that embraced international appeal just like the first convention held in Toronto, Canada, in 1914, when the name changed from Associated Advertising Clubs of America to Associated Advertising Clubs of the World. The advertising industry and Bureau pursued global aspirations. The Bureau eagerly promoted international relations with "advertising organizations in Canada, Great Britain and Continental Europe."

While in Berlin, Appel brought up "disparagement of competitors" relevant to German law defined as "reference to the merchandise of a competitor as inferior." Several examples included "distributing business cards in front of a place of business of a competitor." Appel's clarification of defamation remarkably highlighted the modern Bureau and its monopolizing programs that are bias, disparaging, and based on pay-for-play extortion. Recent Bureau exposés have proven disparagement and filmed operatives pandering higher ratings scores for membership fees.

Appel complimented European countries for their progressive regulation of advertising fraud and wrote, "It thus appears that Germany and Great Britain were in step with, and perhaps ahead of, the United States in regulating advertising." He referred to the Pure Food and Drug Act of 1906, but noted that it was "inadequate, against fraudulent advertising." He also mentioned the *Printers'*

Ink Model Statute "that makes it a misdemeanor to advertise "any assertion, representation or statement of fact which is untrue, deceptive or misleading"."

In 1949, the advertising legend joined eternity at the age of 76. Appel's trailblazing contributions to the advertising industry, consumer advocacy, and ethical business practice are historic. He was a prolific writer and published numerous books including *Golden Book of the Wanamaker Stores* published in 1911; *The Business Biography of John Wanamaker* published in 1930; and *Growing Up With Advertising* published in April 1940. The latter 1940 publication reflected his enthusiastic advertising and mentoring persona, "Get this book – it's got what everybody should know about advertising – some very important history and data, a lot of wise counsel, many sounder-than-ever principles. I want the whole staff to read it – must!" Shockingly, he is not listed in the American Advertising Federation's Hall of Fame. Appel especially deserves enshrinement considering he wrote the *Ten Commandments of Advertising* that sparked the Truth in Advertising Movement and established the Better Business Bureau.

Appel connected ecumenical fervor with consumer advocacy and why Kenner described the 1911 Boston convention as having an "evangelistic spirit" with "more than a hundred advertising clubs" as "truth fires burst into brilliant flames." The Bureau originated from one of those advertising clubs coined a "truth fire" and why its logo is a torch representing everlasting truth.

Appel acknowledged his participation in and importance of advertising history: "It is always hard for one generation to understand another. Crusading for truth in advertising seemed natural back in 1911 when the Associated Advertising Clubs held their convention in Boston. We were going to save advertising. Advertising was going to save business. Business was going to save the world. Fervor, and moral and even religious zeal, was apparent in our speeches."

CHAPTER 12

DR. HARVEY WASHINGTON WILEY

Dr. Harvey Washington Wiley
Chief Chemist Department of Agriculture (FDA) from 1883 to 1912; father of Pure Food and Drug Act 1906; artist: Caryn Cain.

Few offered his exemplary courage, knowledge, and tenacity to fight an uphill battle of corruption during an era of robber barons who controlled the purse strings of Congress. The esteemed Dr. Wiley was considered the "Father of the FDA" and was a renowned consumer advocate, scientist, writer, and chemist. His relentless pursuit of truth and unadulterated food and drugs resulted in regulation of the food and pharmaceutical industries, influenced legislation in the advertising industry, and first warned that smoking caused cancer.

Dr. Wiley inadvertently lit the fuse that ignited a chain reaction of explosive events that forged advertising history. His Pure Food and Drug Act pressed federal charges against Coca-Cola and inspired Samuel Dobbs to join the AACA, which supported Joseph Appel's *Ten Commandments of Advertising* and launched the Truth in Advertising Movement that triggered John Romer's *Printers' Ink* Model Statute and begat the Vigilance Committee, which became the Better Business Bureau. Dr. Wiley polished and refined the Pure Food and Drug Act through the *Barrels and Kegs Case* trial that cemented a lifetime relationship between Coca-Cola and CBBB.

The late 1800s and early 1900s offered no effective laws for food, drugs, or advertising. Accordingly, Dr. Wiley and the advertising industry introduced prosecutorial legislation. Dr. Wiley recognized the harmful impact of adulterated food production on consumer health as a result of the Progressive Era's profiteering industrial revolution enabled by dubious canning procedures and use of preservatives. He forced safe and responsible manufacturing by imposing the Pure Food and Drug Act that regulated ingredients and labeling.

According to the FDA, "All through the 1880s and 1890s, pure-food bills were introduced into Congress--largely through his work--and all were killed." Influential lobbies representing "the food and patent-medicine industries" controlled Congress and astoundingly supported gross corruption despite increasing nefarious results. The Civil War, ignorant doctors, quacks, and Big Pharma created widespread morphine, opium, and laudanum addiction. Additionally, the meatpacking industry produced contaminated meat that was also shipped to U.S. troops during the Spanish-American War; Lieutenant Colonel Theodore Roosevelt and the 1st United States Volunteer Cavalry, "The Rough Riders," were among the soldiers eating such putrid food.

Harvey Washington Wiley was born on October 18, 1844, "in a log farmhouse" and raised on an "antebellum country farm" near Kent, Jefferson County, Indiana. His parents were "Preston Prichard Wiley" (1810-1895) and "Lucinda Weir Maxwell" (1809-1893). The Wiley family "strictly observed Sundays" as members of the Disciples of Christ Church. Fishing was considered a "heinous sin," which probably fueled Dr. Wiley's conversion to a self-admitted agnostic. Wiley's father was "a lay preacher" and "local schoolteacher" who emphasized caution, "Be sure you are right and then go ahead," as well as steadfast bravery that supports "a righteous cause in the face of ridicule." His father was also anti-slavery and ostracized for his beliefs; Dr. Wiley continued his father's abolitionist principles.

In 1863, at the age of 18, Dr. Wiley attended Hanover College, but left in the spring to join the Indiana State troops. The following year, he served in Sherman's Army as "a corporal in Company I of the 137th Regiment Indiana Volunteers"; he was "discharged as ill a year later" having contracted "hookworm." He returned to Hanover College that following spring and in 1867 graduated top of his class; he also earned an "A.M. degree" ("AB" was a graduate degree; "AM" a post-graduate degree similar to a "Masters" or "MBA") from Hanover in 1870. Wiley taught "Latin and Greek" to cover school expenses and earned a medical degree from Indiana Medical College in 1871. In the 1800s, students were required to known Latin and Greek to pass college entrance exams and Dr. Wiley taught such preparatory classes. Between 1872 and 1873, he engaged "post-graduate studies" at Harvard University entering "as a freshman, took seventeen days' continuous examination and became a senior"; he graduated with a B.S. degree three months later.

From 1872 to 1873, he was a professor of chemistry at Butler University in Indianapolis, Indiana. And from 1873 to 1876, he taught chemistry at Indiana Medical College. Dr. Wiley diverted a promising medical practice by entering teaching. Accordingly, "from 1874 to 1883," he accepted a professorship in chemistry with Purdue University, "founded on May 6, 1869," and located in West Lafayette, Indiana, which included "the post of Chief Chemist to the State of Indiana." Additionally, he served "as a professor of physics and military science" at Purdue University from 1876 to1880. He was awarded numerous honorary degrees "including a Ph.D. from Hanover College in 1873, a LL.D. from Hanover in 1898, and a LL.D. in 1911 from the University of Vermont."

While continuing to teach as a professor at Purdue in 1878, at the age of 34, he left for extended studies in Europe. Dr. Wiley was introduced to "the Polariscope" and its amazing analytical abilities. He explored the chemistry of sugar at the Imperial Food Laboratory in Bismarck, Germany, and was a member of the distinguished German Chemical Society. He returned to Purdue and convinced the university to purchase a Polariscope whereby he commenced his investigations into adulterated foods. As a result, Dr. Wiley submitted to the Indiana State Board of Health "the first reports ever made to a State board in the United States." His main interest was to develop a strong "domestic" sugar industry within the United States. Consequently, he wrote a paper in 1881 regarding the "adulteration of sugar with glucose" that represented a precursor to the Pure Food and Drug Act of 1906.

In 1882, Dr. Wiley was offered the position of chief chemist at the Bureau of Chemistry, now known as the Department of Agriculture, "by George Loring, the Commissioner of Agriculture." He accepted the position in 1883 after being snubbed as president of Purdue because he was ""too young and too jovial," unorthodox in his religious beliefs, and also a bachelor." Dr. Wiley was an imposing six feet tall. He dressed and acted like a preacher and was called "Father Wiley" and "preacher of purity." He was a scientific genius and acted unconventional with "a flair for the dramatic." In the modern generation, his noted "infractions" would be deemed aggressively commonplace; for instance, "at Purdue he had been officially reprimanded for riding a bicycle on campus, and in Washington he was the third man to drive a car, the first to suffer a collision."

In 1902, Dr. Wiley organized what was coined the "Poison Squad" composed of "a dozen young men in his department" who "volunteered to eat nothing but what he gave them." The Poison Squad was housed in a boarding area of the agricultural building and for five years Dr. Wiley supervised the food fed to the men. He added various amounts of "borax, benzoate, formaldehyde, sulfites, and salicylates" to the men's meals, which were the same preservatives that manufacturers claimed were "harmless." In 1907, he published his "Squad" results in a 2,000-page pamphlet; it was the same year that the Coca-Cola came under U.S. government scrutiny for misbranding and adulterated foods. Such work facilitated his crusade for pure food and Dr. Wiley became widely respected by consumers. The Franklin Institute awarded Dr. Wiley the Elliott Cresson Gold Medal in 1910, its highest award, for "some discovery in the Arts and Sciences, or for the invention or improvement of some useful machine, or for some new process or combination of materials in manufactures, or for ingenuity skill or perfection in workmanship."

In 1905, Dr. Wiley approached social activist Alice Lakey (1857-1935), the president of the women's "Cranford Village Improvement Association's Domestic Science Unit," for assistance in passing pure-food legislation. Ms. Lakey was also in charge of the Pure Food Committee of the National Consumers League. That same year, she and Dr. Wiley met privately with President Theodore Roosevelt and lobbied him to enact a pure-food law. He told them he would sign the law if they could convince Congress to approve it. Consequently, Ms. Lakey approached the Cranford Village and the New Jersey Federation of Women's Clubs and submitted "over one million" letters to Congress demanding passage of the Pure Food and Drug Act. Ms. Lakey was recorded in the National Archives and "the first woman to be listed in *Who's Who*."

Also, in 1905, author Upton Sinclair published his fictional novel, *The Jungle*, as a serial in *The Appeal to Reason* socialist newspaper, to expose immigration abuse. The following year, *The Jungle* was released in book form and shocked the nation with its gross exposé of meatpacking atrocities that changed history.

On February 21, 1906, unprecedented fallout from the women's temperance movement, *The Jungle*, and Dr. Wiley's long-term scientific experiments convinced Congress to pass the Pure Food and Drug Act. Dr. Wiley was guest of honor and sat in the U.S. Senate's "balcony" to witness the epic moment that President Theodore Roosevelt signed the act into law "on June 30, 1906." Mandates required "testing all foods and drugs destined for human consumption"; "prescriptions from licensed physicians before a patient could purchase certain drugs"; and "label warnings on habit-forming drugs." Whereas regulation of advertising fraud was not included, the act instigated "unintended consequences" that fatefully launched the advertising industry's Truth in Advertising Movement, which ultimately begat the Better Business Bureau.

The FDA conceded that the act was "largely written" by Dr. Wiley and why President Roosevelt ordered respective enforcement under his jurisdiction. In 1909, Dr. Wiley issued an indictment against Coca-Cola for violation of the act.

THE APO$TATE

Dr. Wiley was considered a "chemical fundamentalist" and one of the first consummate consumer advocates for truth in advertising. He knew a law was required to override rampant fraud and enforce consumer protection. The pure food law did not forbid poisonous ingredients, but ingredients were required on labels. At the time the law was enacted, caffeine was not listed by the government as a "poisonous substance." Coca-Cola felt safe in the fact that caffeine was already being used in tea and that its fountain soda, which contained caffeine, would withstand the same scrutiny. To the contrary, Dr. Wiley determined a distinct difference between tea and Coca-Cola and believed the public was being deceived. It was common knowledge that caffeine was an ingredient in tea, but caffeine was natural to tea. Otherwise, caffeine was an added ingredient of Coca-Cola and was being disingenuously promoted as a wholesome drink and sold to children. Coca-Cola was also advertising that its soda was ""guaranteed" under the pure food law." Dr. Wiley warned Coca-Cola to stop disingenuous advertising or he would cancel the company's "serial number." On February 28, 1907, Dr. Wiley harshly responded to a brown-nosing letter from Coca-Cola by waving a foreboding red flag within his message that warned the company's imminent investigation: "I have heard many complaints of the Coca-Cola habit."

Thereafter, in 1907, and prior to Coca-Cola's indictment, Dr. Wiley approached suffragist Martha Meir Allen to join his campaign against misbranded and adulterated foods. In fact, that same year, Allen brazenly met with Coca-Cola's Sales Manager Samuel Dobbs who acted as point man to discuss the women's temperance movement's complaint that its soda contained alcohol and caffeine; Dobbs lost his temper while she remained cool as a cucumber.

"On February 27, 1911," at the age of 66, longtime-bachelor Dr. Wiley married Anna Campbell Kelton (1877-1964) in Washington, D.C. They had two sons, Harvey Washington Wiley Jr. (born May 16, 1912; died 1951) and John Preston Wiley (born February 26, 1914).

The following month, on March 13, 1911, the *Barrels and Kegs Case* trial began and evidenced a turbulent roller coaster ride. The first two native-son lower court decisions were rendered in Coca-Cola's favor, but ultimate ruling was overturned by the U.S. Supreme Court in 1916. Coca-Cola settled out of court in 1917. As a result, Dr. Wiley's efforts were vindicated and the caffeine content in Coca-Cola's formula was lowered.

After the first controversial Coca-Cola trial ended in government defeat in 1911, Dr. Wiley resigned from the FDA on "March 15, 1912." Despite 29 years of dedicated service, Dr. Wiley confronted mounting criticism from longtime congressional and governmental adversaries angry with his handling of the Coca-Cola trial. He was accused of overpaying a chemist $20 dollars a day instead of the usual $9 per day. President William Howard Taft, 27th POTUS from 1909-1913, supported Dr. Wiley, but irreversible damage was done.

Consequently, Dr. Wiley became the director of the Bureau of Foods, Sanitation and Health for the *Good Housekeeping* Institute Laboratories in Washington, D.C., serving from 1912 to 1930. Dr. Wiley had previous history with *Good Housekeeping* and wrote medical articles for its magazine to promote the passage of the Pure Food and Drug Act. In November 1901, he published the article, "Injurious Food Adjuncts: The Part Played by Salicylic Acid in the Preservation of Foods and its Danger." And, in January 1902, he wrote, "Injurious Food Adjuncts: Formaldehyde or Formalin, Which Sometimes Gets Into Infants' Food, and Oftentimes Into Milk and Cream."

Prior to the passage of the Pure Food and Drug Act, *Good Housekeeping* aggressively pursued pure-food legislation. In October 1901, the institute announced it was "launching a national campaign for a national pure food law." Then, in October 1905, the institute introduced "the *Good Housekeeping* Standard of Excellence for Pure Food Products." Interestingly, though, the institute focused on pure food and "rarely addressed the problem of drug purity" and never discussed alcohol. So Dr. Wiley's merger with *Good Housekeeping* was a timely and progressive stepping stone.

Good Housekeeping also incorporated the women's movement in its pure food campaign prior to the enactment of the 19th Amendment and women's right to vote. Women's clubs around the country represented a powerful movement throughout the 1800s. In the early 1900s, local temperance groups galvanized and lobbied Congress to pass pure-food legislation. Dr. Wiley was given ultimate credit for "mobilizing the women's groups" that included the Women's Christian Temperance Union (WTCU) and the General Federation of Women's Clubs.

At *Good Housekeeping*, Dr. Wiley continued to pursue groundbreaking industrial standards. Landmark consumer-oriented legislation and awareness programs were introduced including the renowned *Good Housekeeping* "Tested and Approved" brand seal as "the coveted symbol of responsible industry." Dr. Wiley's tenure at *Good Housekeeping* produced numerous contributions. He wrote 14 books including a collaborative article written with Anne Lewis Pierce entitled, "Swindled Getting Slim," which exposed fraudulent and dangerous cures for obesity. He was also responsible for the enactment of the Maternity Bill in 1921 that curbed the rising infant mortality rate by providing federal funding for "improved infant care." Additionally, in 1927, he was the first to warn that tobacco-related products promoted cancer. His efforts and "mounting evidence" influenced *Good Housekeeping* magazine's decision to discontinue cigarette advertisements in 1952. The U.S. Surgeon General issued a report in 1964 validating Dr. Wiley's cancer warnings.

Dr. Wiley's wife, Anna, was a renowned suffragist and grew up in Oakland, California. Her father was Brigadier General John C. Kelton. Anna won "the Kendal Scholarship to George Washington University" and graduated with a Bachelor of

Science degree in 1897. A year later, she worked as a "secretary to Dr. Wiley" when he was at the Department of Agriculture in Washington, D.C. In 1900, while Dr. Wiley was overseas in Paris, Anna traded her job with the Department of Agriculture for a position at the Library of Congress. Ten years later, destiny brought them back together through serendipitous meeting "on a streetcar." Dr. Wiley told Anna that he carried her picture in his watch since their first meeting, which led to their marriage. Six years later, in November 1917, Mrs. Wiley picketed the White House with 40 other suffragists and was arrested for "obstructing traffic"; she defiantly served a total of 20 days in jail and refused a pardon in order to accompany another suffragist also sentenced to jail for picketing. Mrs. Wiley "served six terms as chairman of the National Woman's party" and continued her efforts on behalf of women's rights after the passage of the 19th Amendment.

Dr. Wiley suffered from heart disease the last year of his life but continued working "with unfailing interest and remarkable vitality." On January 1, 1930, he retired from *Good Housekeeping* and remained "director-emeritus." Then, on June 3, 1930, Dr. Wiley made his last public appearance before a "Congressional committee at a hearing called by the Senate Committee of Agriculture and Forestry to investigate the drug section of the law."

At 2:30 a.m., June 30, 1930, on the 24th anniversary of the Pure Food and Drug Act, Dr. Wiley passed away at his home in Washington, D.C., at the age of 85. The day surely reminded and overwhelmed Dr. Wiley of his lingering animus towards President Theodore Roosevelt for taking credit for the Pure Food and Drug Act that he spent years researching and promoting. Mrs. Wiley remained by his side until death historically welcomed him. Dr. Wiley was scheduled to be buried at Rock Creek Cemetery in Washington, but instead was honored with a "patriot's funeral" at Arlington National Cemetery, Arlington County, Virginia ("Find A Grave" memorial 6619).

Mrs. Wiley's pursuit of women's rights and her participation in the woman suffrage movement undoubtedly influenced Dr. Wiley's affiliation with the temperance movement. Nevertheless, he had always shown special attention to families and healthy foods during his tenures at the FDA as well as at the *Good Housekeeping* Institute. As a result, mothers across the United States held Dr. Wiley in the highest regard. When he left the FDA, a prominent headline read, "WOMEN WEEP AS WATCHDOG OF THE KITCHEN QUITS AFTER 29 YEARS."

On January 6, 1964, at the age of 86, Mrs. Wiley passed away at her home in Washington, D.C., and was interred next to her husband in Arlington National Cemetery. Anna faithfully promoted women's rights and Dr. Wiley's pure-food crusade until her death.

CHAPTER **13**

UPTON SINCLAIR AND THE JUNGLE

Upton Beall Sinclair Jr. (right, beige suit)
Author of *The Jungle* that begat the Pure Food and Drug Act 1906.
Photo by Bain News Service, dated May 4, 1914.
Source: Library of Congress, Control Number 2014696036;
[https://www.loc.gov/resource/ggbain.16059]; public domain.

He was a Socialist and left-wing subversive of his day. He published *The Jungle* to highlight the disgusting working conditions of impoverished immigrants, but, instead, highlighted meatpacking atrocities. As a result, meat sales were cut in half; and the other half apparently did not read his book. In October 1906, Sinclair responded to public ad nauseam in *Cosmopolitan Magazine* and wrote, "I aimed at the public's heart, and by accident I hit it in the stomach."

Federal intervention resulted in two simultaneous laws that same year; the Meat Inspection Act and the Pure Food and Drug Act. President Theodore Roosevelt, 26th POTUS from 1901 to 1909, was already in the midst of promoting a reformist agenda with Congress and previously approached to enact pure-food laws by Dr. Harvey Washington Wiley, Alice Lakey and the women's temperance movement, and *Good Housekeeping* magazine.

Upton Beall Sinclair Jr. was born on September 20, 1878, in Baltimore, Maryland, to parents Upton Beall Sinclair and Priscilla Harden. His father was an alcoholic fueled by his vocation as an alcohol salesman countered by his mother who was a strict Episcopalian opposed to alcohol and caffeine, which aligned with the women's temperance movement that gained traction after the Civil War; all of which turned Sinclair into an avowed agnostic. His parents were poor, but came from wealthy families, which influenced Sinclair's commitment to socialism. The family moved to Queens, New York. At the age of 14, he enrolled at City College of New York on September 15, 1892. He supported his parents and paid for his college tuition by writing "jokes, dime novels, and magazine articles in boys' weekly and pulp magazines," which the trades referred to as "hack writing." In 1897, he graduated from City College at the age of 18. Then, he enrolled at Columbia University to study law and taught himself "Spanish, German and French"; he left after two years because socialism was excluded. Sinclair switched vocation to a "serious novelist" and published four books in four years: "*King Midas* (1901), *Prince Hagen* (1902), *The Journal of Arthur Stirling* (1903), and a Civil War novel titled *Manassas* (1904)."

After publishing *Manassas*, a life-changing event converted Sinclair into a consumer advocate. In 1904, a strike broke out involving "twenty thousand workers in the meat-packing plants of Chicago." The strike, composed mostly of foreign workers, was broken up leaving their respective unions "paralyzed" and forcing them back to unabated horrid conditions. Sinclair was distraught by a newspaper headline questioning, "YOU HAVE LOST THE STRIKE: AND NOW WHAT ARE YOU GOING TO DO ABOUT IT?" Sinclair identified with their plight and contemplated, "What I told the strikers to do was to vote the Socialist ticket, but that didn't seem enough. I had the impulse to go out to Chicago, gather the material, and make that labor struggle the subject of a novel." Accordingly, Sinclair approached publishers of *The Appeal to Reason*, which he described as a "weekly four-page paper" and "hard-fighting organ of the Socialist movement," to advance "a little money for the serial rights." He then went undercover and spent seven weeks in various meatpacking plants to gather comprehensive research for *The Jungle* with his main "source of information" being "the strike leaders and rebel workers"; *The Appeal to Reason* began publishing each completed chapter in weekly episodes.

The Jungle's main characters were Lithuanian immigrants named Jurgis Rudkus and Ona Lukoszaite, his teenage wife. Rudkus worked at a Chicago meatpacking factory and his storyline revealed the sordid atrocities and unsanitary conditions that Sinclair personally witnessed. Sinclair explained that he

UPTON SINCLAIR AND THE JUNGLE

found his characters by crashing a Lithuanian wedding party: "I had everything but the characters for my story, when late one Sunday afternoon I was strolling past a saloon and saw a carriage draw up alongside a dance hall in back. A bride and bridegroom got out, followed by families and guests ... It was a Lithuanian family, and friends of the couple told me about them, including their names."

Sinclair contacted George P. Brett, president of the Macmillan Company and publisher of *Manassas*, to publish *The Jungle*. Brett found *The Jungle* to be too gory and Sinclair was offered publication only if he removed offensive "blood and guts." Sinclair refused. Then, "three or four" additional publishers also declined publication. Destiny stepped in when Sinclair was about to publish *The Jungle* via a pre-order book deal with *The Appeal to Reason*. He was approached for as-is publication by Dr. Sherman Herbert Houston, vice president of Doubleday, Page & Company.

President Theodore Roosevelt received a copy of *The Jungle* from Sinclair and invited the brazen 27-year-old Sinclair to the White House for lunch. Roosevelt's secretary told Sinclair "that he had been receiving a hundred letters a day about the book, urging him to investigate." Powerful special interests and food lobbies controlled Congress, which previously impeded reformation efforts particularly by the FDA's Dr. Wiley. This time, though, public outrage required immediate action. The luncheon was staged as a precursor to legislation with the president accompanied by his "kitchen cabinet." Roosevelt opened conversation by denouncing corrupt meatpackers: "Mr. Sinclair, you don't have to tell me about those packers. I had to eat the meat they prepared for the Army in Cuba." In fact, the food was so bad that Roosevelt financed shipment of supplemental food to feed his Rough Riders.

During the luncheon, Roosevelt enlightened Sinclair regarding his personal battles with "the United States Senate over some of his reform measures." Roosevelt angrily pounded the "luncheon table" and named several senators impeding his efforts while divulging "their political and financial connections." Sinclair noted that Roosevelt never mentioned confidentiality and determined that "Teddy" wanted him to respectively inform the public.

After the luncheon, Roosevelt dispatched his aides to verify Sinclair's story. "Neill and McReynolds" visited the stockyards and corroborated all except one of Sinclair's claims. He wrote, "They had only one uncertainty to report; they had not been able to verify my statement that men who had fallen into lard vats had gone out to the world as Armour's pure leaf lard. I had already warned them that when that happened the families were paid off and shipped back to Lithuania, or whatever European land they had come from."

Sinclair understood that "[Roosevelt's] representatives now wanted the story told but wanted the responsibility to rest on me." He approached C. V. Van Anda, the managing editor of *The New York Times*, to publish

213

THE APO$TATE

Roosevelt's denouncement of discussed senators and his demands for "desperately-needed reforms" in connection with meatpacking complaints. Van Anda jumped on Sinclair's inside presidential scoop telling staffers "*Stop the presses!*" Sinclair's exposé became the next morning's front page headline and declared, "PRESIDENT'S AIDES TALK." The article circulated around the globe and particularly benefited English meatpacking plants that had been at odds with American packers. Adolphe Smith, an "English specialist on the subject of meat packing," and a former stockyard informant for Sinclair, referred the article to *The Lancet*, a prestigious English medical journal. The British were familiar with *The Jungle*, which was distributed in London. In fact, Winston Churchill, as a "newly elected member of Parliament," wrote "a two-part review of the book" in *T. P.'s Weekly* that partly advised, "Let me say at once that people have no right to hold their noses and shut their eyes. If these things are true, all honour to him who has the power and skill to fasten worldwide attention upon them."

Consequently, Sinclair became an international author; he proudly reflected, "*The Jungle* became a best-selling novel in America over a period of many months. It has been translated and published serially and in book form in some sixty languages." He also humbly accepted credit for empowering unions and acknowledged, "Their leaders have paid tribute to *The Jungle*." Sinclair published a subsequent article in *Everybody's Magazine* whereby he presented "a list of the cases where in various states Mr. J. Ogden Armour had pleaded guilty and paid fines for having put on the market cans of foods containing adulterants and preservatives prohibited by law."

The Jungle brought Sinclair fame and fortune. He used the funds to indulge his communist fantasy. In October 1906, he founded a commune in Englewood, New Jersey, called the Helicon Home Colony, which burned down six months later, in March 1907. In the 1920s, Sinclair and his second wife, Mary Craig, moved to Monrovia, California, outside of Los Angeles, where he lived for almost 40 years while engaging government and Hollywood. Sinclair was a "staunch communist" and promoted socialist politics. Most notably, he "founded the state's chapter of the American Civil Liberties Union." He represented the Socialist Party and unsuccessfully pursued public office: in 1920, for the U.S. House of Representatives; in 1922, for the U.S. Senate; and, in 1930, for governor of California. Unlike today's radical Left, the early-1900's Democratic Party denigrated Sinclair and labeled him a "Red" and "crackpot." Additionally, Sinclair "wrote and produced several films" including *The Jungle* (1914), *Oil!* (1927), *The Wet Parade* (1932), and *The Gnomobile* (1937).

Sinclair was a prolific writer and wrote a total of 86 books. In 1942, he published *Dragon's Teeth* (1930's Nazi Germany) for which he won "the Pulitzer Prize for Fiction" in 1943. His last book was *The Autobiography of Upton Sinclair*, published in 1962. But I believe that Sinclair's most poignant achievement came in 1965, when he wrote the foreword for his reprint of *The Jungle*, which was a unique threescore milestone that rightfully boasted, "I have the experience of writing about one of my own books sixty years after it was published." His publications and other works are housed at the Lilly Library at Indiana University.

He was married three times and fathered one son. His first wife was Meta Fuller, from 1902 to 1911; second wife Mary Craig Kimbrough, from 1913 to 1961; and third wife Mary Elizabeth Willis, from 1961 to 1967. Sinclair was longtime estranged from son, David, by his first wife; they reconciled in 1962. Thereafter, in 1967, he and Mary Willis moved into a nursing home in Bound Brook, New York, to be near David; Mary died that same year. On November 25, 1968, Sinclair passed away at the age of 90. He was interred next to Mary Willis in Rock Creek Cemetery in Washington, D.C.

CHAPTER **14**

DR. HERBERT SHERMAN HOUSTON

Dr. Herbert Sherman Houston
Member of First Vigilance Committee; president of AACW;
vice president Doubleday, Page & Company; artist: Caryn Cain.

He published *The Jungle* for Upton Sinclair in 1906 when no one else would and changed advertising history. As a founder of the Truth in Advertising Movement, he participated "in organized advertising for 40 years." He was also a member of the "first board of directors" for the experimental Vigilance Committee of the Advertising Club of New York that opened on March 12, 1912, as the regulatory division of the AACA underwritten by the NYSE. The AACA evolved into the International AACW under his leadership.

His extensive, multi-faceted, and distinguished career in publishing, consumer reform, and international affairs influenced AACA's global transformation and evolution as an educational foundation. Kenner reflected, "Because many advertisers were not equipped to tell the truth well, and lacked adequate information about the good uses and the art of advertising, the Educational

DR. HERBERT SHERMAN HOUSTON

Committee of the association, headed by enthusiastic Herbert S. Houston of New York, laid out programs by which local clubs might work to increase advertising's productivity."

Herbert Sherman Houston was born on November 23, 1866, in Champaign, Illinois, to parents Major Samuel Houston and Emeline Sherman. According to the "International Motion Picture Almanac 1937-1938," he was listed as "Dr. Herbert S. Houston." The world was his family and there was no indication that he ever married and/or had children. In 1888, he earned a bachelor's in philosophy from the University of South Dakota. He continued studies at the University of Chicago and Boston University. In 1916, he earned a Master of Arts from the University of Pennsylvania. The following year, he was awarded a "Doctor of Laws" from the University of South Dakota.

Dr. Houston had a diverse and distinguished career. "The Diamond of PSI Upsilon" elaborated on Dr. Houston's credentials in the article, "Herbert S. Houston's Recent Trip To The Far East"; he was the city editor of the *Sioux City Journal* (1886 to 1892); city editor of the *Chicago Tribune* (1892 to 1895); city editor of the *Outing Magazine* (1895 to 1900); the vice president of Doubleday, Page & Company (1900 until retirement on November 1, 1921); and the president of the Associated Advertising Clubs of the World, from 1915 to 1916. Thereafter, he parlayed AACW prestige into founding *Houston Publishing*, from 1921 to 1924, which produced two monthly magazines, *Our World* and *World Fiction*. Dr. Houston published *Our World* in coordination with Dr. Wallace W. Atwood, president of Clark University and director of the Institute of International Information; *World Fiction* offered an accumulation of "stories from all languages." Then, from 1924 to 1933, he founded and operated, as president, the Cosmos Newspaper Syndicate as part of the Cosmos Broadcasting Company.

As an original vigilance committee member, Dr. Houston participated heavily in the truth movement as it evolved from the vigilance committees into the Better Business Bureau. Dr. Houston was a guest speaker at the famous 1911 Boston convention that launched the Truth in Advertising Movement; afterwards, he supported Romer's *Printers' Ink* Model Statute. Romer wrote a respective article in *Printers' Ink*, Vol. LXXVII, October 5, 1911, No. 1, entitled, "HOUSTON ADDRESSES AD LEAGUE ON DISHONEST ADVERTISING," and discussed Dr. Houston's speech that endorsed the "Printers' Ink plan." At the time, Romer's attorney, Harry Nims, was still in the process of drafting the statute that was completed on October 25, 1911, and published in the following month's issue of *Printers' Ink*.

Dr. Houston made the publication of *The Jungle* possible. Sinclair was forced to self-publish his book due to contentious subject matter involving Chicago's powerful meatpacking industry; he was struggling to pre-sell book purchases to finance publication when Dr. Houston and Doubleday, Page & Company intervened. Sinclair had no idea how they heard about his book, but Doubleday, Page & Company was a large publishing company with scouts planted throughout the printing industry seeking new talent. As a consummate reformer, Dr. Houston probably felt a connection with *The Jungle*.

While World War I raged, Dr. Houston became immersed in international affairs. He authored *Blocking New Wars* in 1918; participated in "the League to Enforce Peace during World War I"; was a member of the Committee of Chamber of Commerce of the United States on Economic Results of the War; attended the Berlin convention in 1929 where he "headed the department of ethics and honesty in advertising"; delivered a series of addresses in Japan in 1931; presented a war debt settlement plan for the International Chamber of Commerce in May 1931; and served as commissioner of the New York World's Fair of 1939. Dr. Houston was also a director of the Motion Picture Research Council and a member of the Commission on International Justice and Good Will of Federal Council of Churches in America.

Dr. Houston was 89 years old when he passed away on May 16, 1955. He was interred at Christ Church Cemetery in Manhasset, Nassau County, New York (Find A Grave memorial 45566954).

CHAPTER **15**

SAMUEL CANDLER DOBBS

The *United States vs. Forty Barrels and Twenty Kegs of Coca-Cola* trial was the second federal case to test the Pure Food and Drug Act of 1906. Trial started March 13, 1911, and settled out of court in the government's favor on November 12, 1917. The rulings from district court, appellate court, and the U.S. Supreme Court ranged from triumph to tragedy for both parties.

Federal accusations first emerged in February 1907, but an indictment was not delivered until October 21, 1909, when a U.S. inspector confiscated a newly delivered shipment of syrup in Chattanooga. The FDA's Dr. Harvey Wiley sought help from Martha Meir Allen (1854-1926) and the powerful "Women's Christian Temperance Union (W.C.T.U.)," located in Marcellus, New York, which by 1911 boasted 245,299 members. As a result, pre-trial dynamics, intended to endear public opinion and sway the jury pool, inadvertently inspired the truth movement.

Coca-Cola sought control of the advertising industry during pre-trial, from initial indictment in October 1909 to trial commencement in March 1911. The company's timely involvement with the truth movement proved to be a brilliant public relations' maneuver and well-placed investment that effectively countered worldwide bad press and loss of revenue. Additionally, Coca-Cola placed its sales manager, Samuel Dobbs, as the president of the AACA from the summer of 1909 to August 1911 and inadvertently linked Coca-Cola with the historic introduction of the *Printers' Ink* Model Statute as a prosecutable advertising law and the Vigilance Committee as the advertising industry's first regulatory organization to enforce the statute; such legacy established Coca-Cola as a lifetime national sponsor of CBBB and Better Business Bureau.

In 1913, Coca-Cola strategically promoted Sales Manager Dobbs to vice president during the ongoing battle of the *Barrels and Kegs Case* lawsuit. His presidency of the AACA established corporate and personal lifetime connections

219

with the elite of Wall Street and the advertising industry. Dobbs became famous for being famous. His iconic name was bandied as a certification for trustworthy advertising. For example, on January 25, 1919, the AAAA placed an advertorial in the *Associated Advertising* magazine (published by AACW) that partly stated, "Resolved by the Executive Board of the American Association of Advertising Agencies that it comments and approves the activities of the Associated Advertising Clubs of the World and specifically comments and approves the work of the Vigilance Committee directed against fraudulent and hurtful advertising and hereby pledges the moral support of the American Association of Advertising Agencies to the Associated Advertising Clubs of the World in its commendable work for the common welfare: The following important executives serve as trustees: Festus J. Wade, President Mercantile Trust Company, St Louis; F.A. Seiberling, President Goodyear Tire and Rubber Company, Akron; Samuel C. Dobbs, Vice-President Coca-Cola Company, Atlanta; David Kirschbaum, President A.B. Kirschbaum, Philadelphia; Henry L. Doherty, President Henry L. Doherty & Company, New York." In turn, the National Better Business Bureau (CBBB) latched onto Dobbs and Coca-Cola with such relationship continuing today.

In 1916, the U.S. Supreme Court issued a final ruling against Coca-Cola in the *Barrels and Kegs Case* whereafter founder Asa Griggs Candler (1851-1929) turned his attention to politics. Asa was elected 41st mayor of Atlanta and served one term from 1917 to 1919. During this timeframe, Charles Howard Candler Sr. (1878-1957), Asa's eldest son, was president of Coca-Cola and dispatched Dobbs to secure a syndicated buyout offer without Asa's knowledge. On September 12, 1919, The Coca-Cola Company of Georgia became The Coca-Cola Company of Delaware and Dobbs was appointed president. The syndicate included Chase National Bank and the Guaranty Trust Company of New York. Later, Dobbs and the syndicate confronted a 500-strong bottlers' association that sued Coca-Cola regarding contracts and ownership of recipe. In 1920, Dobbs resigned after a tangled rise and abrupt fall from grace. After the Crash, Chase Bank was investigated by the Pecora Commission for "unsound loans to investors and issuers of securities to support the activities of their securities affiliates," which suggested inclusion of Coca-Cola's syndicated buyout. The Pecora Commission's conclusive findings produced the Glass-Steagall Act of 1933, the Securities Act of 1933, and the Securities and Exchange Act of 1934.

Samuel Candler Dobbs was "an illiterate farm boy" born on November 8, 1868, in Carroll County, Villa Rica, Georgia. His father was Harris Henry Dobbs; his mother was Elizabeth Frances Candler Dobbs (1849-1922) and the older sister of Asa Candler. Dobbs' sister was Anna B. Dobbs. When 14 years old, Dobbs "assumed charge" of his family's plantation. At the age of 18, he aggressively pursued employment with A. G. Candler and Company, a listed wholesaler of drugs in Atlanta, Georgia, and became Candler's "first salesman on the road." Two years later, in 1888, Dobbs married Mary Ruth Mixon (born August 8, 1869; died December 9, 1941), the daughter of Dr. and Mrs. R. A. Mixon from LaGrange, Georgia. They had a son, Samuel Candler Dobbs Jr. (1899-1973), whom Dobbs described as "curly-headed, blue-eyed," and a daughter, Mildred Dobbs Bird (1902-1956).

The Dobbs' family home was located in Clayton, Rabun County, on Lake Rabun in the "beautiful north Georgia mountains," which is now listed on Barn Inn Road in Lakemont, Georgia. Dobbs described the area as being a three-hour drive from Atlanta. The area includes the Chattanooga River, Tallulah River, and Coleman River; and, "60% of the land is National Forests and State Parks," according to the Rabun County website.

Current Lake Rabun tourist attractions include *The Barn Inn* that was part of Dobbs' former property and "originally was a horse barn built in 1920 for Samuel Candler Dobbs," but the "barn was converted into an Inn in 1984." *The Barn Inn* website provided respective history: "In 1920 Samuel Candler Dobbs purchased approximately 114 acres along Lake Rabun. Mr. Dobbs built a magnificent Riverstone lakeside home, a guest cottage and at the top of the hill, and a Riverstone and timber horse stable with concrete floors and numerous windows. Mr. Dobbs held the property until his death." A "railroad" used to run through Lakemont and was later removed. The local second-generation owner of "Alley's Grocery," Lamar Alley, 79 years old at the time, described the Samuel Candler Dobbses being delivered to their home by way of the railroad. The grocery store acted as the train depot. It changed ownership in 2008 and reopened in March 2009 as "Annie's at Alley's Market & Deli." Lake Rabun's exquisite countryside and gorgeous lake properties have since become a haven for wealthy Atlantans.

The circumstances surrounding Dobbs' employment by Asa Candler may explain his fierce loyalty and driving ambition to prove himself to his uncle, which was evident throughout his early career. Asa initially rejected Dobbs, but a "black porter, a former Candler family slave" coincidentally, and inexplicably, died the next day and Dobbs eagerly took his position. Thereafter, Dobbs earned Asa's trust. He became a staunch advocate of Coca-Cola and highly successful drummer (traveling salesmen who "drummed up trade").

Asa "gained complete legal control of Coca-Cola" in 1888 and by "the end of 1899," Dobbs became sales manager. Dobbs rose quickly within company ranks as a "general office man, road salesman, credit manager, sales manager, advertising and sales manager, and in 1913 vice-president"; he was credited with developing the popular advertising slogan, "Whenever you see an arrow, think of Coca-Cola." Asa took notice of Dobbs and referred to him as "the brains and beauty of the family."

By 1906, the same year that the Pure Food and Drug Act was enacted, Dobbs butted heads with Frank Mason Robinson (1845-1923), Coca-Cola's advertising and marketing genius. Dobbs was young, arrogant, and brazen and failed to unseat the respected Robinson. After all, Robinson invented Coca-Cola's alliterative name and Spencerian script and worked directly with Dr. John Styth Pemberton, the inventor of Coca-Cola's formula. Robinson made Coca-Cola the most popular drink in America. In 1895, Robinson listened to consumers complaining of its "medicinal image" and began advertising Coca-Cola as a refreshing fountain drink. Robinson orchestrated a smart advertising campaign that sold to the masses and catapulted Coca-Cola to national attention. He opened a new category of sales and "flooded the market" using short, direct ads like, "Drink Coca-Cola. Delicious and Refreshing." Most memorably, Robinson caught America's attention by adding "Coca-Cola girls" as seductive entertainment.

Dobbs unsuccessfully countered Robinson at every opportunity. Robinson called Dobbs' advertising methodology, "flash advertising." In 1908, Dobbs argued against the use of electric signage despite the revolutionary Great White Way that entertained the streets of New York City; declined the use of "special Yiddish signs for Jewish Districts" alienating an important segment of society; downplayed overseas marketing despite Robinson setting up bottling plants in "Cuba, Hawaii, and Puerto Rico," which, by 1909, produced lucrative overseas sales; ignored a pleading English marketer offering "forty-five million people" as waiting customers in England in 1911; and refused "repeated entreaties from foreign firms" in 1915. The ever-humble Robinson prevailed mentoring Dobbs along the way while steering Coca-Cola into national notoriety.

But popularity brought liability; Coca-Cola's success drew the attention and ire of Dr. Harvey Wiley, "Department of Agriculture's chief chemist and first commissioner of the Food and Drug Administration." Coca-Cola was aware of the passage of the Pure Food and Drug Act, also known as "Dr. Wiley's Law." Dobbs "referred" to the act as "pure food cranks" and Asa Candler's youngest brother, Judge John Slaughter Candler (1861-1941), appointed associate justice to the Georgia Supreme Court from 1902 to 1906, "complained of "misguided fanatics"." Nevertheless, Judge Candler convinced his brother, Asa, that the law was inevitable, and Coca-Cola should support it to appear "virtuous" and separate it from "'bad' patent medicines." Accordingly, in 1906, Judge Candler traveled to Washington, D.C., to testify on behalf of the act. After passage, Coca-Cola unleashed a series of respective advertising slogans: "*pure* and wholesome"; "the Great National Temperance Beverage"; "Refreshing as a Summer Breeze"; and "it aids digestion and is genuinely good to the taste." During this time, the formula was changed to remove saccharin because Dr. Wiley considered it an adulterant, but remedial activity also secured his scrutiny.

By 1907, federal inspectors advised Dr. Wiley that "Coca-Cola was a habit-forming menace." Consequently, newspaper headlines predicted a lawsuit, "Dr. Wiley Will Take Up Soda Fountain "Dope"." In fact, Dr. Wiley was quietly piecing together a case against Coca-Cola under the Pure Food and Drug Act. He brought in his renowned "poison squad" composed of 12 young male volunteers. According to the Arlington National Cemetery website, "These famous "poison squad" studies drew national attention to the need for a federal food and drug law." Dr. Wiley methodically tested the effects of 100 drinks advertised on the market that listed among their ingredients "cocaine, caffeine, choral hydrates, or opium." Additionally, Dr. Wiley collaborated with Ms. Allen and the surgeon general of the Army to advertise that Coca-Cola was habit-forming and contained alcohol and cocaine. Judge Candler submitted tests that proved minimal alcohol and no cocaine in the formula. Consequently, in November 1907, the Army lifted a ban on Coca-Cola at their base in Cuba, but it took years to rebuild lost business.

About the same time, Dobbs met with Ms. Allen after she continued to circulate propaganda stating Coca-Cola still contained cocaine, caffeine, and alcohol. Their face-off ensued at the Yates Hotel in Syracuse, New York. Dobbs lobbed the opening volley reminding her of Asa Candler's honest character while emphasizing his benevolent reputation as a philanthropist. Ms. Allen dismissed Asa Candler's laurels and double-downed on accusations. Dobbs lost his composure and commenced "screaming" at her asking if she thought he would give poison to his own children who drank Coca-Cola? Ms. Allen calmly responded that she never claimed Coca-Cola was a poison. Dobbs' reply invoked the name of Samuel Hopkins Adams, a renowned muckraker contracted by *Collier's* to investigate Coca-Cola, and stated that Adams found no one was harmed by Coca-Cola. After the meeting, Ms. Allen contacted Adams who contested Dobbs' statements and countered that he found the soft drink to be habit-forming. As a result, rumors continued, and Dr. Wiley's lawsuit festered.

The Coca-Cola Company of Georgia was charged with misbranded and adulterated food products in violation of the Pure Food and Drug Act. The first trial began on March 13, 1911, and ended when Judge Edward Terry Sanford "ordered the jury to return a verdict in favor of Coca-Cola." Judge Sanford determined that the U.S. government failed to prove Coca-Cola was misbranded because it did contain small amounts of "coca and kola." Additionally, he ruled that caffeine was "not an added ingredient" and was part of the original formula.

Dr. Wiley was prosecution's mastermind, but never testified. Despite initial trial defeat, he did influence Coca-Cola to change its marketing strategy and amended the Pure Food and Drug Act. In 1912, the act was amended to add caffeine "to the list of "habit-forming" and "deleterious" substances which must be listed on the label." Additionally, Coca-Cola made it an "unwritten rule" to never advertise any child, younger than 12 years old, drinking Coca-Cola to avoid inference of caffeine addiction by children; tacit policy continued until 1986.

The federal government appealed Judge Sanford's decision. In 1914, the appellate court upheld the decision. At that point, the case was removed from Georgia and submitted to the U.S. Supreme Court. On May 22, 1916, the ruling was reversed by Chief Justice Charles Evans Hughes Sr., who determined that "Coca-Cola was not a distinctive name, but simply the conjunction of two common words." Additionally, Chief Justice Hughes ruled that caffeine should be considered an "added ingredient." The Coca-Cola Company settled out of court on November 12, 1917, pleading "no contest"; settlement included an agreement to cut the caffeine content "by half."

In 1916, the Candler family expressed intentions of selling The Coca-Cola Company of Georgia. Accordingly, in January 1917, a $25 million dollar offer was extended. Howard Candler was previously elected president on January 21, 1916, and "sanctioned the secret sale to the Woodruff Syndicate." Asa retained 90% of the stock and maintained control of the company with no desire to sell. Dynamics changed, though, after the U.S. Supreme Court's upset in May 1916. Asa left Coca-Cola to seek political office. He won city election as 41st mayor of Atlanta in November 1916 and began a two-year term in January 1917. Ultimately, Coca-Cola settled the *Barrels and Kegs Case* in November 1917. A month later, in December 1917, Asa Candler gave his children "all but seven shares of stock" and "all of his real estate holdings." Such transition of power to the Candler children enabled Howard Candler and Dobbs to negotiate a sellout deal without Asa's knowledge.

On July 1, 1919, Dobbs acted as intermediary for Coca-Cola and met with Ernest Woodruff (1863-1944), president of the Trust Company of Georgia, to discuss the Trust Company's purchase offer of $25,000,000. On August 2, 1919, Woodruff made Dobbs a board member of the Trust Company of Georgia. On September 12, 1919, The Coca-Cola Company of Georgia became The Coca-Cola Company of Delaware. The Candler children received "$15 million in cash and $10 million in preferred stock yielding 7 percent interest" and "500,000 shares of its common stock" were publicly sold for "$40 a share." Dobbs was appointed president of The Coca-Cola Company of Delaware and Howard Candler became chairman of the board. Ernest Woodruff received 20,000 shares. There was no mention of Dobbs' financial compensation. Asa did not find out about the buyout until after the fact and was left bitter, angry, and betrayed; he survived a stroke in 1926, but died three years later at the age of 77, on March 12, 1929.

Afterwards Coca-Cola was engrossed in a heated contract battle with bottlers involving the rising cost of syrup caused by WWI that depleted U.S. inventory. Contract controversy pitted bottlers' "bottling rights in perpetuity" against Coca-Cola's respective denial. Coca-Cola invoked the "right to cancel" bottling contracts in February 1920 and distributed a letter notifying contract termination "as of May 1, 1920." The law firm, King and Spalding in Atlanta, represented the bottlers and filed suit on April 16, 1920. Dobbs promised a fight. Eventually both sides agreed to a temporary compromise prior to deadline that allowed $1.72 per gallon for syrup. The bottlers had just as much to lose as Coca-Cola after having "invested over $20 million in real estate, plants and equipment."

The bottlers' trial began in May 1920. The lawsuit was of particular concern because bottlers contended that their 1899 contract with The Coca-Cola Company of Georgia also included rights to the Coca-Cola recipe. On May 31, 1920, the bottlers retracted their "Fulton County" lawsuits and refiled in "Delaware federal court" to move judicial proceedings away from Atlanta, Coca-Cola's hometown. Dobbs frustratingly compared bottlers' endless litigation to "the Sword of Damocles" hanging over his head. Trial ended on June 23, 1920; final ruling was left for judge's discretion. On November 8, 1920, Judge Hugh Morris ruled in favor of the bottlers stating the contract was permanent. Coca-Cola appealed because its trademark and recipe were left in jeopardy. A month later, in December 1920, the U.S. Supreme Court upheld "Coca-Cola's legal rights to the trademark." But, on May 4, 1921, the Court of Appeals affirmed Judge Morris's ruling that forced Coca-Cola to honor the bottlers' original contract. Consequently, the price of syrup was renegotiated and "set at $1.17 ½ per gallon for the parent bottlers, and $1.30 to the actual bottlers, both of which included a 5-cent allotment for advertising."

During the bottlers' trial, Dobbs and Woodruff had a falling out over Howard Candler's overpaid sugar prices, Woodruff's backdoor dealings with the bottlers' association, and Dobbs' overextended advertising budget. Howard Candler, in charge of purchasing, was unable to procure sugar from Coca-Cola's usual cost-effective Cuban sources and substituted pricey suppliers from Java at 20 cents per pound that raised bottling prices. Additionally, while waiting for Judge Morris' final ruling, Woodruff made side deals with the bottlers' association; Dobbs sarcastically complained, "Woodruff is as busy as a mangy dog with fleas, with a great scheme of consolidating The Coca-Cola Company, the parent bottlers and all of the actual bottlers into one big corporation, with the bottlers to take Coca-Cola stock for their holdings and plants." Then Woodruff insisted that Dobbs maintain an annual $1.2 million advertising budget, which Dobbs drastically exceeded before the year's end. Dobbs angrily rebuffed Woodruff questioning his knowledge of the advertising business, and resulted in the Trust Company requesting Dobbs' resignation. On October 4, 1920, Dobbs submitted his resignation finalized at the following month's November board meeting and Howard Candler returned as president.

On April 28, 1923, Woodruff's son, Robert Winship Woodruff (1889-1985), was appointed president of Coca-Cola at the age of 33 and led Coca-Cola for 60 years. Robert Woodruff took Coca-Cola to new heights building on Frank Robinson's initial concept of international sales, overseas bottling plants, and creative advertising. Coincidentally, Wikipedia.org noted, "Woodruff's personal chauffeur was Luther Cain, Jr., father of businessman and 2012 Republican presidential candidate Herman Cain." Luther Cain (1925-1982) influenced his son to begin his business career at Coca-Cola before becoming CEO of "Godfather's Pizza." Herman Cain died on July 30, 2020, from complications of COVID-19.

Wanley's History and Traditions projected a glorified disingenuous backstory of the *Barrels and Kegs Case* trial and Dobbs' involvement with the truth movement. There were blatant discrepancies between Wansley's saintly portrayal of Dobbs versus reality. Obviously, Wansley was obligated to portray Dobbs in a favorable light on behalf of Coca-Cola's long-term national sponsorship of CBBB. Wansley described Dobbs as stalwartly pursuing "truth in advertising" for truth's sake when circumstances contrarily suggested that he exploited the AACA and truth movement for Coca-Cola's intent and purpose. Facts purport that Dobbs schemed a two-prong local and national defense for the *Barrels and Kegs Case* trial; Coca-Cola attorneys moved trial venue to Atlanta for hometown jury-pool advantage while Dobbs led the revered AACA to sway mainstream America. By the same token, the AACA had just formed four years earlier, in 1905, and was only too happy to enlist Dobbs because of Coca-Cola's fame and fortune; AACA's presidency enlisted only those executives who could finance their tenure. Dobbs traveled 45,000 miles at Coca-Cola's expense while serving as president of AACA.

Coca-Cola was aware of possible legal action in February 1907 that led to an indictment in October 1909. During this timeframe, Dobbs broadcast his interest in joining the AACA and was elected president at the AACA's fifth annual convention held in Louisville, Kentucky, in 1909. Dobbs was re-elected the following year at the 1910 convention held at Omaha, Nebraska. Kenner detailed Dobbs' presidency in *The Fight for Truth in Advertising* stating, "The early pages of the truth in advertising saga were written during the two years of the Dobbs leadership of the national advertising association ... He named dishonest advertisers and showed examples of their advertisements; he called a spade a spade." Kenner also detailed how Dobbs attended the famous 1911 convention to pass the reins to a new president: "The truth fires burst into brilliant flames. The "high purpose and singular devotion" of Samuel C. Dobbs, born leader and doughty fighter, had paved the way for a great meeting."

SAMUEL CANDLER DOBBS

The truth movement began with the Boston convention in August 1911 when Dobbs relinquished his presidency of the AACA. Kenner detailed the history of the Bureau's early years and wrote about Dobbs in the timeframe leading up to the convention, but made no further mention of him afterwards, which implied his continued participation as a rank-and-file member. Additionally, Dobbs was not listed as a founding member of the first vigilance committee, which was formed four months after the convention.

Wansley treated the Pure Food and Drug trial as a victory for Coca-Cola even though Coca-Cola ultimately lost the lawsuit and made government-required changes. Additionally, Wansley unfairly lauded Dobbs as a superhero above fellow convention glitterati who actually ramrodded the truth movement: "The challenge of creating high ethical standards in advertising and selling is probably best remembered through the activities of one man. He was Samuel C. Dobbs, sales manager at the time and later president of The Coca-Cola Company." With no intent to diminish Dobbs as a historic personality, it is only fair to emphasize that his participation was limited in comparison to other pioneers' far-reaching contributions to the advertising industry and false advertising legislation.

Loyal trailblazers of the truth movement spent decades fighting for consumer protection after Dobbs left in 1911. They included Merle Sidener, Joseph Appel, John Romer, Harry Nims, and Dr. Herbert Houston among many others. Sidener earned ultimate honor as the primary leader who coined the mantra "truth in advertising," contributed to the creation of the first vigilance committee, orchestrated the name "Better Business Bureau," established a critically acclaimed advertising agency, and continued many honorable contributions throughout his lifetime. Appel was the advertising manager for Wanamaker Stores and introduced his famous *Ten Commandments of Advertising* that provided the guidelines for universal business standards. Romer was the acclaimed editor of *Printers' Ink* and he contracted New York attorney Nims to draft the *Printers' Ink* Model Statute advertising law that inspired the creation of the Vigilance Committee to enforce it. And Dr. Houston loyally participated as a long-time principle member of the AACA and traveled the world promoting education and business integrity; he also produced Upton Sinclair's best-selling fictional novel, *The Jungle*, which sparked the Pure Food and Drug Act and resulted in the indictment of Coca-Cola.

Aforementioned advertising titans were preceded by the esteemed George Presbury Rowell, the father of modern advertising. Rowell founded *Printers' Ink* advertising journal and invented several of the prototypical merit programs adopted by the advertising industry and Bureau.

In fact, an abundance of distorted information encircled Dobbs and his involvement with the truth movement and the Better Business Bureau. Wansley spun a slanted version of Dobbs' involvement at the 1911 convention. Contrary to Wanley's account, Dobbs appeared at the convention to relinquish his title as president in order to return to the *Barrels and Kegs Case* trial that had begun six months earlier. Otherwise, Sidener ramrodded the truth movement later enforced by Romer's *Printers' Ink* Model Statute and Vigilance Committee. Furthermore, the Bureau scrubbed its historical data, which enabled exploitation of consumers. As a result, Dobbs' laurels with the AACA and the Bureau during respective horse-and-buggy years have been blown out of proportion.

Dobbs' collective relationships with Asa Candler, Coca-Cola, AACA, Better Business Bureau, and NYSE opened lucrative doors for him. Handsome Sam was the original "Kardashian" and famous for being famous. After leaving his position as president of Coca-Cola in 1920, Dobbs remained a director of Coca-Cola and active member of the AACW. He parlayed contacts with New York banking and Wall Street elite into a lucrative international investment banking career that categorized him as a "capitalist." To Dobbs' credit, he paid his good fortune forward assisting the educational community as a renowned philanthropist.

As early as 1919, just before being named president of Coca-Cola, Dobbs' participated in the AACW's annual convention held at New Orleans, Louisiana. Prior to the September convention, he attended an executive dinner in June sponsored by the Advertising Club of New Orleans and his speech was quoted in the AACW's monthly magazine, *Associated Advertising*. He was also listed in the magazine's publishing credits as one of the esteemed trustees of the "National Vigilance Committee Plan and Fund" that identified him as "S. C. Dobbs, vice-president, Coca-Cola Co., Atlanta." The other committee trustees included "Festus J. Wade, president, Mercantile Bank & Trust Co., St. Louis; F. A. Seiberling, president, Goodyear Tire & Rubber Co., Akron, Ohio; David Kirachbaum, president, A. B. Kirachbaum Co., Philadelphia; Henry L. Doherty, president, Henry L. Doherty & Co., New York." The committee list was a gilded roster of corporate America's *Who's Who* further emphasizing Dobbs' exemplary success in banking and investments.

A "B2B" business website advertised "Award-Winning Products, People and Organization." There were misstatements: (1) "The National Vigilance Committee (later changed to Better Business Bureau) was founded in Dallas in 1912 by ethical business leaders, with principles based on "The Ten Commandments of Advertising" by Samuel Candler Dobbs of Coca-Cola." (2) "After speaking with other advertising men, Dobbs found widespread agreement with his concerns, and thus formed the Associated Advertising Clubs of America in 1909." These two comments were grossly incorrect. First, the *Ten Commandments of Advertising* were created and introduced by Joseph Appel, who sparked a chain reaction by inspiring Merle Sidener to launch the truth movement that begat the Better Business Bureau. Second, the National Vigilance Committee became the National Better Business Bureau. And, third, Dobbs and Coca-Cola had nothing to do with the formation of the AACA in 1905; Dobbs joined the AACA in 1909. Additionally, the AACA was established by turn-of-the-century advertising glitterati who were members of several exclusive New York City advertising clubs including the Mallet Club, Quoin Club, Sphinx Club, and Poor Richard's Club; none of which Dobbs was previously affiliated.

Dobbs is forever associated with Asa Candler as the founding benefactor of Emory University in Atlanta, Georgia. Asa encouraged Dobbs and others at Coca-Cola to follow his example as a humanitarian and philanthropist. Asa's brother, Warren Akin Candler (1857-1941), was the "tenth president and the first chancellor of Emory University," which influenced Asa's financial support and lifetime devotion to the school. Warren Candler, nicknamed "Shorty," was elected bishop of the "Methodist Episcopal Church, South" in 1898 and acted as "spiritual advisor" to his brother Asa. Bishop Candler was responsible for Asa's financial intervention, which solidified Emory College's present location in Atlanta. According to the New Georgia Encyclopedia website, "Asa Candler wrote a check for $1 million to defray expenses of moving Emory's headquarters from Oxford to acreage he donated in his Druid Hills development in the eastern suburbs of Atlanta." All total Asa donated over $8 million to Emory.

There were also financial motives behind Asa's humanitarian contributions. In July 1914, he donated a million dollars to Emory for a tax write-off due to the newly enacted Revenue Act of 1913 that reinstituted the federal income tax to compensate for lower tariff rates. The act featured a "progressive tax structure," which increased rates along with increased income. The Bradford Tax institute advised, "In 1913, the top tax bracket was 7 percent on all income over $500,000 ($11 million in today's dollars); and the lowest tax bracket was 1 percent." According to author Mark Pendergrast, "In effect, the law forced corporations to pay dividends, which were then taxable to the individual stockholders, but were not deductible at the corporate level, amounting to double taxation." In fact, during the bottlers' lawsuit in 1920, the city of Atlanta enforced the law and won a lawsuit filed against The Coca-Cola Company of Delaware to obtain a list of their stockholders for taxation purpose.

In his later years, Dobbs heavily contributed to Emory University, LaGrange College in LaGrange, Georgia, and Rheinhart College in Waleska, Georgia. The Georgia Encyclopedia website referred to his financial contributions to LaGrange College noting, "The Lamar Dodd Art Center, completed in 1982, is the school's newest structure." But the full extent of Dobbs' generosity will never be known because his biographical information was extremely limited during the 30-year gap between the time he departed Coca-Cola and his death. Random information proved sketchy, but indicated he was a "banker." Records also advised that he held the title "LL.D.," translated as "Legum Doctor" in Latin and "Doctor of Laws" in English, but in the United States "is awarded as an honorary degree only" and is the academic equivalent of a law degree. In 1927, Dobbs was elected a college chairman and was a member of the LaGrange Board of Trustees, which likely resulted in bestowment of his LL.D. title. Otherwise there were no records indicating a formal scholastic degree. The Advertising Federation's supplement to their 1936 Boston convention listed Dobbs' credits as "SAMUEL CANDLER DOBBS, Banker, Atlanta, Georgia, was President, Advertising Federation of America, 1909-1911," and the title to his convention speech stated, "Samuel Candler Dobbs, LL.D." Additionally, in 2015, LaGrange College referenced "Dr. Dobbs" when responding to biographical inquiries.

If it wasn't for LaGrange College in LaGrange, Georgia, there would be very little information available about Dobbs' life after Coca-Cola. In fact, LaGrange College was his wife's alma mater and she was president of the "LaGrange Alumnae Association." Articles referenced her association with the College and Dobbs' philanthropic contributions. LaGrange College's newspaper, *The Scroll*, was "[p]ublished monthly by "Quill Driver's Club" of LaGrange College," and offered insightful snippets that detailed the progression of Dobbs' life. *The Scroll* gratefully acknowledged Dobbs' generous contributions throughout the 1920s and 1930s. Unfortunately, *The Scroll* ceased production between the mid-1930s and 1950 during a critical juncture in Dobbs' life. His wife Mary Ruth and Judge Candler both died on December 9, 1941. Three months earlier, Bishop Candler predeceased Dobbs' wife and the judge on September 25, 1941.

The educational coordinator at LaGrange College kindly researched academic records for any further listing of Dobbs. Search results advised that "the 1939 *Quadrangle*, the College yearbook, is dedicated to him" and "The Board of Trustees Minutes of May 15, 1952 indicates that a resolution of appreciation for Dr. Dobbs was sent to his son and daughter," but the document could not be located "within the minutes"." Otherwise, there was no other information found on Dobbs at the College.

LaGrange College's *The Scroll* and Bulletin published several articles on Dobbs that proved exceptionally informative. The June 1927 edition published the article, "Samuel Candler Dobbs to Deliver Baccalaureate Address," and described his earlier speech delivered on May 30, 1927. The article advised that Dobbs was "a prominent capitalist" and "well-known throughout the South"; that "as an authority on business administration, he has contributed to several magazines and is a lecturer of note"; and that "he is also a member of the Board of Trustees of LaGrange College."

The Scroll's January 1928 edition published the article, "Samuel C. Dobbs

Accepts Post As College Chairman," and noted that Dobbs was elected chairman of the board of LaGrange College on December 9, 1927. The article also referred to Mrs. Dobb's father, Dr. Mixon, as "an outstanding figure in the North Georgia conference." According to the Georgia Encyclopedia, "When Georgia Methodism divided into North and South Georgia Conferences in 1866, LaGrange Female College became the property of the Northern Conference of the present United Methodist Church." In 1898, Warren Candler was appointed bishop by the Methodist Episcopal Church, South and remained a patron of LaGrange College. *The Scroll* published an accompanying article in the same edition entitled, "Atlanta Chapter of the L.C. Alumnae Give Reception for High School Seniors"; Bishop Warren's wife was mentioned: "The Atlanta auxiliary of the LaGrange College Alumnae Association entertained December 27, at the home of Mrs. Warren Candler on North Decatur Road, in honor of the Senior classes of the Atlanta high schools." The article also referred to "Mrs. Samuel C. Dobbs" as the Association's "national president" who attended and "received" students at the event. In classic high-society flair, the article concluded with whimsical, rose-colored nuance: "Mrs. Candler poured tea from the lovely silver service given her on her golden wedding anniversary. The table and rooms were beautifully decorated with cut flowers."

Another Dobbs' speech was found in the LaGrange College Bulletin entitled, "LaGrange College Bulletin, LaGrange, Georgia, The Ancient Landmarks: Address to the Graduating Class by Samuel C. Dobbs, LL.D., August, 1928." The speech was lengthy, heartfelt, and beautifully written. Dobbs eloquently compared landmarks in everyday life with historical significance and religious awareness. He described his family home in Rabun County and described an entertaining, but profound, story about walking his extensive property with an inspector to locate generations-old landmarks to confirm his 1920's property lines; located landmarks were deteriorated posts buried in briars and bushes with markings still legible and legally binding. He referred to his young college-age son gathering the nerve to approach him for permission to join the U.S. military and chastised himself for wanting to prevent his son's enlistment out of concern for his safety. He reminded his high school audience that "more than 56,000 of our boys poured out their blood on French soil." He also discussed the importance of American history as examples for students' future success. And he emphasized the ultimate importance of religion in everyday life.

Dobbs also offered candid insight into his personal and professional life while devotedly referencing Coca-Cola. A brief, but enlightening, paragraph in his speech was most telling, "I can pick up my phone and talk with my farm superintendent up there in the hills of Rabun, or transact business with my broker in New York, or talk with a banker in London, almost with equal ease. There is scarcely a day that I do not talk to someone in New York, consummate important business deals with as much facility as I could if the person to whom I was talking sat at my desk in the Candler Building in Atlanta."

The Scroll's April 1930 issue, named the "Special Alumnae Edition," published an article entitled, "SAMUEL CANDLER DOBBS Newest Club at Tifton, Ga., Is Organized by LaGrange Alumnae." The College gratefully reflected on Dobbs' generosity exclaiming, "Returning Alumnae see on all sides evidences of the love and thoughtfulness of this friend of ours. Our grounds have been enlarged by a western extension reaching to Maidee St. The efficiency of the music department has been greatly increased by the addition of one grand piano and five uprights. Mr. Dobbs' interest and thoughtfulness extends to every department. His gift of a radio to the college family is a constant joy to faculty and students. The newly finished Warren A. Candler Home should luxuriously house presidents and their families for generations to come. For the Alumnae, he is financing the newly made office of Alumnae Secretary." Additionally, the editor noted, "Whatever sum of money our Alumnae can raise, Mr. Dobbs promises to double it."

The last article referring to Dobbs was published by the LaGrange College Alumnae Bulletin and commemorated his death. Before-and-after pictures were posted detailing renovations of the College's Dobbs' Auditorium "before it was remodeled in 1950." The article included a posthumous dedication stating, "This building was named for the late Samuel C. Dobbs, noted philanthropist."

Research into LaGrange College revealed long-standing relationships with Bishop Candler and Judge Candler. The Georgia Legislature "chartered" the LaGrange Female Academy on December 26, 1831, which was bought in 1844 by three Montgomery brothers, "Joseph, Telemachus, and Hugh," who resold the property to "the Georgia Conference of the Methodist Episcopal Church, South, in 1857." A series of name changes occurred, and, in 1934, the school was eventually renamed LaGrange College. Bishop Candler was affiliated with the Methodist Episcopal Church, South, having joined the organization in 1898, and continued to support LaGrange College's growth. Additionally, Judge Candler was listed in "The LaGrange College Bulletin" as a member of the Board of Trustees next to Samuel Candler Dobbs, L.L.S. in 1929. Dobbs left the Coca-Cola Company in 1920, and Asa Candler died in 1929, but LaGrange's articles proved that Dobbs remained close with both of his uncles, Bishop Warren, and Judge Candler after Asa's death.

Additionally, Dobbs donated $100,000 towards building Emory's "first dormitory" and in 1938 donated $1 million to Emory that was placed in a trust. In 1985, Emory University utilized the trust to establish Dobb Professorships "to honor some of the University's best young faculty who have done unusually fine work in both teaching and research early in their careers."

At the age of 68, Dobbs appeared one last time at the Advertising Federation of America's (AFA) 32nd convention, held from June 28 through July 2, 1936, to celebrate the 25th anniversary of the famous Boston Convention of 1911; the Associated Advertising Clubs of America was renamed "Advertising Federation of America" in 1929. Dobbs was among the guest speakers and his address, described as a sermon, was published in AFA's supplemental convention book entitled, *Truth in Advertising: Twenty-Fifth Anniversary*. The style of Dobbs' message implied that he opened ceremonies the same as he did in 1911: "We are assembled here today to celebrate twenty-five years of progress and development in advertising"; it was another historic moment.

When first researching Dobbs' background, like Kenner, there was nothing available regarding his private life other than his involvement in the *Barrels and Kegs Case* as detailed by Wansley. There were no biographies located regarding Dobbs' specific titles and endeavors before and after he left Coca-Cola. Further research into the AACA, Coca-Cola, his wife's alma mater (LaGrange College), and his obituary in the *Atlanta Journal Constitution* indicated a gifted philanthropic life as a capitalist and/or banker, which emphasized the lucrative connections he made through the AACA and Bureau. After resigning as president in 1920, he remained a director for Coca-Cola and became a successful national and international investment banker while escaping to his farm at Lake Rabun on the weekends. Dobbs' banking career after Coca-Cola was enabled by his former position as president of the AACA from 1909 to 1911, creating lifetime affiliations with the NYSE and Investment Bankers Association. It is certain that Dobbs remained a member of the Bureau as an ongoing director of Coca-Cola and maintained his Sphinx connections. His wife's obituary shed further light on their later years and emphasized a happy marriage whereby he supported her involvement in "educational and welfare work among the mountain people." Additionally, it was noted that "Mrs. Dobbs was active for many years in behalf of the Tallulah Fall School for Girls." Dobbs retired at the age of 78, in 1946, and he spent the last four years of his life living full-time at Lake Rabun in Lakemont, Georgia.

Research also discovered Marion Abele Kenan, a former personal assistant of Samuel Candler Dobbs, who passed away at the wondrous age of 98, on June 12, 2005. Her obituary in the *Atlanta Journal-Constitution*, published from June 19 to 21, 2005, stated that she worked for Dobbs "in his business" prior to her commencing employment in 1950 for the Westminster School in Atlanta, Georgia. Otherwise, she maintained confidentiality and did not elaborate about his business. Ms. Kenan represented an unparalleled chapter in history. She was born in 1907, the same year that Coca-Cola began waging war with Dr. Wiley before it was indicted in 1909 for violation of the Pure Food and Drug Act of 1906.

Dobbs' wife, Mary Ruth, 72, was ill for three months before she died on

THE APO$TATE

December 9, 1941. Coincidentally, Judge Candler, 80, also suffered an "extended illness" and eerily passed away the same day. They died in the midst of turmoil and threat of war on American soil. To put history into perspective, two days earlier, December 7, 1941, the Japanese attacked the southern part of the Island of Oahu at Pearl Harbor as well as Malaya, Hong Kong, Guam, Philippine Islands, Wake Island, Midway Island, and torpedoed American ships sailing "on the high seas between San Francisco and Hawaii." The next day, December 8, 1941, President Franklin Roosevelt delivered a 30-minute radio speech that night at 10 p.m. (EST) and as reported by the *Atlanta Journal Constitution's* article, "F.D.R. TO TALK ON JAPANESE ATTACK TONIGHT." Before the next day's dawn, they both met their fates with destiny, Mrs. Dobbs at "a private sanitarium" and Judge Candler at "Emory hospital." Unfortunately, both left this world contemplating the unthinkable - a home front invasion! Such dire circumstances must have weighed heavily on their fragile state of minds. Thousands of military personnel had been killed in one day and the entire United States had begun mobilizing for defense and retribution. The day after they parted this world, on December 10, 1941, the *Atlanta Journal Constitution's* front-page headline read, "JAPANESE ATTACK NAZI-DIRECTED, SAYS F.D.R.; SEES LONG CONFLICT." And another article in that same issue ominously warned, "Hospitals Here Set for Blackout," and described how hospitals as far away as Atlanta were preparing for battery backup in case of a bombing attack. Both were interred at the West View Cemetery on the same day, December 11, 1941. "Funeral service" for Judge Candler was held at 11 a.m. and Mrs. Dobbs at 2 p.m.; Dobbs acted as a pallbearer for Judge Candler.

Dobbs was 82 years old when he passed away on October 31, 1950. His burial site was listed as West View Cemetery, Section B, Fulton County, Atlanta, Georgia (Find A Grave memorial 38970360). He reunited with his wife and the founding crew of Asa Candler, Judge John Candler, and Ernest Woodruff, who were patiently waiting for him at West View. And Saint Peter met him at the pearly gates drinking Coca-Cola with Bishop Candler who honorably resided at the historical Oxford Cemetery reserved for Emory officials and faculty! Howard Candler and Robert Woodruff would later join them adding to the cemetery's gilded roster. In 1953, Dobbs was inducted in the American Advertising Federation's Hall of Fame.

As a footnote to Dobbs' life at Lake Rabun, I called the original Alley's Grocery telephone number hoping to find Lamar Alley on the other end of the line. Alley's Grocery changed owners in 2008 due to Mr. Alley's deteriorating health; he would have been quite elderly if still living. Nevertheless, it was worth a phone call for the happenstance of speaking with him. It was October 8, 2015, and 7:30 a.m., Georgia Mountain Time, and I was calling from Houston, Texas,

Central Standard Time, an hour behind. An elderly woman answered the phone. I asked her if I had reached Alley's Grocery. For a split second, nostalgia happily embraced her. She forgot the moment and excitedly answered, "Yes," but just as quickly composed herself and clarified that the grocery was now owned by others. I identified myself and explained my reason for calling was to speak with Mr. Alley, the former owner of Alley's Grocery; that I was a writer seeking his knowledge of Samuel Dobbs at Lake Rabun. When I pressed to speak with Mr. Alley, she sadly related that he was paralyzed by a stroke and unable to speak. I was devastated. He represented priceless history, yet his memories were forever silenced by a cruel twist of fate.

I asked her if she was his wife and she confirmed with serene authority. Then, Mrs. Alley patiently and mercifully responded to my last-ditch query if she knew Samuel Dobbs? Her encouraging answer stated that although she had never met him, her husband knew him very well from operating the grocery that also served as Lake Rabun's train depot. She confirmed that Mr. Alley was 89 years old, which placed his birth year in 1926. I commented that he sounded 'like a kind and gentle soul' and she tenderly agreed while softly repeating my words as though forwarding my message for him to hear. For the length of our brief and magical conversation, I envisioned Mr. Alley greeting the Dobbs' family outside the grocery as they excitedly stepped off the train. What delightful conversations they must have enjoyed! As I hung up the phone, I listened for history's recollection of an ebbing train whistle slowly pulling away from Alley's Grocery. I felt honored to have spoken with Mrs. Alley, and Mr. Alley's presence during our conversation allowed me to vicariously share a fleeting, but incomparable moment in time with Samuel Candler Dobbs.

CHAPTER 16

VIGILANCE COMMITTEE

The Boston convention of 1911 produced a domino effect encouraging the first advertising law, first vigilance committee, and first national vigilance committee. All three entities fell under the realm of the national advertising association, which started as the International Advertising Association (IAA) in 1904; became the Associated Advertising Clubs of America (AACA) in 1905; the Associated Advertising Clubs of the World (AAWA) in 1914; the Advertising Federation of America (AFA) in 1929; and changed to the current American Advertising Federation (AAF) in 1967.

Despite the excitement sparked by the Truth in Advertising Movement at the 1911 convention in Boston, the advertising industry had no means to regulate false advertising that threatened advertising sales and circulation. Romer solved the lingering problem by contracting New York City employment attorney, Harry Nims, to create a punitive false-advertising law on behalf of the advertising industry.

Romer suggested that the AACA "organize vigilance committees for the purpose of cooperating with local prosecuting officers under the law." The new law became known as the *Printers' Ink* Model Statute. He then approached the AACA to assist with the statute's legislative enactment. Kenner wrote, "In November, 1911, Printers' Ink published this proposed model statute and recommended that through the efforts of the Advertising Clubs it be enacted into legislation in the several states …." Accordingly, the AACA enlisted the Advertising Club of New York to form an experimental Vigilance Committee to invoke the statute as a deterrent against false and misleading advertising.

The Advertising Club of New York's predecessor was the exclusive Sphinx Club. The New York Club's president, William H. Ingersoll, called a meeting in December 1911 and presented the statute and plan. Kenner explained, "Three dynamic speakers were chosen to discuss the subject. Herbert S. Houston, a

VIGILANCE COMMITTEE

publisher, was to speak on the *effect* of dishonest advertising; H. D. Nims, an unfair competition lawyer, was to define its *legal status*; and Richard W. Lawrence, a manufacturer, and of the owners of *Printers' Ink*, was to propose the *remedy*." The Club voted to embrace the statute and assembled the first committee to act as the regulatory arm of the AACA.

The first "Vigilance Committee" membership roster, dated December 1911:

Thomas A. Barrett	Alfred W. McCann, Chairman
A.K. Boursault	Frank Morrison
Mason Britton	H. D. Nims
Clowry Chapman	John Clyde Oswald
Frank Cole	George H. Perry
John J. Dillon	E. H. Randolph
J. George Frederick	H. D. Robbins
William C. Freeman	John Irving Romer
George French	F. J. Ross
J.J. Hazen	F. P. Seymour
Arthur S. Higgins	Charles D. Spalding
Herbert S. Houston	A.E. Sproul
William H. Ingersoll, ex-officio	Edward F. Trefz
J. G. Jarrett	E.E. Vreeland
H. Kirby	Gerald B. Wadsworth
Samuel E. Leith	H. R. Wright
C. H. Lippmann	

The Vigilance Committee opened historic doors on March 12, 1912. Nims was listed as an initial member and placed in charge of investigations. Within six months, the Vigilance Committee investigated "nearly 100 cases of suspected advertising" and set into motion plans to introduce a national organization to oversee expansion of the statute and additional local committees. A year later, the statute was enacted into law in "fifteen states in 1913, and first became law in Ohio." Other advertising clubs around the country followed suit and established vigilance committees.

Then, in 1916, Merle Sidener approached Arthur Sheldon for a new name to replace the sinister-sounding Vigilance Committee. And, the Better Business Bureau was born.

CHAPTER **17**

NATIONAL VIGILANCE COMMITTEE

The Associated Advertising Clubs of America formed the "National Vigilance Committee" in 1912 as its national regulatory division, which dealt exclusively with large advertisers and a nation-wide network of associations that controlled the business industry. It was no coincidence that its chairman represented a "national investment banking firm," and that its benefactor was a governor of the NYSE.

From 1912 to 1925, "the Better Business Bureaus operated under the direction of the National Vigilance Committee," which was a division of the AACA until 1914 when it was renamed the Associated Advertising Clubs of the World. In May 1925, the annual AACW convention was held in Houston and voted to incorporate the National Better Business Bureau of the Associated Advertising Clubs of the World.

After the Vigilance Committee was launched in March 1912, the president of the AACA, George W. Coleman, determined a national organization was needed to support and expand the recently formed local office of the "Vigilance Committee of the Advertising Club of New York." Three months later, in June 1912, he introduced the National Vigilance Committee at the Association's annual convention held in Dallas, Texas.

The National Vigilance Committee began operations "following the convention." Its main purpose was to adjust contentious relations between manufacturing and "dissatisfied purchasers." There were no formal headquarters listed because members were scattered nationally and internationally. Coleman elected Harry D. Robbins, advertising director of a New York investment banking firm, as the National Vigilance Committee's first chairman; he served two years until 1914.

There were 18 "members" of the first National Vigilance Committee:

238

NATIONAL VIGILANCE COMMITTEE

A. M. Candee, Milwaukee, Wis.
Albert G. Clark, Portland, Ore.
Lewis H. Clement, Toledo, Ohio
F. J. Cooper, San Francisco, Cal.
K. S. Fenwick, Quebec, Que.
J. L. Hill, Richmond, Va.
Alfred W. McCann, New York, N.Y.
Hugh McVey, Des Moines, Iowa
Carl Murchey, Detroit, Mich.
Jesse H. Neal, Cleveland, Ohio

William F. Parkhurst, Atlanta, Ga.
H. D. Robbins, New York, N.Y., Chairman
John Irving Romer, New York, N.Y.
R. R. Shuman, Chicago, Ill.
H. H. Stalker, Toledo, Ohio
G. H. Vradenburg, Seattle, Wash.
J. F. Wildman, Toronto, Ont.
J. C. Woodley, E. St. Louis, Ill.

Three months earlier, on March 12, 1912, the first experimental Vigilance Committee began operations in New York City. Robbins and Romer were also listed among its members. The National Vigilance Committee was a division of the AACA that supported the local vigilance committees and pursued large scale offenses that exceeded respective city and state jurisdictions.

On June 21-25, 1914, the AACA was renamed Associated Advertising Clubs of the World at the first international convention held in Toronto, Canada. The AACW nominated Merle Sidener, principal of Sidener, Van Riper & Keeling Advertising Agency in Indianapolis, as "Chairman of the National Vigilance Committee," and H. J. Kenner was appointed "Manager" of the Minneapolis Bureau as of "September, 1914."

In June 1915, the newly appointed AACW president, Dr. Herbert Sherman Houston, re-nominated Sidener as chairman of the National Vigilance Committee and appointed H. J. Kenner as "Manager of the National Committee, and at an expense of not more than $8,000." Sidener requested $15,000 funding from the AACW to establish formal offices at the Association's Indianapolis headquarters. After Armistice Day, November 11, 1918, the Associated Advertising Clubs of the World and the National Vigilance Committee relocated to New York City, which had become known as "the advertising capital of the world."

In 1917, Kenner left the National Vigilance Committee for an advertising position in Minneapolis but returned on "July 1, 1919." He replaced Giles Ferris Olwin, an attorney from Indianapolis, Indiana, as executive secretary of the committee. Olwin was a former partner for 10 years with Judge Enos L. Watson, "father of United States Senator James E. Watson"; one among many elitist connections that represented the gilded scrolls of the National Vigilance Committee and New York Bureau. Golden coattails maintained impregnable ties with the courts, newspapers, Big Retail, Big Business, Big Special Interests, banks, and Wall Street.

Sidener discussed expansion of the National Vigilance Committee at the

AACW's convention held on September 21-25, 1919, in New Orleans. He stated, "This is a big business we are in, and we are required to operate on a large scale." As of 1919, the National Committee was working with "sixteen local Better Business Bureaus and eighty volunteer vigilance organizations." Vigilance work also extended overseas into "Canada, England, France and Australia." Accordingly, the AACW allocated an annual budget of $114,000; funding was raised from "national advertisers" and members.

At the 1920 AACW convention in Indianapolis, Sidener retired as chairman and was replaced by Richard H. Lee. Sidener continued "as a member of the Board of Directors of the National Better Business Bureau" and joined veterans Dr. Herbert Sherman Houston and H. D. Robbins to form a volunteer committee to assist operations of the National Vigilance Committee, which, by then, was managing 30 Bureaus in 30 major cities.

The national headquarters had several names changes. In June 1912, the National Vigilance Committee launched in Dallas; in 1925, the National Vigilance Committee incorporated and became the National Better Business Commission, Inc. of the Associated Advertising Clubs of the World located in Cleveland, Ohio; in 1927, the National Better Business Bureau formally separated from the AACW "to provide for greater specialization and legal safety in its work," which was legal jargon for establishing a separate entity to minimize liability connected to the Bureaus and to facilitate autocratic goals; in 1933, the name changed to the National Association of Better Business Bureaus, Inc.; in 1946, the name changed to the Association of Better Business Bureaus, Inc., located in New York City; and, in 1970, the name changed to the present day Council of Better Business Bureaus, Inc. (CBBB), located in Arlington, Virginia. As of April 5, 2016, CBBB defined itself as "the umbrella organization for the local, independent BBBs in the United States, Canada and Mexico, as well as home to its national and international programs on dispute resolution, advertising review, and industry self-regulation."

By November 2, 1927, James Coats Auchincloss (1885-1976), was all at once the president of the National Better Business Bureau and "governor of the NYSE from 1921 to 1938." Auchincloss offered a superb resume having served in the New York National Guard, Seventh Regiment (1909-1913); was a captain in Military Intelligence during World War I; a New York City deputy police commissioner; and "founder, treasurer, president, and chairman of the board of the New York Better Business Bureau." He maintained close connections with the elite of New York City including the influential Investment Bankers Association. Exemplary members such as Auchincloss shielded the Bureau from prosecution during the Pecora Commission investigations between 1932 and 1933.

NATIONAL VIGILANCE COMMITTEE

James Coats Auchincloss
Governor of NYSE; founder, treasurer, president, and chairman
of the board of the New York Better Business Bureau;
Republican New Jersey Congressman U.S. House of Representatives.
Photo dated January 1963.
Source: *Eighty-Eighth Congress, Pocket Congressional Directory*,
Government Printing Office, p. 89;
[https://en.wikipedia.org/wiki/File:James_C._Auchincloss.jpg];
public domain.

The National Vigilance Committee's decision to break free from the AACW represented initial steps to autocracy and unfettered globalism. The occasion marked the Bureau's liberty celebrated by Auchincloss and his litany of dictatorial titles. In short, Auchincloss was the proverbial Illuminati controlling an extensive corporate and banking network in America whose connections offered international opportunity: "The National Bureau has over a thousand contacts throughout the country for securing the information desired. Besides the forty-one other Better Business Bureaus and the many securities commissions, there are chambers of commerce, rotary clubs, various prosecuting officials, and for the investigation of mining and oil problems, we have at our disposal the assistance of state mining officials, oil inspectors, and geologists." He represented the evolving oligarchy that owned America.

Additionally, the National Vigilance Committee became "well established as a clearing house of information and a national service body." There were 25 national business associations that were members of the National Vigilance Committee. Ten of such members included "National Association of Piano Merchants of America; National Retail Clothiers' Association; National Shoe Retailers' Association; American Newspaper Publishers' Association; Investment

Bankers Association of America; National Automobile Chamber of Commerce; American Pharmaceutical Association; Proprietary Association of America; Canadian Press Association; Canadian Advertisers' Association."

O'Sullivan believed the National Vigilance Committee was formed as a conduit to the NYSE because its governor was also the president of the National Committee and of the New York Bureau. He wrote, "Then the National Better Business Bureau was organized in New York, with funds raised by the governor of the New York Stock Exchange and a leading oil operator. The latter guaranteed a lump sum of $60,000 for the National bureau, with an annual retainer of $7,500; and the Stock Exchange interests provided a total of $100,000 and secured control, the Stock Exchange governor, James C. Auchincloss, being elected president of the National Bureau. The charter of this Bureau was amended so as to include securities within its scope; and everything was set for operation of the National Better Business Bureau in the interests of Wall Street." O'Sullivan was a reliable source as a former newspaper reporter and CSI detective who worked with police departments all over the world.

Three years after O'Sullivan published *Rackets* and the New York Bureau's disgrace by the U.S. Senate, Kenner engaged a well-polished and consumer-oriented narrative that glossed over past Bureau infamy and described the AACW collaborating with the NYSE to raise $100,000 for vigilance committee work. But, between the lines, Kenner confirmed O'Sullivan's assertion that, as of November 2, 1927, Auchincloss was simultaneously juggling three positions as governor of the NYSE, president of the National Better Business Bureau, and president of the New York Bureau. There was no doubt that Auchincloss used his political clout to pull the golden strings that saved the Bureau from indictment during the Pecora hearings.

The development of the National Vigilance Committee was investigated by Logan Billingsley and the Manhattan Board of Commerce with conclusion on June 6, 1932; results provided fodder for U.S. Senate hearings that began earlier in March 1932. Questioning by the Manhattan Board particularly focused on the NYSE's payment of $100,000 to the Bureau to prove collusion between the NYSE and Bureau. Kenner explained that the $100,000 was a contribution towards the development of a national committee to combat a drastic increase in post-war stock scams involving Liberty Bonds whereby "literally hundreds of millions of dollars were being taken from financially illiterate citizens ... It was reliably reported that in one country in the Southwest, where thirty millions of Liberty Bonds had been purchased by residents, fifteen millions of these bonds had been traded, by the end of 1918, for questionable securities - mostly oil stocks." To the contrary, Kenner's patriotic explanation substantiated O'Sullivan's claim that the Bureau's "Before You Invest, Investigate" program did not educate the public, but compounded fraud by promoting a bogus investment program that exploited speculators' patriotism and ignorance. Additionally, Kenner published such statement three years AFTER the Bureau perfected its defensive testimony and excuses respective to securities' investigations by the U.S. Senate and Pecora Commission.

On November 2, 1927, Auchincloss, delivered an address to the Chicago Association of Commerce entitled, "The Better Business Bureau: Its Growth and Work." He acknowledged Bureau trailblazers Sidener and Kenner, the Bureau's legacy of truth, and the *Printers' Ink* Model Statute. Above all, Auchincloss emphasized the Bureau's progressive thinking and marked December 1926 as the watershed date when the National Better Business Bureau "voted to alter its charter to become the National Better Business Bureau, Inc. This act was consummated on February 18, 1927."

As O'Sullivan noted, the Bureau double-downed on self-righteous publicity whenever confronting scandalous press as occurred after Logan Billingsley's exposé, and which explained the timeline and urgency of evolving business standards. One such occasion presented itself just before the U.S. Senate's investigative hearings began in March 1932. A month earlier, in February 1932, the National Association of Better Business Bureaus proffered the Fair Practice Code, which was brief and relatively vague, but impressive: "It is proposed that business men themselves shall abandon and condemn any practices in advertising and selling merchandise, services, securities, property of all kinds which may have: a. The capacity or tendency to undermine public confidence in advertising announcements or other selling representations generally. b. The effect of injuring unfairly the sales or the goodwill of a competitive product or service."

After the Pecora Commission investigation began in January 1933, the Bureau's investigative program, "Before You Invest, Investigate," was discontinued. A worried New York Bureau next confronted the organized-crime trials of Special Prosecutor Thomas Dewey in 1935. The U.S. Senate hearings and Chairman Senator Fletcher had previously accused the Bureau of racketeering and colluding with the NYSE and Investment Bankers Association; allegations insinuated organized crime. So in March 1935, the National Better Business Bureau re-polished its halo and shamelessly published a revised version of its original 1932 "Fair Practice Code" that promoted the following standards:

1. No statement or representation shall be used in advertising which has the capacity or tendency to mislead or deceive the consumer.
2. No statement or representation shall be used in advertising which attacks competitors or which reflects unfairly on competitors' products, services, or methods of doing business.

3. No statement or representation shall be used in advertising which lays claim to a policy or continuing practice of generally underselling competitors.
4. No statement or representation shall be made in advertising which is a "bait" offer, wherein the customer does not have a fair opportunity to buy the advertised article.
5. No statement or representation shall be used in advertising referring to cut prices on trade-marked merchandise or other goods, in such manner as to lead to the public to believe that all of the merchandise sold by the advertiser is similarly low priced, when such is not the fact.
6. An advertiser shall be willing to fully substantiate the accuracy and fairness of any statement which he submits for publication.
7. No advertiser shall use any subterfuge to frustrate the spirit and intent of these Fair Practice Standards, the purposes of which are to prevent advertising which misleads the consumer and to prevent advertising which is unfair to competitors.

Aside from the NYSE and CBBB, Auchincloss participated in politics from 1943 until 1965 as a Republican U.S. Representative for New Jersey's Third District, which reflected the National BBB's and Bureaus' exploitation of national office. In 1946, the National Association of Better Business Bureaus, Inc. was located in New York City as well as the organization's most powerful New York Bureau. The fact that Auchincloss ran as a Republican suggested that he strategically aligned with former Republican Special Prosecutor Dewey who was elected governor of New York also in 1943 until 1955. Auchincloss warned in 1927, "Those of us who are responsible for the policies of the Better Business Bureaus realize that the success of this work is dependent on its sincerity."

CHAPTER **18**

MERLE SIDENER

Merle Sidener
Chairman of National Better Business Bureau; orchestrated renaming Vigilance Committee as "Better Business Bureau"; founding partner of Sidener, Van Riper & Keeling Advertising Agency; artist: Caryn Cain.

He was a one-man advertising extravaganza. The National Vigilance Committee (CBBB) was established in 1912 and he was appointed chairman two years later. In 1916, he engaged sales extraordinaire Arthur Frederick Sheldon to rename the sinister-branded Vigilance Committee as the iconic Better Business Bureau. By 1920, his leadership established the organization's Wall Street and banking connections that contributed to the Crash of 1929. He resigned as chairman in 1920 but continued voluntary management assistance during the New York Bureau's roll-out of the infamous "Before You Invest, Investigate" program in 1922.

THE APO$TATE

Sidener was heavily involved in almost every aspect of the advertising industry. He was president of Sidener, Van Riper & Keeling Advertising Agency (1925); president of the Advertising Club of Indianapolis; a principle member of AACA; launched the Truth in Advertising Movement in 1911; chairman of the National Vigilance Committee from 1914 to1920; chairman of the "Committee on Relation" for the AACW; member of the AACW's National Advertising Commission and "a representative of its Joint Assembly"; vice-president and "charter member of the American Association of Advertising Agencies" from 1928 to 1931; and a member of the "Council of Departmental Activities" for the Advertising Federation of America.

During the late 1920s, Sidener worked to improve "agency-client relations" as an executive committee member of the American Association of Advertising Agencies. The Advertising Hall of Fame website reported that "he helped prepare three important booklets: Buying and Selling Advertising Agency Service, How to choose an Advertising Agency, and Teach Advertisers to Select Advertising Agencies – Not Plans."

Merle Sidener was born on August 7, 1874, in Crawfordsville, Montgomery County, Indiana. Sidener attended Shortridge High School that was founded in 1864 and now listed on the "U.S. National Register of Historic Places." Shortridge became famous for producing the first daily newspaper in the United States called *The Shortridge Daily Echo*. Sidener graduated with a degree from Butler University, which was built in 1855, and located in Indianapolis, Indiana. His wife was Eva M. Sidener (1874-1971).

Sidener grew up in a newspaper-oriented family. His uncle Wallace E. Coons (1867-1935) worked his way up in the newspaper business starting as a printer and became "recognized as one of the outstanding newspaper editors of the state." Coons worked for several newspapers including the old *Argus* weekly, *Argus-News*, *Journal* and *The Journal and Review* in Crawfordsville, Indiana. He worked for the *Journal* until 1914 before it merged with *The Review* of which he was "part owner" to form the *Journal and Review*. Coons was editor of *The Journal and Review* while simultaneously employed as vice-president of *The Journal Review Publishing Company*. He was also member of the Crawfordsville Rotary Club. Sidener was influenced by his uncle. Consequently, Sidener's career and personal convictions followed a similar pattern. In his early newspaper career, Sidener also worked for the *Journal* ("*Old Journal*") as well as *The News* and became the City Editor of *The Indianapolis Star*. Additionally, Sidener was also a dedicated member of the Rotary.

In 1905, Sidener extended a job offer from *The Star* to writer Guernsey Van Riper at the *Louisville Courier-Journal*. Van Riper accepted. Four years later, Sidener and Van Riper went into business together forming the Publicity Corporation on July 22, 1909. Publicity Corp. commenced business on February 20, 1910, and offices were located at "Room 607 Majestic Building on Pennsylvania Street"; their first account was "The National Paving Brick Manufacturers' Association" from 1910 to 1911. Publicity Corp. became "Publicity Counsel" on April 29 and 30, 1914, which changed to Sidener-Van Riper Advertising Company (SVR) on February 23, 1915; and incorporated as Sidener, Van Riper & Keeling on January 4, 1925. According to Indianahistory.org, "Sidener was responsible for business decisions and Van Riper for the agency's editorial and creative aspect." Their company "policy" was to "accept only employment in which we could take pride and satisfaction and be pretty sure to be paid."

SVR ran their first full-page ad in the *Saturday Evening Post* advertising rubber tires for "Kokomo Rubber Company" in 1916 and gained notoriety for the agency. Then, SVR instigated the formation of the American Association of Advertising Agencies, which splintered from the Associated Advertising Clubs of the World in 1917 in order to specifically address the demands of large advertising firms not met in the general assembly. Howard Caldwell joined SVR on April 26, 1919. He left in 1922 along with another SVR employee, Ellis J. Baker, to form "The Howard Caldwell Company" that became Caldwell-Baker Company on February 10, 1923. By 1935, SVR took on national clients like Valvoline Oil Company and American Thermos Bottle Company and "published its first color advertisement for the destination city Hollywood-by-the-Sea, Florida." During World War II (1939 to 1945), SVR created newspaper advertising that "promoted the sale of war bonds and civilian defense."

On August 2, 1911, Sidener encouraged the passion and ethical conviction that begat the Truth in Advertising Movement. The glitterati of the advertising industry attended the AACA's annual convention held at Ford Hall, in Boston, Massachusetts. Sidener introduced the phrase "truth in advertising"; the Advertising Hall of Fame reflected, "He not only launched the campaign, but coined the slogan as well." And Joseph Appel legitimized Sidener's truth movement with his inspirational *Ten Commandments of Advertising*.

Thereafter, a chain of events unfolded. The truth crusade begat the *Printers' Ink* Model Statute that was drafted on October 25, 1911, which enlisted the Advertising Club of New York as a "guinea pig" for the first experimental Vigilance Committee that influenced creation of the Vigilance Committee of New York on March 12, 1912. Surprisingly, Sidener was not listed among the first Vigilance Committee's founding committee members, nor was he listed among the first members of the first National Vigilance Committee that began operating three months later, in June 1912.

The 1909 *Who's Who of Advertising* listed a brief biography of Sidener; he was president of Advertiser's Club of Indianapolis from 1912 to 1914. During this time, he was a member of the AACA. On June 25, 1914, the AACA changed its name to Associated Advertising Clubs of the World (AACW) and elected Sidener as chairman of the National Vigilance Committee at its first international convention held in Toronto, Canada. Sidener was re-elected chairman the following year at the June AACW convention held in Chicago. Sidener-Van Riper Advertising Agency's address was listed at 1206-1207 Merchants Bank Building, Indianapolis, Indiana.

In 1919, Sidener orchestrated the Bureau's introduction into securities and involvement with the NYSE, but he left the National Vigilance Committee's payroll in 1920, while remaining a voluntary consultant. Research indicated that Sidener met with securities officials in Washington, D.C., in mid-June 1919 and then attended the AACW convention on July 10-11, 1919, for the association to act upon respective discovery; Sidener's meeting promoted the Bureau's regulatory involvement in burgeoning securities fraud. The issue of *Editor and Publisher's*, dated June 26, 1919, published the article, "Ad Vigilantes Meet In Chicago July 10-11," which reported, "Merle Sidener of Indianapolis, chairman of the national vigilance committee, was in Washington, a few days ago, attending a meeting of "blue sky" commissioners in their battle of investment frauds, and the conference at Washington further advances this co-operative work." As a result, in 1920, the Cleveland Advertising Club introduced their slogan "Before You Invest, Investigate" that was coined by Salmon P. Halle, identified as a "Cleveland merchant," but the "Cleveland plan" failed to consider that securities were fleeting intangible commodities that could not be guaranteed and/or investigated, which questioned the Bureau's ulterior motive. In fact, the Cleveland plan was inherently fraudulent and invoked crony conspiracy with the brokers and bankers from the NYSE and Investment Bankers Association, yet Sidener promoted the idealistic viewpoint that the Bureau sought to educate the public, thwart public disorientation, and curtail mounting securities fraud. The fact that Sidener legally separated from the Bureau when the program was launched in 1920 suggested a defensive maneuver cognizant of criminal liability in order to shield his partnership in a major advertising agency. Hindsight proved that the Bureau followed a *Roaring Twenties'* reckless mentality and did engage in historic criminal activity that threw the world into financial chaos.

Kenner maintained Bureau loyalty and delusion when reflecting upon the Cleveland plan's purpose 16 years later. He wrote, "The purchasing power of the country was being depleted and future reservoirs of wealth were being impaired. The individual robbed of his savings was discouraged from further thrift, prejudiced against investment in legitimate enterprises, and his mind was poisoned against honest business and the protective power of government." In fact, Kenner wrote such hokum in 1936 only after the Bureau was saved by FDR and his disgraced name was redeemed by procuring a position within the prestigious SEC. Furthermore, his comment actually described the Bureau's criminal behavior that "robbed" investors of savings. By 1936, the Bureau and its caldron of golden coattails had begun their globalist ascent while the rest of the world drowned in misery as a result of the Bureau's Cleveland plan that contributed to the Crash and Great Depression.

In reality, the Great Depression was a by-product of the 1920-21 Depression that erupted after WWI and inspired the Bureau's financial debut on the wings of securities regulation. In 1919, Sidener presided over Bureau affairs that aligned the franchise with its largest member, the NYSE. Strategy aimed to nationalize the Cleveland Bureau's "Before You Invest, Investigate" securities program. Florida Senator Duncan Fletcher accused the NYSE, New York Bureau, and Investment Bankers Association of funneling $815,000,000 million dollars of "foreign securities" through "American banking houses." The Bureau was accused of encouraging risky speculation and operating its investigative program as a clearinghouse to promote questionable NYSE securities to the public as safe investments. Senator Fletcher lambasted the Bureau franchise during U.S. Senate investigations: "The unsavory testimony coming out about the flotation of these securities brings forcibly to mind the existence in this country of the greatest racket ever known in its history, to wit: The hook-up between the New York Stock Exchange, the Investment Bankers' Association, and their puppet, which is known as the Better Business Bureau."

The Bureau's securities investment program continued throughout the contentious Prohibition era. The program was disbanded after the U.S. Senate hearings, which began in 1932, and ended in 1934 with the Pecora Commission's investigative findings that were formally entitled, "Stock Exchange Practices Report of the Committee on Banking and Currency," a.k.a. "Fletcher Report."

Sidener was one of the original golden coattails. His biography portrayed him as a compassionate religious man, which conflicted with his involvement in propagating "Before You Invest, Investigate" that contributed to the Crash. According to the "Sidener Academy for High Ability Students" website, he "founded the Santa Claus fund to finance summer camp for sick children in the Indianapolis area"; "he served as a member of the Board of School Commissioners for four years in the 1930's and was president of that body"; was "active in the Chamber of Commerce and Rotary"; was "a director of the Citizens Gas and Coke Utility"; a director of the YMCA; "member of the Columbia Club"; "founder of the Christian Men Builders Class at the Third Christian Church, which grew to be the largest men's Bible class in the United States"; and "received the Junior Chamber of Commerce 1941 Award of Merit as an "outstanding American."

From June 28 to July 2, 1936, the Advertising Federation of America held its Silver Jubilee that celebrated the 1911 Boston Convention. Sidener and Samuel Candler Dobbs were among the Bureau's surviving 1911 celebrities who attended as special guest speakers. In particular, Sidener's sermon was consumer-oriented and sternly reminded truth in advertising: "There is no twilight zone. Advertisements are either good or bad. They are truthful or dishonest. They are believable or misleading ... Our greatest danger is not in the enemies outside our ranks, but in the free thinkers within ... The publication of advertisements that destroy confidence in all advertising is directly hurtful to the public. For the public has a right to believe advertising."

Sidener's namesake agency continued its journey to greatness. On January 1, 1955, SVR consolidated with Howard, Larkin & Co. to form "Caldwell, Larkin & Sidener-Van Riper, Inc." with Howard Caldwell named president of the agency. In 1963, Caldwell received the *Printers' Ink* Silver Medal "for his contributions to the advertising industry." In February 1964, Caldwell became chairman of the board and "Ed Van Riper" was appointed president. In 1967, Van Riper changed the agency's name to Caldwell-Van Riper, Inc. (CVR). In 1970, Frank J. Wemhoff became president of CVR. "By 1981" the agency was celebrated as "one of the Midwest's largest and Indiana's oldest agencies."

The City of Indianapolis, Indiana, recognized Sidener through education. Three schools were named in his honor: Merle Sidener Middle School 59, Merle Sidener Junior High School, and Merle Sidener Gifted Academy. In 2014, the U.S. Department of Education made the Academy a National Blue Ribbon School that "demonstrated academic excellence or showed significant progress in closing achievement gaps."

Kenner's *The Fight for Truth in Advertising* referred respectfully to Sidener on many occasions. His comments recalled events shared with a dear friend: "He had some new ideas about advertising service, about ways of influencing the minds of men in business, and about reaching the public. He was a strong believer in educational methods in the fight for truth in advertising. After Mr. Sidener had made a good start in applying these beliefs, Elbert Hubbard wrote: "One Merle Sidener of Indiana, a bald-headed, blue-eyed, straight-speaking, true-thinking, incorruptible fighter, is now the head of the vigilance work of the Associated Advertising Clubs of the World. He is bent on destroying the 'graft' of the last of the easy-money men. Also he desires to educate honest merchants and manufacturers who are too enthusiastic, who are afflicted with overstatement in advertising"."

At the age of 74, Sidener passed away "late" Monday evening, May 10, 1948, at his home on North Park Avenue in Indianapolis, Indiana. That same year, the Advertising Hall of Fame was established and Sidener was inducted in 1950. He had been suffering "declining health" the past year and was rendered "bedfast" 10 days before his death. He was interred at Crown Hill Cemetery in Crawfordsville, Marion County, Indiana (Find A Grave memorial 46021301).

Sidener's biographical information was elusive and/or incomplete. I updated Find A Grave's records on October 27, 2015. Research suggested that he had been married, but his private life was as secret as the Sphinx Club. Otherwise, history should acknowledge Sidener's advertising flair and acumen that introduced the Better Business Bureau.

CHAPTER **19**

ARTHUR FREDERICK SHELDON

Arthur Frederick Sheldon
Coined the name "Better Business Bureau"; Founder of
Sheldon School of Business and prolific author; artist: Caryn Cain.

His motto was "He Profits Most Who Serves Best" and he was ultimately known for creating the name "Better Business Bureau." He was a respected "author, lawyer and business scientist" and operated the Sheldon School of Business, Sheldon Publishing Company, and *The Business Philosopher* magazine. His sales concept combined "scientific method and ethical behavior." He was a Rotarian and humanitarian who practiced equality and compassion. His gift of articulation redirected the Truth in Advertising Movement and why grandmasters of the industry sought his all-encompassing expertise.

Arthur "Art" Frederick Sheldon was born in Michigan on May 1, 1868. His wife was Anna Griffiths Sheldon (1871-1958). They had two children: Helen M. Sheldon (1898-1976) and Arthur Frederick Sheldon (1899-1929).

THE APO$TATE

At the age of 34, he founded the Sheldon School of Salesmanship in downtown Chicago, Illinois, which operated from 1902 to 1939. He was a renowned pioneer in the art of high-pressure sales and "emphasized that a salesman should not be merely an order taker but one who was rendering a real service to others." Besides sponsoring correspondence courses, the Sheldon School sold books that catered to business colleges, high schools, Y.M.C.A.'s, and self-help. The school was very successful. In 1904, student enrollment was 150 students per month. When reaching its most popular juncture, in 1915, the school boasted an enrollment of "over 10,000 students from around the world."

In 1908, he moved his printing operations and family to Rockefeller, now known as Mundelein, in Lake County, Illinois, a northern suburb of Chicago. Sheldon bought 600 acres of land and built a school and home. He created the mile-long Mud Lake, established commerce, and employed about 195 local residents, mostly women. He also "persuaded villagers in mid-1909 to change Rockefeller's name to Area, an acronym for his company's motto: Ability, Reliability, Endurance, and Action." His correspondence school swamped the local post office with mail and consequently upgraded operations from fourth to first class. The school ultimately failed when WWI drained the town of manpower and income. In 1921, Sheldon sold the property to the Catholic Diocese that built St. Mary of the Lake Seminary. Mud Lake later changed to St. Mary's Lake.

Sheldon was a prolific writer. His books included *The Science of Successful Salesmanship; A Series of Lessons Correlating the Basic Laws Which Govern the Sale of Goods for Profit*, Chicago, 1904; *Elements in Success*, Chicago, 1909; *The Measure of Value*, Chicago, 1909; *The All-Around and Four Square Man*, Chicago, 1909; *The Art of Selling: For Business Colleges, High Schools of Commerce*, Chicago, 1911; *The Science of Business Building: A Series of Lessons Correlating the Fundamental Principles and Basic Laws Which Govern the Sale of Goods and Services for Profit*, Chicago, 1911; *The Science of Efficient Service; or The Philosophy of Profit Making*, Chicago, 1915; and, *The Science of Business, Being the Philosophy of Successful Human Activity Functioning in Business Building or Constructive Salesmanship*, Chicago, 1917. In the early 1900s, Sheldon's books filled a scholastic void; schools were deficient in the field of sales and were just beginning to add "advertising and the allied branches of marketing education to the curriculums of American universities."

As a Rotarian, Sheldon held personal and professional convictions of friendship and sharing of vocational knowledge. The Rotary was founded by Chicago attorney Paul Harris, on February 23, 1905, during a meeting with "Silvester Schiele, a coal merchant, Gustavus Loehr, a mining engineer, and Hiram Shorey, a tailor." Weekly meetings continued "in turn at the office or home of the members. Rotation was meant to allow each member to acquaint himself with the profession of the others and lead Harris to call his club Rotary," which later became "Rotary International." Sheldon joined the Chicago Rotary Club in January 1908. Sheldon and Harris expanded the organization. The first Rotary Club convention was held in 1910 whereby Sheldon delivered a speech that rendered the organization one of its most celebrated mottos, "He Profits Most Who Serves Best"; he also composed and advertised 800 classifications to encourage rotary membership. Eventually, Sheldon became president of the Chicago Rotary Club. After leaving Chicago, he helped organize the first Rotary Clubs in "London and Manchester," England. The Rotary Club offered a voluntary service that sought to encourage "friendships, promote equality and encourage tolerance and respect among people of all races, religions and socioeconomic backgrounds," according to Ask.com.

Sidener was a member of the Rotary and aware of Sheldon's marketing talents. At the time, Sidener was president of the Advertising Club of Indianapolis, Indiana, and chairman of the Indianapolis-based National Vigilance Committee. Sidener approached Sheldon, "the gifted apostle of service," to summon a new moniker for their expanding Vigilance Committees. Sidener wanted a more attractive commercial name to replace the ominous "Vigilance" that reminded of "night-riders and tar and feathers"; he was a partner of the prestigious advertising agency "Sidener, Van Riper & Keeling," also located in Indianapolis, and understood the influential power and universal appeal of an impressive name.

In early 1916, Sidener invited Sheldon to be a guest speaker at his advertising club's meeting. Kenner also attended and described the momentous event when Sidener and Sheldon made advertising history: "Mr. Sheldon walked to a blackboard in the meeting-room, took up a piece of chalk and, pausing, said: "You have a grip on something fundamental to all business success, not alone to the success of advertising. I suggest you use this name" – and he wrote on the board - "Better Business Bureau." "That's it. That tells exactly what we aim to do," agreed Mr. Sidener."

Sheldon retired to his ranch in "Mission, Texas." He continued to speak on occasion for the Rotary. On December 21, 1935, he passed away at the age of 67 and was laid to final rest at Montrepose Cemetery, Kingston, Ulster County, New York (Find A Grave memorial 47846826). Considering the dynasty that he named, his humble tombstone surprisingly shunned braggadocio and tested time with an equally simplistic epithet inscribed: "BUSINESS. SCIENTIST. AUTHOR. LECTURER. HE PROFITS MOST WHO SERVES BEST."

Six months after Sheldon's death, the Advertising Federation of America held its 25th anniversary convention in Boston, from June 28 to July 2, 1936.

THE APO$TATE

Surprisingly, the AFA made no mention of or tribute to Sheldon in the convention's commemorative publication, *Truth in Advertising; Twenty-Fifth Anniversary*, and guest speaker Sidener completely omitted Sheldon's name. Today, the Better Business Bureau represents one of the most powerful names in history.

CHAPTER 20

FEDERAL TRADE COMMISSION

I mailed a certified complaint letter to the FTC on January 23, 2009, advising awards fraud by the Better Business Bureau. Despite gravity of complaint, I received a generic "Ref. No. 1633992" kiss-off reply on February 10, 2009. The FTC dismissed my awards fraud and deceptive trade practice complaints with the ludicrous excuse, "The Commission does not resolve individual complaints." Apathetic response showed no consideration for my irrefutable evidence that the CBBB and Bureaus were operating an awards racket that fleeced untold millions of dollars every year from untold millions of consumers. Furthermore, I believed that longstanding clandestine FTC and CBBB cronyism rejected my complaint letter and threw consumers under the bus.

The height of hypocrisy and cronyism was underscored by an FTC "opinion letter," drafted August 15, 2011, that responded to CBBB's request letter, dated April 19, 2011, seeking approval for a new digital "accountability program" based on advertising "ethics." According to the FTC, "Under this program, the Council of Better Business Bureaus (the "CBBB") will hold companies engaged in online behavioral advertising ("OBA") accountable for compliance with the "Self-Regulatory Principles for Online Behavioral Advertising" (the "Principles"), released in July 2009 by a coalition of industry associations and administered by the Digital Advertising Alliance ("DAA")." The DAA "was formed through funding and the cooperation of the American Association of Advertising Agencies, the American Advertising Federation, the Association of National Advertisers, the Direct Marketing Association, and the Interactive Advertising Bureau"; all afore listed entities are associated with CBBB.

Accordingly, I question why the FTC was gauging approval of CBBB's OBA program based on advertising standards rather than constitutional law? And why was FTC patting CBBB on its gilded back with a "Statement of Pertinent Facts," which resembled a Bureau-planted propaganda puff piece?

FTC reiterated that "the BBB system seeks to promote ethical business and advertising practices," whereby the FTC sounded more like a cheerleader than a regulator. All the while, CBBB and participating Bureaus continue to operate an online racket that swindles consumers through a bogus awards program promoting evaluated excellence and ethics.

The FTC's advisory letter was a perfect example of a casual rubber-stamped relationship with CBBB emphasized by cozy comments like "subsequent telephone conversations between FTC staff and CBBB representatives." Additionally, FTC acknowledged interaction with CBBB before and after its April 19th letter, which insinuated a perennial open-door policy.

Ultimately, the FTC approved CBBB's OBA program: "For the reasons stated above, FTC staff believes that the CBBB's proposed OBA accountability program is unlikely unreasonably to restrain trade. Accordingly, we have no present intention to recommend a challenge to the program." Needless to say, my stomach turned when reading the FTC's beatification of CBBB's specious accountability program further reiterating how the Bureau leapfrogged its way into a nation state.

Thereafter, the accountability program led to CBBB's participation in the digital transatlantic EU-U.S. Privacy Shield Framework program adopted on July 12, 2016. And, three months later, on October 1, 2016, Obama's DOC administration handed U.S. control of Internet rights to the Internet Corporation for Assigned Names and Numbers (ICANN), which aligned with the EU.

The FTC's long-term embedded partnership with CBBB disingenuously implied that the organization was a federal agency, which it is not. Additionally, FTC cronyism commits conflict of interest and has impeded the Bureau's regulation for almost a century; FTC initiatives promote (express or implied) the Bureau's authoritarian operations as being quasi-governmental by integrating the organization into federal programs that mislead, confuse, and exploit consumers. Accordingly, I believe that the FTC's symbiosis with CBBB makes it complicit in the nonprofit's questionable programs and awards racket whereby preventing strict enforcement of the Federal Trade Commission Act of 1914. Furthermore, since I initially reported awards fraud, the FTC made no effort to investigate the Bureau. Instead, the FTC's inaction condoned and embedded the concept of merit programs without advising consumers of their specious nature, which is tantamount to tendering a false bill of goods to consumers and returning commerce to yesteryear's precarious caveat emptor. In fact, I consider the FTC just as culpable as the Bureau akin to two peas in a shifty pod.

Federal cronyism fueled the Bureau's spectacular metamorphosis into a globalist hypocritical autonomous aristocratic plutocratic autocratic oligarch. In 1928, the Periodical Publishers' Association deemed the National BBB their "agency of assistance" during a conference with the FTC that resulted in the

FTC's crony relationship with CBBB. Then Truman built on FDR's understated relationship with the prestigious New York Bureau and General Manager H. J. Kenner. When governor of New York, FDR maintained a working, but wary relationship with the New York Bureau evidenced by his vague, yet telling reprimand: "No honestly intentional membership corporation should hide its roster; no group of men should be permitted to operate in the dark." Until the 1950s, Bureau memberships were not advertised, and clandestine reverence was sustained by ecclesiastic operations that nuanced the Christian military order of the Knights Templar (1119-1314).

It is the duty of the FTC to uphold consumer protection laws by regulating competition and advertising, but the FTC's centurial relationship with the advertising industry, CBBB, and Bureau franchise question its Obama-era objectivity and ability to judiciously perform legislated duties. My personal experience proved the FTC showed no interest in pursuing my complaint of awards fraud against CBBB and/or Houston Bureau even though I was reporting respective consumer fraud, racketeering violations, and deceptive advertising practice on a global basis.

Research indicated that the DOC and FTC gave CBBB golden keys to the NWO kingdom; FTC federales routinely intermingled with CBBB and its programs. In turn, CBBB partnered with the DOC, FTC, and the EU to enforce transatlantic Internet regulation. Lionized titles were bestowed to FTC personnel in exchange for CBBB's quasi-governmental veneer empowered by respective federal employees' tenured government careers, departmental affiliations, and ambient influence; such cronyism reeked of judicial malfeasance, bribery, collusion, and racketeering. Consequently, after a century of intimidation and disparagement almost every business in the United States is a member of the Bureau and integral to its fifth-column army that steamrolls independent commerce across America. The FTC empowered the Bureau to stretch its tentacles across the Internet to market its online cash cow while ignoring my alleged IRS mandates and RICO abuse. Furthermore, why is a profiteering overlord like CBBB allowed to double-dip as a tax-exempt nonprofit charitable foundation and recipient of government grants? True non-profits are not monopolizing kleptocrats and cyber commandos.

Accordingly, it is my belief that the U.S. Federal government is controlled by a plutocratic shadow government promoting a NWO agenda steered by Illuminati comprised of Obama holdovers and EU sycophants. The NWO has infiltrated governments across the globe to control the masses by levying censorship and ruination against those who oppose them. Repercussions are unconscionable and threaten unparalleled global annihilation of national culture, civilization, and sovereignty. I believe that the CBBB and Bureau franchise are Illuminati minions wielding carte-blanche autocracy.

THE APO$TATE

The Houston Bureau's website posted, "What are the Privacy Shield Principles?" A contentious answer empowered the EU; "Individual Recourse" was defined as "conciliation and/or arbitration services ... to resolve complaints from EU individuals that the parties were unable to resolve on their own ... EU residents have the option of filing complaints directly with their DPA, which will work with the Department of Commerce and the Federal Trade Commission ... to investigate and resolve complaints." The acronym "DPA" was not explained but represents the "Data Processing Addendum" of the EU's "Main Agreement" stipulating that customers will abide by EU "Data Protection Laws and Regulations." It would take another book to fully explain the evolution of the Privacy Shield program. In short, the EU Commission-approved version of the program unfolded in tandem with ICANN's Internet takeover on October 1, 2016, which I believe aligned with EU's intended annexation of America. The United Kingdom, which is the United States' closest ally, voted for Brexit on June 23, 2016, during implementation of the Privacy Shield program. EU initiatives subsequently formed a database of compliant international businesses digitally regulated by the DOC/FTC/Bureau under the sanctimonious aegis of certification while insidiously embedding EU nation-building constructs. Timing suggested that Obama handed U.S. Internet sovereignty to EU cohort ICANN to pave the way for the United States of Europe's land and cyber domination. Brexit threatened EU-NWO evolution by excising its largest member and influencing other member exits. Henceforth, the EU continued to impede Brexit and other populist-leaning European elections to maintain a left-wing globalist stranglehold.

The first three antitrust laws had to be amended to include false advertising. The Sherman Act of 1890 was expanded in 1914 by the Federal Trade Commission Act and the Clayton Act; violation of one violated all three. Then, in 1938, the Wheeler-Lea Amendment was passed to add regulation of false advertising to the Federal Trade Commission Act.

The Sherman Act was signed into law by President Benjamin Harrison on July 2, 1890, and sponsored by Ohio Senator John Sherman (1823-1900), also a former Republican member of the House of Representatives, former secretary of the treasury, and former secretary of state. The law attacked monopolies and prohibited unreasonable restraint of trade, including "plain arrangements among competing individuals or businesses to fix prices, divide markets, or rig bids." Furthermore, "Any combination 'in the form of trust or otherwise that was in restraint of trade or commerce among the several states, or with foreign nations' was declared illegal." Legislative progress was made, but additional market enforcement measures were needed. Accordingly, FTC.gov stated, "By 1899, the Supreme Court had established that the Sherman Act broadly prohibited price-fixing cartels, but the law's application to other forms of interfirm cooperation, and more importantly its application to business consolidations, remained in doubt."

On February 14, 1903, Congress created the U.S. Department of Commerce and Labor that was signed into law by President Theodore Roosevelt Jr. Its investigative division was named the Bureau of Corporations and responsible for regulating Big Business and monopolies. President Roosevelt's predecessor, 25th President William McKinley, was supported by steel, banking, and oil monopolies. On September 6, 1901, McKinley was shot, and he died on September 14, 1901. McKinley's assassination appointed Vice President Theodore Roosevelt as 26th POTUS resulting in a trust-busting crusade led by the Bureau of Corporations. The irony was that Big Business contrived progressive Teddy's powerless vice-presidency to control him and maintain their stranglehold on American business. Titans of industry never dreamed McKinley would be whacked by an assassin and open the door to their worst nightmare.

On March 4, 1913, Democrat Woodrow Wilson was inaugurated 28th POTUS and his revolutionary "progressive legislative policies" restructured the Department of Commerce and Labor and begat the Federal Trade Commission Act and the Clayton Antitrust Act. Prior to Wilson's 1912 election, the Supreme Court introduced the "Rule of Reason" in "*Standard Oil Co. v United States*, 221 U.S. 1 (1911)," which highlighted subjects of "trusts and antitrust" that steered political platforms and post-inaugural reformation measures. Accordingly, on Wilson's inaugural day, the Department of Commerce and Labor separated into two departments, the Department of Labor and Department of Commerce (DOC).

On September 26, 1914, the Federal Trade Commission Act was signed into law by President Woodrow Wilson and created the independent FTC; operations began on March 16, 1915, and absorbed the DOC's Bureau of Corporations, including its duties and personnel. According to FTC.gov, "Like the Bureau of Corporations, the FTC could conduct investigations, gather information, and publish reports. The early Commission reported on export trade, resale price maintenance, and other general issues, as well as meat packing and other specific industries. Unlike the Bureau, though, the Commission could also bring administrative cases." The act banned "unfair methods of competition" and "unfair or deceptive acts or practices" while enforcement was regulated by the FTC. It was further stated, "Its "blue sky" cases, predating the Securities Act, were the start of Federal securities regulation."

The *Printers' Ink* Model Statute uniquely initiated a punitive penalty for deceptive trade. The FTC worked with the AACA, local advertising clubs, and the National Better Business Bureau (CBBB) and Better Business Bureaus to enforce the statute, which was introduced in November 1911 and first passed by the state of Ohio in 1913. The FTC Act did not include advertising at the time and the Bureaus relied heavily on the statute to process lawsuits for false advertising.

The creation of the FTC included construction of the Federal Trade Commission building. President Franklin Delano Roosevelt personally laid its cornerstone and delivered its commemoration: "May this permanent home of the Federal Trade Commission stand for all time as a symbol of the purpose of the government to insist on a greater application of the golden rule to conduct the corporation and business enterprises in their relationship to the body politic." FDR's respective speech is available at [https://www.ftc.gov/about-ftc/our-history]. The FTC building was completed in 1938 and located at 600 Pennsylvania Ave. N.W., Washington, D.C.

The Clayton Act was signed by President Wilson on October 15, 1914, and regulated areas not covered by the Sherman Act. Principle sponsor was Democratic Alabama Representative Henry De Lamar Clayton Jr. (1857-1929). The law's Section 7 "prohibits mergers and acquisitions where the effect "may be substantially to lessen competition, or to tend to create a monopoly"." In 1936, an amendment was added by the Robinson-Patman Act that "bans certain discriminatory prices, services, and allowances in dealings between merchants." Then, in 1976, another amendment introduced the Hart-Scott-Rodino Antitrust Improvements Act, which required "companies planning large mergers or acquisitions to notify the government of their plans in advance."

On March 21, 1938, the Wheeler-Lea Act amended Section 5 of the FTC Act to "prevent unfair methods of competition and unfair or deceptive acts or practices in or affecting commerce" coined as deceptive trade practice. According to FTC.gov, "The 1938 Wheeler-Lea Act contained the first major amendments to the Federal Trade Commission Act. It provided civil penalties for violations of Section 5 orders. (Civil penalties were not available under the Clayton Act until 1959)." The amendment included enforcement over "abuses of advertising; the imposition upon the unsuspecting; and the downright criminality of preying upon the sick as well as the consuming public through fraudulent, false, or subtle misleading advertisements." The FTC's previous restriction, that regulated only business, was removed and added consumer-protection mandates that allowed the agency to "administer a variety of laws on behalf of consumers and business." The new law did not require proof and changed a previous U.S. Supreme Court ruling that held "when challenging deception as an unfair method of competition, the FTC had to show harm to competitors." FTC.gov also stated that "a series of provisions in the new law addressed food and drug advertising, and included the first FTC Act language that authorized pre-complaint injunctions." Sponsors were California Democratic Representative Clarence Frederick Lea (1874-1964), chairman of the House Committee on Interstate and Foreign Commerce, and Montana Democratic

FEDERAL TRADE COMMISSION

Senator Burton Kendall Wheeler (1882-1975).

Today, the DOC is included among the President's Cabinet as legislated by the U.S. Constitution's Article II, Section 2. According to Whitehouse.gov, "The Cabinet includes the Vice President and the heads of 15 executive departments — the Secretaries of Agriculture, Commerce, Defense, Education, Energy, Health and Human Services, Homeland Security, Housing and Urban Development, Interior, Labor, State, Transportation, Treasury, and Veterans Affairs, as well as the Attorney General."

During the formative years of advertising law, a symbiotic relationship developed between the advertising industry, FTC, and Democratic Party whereby FDR's gilded relationship with the National BBB and Bureaus hid mounting impropriety. In fact, the FTC participated in the Bureau's Truth in Advertising Movement; Wansley reflected, "Perhaps the earliest large scale effort along this line was in 1928 when the periodical publishers, in a trade practice conference with the Federal Trade Commission, designated the National Better Business Bureau as their agency of assistance in determining the acceptability of advertising copy." The periodical publishers' trade group eventually split from the AACA but later joined a similar advertising association.

Prior to the Stock Market Crash of 1929, the FTC was in charge of securities regulations. The Bureau promoted a bogus investigative program from 1920 until the Crash under the catchy slogan "Before You Invest, Investigate" that claimed to safely screen securities transacted through the NYSE and Investment Bankers Association while all aforementioned entities disguised questionable pretenses and value of securities. The FTC ignored the triad conglomerate's mounting securities fraud. As a result, excessive abuse of Blue Sky laws, in addition to volatile short selling, contributed to the Crash and Great Depression.

Blue Sky laws were state-level measures to protect consumers from securities fraud. Registration of securities, stockbrokers, and brokerage firms was required to assure legitimate transactions. Unfortunately, the laws exempted securities sold by the Exchanges and shielded the Bureau, NYSE, and Investment Bankers Association even though they were manipulating the sale of securities and violating state laws through interstate sales that perpetrated mail fraud. In fact, Senate investigations revealed that "the Investment Bankers Association told its members as early as 1915 that they could "ignore" blue sky laws by making securities offerings across state lines through the mail."

In March 1932, the U.S. Senate Commission on Banking and Currency initiated securities investigations. A second and more intensive phase engaged the Pecora Commission hearings from January 1933 to June 1934. During such timeframe corrective measures created the Securities Act of 1933 ("Truth in Securities Act") and the Securities Exchange Act of 1934, which established the Securities and Exchange Commission (SEC). Senator Fletcher was chairman of the Pecora Commission and outlined various instances of securities fraud, interrogatories, and corrections in his "Stock Exchange Practices Report of the Committee on Banking and Currency," completed on June 6, 1934, and published on June 16, 1934. His report specifically called attention to securities violations by trusts and pools defined as "concentration of wealth" that were contributing factors of the Crash.

Senator Fletcher died two years after the Pecora Commission ended and the SEC began. He would be turning in his grave if he knew that Kenner and the New York Bureau wormed their way into the SEC's investigative division through their contacts at the FTC. After all, his charges of racketeering against the NYSE, Investment Bankers Association, and Bureau triumvirate fueled the Pecora Commission's Wall Street reform that begat the SEC. In January 1932, a couple of months prior to the commencement of U.S. Senate hearings, Senator Fletcher called the triumvirate "the greatest racket ever known in its history." New York authorities were aware of the triumvirate's underhanded activities. Republican Representative Fiorello La Guardia received formal complaints from New York City businessman E. C. Riegel, president of the Consumers Guild of America, and reported complaints to Democratic Senator Fletcher who reported allegations to Republican President Hoover and Republican South Dakota Senator Peter Norbeck (1870-1936), chairman of the U.S. Senate Banking and Currency Commission. Senator Fletcher replaced Chairman Norbeck and assumed chairmanship of the Pecora Commission when Democrat Franklin Roosevelt was inaugurated POTUS on March 4, 1933. After Senator Fletcher's death, FDR allowed Kenner and the New York Bureau to participate in the new SEC whose creation was inspired by the fraudulent activities of the triumvirate.

On June 30, 1934, Joseph P. Kennedy Sr., father of John F. Kennedy, was appointed the first chairman of the SEC by FDR much to the chagrin of Senator Fletcher who promoted Ferdinand Pecora for the position. Kennedy had been investigated by the Pecora Commission for securities fraud relative to money pools, but FDR ultimately nominated Kennedy as SEC chairman while privately explaining that his decision was based upon his concept of "set a thief to catch a thief." During the early stages of FDR's first administration, the FTC lost power of securities' authority to the SEC. In fact, Section 5, of the Federal Trade Commission Act, previously enforced the Securities Act of 1933, but the Securities Exchange Act of 1934 created the Securities Exchange Commission to replace the FTC's securities' division. Consequently, high-profile executives transferred from the FTC to the SEC, which the New York Bureau exploited.

Two former Bureau presidents, Kenner and Wansley, both insinuated the organization was shielded by the FTC. Kenner described several instances in *The Fight for Truth in Advertising* that indicated the Bureau and FTC operated in tandem; the Bureau would issue complaint and the FTC would faithfully investigate and prosecute. Then Wansley smugly bragged that the FTC's tacit deputation of the Bureau tendered an irrefutable stamp of approval and impunity. He emphasized a 1940 quote by Muriel Tsvetkoff, manager of the San Francisco Bureau, that predicted the Bureau's future autocracy: "No government agency will ever seriously curtail our work ... The reason: consumers will come to the Bureau to complain, or for information in preference to consulting government or prosecuting agencies." Accordingly, Tsvetkoff's comment substantiated my complaint that the Bureau shares a conjugal relationship with the FTC.

History emphasized an embedded U.S. government relationship with the Bureau. Two particular instances involved the FTC, SEC, and U.S. Post Office. George C. Mathews was a former "member of the Federal Trade Commission before he was appointed to the Securities and Exchange Commission." In August 1934, Mathews delivered a speech to the National Association of Better Business Bureaus in Milwaukee, Wisconsin, which partly stated, "The Chief Examiner of the Federal Trade Commission has furnished me with a tabulation showing that over a period of years 389 matters dealing with competitive methods have been referred to the Trade Commission by Better Business Bureaus in leading cities of the country." Another occasion described the Post Office's participation in the Advertising Federation of America's silver anniversary convention held in Boston in 1936. Thomas J. Murray, "[a]ttorney in the Solicitor's Office of the Post Office Department," was among several esteemed speakers endorsing the Bureau and exclaimed: "To your organization, the Better Business Bureaus, newspapers and all kinds of periodicals, we must look for educational campaigns designed to protect the public against the swindler." Kenner described the FTC's guidelines and initial activities in the business arena: "It began conferences with representatives of various industries as early as 1919, to obtain a practical understanding of unfair competition problems, and to provide the means for the formulation of "rules defining, expressing, and prohibiting methods, practices, and acts recognized as unfair, wrongful, invalid, or detrimental to the public or to the industry"."

In 1934, the Securities and Exchange Commission commenced operations and Kenner and the New York Bureau lobbied affiliates of the FTC for insider participation. The Bureau set its crosshairs on Mathews as a former high-profile FTC official who joined the SEC. In August 1934, he was guest speaker at the National Association of Better Business Bureaus, Inc.'s annual convention and his presence confirmed a symbiotic federal relationship: "The records of the Federal Trade Commission will show that cooperation between that Commission and the Better Business Bureaus has existed not only in the administration of the Securities Act, which until the first part of September is to continue within the duties of the Federal Trade Commission, but in the administration of those portions of the Federal Trade Commission law which deal with unfair practices in competition ...." In April 1935, Kenner served as chairman of the committee that drafted "the actual organization and operation of the new department" that became known as the SEC's "Securities Violations Section." Within a year, the New York Bureau established a firm relationship with the SEC. On May 28, 1936, James M. Landis, chairman of the SEC, wrote a letter to James C. Auchincloss, president of the New York Bureau, NYSE, and National BBB, commending the Bureau for its services, and acknowledged, "We look forward to the continuance of our effective cooperation."

The modern FTC openly promotes the CBBB and Bureau franchise underscoring conflict of interest and why the federal watchdog quickly dismissed my respective awards fraud claims. On July 24, 2006, AdAge issued a press release publicizing the appointment of a high-profile FTC officer to oversee NARC that included CBBB: "C. Lee Peeler, deputy director of the FTC's Bureau of Consumer Protection, has been named as the new president-CEO of the National Advertising Review Council." In turn, CBBB's (bbb.org) press release elaborated, "C. Lee Peeler, Esq., is ... Executive Vice President, National Advertising, Council of Better Business Bureaus (CBBB)." In retrospect, NARC was established in 1971 by the Association of National Advertisers, Inc. (ANA), the American Association of Advertising Agencies, Inc. (AAAA), the American Advertising Federation, Inc. (AAF), and the Council of Better Business Bureaus, Inc. (CBBB). Additionally, on October 3, 2017, Thomas Pahl, acting director, FTC Bureau of Consumer Protection, advised, "The FTC regards the Council of Better Business Bureaus' programs under the Advertising Self-Regulatory Council - including the NAD, CARU, ERSP, and NARB - as models in national advertising enforcement. We value all your hard work and partnership in helping protect a free market economy by challenging false and misleading national advertising that harms both consumers and competition."

NARC's mission lauds truth in national advertising but operates on CBBB funds siphoned from Bureau fees garnered from awards fraud. (Members make fortunes from the awards program and return revenue to the Bureau through membership fees and advertising; then the Bureau turnstiles revenue back to CBBB as Bureau fees.) Furthermore, NARC's duties were described as "the body that establishes the policies and procedures for the CBBB's National Advertising Division (NAD) and Children's Advertising Review Unit (CARU), as well as for the National Advertising Review Board (NARB)." Additionally, CBBB self-admitted that "NAD/NARC/NARB's sole source of funding is derived from membership fees paid to the CBBB." Accordingly, I allege that NARC and its subsidiaries are complicit in awards fraud under the fruit of the tree doctrine.

CBBB's annual reports list collective assets and do not itemize fees received from the independent Bureaus. As such, I allege that the CBBB/Bureau franchise system inherently facilitates money laundering of awards revenue. In its

2013 Annual Report, under "Statements of Activities," CBBB disclosed income from the Bureaus, national sponsors, and various programs that include, but do not mention, the integrity awards. In fact, CBBB specifically listed "Bureau dues," "National partner dues," and "BBB programs" under annual report's "CHANGE IN NET ASSETS" revenue column.

As of 2016, the FTC and DOC alarmingly empowered CBBB and grew the Deep State Better Business Bureau. CBBB was involved with Obama's DOC during the handover of the Internet to globalist ICANN. The DOC and FTC created digital privacy programs with the EU and utilize the digital reporting services of the Bureaus. The ICANN handover involved a rapid-fire sequence of events that unfolded as though synchronized with the November 2016 presidential election that expected a Democratic victory. And I believe that the Bureau participated in the ICANN transference along with a litany of progressive nonprofits and globalist mainstream and social media sycophants allied with the Democratic Party's NWO.

On July 12, 2016, "the U.S. Secretary of Commerce Penny Pritzker joined European Union Commissioner Věra Jourová to announce the approval of the EU-U.S. Privacy Shield Framework"; regulated by the DOC/FTC. The EU-U.S. program is a "data privacy" operation promoted as an international job and investment creating venue to "ensure access to the latest technologies, while providing strong privacy protections." In reality, the program facilitated the EU's censorship of the Internet. The DOC began "accepting certifications" for the program on August 1, 2016, and included a self-certification disclaimer: "The decision by a U.S.-based organization to join the Privacy Shield program is entirely voluntary. However, once an eligible organization publicly commits to comply with the Privacy Shield Principles through self-certification, that commitment is enforceable under U.S. law by the relevant enforcement authority, either the U.S. Federal Trade Commission (FTC) or the U.S. Department of Transportation (DOT)." Accordingly, CBBB's National Director Florence Henderson acknowledged a fundamental objective to "enhance privacy protections for EU citizens and provide greater certainty for U.S. companies doing business in Europe."

A month later, the United States government signaled historic forfeiture of Internet rights suggesting a major advance of the NWO. On August 16, 2016, the *Washington Examiner* article, "America to hand off Internet in under two months," reported, "The Department of Commerce is set to hand off the final vestiges of American control over the Internet to international authorities." Effective October 1, 2016, the Internet Assigned Numbers Authority, "responsible for interpreting numerical addresses on the Web to a readable language," was placed under the control of the Internet Corporation based in Los Angeles. Texas Senator Ted Cruz issued a prophetic warning that "the agency could be used by totalitarian governments to shut down the web around the globe, either in whole or in part."

Democratic presidential nominee Hillary Clinton promised a radical socialist agenda that threatened free speech and penalized government critics. The *Federalist* published the article, "The Coming Free Speech Apocalypse," dated August 22, 2016, that reported, "Clinton has promised, if elected, to introduce a constitutional amendment within her first month in office that would effectively repeal the First Amendment by overturning the Supreme Court's *Citizens United v FEC* decision from 2010." Many questions arise concerning the FTC and DOC and their evolving affiliation with CBBB and the Bureau franchise. The DOC does not divulge the extent of its globalist relationship with CBBB's online business reporting services to hide expanding allied autocratic control of virtual commerce. Current trajectory suggests that CBBB will achieve consummate power making Bureau operations impregnable to any and all laws of the land in coordination with globalist initiatives. The Bureau's reporting services are positioned to covertly tether digital airways the same as it shackled land-based industries.

The *Rip-off Report* consumer blog also criticized the FTC and its regulation of the Bureau. The website reiterated my same belief that the FTC is nose-blind when matters involve the Bureau. In fact, we both posed a similar question to the FTC with no response: "Rip-off Report supports and assists all branches of government agencies since 1998, and many times have asked the FTC, why are they not looking into the BBB and the way they do business misleading consumers to do business with bad companies where the BBB hides complaints about their members who are ripping of unsuspecting consumers into doing business with them. To date we have never received a response."

Additionally, *Rip-off Report* performed a "straw poll" that reflected 70% of consumers believed the Bureau was a government agency. Its website questioned, "Why is the BBB listed in local phone books under Government Agencies?" In fact, the Bureau is not and never has been a government agency and was recently sued for false impersonation. Additionally, the website noted a federal umbilical cord: "The BBB is a Franchise operation that is also a non-profit that receives millions in grant money every year from the US Government."

Current "special statutes" have expanded the FTC's venue. FTC.gov advised that "the Commission now enforces an array of credit laws, including the Fair Credit Reporting Act and the Fair Debt Collection Practices Act." Otherwise, the Fair Credit law only applies to licensed agencies and omits the unlicensed CBBB and Bureau franchise further emphasizing respective licensing manipulation since 1930.

My complaints of awards fraud undermined the crony FTC/CBBB/BBB consumer protection narrative. The FTC insinuated an unconditional consumer complaint venue, yet dismissed my individual complaint: "The FTC encourages consumers to file a complaint whenever they have been the victim of fraud, identity theft, or other unfair or deceptive business practices. They can do it online, or by calling the FTC's Consumer Response Center at 1-877-FTC-HELP (1-877-382-4357)."

I was rejected by the FTC and advised that the agency required several individual complaints on a national level. On February 10, 2009, the FTC responded to my awards complaint with a letter labeled Ref. No. 21633992: "Thank you for recent correspondence. The Federal Trade Commission acts in the public interest to stop business practices that violate the laws it enforces. Letters from consumers and businesses are very important to the work of the Commission. They are often the first indication of a problem in the marketplace and may provide the initial evidence to begin an investigation. The Commission does not resolve individual complaints. The Commission can, however, act when it sees a pattern of possible violations developing. The information you have provided will be recorded in our complaint retention system. This computerized system enables us to identify questionable business practices that are generating numerous complaints and may be in violation of the law. Thank you for providing information that may be used to develop or support Commission enforcement initiatives. Sincerely Yours, Consumer Response Center." Accordingly, massive consumer fraud was disregarded by an apathetic generic form letter with no personal signee or signature attached. I realized the FTC's national cover-up after being relegated to "File 13." Greased palms closed ranks around CBBB's lucrative Unholy Grail, the Houston Bureau's *Awards for Excellence*.

The FTC promotes the Bureau's public persona as an immune federal agency. No efforts have been made to advise consumers of the Bureau's nongovernmental status and to correct the Bureau's fraudulent awards program since my notification in 2009. The FTC has no excuse because I was not the only complainant; others offered Bureau fraud-related complaints that invalidated the FTC's professed multiple-complaint mandate. In fact, in 2010, CBBB and the Los Angeles Bureau were splashed across national television by ABC *20/20's* explosive documentary that exposed the franchise's bogus rating score; the documentary included former Attorney General of Connecticut Richard Blumenthal's scathing letter that lambasted CBBB for questionable rating scores and national Torch awards.

Federal cronyism has placed the Bureau above the law whereby encouraging a false pretense of authority and a mirage of superiority that masquerades illicit implication and exaggeration. The FTC has enabled rather than deterred consumer fraud. As a result, the FTC is complicit in the Bureau's indiscretions that hypocritically betray mutual birthrights of consumer protection and truth in advertising. Obama's FTC has disgraced its heritage and mission. Successors knowingly and willingly collaborated with the Bureau's phony awards program that is nothing more than an ingenious marketing gimmick that has monopolized and corrupted the business industry. The FTC has lost its way and must reform or close its doors. Consumers depend upon a judicious FTC to regulate national deceptive trade and deceptive advertising.

In keeping with modern globalist expansion, U.S. Supreme Court Justice Hugo Lafayette Black (1886-1971), nominated by President Franklin Delano Roosevelt, rose through the ranks as a Democratic politician and was considered "a staunch supporter of liberal policies and civil liberties." His generic warning seemed tailor-made to address current FTC cronyism with the Bureau: "There is no duty resting upon a citizen to suspect the honesty of those with whom he transacts business. Laws are made to protect the trusting as well as the suspicious ... The rule of caveat emptor should not be relied upon to reward fraud and deception."

CHAPTER **21**

WORLD WAR I

Gavrilo Princip
Anarchist started World War I; assassinated
Archduke Ferdinand and Archduchess Sophie; artist: Caryn Cain.

"Two rounds from one pistol and the world rocked" when 19-year-old Bosnian Serb Gavrilo Princip (1894-1918) assassinated heir-apparent Archduke Franz Ferdinand of Austria and his wife Sophie, the Duchess of Hohenberg, while on a state visit to the Austrian-Hungarian capital of Sarajevo in Bosnia-Herzegovina. Princip was a member of Mlada Bosna ("Young Bosnia") with a mission to end "Austro-Hungarian rule in Bosnia and Herzegovina" and promote the "creation of Yugoslavia through unification of Bosnia and Herzegovina with Servia." The world suffered over 38 million casualties because he believed Yugoslavia should "be freed from Austria."

On June 28, 1914, Princip shot the Archduke in the neck and the Duchess in the stomach. Archduke Ferdinand bled uncontrollably and refused direly needed medical treatment while frantically begging care for his mortally wounded wife. Both died shortly thereafter and were interred at Artstetten Castle in Austria. On February 4, 1915, the *Duluth News Tribune* article, "Executed for Crimes Causing World War," reported that on Wednesday, February 3, 1915, three of Princip's co-conspirators, Veljko Cubrilovic, Mieko Jovanovic, and Danelo Ilic were executed "in the prison of the court fortress at Sarajevo, Bosnia." Two others had death sentences reduced; Jakov Kilovic received life in prison and Nedji Kerovic was commuted to 20 years. Princip was too young to be sentenced to death and was sent to prison for 20 years; he died of tuberculosis at the age of 23.

A domino-effect led to war's European sparring between Allies versus Central Powers. Allies included the Triple Entente (Russian Empire, the French Third Republic, the United Kingdom of Great Britain and Ireland), Japan, and Italy. The Central Powers included Germany and Austria-Hungary, the Ottoman Empire, and Bulgaria. Both primary alliances added ancillary countries as war progressed. War unfolded in rapid succession; on July 23, 1914, Austria-Hungary delivered to Serbia the July Ultimatum, "a series of ten demands that were made intentionally unacceptable, in an effort to provoke a war with Serbia"; on July 24-25, 1914, Russia ordered "partial mobilization of its armies"; on July 25, 1914, Serbia ordered general mobilization of its military; on July 28, 1914, Austria-Hungary declared war on Serbia; on July 30, 1914, Russia declared general mobilization of forces and Germany responded with an ultimatum for Russia to demobilize, which Russia refused; on August 1, 1914, Germany declared war on Russia; on August 23, 1914, Japan entered the war siding with the Triple Entente hiding ulterior motive to use war's distraction "to expand its sphere of influence in China and the Pacific"; and, on April 26, 1915, the Treaty of London was signed "by United Kingdom of Great Britain and Ireland, the French Republic, the Russian Empire, and the Kingdom of Italy" in order to align Italy with the Triple Entente.

President Woodrow Wilson pursued neutrality during most of the war until the infamous Zimmermann telegram was intercepted by British Naval Intelligence on January 9, 1917. Eight days later, Britain's Political Section decrypted the secret transmission sent by the German Kaiser, "I order that unrestricted submarine warfare be launched with the greatest vigor on February 1. You will immediately take the necessary steps." British Intelligence intercepted a second signal on January 16, 1917, known as the Zimmermann Telegram, that was "an internal diplomatic communication issued from the German Foreign Office ... that proposed a military alliance between Germany and Mexico in the event of the United States entering World War I against Germany." The telegram was the final indignity after Germany engaged ocean warfare sinking British and American shipping vessels including the *William P. Frye* (U.S.), the *Lusitania* (U.K.), and the *Housatonic* (U.S.). On April 4, 1917, the "U.S. Senate voted 82 to 6 to declare war against Germany" and the U.S. House of Representatives agreed "by a vote of 373 to 50." Two days later, April 6, 1917, the United States entered WWI.

Only 100,000 troops volunteered, which forced conscription. By the end of the war, there were more than two million soldiers in the American Expeditionary Forces. A fully employed workforce prior to the war hindered the armed forces ability to staff its ranks and the United States struggled to retool wartime industries.

President Wilson engaged the media to create an advertising campaign to sell the American public on the war effort. In 1917, *Kansas City Independent* newspaper publisher George Creel (1876-1953) was approved by the president to spearhead the "Committee on Public Information (CPI)"; in 1920, Creel published the book, *How We Advertised America*. Accordingly, author Stephen Fox wrote, "In only two years the total annual volume of advertising *doubled*, from $1.5 billion worth in 1918 to just under $3 billion in 1920." Henceforth, WWI cemented the advertising industry's relationship with the federal government.

Congress enacted the First Liberty Bond Act on April 24, 1917, which approved the sale of Liberty Loans and/or War Bonds by the U.S. Treasury. Liberty Loan pins were patriotically worn to promote the sale of the bonds to finance the war effort. The advertising industry designed several advertising campaigns for the war department. A particular 1918 Liberty Loan advertising poster featured the slogan "If You Can't Enlist – Invest." No doubt that the Bureau's 1920 slogan "Before You Invest, Investigate" was a Liberty Loan knock-off.

Liberty Bonds marked the first eye-opening collaboration between the War Department and advertising industry. *Printers' Ink* led the charge and aggressively promoted sale of Liberty Bonds through articles and advertising. In fact, *Printers' Ink*, Vol. CV, October 3, 1918, No. 1, was jam-packed with ads and war stories that were meant to subliminally sell Liberty Bonds. Advertising included soldiers holding "bulletins" that advertised bonds; one example stated, "Sergeant Jim Says: "The only way we fellers in khaki can judge you folks at home is by the way you come across for Liberty Bonds"."

Printers' Ink also patriotically supported *Stars and Stripes* described as the "newspaper of the American Expeditionary Force, in Paris" and "was edited by Guy T. Viskniskki." The newspaper's military masthead was impressive: "The Official Publication of the A.E.F.; Authorized by the Commander-in-Chief, A.E.F.; By and for the soldiers of the A.E.F.; Published every Friday in Paris, France by members of the A.E.F." *Printers' Ink* published the article, "Advertising Space Sold by the Inch," which discussed printing and overseas delivery of *Stars and Stripes*; that it "was delivered on the day of publication to the men in the front line in Argonne by American pilots flying Liberty planes. Two thousand two hundred copies done up in bundles of ten were scattered along the line from the western edge of the Argonne forest itself to Brieulles on the Meuse. Some fell 1,000 feet, others were dropped from airplanes that almost grazed the tops of the trees. The soldiers ran pell-mell for the papers as they fell – the rush being similar to the crowds that gather about the bargain counter at department stores."

Liberty Bonds were redeemable same as cash, which invited scammers to conjure elaborate schemes to steal them from consumers. Like bees to honey, the National BBB and Bureau franchise leapt at the opportunity to work with the U.S. Federal Government and advertise their business services. Thereafter, in 1928, the Periodical Publishers Association promoted the National BBB to the FTC as their "agency of assistance in determining the acceptability of advertising copy." The Bureau triangulated its celebratory title into disingenuous authoritarian quasi-governmental empowerment.

Advertising took on new power and prestige during WWI with innovative advertising that drew on raw patriotism. The most famous political artist was James Montgomery Flagg (1877-1960) who contributed the famous depiction of Uncle Sam and "I Want YOU for U.S. Army" war recruitment poster. Flagg used himself as "a model" for the aged version of "Uncle Sam."

In fact, the iconic "Uncle Sam" was Sam Wilson (1766-1854), a post-American Revolutionary War meatpacker. Wilson was 15 years old when he participated in the American Revolution. His duty was to protect food supplies and prevent poisoning by the enemy. On March 8, 1793, Sam and his brother Ebeneezer opened E & S Wilson slaughterhouse in Troy, New York. During the War of 1812, when the British burned Washington, D.C., almost to the ground, Sam provided barrels of food for the soldiers stamped "U.S." that "gained him the moniker of "Uncle Sam", which then became a symbol for the United States." Samuel "Uncle Sam" Wilson died at the seasoned age of 87 and was laid to rest in Oakwood Cemetery, Troy, Rensselaer County, New York (Find A Grave memorial 1114).

In June 1917, 14,000 U.S. soldiers with the American Expeditionary Forces began arriving in France under the command of General John Joseph "Black Jack" Pershing (1860-1948). The Bureau saw many of its employees drafted, causing several offices to temporarily close. Kenner wrote, "Most of the vigilance staff men had left for war service, during 1918."

The war influenced technological development, military service, and daily life. Blacks migrated to the North causing a labor deficit offset by commercial substitution including "labor-saving appliances" and "power farming equipment." Additionally, "the Government insisted on a separate sleeping unit for every soldier in the barracks" because of the deadly Spanish Flu pandemic. As a result, twin beds became popular as well as divorce. Furthermore, "national daylight saving was put into effect in 1918," according to *Printers' Ink*, "as a means of providing incentive for the home gardening movement and to save on electricity."

A ceasefire armistice was signed on November 11, 1918, in Compiègne, France. Occasion was celebrated as Armistice Day, which was effective the ""eleventh hour of the eleventh day of the eleventh month" of 1918." On June 28, 1919, the Treaty of Versailles (Versailles, France) officially ended the First Great War.

Memorial Day (Decoration Day) honors only fallen soldiers, and Veterans Day (Armistice Day) honors all veterans. On May 5, 1868, General John Logan, "national commander of the Grand Army of the Republic," introduced Decoration Day to honor slain Civil War soldiers. General Order No. 11 declared, "The 30th of May, 1868, is designated for the purpose of strewing with flowers, or otherwise decorating the graves of comrades who died in defense of their country during the late rebellion, and whose bodies now lie in almost every city, village and hamlet churchyard in the land." Inspired by the Korean War (June 25, 1950 until July 27, 1953), Congress passed Public Law 380 on June 1, 1954, which changed Armistice Day to Veteran's Day and honored all wars and all soldiers, living and dead, with commemoration celebrated every November 11th. On June 28, 1968, Congress passed the National Holiday Act (Public Law 90-363) which took effect January 1, 1971, and changed Decoration Day to Memorial Day and reset federal holiday observances to Mondays. The act "was intended to ensure three-day weekends for federal employees by celebrating four national holidays on Mondays: Washington's Birthday, Memorial Day, Veterans Day, and Columbus Day."

WWI acknowledged and entrenched the importance of advertising. The U.S. Federal Government aligned with the advertising industry and "sold the war to the working men" by "mobilizing the nation's resources for war" including Selective Service enrollment. *Printers' Ink* reflected, "Both the Government and associations of business men sponsored campaigns to inspire the laboring man to speed up production of needed materials. Advertising was used to raise shipyard volunteers, then to impress upon these 300,000 workers the importance of the task in which they were engaged. It was used to encourage conservation of coal and gasoline and food and other vital supplies."

CHAPTER **22**

PROHIBITION

Demand for regulation of intoxicating liquors began to emerge after the American Revolution ended on September 3, 1783, at the signing of the Treaty of Paris. The following year, Dr. Benjamin Rush (1746-1813), Founding Father of the United States, signer of the Declaration of Independence, and esteemed member of the Continental Congress, published *An Inquiry Into the Effects of Ardent Spirits Upon the Human Body and Mind*. Five years later, in 1789, two hundred farmers united in Connecticut and formed a temperance group "to ban the making of whiskey." Alcoholic consumption had evolved in the colonies ranging from light alcohol such as cider to heavier beverages like rum and whiskey producing a drunken backlash counterproductive to the welfare and growth of a new nation.

Temperance organizations grew powerful after the Civil War and caused economic repercussions that relied upon taxation of alcoholic beverages. War's end included the assassination of Lincoln at Ford's Theater, which was particularly relevant because "Temperance Theater" was a driving force prior to the Civil War and promoted an underlying message of abstinence. One of the most popular temperance plays was W. H. Smith's *The Drunkard* in 1841 that featured "144 shows" in Boston before proceeding to rave reviews on Broadway.

In a similar manner, Lincoln was the ultimate playwright using the Civil War to press his abolitionist convictions. After Lincoln's assassination, a beleaguered, war weary, and divided nation turned away from his Emancipation Proclamation that he unleashed after exploiting the blood-soaked banks of Antietam Creek (outside of Sharpsburg, Maryland), which marked military history's bloodiest day, on September 17, 1862, with combined Union and Confederate "dead, wounded, or missing" soldiers estimated at 22,717. Reconstruction diverted a traumatized nation back to religion and temperance values while dealing with an aftermath of soldiers' disease consequent to morphine and alcohol addictions. Consequently, the Progressive Reformation Era produced dramatic innovations in technology, communications, and transportation.

Federal prohibition legislation was not initiated until the United States declared war against Germany on April 6, 1917. In fact, Prohibition did not take effect until a year after WWI ended. The spirit of war, onset of longer work hours in the factories, and a powerful nationwide temperance movement influenced the proposal of the 18th Amendment on December 18, 1917, to ban the "manufacture, sale, or transportation" of alcohol, but provided exclusion for consumption and private possession. The 18th Amendment was eventually ratified (passed by all states) by Congress on January 16, 1919, and took effect January 17, 1920.

In the interim, WWI wreaked havoc creating global food shortages, particularly grain. War officially ended on Armistice Day, November 11, 1918. A week later, November 18, 1918, Congress ratified the temporary Wartime Prohibition Act, which took effect June 30, 1919, and banned alcohol content over 2.75% as a measure to preserve grain used in the production of alcohol.

Thereafter, the National Prohibition Act, also known as "Prohibition" or "Volstead Act," was implemented as the prosecutorial arm of the 18th Amendment to exact penalties and define the realm of intoxicating liquors. The Volstead Act suffered contentious passage; on June 27, 1919, the act was introduced by the U.S. House of Representatives; on July 22, 1919, the act was approved by the U.S. House of Representatives; on September 5, 1919, the act was approved by the U.S. Senate; on October 27, 1919, the act was vetoed by President Wilson; on October 27, 1919, the act was overridden by the House; and, on October 28, 1919, the act was overridden and approved as law by the Senate.

Wayne Bidwell Wheeler (1869-1927), an attorney from Ohio and a prohibitionist with the Anti-Saloon League, "conceived and drafted" the Volstead Act (H.R. 6810) of 1919 "to provide the government with the means of enforcing Prohibition" and executing penalties. The act was named after its legislative sponsor, Minnesota Republican Representative Andrew John Volstead (1860-1947), chairman of the House Judiciary Committee. Volstead served in office from March 4, 1903 to March 3, 1923, and lost re-election in 1922.

The Volstead Act partly read, "TITLE II. PROHIBITION OF INTOXICATING BEVERAGES. SEC. 3. No person shall on or after the date when the eighteenth amendment to the Constitution of the United States goes into effect, manufacture, sell, barter, transport import, export, deliver, furnish or possess my intoxicating liquor except as authorized in this Act, and all the provisions of this Act shall be liberally construed to the end that the use of intoxicating liquor as a beverage may be prevented."

The act's penalty clause Section 29 partly read, "Any person who manufactures or sells liquor in violation of this title shall for a first offense be fined not more than $1,000, or imprisoned not exceeding six months, and for a second or subsequent offense shall be fined not less than $200 nor more than $2,000 and be imprisoned not less than one month nor more than five years."

And the act's medically exploited Section 7 inadvertently encouraged a medical hooch industry in-between sanctimonious lines: "No one but a physician holding a permit to prescribe liquor shall issue any prescription for liquor. And no physician shall prescribe liquor unless after careful physical examination of the person for whose use such prescription is sought, or if such examination is found impracticable, then upon the best information obtainable, he in good faith believes that the use of such liquor as a medicine by such person is necessary and will afford relief to him from some known ailment. Not more than a pint of spirituous liquor to be taken internally shad be prescribed for use by the same person within any period of ten days and no prescription shall he filled more than once. Any pharmacist filling a prescription shall at the time endorse upon it over his own signature the word "canceled," together with the date when the liquor was delivered, and then make the same a part of the record that he is required to keep as herein provided."

The U.S. Treasury Department, Bureau of Industrial Alcohol, issued "Prescription Forms for Medicinal Liquor" to doctors allowing prescriptions for a pint of "medicinal alcohol" to each "patient" every week-and-a-half at the cost of about $3.00 per prescription. In 1932, Dr. Arthur Dean Bevan, University of Chicago, reported that enterprising doctors sold their allocated 400 prescriptions per year for medicinal bootlegging. Pharmacists similarly profited for filling each prescription, and, also forged bogus prescriptions to circumvent the doctor as a middleman. Additionally, nonmedical entrepreneurs (businessmen) built breweries to support a growing medical industry while pharmacists jumped on the bandwagon to expand business operations. In fact, pharmacist Charles Walgreen greatly expanded his business during Prohibition.

Section S3 double-downed on Section 7 making a mockery of the Hippocratic Oath: "After February 1, 1920, the possession of liquors by any person not legally permitted under this title to possess liquor shall be prima facie evidence that such liquor is kept for the purpose of being sold, bartered, exchanged, given away, furnished, or otherwise disposed of in violation of the Provisions of this title .... But it shall not be unlawful to possess liquors in one's private dwelling while the same is occupied and used by him as his dwelling only and such liquor need not be reported, provided such liquors are for use only for the personal consumption of the owner thereof and his family residing in such dwelling and of his bona fide guests when entertained by him therein; and the burden of proof shall be upon the possessor in any action concerning the same to prove that such liquor was lawfully acquired, possessed, and used."

The Increased Penalties Act, also known as the "Jones-Stalker Act" or "Jones Act," became effective on March 2, 1929. The Jones Act worked in tandem with the Volstead Act and increased penalties: "CHAP. 473. An Act to amend the National Prohibition Act, as amended and supplemented. Be it enacted by the Senate and House of Representatives of the United States of America in Congress assembled, That wherever a penalty or penalties are prescribed in a criminal prosecution by the National Prohibition Act, as amended and supplemented, for the illegal manufacture, sale, transportation, importation, or exportation of intoxicating liquor, as defined by Section 1, Title II, of the National Prohibition Act, the penalty imposed for each such offense shall be a fine not to exceed $10,000 or imprisonment not to exceed five years, or both."

The Jones Act was a last-ditch attempt to save Prohibition by Republican Senator Wesley Livsey Jones (1863-1932) of the state of Washington and Republican Representative Gale Hamilton Stalker (1889-1985) of the state of New York. Honorable intentions gravely underestimated national impact and/ or creative countermeasures by thirsty Americans. The Jones Act was based on the precarious assumption that assessing greater penalties for bootlegging would curtail the illegal sale and production of alcohol. In fact, the opposite effect occurred. The term bootlegging arose from hiding a flask of alcohol in a boot that was common footwear at the time. There was no "stop and frisk."

Out-of-touch armchair politicians failed to recognize the extent of desperation; that the poor had nothing to lose especially after the Crash when lucrative bootlegging surpassed the repercussions of a felony as a means of survival. In fact, entire neighborhoods engaged basement bootlegging. Prohibition agents were hauling moonlighting yesteryear soccer moms into jail.

On March 3, 1929, The *New York Times* article, "Coolidge Signs Bills for Stiff Dry Penalties; Two Are Arrested at Capital Under New Law," heralded the introduction of the Jones Act, which became effective the day before. The article documented the act's first unfortunate victims. There were many offenders, but two particular men were arrested during "liquor raids" held in Washington, D.C., prior to the following day's inaugural ceremonies for Herbert Hoover. According to The *New York Times*, "Eugene Liverpool and James Turner, both colored" were "probably the first arrested in the country after the Jones act became effective." Increased penalties listed a maximum $10,000 fine and five years' imprisonment, or both. Furthermore, law enforcement received a "$3,000,000.00 additional prohibition appropriation, available July 1." Hoover's presidency marked an intensified regulation of Prohibition.

A few days later, March 8, 1929, the *St. Louis Globe Democrat* article, "Fifteen Dry Law Violators Sentenced," highlighted lighter sentencing because Volstead violations had occurred before the "drastic" Jones Act became effective. Prohibition agent Merritt D. Padfield performed a sting operation that indicted "fifteen bartenders and saloon keepers" for "illegal sale and possession of intoxicants." The most extreme sentencing of the group was six months in jail and the largest fine was $1000 with the majority of assessed fees being $450. Violators benefited from the lag time in-between the Volstead Act and the effective date of the Jones Act that resulted in a substantial difference in jail time and fines.

Prohibition initially worked, but was defeated by bootlegging, the Depression of 1920-1921, and rise of organized crime. Prohibition especially targeted the "working-class poor" as the predominate class responsible for liquor running and production of moonshine. The workforce was swamped with returning soldiers and the economy tanked. Bootlegging and organized crime resulted from desperation, rebellion, and opportunity. No one was spared from Prohibition's explosive scatter-shot. A crime spree ravaged politics, courts, and police. Bootlegged alcohol poisoning caused needless fatalities from tainted hooch as a result of adding dangerous chemicals to assimilate booze buzz. Jails overflowed. Ruthless gangsters emerged as national celebrities with copycat thugs stalking every street corner. Draconian law converted millions of Americans into felonious "liquor runners." Otherwise, the wealthy continued life as usual stocking whatever wine, liquor and beer could be brewed, bought, and/or bribed, including POTUS. According to 1920-1930.com, "President Harding kept the White House well stocked with bootleg liquor, though, as a Senator, he had voted for Prohibition."

The *Denver Post* published cartoonist Fay King's serial comic strip, *Fay Likens Higherups and 'Pullmen' to Gangsters and His Clan*; a side-by-side comparison featured "Underworld" thugs dressed in gangland attire next to "Upperworld" businessmen wearing suits. King attached an article that described two colliding worlds using different means to achieve the same goal: "When a racketeer's territory is threatened he calls on his mob to pull guns and save him. When a higherup's business, professional or social career is threatened he calls on his pals with "pull" to save him. It amounts to very much the same thing if you view it without bias or partiality ... We heartily condemn the gangster and his gunmen, but the higherup and his pull-men are sometimes no better." King associated the term "racketeer" with mobsters and organized crime and may have been referring to the Bureau. Senator Duncan Upshaw Fletcher renounced the Bureau as a racket in the U.S. Senate on January 25, 1932; King published his cartoon on March 2, 1932.

Critics accused the Bureau of performing gangland-style activities that included bully tactics, extortion, special favors, and membership demands. Disparagement and ruinous results caused emotional distress and loss of business and livelihood. In fact, Frank O'Sullivan, author of *Rackets*, accused the Chicago Bureau of targeting his publishing business and causing him heart problems; he died at the age of 53. Another occasion found me searching for a particular article that described the Bureau's bully tactics against independent small loan companies; the article was located under a blockbuster headline about gangland murders. The front page of the *St. Louis Globe-Democrat*, dated February 22, 1929, featured the headline, "'DEATH CAR' IN CHICAGO GANG MASSACRE FOUND." Just below the article was a captioned sub-article, "Business Bureau Explains Its Stand on Small Loan Act." My immediate reaction was tantamount to "a picture is worth a thousand words"; although the articles were separate from each other, the Bureau was historically recorded next to an overshadowing and incriminating screenshot of gangland activities. Aside from awkward optics, the Bureau's public-relations machine issued the article to counter critic's allegations that the Bureau manipulated Missouri's pay day loan industry on behalf of influential financial members.

The Missouri Uniform Small Loan Law was first enacted in 1891 and "declared invalid any chattel mortgage given to secure a usurious loan." Chattel mortgages were used to secure small loans with household goods (furniture) until the integration of payday loans. Lenders became known as "salary buyers." Interest rates fluctuated for several years with Bureau members raising rates to 3 1/2%. The 1929 amendment settled rates at 2 ½%. By 1939, the rate increased to 3% while adding extra investigation and "extra hazard" fees.

The Bureau's payday-loan members were referred to as "42 Per Centers" meaning they collectively charged 3 1/2% interest per month or 42% per year. Critics alleged antitrust violations. The Bureau published the *St. Louis Globe-Democrat* article to deny, discredit, and divert allegations regarding the Missouri Uniform Small Loan Act of 1929: "Answering criticism on the score that a number of licensed lenders in the city are members of the Better Business Bureau, Harry W. Riehl, the general manager of the bureau, asserted it "both untrue and ridiculous to say that such memberships were accepted to combat salary buyers or for any other ulterior purpose"." Yet Riehl questionably admitted, "The Bureau does have among its members licensed lenders, seventeen in number at present, who constitute 2 per cent of the membership of the bureau and 10 per cent of the members whose business specifically is that of lending money."

WWI's influx of returning soldiers substantially increased Bureau ranks and militarized the Bureau with wartime skills. Branch offices were strategically positioned similar to battle zoning and placed in major cities throughout the United States. The Bureau self-indulgently transformed into a presumptive quasi-governmental organization to embed empire, practices, and authority. A confused public assumed the Bureau was a government agency encouraged by respective false authoritative implication.

Temperance movements railed against the evils of alcohol and "moral decline" beginning with the Women's Christian Temperance Union (WCTU), formed in 1873. Twenty years later, the Ohio Anti-Saloon League launched on May 24, 1893. That same year, the Anti-Saloon League in Washington, D.C., also organized. In 1895, the Ohio and Washington organizations merged and renamed the "Anti-Saloon League of America" (ASL). The ASL engaged intensive lobbying efforts against saloons and endorsed whatever political candidate was sympathetic to their cause. According to Ohiohistorycentral.org,

"The Anti-Saloon League's primary publication was the *American Issue*, but published numerous other tracts as well. During the League's heyday, it issued more than forty tons of anti-liquor publications every month." The temperance movement's most renowned advocate was Carrie Amelia Moore Nation (1846-1911), self-addressed as "Carry-A-Nation." She was an imposing figure at six feet tall and invented the term "hatchetations" that involved "breaking saloon windows and mirrors and destroying kegs of beer or whiskey with a hatchet." Her convictions were influenced by the death of her first husband from alcoholism. History painted her as the fiery epitome of Prohibition.

Prohibition proved to be the motherlode of unintended criminal consequences and insidious decadence that spread into every corner of society. Archives.gov advised that "by 1925 in New York City alone there were anywhere from 30,000 to 100,000 speakeasy clubs." And, on June 14, 1930, the *St. Louis Post Dispatch* cited an investigation performed by the staff of the *Daily News*, which concluded that the City of Chicago had "6000 speakeasies" selling "beer, whisky and gin." The *Daily News* conservatively estimated that "$5,785,000 is paid weekly to gangsters through operation of speakeasies, gambling houses and handbooks, disorderly houses and extortion schemes." Additionally, it was stated, "Including the speakeasies, some 15,000 places in the city which are outlets for alcohol, drug stores which peddle gin, cigar stores which peddle gin, and beer flats with gin or yockey-dock (a caramel-colored whisky imitation)." Accordingly, a panacea of debauchery spewed from the sale of illicit liquor forging "an alliance between crime and politics," which encouraged wide-spread police and judiciary corruption with no concern for collateral death and destruction. Even doctors succumbed to the temptation of easy money generated from a prescription pad.

On March 5, 1929, the *St. Louis Globe Democrat* article, "6 Months, $1000 Fine For Ex-Police Chief," reported former Johnson City Chief of Police Hezzie Byrne, former State Attorney Arlie Boswell, and former Williamson County Coroner George Bell were indicted for "liquor law violation conspiracy" in what was referred to as "the Boswell trial" in Danville, Illinois; other non-official conspirators included Pete Selmo and Dominic Loni. Byrne was sentenced to "six months in the Franklin County Jail." And Boswell received the most severe penalty and was "sent to the penitentiary."

On June 17, 1930, the *St. Louis Post Dispatch* article, "Prohibition Agent Killed, Aid Shot, Two Others Hurt," honored the stolen life of enforcement agent P. L. Flinchum. Storyline described a "running pistol fight" whereby Flinchum and several agents chased "an automobile they suspected to be loaded with liquor." In true Bonny and Clyde fashion, the "liquor runners" shot at agents through their "rear window." Flinchum was shot in the head causing the car to veer off the road and crash into a tree injuring the other agents; he left behind a wife and "two small children."

On February 3, 1932, the *Denver Post* article, "Doctor Assails Bootlegging in Prescriptions," interviewed University of Chicago's Dr. Bevan. He warned that "90 per cent of liquor prescriptions issued by doctors in the country are "bootlegging prescriptions"" and were "bootlegging prescriptions in the sense that they are not issued for medical purposes but to be used as a beverage." Dr. Bevan stated physicians could make "about $1,200 a year" selling their annual quota of 400 prescriptions, which considerably boosted their salaries since "the lower half make less than $2,500 a year." His comments referred to the Volstead Act's Section 7.

On March 5, 1932, the *Denver Post* article, "Mayor And Police Chief Are Arrested," referenced Mayor George R. Dale and Chief of Police Frank Massey, of Muncie, Indiana. The men "were arrested by deputy United States marshals" and indicted along with 39 others "in a conspiracy to violate the national prohibition act."

According to author Ralph Blumenthal, "Prohibition's toll was grim. One hundred seventy-eight civilians and ninety-two federal agents killed. More than half a million people convicted of alcohol violations and fined more than $80 million ... More than 200,000 jailed. And more than $200 million worth of property seized."

Many of those who initially clamored for the passage of Prohibition later opposed it. After a decade of Prohibition, the temperance movements reversed gears requesting an end to one of history's worst mistakes. On February 18, 1929, the *St. Louis Globe Democrat* article, "Temperance Body Seeks to Modify Prohibition Law," reported the Church Temperance Society and "fifteen hundred Episcopal clergymen" engaged a campaign to modify the Volstead Act with a "more practical legislation in the interest of temperance." The Society complained that "all but a few of the fanatical extremists – who would rather brand any drinking as a crime than reduce the actual amount of drunkenness – will prefer the honorable course of modification to the cowardly hypocrisy of nullification."

Herbert Clark Hoover (1874-1964) ran on a dry platform. He was inaugurated 31st POTUS, on March 4, 1929, and immediately clamped down on Prohibition sending a swarm of federal agents into the streets. His inauguration followed the passage of the Jones Act a couple of days earlier.

To the contrary, Franklin Roosevelt (1882-1945) ran on a wet platform in 1932 promising to repeal Prohibition. After FDR's inauguration as 32nd POTUS, on March 4, 1933, the U.S. Congress quickly passed the Cullen-Harrison Act on March 21, 1933, legalizing beer and wines with 3.2% alcohol content that undermined the Volstead Act's 0.5% limit. The act was sponsored by New York Democratic Representative Thomas Henry Cullen (1868-1944) and Mississippi Democratic Senator Byron Patton Harrison (1881-1941). On December 5, 1933, the 21st Amendment repealed the 18th Amendment (the only Amendment to be repealed to date). But remnants of Prohibition still remain today; several states maintain "Blue Laws" that "restrict alcohol sales in certain cities."

CHAPTER **23**

BEFORE YOU INVEST, INVESTIGATE!

The Bureau devised an investigative program that boasted safe screening of NYSE securities consequently promoting risky stock speculation while manipulating consumer-oriented Blue Sky state licensing laws to hide respective illicit transactions.

O'Sullivan's *Rackets* documented the Bureau's nefarious participation in the Stock Market Crash and whose cast of characters exemplified the glamorous corrupt frenetic evasive precarious bootlegging machine gun-riddled *Roaring Twenties*. His storyline captured the pivotal juncture in history, seven years after formation, when the Bureau's birth mission began to morph from a doctrine of truth to profit, and when the advertising industry melded with Wall Street and banking. He described the early 1930s as a punitive period that sought fire-and-brimstone accountability, including the U.S. Senate Banking and Currency Commission in 1932, which became the "Pecora Commission" in 1933; the formation of the SEC in 1934; and Special Prosecutor Thomas Edmund Dewey's New York City crime trials that prosecuted money pools, swindlers, and kingpins in 1935. O'Sullivan celebrated Logan Billingsley and others for exposing the Bureau's deceptive advertising and trade practices that included securities fraud, mail fraud, operating illegally without a license, racketeering, and collusion with the NYSE and Investment Bankers Association, which inspired historic legislative reform. The Bureau's complicity in the Crash was buried by FDR through his SEC and is only known today because of *Rackets*. Esteemed Democrat Chairman/Senator Duncan Fletcher deserved beatification for pursuing the Bureau for racketeering and Blue Sky securities fraud. Fletcher's exceptional and ethical bipartisan statesmanship changed American history as outlined in his *Stock Exchange Practices Report*, published on June 16, 1934.

O'Sullivan documented the Bureau's globalist epiphany that begat "Before You Invest, Investigate" as its first scam. Trusting speculators relied on the

Bureau's endorsement of supposedly screened NYSE securities while unaware that the Bureau manipulated Blue Sky licensing laws to prevent prosecution of its enterprising securities racket with the NYSE and bankers. It was a turbulent time: WWI had just ended; the Spanish Flu (*influenza A (H1N1)*) pandemic ravaged the world; unemployment was rampant; the 1920/1921 Depression sunk the economy; and, stock fraud was swirling.

WWI closed many Bureau doors. The organization engaged survival mode and internally corporatized through the NYSE while maintaining external Puritan pretenses. O'Sullivan wrote, "It was in 1919 that a change came o'er the spirit of the Better Business Bureau's dream. A wonderful new field of activity was opened up. It was a year of boom in the stock market. Americans had begun to invest and to speculate in securities as never before in their history. The demands of the great war had loosened their purse strings for the purchase of Liberty bonds … Office boys and girls learned how to speculate, and none foresaw the day of retribution, to come in 1929, when office desks were to be flooded with tears as the bottom dropped out of the stock boom … That was the time chosen by the Better Business Bureaus to enter the financial field, under the misleading slogan, "Before you invest, investigate," which replaced the former slogan, "Truth in advertising … So the Better Business Bureaus jumped into the breach, to act as investigators … while tacitly approving the offerings of its members and subscribers. And the Stock Exchanges were among its members."

In 1936, Kenner published *The Fight for Truth in Advertising* in conjunction with the Advertising Federation of America's 25th Silver Anniversary celebration of the 1911 Boston Convention, which sparked the Truth in Advertising Movement. In reality, Kenner's book was a rebuttal to *Rackets*. Kenner's style and point of view favored the Bureau, but his defense inadvertently corroborated O'Sullivan's allegations. He was a loyal company man and faithfully accepted and executed national directives as part of the greater good. As manager of the prestigious New York Bureau, Kenner was personally targeted by critics for the group's collaboration with the NYSE and Investment Bankers Association in addition to a litany of other criminal allegations. Most significantly, Kenner's comments were written after the Bureau was run through an intensive investigative gauntlet by the U.S. Senate and Pecora Commission. Accordingly, his statements reflected polished revisionist history.

On January 10, 1919, H. G. S. Noble, president of the New York Stock Exchange, began issuing warnings to the public against stock-swindling. Kenner quoted Noble: "While legislation is being prepared by the Capital Issues Committee, in collaboration with the administration and other governmental departments, the management of the Stock Exchange is apprehensive that before adequate protection is provided by law many investors may be irretrievably harmed." The following month, on February 17, 1919, Noble held a meeting at the Chamber of Commerce of New York for the "presidents of the leading financial and industrial interests in Wall Street." He read a letter from then Secretary of the Treasury Carter Glass (1858-1946) who stated, "I am genuinely glad to note that the New York Stock Exchange is starting a general movement to check vicious operations in worthless and fraudulent securities, pending enactment of suitable legislation by Congress."

Five months later, and just before the AACW convention held in Chicago on July 10 -11, 1919, Merle Sidener, chairman of the National Vigilance Committee, met with Washington officials regarding the alarming increase of securities fraud.

In 1920, the Cleveland Advertising Club introduced the "Cleveland Plan" and respective slogan "Before You Invest, Investigate." Kenner explained, "This phrase was suggested by Salmon P. Halle, a Cleveland merchant who knew the value of expressing ideas tersely." The idea was to approach "wage-earners through the industrial plants" and "to protect wage-earning investors especially – before they parted with their money." Bottom line, the Bureau wanted first crack at workers' money by steering speculative buying power towards supposedly Bureau endorsed NYSE securities. Additionally, the investigative program's venues were explained as functioning "in cooperation with the investors' information departments of newspapers and financial periodicals, and distributed facts through savings institutions, investment bankers, commercial banks and trust companies, life insurance companies, industrial companies, and other institutions." Sidener and the National Better Business Bureau systemically approved the program and slogan that the New York Bureau adopted in 1922.

Also, in 1920, in coordination with the Cleveland plan, the New York Investment Bankers Association directed its attorney, George W. Morgan, to "draw a state law which provided special powers enabling the Attorney General to investigate suspected fraudulent transactions in securities." The Investment Bankers' statute was enacted in 1921 but was not enforced until 1923 when respective funding became available due to the Depression of 1920/1921. Dynamics mirrored *Printers' Ink* Editor John Romer contracting employment attorney Harry Nims to draft the *Printers' Ink* Model Statute in 1911 for state regulation of fraudulent advertising.

The Investment Bankers' statute was basically a sanctimonious scam underpinning an ingenious public relations ploy. Kenner's wily gloss-over described the Investment Bankers' statute: "The Act was not a licensing, nor a registration, blue-sky measure. It was a statute aimed directly at fraud without unnecessarily placing hobbles on honest business in order to catch crooks. It was a new type of fraud-fighting legislation." In other words, the law was meant to protect the NYSE and minions. The statute issued superficial authority to the Bureau's

"Before You Invest, Investigate" program as impetus to convince consumers to use the service while overlooking the impossibility of endorsed safe securities whose provenance was the bias brokers and bankers who manipulated Blue Sky state licensing laws to peddle said securities. As a result, the statute singlehandedly empowered a racket, legitimized and promoted the Bureau's fake investigative program, enabled abuse of Blue Sky laws, and granted offenders immunity. Kenner related that speculators mostly relied upon stock promoters for securities information, which supposedly instigated formation of "Before You Invest, Investigate" to ferret out "worthless certificates." Except, one scam begat another, the Bureau's investigative scam exploited consumer trust to promote worthless NYSE securities protected by the Investment Bankers' statute scam.

The National Better Business Bureau worked with the triumvirate of the New York Bureau, NYSE, and Investment Bankers Association. The group drafted and weaponized the Investment Banker's statute to empower the Bureau-friendly New York Attorney General to pursue securities violations against competitors while overlooking the quadraplex's fraud.

In 1921, Sidener stepped down as chairman of the National Vigilance Committee at the AACW convention in Atlanta. Loss of his leadership apparently created an operational vacuum because the AACW brought Sidener back to participate in a voluntary management committee that also included Vigilance Committee founding members Dr. Houston and H.D. Robbins. I emphasize the term "voluntary" because paid services tendered legal liability. Additionally, I question the religious Sidener's departure just as the Bureau's investigative program commenced; that he may have determined a nefarious trajectory involving the Bureau's questionable relationship with the NYSE and Investment Bankers Association as later proven by New York authorities and the U.S. Senate.

On January 25, 1932, Senator Fletcher addressed the U.S. Senate and described the Bureau hook-up with the NYSE and Investment Bankers Association as a racket. He exposed the Bureau's sordid relationship with NYSE and bankers and their respective manipulation of Blue Sky consumer protection laws: "The actual line-up existing, and which you verify by an examination of witnesses coming before you, is simply this: The New York Stock Exchange and the Investment Bankers' Association, with the aid of their puppet, the so-termed Better Business Bureau,-the income of the latter being derived from donations contributed by the former,-first, secured the passage in some forty-odd states, of that which we know as 'the blue sky law,' and you must be familiar with it. This law exempts securities listed on the Exchanges, and thus permits the crooked banker and the crooked broker to sell listed securities at any price obtainable, regardless of actual value, to the unwary sucker; and no matter how utterly worthless that stock may be in actual money, those bankers and brokers cannot be charged with fraud or the offense of obtaining money under false pretenses. You must pay tribute to one of the organizations or go to jail."

A year later, O'Sullivan published *Rackets* and connected the dots between "Before You Invest, Investigate" and the Crash. O'Sullivan condemned the program as a racket that "lent more than tacit support to promotions that were listed on the Stock Exchanges, as if all these were beyond criticism." He wrote, "The nation was about to go mad with the craze for speculation, and the prices of stocks were soon to mount to unheard-of figures in the era of unprecedented "prosperity". That was the time chosen by the Better Business Bureaus to enter the financial field, under the misleading slogan, "Before you invest, investigate," which replaced the former slogan, "Truth in advertising"." Furthermore, O'Sullivan directly accused the Bureau of conspiring securities fraud with members: "So the Better Business Bureaus jumped into the breach, to act as investigators, "without charged to the public," and to perform its favorite function of criticizing and censoring outsiders, while tacitly approving the offerings of its members and subscribers. And the Stock Exchanges were among its members." Furthermore, O'Sullivan indicted the Bureau stating that "…the public was enabled to learn of the manner in which the New York stock Exchange had used the Bureau as its tool in the approval of all "listed stocks," and in a campaign of disparagement against all securities that competed with the Exchange for the investment of the people's available cash. Thus, the Better Business Bureaus encouraged the wild orgy of speculation that ended with a crash which impoverished the nation."

While the Bureau entered securities, General Motors established General Motors Acceptance Corporation (GMAC), which first introduced consumer credit in 1919. Millions of consumers were able to buy cars that they could not afford otherwise. The automobile industry empowered an emerging middle class and opened new opportunity for advertising, business, and travel. According to author David E. Kyvig, "By the mid-1920s one of eight U.S. workers was somehow involved in the production, sales, service, and fueling of automobiles."

The *Roaring Twenties* invited wayward wealth that led up to the Stock Market Crash and Great Depression that lasted from 1929 to 1939. Big Business and the NYSE controlled the wealth of America; Bureau honchos followed gilded breadcrumbs and basked in moneyed afterglow. Advertising and securities' fraud were rampant fueled by desperation, incorrigible avarice, and organized crime. The Great Depression finally ended with the onset of WWII and inducted the Better Business Bureau into the Deep State.

CHAPTER **24**

STOCK MARKET CRASH

On *Black Tuesday*, October 29, 1929, a record-setting total of "16,410,030 shares" were traded with a loss of "$14 billion" in one day and "$30 billion in a single week." As such, Senate.gov reported, "It was a record that would stand for 39 years." And the Crash continued to bottom. Blacktuesday.org reflected, "On July 8, 1932, the Dow closed at 41.22. The market had completely collapsed and lost 89% from Black Tuesday to this day." Between 1930 and 1933, Federal Reserve Education advised that "nearly 10,000 banks failed." Hindsight blamed, "Wall Street and the banking community." All the while, the Better Business Bureau loomed as the complicit elephant in the room. The secret society's distinguished swells and Freemasons projected a golden shield that deflected accountability as entitled robber barons and titans of industry who built America. Furthermore, the Bureau had no constraints and fell between the cracks of regulation because it was not licensed, was not a bank, and was not a broker. It was astounding that Democratic Senator Duncan Fletcher led the charge against the Democratic Bureau's securities and racketeering fraud compounded by incoming Democratic President Franklin D. Roosevelt, a Freemason and the guardian angel of the New York Bureau.

Freemasons or Masons were stonemasons and builders whose trade standards essentially regulated respective business interaction and played an integral part in the evolution of America and Medieval Europe. Some historians believe that Freemasons evolved from the Knights Templar Order. The Templars scattered into other secret societies after 1314 when the order was disbanded, and its Grand Master was burned at the stake. Otherwise, the earliest recorded masonic document was "the Regius Poem, printed about 1390." Today, a Freemason is often referred to as a Templar.

The Knights Templar were a Catholic military order and emerged in 1119. Consequently, the Templars established the first banking and loan system vicariously adopted by wayward *Roaring Twenties'* minions, including the NYSE, Investment Bankers Association, and Better Business Bureau. The Templars' demise commenced on Friday, October 13, 1307, which explains the significance of the number 13, when the corrupt conniving cowardly King Philip IV of France schemed to destroy the order and steal their treasure rather than repay his heavy debt. Crooked Philip IV dredged false charges, including heresy, to substantiate and invoke Templars' arrest, torture, confession, and execution. Grand Master of the Knights Templar Jacques de Molay was held captive and tortured for seven years and killed on March 18, 1314. Molay refused to acquiesce to the king's false charges, proclaimed his innocence, and was burned at the stake with hands clasped in prayer while facing the Notre-Dame de Paris ("Our Lady of Paris") Catholic cathedral. (Notre-Dame was dedicated to the Virgin Mary and built between 1163 and 1345, but almost burned to the ground 674 years later, on April 16, 2019.)

The fraternal (no women) Order of Freemasons was not specifically a Christian organization like the Templars, but the Order did incorporate Christian principles in rites and decorum. Some historians dispute Freemasonry's ancestral link to the Knights Templar; that Freemasonry emerged in the latter part of the 1300s, long after the earliest Templars met their maker. To the contrary, history reflects that some of the Knights Templar escaped the treachery of Philip IV and joined other secret orders, including the Hospital, Teutonic Knights, Knights of Christ, and Order of Montesa (Spain). Templars also became explorers and/or pirates, whose adventures possibly included the discovery of America. In fact, the skull and crossbones' flag, a.k.a. the "Jolly Roger," was attributed to Templar King Roger II of Sicily. Additionally, 14 American presidents were Freemasons including George Washington, James Monroe, Andrew Jackson, James Polk, James Buchanan, Andrew Johnson, James Garfield, William McKinley, Theodore Roosevelt, William Taft, Warren Harding, Franklin Roosevelt, Harry Truman, and Gerald Ford.

In addition to Blue Sky violations, short selling (speculating on extended credit) caused the Crash. According to writer Richard Lambert, "By August 1929, brokers were routinely lending small investors more than two-thirds of the face value of the stocks they were buying. Over $8.5 billion was out on loan, more than the entire amount of currency circulating in the U.S. at the time." In 1931, Republican President Herbert Clark Hoover accused Democrats of manipulating short selling to make his administration seem incompetent. The Great Depression particularly affected the farming industry and caused a severe decline in the pricing of produce. Speculators took advantage of farmers' misfortune "by selling agricultural products short, correctly assuming that prices would fall." Hoover approached the NYSE to stop short selling under threat of regulation but was ignored.

In the interim, the New York Bureau hunkered down with the NYSE and Investment Bankers Association. O'Sullivan wrote, "The Wall Street interests are believed to be the chief supporters of the Better Business Bureau of New York City. "Wall Street interests" are typified in the public mind by the New York Stock Exchange, with its two chief elements, the stock brokers and the speculators"." He claimed that the Bureau abused its trusted reputation to promote high-risk NYSE stock investments through its phony investigative securities program, "Before You Invest, Investigate."

In September 1931, New York authorities pressed federal charges against the New York Bureau, NYSE, and Investment Bankers Association. It was the straw that broke the camel's back; Blue Sky securities' fraud compounded abusive short selling. New York's federal charges landed with Florida Democratic Senator Duncan Fletcher who held President Hoover's confidence. Senator Fletcher convinced Hoover to pursue stock-exchange investigations. As a result, Wall Street history was made.

On March 2, 1932, the U.S. Senate passed Resolution 84 "authorizing the Committee on Banking and Currency to investigate "practices with respect to the buying and selling and the borrowing and lending" of stocks and securities," according to Senate.gov. The committee was led by Republican Chairman/Senator Peter Norbeck, former governor of South Dakota, and Vice Chairman/Senator Fletcher.

On April 11, 1932, hearings began. Democrats criticized proceedings as an attempt to pacify deepening angst of the Great Depression. Unfortunately, the committee proved toothless and witnesses evaded investigations because S.Res. 84 did not authorize subpoena power.

On November 8, 1932, presidential and senatorial elections produced FDR's Democratic sweep. According to Senate.gov, "Senate Democrats scored one of the greatest electoral victories in their party's history."

On January 24, 1933, Chairman Norbeck retained former New York Deputy District Attorney Ferdinand Pecora (1882-1971) as chief counsel for the U.S. Senate Banking and Currency Committee. Pecora was only supposed to write a final committee report, but he discovered investigations were incomplete and requested that Chairman Norbeck allow him another month to complete.

On March 4, 1933, FDR was inaugurated 32nd POTUS. Democrats also won the U.S. Senate's majority and Senator Fletcher assumed chairmanship of the U.S. Senate Banking and Currency Commission. FDR encouraged Pecora to continue expanding investigations.

On April 4, 1933, Chairman Fletcher led the passage of Senate Resolution 56 by the "Seventy-third Congress" to assist Pecora by adding banking investigations and subpoena powers to amend the toothless ineffective S.Res. 84. The congressional headline for S.Res. 56 was entitled, "INVESTIGATION

THE APO$TATE

OF BANKING BUSINESS AND SECURITY EXCHANGE," and granted authority "to investigate the matter of banking operations and practices, the issuance and sale of securities, and the trading therein."

On June 8, 1933, Chairman Fletcher orchestrated another amendment to S.Res. 84 and added Senate Resolution 97 (Seventy-third Congress) to facilitate investigations involving income tax. Fletcher explained scope and reason for S.Res. 97 in his final report that partly stated, "Such legislation shall be made with a view to recommending necessary legislation, under the taxing power or other Federal powers.[1]" His respective footnote explained, "It should be noted that the above Resolution No. 97 had for its primary purpose the bestowal of increased power upon the Committee or any duly authorized subcommittee thereof to investigate any particular transaction or transactions as well as "practices" as had been incorporated in previous resolutions in order that the Committee might not have its hands tied while going into income-tax transactions of firms or individuals ...."

Pecora uncovered widespread banking and securities fraud. Early hearings included testimony from Richard Whitney, president of the NYSE, and Charles Mitchell, chairman of National City Bank of New York (now Citigroup), which at the time was the nation's second largest bank after Chase National Bank (now JPMorgan Chase & Co.). Former Chairman Norbeck claimed National City Bank was responsible for the Crash "because of "its recognized leadership in the orgy of speculation which led to the business collapse"." Tulane Law Review highlighted "abusive securities practices and conflicts of interest that occurred at National City, Chase, and their securities affiliates during the 1920s and early 1930s" including "unsound and deceptive practices," "high-risk securities," "ill-advised loans" and "speculative securities." Chairman Norbeck's allegations fell in line with Senator Fletcher's earlier indictment of the Better Business Bureau as a puppet of the NYSE and Investment Bankers Association whose membership scroll likely included National City Bank. Kenner confirmed in *The Fight for Truth in Advertising* that the "Investment Bankers Association of America" was "well established" and worked in "close cooperation" with the National Vigilance Committee.

In fact, the National Vigilance Committee's formation in 1912 solidified banking connections by appointing Harry D. Robbins as its first chairman. Kenner described Robbins as "then advertising director for a national investment banking firm, who had been especially active in the vigilance work of the New York club"; Kenner omitted the name of the investment bank questioning if it was National City Bank? The incriminating answer lies within the membership scrolls of the Vigilance Committee and National Vigilance Committee. There is no doubt that the NYSE and Investment Bankers Association assisted the AACA and that the National Vigilance Committee of the Associated Advertising Clubs was the AACA's enforcement arm. Furthermore, Kenner noted, "George W. Hodges, former president of the Investment Bankers Association" participated in "a series of conferences ... to discuss stock-swindling evils," dated April 8, 1922. As a reminder, Kenner wrote *The Fight for Truth in Advertising* two years after the Pecora Commission ended and FDR appointed him to an SEC crime commission, and one year after Thomas Dewey's crime trials commenced; his book was a testament to Bureau cover-up, connections, and championing the reputations of New York's high society, NYSE, and banking community.

The Investment Bankers Association of America (IBA) also formed in 1912, which questioned a connection with the AACA's Vigilance Committee and National Vigilance Committee that were established the same year and seemingly tracked IBA's securities' affiliations and footsteps; many bankers and brokers were members of the AACA. Eventually, IBA rebranded and merged several times to become today's Securities Industry and Financial Market Association (SIFMA). SIFMA described itself as "the leading trade association for broker-dealers, investment banks and asset managers operating in the U.S. and global capital markets ... we advocate on legislation, regulation and business policy, affecting retail and institutional investors, equity and fixed income markets and related products and services." Additionally, SIFMA manages "more than $185 trillion in assets and ... clients include mutual funds and retirement plans, as well as banks and brokerage firms," according to Investopedia.

In retrospect, IBA formed when American Bankers Association (ABA) refused an upstart group's request to open "an investment banking section." Then, in 1913, the Association of American Stock Exchange Firms (ASEF) organized to represent financial interests. In 1918, IBA established the Municipal Securities and Government Bonds Committees. In 1971, IBA merged with ASEF to form the Securities Industry Association (SIA). In 1976, IBA's Municipal Securities and Government Bonds Committees incorporated to form the Public Securities Association (PSA). In 1997, PSA changed its name to The Bond Market Association (TBMA). And, in 2007, SIA merged with TBMA to form SIFMA.

On May 4, 1934, the Pecora Commission ended. Collective hearings in the U.S. Senate produced the Glass–Steagall Banking Act of 1933, the Securities Act of 1933, and the Securities Exchange Act of 1934. In a nutshell, the Glass-Steagall Act established separate commercial and investment banking; the Securities Act established penalties for filing fraudulent securities information; and the Securities Exchange Act created the Securities and Exchange Commission (SEC) to regulate stock exchanges. The Glass-Steagall Act was sponsored by Virginia Democratic Senator Carter Glass and Alabama Democratic Representative Henry Steagall and signed into law by FDR on June 16, 1933. The act "separated commercial banking from investment banking," empowered the Federal Reserve System by increasing its regulation of banks, and "created the Federal Deposit Insurance Corporation (FDIC), which insures bank deposits with a pool of money collected from banks."

Then, on June 6, 1934, Chairman Fletcher completed his 394-page "Stock Exchange Practices Report of the Committee on Banking and Currency," published June 16, 1934. Fletcher's "Stock Exchange Practices Report" announced newly engaged corrective measures and detailed how Wall Street, Big Business, and Big Banking gamed the financial system and the public. The Fletcher Report's closing paragraph was a certification: "This Committee, actuated by a genuine desire to be helpful in solving our economic difficulties, has conducted, without animus, this comprehensive inquiry into our financial institutions. Legislation has been enacted, designed to eradicate those factors which may adversely affect our economic conditions. Further legislation may be necessary to fully accomplish this purpose. Certain it is that legislation done cannot completely eliminate these disturbing elements. The undivided cooperation of industrialist, financier, and investor, with a mutual recognition of their reciprocal rights and duties, is indispensable to a fulfillment of this desired end. Respectfully submitted, Duncan U. Fletcher, Chairman Senate Committee on Banking and Currency."

New York City is an international port that blends investments, banking, and advertising. History reflected that investment banking began with merchant trading as explained by Emory University: "The merchant banks lent to a range of monarchs, royalty, and the papacy, usually gaining privileges, access, and side payments in return. Famous examples include the Medici of Florence from the late 14th and 15th century and the Fuggers of Augsburg rising to the fore in the mid-15th to 16th centuries. The major British houses start with the Barings in 1763 and Rothschilds later in the 18th century, followed by a string of others over the early to mid-19th century: Schroders (aka Schröders), Hambros, Kleinwort, Morgan, and others."

Black Tuesday's ominous aftermath led to grim consequences. Author Charles Geisst clarified, "Although a few traders committed suicide after losing everything, the actual number was fairly low. That did not stop Will Rogers from telling the story about the New York hotel clerk who asked incoming guests whether they wanted a room "for sleeping or for jumping"."

Research revealed several fatalities:

The *St. Louis Post-Dispatch* article, "Bank Closes After Suicide," dated June 30, 1930, reported Executive Vice President Richard P. Asbury, 65 years old, committed suicide causing his bank to close.

The *St. Louis Globe Democrat* article, "Man Leaps Twenty Stories to Death," dated July 23, 1930, reported Herbert L. Wittnebel, a "Brooklyn business man, fell from the roof of the twenty-story Paramount Hotel in West Forty-sixth Street"; his death was ruled a suicide. He was "an official of the Commonwealth

Color and Chemical Company" and owned a summer home on Long Island Sound.

The *New York American* article, "Work 'Counsel' Ends Own Life," dated October 1, 1931, reported Rose Boyd, 43 years old, "had offices as an "employment counselor" at 80 Wall st. shot and killed herself" at her home. Several suicide notes indicated she was upset over "recent business losses."

Another *New York American* article, "15-Story Fall Kills Broker," dated October 1, 1931, reported Bert A. Rosenthal, coffee broker for S. Rosenthal and Sons, jumped "from a window in his office on the 15th floor of 82 Beaver st., landing on the "L" tracks at Pearl and Beaver sts." Police had to turn power off the tracks to "extricate the body."

President Hoover did not glean any credit for initiating the U.S. Senate investigations and/or subsequent historic Wall Street reform. The Crash exploded eight months after he was inaugurated on March 4, 1929. Supreme irony incriminated the former secretary of commerce for the historic implosion of U.S. commerce. In addition to Blue Sky abuses and short selling, Hoover blamed the Hispanic population for taking jobs and taxpayer money. Hoover launched the "Mexican Repatriation" program, which "forced migration of approximately 500,000 to 2 million people to Mexico" and lasted "until 1936" under FDR's administration.

On December 7, 1941, the Japanese attacked Pearl Harbor and FDR similarly enacted a roundup of Americans with Japanese ancestry dispersed to internment facilities within the United States until the end of WWII. In fact, FDR had good reason for taking such drastic action. Microbiologist Surgeon General Shirō Ishii (1892-1959) was captured and imprisoned for threatening the United States with germ warfare. In 1946, Dr. Ishii received immunity from a Tokyo war-crimes tribunal in return for providing information on his experimentations. One report stated that he was later brought to Fort Detrick in Maryland, known for its biomedical facility, and another report placed him "in South Korea in 1951 ... at the same time that North Korea was alleging the US had used biological warfare in the Korean War."

Additionally, after Pearl Harbor, research suggested that FDR inducted the Better Business Bureau into the Deep State under the First War Powers Act of 1941 to monitor Japanese American activity and enemy agents including Issei (non-citizen/Japanese-born), Nisei (citizen/second generation), and Sansei (citizen/third generation). FDR intended to form a new surveillance agency in 1941 as implied by Wansley in History and Traditions. Instead Senator Truman convinced Congress to cost-effectively substitute the Better Business Bureau whose reporting services were already operating nationwide. In 1947, President Truman retooled the Bureau's spyster footprints to create the CIA.

Hoover was only remembered for producing "shacktowns and homeless encampments" called "Hooverville[s]" as well as cardboard blankets called "Hoover blankets." The largest shacktown was the Seattle Hooverville, which operated from "1931 to 1941," and spread over "nine acres of public land ... [and] housed a population of up to 1,200, claimed its own community government including an unofficial mayor, and enjoyed the protection of leftwing groups and sympathetic public officials until the land was needed for shipping facilities on the eve of World War II," according to the University of Washington.

Blue Sky laws regulated the sale of securities and were defined as "state level anti-fraud statutes enforced by the individual states' attorneys-general," according to Investopedia.com. Provisions required that all securities and brokers be registered in a respective state or prove exemption from registration. Banking Commissioner Joseph Norman Dolley (1860-1940) introduced the first Blue Sky laws in the state of Kansas in 1911, same year as the Truth in Advertising Movement and the *Printers' Ink* Model Statute. The name was used as early as 1906, according to the *Oxford English Dictionary*, but the original source cannot be confirmed. Dolley popularized the term "Blue Sky" when he "observed that certain fraudulent investments were backed by nothing but the blue skies of Kansas." U.S. Supreme Court Justice Joseph McKenna first cited Blue Sky laws in *Hall v. Geiger-Jones Co.*, 242 U.S. 539 (1917), which "addressed the constitutionality" of the laws.

In August 1919, the Better Business Bureau of the Cleveland Advertising Club coordinated with local Cleveland newspapers to refuse any stock advertising that was not approved by Ohio Blue Sky commissioners. Stock gypsters were proffering securities through the mail in states where they did not have licensing. So the National Vigilance Committee "issued a bulletin to all vigilance committees" suggesting they set up similar agreements with their local newspapers. The National Committee and local Bureau interaction with newspapers formed an impregnable alliance that resulted in allegations of cronyism after the Stock Market Crash. By the time the Securities Act of 1933 was introduced, 47 states enforced Blue Sky laws with exception of Nevada.

O'Sullivan claimed that the Bureau abused its trusted reputation to promote "Before You Invest, Investigate" as a safe securities screening program on behalf of the NYSE and Investment Bankers Association. He wrote, "The Better Business Bureaus ... lent more than tacit support to promotions that were listed on the Stock Exchanges, as if all these were beyond criticism – and thus encouraged the craze for stock speculation between 1919 and 1929, that ended with a crash and threw the country into a state of depression unprecedented in its history." O'Sullivan believed that the Bureau's phony investment program was among several erratic factors that caused the Crash: "Thus the Better Business Bureaus encouraged the wild orgy of speculation that ended with a crash which impoverished the nation."

Investors were uneducated regarding security investments and O'Sullivan alleged the Bureau exploited consumer ignorance to establish a securities racket with the NYSE: "It was 1919 … a year of boom in the stock market…Men who couldn't have told you in 1914, to save their lives, what a stock ticker look like, were now found in brokers' offices reading the tape … Office boys and office girls learned how to speculate, and none foresaw the day of retribution, to come in 1929 … That was the time chosen by the Better Business Bureaus to enter the financial field, under the misleading slogan, "Before you invest, investigate," which replaced the former slogan, "Truth in advertising." It was a good deal like the doctor's advice, "Be careful." What facilities had the average amateur speculator for investigation? Any investigation he could make would be nothing but the farce of asking a broker, a lawyer, or a banker for advice, with all of them equally ignorant and equally helpless. So the Better Business Bureaus jumped into the breach, to act as investigators … approving the offerings of its members and subscribers. And the Stock Exchanges were among its members."

Kenner explained why the Bureau became involved in securities investigations, but he omitted underlying profiteering motive that exploited the stock-market fad. The program was designed to grab workers' money before they had time to spend it by diverting speculation to Bureau/NYSE/Investment Bankers' manipulated securities. The Cleveland Advertising Club had introduced the "Before You Invest, Investigate" slogan or Cleveland plan, as a program for workers in the industrial plants. The slogan was advertised "on special posters in industrial plants, by circulars, and through the newspapers, so the individual worker would be informed that, when approached by a stock salesman, he could get information on the offering from a reliable source." Workers were also issued a list of questions to ask; "This gave him time to "think it over" before he made a commitment. Impulsive buying, under the spell of a suave salesman's glamorous word-pictures of future profits, accounts for many vanished millions of savings."

O'Sullivan also alleged that the New York Bureau and National Better Business Bureau acted with bias and in bad faith colluded with the NYSE as their benefactor and organization's most powerful member: "Then the National Better Business Bureau was organized in New York, with funds raised by the governor of the New York Stock Exchange and a leading oil operator. The latter guaranteed a lump sum of $60,000 for the National Bureau, with an annual retainer of $7,500; and the Stock Exchange interests provided a total of $100,000 and secured control, the Stock Exchange governor, James C. Auchincloss, being elected president of the National Bureau. The charter of this Bureau was amended so as to include securities within its scope; and everything was set for operation of the National Better Business Bureau in the interests of Wall Street."

Kenner essentially confirmed O'Sullivan's allegation of collusion between the Bureau organization and NYSE: "This was the situation when the bureau's founders – representative of the business community – had accepted the offer of the governors of the New York Stock Exchange to provide funds for the expenses of the organization during a year's try-out of its efficiency. In the first eight months, the Exchange contributed a total of $64,000. The bureau's directors then, believing that the practicability of the effort had been demonstrated, solicited financial support from business firms generally to make the institution permanent. Addressing the Association of Stock Exchange Firms, at a meeting in March, 1923, Seymour L. Cromwell, president of the New York Stock Exchange, told the reasons for the establishment of this work by the joint action of numerous financial groups in the community, and said that the Stock Exchange had been ready to contribute as much as $100,000 to this project for its first year."

The Crash and subsequent Great Depression closed several Bureau doors. Kenner eloquently wrote of the demise of one such Bureau: "Where a Better Business Bureau has existed and then ceased to function, as has happened, especially due to the rigors of the late depression, it has been missed. At Louisville, Ky., in 1934, the business community allowed the local bureau to close its doors." He also noted that the Bureau in Buffalo, New York, closed and reopened 18 months later.

Rackets provided a treasure trove of long-hidden facts and occurrences that largely revolved around the Crash. O'Sullivan's chronicles described in 1933 detailed the Pecora Commission in its embryonic stage. He recorded historical characters, organizations, and events as they were happening, and documentation coincided with actual recorded facts.

After the Crash, investigations were called upon to review the Bureau's nefarious securities and banking connections. O'Sullivan wrote, "Since the collapse of the Stock Exchange boom in 1929, there has been continued criticism of the connection of the Exchange with the Better Business Bureau system." Criticism was also lodged by the Manhattan Board of Commerce, the New York Reform Committee, the Bronx Chamber of Commerce, the Syracuse Chamber of Commerce, and the Consumers Guild of America.

O'Sullivan summarized allegations and charges that were brought against the New York Bureau, NYSE, and Investment Bankers Association by several New York authorities. Respective information was forwarded to New York Representative Fiorello La Guardia that resulted in Senator Fletcher's indictment of the Better Business Bureau. Additionally, short selling ravaged the stock market. Collective fraud established the U.S. Senate Committee on Banking and Currency authorized by Senate Resolutions 84, 56, and 97 to pursue historic Wall Street reform.

The New York Bureau was interconnected with the NYSE, the SEC, the Curb Exchange, the Chamber of Commerce of New York State, and the Investment

Bankers Association, to name only a few of New York City's 1920's/1930's titans of industry. Kenner divulged that, on November 2, 1927, James C. Auchincloss juggled three prestigious positions as "president of the National Better Business Bureau, Inc.," as "a governor" of the NYSE, and "also president of the New York bureau." And, Kenner referenced a New York Bureau meeting held in May 1936 that highlighted the Bureau's affiliation with the Investment Bankers Association whereby he acknowledged, "Trowbridge Callaway, formerly president of the Investment Bankers Association of America, and recently president of the Better Business Bureau of New York City." Additionally, Kenner reported that the National Bureau hired a former judge, Frank C. Brooks, from Minneapolis to "defend the law," which suggested that the franchise was court friendly. And, without a doubt, the New York Bureau's members included the state's most prominent businessmen connected to the NYSE and various elite organizations.

The Bureau was considered an affiliate of the NYSE. Critics, businessmen, and statesmen challenged the Bureau's questionable authority, tactics, and investigative services that disingenuously endorsed and promoted NYSE products as safe investments. O'Sullivan warned that "the Better Business Bureau, as a tool of the Stock Exchange in the approval and promotion of listed stocks, has been the subject of condemnation on the floor of the United States Senate, which is investigating Stock Exchange methods; and the further fact that many suits for damages to business men have been filed against the Bureaus, demonstrate beyond the possibility of doubt that the Bureau system, as at present operated, constitutes a decided menace to business and no longer merits the public confidence and support that were accorded to it when it was first established."

O'Sullivan envisioned the decline of the Bureau: "The year 1930 saw the beginning of the end of Bureau prestige. Up to that time, the activities of the Bureaus had been taken rather seriously." To the contrary, the Bureau dodged Pecora's silver bullet because it was shielded by FDR and a litany of distinguished *Who's Who* across the country. In 1935, Dewey's organized-crime trials spooked the New York Bureau resulting in gilded publicity ploys like Kenner's book and participation in FDR's new SEC. And, in 1938, the New York Bureau donned its deflective golden halo when Richard Whitney (1888-1974), president of the NYSE from 1930 until 1935, pled guilty to embezzlement and served three years and 10 months in Sing Sing prison. According to Wikipedia. org, "He stole funds from the New York Stock Exchange Gratuity Fund, the New York Yacht Club (where he served as the Treasurer), and $800,000 worth of bonds from his father-in-law's estate."

CHAPTER 25

LOGAN BILLINGSLEY

Logan Billingsley
Bootlegger extraordinaire; chairman of the Manhattan
Board of Commerce and president of the Bronx Chamber
of Commerce; New York real estate developer; exposed Better
Business Bureau's phony "Before You Invest, Investigate" securities program that
instigated U.S. Senate Committee on Banking and
Currency/Pecora Commission investigations; artist: Caryn Cain.

As chairman of the Manhattan Board of Commerce and "president of the Bronx Chamber of Commerce from 1928 to 1932," he was the central figure leading the charge against the Bureau, Investment Bankers Association, and NYSE for alleged securities fraud that contributed to the market collapse. Nobody was better qualified than Logan as a redeemed ex-bootlegger to rat out the Bureau. His yesteryear interludes with the law were poverty-driven and he was one among many who resorted to testing Prohibition as a desperate means of survival. To the contrary, the Bureau's activities were intentional, underhanded, disparaging, and capitalistic.

By the 1920s, age blessed Logan with wisdom and a yearning for genuine rehabilitation when he and his brother Sherman found burgeoning opportunity in the advertising capital of the world. The brothers quickly adapted to the throes of organized crime that flooded the marauding streets of New York City during the *Roaring Twenties*. But they also parted ways. Logan cleaned up his life and gave back to the City, reinventing himself as a respected real estate developer. To the contrary, Sherman embraced his colorful past and opened the Stork Club that welcomed the criminal element flourishing in the sordid life of the speakeasy.

When New York City's financial district fell to rack and ruin, the saloons, theater, and organized crime prospered. Sherman made millions while Logan lost his burgeoning realty business. The Stork Club offered writer's nirvana that entertained gossip and media headlines. Breakaway drama blended a turnstile of Hollywood stars, journalists, reformers, city and government honchos, and crime lords. Sherman's club shot to popularity nurtured by mayhem and machine guns.

The speakeasies and saloons played cat-and-mouse with federal agents until Prohibition's repeal returned alcohol as the cat's meow on "December 5, 1933," but organized crime adapted and infiltrated the alcohol industry as legal proprietors. The 18th Amendment created organized crime and the 21st Amendment spread it. Underground syndicates scrambled to muscle owner's interest in speakeasies and saloons to use them as legal store fronts for illegal activity. Consequently, daily threats, bribery, kidnapping, and murder were commonplace. Salvation came in 1935 when Special Agent Thomas E. Dewey's Mafioso trials stabilized New York City.

Logan shot an arrow into the heart of Bureau operations targeting its lack of authority as an unlicensed investigator and ended its popular "Before You Invest, Investigate" program as a bogus puppet-stringed NYSE promotional scheme. He gathered support from New York's Attorney General and Secretary of State to confirm the Bureau's violation of the state's "Section 70 Business Law" that required that the organization immediately secure a license or face criminal prosecution. Then he introduced a wide variety of fed-up city, state, and federal authorities to indict the Bureau culminating with Senator Fletcher's denouncement of the Bureau as an "intimate connection of the New York Stock Exchange" participating in "the greatest racket ever known in its history."

The esteemed Senator called attention to underhanded collaboration between the Bureau, the NYSE and the New York Investment Bankers Association that duped millions from pre-Crash speculators. His speech regarding "the crooked banker and the crooker broker" ("Senate Congressional Record, Volume 75, No. 32, Page 2709") described how the triumvirate colluded to gainfully manipulate Blue Sky laws in various states contrary to the law's consumer-protection purpose.

The Blue Sky laws were investment-centered consumer state laws. The U.S. Securities and Exchange website offered a basic overview: "In addition to the federal securities laws, every state has its own set of securities laws—commonly referred to as "Blue Sky Laws"—that are designed to protect investors against fraudulent sales practices and activities. While these laws do vary from state to state, most state laws typically require companies making offerings of securities to register their offerings before they can be sold in a particular state, unless a specific state exemption is available. The laws also license brokerage firms, their brokers, and investment adviser representatives."

To the contrary, the triumvirate distorted the law and set up a bogus promotional investment scheme that operated on the wings of impunity. The Bureau sponsored a bogus investigative program that ludicrously vetted risky Blue Sky-registered securities through the same NYSE-affiliated bankers and stockbrokers that sold them. The Bureau, NYSE, and bankers evidenced premeditated criminal intent when registering sketchy securities in various states under Blue Sky laws as a legislative shield against liability. Accordingly, the Bureau betrayed its mission and consumer trust with its bogus "Before You Invest, Investigate" program that lured gullible speculators under premise of safe investments.

Logan Billingsley was born on "December 20, 1882," in Enid, Oklahoma. His dirt-poor family originally hailed from Tennessee, moved to Kentucky, and eventually settled in Anadarko, Oklahoma, where Logan developed a life-long relationship with the Anadarko Indian tribe. His father was Robert W. Billingsley (July 18, 1864 – May 14, 1918), born in "Claiborne County, Tennessee"; his mother was Emily Collingsworth; they married in 1882. Logan was born later that same year; other siblings included Robert Jr. (1887 - 1906), Charlotte ("Lottie"), Ora (July 19, 1890 - September 1969), Frederich (born June 1892), Pearl (born 1894), and John 'Sherman' Billingsley (March 1896 - October 4, 1966).

He was described as "six feet tall, straight as a poker, with wavy black hair, fair skin and an icy nerve seemingly impervious to fear." He was married three times. His first wife was Chloe Wheatley (born May 1886) and they had one son, Glenn. His second wife was Hattie Mae and they also had one son, Logan Jr. His third wife was Francis Longworth (December 5, 1912 - February 14, 2002) and they had three sons, Jerry, Robert, and Frank.

Family genealogy melded with Hollywood. In 1941, Logan's first son, Glenn, married Barbara Lillian Combes (1915-2010) of *Leave It To Beaver* fame (show debuted in 1957); they begat two sons, Glenn Jr. (born in 1945) and Drew.

Moreover, Glenn Sr. was a restauranteur and operated several businesses including *Billingsley's Restaurant* in Los Angeles. Glenn Sr. and Barbara divorced in 1947. Then, Glenn Sr. moved to Palm Springs; the local library's genealogy department advised that no obituary information was available because he was cremated. Glenn Jr. married Karen and they resided in Pomona, California, near Los Angeles. Barbara Billingsley died at the age of 94 from polymyalgia rheumatica (complication of rheumatoid arthritis), and Glenn Jr. and Karen took over her *Billingsley's Restaurant*. I called the restaurant on February 1, 2016, and was told that Glenn Jr. sold the business shortly after Barbara's death.

Logan found early success through the lucrative sale of alcohol and stuck with it in various aspects throughout his early adulthood. He was influenced by his father's proclivities specializing in real estate and gambling. His father, Robert, chased homesteading opportunities in new territories like Kentucky and Oklahoma and was a talented poker player and gambler. By the time Logan was 25, he was a proficient bootlegger, gambler, and acquitted murderer (justified self-defense). Bootlegging was a poor man's rich game and put food on the table for many a starving family.

On June 1, 1930, the *St. Louis Globe Democrat* published the article, "Gets 18 Months and $1500 Fine for Liquor Making," whereby "several defendants" pled guilty "to the manufacture of liquor" in the basement of their homes. Defendants stated that "it was better to make liquor than to steal" and that "bootlegging was the only profitable occupation under present economic conditions." The travails of Prohibition posed constant hazards of rival competition, loss of property, imprisonment, or death. Furthermore, Prohibition's eventual repeal emphasized its unrealistic inception that criminalized human frailty and plight.

The backstory to Logan's first marriage was intriguing and scandalous. His unfortunate early life set him up for disparagement in his later life. In "June 1904," at the age of 22, Logan had a scandalous affair with "Chloe Wheatley" that left her pregnant. Her outraged father, "Andrew," attempted a shotgun wedding, but Logan refused to marry Chloe, which sparked an argument that resulted in Andrew's death. Logan claimed that Andrew attacked him with "two large knives" and he drew his ".45 double-barrel pistol" shooting Andrew "through the heart." Consequently, Logan was hauled into the county jail and charged with murder. His father moved into town and remained by his side. The first trial convicted him of murder, but an appeal and second trial quickly acquitted Logan on grounds of "self-defense." Robert Billingsley sold the family farmhouse to pay legal bills. Then, Chloe had baby Glenn and Logan married her.

In 1907, while still in Anadarko, Logan gave younger brother Sherman "a little red wagon" and initiated him into smuggling at the tender age of 10.

THE APO$TATE

Logan gifted Sherman the wagon as a cover up for his own bootlegging business that sold beer to grateful Anadarko Indians who were "forbidden alcohol." He lined the bottom of the wagon with beer bottles, covered the stash with a blanket and then sat baby Glenn on top as innocuous camouflage. Logan then instructed Sherman to roll the wagon and baby to waiting Indian customers. Sherman pocketed "fifty cents a bottle" in addition to turning a profit by reselling the empties back to the "saloons."

In January 1912, the family moved to Oklahoma City, which offered a wide array of gambling houses, brothels, bank robberies, bootlegging, and opium dens. Logan went to school at "the University of Oklahoma" and worked "in the Indian service." He returned to his wiles resulting in more lucrative income. Citizens were allowed "a gallon a month," so Logan bought the allotments and resold them "by the pint or by the drink."

In the same timeframe, Logan opened the *Night and Day Drugstore* gambling house that sold whiskey. Occasion introduced Sherman to club life and Logan found himself in and out of jail for "operating a gambling house."

In 1914, Logan, Sherman and their father opened the *Stewart Street Pharmacy* in Seattle, Washington. But it was really a storefront for selling alcohol as was prevalent in the day. The tide turned again when Sherman was arrested for selling liquor to an undercover agent. Sherman's family hired former district attorney George F. Vanderveer to successfully represent him and he avoided the slammer.

By 1916, the Billingsley brothers were running the "city's largest bootlegging ring" in Seattle while competing against a former detective with city hall connections. Again, Logan found himself in the middle of murder. At the time, Sherman had married and gone out of town. Two other brothers, Fred and Ora, joined Logan to run the "family" business. On the evening of July 25, 1916, two policemen appeared at the Billingsley's warehouse. Logan's Japanese security guard mistook the men for burglars and a firefight ensued resulting in the death all three men. Mayor Hiram C. Gill ordered the arrest of the Billingsley brothers. Logan escaped to San Francisco but was caught and returned to Seattle.

Logan dodged a prison sentence through a plea deal. He pled guilty to violating liquor laws and agreed to testify against the corrupt mayor; that he paid the mayor $4,000 to return his business records. The jury returned a "not guilty" verdict. Otherwise, the brothers (excluding Sherman) faced prison time for earlier offenses and respective guilty pleas: Ora received 30 days in prison; Fred was given six months; and Logan was issued 13 months and appeared at McNeil Island penitentiary in May 1918.

Ora and Fred returned from prison and opened a grocery and cigar store in Detroit, Michigan; as usual, they sold liquor out the backdoor. Logan headed back to Seattle prior to entering prison to tie up legal loose ends. And Sherman joined Ora and Fred in Detroit. Their father, Robert, had been visiting Sherman, Fred, and Ora and was killed "by a streetcar" on May 14, 1918. The Billingsley patriarch was returned home and buried in Anadarko.

By 1920, Logan had relocated to New York City and found his calling as a successful real estate developer. He later expanded his business to Miami, Florida. In 1924, Logan married Hattie Mae Key, a "descendent of Francis Scott Key"; they divorced in 1926. Their son, Logan Jr., was sickly and died at a young age. During this timeframe, Logan became a reputable real estate mogul and built "many apartment houses" in the Bronx area of New York City. In 1924, he built the Theodore Roosevelt Apartments (Roosevelt Gardens) located at 1455-1499 Grand Concourse, Bronx, New York. And, in 1927, he extended the Grand Concourse from East 161st Street to East 138th Street. Then, in 1928, he was appointed president of the Bronx Chamber of Commerce.

Sherman joined Logan in New York City in early 1920 and never left. After a transition period involving several more liquor-related arrests and prison stints, Sherman procured a real estate license in 1926 and followed Logan into the lucrative real estate market. Eventually, Sherman returned to the nightlife. In 1929, Sherman opened a speakeasy on West 58th Street, which was shut down by "Prohibition agents" in 1931. He reopened another speakeasy on East 51st Street. When Prohibition ended, he opened the Stork Club in 1934 that continued operations until 1965. According to Untapped Cities, the Stork Club "was the place where actors, novelists, government figures, directors, American troops, American culture-creators, and New York's fanciest and wealthiest gathered."

The Club hit pay dirt when Walter Winchell (1897-1972), host of a WABC radio show and New York's premier gossipmonger of the column "Walter Winchell on Broadway," plugged the nightclub as "New York's New Yorkiest place on W. 58th." A star was born and the Stork Club became an overnight sensation drawing famous celebrities like Marilyn Monroe and Joe DiMaggio, Frank Sinatra, the Kennedys, Eva Gardner, Lucille Ball and Desi Arnaz, Bob Hope, Elizabeth Taylor, Judy Garland and Vincent Minnelli, Lauren Bacall and Humphrey Bogart, Ernest Hemmingway, and Spencer Tracy.

Sherman's partners in the Stork Club, Henninger and Patton, turned out to be a front for the mob. Without Sherman's knowledge, they sold their joint 30% ownership and distributed 10% individual shares to George Jean "French" De Mange, Owney Madden, and William V. "Big Bill" Dwyer. Sherman had to fight his way back to 100% ownership. Organized crime had begun investing in speakeasies and saloons and the Stork Club was on the mob's short list. Kingpins like Dutch Schultz and Legs Diamond wanted a cut of the Stork Club; Sherman was kidnapped and threatened by Mafioso wise guys.

The Stork Club officially closed on "October 4, 1965." Sherman sold the building to William S. Paley (1901-1990), who "built Columbia Broadcasting System (CBS)." Paley leveled the building to build a park in memory of his father, Samuel, whom he owed his remarkable radio heritage. In its heyday, the Stork Club gave both Logan and Sherman sterling street cred. By the same token, its ominous connections brought reminder of a tainted past and compromised Logan in his gritty battle with the Bureau.

After the Crash, Logan jumped into corrective action and established the Chamber's subsidiary Manhattan Board of Commerce to attract business. The Board authorized the creation of the Stock Exchange Reform Committee with "over 100,000" members throughout the country. Additionally, Logan "served on Mayor James J. Walker's Planning Committee for the City of New York, and was chairman of a mayoral committee that competed for the selection of New York City as the site of the World's Fair." The City of Chicago had planned a similar extravaganza and won the toss-up, consequently hosting the 1933 World's Exposition. Furthermore, according to Forgotten New York, "In 1927, [Logan] spearheaded a plan to lengthen the Grand Concourse from East 161st Street to East 138th Street."

The Bureau took notice of Logan's rise to power. Operatives had no control over his business affiliations, which included the Bronx Chamber of Commerce and the Manhattan Board of Commerce and its subsidiary the Stock Exchange Reform Committee; all affiliations promised to be combative regulatory organizations against the Bureau. Accordingly, the Bureau schemed to discredit Logan and his organizations by publicizing his sordid past and family ties to the infamous Stork Club. Had this drama unfolded between 1935 and 1936 when the Dewey crime trials were raging, the Bureau would have kept silent to avoid being dragged into court with the other ruffians of organized crime.

O'Sullivan provided evidence that the Bureau controlled New York City and chambers of commerce by publishing one of the Bureau's intercepted bulletins: "We have 246 publications alone, carrying our message to the public – all helping us. We give the story to the public in such a way that they single out the man who attempts to us the tactics we have talked about, and attribute our warning to that particular individual. We have completely crippled several businesses by publicity. In one instance we sent information and suggestions to every Chamber of Commerce in the United States; as a result two local firms were forced into bankruptcy." Consequently, the bulletin represented irrefutable proof of the Bureau's bully tactics that engaged defamation same as occurred against Logan.

The Bureau lobbed the first resounding punches, but Logan returned to K-O the Bureau with an alliance of state and federal reinforcements. In "April 1930," the Bureau engaged a mock investigation resulting in a smear campaign against Logan that splashed his criminal past across newspaper headlines.

Additionally, the Bureau denounced his Manhattan Board of Commerce as a "racket" and demanded corporate documents. Logan refused to produce documents for fear of a setup because the Bureau owned the courts. Then, Logan filed a defamation lawsuit. The New York Bureau responded by charging Logan with contempt. Logan jumped bail and was captured in Atlantic City. A Bronx judge waived jail time and rendered a fine after Logan claimed a nervous breakdown. In "January 1931," Logan withdrew his lawsuit against the New York Bureau, but it was a stall tactic and Kenner was in for a rude awakening.

All the while, E. C. Riegel, president of the Consumers Guild of America, had been investigating the New York Bureau and was preparing federal charges. Logan was waiting for Riegel's results, which proved damning. Consequently, Logan turned the tables on the Bureau and struck back with a vengeance. His Bronx Chamber of Commerce filed a complaint against the New York Bureau with the state of New York's attorney general alleging that "the Better Business Bureau was a camouflaged detective agency, and should be compelled to take out a detective agency license." On December 21, 1930, Republican New York Attorney General Hamilton Ward processed the complaint and ruled in the Chamber's favor citing Section 70's general business law. Ward was supported by Democratic New York Secretary of State Edward Flynn who issued a follow-up licensing demand on January 2, 1931. Then Riegel struck and filed securities fraud and racketeering charges against the New York Bureau. Riegel's accusations added to egregious claims of short selling, which convinced President Hoover and Senator Fletcher to convene U.S. Senate Banking and Currency Commission hearings. Logan received ultimate vindication when Senator Fletcher proclaimed the Bureau a racket.

After the Crash, one of the worst examples of a "dirty judge" involved the resignation of County Judge W. Bernard Vause of Brooklyn, New York, who was indicted for "grand larceny, mail fraud and perjury." The *St. Louis Post Dispatch* published the article, "Ex-Judge On Trial For Mail Fraud Weeps In Court," dated June 17, 1930, which reported, "Vause is charged with fraud in connection with the $400,000 crash of the Columbia Finance Corporation. A heavy stockholder in Columbia, he also faces a Federal indictment for perjury, and a New York Country indictment for grand larceny in connection with the case." The article also noted that the judge "attempted to bribe a psychiatrist" and "attempted to have an operation for appendicitis performed on himself to force delay of the trial."

On June 1, 1930, the *St. Louis Globe Democrat* published their New York affiliate's article, "$25,000,000 Bond Swindles in 1930," stating, "The public paid approximately $25,000,000 to bucket shop operators and dealers in fraudulent securities during the first five months of the present year." Furthermore, the article revealed that the money "muleted from the public ... was obtained by 333 corporations, individuals and partnerships, against whom ninety-two temporary and final injunctions were obtained in the Supreme Court." Assistant Attorney General Watson Washburn prosecuted the case and forwarded a final report to New York Attorney General Hamilton Ward. Washburn's report advised, "[T]hat during the five months' period eight actions involving stocks listed on the New York Stock Exchange were instituted." Be it reminded that during this time, the Bureau was operating its bogus NYSE-affiliated "Before You Invest, Investigate" program.

On December 26, 1930, Attorney General Ward indicted the Bureau for operating without a license. Ward participated in the prosecution of large-scale securities fraud after the Crash and felt the Bureau was similarly involved, but the franchise was shielded by its golden membership scroll. The Bronx Chamber of Commerce, an affiliate of Logan's Manhattan Board of Commerce, provided Ward an opportunity to prosecute the New York Bureau.

A year later, on December 16, 1931, Logan submitted, "The Billingsley letter," addressed to the Syracuse Chamber of Commerce and "challenged" Richard Whitney to a debate before Chamber officials. Whitney declined. O'Sullivan quoted Billingsley, "We are endeavoring to bring about a Senatorial investigation of the Stock Exchange. Through secret processes, we find that the Stock Exchange is even corrupting the public press, and that the publishers of important newspapers do not know that their papers are compromised by the Exchange, through its hook-up with the Better Business Bureau, and that their papers have been used by this combination to unload fifty billions of dollars' worth of blue sky on the public. All of these facts we expect to prove before a Senatorial investigation – which is not far distant."

Over the following year, the Manhattan Board continued to press the issue. Once Senate investigations commenced, Billingsley intervened again and advised the committee to delve deeper into NYSE corruption. O'Sullivan reflected on the occasion: "As the Senatorial committee began its investigation of the Stock Exchange, in March, 1932, Mr. Billingsley urged that there be a "thorough and searching investigation of all the ramifications of the Exchange," instead of the limited inquiry into the practice of "short-selling" which the committee had launched. He was emphatic on this point, saying: "Many of our citizens have lost their life savings through speculating in stocks and bonds, and kindred securities, believing they were dealing in legitimate investment securities. For instance, more than $50,000,000,000 have been wiped out through depreciation over a short period of months, and people are dazed by this situation and seek to discover the cause thereof. They are depending on you gentlemen of the United States Senate to investigate and find out what it is all about"."

The Manhattan Board of Commerce led a two-year probe into the crony relationship between the New York Bureau and the NYSE. On June 6, 1932, F.

Odell Adams, secretary of the Manhattan Board of Commerce, forwarded a letter to Richard Whitney, questioning the NYSE's collusion, bribery and corruption with the New York Bureau and H. J. Kenner. Whitney was already being pursued by U.S. Senate investigations and ignored Adams. Kenner also ignored Adams.

O'Sullivan quoted Adams' questions as follows:

"1. When the Stock Exchange pledged $100,000 to the Better Business Bureau, did it have any agreement with H. J. Kenner that all listed securities would be recommended to the public by the Bureau as good investments, no matter how worthless or how much inflated the prices might be?

"2. Did the $100,000, which the Stock Exchange paid the Bureau, pay for an arrangement by which the Bureaus of the entire country would sponsor blue-sky legislation, purposely framed so as to exempt all securities listed on the Exchange, thereby permitting your members to sell at any price obtainable, without fear of prosecution for fraud?

"3. Did Mr. Kenner further promise you that the entire Bureau system would be used to clog-up the courts all over the United States with petty larceny stock promotion cases, so that these courts would not have sufficient legal machinery left with which to regulate manipulations of the Exchange?

"4. Did H. J. Kenner tell the Stock Exchange that the principal newspapers were members of his Bureau system, and that he could and would use these newspapers, coupled with the legal machinery of the country, to jail anybody and everybody who interfered in any way whatsoever with the activities of the New York Stock Exchange?

"5. We quote from a Stock Exchange letter to one of its members, dated June 26, 1923, as follows: "We would like to bring to the active support of the work of the Bureau those individual members of the Exchange who are unattached. We would be very glad, therefore, if you would give serious consideration to the work and aims of the Bureau" – and ask you if this question has any significance with respect to the payment of $100,000 to the Bureau?

"If your answers to the above questions are 'No,' then, in the name of common sense, will you please explain why the Stock Exchange gave the Better Business Bureau $100,000, when the yearly membership fee of the Bureau is only $25?"

THE APO$TATE

In September 1931, E. C. Riegel filed "formal charges against the Better Business Bureau" with various U.S. departments. He demanded that the Bureau be licensed and that the "Before You Invest, Investigate" program be investigated.

Logan initiated a pile-on that included a litany of additional complaints and highlighted various lawsuits filed against several Better Business Bureaus for fraud and defamation. The Manhattan Board of Commerce's allegations were forwarded to Congressman LaGuardia who passed claims to Senator Fletcher. O'Sullivan respectively wrote, "Mr. Billingsley's prediction came true, for investigation of the New York Stock Exchange by a committee of the United State Senate started on March 4, 1932. Congressman La Guardia of New York was among the first to submit some of the proof referred to in the Billingsley letter, and the probe by the Senatorial committee is still in progress." It was noted that "over the years" the Bureau's "file" on Logan mysteriously "disappeared," but the Bureau remains on Congressional record for being declared a "racket" the same as it accused the Manhattan Board.

Fiorello Enrico (Henry) LaGuardia was a veteran of WWI and a bipartisan Republican elected to the U.S. House of Representatives for the 20th District of New York from March 4, 1923 to 1933. Then, he was elected the 99th mayor of New York, serving three terms from 1934 to 1945. He stood five feet tall and his nickname was "Fiorello" or "Little Flower." LaGuardia maintained strong ties with FDR and employed FDR's New Deal dynamics to assist impoverished immigrants and reform Tammany Hall corruption. He was known for leading "a coalition opposed to Tammany Hall" after incumbent leaders tried to "block" FDR's Democratic nomination for the presidency in 1932. According to Wikipedia.org, "Roosevelt heavily funded the city and cut off patronage for La Guardia's enemies."

Despite the Bureau's censorship, Logan was supported by the influential Congressman LaGuardia who would be one of the greatest and most powerful mayors of New York and held the ear of FDR, considered to be one of the greatest presidents in U.S. history. Logan had the clout and connections to turn the table on the New York Bureau and fraud-shame the organization in the U.S. Senate. Unfortunately, as time passed, Bureau sycophants distorted Logan's tremendous contributions to society by branding him a murderous bootlegger to bury the Bureau's historic securities fraud and racketeering. He was a bootlegger, but not a murderer. And the Bronx owes Logan a debt of gratitude.

While battling Logan and Riegel, the Bureau unleashed a desperate public relations' smoke screen to deflect fallout. Kenner was accused of soliciting crony newspapers to spin state and federal racketeering accusations against the Bureau into the Bureau's fight against rackets. It was the ole' throw the scent of the trail trick. Instead, the Bureau's PR campaign backfired and emphasized the Bureau's diabolical collusion with newspapers. My research of newspapers in the 1920s and 1930s indicated media censorship was engaged to suppress derogatory ink against the Bureau.

The Bureau's feigned discovery of Logan's criminal record was disingenuous, to say the least, but provided an excuse to engage public excoriation of his personal life. Logan's background was never a secret, but he did not wear it on his sleeve. Before he reached New York, his life embraced bootlegging, gambling, and the illegal sale of alcohol. He was constantly at odds with the law. Otherwise, his background added to his aura and charm. His colorful past drew celebrity acclaim tempered by his subsequent rehabilitation and successful real estate career. Logan had long since redeemed himself as a pillar of society. He emerged as a respected real estate mogul and mingled with the elite of New York. Furthermore, his connection to the *Stork Club* added flair because it was considered a Manhattan landmark.

Logan exposed the Bureau's NYSE jugular, widespread chicanery, and participation in the Crash. He diligently set about rebuilding the city to encourage new business and jobs. To the contrary, the Bureau played Nero's fiddle while organized crime ravaged New York City.

Public response exceeded expectation when an appreciative New York City disregarded the Bureau's publication of Logan's criminal background and unified behind his leadership. Undaunted New Yorkers were already conditioned by the atrocities of gangland crime and Mafioso kingpins, and Logan's reputation was tame by comparison. Thereafter, he successfully convoluted the Bureau's allegations by exposing the franchise's racketeering, collusion, and organized securities fraud with the NYSE. A litany of defamation and corruption lawsuits lodged against various Bureaus supported the vanguard of Logan's claims. And a fed-up chorus of city, state, and federal authorities validated his allegations when referring to the Bureau as "milk bottle thieves," a "proficient liar," and a "racket." As a result, Logan earned his wings as a respected businessman, Bronx developer, and influential leader of two major chambers of commerce.

A snapshot of Logan's chaotic marital life, criminal background, and murder of two policemen seemingly supported Bureau accusations. To the contrary, a 1930's newspaper article detailed in-depth circumstances, witnesses, and testimony that either exonerated or tempered the most outlandish charges. Logan was born into a flawed environment that resulted in his rebellious youth, but he evolved into a dignified public figure.

Logan and Sherman were estranged in their later years. Sherman went on to make and lose a fortune through the Stork Club while fending off a litany of gangsters and crooked politicians, police, and judges. He saw his beloved Stork Club leveled and died broke. And Logan's real estate business in the Bronx was devastated by the Crash. After his duel with the Bureau, Logan left New York City for good. To his credit, Logan left indelible marks; the Bureau was exposed,

THE APO$TATE

and the Bronx was reborn. Logan returned to his home state of Oklahoma as a distinguished man with noble convictions. He became a wealthy home builder and office park developer in Westchester, Oklahoma. On February 1, 1952, Logan established the "National Hall of Fame For Famous American Indians," located at "132 ½ W Bdwy, Anadarko, Oklahoma," and served as its "executive director." He belonged to the Oklahoma Historical Society, and was a member of "the Association of American Indian Affairs and the New York Historical Association." Additionally, he supported the "Southern Plains Indian Museum," also located in Anadarko.

Ill health plagued an elderly Logan. He suffered from diabetes and heart disease. Logan lived in the quaint town of Mount Kisco, New York, in Westchester County. He passed away on August 3, 1963, after being hospitalized for several weeks. He was 80 years old. Logan asked his wife Francis to bury him in the Billingsley family plot at Memory Lane Cemetery in Anadarko, Caddo County, Oklahoma, next to his father and brother, Richard, who had died at the young age of 19 from influenza.

Out of curiosity, I called the "National Hall of Fame For Famous American Indians" in Anadarko and spoke to an elderly volunteer who kindly related that Logan was highly respected by local residents; that he had built the area with successful real estate ventures. She proudly described the many native Indian statues that he financed for the museum that was still visited by passing travelers. Logan made good on his promise as a child and left the Anadarko Indians a legacy that made them proud.

CHAPTER **26**

EDWIN CLARENCE RIEGEL

E. C. Riegel
Prolific author; renowned economist; president of Consumers Guild of America; initiated Wall Street reform; brought federal charges against Better Business Bureau that contributed to launch of U.S. Senate Committee on Banking and Currency and Wall Street reform;
artist: Caryn Cain.

The obscure author of *Barnum and Bunk* and president of the Consumers Guild of America was an eccentric revolutionary consumer advocate and obscure financial genius who filed charges of racketeering and securities fraud against the New York Bureau. Henchmen long since buried his damning Bureau accusations, but O'Sullivan's spirit reminded his participation in extraordinary and buried Wall Street history. Otherwise, Riegel would have passed unheralded into restless perpetuity, and the wordless sins of an iconic hypocrite would have forever remained elusive. It was not until after his death that his work was recognized for its exemplary achievement and public contribution. As a result, history is forever enriched and informed.

O'Sullivan featured Riegel in his most formidable publication, *Rackets*. Both men lived in the day and provided a similar narrative that detailed scandalous indiscretions of the early Better Business Bureau.

Riegel was a proud arch nemesis of the Bureau and stood for "free exchange" opposed to the organization's big-business interests that aligned with government at the expense of consumers. According to authors Spencer MacCallum and George Morton, "He traced the massive build-up of government in this century directly to businessmen seeking unfair trading advantage. He saw the league of big business, government, and finance as tending to bring about an aristocracy in America, a privileged class that was diametrically at odds with his ideals of democracy and justice." In fact, Riegel and other New York authorities exposed the collaborative relationship between the Bureau and the NYSE from 1919 until after the Crash that resulted in a securities-fraud investigation by the U.S Senate between 1932 and 1934. *Rackets* documented Riegel's historical involvement, which forced sweeping reforms on Wall Street.

Edwin Clarence "E.C." Riegel was born on June 18, 1879, in Cannelton, Indiana. His Swiss-German family name was "Zuckriegel." Riegel's father was unnamed, but he was a treasurer for Perry County. His mother's name was Kathryn Dusch and she was an accomplished musician. His only sibling was an older brother named Oscar. Around the age of 15, about 1894, he headed for the excitement of New York City. Reigel married Blanche Ellis Beach in 1905, but wedlock digressed into an amicable divorce in 1912. He never earned a scholastic degree. Nevertheless, he was inherently well-bred and intermingled in high society as a self-described "non-academic student of money and credit."

He refused to work for others and remained a "libertarian" and free spirit in keeping with his convictions promoting free trade. His numerous books and projects were financed through temporary retail sales jobs easily procured due to his "distinguished personal bearing."

As was common in the day, Riegel used his initials because he did not like his middle name. A respective occasion was described when he applied for a Social Security card and argued with officials when firmly instructed to write out his full name. He finally complied by sarcastically writing, "Edwin Controversy Riegel," as a personal protest against an overbearing government. (MacCullum advised that he retained Riegel's original Social Security card.) Later in life, Riegel became known to close friends as "Uncle Ned." Considering the serious nature of his publications and historical confrontations, his familial nickname seemed trite and out of character.

As a prolific writer, he published several significant books, pamphlets, and over 150 essays. Listed by date, his publishing credits included *The Credit Question* in 1926; *Barnum and Bunk: An Exposure of R. H. Macy & Co.* in 1928; *The Yellow Book, The Three Laws of Vending* and *Main Street Follies* between 1928 and 1930; *The Indictment of the Better Business Bureau Conspiracy* in 1931; *The Camorra of Commerce* in 1932; *The Meaning of Money* in the mid-1930s; *The Valun Discourses and Monologue* also mid-1930s; *Roosevelt Revalued* in 1936; *Are You Better Off?* in 1936; *Brain Trussed* in 1936; *Franklinstein* in 1936; *Quarantine the Aggressor in the White House* in 1941; *The Fifth Column in America* in 1941; *Dollar Doomsday* in 1941; *Private Enterprise Money* in 1944; *New Approach to Freedom* in 1949; and *Flight from Inflation* in 1953. The recurring theme of Riegel's books focused on monetary policies that encouraged financial recovery by encouraging small business, "individualism," and "separation of money and state."

The Indictment and *The Camorra* were particularly significant as substantial Bureau-related complaints that pre-empted and/or coincided with U.S. Senate investigations and O'Sullivan's *Rackets* in 1933, when FDR's Pecora Commission took over President Hoover's U.S. Senate hearings. Riegel's two books, especially *The Camorra*, documented the Better Business Bureau's racketeering relationship with the NYSE and Investment Bankers Association. According to MacCallum and Morton, *"The Camorra* is a responsibly documented expose of the role of the Better Business Bureau, after 1922, in collusion with the Investment Bankers Association and the New York Stock Exchange, to protect the Bureau's members from competition. Prominent among its members were Wall Street brokerage firms and companies listed on the Exchange." And the year 1922 was especially relevant because the New York Bureau launched the bogus "Before You Invest, Investigate" securities program.

The Camorra also incredibly documented the Better Business Bureau's participation in President Hoover's "Neighborhood Enforcement Policy" that was a euphemism for the "Mexican Repatriation" program initiated in 1928. Hoover's program operated on the premise "that jobs and charity should be reserved for Americans, and that non-citizens should return to their home countries." According to National Archives, "In the late 1920s, about 60,000 people would enter the U.S. annually from "non-quota" countries, primarily Mexico, and many of them stayed for years. (The 1924 Immigration Act had established strict quotas for immigration from Europe, Asia and Africa, but did not limit immigration from North or South America.) As long as migrants had a visa and a job, they could stay as long as they wished. Any migrant without a valid visa could be deported at any time, and any migrant, temporary or permanent, could be deported if they became a public charge." Consequently, the Bureau established a *Roaring Twenties'* military connection with Hoover that segued into the Bureau's Deep State induction by FDR in 1941 to covertly monitor Japanese American movement after Pearl Harbor. FDR initiated Japanese American internment comparable to Hoover's Mexican Repatriation.

In 1928, Riegel formed the Consumers Guild of America that was later succeeded by The Valun Institute for Monetary Research in the 1940s. The Guild was what the Bureau was supposed to be. MacCallum elaborated, 'The purpose of the Consumers Guild was to simplify buying and raise the dignity of the consumer, and it opposed anything that would suspend or restrain the consumer's right of bargain."

In 1930, Riegel commenced a year-long investigation of the New York Bureau and its nefarious relationship with the NYSE contributing to the Stock Market Crash and Great Depression. O'Sullivan documented Riegel's allegations as well as those of Logan Billingsley whose joint complaints were adjudicated by Senator Fletcher in U.S. Senate chambers in January 1932, two months prior to launch of the Banking and Currency Committee investigation that began March 2, 1932, and ended July 2, 1934. Riegel published "a pamphlet" (paperback book) entitled, *The Indictment of the Better Business Bureau Conspiracy*, around 1933, which questioned the Bureau's disingenuous sales tactics linking to membership sales prior to the Crash. Riegel described an ""operating program" presented by the manager of the National Better Business Bureau that was presented to his Board of Directors in 1929." O'Sullivan quoted Riegel's description of the National Bureau's scheme for soliciting funds: "From our experience," – said the National Bureau manager, - "we believe the most substantial method of attaining and retaining financial support is by continually tying in our solicitation with the operating program of our Commercial and Financial Departments. By this method those appealed to for funds have the practical demonstration of Bureau service, as it relates to their specific business. They can see an economic value of selfish interest ... This method provides the Extension Department (the solicitors) with a constant flow of sales material at regular intervals, keeps our subscribers old, and provides the means to sell prospective subscribers."

Riegel believed that the Bureau collaborated with the NYSE by using its investigative programs to encourage speculation in Wall Street securities that were "exempted from the blue-sky laws." Professor Charles R. Geisst explained Blue Sky laws as, "During World War I, some western states had passed what were known as blue sky laws, which required an investment banker to register the securities it wanted to sell in the state with the appropriate state securities authorities."

In accordance with Riegel, O'Sullivan lambasted the Bureau's highly acclaimed mantra "Before You Invest, Investigate!" as a disingenuous investment program that insinuated safe speculation in NYSE stocks and contributed to the snowballing catastrophe, which came to a crashing halt on "Black Tuesday," October 29, 1929. O'Sullivan summarized that the NYSE worked in cahoots with the New York Bureau to disparage any "unlisted" securities outside their purview: "The Stock Exchange is interested in maintaining the prestige of the stock which it lists, and the Better Business Bureau, while approving all such listed stocks and Stock Exchange promotions, frowns upon unlisted securities, casts upon them the limelight of their "investigations," and creates in the public mind the impression that stock issues not listed on the Exchange should be regarded with suspicion and doubt."

It seems unfitting that Riegel was rendered decrepit by Parkinson's disease. He was no longer able to type and could not complete the manuscript for his final book. MacCallum stated that he met Riegel in 1953 and that he died later that year at the age of 74. His grandfather knew the family who retained Riegel's possessions and intellectual works. MacCallum paid $500 to secure such property and, with the editing assistance of George Morton, completed *Flight From Inflation*.

CHAPTER 27

SENATOR DUNCAN FLETCHER

Senator Duncan Fletcher
Democratic Florida Senator and Chairman of Pecora Commission; indicted Better Business Bureau in U.S. Senate Chambers; artist: Caryn Cain.

He was a gift to humanity from the state of Florida and lived an extraordinarily distinguished career. Only a statesman of his outstanding caliber and gravitas could accuse the Bureau of being a racket. The Senator condemned the Bureau's tripartite relationship with the NYSE and Investment Bankers Association and alleged that they manipulated "Blue Sky" exemptions for questionable Wall Street listed securities that were whitewashed through the Bureau's bogus "Before You Invest, Investigate" program. The Senator validated complaints of Bureau-related securities fraud initiated by Logan Billingsley, president of the Bronx Chamber of Commerce, and E. C. Riegel, president of Consumers Guild of America.

Billingsley and Riegel funneled complaints to New York Congressman La Guardia who presented complaints to Senator Fletcher who advised President Hoover.

Duncan Upshaw Fletcher was born on January 6, 1859, in Americus, Sumter County, Georgia. After attending public school and graduating from the Gordon Institute in Barnesville, Georgia, he studied law at Vanderbilt University in Nashville, Tennessee, and graduated in 1880. The following year, he was admitted to the bar and began practicing law in Jacksonville, Florida. His wife was Anna Louise Paine (1861-1941) from New York. They had a daughter, Louise Chapin Fletcher Kemp (born in Florida 1887; died in Florida, June 24, 1959).

In 1887, Fletcher shifted into politics and won election to the city council. He was elected to the "State house of representatives" in 1893 and served two terms as mayor of Jacksonville from 1893 to 1895 and from 1901 to 1903. According to the Florida International University Library, Fletcher also served "as chairman of the board of public instruction of Duval County from 1900-1907; as president of the Gulf Coast Inland Waterways Association in 1908, and, later, of the Mississippi to Atlantic Waterway Association."

On March 4, 1909, Fletcher began a brilliant political career as Florida's Democratic United States senator serving until 1936. While senator he was also "chairman, Committee on Printing (Sixty-third and Sixty-fourth Congresses), Committee on Commerce (Sixty-fourth and Sixty-fifth Congresses), Committee on Transportation Routes to the Seaboard (Sixty-sixth Congress), Committee on Banking and Currency (Seventy-third and Seventy-fourth Congresses); president of the Southern Commercial Congress 1912-1918." In 1913, President Woodrow Wilson appointed him "as chairman of the United States commission to investigate European land-mortgage banks, cooperative rural credit unions, and the betterment of rural conditions in Europe." In 1916, he served as "a delegate to the International High Commission at Buenos Aires, Argentina."

Towards the end of his life, Senator Fletcher was embroiled in securities investigations and Wall Street reform consequent to the Crash. Investigations included short selling and Blue Sky law violations as perpetrated by the Bureau, NYSE, and Investment Bankers Association. The Bureau's "Before You Invest, Investigate" program was charged with exploiting Blue Sky laws to promote worthless NYSE securities. Blue Sky laws required that parties register all securities, firms, brokers, and investment advisers, but registration also shielded parties from liability.

Senator Fletcher acted upon allegations initiated by Riegel and Billingsley in New York City. After a year-long investigation, Riegel filed charges "before five departments of the United States Government in September, 1931" against the "Better Business Bureau system" and Billingsley followed up in December 1931. The senator worked with La Guardia, Republican representative for New

THE APO$TATE

York's 20th District, from March 4, 1923 to March 3, 1933, to adjudicate claims by Riegel and Billingsley. Riegel specifically connected the Bureau's fake NYSE-affiliated investigative security program to the Crash and Great Depression. To his credit, Democratic Senator Fletcher acted with exceptional objective bipartisan fairness to indict the Democratic Bureau whose members included the elite of every major association in New York and throughout America. Senator Fletcher had the ear of Republican President Hoover and his advice established the U.S. Senate Banking and Currency Commission.

On September 4, 1931, the United Press in Washington, D.C., broke the story of Riegel's intent to file charges against the Bureau; its dispatch read, "Charges of unlawful practices by the Better Business Bureau and member organizations, including the New York Stock Exchange, have been made in printed statements sent to various government agencies by the Consumers Guild of America, Inc. The statement was signed by E. C. Riegel, President, and asserted that briefs and evidence supporting the charges would be filed at a later date. The statement was sent to the Federal Trade Commission, the Department of Justice, the Federal Reserve Board, the Post Office Department, and the Federal Radio Commission. Riegel's statement charged that the Better Business Bureau organizations were engaged in unfair trade practices, promoting gambling on the Stock Exchange, using the mails to defraud, and encouraging unfair trade practices and attempting to restrain radio communication."

Accordingly, on September 31, 1931, Riegel filed charges: "We shall file briefs and evidence showing that the accused system, while professing to fight fraud is itself the greatest of all frauds; that under the slogan, 'Truth in Advertising,' it has been the most proficient liar; that under the motto, "Before you invest, investigate,' it has resisted investigation of the securities-selling houses that are its secret patrons; that it has resorted to slander, libel, and blackmail to promote its conspiracy to defame the names and restrain the trade of non-members who compete with members. We shall show that its crowning achievement has been to help the New York Stock Exchange to sell the American people fifty billions of dollars' worth of blue sky, that faded and left the nation with the present drab horizon."

Billingsley, was also "Chairman of the Board of the Manhattan Board of Commerce," and followed Riegel's charges by challenging the NYSE's Richard Whitney "to a debate before the Syracuse Chamber of Commerce on December 16, 1931, but the challenge was declined." O'Sullivan provided a clip from Billingsley's letter addressed to the Syracuse Chamber: "We are endeavoring to bring about a Senatorial investigation of the Stock Exchange. Through secret processes, we find that the Stock Exchange is even corrupting the public press, and that the publishers of important newspapers do not know that their papers are compromised by the Exchange, through its hook-up with the Better

Business Bureau, and that their papers have been used by this combination to unload fifty billions of dollars' worth of blue sky on the public. All of these facts we expect to prove before a Senatorial investigation – which is not far distant."

Thereafter, Billingsley feared that the Bureau "would interfere with the investigation of the Stock Exchange, its ally and supporter" and forwarded respective inquiry to Congress. He received a reply from "Representative A. J. Sabath, of the Fifth District, Illinois." Sabath addressed his response letter, dated May 21, 1932, from "Congress of the United States, House of Representatives, Washington, D.C.," to "Mr. Logan Billingsley, Chairman, Board of Directors, Manhattan Board of Commerce, 9 West, 170th Street, New York City," that read in entirety:

"My dear Mr. Billingsley: I am just in receipt of your letter of May thirteenth asking me if I know of any instances where propaganda methods are being used by managers of the Better Business Bureau system to block the investigation of the New York Stock Exchange.

"It has come to my attention that the principal newspapers of the country have their names printed on the stationery of the various Better Business Bureaus, and, whether they know it or not, this makes possible the stage-setting for powerful propaganda.

"I note that these Better Business Bureau letters, with the names of important newspapers on the margin of the letterhead, are seen by Members of Congress, the Department of Justice, the Post Office Department, and the Federal Trade Commission.

"Personally, I doubt that the newspaper publishers sanctioned the use of their names to block Senatorial investigations, and, more particularly, the present investigation of the New York Stock Exchange; but they have laid themselves wide open to be misunderstood by having their names listed on the stationery of an organization, along with the names of such men as Richard Whitney and James C. Auchincloss.

"For instance, if I received a letter from the New York Better Business Bureau, or any other Bureau, telling me that they had the protection of America's newspapers, and that I might be sprayed with derogatory publicity if I interfered with anything pertaining to them, I might pay little or no attention to it. But, on the other hand, if I received a very innocent-looking letter from the Better Business Bureau, asking me about banking conditions in my home state, and the bureau letterhead carried the names of half-a-dozen important newspapers, I could very naturally assume that this Better Business Bureau had enormous newspaper influence.

"I see powerful propaganda possibilities, coupled with great protection to the New York Stock Exchange, through the Better Business Bureau hook-up.

"If the Stock Exchange group gave $50,000 to the Better Business Bureau,

THE APO$TATE

they undoubtedly had something up their sleeve. $50,000 is a lot of money to give away for nothing. Very truly yours, (Signed) A. J. SABATH ... AJS:H"

On January 25, 1932, the eloquent Senator Fletcher lambasted the Bureau as a racket on the floor of the U.S. Senate and built on Riegel's Blue Sky-related allegations. O'Sullivan described Senator Fletcher's historic indictment: "From the nature of the charges freely made against the Better Business Bureau system, many of which have been corroborated by independent investigation, the assertion made by Senator Fletcher of Florida on the floor of the United States Senate that the Better Business Bureau has become a racket appears to have been fully justified." Senator Fletcher spoke to colleagues, but he dutifully warned the nation: "The unsavory testimony coming out about the flotation of these securities brings forcibly to mind the existence in this country of the greatest racket ever known in its history, to wit: The hook-up between the New York Stock Exchange, the Investment Bankers' Association, and their puppet, which is known as the Better Business Bureau. The actual line-up existing, and which you can verify by an examination of witnesses coming before you, is simply this: The New York Stock Exchange and the Investment Bankers' Association, with the aid of their puppet, the so-termed Better Business Bureau, ---the income of the latter being derived from donations contributed by the former, ---first secured the passage in some forty-odd states, of that which we know as 'the blue sky law,' and you must be familiar with it. This law exempts securities listed on the Exchanges, and thus permits the crooked banker and the crooked broker to sell listed securities at any price obtainable, regardless of actual value, to the unwary sucker; and no matter how utterly worthless that stock may be in actual money, those bankers and brokers cannot be charged with fraud or the offense of obtaining money under false pretenses. You must pay tribute to one of the organizations or go to jail." O'Sullivan noted, "The remarks of Senator Fletcher may be found in the Senate Congressional Record, Volume 75, No. 32, Page 2709."

Furthermore, according to O'Sullivan, Senator Fletcher incriminated the banking industry: "The daily press shows that more than $815,000,000, in foreign securities that were floated under the chaperonage of American banking houses are now in default"; that "millions of dollars were pocketed by these bankers in 'commissions,' etc., in disposing of these securities to the American suckers, and there is no doubt that our present suffering is due in a large measure of the effects of this robbery."

On March 2, 1932, the U.S. Senate passed Resolution 84 authorizing respective investigation of the buying and selling of stocks and securities. Accordingly, on March 4, 1932, Chairman Norbeck opened the U.S. Senate's Banking and Currency Commission's investigations into the Crash. After almost a year of unproductive hearings, Chairman Norbeck "hired a new chief counsel, former New York deputy district attorney Ferdinand Pecora. Norbeck called him a "happy discovery"."

In latter March 1932, the National Better Business Bureau Commission, Inc. histrionically responded to Senator Fletcher's scathing rebuke of the Better Business Bureaus and launch of U.S. Senate investigations by introducing the "Standards of Practice of the Association of National Advertisers and the American Association of Advertising Agencies." Such lionized title was a desperate publicity stunt emphasized by timing and context and meant to deflect charges against the New York Bureau's tainted "Before You Invest, Investigate" securities program and questionable Wall Street and banking relationships.

On March 4, 1933, Democratic President Franklin Delano Roosevelt took office. A Democrat-controlled Senate replaced Republican Senator Norbeck with Democratic Senator Fletcher as Chairman of the U.S. Senate Banking and Currency Commission. Three months earlier, in January 1933, and prior to his pending departure, Norbeck appointed former New York Chief Assistant District Attorney Ferdinand Pecora as the fourth chief counsel of the Commission.

On June 6, 1934, the Pecora hearings ended and Chairman Fletcher completed the 394-page long "Stock Exchange Practices Report of the Committee on Banking and Currency," a.k.a. the "Fletcher Report"; published on June 16, 1934. The Fletcher Report blended accusation, explanation, and corrective measures; prevailing emphasis was "concentration of control of wealth" by investment trusts and pools.

Chairman Fletcher acknowledged legal and illegal pools. He wrote: "Attempts have been made to differentiate between "beneficent" pools and "nefarious" pools. It is claimed that pools operated for the purpose of stabilizing market prices during periods of secondary distribution, or while liquidating blocks of stock held by estates or creditors are "beneficent" pools; whereas pools operated merely for the purpose of raising the price of securities so that the participants might unload their holdings at increased prices have been characterized as "nefarious" pools."

Additionally, Chairman Fletcher highlighted misrepresented pools and securities: "The testimony before the Senate subcommittee again and again demonstrated that the activity fomented by a pool creates a false and deceptive appearance of genuine demand for the security on the part of the purchasing public and attracts persons relying upon this misleading appearance to make purchases." Accordingly, Senator Fletcher incriminated the Bureau's "Before You Invest, Investigate" securities program that attracted consumers through duplicitous promise of stringent investigation to guarantee safe securities.

Broad reform was detailed as a safeguard to prevent relapse and move the economy forward. New legislation was identified including the Glass–Steagall Act or Banking Act of 1933, the Securities Act of 1933 or "truth in securities law," and the Securities Exchange Act of 1934.

The Better Business Bureau was not mentioned in Chairman Fletcher's final report because it was neither a bank nor a security firm even though it did business with both as a parasitic free-floating autocrat. Many of its members in the NYSE and Investment Bankers Association were investigated, though, and revealed a glimpse into the secret society's Prohibition-era network.

Chairman Fletcher exposed many household names beginning with the year that the Bureau entered the lucrative field of securities. His report stated, "During the year 1920, 105 stockholders listed on the New York Stock Exchange were subject to one or more syndicate, pool, and/or joint accounts which member firms or partners thereof managed, and in the profits or loses of which they participated.[90]" The "90" footnote listed all respective stockholders: "Alleghany Corporation; Allegheny Corporation preferred; American Commercial Alcohol; American Ice; American Sugar Refining Co.; American Tobacco; Archer Daniels Midland Corporation; Aviation Corporation; Beatrice Creamery; Bendix Aviation; Bethlehem Steel; Borden Co.; Bullard Co.; Bush Terminal; Campbell Wyant Foundry Co.; Celotex Co.; Chicago, Milwaukee & St. Paul R.R. preferred; Cerro de Pasco; Childs & Co.; Chrysler Co.; Clark Equipment Co.; Cluett Peabody Co.; Columbian Carbon Co.; Commonwealth & Southern Congress Cigar Co.; Consolidated Cigar; Consolidated Gas Co.; Continental Can Co.; Continental Motors Co.; Cream of Wheat Corporation; Crosley Radio; Curtis Aeorplane Co.; Curtiss-Wright Co.; Eastern Rolling Mills; Ellington Schild, Firestone Tire common; General American Tank Car Co.; General Cable; General Cigar Co.; General Refractories; Gimbel Bros.; Gold Dust; Goodrich & Co.; Gotham Silk Hose; Grand Union Co.; Columbia Graphophone Co.; Indian Refining Co.; International Match preferred; International Telephone & Telegraph Co.; Kreuger & Toll; Kroger Grocery; Lehn & Fink Products; R. H. Macy & Co.; May Department Stores; Marmon Motor Co.; McGraw-Hill; McKeason & Robbins; Mengel Co.; Mexican Seaboard Oil; Miami Copper; Michigan Steel Corporation; Mid-Continental Petroleum Co.; Minneapolis Moline common; Minneapolis Moline preferred; Missouri, Kansas, Texas R.R. Common; Monsanto Chemical; Montgomery Ward & Co.; Munsingwear Murray Corporation of America; National Cash Register Co.; National Dairy Co.; North German Lloyd; Oppenheim-Collins Co.; Packard Motor Co.; Phelps Dodge Co.; Pillsbury Flour Mills; Pittsburg & W. Va. R.R.; Purity Bakeries; Radio Corporation; Radio Corporation "A"; R. J. Reynolds Tobacco Co.; Safeway Stores, Inc.; Servel, Inc.; Sharon Hoop; Simms Petroleum; Southern Puerto Rico Sugar; A. G. Spalding & Bros.; Spang Chalfante Co.; Standard Gas & Electric Co. preferred; Standard Oil of California; St. Louis-San Francisco R. R. Co.; Studebaker; Teloutograph; Underwood-Elliott-Fisher Co.; Union Carbon & Carbide Co.; United Carbon;

U.S. & Foreign Securities; U.S. Rubber Co.; U.S. Smelting & Refining Co.; Utility Power & Light "A"; Walworth Co.; Weber & Heilbroner, Westvaco Chlorine Co.; L. A. Young Spring & Wire Corporation; Zenith Radio (pt. 17, p. 7949)."

By October 29, 1929, Samuel Candler Dobbs, former president of the AACA from 1909 until 1911, had become a wealthy influential investment banker self-admittedly doing business in New York City and overseas after resigning his position as president of Coca-Cola on October 4, 1920, but he remained on Coca-Cola's Board of Directors. Also, in 1920, the National Vigilance Committee, a branch of the AACA (renamed the AACW), systemically launched the "Before You Invest, Investigate" securities program. Dobbs continued a long-term membership and advisory relationship with the National Vigilance Committee and New York Bureau that suggested investments were involved. Chairman Fletcher specifically named Coca-Cola Co. regarding investment trusts and pools; Dobbs was not named, but was indirectly implicated due to his background and affiliation with Coca-Cola: "In 1932, two issues listed on the New York Stock Exchange were subject to one or more syndicate, pool, and/or joint accounts in which the member firms or partners thereof had an interest and which they managed.[95]" The "95" footnote stated: "Coca-Cola Co., S.S. Kreage Co., (pt.17, p.7050)." Accordingly, Dobbs was likely among many Illuminati pulling golden strings to distance themselves, their companies, and the Bureau from Senate investigations. It was all for one and one for all. If the Bureau went down, so did they.

Chief Counsel Pecora exposed abusive banking and securities practices that aligned with relative claims by Billingsley and Riegel regarding the NYSE, Investment Bankers Association, and Bureau. Chairman Fletcher and other committee Senators alternated with Pecora's detailed interrogation of the elite of Wall Street and Big Banking that included "Richard Whitney, president of the New York Stock Exchange, George Whitney (a partner in J.P. Morgan & Co.) and investment bankers Thomas W. Lamont, Otto H. Kahn, Albert H. Wiggin of Chase National Bank, and Charles E. Mitchell of National City Bank (now Citibank)," according to Wikipedia.org.

In November 1929, former newspaper publisher, former 47th U.S. secretary of the treasury from 1918 to 1920, and Virginia Democratic Senator Carter Glass pointed damning blame: "Mitchell more than any 50 men is responsible for this stock crash." In 1933, Mitchell resigned from National City Bank when he "was arrested and indicted for tax evasion by then Assistant U.S. Attorney Thomas E. Dewey." He was found not guilty, "but the government won a million-dollar civil settlement against him."

Several high-profile industrial, financial, and banking celebrities were subpoenaed to assure publicity for the hearings. Those who were cross-examined were either a member of the Bureau or its national dashboard and represented a gilded scroll of uber globalists. It was the first time that the Bureau's extensive underground network was exposed in an era where memberships were not advertised, and the secrecy of the Sphinx Club still reigned. The extent of multilayered power and wealth emanating from testimony was incomprehensible and emphasized egregious abuse of the financial and banking systems that created the Crash.

Chief Counsel Pecora and Senator Fletcher unearthed the lucrative secrets of Wall Street's hallowed halls. Pecora interrogated a litany of NYSE swells and determined that steep discounts were issued to powerful insiders including former U.S. President Calvin Coolidge and U.S. Supreme Court Justice Owen J. Roberts. Senator Fletcher revealed, "The "preferred list" in Standard Brands stock contained various names which did not appear on the "preferred list" in Alleghany Corporation stock. These included F. H. Ecker, president of the Metropolitan Life Insurance Co., which company was a heavy purchaser of securities for Norman H. Davis, for Calvin Coolidge, and for Bernard M. Baruch, the financier." And, Pecora opened a global can of worms when discovering "that National City sold off bad loans to Latin American countries by packing them into securities and selling them to unsuspecting investors … that Mitchell and top officers at National City had received $2.4 million in interest-free loans from the bank's coffers."

Senator Fletcher was co-sponsor of the "Fletcher-Rayburn" bill that introduced the Securities Exchange Act of 1933. Fletcher and Democratic Texas Congressman Samuel Taliaferro Rayburn (1882-1961) presented the bill drafted by James M. Landis, Benjamin Cohen, and Thomas Corcoran. Landis was appointed commissioner of the Securities and Exchange Commission by FDR.

O'Sullivan referred to the Pecora Commission as "the banking committee under the chairmanship of Senator Peter Norbeck" because its famous name had not been coined at the time of *Rackets'* publication. Consequently, I believe that *Rackets* was published just before Ferdinand Pecora assumed investigations on January 24, 1933. In fact, O'Sullivan quoted Senator Norbeck on January 10, 1933: "We are trying to find out to what extent the American investor has been played for a sucker, with the help of American bankers and the Stock Exchange." *Rackets* was hugely historical and provided a remarkable and obscure backstory that described the posturing and conflict that led to the U.S. Senate and Pecora Commission hearings. O'Sullivan's gumshoe efforts caught the Bureau red-handed and left posterity a documented account of the advocate's incalculable fraud that brought America to its knees.

Senator Fletcher's far-reaching contributions instigated historic Senate investigations and Wall Street reform. Unfortunately, the Bureau was excused with a slap on the wrist that O'Sullivan contributed to high-profile membership and elite business connections: "These individuals are exemplars of business ethics and personal integrity, and constitute both the Bureau's foil against suspicion and its vestment of leadership. To understand the Bureau, however, one must approach it through the back door rather than the front."

Fate brought Peter Norbeck and Duncan Fletcher together in 1933 to reform Wall Street and death separated them three years later. On June 17, 1936, Senator Fletcher was at home and died of a heart attack while preparing to leave for the "Capitol"; he was 77 years old. And, on December 20, 1936, Senator Norbeck died of oral cancer at his South Dakota home; he was 66 years old. Fletcher "was the longest serving U.S. Senator in Florida's history" serving from 1909 to 1936. He was laid to rest at the Evergreen Cemetery in Jacksonville where he first began practicing law in 1881. Fletcher gifted posterity the Everglades National Park as his legacy that he founded and was signed into law by FDR on May 30, 1934.

CHAPTER 28

FRANK DALTON O'SULLIVAN

Frank Dalton O'Sullivan
Author, publisher, CSI detective; published *Rackets* to expose
the New York Better Business Bureau's racket with the NYSE
and Investment Bankers Association; artist: Caryn Cain.

An unsung hero! A writer, publisher, consumer advocate, criminologist, historian, and businessman supporting the principles of limited government and free trade! He published *Rackets* at the commencement of the Pecora Commission, which inspired and assisted respective investigations into securities fraud and racketeering by the New York Bureau, NYSE, and Investment Bankers Association. O'Sullivan's 1930's accusation, "You're an iconoclast. You never help the little fellow that is struggling to exist," prophetically immortalized the Bureau as an oppressive globalist. He communicated as a victim and renowned critic of the Bureau comparing its plenary authority, restraint of trade, and bully tactics to organized crime. *Rackets* exposed the Better Business Bureau as "the greatest racket ever known in its history."

O'Sullivan wrote that he was an Easterner and moved to Chicago in 1914. Research implied that he was home-schooled, highly educated, and appreciated Greek Classics. Without a formal academic degree, he measured his expertise through achievements and contributions: "I have sold over 300,000 educational books throughout the world. I have written and published 26 books. I have edited hundreds of large manuscripts and thousands of short stories and articles for customers. I have written speeches, lectures, and talks for some of the most prominent men in this country. I have written reams of newspaper and editorial copy. I now write the editorials and lead articles for a number of trade and important publications. I write advertising copy, sales letters, booklets, broadsides, catalogues – everything to build and boost business."

Towards the end of his short life, he focused on the Better Business Bureau, NYSE, and organized crime. I believe that *Rackets* was his magnum opus and exposed the Bureau's extensive nefarious operations as a racket and what should have been the scandal of the century, but publication was muffled by the Great Depression. O'Sullivan listed "earmarks of which a racket may be recognized" that are still relevant today: "1. A secret membership, based on selfish interest. 2. Secrecy in operation, without license or authority. 3. Autocratic management and control of funds. 4. Persecution of "outsiders," or non-contributors. 5. Use of unfair and illegal methods and practices. 6. Promotion of selfish interests. 7. Disregard of the public welfare. 8. Association with stock gamblers to delude the public."

My extensive research verified *Rackets*' narrative; authenticity was imperative because the smallest incongruity would alter history. O'Sullivan's obscure storyline proved that the Bureau fell victim to 1920's organized crime and profiteering. His priceless chronicles offered incredible panoramic opportunity to experience a bygone era and answered lingering questions. How did the Bureau grow so powerful? And, why wasn't it licensed? *Rackets* was the gift that kept giving and bridged time to explain that its gilded membership scroll and control of the court system empowered its rise and autocracy.

O'Sullivan's comments also bridged time with modern complaints: "Membership in the Bureau is all that is required to place the member, apparently, on a higher plane than his competitors. They and their practices are subject to Bureau investigation, suspicion, and harassment, while the member is not." Even his sarcasm was spot-on; that "alleged news ... gave the Bureau manager an opportunity to break into print" suggesting that the Bureau was a publicity hound proffering fake news.

Defiance cost O'Sullivan his life. He died six years after *Rackets* was published. In fact, *Rackets* was his testament to the Bureau's abuse and corruption. He included a complaint letter in *Rackets* written under his pseudonym, "Don Sullington," wherein he described the Bureau's relentless harassment that made him seriously ill, but "he refused to be scared and fought back." No doubt that I was fortunate to have found *Rackets* considering its elusive out-of-print decade's differential. I shared O'Sullivan's anguish, supported his mission, and accepted the same burden of reporting consumer fraud. My book continues where his left off. I discovered comradery with O'Sullivan having treaded a similar path and shared his writer's conviction as another targeted victim of the Bureau.

His words escaped the grave to find me. I was ecstatic when serendipitously finding Wansley's History and Traditions but was euphoric when discovering *Rackets*. Although Wansley's report was a Bureau-slanted version of O'Sullivan's narrative, his review aligned with *Racket's* exposé of Bureau events. O'Sullivan's 1930's allegations, evidence, and witnesses provided irrefutable history that astonishingly supported my 2008 complaints against the Bureau. He walked a similar path long ago having been unmercifully harassed by the Chicago Bureau at his business, The O'Sullivan Publishing House. As a result, he publicized the organization's hypocrisy, fraud, and gangland tactics. His words proved prophetic and are as true today as they were yesterday.

He exposed greedy stockscrubbers, money changers, and stockbrokers who created the greatest financial catastrophe on American shores. Who better than O'Sullivan, an experienced gumshoe and newspaper reporter, to compile hidden scandalous details; to reveal shocking criminal allegations against the Bureau regarding its dubious connections with Wall Street and prominent bankers before and after the Crash.

Long before the Pecora Commission, O'Sullivan documented the Bureau's evolution into securities. He believed the wealth of Wall Street seduced the Bureau into forsaking its reason for existence. The misleading concept of safe securities promoted by the deceptive slogan "Before You Invest, Investigate" proved lucrative for the Bureau during the heyday of the *Roaring Twenties*.

O'Sullivan indicted the Bureau as an accomplice of Wall Street fraud. He explained, "Thus we find that the New York Stock Exchange became an active promoter of the Better Business Bureau system when, in 1919, it was decided that the system should have a financial department. James C. Auchincloss, governor of the Stock Exchange, is reported to have raised $50,000 in "the Street" for the National Better Business Bureau and induced the banks to lend another $50,000; and having thus secured $100,000, the largest contribution to its funds, he was elected president of the National Bureau, with a relative as financial manager. The Curb Exchange and the Chamber of Commerce of New York State were also lined up in support of the Bureau system, through the influence of the Stock Exchange; and the Investment Bankers' Association was likewise enlisted in its favor, and supplied the Bureau with the services of its legal counsel." Accordingly, O'Sullivan connected financial dots between Wall Street and the Better Business Bureau. He also condemned the Bureau for promoting deceptive investigative services: "What facilities had the average amateur speculator for investigation? Any investigation he could make would be nothing but the farce of asking a broker, a lawyer, or a banker for advice, with all of them equally ignorant and equally helpless."

Frank Dalton O'Sullivan was born on May 23, 1886, in Manston, Wisconsin. He was a prolific writer, newspaperman, editor, publisher, mentor, detective, criminologist, historian, patriot, activist, and renowned Bureau critic. He was a pioneer of the science of crime scene investigations, later coined "C.S.I." His numerous publications and worldwide police affiliations provided unquestionable bona fides despite being home-schooled and apprentice-trained. He competed professionally with the best of degreed experts and was scholastically articulate, impeccably groomed, and passionately political.

His father, John, was born in Ireland and immigrated to the United States in the latter 1800s. Between 1850 and the 1900s, John was among a small group of Irish immigrants who settled in Wisconsin. In the early 1900s, Wisconsin was recognized as being "predominantly Republican," which explains O'Sullivan's firm support of small business, free trade, and the Second Amendment. Wisconsin also participated in the nation-building Progressive Reformation Era that supported consumer reform under the leadership of Robert M. LaFollette Sr. (1855-1925), 20th governor of Wisconsin from January 7, 1901 to January 1, 1906, and senator from January 2, 1906 to June 18, 1925.

O'Sullivan's state heritage and conservative patriotic comments would qualify him as a modern-day Trump supporter with a-very-proud membership in the National Rifle Association (NRA). He promoted the police and chastised a fickle society for disrespecting the thin blue line: "As I write this sketch today, I venture there are not ten people in Chicago who could tell you that the name of the officer who fell a victim of the assault of this gang of thieves and murderers was Sergt. Charles Cohen. Yet, if Cohen had bolted for safety just before the machine gun aimed at his heart spoke, he would be branded as a coward and his name would be on the lips of the populace."

He moved to the Bluegrass state of Kentucky before he married around 1908 when he was about 22 years old. His wife, Janey, was born in 1888 and two years younger. Two of his three children were born in Kentucky; son, Dehoney, was born June 6, 1910; daughter, Janey, arrived in 1912; and another son followed their relocation to Illinois. O'Sullivan and family moved to Chicago in 1914 where he opened a literary workshop for writers. U.S. Census records listed his family residence in Chicago, Cook County, Illinois. In 1916, he launched The O'Sullivan Publishing House; only divine destiny could have matched the same year when the Vigilance Committee was renamed the "Better Business Bureau."

The daunting prospect of marriage and children inspired O'Sullivan to re-evaluate his career path. He quit his job as a newspaperman and sought opportunity in criminal science, which he considered avant-garde and lucrative: "In 1908 I had an idea. The thought embraced a series of technical instruction lectures for the less informed detectives. I resigned my position and took up research work, interviewing leading detectives, police officials, and all others who might possess knowledge of the kind I wanted. I drew upon the accumulated experience of famous detectives of criminality from the early days of Allan Pinkerton to the recent wonderful work of men like Joseph A. Faurot, George S. Dougherty, and others."

O'Sullivan considered Chicago to be the "second metropolis" of the United States and the "crime capital of the world." He was one of the first C.S.I. scientists who worked with detectives and chiefs of police around the world for "twenty years." Crime scene investigation was promoted because it recognized the significance of retaining irrefutable prosecutorial evidence. Criminology was a developing science in the 1920s and was not included in collegiate academia. Accordingly, he discussed home schooling as an alternative that aligned with his background and explained his diverse knowledge of world history including mythological and Greek classics. He promoted the detective profession as a productive, successful, and cost-effective alternative to the more time-consuming and expensive careers such as law and medicine.

He believed criminology was an attractive vocation and required by police to combat the rise of organized crime: "The detective profession is one of the most honorable and profitable of the professions." O'Sullivan promoted "CSI" training as a critical aspect of police work and considered it to be an imperative process required to retain irrefutable indictments and prosecution of the "Hoodlum – Gangster - Racketeer" committing crimes against unarmed citizens.

O'Sullivan also thought that every citizen should be armed to fend off gangsters who inundated early-1930's Chicago. He advised, "Gangsters should be shot at sight! They are more dangerous to the community than the horse or cattle thief of pioneer days. All are potential murderers ... Every reputable citizen with a home, a business, or property to protect should be armed with a 45 Colt and instructed in its use."

He described himself as a "working newspaperman." His experience as a newspaper reporter was evident in his flair for descriptive, inquisitive, and intellectual writing. And he remained devoted to criminology and teaching: "For more than twenty years my pen and mind have been active in the interests of those seeking opportunity and advancement in the detective profession."

In 1910, he was editor of the *Business Philosophy* magazine. Insight was his specialty. He offered more than the average writer and delved into the nooks and crannies that others ignored: "Today, as I glance at the piles of manuscript ready for the press, I cannot help but feel that I was forced to search far and wide and pursued the quest into many unscented crime spots. I have helped to find the lost and to identify the dead. I have dug deep into the archives of musty records of marriages, births, and deeds. I have scaled the mountainside of adventure, and gone down into the tomb of mystery and mingled with the bones of skulls of those who once reflected power or engendered hate. I have rejoiced with the successful crime investigator and wept with the failures. I have drunk from the golden goblet with the man who does things, and from the cup of despair with the man who "nearly succeeds." ... What stimulated me in my efforts should furnish others with strength of purpose for the struggle against the eroding sameness of the workaday of the unprepared. Such at least was the hope and purpose that I had in mind."

In 1916, and true to his literary objectives, he established The O'Sullivan Publishing House in Chicago, Illinois. O'Sullivan listed several company addresses in his books including Chicago-Clark Building, 536 S. Clark St., Chicago (1928); Railway Exchange Building, Chicago (1932); and his last location at the Southern Pacific Building, 35 West Jackson Blvd., Chicago (1936).

The O'Sullivan Publishing House behaved like a thermometer responding to the ups and downs of a volatile economy. Book style and quality reflected the prosperity of the *Roaring Twenties* versus the austerity of the Great Depression. Packaging design produced from 1917 to 1928 at the Chicago-Clark Building produced impressive 8 x 11-inch hardcopies with gold lettering on two-toned green and brown cloth-covered boards. His 1933 publications changed to smaller 5 ½ x 7 ½-inch paper-backed books described as magazines and produced at the Railway Exchange Building. They were plain, unillustrated, and cover-bound with heavy-weight poster board in earth-tone colors of gold and umber. The book title and author were printed on a 4 x 3-inch label with a double-lined border and glued to the upper half of the front cover. Downgraded publishing operations aligned with economic statistics that manufacturing output "decreased by one third" between 1929 and 1933.

He expected conflict from the upcoming repeal of Prohibition in 1933 that would create beer wars with organized crime taking over legitimate breweries. New York Governor Franklin Delano Roosevelt won the 1932 presidential election based on repeal of Prohibition that inspired organized crime to transition from bootlegging into legitimate beer production. O'Sullivan reflected, "Within ten days after the 1932 national election, a group of Chicago men, one at least of whom was reported as 'fairly well-known in gang circles,' was reported

THE APO$TATE

to have taken a most significant step, and one unprecedented in the history of the beer industry. This group applied to the Secretary of State of Illinois for articles of incorporation for no less than twelve new brewing companies ... All the earmarks of the gangs were present ... To the man in the street it certainly looked like the beginning of a conspiracy to 'muscle in' on the anticipated profits of brewing in the near future."

Between 1933 and 1936, economic improvement slowly gained traction with the introduction of FDR's "New Deal" domestic programs. The O'Sullivan Publishing House relocated to the Southern Pacific Building and, in 1936, reverted to printing smaller hard-cover copies again with colorful and entertaining dust jackets that signaled an improving, but still fragile economy. Then the Great Depression took a turn for the worse and spiraled into the Recession of 1937/1938 that jolted the economy almost to 1929 levels. According to Wikipedia.org, "The American economy took a sharp downturn in mid-1937, lasting for 13 months through most of 1938. Industrial production declined almost 30 percent." There were no other O'Sullivan publications located after 1936 to decipher ongoing repercussions.

O'Sullivan authored many books through The O'Sullivan Publishing House. Those titles located included *The Poison Pen of Jersey* (1936); *Rackets* (1933); *Enemies of Industry* (1933); *Crime Detection* (1928); *Lectures on Preparatory Scientific Detective Instructions* (1922); *Under The Yoke*, Lansing, Ltd., Publishers, (1921); *Enemies of the Underworld* (1917); *The Science of Criminology*; *The Detective Adviser*; *Preparatory Lectures on Detective Science*; *Lectures on Applied Criminal Psychology*; *Applied Psychology and Its Relation to Crime*; *The Defense Pleads Insanity*; *Successful Telephone Selling*; *The American Merchant*; *Fighters Behind the Lines*; and *The Primrose Path*.

In 1915, he wrote *In the Orchard of Forbidden Fruit* under the pseudonym "Don Sullington" because scandalous subject matter involved prostitution. I own several of O'Sullivan's first editions and found him remarkably refreshing, visionary, talented, professional, genuine, fair, and outspoken, particularly regarding unrestrained free trade. His word was honorable, and he interwove business integrity with history's majesty.

O'Sullivan was relatively unknown to the public with the exception of the Bureau who knew him as their worst nightmare. He and Kenner crossed swords rebuking each other between the lines of each other's dueling books sharpened by edgy experience honed as newspaper reporters. *Rackets* provided an incriminating account of Bureau indiscretions that targeted Kenner. In 1936, Kenner wrote *The Fight for Truth in Advertising* as fanfare for the Advertising Federation of America's (AACA) twenty-fifth anniversary convention that, in reality, was a rebuttal to *Rackets*. Kenner felt redeemed and empowered after procuring an SEC appointment from FDR, which salvaged the New York Bureau's soiled reputation after the Pecora Commission debacle that labeled the organization an NYSE puppet and a racket.

He was a historian who romanced the ages and proudly supported America's evolution. Patriotic words reflected love of country: "When a band of storm-tossed adventurers landed in 1620 upon the rock-bound coast of New England, it was to found a community destined to become the corner-stone of a mighty nation." He reminisced of America's complicated past swept into the Progressive Reformation Era of unparalleled industrial and technological innovation. Sanctimonious reformers like the Bureau were deemed "nefarious" bottom feeders and created issues for their own ill-gotten gain at the expense of independent businesses and manufacturers. It is only fair that karma now enshrines O'Sullivan's historical imprint to hold a miscreant Bureau accountable. He never dreamed that his allegations would resurface almost 100 years later to validate another victim's respective complaints against the same globalist hypocrite; his documented travails provided a gateway to the Bureau's scandalous past.

In 1928, O'Sullivan published *Crime Detection* that was 667-pages long and a voluminous accomplishment in his day. The book was designed to be an academic textbook and supplied self-taught directives, field reports, police supervisors, and crime stories; years of criminology experience was evident and underscored his affiliation with various police departments. He also devoted an entire chapter to the nameless denouncement of reformers but was obviously referencing the Bureau: "This country is overrun with self-appointed reformers, men who as a rule have failed in everything else on top of the earth, and as a last dying effort, started in the reform racket. They want to become benefactors to humanity – and incidentally keep from starving to death." At the time of publication, he had been operating The O'Sullivan Publishing House for 12 years and had a longstanding relationship with police. Additionally, his newspaper background kept him in touch with the pulse of the city and small businessmen. All aforementioned affiliations complained to him of Bureau intimidation and "muscle" methods.

O'Sullivan denounced disingenuous reformers, which underscored his complaint against the Bureau: "Reform organizations may be good things, they may be municipal necessities – but they should be made to prove their worth. If the men who conduct them are so earnest and sincere concerning the welfare of society in general and the criminal element in particular, then they should supply their services without cost to the credulous business man who has not the time to look into such affairs ... The business of "reform," be it known, is a profession or trade, and the majority of men who specialize in that line have no other visible means of support. Reforming is their exclusive business."

He worried that the Bureau would respond by suing him for defamation as expressed in his endearing backwoods' Kentucky humor: "Wonder when this is published if the reformers will get after me with a stick? If they do, I will tell them what a wise old editor told me when I was a cub. He said: "Boy, when you throw a stone among a pack of dogs, it's the hit dog that howls"."

O'Sullivan was a pioneer in criminal profiling, sociological criminology, and procuring crime scene evidence. He predicted science technology now considered standard procedure in modern investigations. *Crime Detection* showcased O'Sullivan as a visionary ahead of his time and attempting to update his generation. It also emphasized O'Sullivan as an unpretentious intellectual. He taught detectives to be humble and open-minded and advised that "the most unsuccessful detective was too wise in his own conceit ... that he could not be successful until he changed his tactics and learned to listen to, believe in, and profit by the experience of others ... the successful men of today were the "fools" of yesterday who had listened to reason and profited by the experience of others. Thus, the "fools" of twenty years ago are the sages of today."

He advocated crime scene investigation and discussed intricate testing procedures, blood work, and criminal profiling. He acknowledged working relationships with several police departments: "Chapter LXXVIII: How to Cope with Present-Day Crime" saluted police, detectives, and police chiefs and included their photographs. His "Author's Note" stated, "In my opinion this is one of the most interesting chapters in the entire book." Additionally, he honored police and supported their cause: "[T]he proper way to cope with present-day crime and the criminal is to have policemen so plentiful in all sections of the city – in fact, all cities – that crooks will hesitate before venturing forth bent on crime. The job immediately ahead for the police forces of America is to see that they are given greater facilities for suppressing crime – facilities that are badly needed in order to cut down the menace from the criminal classes."

O'Sullivan operated under the belief that the police departments he worked with, or had knowledge of, were none too happy with the Bureau. Vigilance men overstepped their bounds and made local police look incompetent; police felt that the Bureau exploited police department budget issues to promote their services as the best.

He predated modern complaints against the Bureau alleging what has now been coined "pay-for-play." O'Sullivan ridiculed Bureau memberships and sales tactics while mentioning questionable Bureau bulletins: "In Chicago, New York, Philadelphia and other large centers of population business men and philanthropists contribute annually something like one million dollars a year in each city to the alleged reform element. And what do the cities get in return for this lavish outlay? Nothing except a few scrambled reports of what has transpired, reams of criticisms, nothing in a constructive way."

Prior to the publication of *Rackets*, Joy Morton requested that O'Sullivan help him with an autobiographical project. In April 1932, Joy Sterling Morton (1855-1934), founder of Morton Salt, whose father, Julius Sterling Morton, founded "Arbor Day" in 1872, contacted O'Sullivan at his "literary workshop" located at the time in the Railway Exchange Building (now "the Santa Fe Building"), at 224 South Michigan Avenue, Chicago, Illinois. Morton also officed in the "Chicago Style" building as chairman of the Standard Office Company that financed the Railway Exchange Building's construction in 1903. He noticed O'Sullivan through his stationery that advertised he was a "biographer."

After weeks of research at Morton's Thornhill estate, O'Sullivan presented a hurried manuscript entitled, *Seventy-Five Years in the Midwest*. He tried to convince Morton to publish a biography instead of a "private edition," but the other editors, including Morton's wife, convinced him to decline. O'Sullivan humorously responded: "If too many cooks spoil the broth, it is just possible that too many editors may also spoil a book," according to Professor James Ballowe. Morton's autobiography was never completed.

Rackets provided incredible insight into Bureau operations during the 1920s and 1930s. O'Sullivan accused the The year 1933 was epic. O'Sullivan published *Rackets: Including the Practices of the Better Business Bureau System* and *Enemies of Industry: Gang Invasion of Business and Industry*. He directly incriminated the Bureau with a scathing review and shocking exposé of securities fraud and collusion leading up to the Pecora Commission. Later that year, he published *Enemies of Industry* that was directed at organized crime, gangsters, and beer wars. He also included an interview with Fred Pabst of the Pabst Brewery in Chicago. As expected, FDR was inaugurated 32nd POTUS and repealed Prohibition with the 21st Amendment that was ratified December 5, 1933. Then, Chicago's Century of Progress World's Fair opened May 27, 1933, and closed October 31, 1934, bringing a new wave of crime and corruption.

Bureau of racketeering and described its cronyism with the NYSE before and after the Crash. He chronicled major critics including the New York Reform Committee, the Manhattan Board of Commerce, and the Consumers Guild of America who collectively contributed to the Bureau's indictment by the U.S. Senate for securities fraud, racketeering, and influencing radio communication. The Bureau's defense was lame at best and alleged that critics were of dubious character and/or held ulterior political motive. To the contrary, critics were distinguished New York authorities in addition to Rep. La Guardia and Chairman/Senator Fletcher of the Pecora Commission.

The Bureau questioned the validity of Logan Billingsley's New York Reform Committee and the Manhattan Board of Commerce, its most vocal critics after the Crash. But both organizations were legitimate and officially recognized consumer reform committees. The *Brooklyn Daily Eagle* wrote the article, "Asks

THE APO$TATE

Senate Probe Probers," dated February 9, 1933, which referenced Billingsley's organizations seeking Senate investigation into NYSE securities abuse: "The Stock Exchange Reform Committee, functioning under the auspices of the Manhattan Board of Commerce, was created in 1930. James P. Meehan of New York is general chairman of the committee, which set up as its first objective a far-sweeping inquiry into the Stock Exchange and market practices."

Enemies of Industry detailed the historic occasion of O'Sullivan interviewing Pabst who was also a visionary looking beyond Prohibition, gangsters, and beer wars to correctly predict the ongoing evolution of the alcohol industry through consumerism and restaurants. O'Sullivan and Pabst discussed Prohibition's imminent repeal that was expected to occur because "prominent Democrats ... helped Franklin D. Roosevelt win in 1932 on a wet platform."

Pabst made practical business sense and his intuition was spot-on when he suggested a new approach for licensed alcoholic sales within the realm of legitimate retail, recreational, and entertainment industries. He offered a viable solution for the alcohol industry after the massive failure of Prohibition, which created bootlegging, organized crime, and reduced federal revenue that compounded and prolonged the Depression. Pabst suggested, "Beer should be sold through the same outlets that dispense food ... These outlets, which should be duly licensed, include all reputable hotels, restaurants, groceries, and drug stores that serve food ... this being the function of a proper licensing system."

In respect to his interview with Pabst, O'Sullivan worried about organized crime's lingering foothold supported by racketeers protected by corrupt politicians. O'Sullivan forewarned, "Racketeering has become gangsterized." Furthermore, he warned, "Capone gang's "board of directors" have been active for some time by gun and "muscle" methods, as a preliminary to the seizure of control of the beer industry. The gang is said to hold options on two large local breweries ... and it expects ... to supply all the beer that is to be consumed in Chicago. How will the legitimate brewers ... meet this gang competition, except by force - and what a state of affairs may be expected in the city then!"

O'Sullivan similarly quoted a "government agent" as saying, "The hoodlums foresee themselves selling beer on 'muscle' and eliminating competition by fear. They expect to charge their own price, and make retailers take it." After all, O'Sullivan was talking about Chicago society being mesmerized by Alphonse Gabriel Capone (1899-1947) whose two favorite sayings were: "I am just a businessman, giving the people what they want" and "All I do is satisfy a public demand." O'Sullivan's *Enemies of Industry* was among many critics of Prohibition and was published in mid-1933 before the 21st Amendment was ratified on December 5, 1933, repealing Prohibition and the 18th Amendment.

The Chicago World's Fair, also known as the "Century of Progress Exposition," was the second world's fair to be held in Chicago; the first opened in 1893 and was called "World's Columbian Exposition." The World's Fair was an attempt to clean up Chicago's gangland image and promoted "technological innovation" as its theme. Its motto, "Science Finds, Industry Applies, Man Adapts," was represented by a statue named the "Fountain of Progress" that portrayed "two humans, male and female, being pushed ahead by a giant robot resting its steel hands on their backs."

O'Sullivan referenced the 1933 World's Fair in *Enemies of Industry* and wrote about Chicago's corruption while inferencing the Bureau. He described a group of questionable reformers labeled the "Secret Six" that "resembles the Better Business Bureau racket in that it operates without license or bond and is supported by the contributions of well-meaning business men ... it brought public ridicule upon itself by the methods of its managers and operatives; and it practically collapsed immediately after the elections of November, 1932." Furthermore, O'Sullivan elaborated, "The director of the "Secret Six," an industrial engineer, has been selected as head of the police force for the Century of Progress exposition of 1933. If he measures up as well in that job as he did with the "Secret Six," Chicago's second world's fair may become a happy hunting-ground for crooks and pickpockets." During the time period of March 1929, Wikipedia.org corroborated the Secret Six with an idealistic description as "a group of crime-fighting Chicago businessmen ... who were working behind the scenes to bring Capone down," but O'Sullivan's account provided a grittier film noir version.

Despite good intentions supporting the World's Fair, crime grew rampant due to underlying organized crime. On February 15, 1933, according to Wikipedia.org, "Corrupt Chicago Mayor Anton Cermak was riding in an open car with President-elect Franklin D. Roosevelt (FDR) in Miami, Florida, when Cermak was hit with sniper bullets. He died three weeks later. Speculation for years afterward was that Cermak had always been the sniper's real target, not FDR, the president-elect."

In 1936, O'Sullivan published *Poison Pen of Jersey* and railed against the best-selling book, "*100,000,000 Guinea Pigs: Dangers in Everyday Foods, Drugs, and Cosmetics,*" published in 1933 by authors, Arthur Kallet (1902-1972) and Frederick John Schlink (1891-1995). O'Sullivan's *Poison Pen of Jersey* metaphorically referred to Schlink as "poison pen" and his company, Consumers' Research, Inc., as "Jersey" because corporate offices were located in Washington, New Jersey. Schlink was the ringleader of the group writing all product reviews. O'Sullivan worried that Schlink would tarnish all product manufacturing and hurt honest business owners amidst a crusade to root out the unscrupulous few. He may have been right that "reformers" were posturing for a buck and taking advantage of an open consumer market, but Schlink carried weight due to his distinguished credentials. He was later succeeded by the crown prince of

THE APO$TATE

consumer advocacy, the esteemed Ralph Nader, born February 27, 1934, in Winsted, Connecticut, whose contributions are too numerous to list. Suffice to say that Nader was listed among the "100 Most Influential Americans in the Twentieth Century."

In fact, consumers were being victimized by fraudulent products causing atrocities in the marketplace. The public was already wary of horrific meat-packing abuse as a result of Upton Sinclair's eye-opening *The Jungle* in 1906. Accordingly, Schlink quickly gained the public's attention regarding product fraud in *100,000,000 Guinea Pigs*. Besides being the technical director for Consumers' Research, Inc., Schlink was an acclaimed research pioneer and accomplished engineer holding impressive credentials and experience that supported his publications; he held a "bachelor's degree in mechanical engineering from University of Illinois in 1912," "worked as an associate physicist and technical assistant to the director at the U.S. Bureau of Standards from 1913-19," and earned a second degree in mechanical engineering also from University of Illinois in 1917.

In retrospect, Schlink co-wrote *Your Money's Worth* with Stuart Chase in 1926. The book's bestselling success led to the establishment of Consumer's Research, Inc. in 1929, as "a consumer product-testing organization" to report truthful product information. Thereafter, Consumers' Research, Inc. produced *Consumers' Research Bulletin*, a monthly magazine, which set the stage for *100,000,000 Guinea Pigs* in 1933. Then, in 1936, Schlink's co-author, Arthur Kallet, and several strikers left Consumer's Research, Inc. to form Consumer Union and published *Consumer Reports*, which continues today.

Schlink's book angered O'Sullivan who denounced it as a "scurrilous" publication. O'Sullivan considered Schlink to be a "Communist" who "always had an eye on Russia and likes to furnish Moscow with material for exultation over the economic and government conditions in America." Accordingly, O'Sullivan referenced an alleged anti-American Consumer's Research bulletin, dated June 1935, which published the article, "American City Has Ordinance To Poison Inhabitants." O'Sullivan felt compelled to defend American business and manufacturing and wrote *Poison Pen of Jersey* as a rebuttal to *100,000,000 Guinea Pigs*.

Poison Pen formally introduced O'Sullivan as a manufacturer's defender. He considered Consumers' Research to be an opportunistic fraud and guilty of fearmongering. He included a lengthy commercial message on his book's back cover dust jacket that trounced "self-appointed critics and libellants of advertised products" engaged in "poisoning the public mind."

O'Sullivan infused his professional credibility as an editor to substantiate the muckraking of Schlink as a highly credentialed technical director and bestselling author. *Poison Pen's* back dust cover also provided O'Sullivan's resumé as if to emphasize his literary expertise: "Note: It is somewhat unusual for an author to be the head of a publishing business, but in the case of the author of

'The Poison Pen of Jersey,' it came about in a natural way. In 1914 he established and became the head of The Literary Workshop, Chicago, as an aid to authors. So many good manuscripts were submitted to him for revision that he found it advisable to organize a publishing business, and in 1916 he established The O'Sullivan Publishing House, of which he is the editorial director."

The O'Sullivan Publishing House also produced *The Lance* for several years throughout the 1930s that routinely criticized the Bureau and whose surviving copy is apparently now stored under lock and key by the Bureau to hide truth's exoneration. In fact, *The Lance*'s existence was publicized when mentioned in Wansley's 1971 address delivered to the business school at Washington University, St. Louis, Missouri. Wansley complained, "Probably the most notorious attack was in "The Lance" published by Frank Dalton O'Sullivan in Chicago." Wansley's address originally included a 1933 copy of *The Lance* as "Exhibit 6," but the Boston Bureau, who published Wansley's address on its website, did not include a respective access link. After researching information provided in Wansley's address, I had no doubt that he revised history to favor the Bureau.

Kate Whelan, O'Sullivan's "long-time assistant," supported him in his crusade against the Bureau. The Bureau loathed O'Sullivan and Whelan due to their continuous criticism through *The Lance* and his books. Furthermore, Wansley did not mention *Rackets* in *History and Traditions*. Circumstances insinuated that Wansley knew *Rackets* was a smoking gun capable of destroying the Bureau's pristine image; omission implied that everything O'Sullivan detailed in *Rackets* was true. O'Sullivan and Whelan presented a formidable team that I understood to be a trusted relationship based on a joint mission to undermine the Bureau as a mutual mortal enemy.

Whelan must have joined The O'Sullivan Publishing House during fledgling years since its start-up date in 1916. They were WWI years (1914-1918) when women entered the workplace and assisted military service on the home front. In fact, women participated en masse during WWI resulting in the ratification of the 19th Amendment on August 26, 1920, as appreciation and reward for military-related service. History.com stated, "In 1917, America entered World War I, and women aided the war effort in various capacities that helped break down most of the remaining opposition to woman suffrage."

The Chicago Bureau terrorized O'Sullivan's publishing business during the Great Depression, resulting in his deleterious loss of business and severe medical issues. On Friday, January 13, 1939, O'Sullivan died of a heart attack at his Chicago home on 4655 Monroe Street. He was 53 years old. The next day, the *Chicago Daily Tribune* published his obituary advising funeral services were scheduled on Monday, January 16, 1939, at the chapel of Resurrection Church on 2346 Madison Street. According to Illinois "Deaths and Stillbirths Index, 1916-1947," O'Sullivan was laid to rest at Mt. Carmel Catholic Cemetery in

THE APO$TATE

Hillside, Illinois; one of 15 cemeteries in Proviso Township that is one of 30 townships in Cook County, Illinois, as of 2010. He was survived by his wife, Janey, 51 years old, and two sons and a daughter. One of his two sons, Dehoney, was about 29 years old and his daughter, Janey, was about 27 years old.

Whelan responded with raw anger and unbridled defiance. She blamed the Bureau for O'Sullivan's death in accordance with O'Sullivan's respective sentiments expressed in *Rackets* that the Bureau had made him seriously ill. She continued to produce *The Lance* using reprints of O'Sullivan's articles as though to keep his message alive, but with O'Sullivan gone, the Bureau pounced at the first opportunity. Whelan called the Detroit Bureau manager a "Racketeer" and the Bureau gathered a national war chest for legal retribution. Whelan never stood a chance. The Bureau was inducted into the IC community that owned Court Street. She apparently paid a judgment and vanished, closing the final chapter to O'Sullivan's crusade against the Bureau.

Contrarily, the Bureau never sued O'Sullivan despite his inflammatory allegations including racketeering. O'Sullivan's impregnable shield was forged by Logan Billingsley and the Manhattan Board of Commerce, E. C. Riegel and the Consumers Guild of America, the Pecora Commission, Representative Fiorello La Guardia, and Senator Duncan Fletcher. But WWII followed O'Sullivan's death and supporters dispersed or died. Furthermore, Pearl Harbor happened, and FDR inducted the Bureau into black ops via the First War Powers Act. Whelan confronted the progenitor of the Deep State Better Business Bureau that attacked me decades later.

As the leading critic of the Bureau throughout the 1930s, O'Sullivan complained of its unfair corrupt business ploys and practice. Because of him, evidence is available to document missteps in advertising history. Otherwise, the Bureau's public-relations machine tried to sweep all dirt under the rug to maintain its hallowed reputation. He accused B-men of Mafioso tactics "by the issuance of defamatory reports on such individuals, firms, and corporations as fall under their displeasure" or if they refused membership whereby infringing upon the rights of small business. O'Sullivan proudly criticized the Bureau adeptly dispensing meaningful contempt: "The Better Business Bureau system is like a snake in the grass, endangering the path of progress. Its methods of investigation resemble those of the Ku Klux Klan. It acts on suspicion and wears a hideous robe of secrecy."

I would have liked to have met O'Sullivan. Instead, I honor him and thank him for his indomitable courage, documentation, vision, and guidance. *Rackets* anointed his battle with the Bureau with an ending prayer that "we must invoke the Lord to protect us against our "protectors"," but *Rackets'* ending message memorialized the Bureau's fraud: "We have other information, besides that given in this book regarding the operations of the Better Business Bureau."

CHAPTER **29**

HURNARD JAY KENNER

H. J. Kenner
First Vigilance Committee paid employee;
New York Better Business Bureau general manager.
Photo dated before July 1919.
Source: AACW, Associated Advertising,
July 1919, P. 36, Vol. 10, No. 7;
[https://babel.hathitrust.org/cgi/pt?id=iau.31858034256317;
view=1up;seq=274, Pg. 36]; public domain.

He was the controversial general manager of the New York Bureau, from 1926 to 1947, and orchestrated the induction of the Better Business Bureau into the Deep State. His 1936 book, *The Fight for Truth in Advertising*, was sponsored by the Advertising Federation of America (formally AACA) and offered incredible insight into the history of the advertising industry and Better Business Bureau. He was the first paid manager for the Vigilance Committee and National

THE APO$TATE

Vigilance Committee. Additionally, he chaired the committee that formed FDR's Security Violations Section for the SEC and managed the Bureau's largest and most prestigious New York branch office during infamous American history that experienced WWI, Prohibition, organized crime, *Roaring Twenties*, Stock Market Crash and Great Depression, Pecora Commission, Dewey mob trials, Pearl Harbor, and WWII. He represented scathing reminder of a foreboding timeline that witnessed his arrest and federal indictment of the Bureau franchise.

History was not kind to H. J. Kenner. He deserved better. I believe that he was an honest intense passionate businessman who meant well but drank the company Kool-Aid that blurred right from wrong. Consequently, critics painted him a villain, and the U.S. Senate dubbed his New York Bureau a crooked racketeering puppet of the NYSE. He absorbed disparaging impact for questionable activities resultant of an impregnable tripartite relationship between the New York Bureau, NYSE, and Investment Bankers Association.

I discovered Kenner through Wansley's speech, *History and Traditions,* that was delivered to Washington University's now defunct Institutes for Organizational Management. Without *Rackets*, I would have succumbed to Wansley's bias one-sided revisionist narrative. Nevertheless, Wansley's glossy propaganda piece inadvertently and incredibly provided invaluable references that detailed a lost timeline and unearthed the Bureau's buried skeletons. Furthermore, if not for O'Sullivan, the Bureau's nefarious yesteryear would have remained a redacted footnote in history. Kenner's book whitewashed organizational iniquities and paint-brushed the advertising industry's noble deployment of the Bureau to regulate out-of-control advertising fraud. Both Kenner and O'Sullivan jointly documented the Bureau's victorious rise, scandalous fall, and globalist deviation.

Kenner was the central figure in a remarkable cast of formidable characters during the Bureau's founding years. Wansley applauded him for his work and extraordinary efforts: "Probably no one single individual had more impact on the drive for more truth in advertising than H. J. Kenner, the first BBB manager. His awareness of the problem was crystallized in his book, *The Fight for Truth in Advertising*, published in 1936 by Round Table Press, Inc. of New York City." Kenner's book took on new meaning when I fortuitously discovered O'Sullivan's telltale *Rackets*. I realized spectacular conjugal history in my possession; that Kenner and O'Sullivan were polar opposites and public enemies locked in mortal combat; that their books represented an extraordinary literary pas d'armes (duel).

The Dewey mob trials began in 1935 and set the New York Bureau into defense mode. Two years earlier, the Pecora Commission had just started, and O'Sullivan published *Rackets* to call the commission's attention to the Better

Business Bureau's racketeering relationship with NYSE and Investment Bankers Association. Then FDR stepped in and gilded the tarnished image of Kenner and the New York Bureau. Consequently, an empowered Kenner published *The Fight for Truth in Advertising* that served dual purpose of inoculating golden coattails against organized-crime implications and staunching O'Sullivan's respective allegations and revelations that threatened to catch the litigious attention of Special Agent Thomas Dewey. The Advertising Federation of America promoted Kenner's book as an adjunct to its silver anniversary commemorative book, *Truth in Advertising*, but, in reality, Kenner's book served ulterior motive to encase the Bureau in a sanctimonious Teflon shield to deflect organized crime's collateral damage by promoting venerable advertising history, ethics and regulatory actions, and government affiliations.

Kenner called attention to the term "muckraker." He unquestionably referred to O'Sullivan when describing Bureau attacks from "detractors," "destructionists," "fanatics," "cynics," and "business-baiters" who involved politicians to spread "scurrilous slander in printed pamphlets." (In reality, all afore listed terms described the Bureau.) O'Sullivan published *The Lance* to expose the Bureau's indiscretions substantiated by local, city, state, and government officials, newspaper articles, and historical documentation. Kenner backhandedly referred to *The Lance* as slanderous, which is questionable considering no one from the Bureau ever sued O'Sullivan for defamation. Both *Rackets* and *The Lance* were insulated by police who worked with O'Sullivan as a C.S.I. detective.

Kenner's personal information was practically nonexistent and comparable to blink-and-you-miss anecdotes, yet a sprinkling of breadcrumbs enabled an extensive biography. He walked among the most famous of advertising elite and established historical Bureau milestones and pivotal relationships that staged the organization's globalist empire. His obscurity underscored liability because he documented true events that inherently questioned the modern Bureau's ethics. Personal information was assembled from random sources including *Printers' Ink*, *Rackets*, *The Fight for Truth in Advertising*, *Associated Advertising* Magazine, Advertising Federation of America's *Truth in Advertising: Twenty-Fifth Anniversary*, B. Charles Wansley, *The Business History Review* (Volume 83, No. 1), archived newspaper articles, Tiki-Toki.com, and James C. Auchincloss's *The Better Business Bureau: Its Growth and Work*.

It would be difficult to prove if Kenner was pushed or fell on his Templar's sword to hide the Bureau's checkered past. Either way, he was relegated to ambiguous shadows and forgotten by modern power-grabbing globalists who attained autocracy because of his contributions, achievements, and sacrifices. The American Advertising Federation/AAF (successor to the Associated Advertising Clubs of America/AACA, Associated Advertising Clubs of the World/AACW, and Advertising Federation of America/AFA) shamefully omitted Kenner's name in its venerable Advertising Hall of Fame launched in 1948, a year after he retired. Kenner was overlooked as a distinguished advertising pioneer, first-hired vigilance employee, first national manager, and witness to the historic naming of the Better Business Bureau. Additionally, Kenner's background prior to the Bureau was a "newspaper man and advertising manager," so the AAF had no excuse for omitting him from its gilded advertising scrolls. A random advertising commendation listed his recognition in 1955 at the "BBB annual convention" held in Minneapolis, Minnesota.

Kenner's banishment to the Twilight Zone buried damning dirt. Altered Bureau history modified national history with wily deviations misleading current consumers. I experienced the Bureau's mystical mirage during trial; jurors were unaware of its past and present iniquities and, consequently, rendered an unfair verdict; had the truth been known, results would have been different. My encounter served only the smallest example offset by the Bureau's centurial history and chameleon initiatives that profoundly changed national advertising, commerce, law, finance, and defense. Nevertheless, the Bureau's sinister proclivities contributed to the Crash and Great Depression, introduced modern deceptive promotional schemes, and set the stage for contemporary Deep State intelligence surveillance. Good or bad, Kenner was at the helm of the Bureau's history and was a dedicated company man who earned remembrance. I credit Wansley for acknowledging Kenner and inspiring my treasure hunt that searched every nook and cranny to reconstruct his life with nothing deemed too trivial.

Hurnard Jay Kenner called himself "H. J." probably to avert anti-German sentiment that flourished in the throes of WWI. According to Alphahistory.com, "In the years prior to 1914, Kaiser Wilhelm II and his government adopted policies, both foreign and domestic, that contributed to rising tensions in Europe." My grandfather, a train conductor from Palestine, Texas, was also German and, for the same reason, went by "A. D." that stood for Adolphus Dweese. In fact, there were many acronymic German names that I discovered when researching the Bureau, which emphasized the extent that German Americans contributed to the Progressive Reformation Era that built America.

Kenner was born on September 1, 1887, in Chicago, Illinois. The 1920 U.S. Census records listed his father from Illinois and his mother from Kentucky; otherwise, their names and birth dates were not available. He was "educated in the Chicago public schools, and a student at the University of Chicago." His wife's name was Frae McCarty. They had a daughter named Frances and a son named Huenard. The Census listed their residence as "New Rochelle, Ward 1, Westchester, New York." In 1946, the family moved to Manhattan during his final year as general manager of the New York Bureau, from 1926 until 1947.

A genealogy search on Ancestry.com indicated the name "Kenner" is

"German and Jewish (Ashkenazic): from Kenner 'connoisseur' (from kennen 'know'), hence a nickname for someone considered to be knowledgeable or an expert of some kind; it may also have been used to denote a 'know-all'." Additional ancestral data stated, "German: habitational name for someone from Kenn, near Trier. German: topographic name for someone living near a water pipe or channel, from Middle High German kener 'water channel', 'drainage pipe'." The name "Hurnard" suggested origin from England. A search under "UK Incoming Passenger Lists" indicated that a majority of about 50 records dating back to 1820 departed from cities in the UK, including London, Plymouth, Bristol, Southampton, and Liverpool. A recreated genealogy might describe his heritage as third generation German, Jewish, and English whose ancestors immigrated to U.S. shores in the early 1800s.

By 1914, the AACA was realizing financial stability and sought universal advertising solidarity. The AACA held the industry's first international convention in Toronto, Canada, and changed its name to the Associated Advertising Clubs of the World (AACW). That same year, in September, the AACW hired Kenner, 26 years old, as the first employee and full-time manager of the "Vigilance Committee of the Minneapolis Advertising Club" (Minneapolis, Minnesota). The year before he joined the Bureau, on March 20, 1913, he was described as "Secretary H. J. Kenner" for a "boosters" group holding a retail-related "commercial club banquet at Devils Lake, North Dakota." Supportive documentation expounded on his booster position and reported that he "spent his early career as a merchant in North Dakota, serving as an officer for a local merchants association."

In June 1915, Kenner was hired as the first manager of the National Vigilance Committee that later established an office with the AACW headquarters in Indianapolis, Indiana. Kenner described his title as "secretary," but the president of the National Better Business Bureau, James C. Auchincloss, described his national position as "Manager." Additionally, Merle Sidener was reappointed chairman of the National Vigilance Committee by Dr. Herbert Sherman Houston, the newly elected president of the AACW. Sidener asked for $15,000 to establish a fully staffed office for the National Vigilance Committee in the AACW's headquarters. Sidener expressed that he wanted "to make investigations, to assist local clubs in the vigilance activities, to develop more bureaus with paid managers, and to enlarge educational functions of this new service."

Also, in June 1915, Kenner described one of the first cases pursued by the National Vigilance Committee involving the *Printers' Ink* Model Statute. He wrote, "A prominent retail clothier advertised a half-cotton sweater as all-wool. When asked to cooperate by changing the description he refused. "Stay out of this store on any such business," this merchant warned the earnest young vigilance secretary, H. J. Kenner. Impressed, but not intimidated, the secretary returned the next day, when the misrepresentation continued, to purchase the advertised garment. And, with the full backing of his committee, he called on the public prosecutor and lodged a complaint of false advertising. The advertiser was convicted and fined."

Additionally, in November 1915, Kenner described attending a conference, held by invitation, for the new Federal Trade Commission's "first chairman" Joseph M. Davies. The year before, on September 26, 1914, President Woodrow Wilson signed into law the Federal Trade Commission Act of 1914 that established the Federal Trade Commission. Organized advertising supported the act as a consumer-protection measure, so Davies invited the AACW's president, Dr. Houston, to participate in the conference and discuss "untrue and misleading advertising as an unfair method of competition prohibited by the new law."

Working for Sidener was Kenner's big break and anointed him a celestial witness to unparalleled history. In the spring of 1916, at an Indiana Advertising Club meeting, Sidener approached guest speaker Arthur Frederick Sheldon, founder of Sheldon Schools of Salesmanship in Chicago, to rename the Vigilance Committee and remove its tar-and-feather connotation. Sidener was simultaneously president of the Indiana Advertising Club as well as chairman of the National Vigilance Committee. Sheldon suggested the name "Better Business Bureau" and Sidener immediately approved the momentous moniker. As destiny foretold, Kenner was also present and, as manager, was responsible for recording official business. His reporter's descriptive eye documented the historic event as a profound turning point for the organization, and he integrated the name Better Business Bureau into the bedrock of America. George W. Coleman, president of the AACA from 1911 to 1912, and founder of the National Vigilance Committee in 1912, complimented Kenner's far-reaching transformative contributions and achievements when advising that "the Vigilance Committees merged into Better Business Bureaus under the inspiring leadership of H. J. Kenner."

President Woodrow Wilson was the honorable guest speaker at the AACW convention of 1916. Kenner described the assembly as "a great gathering of advertising men on the plaza of Independence Hall, Philadelphia, at their annual convention meeting, in June, 1916." He quoted Wilson: "The only thing that ever set any man free, the only thing that ever set any nation free, is the truth."

During the same timeframe, Kenner participated in a Bureau sponsored playlet entitled, "On Sale - $9.98," that traveled around the country promoting the advocate's new name and venerable mission to enforce truth in advertising. He described its essence as "the skit depicted a consumer's experience with a false clothing advertisement, the winning of a recalcitrant merchant to truth principles, and the cooperation of a newspaper in putting those principles into effect"; purpose declared, "This playlet, with changes in the lines to localize it, was presented later to large audiences by the advertising clubs in Indianapolis, Cincinnati, Minneapolis, and other cities, to help "sell" the idea of the new Better Business Bureau work." The cast was comprised of presidents of various advertising clubs. Kenner's character was named "Will Everwork, Bureau Manager" and he listed his formal title as "Secretary, National Vigilance Committee."

Kenner remained with the National Vigilance Committee for "two years" from 1914 to 1916. The following year, he left the National Vigilance Committee and ventured into "retail advertising" in Minneapolis. Thereafter, he accepted an executive management position with "Northwestern Knitting Co.," also located in Minneapolis.

During his absence, the AACW's annual convention was held in "St. Louis in May, 1917." Outgoing president Dr. Herbert Sherman Houston appointed William C. D'Arcy, principal of D'Arcy Advertising Agency (represented Coca-Cola Company), as president of the AACW. D'Arcy requested that Sidener continue as chairman of the National Vigilance Committee that had begun working with various state securities commissions investigating Blue Sky securities fraud.

On January 10, 1919, H. G. S. Noble, then president of the NYSE, issued a statement requesting "a broad national campaign to expose stock-swindling operations and in this way protect the security-buying public."

On February 17, 1919, a meeting was held at the Chamber of Commerce of the State of New York that resulted in the formation of the "Business Men's Anti-Stock Swindling League." Kenner advised that Noble read a letter at the meeting from 47th Secretary of the Treasury Carter Glass that was addressed to Secretary of the Committee Jason Westerfield and expressed his support for regulation of securities fraud. Thereafter, Senator Glass, representing the Democratic Party for the state of Virginia, and serving from 1920 to 1946, co-sponsored the Glass-Steagall Act of 1933 that established the Federal Deposit Insurance Corporation (FDIC) and separated commercial and investment banking. As usual, the Bureau engaged stolen thunder to embed and/or empower its operations by exploiting the distinguished Senator Glass.

On "July 1, 1919," Kenner returned to his former position as manager of the National Better Business Bureau that had since relocated to New York City. The AACW financed the National Vigilance Committee and expansion of local Bureaus into investigations of securities fraud and Kenner orchestrated the roll out. The association's magazine, *Associated Advertising*, reported, "Mr. Kenner's coming is of special significance just at this moment, when the association has entered upon the program for the large expansion of vigilance work. In connection with the broader movement that will be financed with the special fund of $141,000 which is being raised for vigilance work." The *Associated Advertising* article reflected an earlier piece published by *Editor and Publisher* magazine that described a meeting between Merle Sidener, chairman of the National Better Business Bureau, and ""blue sky" commissioners" in Washington, D.C., in June 1919.

During September 21-25, 1919, Kenner rejoined the National Vigilance Committee and participated in the annual AACW convention held in New Orleans, Louisiana. He delivered a speech on September 24th entitled, "Bricks That Build Walls of Confidence."

The following year, in 1920, the Better Business Bureau of the Cleveland Advertising Club launched the "Cleveland Plan" that promoted the motto "Before You Invest, Investigate" securities investigation program that was systemically approved and adopted by Sidener and the National Bureau. Kenner detailed the background and introduction of the investigative securities program in his book.

In 1926, at the age of 39, Kenner was appointed general manager of the prestigious New York Bureau and became deeply involved with the NYSE. New York City was a hotly contested war zone in the latter years of the *Roaring Twenties* and was infested with organized crime and securities fraud. As a result, Kenner was caught in the middle of a firestorm that erupted after the Crash and he suffered the brunt of critics' angst. The New York Bureau, NYSE, and bankers were investigated during the U.S. Senate hearings in 1932 that became the Pecora Commission in 1933. Senator Fletcher denounced the Better Business Bureau as a puppet and player of the NYSE/Investment Bankers Association racket. Consequently, Kenner shrewdly aligned with securities reformation forces. In 1934, Kenner jumped on the newly minted SEC bandwagon as a publicity ploy to redeem the Bureau's name.

Prior to assuming management of the New York Bureau, Kenner wrote an article in November 1926 that led to a happenstance meeting and enduring friendship with FDR. He published "The Danger Line in Real Estate Mortgage Bonds" in the *Industrial Digest* that focused on "security gyps" operating in the mortgage trade in post-World War I years. A month later, Kenner attended a meeting sponsored by the American Construction Council of New York City where he met Franklin Delano Roosevelt, president of the Council, who discussed the tenants of establishing real estate standards that meshed with Kenner's article. Two months later, in February 1927, FDR "announced an agreement among six large real estate mortgage bond companies which had pledged themselves to observe certain principles in the conduct of their business." Consequently, "a code of practice, by which most of the real estate mortgage bond companies agreed to abide" was established. Thereafter, Kenner developed a strategic and long-term friendship with FDR as he advanced within the ranks of the Democratic Party, was inaugurated 44th governor of New York on January 1, 1929, and was inaugurated 32nd POTUS on March 4, 1933.

In retrospect, FDR was previously defeated when running for vice president six years earlier in the 1920 presidential election. Kenner and the New York Bureau attached itself to the Democratic Party under the guise of organized advertising. The 1924 Democratic National Convention (DNC), "also known as the Klanbake," was held in "Madison Square Garden in New York City from June 24 to July 9, 1924," and broke a record as "the longest continuously running convention in United States political history" that required a record-breaking "103 ballots to nominate a presidential candidate."

The 1924 convention also presented historic occasion as the first time that women delegates were accepted and the first time a woman was nominated for vice president of the United States. The 19th Amendment was ratified four years earlier on August 18, 1920, giving women the right to vote. Lena Jones Wade Springs (born March 23, 1883; died May 17, 1942) was a suffragist from Pulaski, Tennessee, and married to Colonel Leroy Springs. In 1922, Springs was appointed a Democratic National Committeewoman. And, in 1924, she was named chairman of the Credentials Committee and among 30 candidates nominated for vice president. As a South Carolina delegate, Springs received "over 50 votes from delegates of a dozen states and the Canal Zone." She was described as "beautiful," "level-headed," and charming; and publicized by a particular newspaper "as the hit of the convention." The attending band spontaneously played "Oh, You Beautiful Doll" as she presented a report from the Credential's Committee.

New Yorker John W. Davis was ultimately nominated as the Democratic presidential candidate and Nebraskan Charles W. Bryan was chosen candidate for vice president. On November 4, 1924, the Democrats were defeated by Republican President-elect John Calvin Coolidge, Jr. and Vice President-elect Charles Gates Dawes. Coolidge won as incumbent 30th POTUS. He had been vice president under 29th President Warren Gamaliel Harding and assumed the presidency upon Harding's death from a cerebral hemorrhage on August 2, 1923. (I question if Harding died from the White House's hidden hinky hooch during Prohibition? In fact, many people died from poisoned "alky.")

The New York Bureau's long-term relationship with FDR was emphasized by the Advertising Federation of America's publication that posted "MESSAGE FROM HIS EXCELLENCY" as an opening page commendation in *Truth in Advertising: Twenty-Fifth Anniversary*. Historical footnote stated: "The message from the President was addressed to Edgar Kobak, Chairman of the Board, Advertising Federation of America, and read at the opening general session on Monday, June 29, by President Chester H. Lang."

O'Sullivan wrote that Kenner's Bureau was "almost a department of the New York Stock Exchange" and "since the collapse of the Stock Exchange boom in 1929, there has been continued criticism of the connection of the

THE APO$TATE

Exchange with the Better Business Bureau system." In September 1931, Riegel filed formal charges "against the Better Business Bureau" with the United States Government. Additionally, Wall Street short selling was singled out for scrutiny by populist advocates, such as Huey Long and Father Charles E. Coughlin, who riled public angst against corporate greed and elitism. Thereafter, on March 4, 1932, President Hoover, at the behest of Senator Fletcher, invoked the U.S. Senate to begin what evolved into an extensive two-year investigation of the NYSE, banks, and brokers.

Kenner and the New York Bureau's "Before You Invest, Investigate" program and racketeering relationship with the NYSE and Investment Bankers Association contributed to the incendiary charges that sparked the U.S. Senate investigations. Prior to the Senate's incrimination, the Bureau organization was disciplined and/or indicted by several governances including New York Attorney General Hamilton Ward, New York Secretary of State Edward Flynn, Illinois Representative A. J. Sabath, Missouri Secretary of State Charles U. Becker, and Judge Edward J. Jeffries, Recorder's Court, Detroit Michigan. But the Bureau's affiliation with FDR ran deep and prevented prosecutorial statesmen and officials from exposing the Bureau's sanctimonious corruption that threatened the secret society's gilded membership. The Depression lingered and FDR had no intention of upsetting productive commerce that was direly needed to reboot the economy.

O'Sullivan listed a series of newspaper articles whose incriminating headlines evidenced the Bureau's fall from grace. I found four of the seven articles he provided with the renegades evading perpetuity just so fate could peak my curiosity and leave me wondering what I missed. Fortunately, O'Sullivan and Kenner discussed most of the respective topics in their books. I listed all of O'Sullivan's "'undesirable' publicity" articles because headlines paraphrased original narratives and offered insight into any misplaced history. Research revealed additional trivia, documentation, and news clippings that enlightened Kenner's mindset and professional career while reiterating the New York Bureau's kingpin status within the boiling cauldron of organized crime during the tempestuous Prohibition era.

The *New York Herald-Tribune* article, "Better Business Bureau Head Under Bail in Suit – Kenner Freed on $5,000 Bail," dated January 12, 1928, reported that the Iroquois Trust Company of Illinois filed a lawsuit against the New York Bureau and Kenner in the amount of $1,300,000.00 "for alleged damages to its reputation." Kenner's consequent arrest and handcuffed perp walk "was based on the claiming of "personal" injuries." Iroquois Trust complained that "it was libeled in a "false and malicious" article by Kenner that was delivered to newspapers" on December 26, 1927. The New York Bureau also distributed the article to the state of New York's attorney general under the guise of illicit business activities. As a result, Attorney General Albert E. Ottinger (born 1878; died 1938) "obtained a temporary injunction against the sale in New York of shares and trusts in the Iroquois Trust Company and the projected Iroquois National Bank of New York...." The lawsuit's resolution was not disclosed, but O'Sullivan documented several successful defamation cases against the Bureau that implied similar victory for Iroquois Trust. Kenner's stunning arrest vindicated O'Sullivan and exposed the Bureau's deceptive practice of contriving false claims as advertising gimmicks to bait headlines and remain relevant.

At the end of his second term, on January 1, 1929, Ottinger left the attorney general's office to run against FDR as governor of New York but was defeated in a historically close election. Republican Hamilton Ward replaced Ottinger as attorney general.

The *New York Evening World* article, "Thief Caught - He Charges Better Business Bureau Ordered Burglary – Is Found Rifling files in Stock Fraud Case," dated January 26, 1929, reported that advertising agent James Wallace caught 35 year old Bronx resident and "known criminal" Fred Stanley burglarizing filing cabinets in his 18th floor office located at No. 220 West 42d Street. Wallace filed a complaint with the Jefferson Market Court on January 25, 1929, claiming Stanley admitted to him that Deputy Assistant Attorney General William Mulholland and the New York Bureau's "operative" Frank Reidy contracted Stanley to steal "certain papers" belonging to Joseph Morris who shared Wallace's office. Mulholland and Reidy "denied that they knew or had hired Stanley saying their offices "never employ such tactics"." They claimed Morris and his partner Charles Beadon, publishers of *Trend of the Market* (later renamed *Stock Market Reporter*), were under an injunction by Mulholland's office from "boosting certain stocks"; that Morris, Beadon, and others had been "arrested by postal authorities for using the mails to defraud."

As it turned out, Beadon was targeted by the New York Bureau's "Before You Invest, Investigate" program as its first case involving securities fraud for promotional purposes. Kenner's revised version of the story in *The Fight for Truth in Advertising* conveniently overlooked the *New York Evening World's* 1929 article that implied the New York Bureau was the actual culprit and perpetrated an early rendition of Watergate.

The same month that "Before You Invest, Investigate" began, Beadon was running a stock promotion "employing high-pressure salesmen, which had offices in New York and ten other eastern cities." Beadon was no different than other stockbrokers doing the same thing, and circumstances were nothing more than the New York Bureau's typical stolen thunder tactic that seized or fabricated a grandiose photo opportunity to publicize its services. Additionally, Beadon was a competitor. Accordingly, Kenner perpetrated false advertising that criminally disparaged Beadon as "head of the promotion" and that he "planned to unload several million dollars of shares of the enterprise – the International Radio Corporation." Kenner transformed Beadon's business into a national stock conspiracy that abused radio communications: "Beadon and his colleagues had a small plant in Newark, N. J., for producing radio-receiving apparatus and expected to reap a harvest by exploiting the public's eager curiosity about the infant radio industry which was just getting on its feet." As a result, Kenner ruined Beadon's business by publishing a warning bulletin and "the corporation was forced into bankruptcy by its stockholders." It was Bureau humbuggery at its finest and personified "the pot calling the kettle black." Kenner and the New York Bureau were reported to the Federal Radio Commission for restraint of radio communications in 1931 and indicted by the U.S. Senate for securities fraud in 1932.

Beadon was not charged, though, which meant the New York Bureau filed unsubstantiated claims. Kenner passed the buck and blamed failure to prosecute on lack of enforcement of the Investment Bankers' statute: "The promotion was nipped in the bud; but no action was by public prosecutors, either state or Federal followed. They were not yet organized and equipped, at New York City, to engage in active war on questionable stock vendors." The statute was not enforced until after 1923 and was ignored during Ottinger's two-term administration from 1925-1928, which further explained why Mulholland, an Ottinger hold-over, and Reidy targeted Beadon a second time in the 1929 Stanley burglary to compensate for earlier dismissal of charges. The newspaper article made no mention of the statute or its connection to the "Before You Invest, Investigate" program. And Kenner's revisionist spin, touted in *The Fight for Truth in Advertising*, used the 1922 Beadon narrative to gild the New York Bureau's investigative program while omitting the questionable 1929 Stanley burglary that indicated a cover-up.

To the contrary, O'Sullivan accused the "Before You Invest, Investigate" program of exploiting Blue Sky licensing laws to gainfully promote worthless NYSE securities under a canopy of contrived immunity. He quoted Senator Fletcher's 1932 overview of the Blue Sky securities racket operated by the Bureau, NYSE, and Investment Bankers Association: "This law exempts securities listed on the Exchanges, and thus permits the crooked banker and the crooked broker to sell listed securities at any price obtainable ... those bankers and brokers cannot be charged with fraud ...."

The Beadon case cemented a crony relationship between the triumvirate of the New York Bureau, NYSE, and Investment Bankers Association who collectively manipulated the Office of the New York Attorney General. The genesis of the New York Bureau's investigative program aligned with the New York licensing statute drafted by the New York Investment Bankers Association and enacted in 1921; the statute authorized the attorney general "to investigate suspected fraudulent transactions in securities." The statute also allowed the Bureau to undermine competitors like Beadon. The New York Bureau was incorporated in June 1922 and began its investigative program two months later in August 1922 to enforce the new securities statute in a déjà vu remix of the *Printers' Ink* Model Statute whose false advertising mandates were enforced by its predecessor, the New York Vigilance Committee.

Reviewing case facts almost 90 years later, my first impression screamed "Bureaugate." Reidy, a Kenner protégé, evidenced a crony relationship with Assistant Attorney General Mulholland, suggesting a coordinated albeit bungled burglary. Hamilton Ward had just replaced Ottinger on January 1, 1929, and was in office less than a month. Ward probably relied upon Mulholland while busy establishing his administration without realizing his assistant's underhanded proclivities with the New York Bureau, which involved an attempt to get convictable goods on Beadon by committing espionage and theft. Additionally, Mulholland had access to underworld connections and jailbait like Stanley to covertly burglarize Wallace's office. Expendable Stanley was the perfect patsy because if he got caught no one would believe him as a convicted con sporting a lengthy rap sheet that included petty larceny, grand larceny, multiple parole violations, and a prison-stint at Sing Sing. Otherwise, reality dictated no reason for a street thug like Stanley to be stealing worthless securities documentation.

The *New York World* article, "Better Business Bureau Criticized – General system Opposed – Report Attacks Activities of Paid Managers," dated September 15, 1930, described the results of an investigative report by the Manhattan and Bronx Chambers of Commerce that exposed the Bureau's hypocritical regulatory practice. The report concluded that "there is "no mechanism designed to project ideals or elevate standards" in the Better Business Bureau system as a whole." In fact, the article incriminated Kenner, "The New York bureau, the report finds, "appears to have been organized solely by the initiative of the general manager." Furthermore, the article's prophetic conclusion indicted the Bureau: "The Better Business Bureau system in general is attacked chiefly on the grounds of its method of operating, which the report says, is "to strike not with the methods of the crusader but with the weapons of the secret clan"."

The article marked the beginning of allegations that forced the New York Bureau into hearings by the U.S. Senate Banking and Currency Commission. Consequent criminal charges epitomized the Bureau's scandalous fall from grace. O'Sullivan prognosticated, "The year 1930 saw the beginning of the end of Bureau prestige. Up to that time, the activities of the Bureaus had been taken rather seriously."

Logan Billingsley undoubtedly inspired the *New York World's* article considering that he was the founder of the Manhattan and Bronx Chambers of Commerce. The *New York World* represented one of the few remaining publishers who defied the Bureau's overreach. After the Crash, Billingsley organized the Manhattan Board of Commerce, an affiliate of the Bronx Chamber of Commerce, to spark new business and real estate development in the Bronx. The New York Bureau perceived encroaching competition, and, in April 1930, vindictively attempted to discredit Logan and dissolve the Board by publicizing his past indiscretions as a convicted bootlegger and involvement in the murder of two policemen in Seattle, Washington. Logan responded with a defamation lawsuit but withdrew charges when the Bureau demanded the Manhattan Board's business records. He feared evidence tampering relative to the Bureau's cronyism with the court system. His retreat was temporary, planned, and allowed time to assemble allies for the Bureau's epochal slap-down. On Dec 26, 1930, Attorney General Ward, supported by Secretary of State Flynn, indicted the Bureau for operating illegally without a license. In September 1931, the Consumer Guild of America's Riegel filed multiple fraud charges against the BBB system with the U.S. Federal Government. On January 25, 1932, Senator Fletcher delivered historical and scathing condemnation of the Bureau in U.S. Senate chambers that laid groundwork for the formation of the U.S. Senate's Banking and Currency Commission under President Hoover that became known as the Pecora Commission under FDR. Then, on June 6, 1932, the Manhattan Board victoriously re-emerged after a two-year investigation and presented a litany of criminal accusations supported by all aforementioned state and congressional officials that spearheaded securities-fraud charges against the Bureau organization and its bogus "Before You Invest, Investigate" program involving its crony racketeering relationship with the NYSE and Investment Bankers Association.

The *Cincinnati Post* article, "Unfairness Charged – Better Business Bureaus Accused," dated September 3, 1931, was not located, but the headline is self-explanatory.

The *Birmingham, Alabama Post* article, "Sale of Blue-Sky to United States People Charged – Riegel's Statement Charges the Better Business Bureau with Unfair Trade Practices, Promoting Gambling on the Stock Exchange, Using the Mails to Defraud," dated September 4, 1931, was also not located, but the headline is self-explanatory.

O'Sullivan particularly elaborated on the Bureau's Blue Sky fraud and related racketeering operations with the NYSE and Investment Bankers Association, which many authorities attributed to the Crash. Occasion involved the participation of renowned economist Riegel whose Consumers Guild of America supported Billingsley and the Manhattan Board of Commerce's allegations against the New York Bureau. Riegel spent a year investigating the Bureau and the *Birmingham, Alabama Post* article acknowledged his results. He filed federal charges against the New York Bureau in September 1931 resulting in the U.S.

Senate Banking and Currency Commission after Senator Fletcher forwarded charges to President Herbert Hoover. Fletcher denounced the Bureau's "Before You Invest, Investigate" program as a racket that encouraged side-winding stock speculation, exploited Blue Sky laws, and violated postal laws for mutual-benefit with the NYSE and Investment Bankers Association. FDR whitewashed the New York Bureau's crimes by appointing Kenner to the SEC.

The *Denver Post* article, "The Denver Better Business Bureau took it on the chin Saturday, when the fraud case it sought to build up against the International Guarantee Thrift Syndicate collapsed completely," dated March 3, 1932, was also not located, but the headline is self-explanatory.

The *Pittsburgh National Labor Tribune* article, "Better Business Bureau Bunk and False Pretenses," dated March 31, 1932, evidenced another courageous newspaper daring to publish negative Bureau press. The article lambasted the Pittsburg Bureau "as an institution pretending to ferret out advertising frauds and other rackets." G. H. Denniston, the manager of the Pittsburg Bureau, appeared before Magistrate Leo Rothenberg at the Central Police Court and filed a false claim involving fake perpetrators to garner publicity for the Bureau. At the same time, the Bureau ignored egregious fraud created by its influential members. The article reported that "charity racketeers took $1,000,000.00 from Pittsburgh during 1931, but this man Denniston made no charge against the big advertising racketeers, with their false claims in their advertisements." The Bureau was exposed for ignoring false advertising committed by two of its influential members: "A large department store" advertised "for 800 girls" after a massive layoff. The women were never hired or compensated but were tricked into reporting for interviews to appear as "shoppers." A second example detailed another large store falsely advertising suits for $21.50 that in reality cost twice as much. Additionally, the article reminded of an earlier occasion whereby Denniston filed false charges alleging the City of Pittsburgh had been defrauded $8,000,000 by "racketeers or fake stock salesmen." When Denniston was pressed to name victims to prove his allegations, he admitted, "It was just an advertising scheme." O'Sullivan described deception as "an opportunity to break into print, in typical Bureau style."

O'Sullivan also listed additional complaints questioning ethical business practice by the Bureaus of St. Louis, Missouri, Denver, Colorado, and Chicago, Illinois. Allegations included Francis E. Williams, attorney for the St. Louis Bureau; O'Sullivan advised that he "attempted to plant himself in a position to influence court decisions by appointment as amicus curiae (friend of the court) in cases in which the Bureau was interested."

On June 6, 1932, F. Odell Adams, secretary of the Manhattan Board of Commerce, sent a formal inquiry to the NYSE's Richard Whitney. Adams spent two years investigating the Bureau's relationship with the NYSE and presented

Whitney a list of questions that included Kenner at the epicenter of investigative proceedings. Both Whitney and Kenner brushed off the Board's inquiries. O'Sullivan noted that Congressman La Guardia of New York was the arraigning authority and that "the probe by the Senatorial committee is still in progress."

O'Sullivan published *Rackets* in early January 1933 just as the Pecora Commission began that same month; he predicted the Bureau's escape from accountability. The mystic Sphinx dodged a silver bullet only because its gilded membership included every golden coattail, national association, bank, and exchange located in New York City. The Bureau's indictment by Senator Fletcher in the U.S. Senate was meant to record respective hardcore criminality to assure some measure of retribution; any other crook committing the same offenses would have been imprisoned with the keys thrown away considering the magnitude of historical theft, fraud, and consequences. Even Kenner attempted to prosecute stockbrokers committing lesser offenses. Nevertheless, the franchise's "Before You Invest, Investigate" was shut down, which confirmed apparent wrongdoing.

FDR's "First New Deal" (1933-1935) sought to bring securities and exchanges under the government umbrella in order to reform stock exchanges and regulate sale of securities. Blue Sky laws proved pathetically ineffective. Accordingly, FDR assembled an advisory legal team to form the first securities regulatory agency and included James McCauley Landis (1899-1964), a Harvard lawyer and law professor; Benjamin Victor Cohen (1894-1983), a Harvard lawyer; and Thomas Gardiner Corcoran (1900-1981), also a Harvard lawyer. Roosevelt placed Landis in charge of the FTC's new securities division. Landis earned an impressive resume under FDR and served with the FTC from 1933 to 1934; was commissioner of the SEC from 1934 to 1937; and he assumed Joseph Kennedy's position in 1935 as chairman of the SEC serving until 1937.

On May 27, 1933, the Securities Act of 1933 became law and regulated "original issues" in what is called the "primary market." Description of the law stated, "An act to provide for the regulation of securities exchanges and of over-the-counter markets operating in interstate and foreign commerce and through the mails, to prevent inequitable and unfair practices on such exchanges and markets, and for other purposes."

On June 6, 1934, the Securities Exchange Act of 1934 (a.k.a. Fletcher-Rayburn bill) was enacted to regulate "secondary trading of securities" and/or "aftermarket" securities including "stocks, bonds, options, and futures" in addition to mortgage transferals. The SEC received the "power to approve stock exchange rules, prohibit manipulative trading practices, regulate corporate proxy practices and increase disclosure requirements." The act also established the Securities and Exchange Commission. Landis assigned his former cohorts, Cohen and Corcoran, to draft the constructs for a new securities division. The Fletcher-Rayburn bill was introduced on February 10, 1934, and sponsored by

Senator Fletcher and Democratic Texas Congressman and Speaker of the House of Representatives Samuel Taliaferro Rayburn. Corcoran was influential in making Rayburn the Speaker of the House in 1937. In return, Rayburn introduced Corcoran to "the Texas oil industry."

The Fletcher-Rayburn bill created immediate controversy. Richard Whitney aggressively contested the bill's reform mandate and control of the stock exchanges on behalf of the NYSE. Thereafter, the FTC announced that it would not enforce the bill. As a result, Democratic Virginia Senator Carter Glass introduced an amendment to the bill that would form the SEC as a new agency outside the FTC, and, which also separated securities regulation from the FTC.

The SEC had multi-faceted powers that included regulation of the securities exchanges, over-the-counter markets, registration of securities, members of the exchanges, and issuers of stocks. FDR influenced the appointment of Joseph Patrick Kennedy Sr. (1888-1969) as SEC chairman on June 30, 1934; he was offered a five-year contract but only served one year and left in 1935 to direct the Maritime Commission, which "built on his wartime experience in running a major shipyard." Landis was initially favored as chairman, but FDR chose Kennedy who supported FDR while running for president. Additionally, after Prohibition, Kennedy started a lucrative liquor business with FDR's son, Congressman James Roosevelt II, and established Somerset Importers that was the exclusive distributor for "*Haig & Haig* Scotch, *Gordon's* Dry Gin and *Dewar's* Scotch."

Kennedy selected Landis and the Pecora Commission's lead prosecutor Ferdinand Pecora among a team of commissioners to build the SEC. Landis was placed in charge of regulations and reports and Pecora handled investigations but resigned after six months. Then, Landis brought in reinforcements from the FTC to complete the assembly of the SEC. Three divisions were created including the Examination Division (Registration Division), Trading and Exchange Division, and Legal Division, which worked with the Justice Department.

The Crash did not happen overnight; Wall Street titans fought encroaching doom over several months. The New York Bureau and its illustrious membership were heavily involved from start to finish. When the jig was up, golden coattails deflected culpability through standard disingenuous modus operandi that established a lionized committee as a virtuous optical illusion to dodge complicity. Kenner reflected with gilded hypocritical hindsight: "Early in 1929, the National Conference on Prevention of Fraudulent Transactions in Securities had been formed, organized to unify the activities of leading commercial, financial, and government groups in their fraud-fighting activities." Kenner coined the organization as the "National Fraud Conference." But the organization should have been alternately called the "National Fraudsters Conference" because it was comprised of 17 elite national members of the

National BBB and/or affiliates of the New York Bureau, who were the same culprits that contributed to the Crash. Yet, true to form, Kenner glossed over culpability and crimes to revisionistically write, "These groups had long been cognizant of the need for a national clearing house of facts about illegal securities transactions and lawless vendors." Furthermore, tongue-in-cheek objective was "to develop further cooperation between state and Federal agencies and business organizations engaged in truth in securities work."

> Members of the National Fraud Conference:
> American Association of Personal Finance Companies
> American Bankers Association
> Associated Stock Exchanges
> Boston Stock Exchange
> Better Business Bureau of New York City
> Chamber of Commerce of the United States
> Chicago Stock Exchange
> Investment Bankers Association of America
> Mortgage Bankers Association of America
> National Association of Better Business Bureaus, Inc.
> National Association of Owners of Railroad & Public Utilities Securities
> National Association of Real Estate Boards
> National Association of Securities Commissioners
> National Better Business Bureau, Inc.
> National Conference of Commissioners on Uniform State Laws
> New York Curb Exchange
> New York Stock Exchange

The National Fraud Conference instigated the founding relationship between the Better Business Bureau franchise and the SEC, underpinned by the FTC's entrenched cronyism with the National BBB. Furthermore, the conference assembled in early 1929 when Wall Street was spiraling, and sanctimoniously shrouded the same guilty parties running for cover after the Crash.

In May 1929 and May 1930, the National Fraud Conference held two meetings in Washington, D.C., but the conferences were compromised from the get-go because ongoing securities fraud made the Crash inevitable. As always, dirt was swept under the rug while robber barons played musical chairs. In April 1935, the conference met in Washington with the SEC and newly instated Chairman Landis to inform their activities. Of course, the National BBB and New York Bureau (Kenner) attended the conference to offer their voluntary assistance. And, Landis "accepted" their assistance. Consequently, Kenner slithered his way into the SEC.

Kenner's friendship with FDR brought him favored status and executive branch-approval to participate in the SEC's respective programs. His participation in the SEC was classic stolen thunder. The New York Bureau latched onto SEC merit and clout by volunteering services and personnel. Kenner described his involvement as chairman of a development committee whose mission was to design an SEC regulatory department: "The Commission accepted the offer, and a committee was appointed under the chairmanship of H. J. Kenner, to outline a plan for the actual organization and operation of the new department. A program was presented to the Commission and approved." The department was named "Securities Violations Section of the Securities and Exchange Commission" and involved the Bureau publishing reports called "Bulletins" distributed to "law-enforcement agencies throughout the United States and to voluntary organizations engaged in securities fraud-prevention work." The Bulletins, first distributed on June 15, 1935, reported individuals "engaged in the sale of securities by allegedly fraudulent methods."

After Kenner's committee was established, Landis sent an appreciative missive to James Coats Auchincloss, president of the New York Bureau, on May 28, 1936, which cemented a close association between the SEC and Better Business Bureau organization. Landis wrote, "The Securities and Exchange Commission appreciates the assistance rendered by the Better Business Bureau of New York City in the Commission's efforts to suppress fraudulent dealings in securities. We sincerely hope that there will be no curtailment of your activities in this respect and we look forward to the continuance of our effective cooperation." So, in one fell swoop, FDR dispatched the SEC to whitewash the Bureau's tarnished image from unfettered *Roaring Twenties'* organized crime. After all, FDR was desperately trying to kick-start new business, and the New York Bureau was the kingpin of business. It was ironic that the Bureau helped start the Great Depression that needed the Bureau's business membership to end it.

Kenner's *The Fight for Truth in Advertising* was written to take advantage of the Bureau's newfound SEC affiliation that offered redemption and a ticket to ride back into the securities field. As a result, the real truth involving one of America's greatest national tragedies was quietly buried, dismissing condemnation by Senator Fletcher and the U.S. Senate that the Bureau was "the greatest racket ever known in its history."

O'Sullivan's reference articles described a quixotic and scandalous Kenner:

The *Aberdeen Weekly American* article, "Boosters Rule at Devil's Lake," dated March 21, 1913, described Kenner attending a meeting of the Grand Fork's Commercial Club held at Devils Lake, North Dakota, on March 20, 1913. The article was a puff piece and was probably arranged by the New York Bureau to promote Kenner: "The affair was largely a result of the effort of Secretary H. J.

Kenner, working in conjunction with officials of the club."

The *Duluth News Tribune* article, "Would Discard 'Caveat Emptor': H. J. Kenner of Minneapolis Speaks to Duluth Ad Men and Retail Merchants," dated February 3, 1915, recreated the Bureau's horse-and-buggy era when identifying Kenner's title as "H. J. Kenner, secretary of the vigilance committee of the Minneapolis Ad Forum." Personal mention ear-marked history a year before the organization changed its name to the Better Business Bureau. Kenner had just begun his career with the Bureau and his comments reflected youth's idealism and innocence. His comment, "We believe that untruth, trickery, or any sort of deception in advertising is a slow method of committing business suicide," particularly caught my attention because he defined the stark difference between a stalwart Puritan Old Guard Bureau versus the modern globalist NWO Bureau. Kenner also sounded like O'Sullivan before corporate corruption took its toll.

The *Kansas City Times* article, "Truth Is The Rule In Ads," dated November 10, 1915, and subtitle, ""Advertising Fakers Are Passing," H. J. Kenner says," depicted Kenner's Puritan early years. The comment, "Seeking to Protect the Public Against Dishonest Advertising," summarized Kenner's youthful idealism. The article also rated historical mention by defining the vigilance committee as "the better advertising movement." Additionally, a historical milestone was emphasized when referring to Kenner as "secretary of the National Vigilance Committee of advertising clubs"; he was the committee's first paid manager and/or secretary. I believe this article best described Kenner as the reformer he wanted to be and how the Bureau embedded its legacy: "Honest advertisers and intelligent readers are demanding that the deliberate falsehoods, the half-truth and the petty deceit be weeded out of the field of publicity."

The AACW's *Associated Advertising* magazine, July 1919 edition, published the article, "H. J. Kenner Returns to Vigilance Department Work." Kenner's corporate trajectory was highlighted, which prepared him to command the secret society's most prestigious and strategic branch office, the New York Bureau, seven years later. The write-up also reflected Kenner's unsettled private life after WWI that, although presented in favorable light, underscored trying times: "Mr. Kenner left the association to enter retailing in Minneapolis, and later went with the Northwestern Knitting Co., to take charge of work for that organization, for which his training had especially fitted him. His experience in both those business connections in Minneapolis has been of especial value as further training for the service which he is re-entering."

The *Duluth News Tribune* article, "Kenner Acts As A Watchman," dated February 8, 1920, provided the subtitle, "Vigilance Official Re-Enlists With Associated Advertising Clubs of World," and incorporated much of the *Associated Advertising's* July 1919 article. Kenner's rise within the early Vigilance Committee was reviewed when the committee was still a division of the AACW.

Even though the organization changed names in 1916, the article still connected Kenner to the Vigilance Committee reporting, "His brilliant record in Minneapolis resulted in an invitation to join the headquarters staff, to serve as secretary of the National Vigilance Committee, and to help other cities organize more effective vigilance work."

In the fall of 1936, Kenner wrote *The Fight for Truth in Advertising* that glorified the Old Guard Vigilance Committee and its evolution into the Bureau. His book's narrative ended with the Advertising Federation of America's 1936 Boston convention with underlying intention to celebrate the advertising industry's silver anniversary of the AACA's 1911 Boston convention. The AFA's 1936 convention supplement, *Truth in Advertising; Twenty-Fifth Anniversary*, bundled several speeches into proselytizing sermons written by Old Guard Bureau and advertising elite who were also included in Kenner's storyline. Kenner was specifically mentioned as "H. J. Kenner, in his excellent book, "The Fight for Truth in Advertising"." His book was still in a pre-publication stage at the time of the AFA publication as determined from Kenner's last dated entry with drafts obviously reviewed by association officials. In turn, Kenner commemorated the AFA in his "Acknowledgments" page that advised he was chairman of "The Committee on 'History of the Truth in Advertising Movement' of the Advertising Federation of America" and undersigned as "H. J. Kenner, New York, N.Y., October 1, 1936."

The full title of Kenner's book was, *The Fight for Truth in Advertising: A Story of What Business Has Done and Is Doing to Establish and Maintain Accuracy and Fair Play in Advertising and Selling for the Public's Protection*. Back in the day, authors wanted the whole kit-and-caboodle known up front by framing their message within the title. The AFA sponsored Kenner's book as a follow-up to their convention held in Boston, between June 28 and July 2, 1936, at the historic Faneuil Hall, a.k.a. "the Cradle of Liberty." Faneuil Hall was named after and built by merchant Peter Faneuil (pronounced "fænəl") in 1742 and located on Freedom Trail at Dock Square "bounded by Congress Street, North Street, and Union Street."

As manager of the New York Bureau, Kenner celebrated the AFA's silver jubilee in *The Fight for Truth in Advertising*. He defined its message:, "Declaring renewed faith in the principles which above all others vitalize advertising, the Advertising Federation of America, at its 1936 convention, at Boston, adopted resolutions intended to clarify in the public mind the truth *about* advertising and pledged itself also to use its influence, through related and constituent bodies, to the end that the Better Business Bureaus "be given adequate financial aid and hearty support in the constructive work they are doing"." Accordingly, Kenner confirmed the Bureau owed its existence to the advertising industry.

Kenner wrote his book during the New Deal era and chronicled the evolution of the advertising industry and Better Business Bureau. Over all, he invigorated the franchise after the decimating Pecora Commission investigation and defined the Bureau as a powerhouse with extensive connections in every elite political circle and facet of business. Kenner put the Bureau back on its pedestal while glossing over the Bureau's scandals. He participated in and publicized the consolidation and chartering of fair business practice now incorporated in FTC legislation, advertising, business, and cinematic industries; business codes evolved into member accreditation guidelines now known as "BBB Standards for Trust." But, as with any autocracy, I believe that the modern Bureau marginalized the U.S. Constitution in favor of its bias insular standards.

During the course of writing, Kenner emphasized his talent for incorporating entertaining figures of speech to describe offenses and offenders, such as "manufacturing magnificence," "oil pirates," "wolf packs," "financial parasites," "security gyps," "minions of Wall Street," "snooping rats," "sucker-money," "land sharks," "white-collar bandits," "ghoulish gentry," and "tipster-sheet and boiler-room operators"; descriptions could have also described the Bureau.

The Fight for Truth in Advertising remains an incredibly important vestige of the Bureau's early history. The storyline reads like an innocuous chronology of the Bureau's celebrated evolution but ends with a thrashing blow to critics as though always intended as the objective for publication. Kenner flexed Bureau muscle while boasting regulatory victories. He also focused covert crosshairs on O'Sullivan and *Rackets for* exposing the Bureau as a crony NYSE puppet that was engaged in racketeering and securities fraud.

Wansley's address, *History and Traditions*, glossed over the Bureau's Pre-Crash escapades highlighted by O'Sullivan and suppressed by Kenner. Being a former Bureau president, Wanley wrote a Bureau-friendly narrative: "In their long history the BBBs have been the targets of both critical attacks and accolades. Early attacks included the example shown in "Exhibit 4" which the Manhattan Board of Commerce and the Bronx Chamber of Commerce issued the first report of the "Committee to Investigate Better Business Bureaus"." Wansley did not describe the "attacks," but was referring to Logan Billingsley who orchestrated the take-down of the Better Business Bureau. Billingsley was supported by the Manhattan Board of Commerce, the Bronx Chamber of Commerce, Stock Reform Committee of New York, Syracuse Chamber of Commerce, and Consumers Guild of America. Kenner responded with character assassination against Billingsley that represented low hanging fruit since he was a former convicted bootlegger with nuances of yesteryear murder attached to his name. Kenner also attacked his brother, Sherman Billingsley, owner of the infamous *Stork Club* in Manhattan; he forgot to mention that Sherman's patrons included FBI Director J. Edgar Hoover (1895-1972).

Unfortunately, the Boston Bureau did not include links to Wansley's noted exhibits, which was akin to an accusation without evidence. I hoped that a copy of his address, including exhibits, was archived by Washington University's Institutes for Organization Management where Wansley delivered his 1971 address, but the department no longer existed, and the University did not store respective historical records.

Kenner considered critics as "spreading scurrilous slander in printed pamphlets" that referred to O'Sullivan and his pamphlet, *The Lance*. Nameless pointed accusations confirmed that Kenner and O'Sullivan were mortal enemies. A Battle Royal may have escalated had it not been for O'Sullivan's early demise less than three years after Kenner's publication of *The Fight for Truth in Advertising*. In fact, O'Sullivan's assistant, Kate Whelan, did escalate his previous criticism of the Bureau as evidenced by her ongoing publication of *The Lance* that developed into a lawsuit shortly after O'Sullivan's death in 1939. Whelan accused Detroit Bureau President Harry Leslie McEldowney of being a "racketeer." He retaliated by gathering a "war chest" from Bureaus around the country including Kenner's New York Bureau, and filed a lawsuit in Chicago. McEldowney won the lawsuit, ruined Whelan, and closed *The Lance*, which were no great feats considering the Bureau owned the courts. Nevertheless, O'Sullivan's valiant crusade against the Bureau ended.

As manager of the most powerful Bureau, Kenner rubbed shoulders with the elite of New York and Washington, D.C., which included prominent newspapers, banking, NYSE, FTC, SEC, courts, political lobbies, and local authorities. Such empowerment reflected in his statement, "This writer has had no desire to defend, whitewash, or glorify business, or any of its branches, through the medium of this volume. Yet he has tried to show, by individual instances, how the protective agencies of business have functioned, in a pattern of activity nationally coordinated. This has meant that their factual and moral powers have been integrated with, and have supplemented, the legal power of government so as to help preserve, and to give stronger effect to, fundamental principles upon which economic, social, and political progress must be based." I believe Kenner's use of the word "defend" was directed at O'Sullivan as confirmed by his additional references to "muck-rakers" and "propagandists." Furthermore, Wansley specifically wrote that O'Sullivan's *The Lance* was "probably the most notorious attack."

There had been no hint of Kenner's pending reprisal in *The Fight for Truth in Advertising* until the final chapter titled, "CHAPTER XX: *Conclusion*." Accordingly, Kenner generically castigated critics of the Bureau: "This volume relates some evils of business and various depredations of those who prey upon the public, and holds a brief also against the avoidable errors and laxities of careless business. However, this writer cannot see why the existence of these should constitute, at any time, a just cause for indictments of business generally or of its branches by self-serving propagandists in private life, or by misguided, over-reaching individuals in public life. The public itself must, and undoubtedly will, at some early or late stage of consideration of the situation, exercise its common sense and love of fair play to administer sound correctives of its own, rebuking the muck-rakers."

Kenner unwittingly supported several of O'Sullivan's allegations and description of the Bureau network to the extent that he acknowledged respective issues occurred. He elaborated, "The Better Business Bureaus are not operated as a national system. Each organization is entirely autonomous and is responsible to local business men, their ideals and standards, for the right conduct of its affairs. Yet, the bureaus in this country and in Canada have at all times exerted their collective moral force against wrong acts, and faults of procedure, among their associated units. They have acted swiftly when individual bureaus have shown black sheep proclivities."

On the other hand, O'Sullivan sternly warned, "The so-called Better Business Bureaus are cunningly organized corporations, "not for profit," and with individual liability limited under laws governing educational, benevolent, and religious institutions. They are without one scintilla of legal authority to regulate, censor, police, or supervise the business of a single citizen or concern in the whole country that does not belong to their Bureau; therefore any act of their contrary to vested rights is unlawful ... The Bureaus are not licensed, bonded, empowered or legally authorized by either State or Federal Government, to act as regulators, supervisors, censors, or dictators, over business or the conduct of business enterprises outside of their own membership. Still, they usurp the rights and authority of licensed and bonded detective agencies and investigation bureaus."

The Fight for Truth in Advertising is an authentic history book that portrays the Bureau's real-time development through its affiliations with federal branches of the government that inspired a lasting quasi-governmental façade. Kenner described the Bureau's march into major cities throughout the United States and Canada while stewards tackled a wide range of fraudulent advertising in conjunction with local, state, and federal officials to procure convictions that also exponentially empowered their reputation. And, the larger the Bureau grew, the more federal entities relied upon its entrenched forces that had expanded across the country. The Depression of 1920-21 followed WWI and lasted for seven far-reaching months. Kenner confirmed that returning troops created a surge in the civilian labor force, and that many veterans became vigilance men. The decade started slow, but years transitioned into the prosperous *Roaring Twenties* or ""*Années folles*" ("crazy years" in French)." The Bureau's military acumen strategically positioned offices in every major city to warrant the government's continued partnership. Thereafter, marketing expertise utilized every rising-star opportunity to embed the Bureau as a respected household name.

Kenner specifically retraced the years that O'Sullivan discussed in *Rackets*. He elaborated the Bureau's respective point of view and gave example after example of scandals and scams as though to undermine O'Sullivan's criticism of the Bureau; reams of credentialed organizations, legislators, and federal committees supporting the Bureau were listed. But, after reading both books side by side, they each made perfect sense. The epochal literary duel between Kenner and O'Sullivan epitomized Big Business versus the corner drugstore, although Kenner unwittingly verified many of O'Sullivan's accounts and accusations especially involving the NYSE, Investment Bankers Association, SEC, and FTC.

Both Kenner and O'Sullivan wrote about the same explosive decades of the 1920s and 1930s, which saw the Bureau evolve into a superpower. O'Sullivan was a victim of the Bureau and worried about an encroaching, intimidating, unregulated, and unlicensed bully. On the flipside, Kenner was a loyal company man protecting the Bureau's vested interests and globalist expansion. He acknowledged that the Bureau wasn't perfect but maintained virtuous optimism: "[I]t has benefited by the trials and errors of former days. Tomorrow it will make new gains."

Kenner painstakingly detailed the Bureau's early years providing a rare historical accumulation of facts including names, dates, events, and documents. He organized the Bureau's mission into a Biblical form preserving its Old Testament legacy for future generations. It was critical that he documented Bureau history as he did because incongruities are occurring decades later due to dearth of information. Kenner's original insight has faded with the wind and information is being perverted. Fundamentals that he outlined as mission critical are now being distorted, changed, and/or denied. Additionally, the Bureau no longer promotes its historical legacy resulting in outdated material, which misinforms consumers.

Corporate New Guard successors distanced themselves from the traditionalist Old Guard Bureau. Dearth of information enabled cover-up. The current generation knows nothing about the Bureau, yet instantly recognizes its iconic name. Consumers have been conditioned to believe whatever the Bureau presents via press releases, events, and staged propaganda. The Bureau maintains over a century of museum-worthy documents, pictures, and records that are locked away in its secret vaults restricted from public access. Gumshoe efforts can only go so far, though, and then blank spaces become black holes. Golden coattails owe consumers fair disclosure having evolved into a too-big-to-fail global enterprise as a result of consumer trust.

The twenty-first-century Bureau relegated Kenner to virtual obscurity even though his leadership and guidance were integral to its evolution and the early Truth in Advertising Movement. He deserved a distinguished bookmark rather than a passing footnote. Much of Kenner's life was wrapped up in Bureau affairs. He insinuated a great deal of information was left out when stating, "Even though it seems to contain much detail, this volume is really little more than an outline. There are phases which have been omitted. If all that business has done to curb commercial and financial evils were included, even in outline, this book would have to be much larger than it is."

Kenner made sporadic references to his various positions in the Bureau, but he never elaborated directly on his career in *The Fight for Truth in Advertising*. He spoke as the Bureau's narrator contending with "masqueraders," "wolves in sheep's clothing," "security gyps," "fakers," and "tricky trading." Sifting through the book's pages for any personal reference and/or bit of information was similar to picking a needle out of a haystack. He remained ultimately focused on the Bureau. The book's "Acknowledgments" page read like a VIP list of Illuminati featuring New York's publishing and advertising elite that emphasized Kenner's authority and identified Bureau power players of that era. Such high-profile membership validated O'Sullivan's claims of how and why the Bureau evaded U.S. Senate indictments relative to U.S. Senate investigations between 1932 and 1934. Kenner's book could be construed as a lost "classic" because he included information that the Bureau would prefer to be buried and why he and his book are no longer mentioned. His narrative provided incomparable insight into Old Guard methodology and affairs. He also stated dogma that undermined modern Bureau programs such as the current awards program and ratings system.

At the age of 60, and, after 33 years with the Bureau, Kenner retired "at the end of 1947." His last contact with the Bureau was in 1955 when he was 68 years old. One can only imagine the incredible conversations that transpired among colleagues who experienced the rebellious Prohibition years. The website, Tiki-Toki.com, featured a chronological Bureau timeline with his name and picture beside the accolade, "1955 ... Minneapolis hosts a "homecoming" meeting for all the Better Business Bureaus at the BBB annual convention. Mac Martin, H.J. Kenner, and others are recognized as trailblazers in the organization. Kenner receives a unique status as the only employee of all Bureaus due to his work in Minneapolis and New York City." An incomparable era ended with Kenner's retirement. He dutifully faded into the welcoming Sphinx sunset.

Hurnard Jay Kenner died Monday, January 8, 1973, at his family home in Tuscola, Illinois. He was 85 years old. True to the ways of an elusive Sphinxster, his burial site was not published. His name has become a distant memory rarely mentioned outside of scholarly contributions, but history cannot deny the legacy that he left behind as the dedicated general manager of the New York Bureau that began as a humble experiment to uphold truth in advertising. He led the organization during a tumultuous period that included WWI, *Roaring Twenties*, Prohibition, Stock Market Crash and Great Depression, the Pecora Commission, and WWII. Kenner was the essence of horse-and-buggy advertising and solidified the dynastic rise of the Better Business Bureau.

CHAPTER **30**

JOHN JAMES BENNETT JR.

John James Bennett Jr.
Democratic New York Attorney General from 1931 to 1942;
buried Republican predecessor's decree to license
the Better Business Bureau; artist: Caryn Cain.

He was the man whom the Bureau truly owes a staggering debt of gratitude. The Bureau became what it is today because of him. He empowered the Bureau with unconditional freedom by eliminating his predecessor's licensing ultimatum. If not for him the Bureau would have been tightly regulated like other consumer reporting agencies and denied free-ranging imperialistic sovereignty that begat global stature; the FTC would have maintained its mandated disciplinary profile; the Bureau's nonprofit operations would have remained limited and benign; Congress would have established an alternate federal reporting agency to replace the Bureau's reporting services as was considered before the Bureau's 1941 Deep State indoctrination; and a modern world would have escaped the wrath of the Bureau's bogus awards and bias rating scores that have monopolized the marketplace and threatening digital airways. In fact, Bennett created a monster and unbridled leviathan gobbling power and prestige with every influential opportunity.

His intervention enabled the Bureau's cronyism with the FTC that has encouraged and vastly expanded its globe-trotting services. The FTC was created to regulate deceptive trade and to protect consumers, but the agency muddied boundaries by its crony relationship with the Bureau franchise. Preferential collaboration serves to empower the Bureau above all others, which suggests impropriety due to the FTC's supposed strict impartial mandate. Consequently, the Bureau has been allowed unprecedented leeway to control the business industry. The centurial Bureau has refined an impregnable legal infrastructure that effectively eliminates liability and right of consumer redress and is shielded by U.S. laws of free speech, yet its programs strangle and intimidate free trade. Bennett inadvertently incentivized the Bureau's monopolistic self-serving operations that now reach into the courts and impede individual justice.

John James Bennett was born on March 2, 1894, in Brooklyn, Kings County, New York. Of course, his father was John James Bennett Sr. and his mother was Kathryn O'Brien. He was a Roman Catholic and attended St. Francis High School. In 1923, he graduated from Brooklyn Law School. And, on "September 4, 1923," he married Evelyn Ann Cogan (1899-1955) also from Brooklyn. They had four children: Mary Louise (born September 28, 1924), John James Bennett III (born April 10, 1927; died April 22, 2005), Joan (born January 31, 1931), and Evelyn (born August 21, 1934). Over the next seven years, until 1931, Bennett taught as a professor at Brooklyn Law School while also practicing law. Bennett was awarded honorary LL.D. degrees from St. Lawrence University in Canton, NY; St. John's University in Brooklyn, NY; and, Manhattan College in the Bronx, New York City.

Bennett offered impressive military credentials and a stellar civil dossier that invited a promising political future. During WWI, he served in the U.S. Army 308th Infantry, 77th Division, and later served with the Air Service. He returned to the war front in latter 1943 during WWII and served as a lieutenant colonel with the Supreme Headquarters Allied Expeditionary Force (SHAEF) in European Theater Operations under Supreme Commander U.S. General Dwight D. Eisenhower. Bennett was a member of several organizations: the "Elks Knights of Columbus, American Legion (Post Commander, County Commander, State Commander, Department of New York), President of the American Legion Mountain Camp, and Democratic Corporate Counsel for the City of New York."

While state commander of the American Legion, Bennett caught the

JOHN JAMES BENNETT JR.

attention of Brooklyn political boss, John Henry McCooey (1864-1934), "chair of the Kings County Democratic Party from 1910 to his death in 1934." McCooey "joined Tammany Hall in 1925" and in 1932 was elected to the New York Democratic National Committee. He supported Al Smith as candidate for the 1932 presidential election, but when the nomination was handed to Roosevelt, both he and Smith fell in line behind him. McCooey supported Bennett as attorney general, which invited a connection to the New York Bureau and their extensive membership affiliations throughout New York City. On September 19, 1930, The *New York Times* published the article, "BENNETT REPORTED M'COOEY CANDIDATE; State Legion Head Is Said to Be His Choice for Nomination for Attorney General. CURTIN ALSO AN ASPIRANT But Up-State Leaders Are Opposed to Naming of City Man Since Graft Disclosures." The article was another example of how newspaper headlines paraphrased their respective stories.

In the day many renowned critics and city officials alleged the New York Bureau operated lawlessly. The New York Bureau and its affiliates were compared to organized crime that largely controlled political elections in New York City during the *Roaring Twenties* and early 1930s. It was not until 1935 that Special Agent Thomas E. Dewey rounded up New York kingpins and the Bureau joined the SEC to contrive a hallowed "halo" to dodge Dewey's dragnet.

Kenner and the New York Bureau deflected the state of New York's bi-partisan prosecutorial demands for licensing by electing Bennett as a "Bureau-friendly" Democratic attorney general. The Bureau supported Bennett in the 1930 state election against incumbent Republican Attorney General Hamilton Ward Jr. (1871-1932), a former captain in the Spanish-American War of 1898, former "Commander-in-Chief of the United Spanish War Veterans," and attorney general for state of New York from January 1, 1929 to December 31, 1930. Electing a crony politician was common practice in the early 1930s during the heyday of organized crime in New York City.

At the time, FDR was the incumbent 44th governor of New York (from January 1, 1929 to December 31, 1932) and was elected POTUS in the 1932 election. Kenner and the New York Bureau maintained a cordial working relationship with FDR before and after his ascension to POTUS. The New York Bureau mixed heavily in Democratic circles and always supported FDR. In fact, FDR provided the Advertising Federation of America a "MESSAGE FROM HIS EXCELLENCY" for its 25th anniversary supplement, *Truth in Advertising*, distributed at its respective convention held at Boston in 1936. The AFA was one of several successors to the famous Associated Advertising Clubs of America that launched the first vigilance committee that became the Better Business Bureau.

Governor Roosevelt nominated Democrat Edward Joseph Flynn (1891-1953), a Bronx attorney and close friend, as secretary of the state of New York who served in office from 1929 to 1939. Flynn offered bi-partisan support to the attorney general's office.

O'Sullivan acknowledged the failed attempt to license the Bureau and that the Bureau avoided licensing by electing Bennett. He wrote, "An attempt was made in 1930 to compel the manager of the Better Business Bureau of New York City to take out a detective license. The Bronx Chamber of Commerce informed the then Attorney General of New York State, Hon. Hamilton Ward, that the Better Business Bureau was a camouflaged detective agency, and should be compelled to take out a detective agency license." Ward agreed with the Bronx Chamber of Commerce and issued a legal decree stating, "My conclusion is that the Better Business Bureau of New York is carrying on the business of investigation for hire or reward, and should be licensed under Section 70 of the general business law." Additionally, he warned, "This brings up a grave situation, which is troubling me in various other connections; namely, the right of a membership corporation, as such, to receive substantial revenues and carry on what is in effect a business enterprise, even though all or almost all of such income is paid out in salaries ..." O'Sullivan agreed and poignantly stressed, "The legal point thus raised by Attorney General Ward is worthy of consideration by all who are convinced that the Better Business Bureaus have exceeded the powers of a private organization, abused their privileges, usurped the functions of detective agencies, and should either be licensed as such or put out of business." Accordingly, both Ward and O'Sullivan substantiated my contemporary complaint that the Better Business Bureau Foundation is a profit-oriented enterprise masquerading as a charitable non-profit.

On January 2, 1931, two days after Ward left office, Flynn reiterated the former attorney general's demand, "If it is your intention to continue operations, it will therefore be necessary to make an immediate application for a license as a private detective or investigator under the stature, for which purpose I enclose proper form. Unless you make such application within a reasonable time, it will be my duty to institute criminal prosecution against you for violation of such statute."

Bennett ultimately routed Ward's licensing decree. He took office five days after Ward's licensing demand. Attorney General Bennett was in office from January 1, 1931 to December 31, 1942. During his five terms, the licensing mandate disappeared. O'Sullivan reflected that "no license was taken out by the New York Bureau, and the question has never been settled in court."

Prior to Bennett's second re-election, Ward died of pneumonia on October 8, 1932, in Buffalo, New York, further preserving the Bureau's licensing cover-up and why it remains unregulated to present date. Ward made mentionable history with his valiant attempt to regulate the Bureau, but dirty politics prevailed.

O'Sullivan believed the Bureau manipulated their invincible network of intercity connections to nominate Bennett as attorney general for the state of New York. Just like organized crime, the Bureau was a secret high-profile insular society bound by the indisputable decrees of a ruling commission, which made it impossible to hold them accountable or convict them of blatant indiscretions.

Bennett's mission was to cement the Bureau's autonomy. He was the answer to the centurial question of why and how the Bureau escaped licensing required by every other consumer credit agency. O'Sullivan explained, "But a new Attorney General came into office in New York State almost immediately; and it is said this new official had formerly been employed in the office of a large contributor to the Bureau funds. Anyway, without notice to the Chamber of Commerce, he reversed the decision of his predecessor, no license was taken out by the New York Bureau, and the question has never been settled in court." All peripheral information and circumstances suggested that the "large contributor" to whom O'Sullivan was referring was relative to Bennett's former employment as "Democratic Corporate Counsel for the City of New York." Skullduggery ran deep during the Prohibition era; rigging elections, obstructing justice, and making underhanded deals were expected.

O'Sullivan questioned if the Bureau could qualify for a license, but that a license was necessary to enforce Bureau accountability and provide public recourse. He asked, "Could they measure up to the requirements specified by law, in order to obtain licenses to operate as private detectives?" As a reminder, O'Sullivan was a criminologist and a detective who worked with police departments all over the world; he was a CSI and investigated and documented crime scenes; and, he wrote *Crime Detection*, a criminology textbook. O'Sullivan raised a valid point regarding holding the Bureau accountable for its actions when rhetorically asking: "Could damages be collected from the Bureaus in cases where the innocent victims sought redress through the courts, and secured judgment? No, but a private detective, licensed and bonded, can be successfully sued on his bond for any malicious, willful, or wrongful act – and that fact probably explains the unwillingness of the Bureaus to admit that they are subject to license and bond as detective agencies."

In 1938, during his last term as attorney general, Bennett served as "a delegate to the New York State Constitutional Convention 4th District." And two years later, he was a delegate to the Democratic National Convention "in Chicago, Illinois from July 15 to July 18, 1940." In 1942, Bennett ran against Republican Thomas Edmund Dewey for governor of New York. Dewey had attained celebrity status after successfully convicting several crime bosses between 1935 and 1937 and easily won the election.

According to *Political Graveyard's* website, he was also a member of the "American Bar Association; American Legion; Phi Delta Phi; Catholic War Veterans; Veterans of Foreign Wars; Elks; [and] Eagles" and "served as Deputy

THE APO$TATE

Mayor of New York City, Corporation Counsel of the City of New York, Chief Justice of the Court of Special Sessions, and Chairman of the New York City Planning Commission."

On "October 4, 1967," Bennett died of a heart attack at his home in Brooklyn, New York; he was 73 years old. His interment was at Holy Cross Catholic Cemetery in Brooklyn (Find A Grave memorial 13982236). His gravesite was difficult to locate because he was interred under "Cogan," which was his wife's maiden name. She was 56 years old when death took her 12 years before him and interred next to her mother and father. He was placed by her side with his name added to their family tombstone.

CHAPTER **31**

THOMAS EDMUND DEWEY

Thomas Edmund Dewey
New York special prosecutor engaged crime trials in 1935 that jailed New York City's Mafia kingpins; 47th governor of New York.
Photo dated January 1, 1948.
Source: U.S. Library of Congress's Prints and Photographs division; [https://en.wikipedia.org/wiki/Thomas_E._Dewey]; public domain.

He was the special prosecutor who removed organized crime from the streets of New York City, but he is best known for the famous *Chicago Daily Tribune* "Dewey Defeats Truman" photograph held by President-elect Harry Truman after Truman won the 1948 election. He was a Republican abolitionist and introduced civil rights into the New York City workforce that spread nationwide. Additionally, he encouraged women in the legal field and hired Eunice Roberta Hunton Carter, an African American lawyer, to assist him with the Mafia crime trials. She spearheaded investigations and convinced prostitutes in the women's court to testify against "Lucky" Luciano. After his successful tenure as special prosecutor, he was appointed county district attorney of New York (1938-1941) and then elected governor of New York (1943-1954).

Thomas Edmund Dewey was born on March 24, 1902, above his grandfather's store in Owosso, Michigan. His father was George Martin Dewey, the publisher of the *Owosso Times*, and his mother was Annie Thomas. On June 16, 1928, he married Frances Eileen Hutt (1928-1970), a stage actress from Sherman, Texas. They had two sons, Thomas Edmund Dewey Jr. and John Martin Dewey. From 1939 to 1971, the family spent weekends at their farm named ""Dapplemere" located near the town of Pawling some 65 miles (105 km) north of New York City"; Dapplemere was a rural farm in the wealthy area of Quaker Hill.

Like his father, Dewey held an interest in the media. When he was 13 years old, he operated a "news agency" and "hired nine other boys to sell newspapers and magazines door to door." Then he was "editor-in-chief" of the "Central High School yearbook" called the *Spic*. He attended the University of Michigan and wrote for the school's student newspaper, *The Michigan Daily*, and graduated in 1923 with a bachelor's degree. Two years later, he earned a law degree from Columbia University and was "admitted to the New York bar" in 1926.

In his early years Dewey was a federal prosecutor and a private-practice lawyer. Then, according to the Shiawassee District Library, "From 1931 to 1933 he served as chief assistant to the U.S. attorney for the southern district of New York, and from 1933 to 1935 as special assistant to U.S. Attorney General Homer Stille Cummings."

Republican Dewey was appointed a special prosecutor for the state of New York in 1935 by Democratic Governor Herbert H. Lehman and served until 1937. He was specifically appointed to eliminate organized crime in New York City. Dewey's initial efforts focused on indicting kingpin Dutch Schultz until he was murdered by the Mafia Committee and Charles "Lucky" Luciano in 1935. All total he convicted "72 of the 73 people he brought to trial" including Luciano. On June 7, 1936, Luciano was sentenced to "30 to 50 years" for extortion and "62 counts of compulsory prostitution." Dewey had a reputation for impeccable honesty and became known as the "gang buster." He could not be bought like the others.

In 1936, Dewey assisted the conviction of Richard Whitney, "the former president of the New York Stock Exchange, for embezzlement." A year later, Dewey was elected "District Attorney of New York County (Manhattan)."

In 1938, Dewey unsuccessfully challenged incumbent Governor Lehman, who previously appointed him special prosecutor. He ran for governor again in 1942 and won against Democratic opponent former New York Attorney

General John J. Bennett Jr. who replaced Republican Hamilton Ward Jr. as attorney general in 1931. Karma repaid Bennett "for revers[ing] the decision of his predecessor."

Dewey was elected 47th Republican governor of New York, serving from 1943 to 1955, and continued his promotion of civil rights for African Americans. He enacted the historical Ives-Quinn anti-discrimination bill on March 12, 1945, that prohibited "racial and religious discrimination from employment." New York Public Radio's WNYC.org stated, "New York became the first state to enact legislation curtailing the practice of discriminating against job applicants and employees on the basis of race, religion, or creed."

The Ives-Quinn bill was signed into law 82 years after Republican President Lincoln enacted the historical Emancipation Proclamation on January 1, 1863, which applied only to "rebellious southern states" as a measure to cripple the Confederacy, and freed the slaves giving them the right to vote for the first time in history. Civilwar.org stated, "Five months after the Proclamation took effect; the War Department of the United States issued General Orders No. 143, establishing the United States Colored Troops (USCT). By the end of the war, over 200,000 African-Americans would serve in the Union army and navy." Dewey's actions highlighted the fact that the Republican Party has always promoted civil rights for African Americans.

Dewey ran as the Republican candidate against Democrat Franklin Roosevelt in 1944 and lost to Democrat Harry S. Truman in 1948, in "perhaps the greatest political upset in American history." Dewey was expected to win the latter election evidenced by the famous picture of President-elect Truman triumphantly holding the *Chicago Daily Tribune* with its headline mistakenly blaring: "DEWEY DEFEATS TRUMAN." Thereafter, Dewey retired on September 7, 1954, at the end of his gubernatorial term.

In 1955, he entered private law joining the firm of Ballantine, Bushby, Palmer & Wood. He became partner and the law firm "became Dewey, Ballantine, Bushby, Palmer & Wood." In 1990, the firm renamed itself Dewey Ballantine and later formed a limited liability partnership as Dewey Ballantine LLP. According to Wikipedia.org, "On October 1, 2007, Dewey Ballantine merged with LeBoeuf, Lamb, Greene & MacRae to form the combined firm of Dewey & LeBoeuf LLP. The combined firm had over 1,400 attorneys in 27 offices around the world" and was located in "Midtown Manhattan." Dewey & LeBoeuf went bankrupt in 2012 and was considered "one of the biggest collapses of a law firm in the nation's history." The firm's founding predecessor, "Root, Clark & Bird," established in 1909, prospered during the Depression by concentrating on bankruptcies.

In 1968, President Richard Nixon offered Dewey positions as chief justice of the United States and/or secretary of state, but he declined both. Most likely his refusal of further government service was due to his wife's illness and six-year battle with breast cancer, which she succumbed in the summer of 1970. Later that same year, Dewey began a serious relationship with actress and singer Kitty Carlisle (1910-2007).

Destiny intervened on March 16, 1971. At the age of 66, Dewey died from a "massive heart attack" following a round of golf while vacationing in Miami, Florida. President Richard Nixon and former Vice President Hubert Humphrey attended his funeral in Pawling, New York.

CHAPTER **32**

EUNICE ROBERTA HUNTON CARTER

Eunice Roberta Hunton Carter
Member of Dewey's Famous "Twenty Against The Underworld";
among first Black women lawyers to champion equal rights in workforce.
Photo dated about 1935.
Source: *National Archives* [http://onehistory.org/faceb.htm];
public domain.

President Theodore Roosevelt was known as the "trust buster" and she was known as the "mob buster." She was one of New York's most celebrated first female African American attorneys. Dewey's prosecutorial success against mobster Salvatore Charles "Lucky" Luciano (1897-1962), head of the Genovese crime family, was largely credited to her. In return, Dewey supported her efforts to establish the first workplace civil rights and equal opportunity laws. African

THE APO$TATE

Americans lost their government support when President Abraham Lincoln was assassinated on April 14, 1865, at the end of the Civil War. As a result, his Emancipation Proclamation proved a dismal failure during the Reconstruction Era. A post-war backlash of southern extremism, retaliation, and discrimination emerged and was fueled by the "Ku Klux Klan" that was founded by six former Confederate soldiers on December 24, 1865.

Eunice Roberta Hunton Carter was born on July 16, 1899, in Atlanta, Georgia. In 1906, after the Race Riot, the family moved to Brooklyn, New York. Her parents were progressive educators and social reformation activists "William Alphaeus, Sr. and Addie Waite Hunton." Her father was "founder of the black division of the Y.M.C.A." And, her mother was a renowned activist for the National Association for the Advancement of Colored People (NAACP) and Y.M.C.A.; she visited France during WWI to monitor Black servicemen. Her brother was author and social activist W. Alphaeus Hunton Jr. who worked with the Council on African Affairs. In 1924, she married dentist Lisle Carter and they begot son Lisle Carter Jr.; the family resided in Harlem.

Carter inherited and built on her parents' legacies that underpinned African American history. She attended Smith College in Northampton, Massachusetts, and "graduated cum laude with both undergraduate and graduate degrees," in 1921. While pursuing her master's degree at Smith College, she was befriended by Republican Massachusetts' Governor Calvin Coolidge, later elected 30th POTUS from 1923-1929, which cemented her political future. During the 1920s, she attended the Pan-African Congress and worked with the United Nations. She was the first African American woman to earn a law degree at Fordham University Law School, a Catholic Jesuit University in New York City. In 1934, she was the first African American woman to pass the New York State Bar Exam. That same year, she was "nominated by the Republican Party to represent New York's 19th District in the State Assembly." Then, in 1935, following the Harlem Race Riot, she was appointed by New York Mayor LaGuardia as "secretary on the Committee on Conditions in Harlem." But her life and career changed forever when she prosecuted prostitution cases for New York City's "Women's Court."

Carter instigated what has been described as the "largest prosecution of organized crime in U.S. history." Her profound legal efforts contributed to purging gangland activity in New York and provided precedence for future generations of prosecutors against organized crime. She faced enormous challenges having to prove large-scale racketeering before the "Racketeer Influenced and Corrupt Organizations (RICO) Act" existed. The law was later enacted on October 15, 1970, and immortalized in February 1985 during the renowned "Mafia Commission Trial" between February 25, 1985 and November 19, 1986; trial was led by New York City's esteemed Mayor Rudolph ("Rudy") William Louis

Giuliani. At the time, Giuliani was "U.S. Attorney for the Southern District of New York" and a federal prosecutor. He indicted 11 Mafia kingpins from five New York crime families and ultimately sentenced eight on January 13, 1987.

She showed Dewey how to strategize the case against Luciano. As a young female attorney from Atlanta, Georgia, she was relegated to New York's "Women's Court" that processed prostitution cases. She determined alarming peculiarities; that as soon as streetwalkers were brought in, they were let go. Carter discovered a connection with the Mob when realizing all the prostitution cases involved the same "lawyers, bondsmen and alibis." *Time magazine* reported, "As it turns out, the investigation revealed that mob figures were providing these services to the prostitutes in exchange for 50 percent of their take, which brought in millions for the underworld."

Carter approached Dewey with her findings that indicated organized crime's prostitution-related connections within the New York judicial system. Dewey consequently brought her into his prosecutorial team that he coined, "Twenty Against The Underworld." She convinced Dewey to personally prosecute the trial instead of her because he was nationally famous from the Dutch Schultz trials and his headlining presence would connect organized crime to Luciano.

After orchestrating a raid on "200 brothels" in New York City, Carter applied her skills and notoriety earned in Women's Court. She persuaded 68 of the arrested "125 prostitutes, madams and bookers" to testify against Luciano who was convicted of "compulsory prostitution" and received a prison term of 30 to 50 years. Her leading witness, Cokey-Flo Brown, made the prosecution's case when she stated Luciano intended to "organize cathouses just like the A&P [supermarket chain]."

In 1937, Carter was appointed by Dewey, then district attorney, as "head of the D.A.'s Special Sessions Bureau." The following year, Dewey placed her in charge of "the Abandonment Bureau of Women's Courts" to become the first African American assistant district attorney of New York. Carter "served as Assistant District Attorney of New York County for ten years." She returned to private legal practice in 1945. Carter continued to participate as an advocate for women on the home front while expanding into international affairs. In 1947, she attended "the first International Assembly on Women in Paris" and was "a consultant to the Economic and Social Council of the United Nations' International Council of Women." In 1955, she was "elected to chair the International Conference of Non-Governmental Organizations." Two years later, she attended the United Nation's "Commission On the Status of Women" held in Geneva, Switzerland, and was "elected 'Chairman' of the Conference of International Organizations in Consultative Status with the United Nations."

She avoided the limelight that followed the Dewey crime trials and pursued her parents' activist footsteps. Carter participated in the NAACP, National

Urban League, the Young Women's Christian League (Y.W.C.A.), and "served as legal advisor to the National Council of Negro Women and field representative for the Manhattan Office of Civilian Defense." She was a lifetime humanitarian and served as an outstanding role model for African Americans and all women. Her passion, wisdom, and strength enriched everyone in her presence.

Yale law professor Stephen L. Carter called his grandmother "Nana in New York" because New York City was her beloved home. He remembered, "She had shelves and shelves of books ... And she had a twinkling smile." On January 25, 1970, at the age of 70, Eunice Roberta Huntington Carter passed into the annals of celebrated history.

CHAPTER **33**

DUTCH SCHULTZ

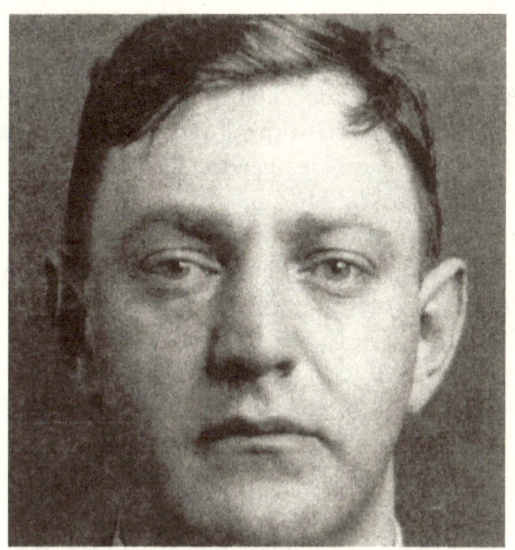

Arthur Simon Flegenheimer (Dutch Schultz)
American mobster contributed to Dewey crime trials.
Photo: June 18, 1931 police mugshot.
Source: File: Schultz dutch mug.jpg; Wikipedia Commons; [https://en.wikipedia.org/wiki/Dutch_Schultz#/media/File:Schultz_dutch_mug.jpg]; public domain.

He was one of New York City's most notorious gangsters ramrodding organized crime in the 1920s and 1930s. Bootlegging and the "Italian lottery" numbers racket were his specialties. Schultz was acquitted twice on tax evasion charges. After the second trial, New York Mayor LaGuardia exiled him from New York City. In the interim, Schultz determined to kill Special Agent Thomas Edmund Dewey to end legal harassment once and for all, but the Mafia Commission intervened and killed Schultz to save Dewey and keep the peace.

German Jewish mobster Arthur Simon Flegenheimer was born August 6, 1902, in the Bronx, New York City. His parents were Herman and Emma (Neu)

THE APO$TATE

Flegenheimer. His wife's name was A. Martha Geiss (1895-1937), and their two children were Anne Davis Flegenheimer and John David Flegenheimer.

It was questionable whether his father abandoned the family or died, as was reported in the 1910 U.S. Census. A fatherless Flegenheimer dropped out of the eighth grade to support the family and worked odd jobs as "as a feeder and pressman for the Clark Loose Leaf Company, Caxton Press, American Express, and Schultz Trucking in the Bronx." From those jobs he moved into burglary and was caught and sentenced to prison on Blackwell's Island (Roosevelt Island). After being paroled on December 8, 1920, he returned to Schultz Trucking and began transporting hard liquor from Canada. The owner's youngest son's nickname was "Dutch" and Flegenheimer latched onto the name calling himself "Dutch Schultz." During one of the Canadian deliveries, Schultz shot and killed his first victim. An argument ensued, and he quit the trucking company.

Schultz later became partners with gangster Joey Noe at the "Hub Social Club" speakeasy in the Bronx. Noe operated the only non-Italian gang in the city and ran beer and rum to clubs In Upper West Side Manhattan. Schultz kept an apartment on 5th Avenue and became a local celebrity. His multimillion-dollar empire was maintained through political control and bribing police officials; paid voters were trucked in during elections to assure that accommodating politicians remained in office. On October 16, 1928, Noe was shot several times and died November 21, 1928. Schultz blamed "Legs" Diamond who was later shot five times and survived. In 1931, Legs was murdered by either police or Irish mobsters.

After Prohibition flat-lined his bootlegging operations, Schultz moved into illegal gambling and slots machines. He established the Metropolitan Restaurant & Cafeteria Owners Association and consolidated all the local unions. The association was supported by "tributes" and "fees" extorted from restaurant owners who, if they refused, would be beaten and their restaurants attacked with smoke bombs. He started a lottery in Harlem, which was "Legs" Diamond's territory and sparked a turf war. The lottery became hugely successful. It was a rigged numbers' racket like "Pick 3" with the winning ticket paying "600 to 1." He made two million a year and never paid taxes. By 1932, Schultz was considered the richest "ganglord" in New York City until special prosecutor Dewey arrived in 1935.

Dewey closed in on Schultz's numbers' racket indicting him twice for tax evasion using the same approach that convicted Al Capone (1899-1947) for tax evasion in 1931. A hung jury released Schultz in the first trial. In late 1935, Schultz was acquitted in a second trial that had changed venue to Malone, a small town in upstate New York. Prior to trial, Schultz spread money around while hobnobbing with the townspeople to buy their votes. Mayor LaGuardia was incensed and ordered Schultz "arrested on sight" if he entered New York City.

DUTCH SCHULTZ

Consequently, Schultz relocated his operations to New Jersey. Legal expenses had weakened his business and that of his "associates" including Luciano. Schultz feared continued harassment from Dewey so he approached "The Commission," headed by Luciano, requesting approval to kill Dewey. Before the meeting, Schultz converted to Catholicism to impress Luciano, a Catholic. Unbeknownst to Schultz, The Commission determined he was a loose cannon and planned to take over his numbers' racket. Luciano had no intentions of killing Dewey, which he felt would bring the wrath of New York City down on the Mob. When The Commission refused to order a hit on Dewey, Schultz went behind their backs to contract his assassination. Wayward word got back to Luciano.

On October 23, 1935, at 10:15 a.m., assassin Charles Workman gunned down Schultz and his crew, including his accountant, henchman and bodyguard, while dining at the Palace Chophouse on 12 East Park Street in Newark, New Jersey. Two shots were fired at Schultz; one bullet hit him below the heart and "ricocheted" throughout his stomach until exiting his lower back. Workman used "rust-covered" bullets with intent to cause blood poisoning and guarantee a kill-shot one way or the other. Schultz and the others were transferred to a hospital where they all later died. Workman was convicted of Schultz's murder and sentenced to 23 years in "Sing Sing Correctional Facility" located in Ossining, 30 miles north of New York City.

Schultz died on October 24, 1935; he was 34 years old. Cause of death was attributed to peritonitis, an infection in the lining of the stomach that when reaching the bloodstream causes organ failure and death. In other words, Schultz was whacked by a rusty bullet. Because of his conversion to Catholicism, albeit for murderous intentions, he received "Last Rites" before his death. Schultz was buried at the Roman Catholic cemetery of "Gate of Heaven" located in Hawthorne, New York, 25 miles north of New York City. It was the Mafia way that even if a gangster did not live a righteous life, relatives laid their tarnished souls to rest in hallowed ground hoping for respective absolution and eternal salvation.

PART THREE

CHAPTER **34**

WORLD WAR II

German dictator Adolf Hitler (1889-1945(?)) rose from the unsettled ashes of WWI to spark WWII. He wanted Poland and made an agreement with Russian dictator Joseph Stalin (1878-1953), leader of the Union of Soviet Socialist Republics (USSR) from 1929 to 1953, to solidify Russian allegiance and included "secret protocols" outlining Polish spoils of war. The German-Soviet Nonaggression Pact (also Hitler-Stalin Pact), dated August 23, 1939, was signed by Nazi Foreign Minister Joachim von Ribbentrop and Soviet Foreign Minister Vyacheslav Mikhaylovich Molotov "in the presence of Stalin, in Moscow." Germany would take the "western third of the country" with the USSR taking the "eastern two-thirds." On August 31, 1939, Germany attacked Poland. Consequently, "Great Britain and France declared war on Germany on September 3, 1939." As war progressed, Hitler wanted Romania's oil fields that were being threatened by Stalin. So, on June 22, 1941, Hitler ended the German-Soviet Nonaggression Pac by attacking the USSR in "Operation Fritz," which Hitler tagged "Operation Barbarrosa" in honor of "Holy Roman emperor Frederick Barbarrosa (reigned 1152-90), who sought to establish German predominance in Europe." Stalin's Red Army later defeated Hitler in the Battle of Stalingrad "from August 1942 to February 1943." Then the United States entered WWII: on December 7, 1941, Japan declared war on the U.S.; on December 8, 1941, the U.S. declared war on Japan; on December 11, 1941, Germany declared war on the U.S.; and, also December 11, 1941, the U.S. declared war on Germany. Ultimately, on May 7, 1945, Nazi Germany surrendered to allied forces in Reims, France, and WWII concluded on September 2, 1945, aboard the USS *Missouri* battleship docked in Tokyo Bay. Collective casualties totaled between "40,000,000 and 50,000,000 deaths," including Holocaust victims, making it "the bloodiest conflict, as well as the largest war, in history."

THE APO$TATE

The first half of the 1900s was a roller coaster ride from one cataclysmic event to the other while highlighting the importance of the advertising industry as a regulatory social media. America suffered through WWI (1914-1918), the "forgotten" Depression (1920-1921), the 18th Amendment and Prohibition (1917-1933), the Stock Market Crash (October 29, 1929), the Great Depression (1929-1939), and WWII (1939-1945).

In fact, WWII provided the perfect opportunity for the Bureau to redeem its disgraced reputation and restore financial stability. FDR inducted the Bureau into the Deep State while the advertising industry covered Main Street. Accordingly, former California Bureau President Wansley quoted Muriel Tsvetkoff, the manager of the San Francisco Bureau in 1940: "No government agency will ever seriously curtail our work ... The reason: consumers will come to the Bureau to complain, or for information in preference to consulting government or prosecuting agencies."

The United States did not enter the war until Pearl Harbor, but FDR assisted allies wherever possible. On December 9, 1940, England's Winston Churchill approached FDR for financial aid above and beyond the "cash and carry" rules mandated by the Neutrality Acts of 1935, 1936, 1937, and 1939. FDR responded via a "Fireside Chat" and warned, "If Great Britain goes down ... the Axis powers will control the continents of Europe, Asia, Africa, Australasia, and the high seas – and they will be in a position to bring enormous military and naval resources against this hemisphere. It is no exaggeration to say that all of us, in all the Americas, would be living at the point of a gun ... We must be the great arsenal of democracy."

FDR presented and pushed through Congress "the Lend-Lease Act" that he signed into law on March 11, 1941. The act, according to History.co.uk, "[P]ermitted the lending, leasing, selling, or bartering of arms, ammunition and food to "any country whose defense the President deems vital to the defense of the US"." In essence, the United States worked the sidelines of war as a non-belligerent and supplied Allies materials and armaments without requiring immediate payment.

Research suggested that FDR brought the Better Business Bureau into the Deep State after Pearl Harbor as part of the War Powers Act of 1941. The Japanese attack "was the result of the greatest intelligence failure in American or perhaps all military history." The government promoted the Bureau's public mission as regulating Liberty Bond fraud when its covert mission was monitoring Japanese movement within the United States.

The Deep State began during the Reconstruction years after the Civil War. The "Office of Naval Intelligence (ONI)" was established in 1882; the "Federal Bureau of Intelligence (FBI)" in 1908; and the Army's "Military Intelligence Division (MID)" from May 1917 to March 1942. FDR expanded IC operations:

he established the office of the "Coordinator of Information (COI)" on July 11, 1941; weaponized the Bureau's domestic reporting services after Pearl Harbor under the "First War Powers Act" enacted on December 18, 1941; expanded the Bureau's intelligence monitoring under the "Second War Powers Act" passed on March 27, 1942; and replaced the COI with the "Office of Strategic Services (OSS)" on June 13, 1942. After FDR's death on April 12, 1945, President Truman continued to expand the IC: he issued "Executive Order 9621" to abolish the OSS on September 20, 1945; launched the "Strategic Services Unit (SSU)" on October 1, 1945; established the "Central Intelligence Group (CIG)" on January 22, 1946; and created the "Central Intelligence Agency (CIA)" on September 18, 1947.

Senator Harry Truman was in charge of a senatorial committee after Pearl Harbor that was exploring the possibility of regulating the advertising industry as part of the nation's "wartime economy." Federal propaganda was only partially true; in reality, FDR wanted another IC agency to monitor Japanese movement within the United States. He ultimately chose the Bureau because of its means-tested self-regulatory reporting services and strategic positioning in major cities throughout the United States. Furthermore, Kenner and the New York Bureau held an impregnable link with FDR that facilitated the Bureau's Deep State induction as an underground reporting agency. Thereafter, Senator Truman became FDR's vice president in 1944, and his affiliation with the Bureau treaded footprints for his subsequent presidential establishment of the CIA through the National Security Act of 1947.

Wansley wrote, "After hearing testimony on the effective self-regulatory work being done by the advertising industry and the Bureaus, the committee recommended that no emergency regulation of advertising be undertaken. That recommendation was followed by Congress." Otherwise, the Bureau would have been ruinously undermined if the U.S. had established a national reporting agency. As a result, the advertising industry established a symbiotic relationship with the U.S. War Department providing talent, expertise, and ad space that continues today.

According to my research, the Bureau operated within FDR's Deep State from 1941 to 1945; from the date of the First War Powers Act to the date when the Supreme Court ruled Japanese internment was unconstitutional in *Endo v. the United States*, on December 18, 1944; all internment camps were closed by March 1946. Thereafter, in 1976, President Gerald Ford repealed FDR's E.O. 9066. And, in 1988, Congress enacted the Civil Liberties Act "awarding $20,000 each to over 80,000 Japanese Americans as reparations for their treatment." Today, liberal scholars hide the reason why FDR took drastic action against Japanese Americans to prevent internal sabotage from discovered fifth-column germ warfare treachery. FDR was proven right by the deadly 2020 pandemic that was caused by the highly contagious COVID-19 coronavirus that allegedly originated from the Chinese Communist Party's Biosafety Level 4 (BSL-4) biolab in Wuhan.

U.S. intelligence failed to report Pearl Harbor. Consequently, FDR sought immediate militarized surveillance services that the Bureau provided through local offices dispersed in major cities across the nation. The First War Powers Act was enacted on December 18, 1941, and expanded American military and surveillance that included the Bureau. On February 19, 1942, FDR signed "Executive Order 9066" to prevent espionage and relocated about 117,000 Americans with Japanese ancestry, to "facilities in Montana, New Mexico, and North Dakota." Canada and Mexico followed suit. In March 1942, the civilian-run War Relocation Authority was established under the U.S. Department of Agriculture. Then, on March 29, 1942, the Second War Powers Act was passed to strengthen the presidency, allow acquisition "of land for military or naval purposes," and suspend parts of the Hatch Act of 1939 that restricted political activity by federal officials.

The U.S. government formed the Defense Plant Corporation (DPC) in 1940 that cobbled business, finance and advertising. According to Bloomberg View, "Government-financed capital spending accounted for only 5 percent of the annual U.S. investment in industrial capital in 1940; by 1943, the government accounted for 67 percent of U.S. capital investment." As a result, the economy improved through the creation of new innovative products and established the aerospace industry. The DPC was run by a committee that included William Knudsen, president of General Motors Company; Donald Nelson, vice president of Sears, Roebuck & Company; and Ralph Budd, president of Chicago, Burlington and Quincy Railroad.

Many products were unavailable during WWII, but businesses continued advertising their wares to maintain their corporate presence under an aegis of patriotism. *National Geographic* reported, "According to Inger Stole, a communications professor at the University of Illinois at Urbana-Champaign, companies advertised these products to "keep their brand names in the public consciousness. They knew that once the war was over, it was very, very important that the public [not forget] the brand names"."

WWII forced the advertising industry closer to the federal government resulting in the "War Advertising Council" to assist FDR. In February 1942, the War Council incorporated in New York and developed public service advertisements ("PSAs") for enlistment, sale of war bonds, and conservation. In particular, two famous PSA's were introduced: "Loose Lips Sink Ships," from 1942 to 1945, which supported sale of war bonds; and, Smokey the Bear's famous warning, "Only You Can Prevent Forest Fires," from 1944 to present, which originated from the fear that the Japanese might bomb the West Coast

WORLD WAR II

and create forest fires (today's version is "Get Your Smokey On"). According to author Stephen Fox, "Ultimately, the industry donated about a billion dollars' worth of space and time to the war effort, and many conventional product ads included war messages, some of them dubious assertions of how the product was helping win the war."

FDR requested that the War Advertising Council continue its services during peacetime. The War Advertising Council renamed itself the Advertising Council and continued ad campaigns that included PSAs for the American Red Cross (1945-1996), Polio (1958-1961), "Keep America Beautiful" (1961-1983), Peace Corps (1961-1991), United Negro Fund "A mind is a terrible thing to waste" (1972-present), "Take a bite out of Crime" (created in 1978-present), "Friends Don't Let Friends Drive Drunk" (1983-present), "Vince and Larry, the Crash Test Dummies" (1985-present), "AIDS Prevention" (1988-1990), "Domestic Violence" (1994-present), "I am an American" resulting from September 11, 2001 terrorist attacks (2001-present), "Autism Awareness" (2006 to present), and "Whether you have COVID-19 or not, stay home!" (March 2020).

Today the Advertising Council is known as the Ad Council. Its website message advises, "The Ad Council marshals volunteer talent from the advertising and communications industries, the facilities of the media, and the resources of the business and non-profit communities to create awareness, foster understanding and motivate action."

CHAPTER 35

BUREAU LAWSUITS

A spontaneous combustion of complaints and lawsuits were lobbed at the Bureau following the introduction of two disingenuous pay-for-play merit programs. CBBB launched the awards in 2000 and the ratings system in 2009. Both programs were interlinked marketing gimmicks that rode the gilded wings of the Bureau's venerable reputation. Deception was hidden behind the bellwether of truth's scam-buster façade. The organization reached a sink-or-swim turning point and chose to transform its floundering archaic brick-and-mortar operations into a lucrative cost-effective dazzling monopolizing state-of-the-art smoke-and-mirrors' online business surveillance system. A virtual portal dramatically slashed operational expenses; offered unlimited financial opportunity and universal consumer trade; incorporated a centurial history of means-tested advertising expertise; guaranteed despotic control of the marketplace; and commercialized sanctimonious hocus pocus to dodge a pesky oath to truth in advertising. The Bureau literally banked on covert keyboard operations that lionized paper merit for money-grubbing pawns at the mystical speed of digital touch.

I can attest to the Bureau's penchant for bully tactics and controlling the courts as highlighted by O'Sullivan in *Rackets*. In 1929, O'Sullivan documented the Manhattan Board of Commerce's complaint against the NYSE and the New York Bureau for manipulating the court system. In fact, the Manhattan Board specifically asked Whitney, "Did Mr. Kenner further promise you that the entire Bureau system would be used to clog up the courts all over the United States with petty larceny stock promotion cases, so that these courts would not have sufficient legal machinery left with which to regulate manipulations of the Exchange?"

Consumers know little about the Bureau except for brainwashed word-of-mouth hearsay passed to them from previous generations. Lack of information was deliberate and created whitewashing flexibility to promote modern initiatives that marketed a pristine brand image endorsing idealistic awards and rating programs. Research proved that mounds of dirt were swept under the rug. The twenty-first-century Bureau feverishly scrubbed shocking criminal proclivities exposed by O'Sullivan. Moreover, contemporary authors' historical chicken scratch repeats inaccuracies and slants narrative to aggrandize the Bureau. Accordingly, I believe that O'Sullivan traveled time to find me and breathed life into our joint mission to educate consumers and stop the Bureau. The fact that I fell into his same conundrum and discovered his "out of publication" book is beyond the pale. I do not believe in coincidences and feel that I was chosen to finish what he began. The Bureau rose from phenomenal advertising history that aligned with unparalleled American history, yet its brick-and-mortar offices and websites suspiciously omit all references to the nonprofit's founders and horse-and-buggy days.

The advertising industry's centurial Truth in Advertising Movement experienced a rebirth with the Bureau's virtual makeover. Only this time, the Bureau was the offender, not the enforcer. Furthermore, the advertising industry was protected by me and others launching individual crusades to hold the Bureau accountable for promoting deceptive trade that betrayed its birth mission of truth.

Several lawsuits have knocked Bureau doors, but none of them knew the likes of what I experienced during what was supposed to be a private employment trial. The Houston Bureau morphed into a skulking predator working the sidelines of my civil lawsuit and unlawfully forced its way into court proceedings in a staged effort to destroy me and my evidence against its *Awards for Excellence*. The hypocritical Houston Bureau previously convoluted and dismissed my complaint of awards fraud against their wealthy member under counterfeit excuse that its corporate policy prohibited involvement in "employer/employee" civil matters. Thereafter, the Bureau's wishy-washy de facto policies, double standards, and unconstitutional overreach violated my First Amendment right of free speech and 14th Amendment rights of due process and equal protection of law.

Irrefutable records will prove that the Bureau aggressively protected and promoted my former employer, an incorrigible liar and thief, as a distinguished award-winning member while defiantly continuing a fake awards program that scammed millions of consumers every year. In fact, the two shylocks joined forces to silence me. They feared my award complaints would go public with the potential to drag them both down and expose the Bureau's Unholy Grail as a specious cash cow that milks a venerable legacy and thrives on virtual exaggeration.

The Pinnacle represented the Bureau's ultimate endorsement and guarantee of unsurpassed excellence. To the contrary, the Pinnacle's crystal pyramid is a sensational hoax with no means for evaluation to substantiate its Herculean glamorous prestigious incomparable grandiose revered superstar sovereignty.

Accordingly, the Houston Bureau, CBBB, and Houston Foundation should be investigated and prosecuted for defrauding the public! Unfortunately, the state and federal agencies responsible for marshalling deceptive trade are crony affiliates of the Deep State Better Business Bureau.

I became a whistleblower to stop massive consumer fraud, but I had no idea of the extent of gilded deception and seditious deep pockets. During the interlude between reporting awards fraud in 2008 and publishing *The Apostate* in 2020, I was shocked to learn that several lawsuits and scandalous exposés empowered the Bureau and embedded its bogus programs as society's unequivocal barometers to gauge quality. Globalist judicial discretion imposed the First Amendment's immunity and repurposed law to marginalize the Bureau's restraint of trade, deceptive trade practice, and defamation. The BBB had become indomitable.

Several yesteryear tussles initially tugged the Bureau's stranglehold and reminded invaluable insight overlooked by recent lawsuits. Modern legalese should pay attention to dusty paged achievements. Just because voices were silenced does not mean respective legacies are meaningless. Unfortunately, the Bureau's early 1900's landmark lawsuits were ignored and globalist activist judges have since hijacked and corrupted the modern court system.

The Bureau aggressively exploited globalist court rulings to immunize its specious programs. Our protracted employment lawsuit offered exceptional insight giving me a front row seat to the overriding buffoonery of a lying conniving overreaching colluding malfeasant micro-manipulating bully that an earlier century would have indicted for defamation and deceptive trade practice. During the course of our lawsuits, the Bureau inoculated itself through a globalist court verdict, which interwove free speech with defamation to legitimize bias baseless rating scores. And convoluted consequences now threaten to consecrate misleading meritless awards.

O'Sullivan described several complaints, scandals, and lawsuits that accused the Bureau of deceptive trade, defamation, securities fraud, and racketeering. He was an outspoken critic because the Chicago Bureau unmercifully harassed him and his publishing business; angry requital drove him to publish *Rackets*. His experience as a C.S.I. detective was evident in his exceptionally thorough narratives that cited various newspaper articles, incidents, and authorities. The Bureau's silence after *Rackets* was deafening considering O'Sullivan's comments were published at the start of the Pecora Commission in 1933 and prior to Dewey's organized-crime trials that began in 1935. I believe that Dewey would have also prosecuted the Bureau, but he declined as a favor to golden coattails and political puppet strings attached to FDR.

A review of several lawsuits will explain the gravity of the Bureau's interference in my employment trial. Besides O'Sullivan, I was not the only victim with a torch target on my back. There were several significant lawsuits involving the Bureau that occurred over the past century. The earliest court battles denounced the Bureau, but the BBB's latest buzz built its empire. The *Somber Thirties* decade was desperate, angry, and punitive. Wall Street was spanked. And Dewey jailed organized crime bosses while the disgraced New York Bureau hid behind a gilded membership and FDR's friendship. It was a tumultuous era of prostitution, speakeasies, bootlegging, rackets, gambling, and machine-gun mayhem, which influenced the sinister metamorphosis of the sanctimonious Bureau.

On January 12, 1928, the *New York Herald Tribune* published the article, "Better Business Bureau Head Under Bail in Suit." Storyline reported that, on January 11, 1928, H. J. Kenner, general manager of the New York Bureau, was arrested for defamation and released after posting a $5,000 bond. Kenner was charged with defaming the Iroquois Trust Company of Illinois; said entity filed a lawsuit alleging that "it was libeled in a "false and malicious"" article prepared by Kenner that was delivered to newspapers on December 28, 1927. In fact, Kenner did write and distribute a report that described New York Attorney General Albert E. Ottinger (1878-1938), in office "from 1925 to 1928," as having "obtained a temporary injunction against the sale in New York of shares and trusts in the Iroquois Trust Company and the projected Iroquois Trust National Bank of New York." The lawsuit requested $1,300,000 in damages and was signed by John C. Gray, president of Iroquois Trust; Wilson H. Mears, manager of stock sales Iroquois Trust; and Harrison M. Parker, advertising and sales manager of Iroquois Trust. No further information was located regarding outcome.

In 1929, the Service Purchasing Company sued the St. Louis Bureau for harassment against "salary buyers." A David vs. Goliath battle ensued pitting the Bureau's monopoly of newly enlisted big-lender members demanding higher interest rates against independent lenders charging lesser more cost-effective rates. The lawsuit highlighted Missouri's tumultuous history involving small loans that contended with the Bureau's aggressive overreach into consumer financing.

In retrospect, a series of Missouri lender laws dating to 1891 reflected low interest rates fluctuating between 1% and 2% per month and were enacted to regulate racketeering loan sharks. The state's nineteenth-century lending system utilized chattel mortgages, a vestige of early English law, which borrowed on a basis of secured interest or collateral. In 1891, Missouri passed its first small loan law that "declared invalid any chattel mortgage given to secure a usurious loan." The law was enacted to remedy "the existence of a racket in small chattel mortgages" that confused bona fide purchasers with "straw parties" representing lenders. The landmark lawsuit, *Smith v. Mohr* (64 Mo. App. 39, 1895), exposed illicit lending and racketeering patterns: "The defendant paid $50 for a $125 chattel loan for 10 months and the evidence showed the alleged bona fide purchaser was really a straw party for the plaintiff." Six years later, the 1897 act was

THE APO$TATE

introduced and "made it a crime to charge more than 1 per cent per month on loans of $500 and less secured by chattel mortgage on household goods."

Thereafter, the loan industry was reshaped by the 1899 and 1927 Small Loan Acts. A few illicit lenders began repackaging chattel mortgage loans into high interest "wage assignments" using employment as security for loans, now referred to as "pay day loans." The 1891 and 1897 acts encouraged low monthly interest rates, but the 1899 act made it a crime "to charge more than 2% per month." Then the Bureau launched its "Before You Invest, Investigate" securities program and its powerful lobby manipulated interest rates. Lenders (members of the Bureau) complained that low interest impaired business and the 1927 Small Loan Act was enacted to raise the interest ceiling to 3½% per month or 42% annually. Then on, ever-changing laws and rates benefited business over borrowers.

The Russell Sage Foundation, a New York philanthropic foundation established in 1907, influenced enactment of the Small Loan Act of 1927, which took effect on July 1, 1927. Participating venders were called "42 Per Cent Lenders." The same year, after passage of the act, Frank Brooks Hubachek, replaced his father, Frank R. Hubachek, as general counsel for Household Finance Corporation (HFC), from 1927 to 1967. The elder Hubachek, while representing HFC, worked with the Russell Sage Foundation to draft the Small Loan Act. HFC was among the 42 Per Cent Lenders seeking Bureau membership as an underground movement to enforce higher rates offered by the new law.

Seventeen 42 Per Cent Lenders joined the St. Louis Bureau in an alleged attempt to monopolize the loan market and disparage smaller independent lenders from undercutting the Small Loan Act's maximum 3½% monthly rate. The backstory revealed that around "May 1928," Charles R. Napier, a prominent Chicago lawyer representing the American Industrial Lenders' Association and the Russell Sage Foundation, approached Harry W. Riehl, general manager of the St. Louis Bureau, to fight competition from more cost-effective independent "money-lending institutions" known as "salary-buyers." The independents were represented by Charles M. Hay, attorney for the Missouri-Kansas-Texas Railway Clerks Association. Hay supported the Brogan Bill, which, at the time, was circulating in "Senate Committee hearings." The bill promised to reduce the Small Loan Act's high 42% annual ceiling and 3½% monthly interest rates to a lesser borrower-friendly 18% annual and 1% monthly charges.

Then the American Industrial Lenders' Association paid the St. Louis Bureau a down payment of $2500 (with more "promised") to create trouble for the salary-buyers "who were hauled into court and harassed in every possible way." Thereafter, the Service Purchasing Company, one of the disparaged independent salary-buyers, alleged a conspiracy and sued Riehl and the St. Louis Bureau for defamation. On February 22, 1929, the *St. Louis Globe-Democrat* ran two conjoined articles, "42 percent Lenders Hold Membership in Business Bureau," and, "Attorney of Lenders Defends 42 Per Cent Small Loan Charge," which exposed the American Industrial Lenders' Association's previously undisclosed relationship with the Bureau. Bad publicity mounted and a few weeks later, on March 30, 1929, the Bureau settled the lawsuit out of court paying "$20,000.00" in damages. Additionally, the disgraced St. Louis Bureau lost "more than one-third" of its members.

Missouri attorney Clark G. Hardeman also submitted a scathing accusatory letter to the St. Louis Bureau. Hardeman pursued the Bureau's complicit money trail: "I charge that you did these acts because you were paid money by members of the Missouri Industrial Lenders' Association. Where did the $71,068.41 that you raised and collected in 1930 go? The public will be very much interested in knowing into whose pockets those thousands went."

On June 9, 1930, the *St. Louis Post Dispatch* published notice of legal action taken against several Bureaus for restraint of trade: "A total of fifty-eight suits have been filed against twenty-four Better Business Bureaus." Damages were "estimated to amount in the aggregate to $15,000,000." Bureau members were held liable with an individual penalty fee assessed at "$240,000.00." O'Sullivan further explained that "many of the members ... were unable to pay their share ... [and] in several instances, the homes and life savings were taken from them to satisfy the judgment."

Charges were filed on the legal authority of *Deitrich Loewe et al. v. Martin Lawlor et al.*, also known as the "Danbury Hatters Case." The U.S. Supreme Court rendered two decisions: *Loewe v. Lawlor* (208 U.S. 274) "on February 3, 1908"; and *Lawlor v. Loewe* (235 U.S. 522) "on January 5, 1915"; both decisions ruled violation of Section 7 of the Sherman Anti-Trust Act of July 2, 1890. Opinion for 208 U.S. 274 declared, "Every contract, combination in the form of trust or otherwise, or conspiracy, in restraint of trade or commerce among the several States, or with foreign nations, is illegal." And court opinion for 235 U.S. 522 upheld validity "of a verdict for damages resulting from a combination and conspiracy in restraint of trade under § 7 of the Anti-Trust Act."

The Danbury Hatters Case determined that "men joining organizations and paying dues to them, are bound by their constitution; they are responsible for the results of the acts of the organization or its officers, even though, under the constitution of the organization, their officers are forbidden to do any but lawful acts; they pay dues and could be, and were, informed of what was going on, through the published journals and bulletins."

In retrospect, Dietrich E. Loewe, a fur hat manufacturer in Danbury, Connecticut, opposed the formation of a union. He declared his place of business an "open shop" opposed to a unionized "closed shop." When he hired scabs to replace "striking workers," the United Hatters of North America (UHU) organized a boycott of his hats in several states causing severe loss of business. The American Federation of Labor (AFL) worked with UHU to convince "retailers, wholesalers and customers not to buy from or do business with Loewe." In 1902, Loewe filed a lawsuit against UHU. In 1908, the U.S. Supreme Court determined violation of interstate commerce ruling against the union and strikers; and, in 1915, issued a damage judgment. In 1917, the case settled "for slightly over $234,000 (approx. $3.9 million in 2009 currency)." AFL collected "$216,000 in voluntary contributions" from its members. And UHU held "Hatters' Day" requesting each member contribute "an hour's pay."

In 1932, the law firm Ginsburg and Ginsburg filed a successful $75,000 defamation and "price-fixing" lawsuit against the Denver Bureau in the District Court of Denver, Colorado. The complaint charged a conspiracy involving the Denver Bureau; two Bureau agents, Daniel J. Sparr and F. C. Montrose; and a group of "local dyers and cleaners" seeking to "drive a competitor out of business unless he complied with their specific demands" to join the Denver Bureau's membership. On February 9, 1932, the *Denver Post* published an article exposing an antitrust violation by the Denver Bureau and partly stated, "Denver's cleaning and dyeing business is seething over a plan devised by representatives of the Better Business Bureau to form an organization which they declare will raise prices and standards of local cleaners, and eliminate competition." The owners of the Gigantic Cleaners, Mr. and Mrs. M. Orlinsky, refused to comply and refused membership in the Bureau. Sparr and Montrose threatened to "throw the Gigantic Cleaners out of business, and make it so disagreeable for other cleaners that they would be glad to join." O'Sullivan compared the Denver Bureau's harassment to the Mafia: "There is very little difference between the tactics of Sparr and Montrose, in their approach to the independent cleaners of Denver, and the gang tactics of the Capone mob in Chicago in coercing speakeasy proprietors to buy their "alky" products and their $55 beer."

A private detective investigating the case filed a report that described the Bureau's typical whitewashing methods. He wrote, "We find that the Bureau operatives would have the public believe that they were just innocently and conscientiously trying to standardize a certain business industry, stimulating ethics and truth in advertising, and that they were doing all of this for no profit whatever to themselves, notwithstanding the fact that Daniel Sparr made the very careless and serious mistake of admitting to the *Denver Post* representative that he was being paid $1,500 for this job, and practically admitting that he was using high-powered methods in order to put over the project."

Consequently, the Court found the Denver Bureau guilty of restraint of trade. The Bureau was forced to return "upwards of $3,000 in notes" collected from their co-conspirators. Sparr and Montrose audaciously approached the Denver Bureau manager, Perry N. Moore, to compensate them for "commissions for their work regardless of the fact that they were compelled to return some of the moneys collected."

The Bureau exploited its newspaper heritage implying sinister repercussions against anyone attempting to expose its operations. O'Sullivan wrote, "Hence Bureau managers were able heretofore to bulldoze and terrorize their victims by threatening to invoke their pretended newspaper support." Several notable businesses were victimized by the Bureau's fabricated claims of suspicious "advertising methods" and included "R. H. Macy & Co., the Bulova Watch Co., the American Tobacco Company, and the Firestone Tire and Rubber Company." It was further stated, "The investigators did find definite cases where bureau managers "caused the advertising of certain corporations (which were competitors of their large contributors) to be temporarily discontinued; but after investigations were made, the publisher in each instance found that he had been tricked by the Bureau manager, and the advertising in question was immediately accepted by the newspaper"." O'Sullivan listed "Paf Manufacturing Company, of Greenville, Ill., and M.H. Rhodes, Inc., of Hartford, Conn." as two particular companies suffering Bureau harassment. The Bureau's behavior became so abusive that newspapers "categorically" denied "that they have authorized Better Business Bureau managers to use their names, influence, and prestige in furtherance of bureau activities."

The backstory of M. H. Rhodes was of particular interest because it involved the Bureau being accused of defamation due to special membership interests. The electrical manufacturer moved its operations from St. Louis, Missouri, to Hartford, Connecticut. Upon arrival, Rhodes visited the local Bureau. While waiting for the manager, he noticed a stack of "printed reports" about to be mailed. Upon further review, he discovered such literature named him and his company in a disparaging manner using "damaging and libelous statements." Rhodes secured the manager's approval not to mail the reports, but they were mailed anyway. It was suggested that a wealthy competitor of Rhodes influenced the Bureau's derogatory actions. Thereafter, Rhodes complained to the attorney general of Connecticut who exonerated him and determined his "business in perfect shape." But harassment continued and his business and customers suffered severely. A meeting was called between Rhodes and the Bureau and arbitrated by the mayor of Hartford. Arbitration verdict determined the Bureau acted wrongfully and was "interfering with legitimate business."

In 1931, Pittsburg Bureau and Manager G. H. Denniston planted a false story to gain public attention and was caught red-handed by "the Superintendent of Police of Pittsburgh, Peter P. Walsh."

On March 31, 1932, the *Pittsburgh National Labor Tribune* wrote the article, "Better Business Bureau Bunk and False Pretense," which described Denniston claiming "racketeers or fake stock salesmen had taken out of the city

$8,000,000 through the sale of fraudulent securities, fake stocks, etc." Public outrage resulted with a demand for more stringent Blue Sky laws. Backlash also denigrated the Pittsburgh police department. Consequently, Police Chief Walsh interrogated the Pittsburgh Bureau and determined Denniston lied. The Bureau admitted, "It was just an advertising scheme."

Additionally, "Better Business Bureau Bunk and False Pretense," detailed another Denniston escapade involving his false claims that charged "charity racketeers took $1,000,000 from Pittsburgh during 1931." The article specifically derided the Bureau as "an institution pretending to ferret out advertising frauds and other rackets." Denniston was called before Magistrate Leo Rothenberg "in Central Police Court," but the case was dismissed because there was no proof to verify his statements.

Another Denniston scam caught the Bureau ignoring an influential retailer and Bureau member deceiving consumers. The store disingenuously advertised for "800 girls" during a time of layoffs and used their appearance seeking employment to masquerade as shoppers "crowding the store." It was considered a "dastardly trick" and Denniston was questioned for ignoring the store's illicit actions. The *Pittsburgh National Labor Tribune* wrote, "Denniston, head of the so-called Better Business Bureau, refuses to go after these big merchants, because they are contributors to the maintenance of the Better Business Bureau. A glance through the newspapers, with the outrageous deceptive claims made by large advertisers, is sufficient to prove the worthlessness of the so-called Better Business Bureau."

Even Bureau attorneys were caught committing fraud. As previously mentioned, court records showed that Francis E. Williams, attorney for the St. Louis Bureau, tried to sway court decision on behalf of the Bureau. In fact, I claimed the same offense was committed by the employer's (Houston Bureau's) attorney during my 2015 trial.

"Bulletins" were the forerunners of the current online "BBB Reliability Reports" and used as a smear tactic to intimidate members, encourage purchase of expensive memberships, and/or to disparage competition. O'Sullivan described the publications as "containing reports of their activities, presented in the most favorable light possible" and "the medium used for criticism and censorship of advertising." He cited "a case" where a bulletin "charged that several of the largest retail drug companies of Chicago were misrepresenting their goods in local advertisements, and the people of the city were asked to believe that such popular stores as those of the Walgreen, Economical, and Owl companies could not be depended upon to furnish the bargains they advertised. One offer in particular was criticized – that of a $5 imitation pearl necklace for $1, which the Bureau intimated was just a scheme to catch the unwary." In reality, popular demand increased production, which led to lower pricing and "justified" the store's advertised cost. The store was exonerated, but the Bureau misled the public and "blackened" its name.

O'Sullivan advised, "A system of numbers was applied to them, reminding one of the manner in which convicts in penitentiaries are numbered." He listed Mandel Bros as "No. 17750"; the Spiegel Furniture Company as "three numbers, 17444, 17204, and 17558"; the L. Fish Furniture Company as "No. 17622"; Strauss & Schram as "No. 17185"; M. Fine & Sons as "Case No. 17191"; Becker, Ryan & Co. as "No. 17548"; the Kennedy Furniture Company as "No. 17219"; and Dunn Brothers as "No. 17916." Such numeric system tapped an ancestral link to George Presbury Rowell's rating methodology that he invented for his *American Newspaper Directory* that was the forerunner of the Bureau's rating system. But Rowell performed verified evaluations whereas the Bureau proffered bias opinion. O'Sullivan advised the listed records were filed under "offenders" with no apparent reason "other than that of possibly refusing to contribute to the funds of the Better Business Bureau"; his dry humor summarized their collective misfortune, "Thus "birds of a feather are in the files together"."

Another occasion exemplified stolen thunder whereby the Bureau ceremoniously injected itself in contentious matters for publicity sake. On January 11, 1933, a "Chicago newspaper" wrote an article about a "Chicagoan" accused by a North Carolina grand jury of being a loan shark and "head of a national chain of loan companies." The Chicago Bureau offered its records as background information on the accused. O'Sullivan noted, "There was certainly nothing in these facts to incriminate the individual." And reality proved that the Chicagoan was "simply an expert and successful accountant." But the Chicago Bureau used the occasion as "an opportunity to break into print, in typical Bureau style."

Membership affiliations were highlighted in a case involving H. O. Stone & Co., a prestigious Chicago "real estate investment house." In 1932, the company failed while holding liabilities valued at $15,000,000. Criminal indictments led to prison terms ranging from 2 to 20 years for "five executives of the company" for knowingly selling worthless securities. O'Sullivan was unable to confirm if H. O. Stone & Co. was a member of the Bureau because "the membership list is carefully guarded as a Bureau secret." His underlying point was that the disgraced company "was one of the presumably high class and reputable type of business houses that support Better Business Bureaus, and are supposed to entitle them to public confidence." Furthermore, O'Sullivan questioned why the Bureau was not concerned about H. O. Stone's dirty dealings and neglected to respectively warn the public; that it was "asleep or winking with both eyes."

In retrospect, the Bureau dodged several silver bullets:

On December 26, 1930, New York Attorney General Hamilton Ward ruled that the New York Bureau be licensed.

THE APO$TATE

On January 2, 1931, New York Secretary of State Edward Flynn reiterated the New York Bureau's requirement to be licensed.

In October 1931, Kenner reported in his 1936 book that the Bureau drafted radio standards, but he did not list the original standards to prevent incriminating and comparative history. Kenner's gilded pen reflected, "At Boston, in 1931, standards were drawn up by the Better Business Bureau to apply to undesirable radio advertising and were adopted, in October, by seven principal local stations, WDZA, WEEI, WHDH, WLEX, WLOE, WNAC, WSSH." In fact, in September 1931, Consumer Guild of America's E. C. Riegel filed several charges against the Better Business Bureau with various federal agencies that included the Federal Radio Commission for restraint of radio communication, which impugned the Bureau's 1931 radio standards; allegations landed with Senator Fletcher. The totality of Riegel's charges alleged "unfair trade practices, promoting gambling on the Stock Exchange, using the mails to defraud, and encouraging unfair trade practices and attempting to restrain radio communication"; he characterized the Better Business Bureau as a proficient liar. On the flip side, Kenner's 1936 book did list the Bureau's revised eight standards for broadcasting entitled, "Excerpts from Code of the National Association of Broadcasters, Adopted 1935," after the excoriating Pecora Commission hearings from 1933 to 1934, and after Kenner aligned with the prestigious SEC in 1935.

On January 25, 1932, Senator Duncan Fletcher entered into Congressional record an indictment of racketeering against the Better Business Bureau.

On January 15, 1933, Stock Exchange Reform Committee Secretary James Cahill filed charges against the Bureau with the Department of Justice, Washington, D.C. Additionally, Cahill noted that "the professional managers of these Better Business Bureaus contend that their system is maintained by reputable business firms and for the sole purpose of "protecting the public against fraudulent investments," and that this alleged protection is given to the public "free of charge"." Cahill took offense to the Bureau's inference of providing free services by noting that "if there were no other evidence of deception except the deceptive phrase 'free of charge,' coupled with the past performance of the Bureau's principal sponsors, we would feel amply justified in labeling the entire system a racket."

And, on January 24, 1933, former New York Deputy District Attorney Ferdinand Pecora took over securities investigations as chief counsel for the U.S. Senate Banking and Currency Committee.

During the interim, the New York Bureau desperately commenced laying deflective smoke screens through crony newspapers prior to Cahill's expected racketeering allegations and the U.S. Senate's ongoing investigations that were about to gain head winds through the Pecora Commission. On December 30, 1932, the *San Francisco Examiner* published the Bureau-instigated article, "Sellers of Wooden Nutmegs Are Not All Vanished," and advised the public "not to purchase frivolous commodities or merchandise as "wooden nutmegs"." Four days later, January 3, 1933, the *New York American* published another Bureau article, "Stock Tipster Racket Again Being Worked," wherein advising "the public to beware of "tipster sheet crooks"." A month later, February 5, 1933, a "Chicago newspaper" published a Bureau article warning against "the endless-chain selling racket" of sundry sales items such as "bill-folds, fountain pens, cigars, hosiery, lingerie, pocket lighters, soft drinks, and tickets to the 1933 Chicago World's Fair." Reality dictated that afore listed commentaries were among a slew of Bureau-generated articles published to deflect pending criminal charges.

O'Sullivan died in 1939, the same year that *McCann v. The New York Stock Exchange et al* delivered a landmark appellate decision, which applied a truth exemplar to legitimize the Bureau's unfettered Bureau. As a result, B-men added a new ploy to their growing bag of fuzzy tricks that hid disparagement behind twisted truth. Such a ruling would have devastated O'Sullivan considering his contentious relationship with the Bureau and intimate knowledge of the organization's controversial past that he documented and criticized. *McCann* was the first among several lawsuits that incrementally decimated defamation and established the Bureau's autocracy. The modern Bureau expanded *McCann's* truth exemplar to include the First Amendment's right of opinion to legitimize its specious rating program.

On November 13, 1939, Circuit Judge L. Hand, Circuit Court of Appeals, Second Circuit, established sovereignty of truth and succinctly set the legal standard that there was no liability for publishing true facts. Lawsuit complaint stated, "The defendant, Better Business Bureau of New York, in conjunction with the New York Stock Exchange, its officers and members, and a large number of other persons, conspired to drive the plaintiff out of business in order to rid themselves of his competition." As requital for Bureau injustice, the plaintiff unsuccessfully attempted to enter "an editorial in *Printers' Ink* which very mildly criticized the Bureau, and suggested possible changes in its methods."

Gene McCann was a New York stockbroker who claimed the New York Bureau intentionally divulged his earlier youthful misconduct to ruin his reputation and business on Wall Street. Judge Hand supported the Bureau ruling that it didn't matter the reason for publishing the plaintiff's background because the information was based on true occurrence; that the stockbroker's previous offenses were "several and grave" as though justifying the Bureau's divulgement; that "no person or firm is liable, regardless of the purpose with which it is published, for publishing facts that are true." The court conceded that the Bureau omitted important factors including McCann's criminal behavior occurred during his youth when he was "eighteen and twenty-four years old" and that the

Bureau acted in a manner with intention to leave a false impression against McCann when broadcasting "letters and leaflets that he was a person unreliable morally and financially, with a record of criminal convictions." But final decision focused on the fact that the statements themselves were true and the Bureau had no responsibility to "palliate" or excuse McCann's past indiscretions.

Unfortunately, McCann was about seven years too late to successfully sue the Bureau. Had McCann sued during the Pecora Commission investigations, he would have received a favorable ruling supported by kindred spirits like Logan Billingsley, E. C. Riegel, Attorney General Hamilton Ward, Senator Duncan Fletcher, and Frank O'Sullivan. By the time McCann did sue, the Bureau was impregnable due to FDR's presidential endorsement and Kenner's SEC clout.

In May 2010, Incorp Services Inc. of Henderson sued "the Better Business Bureau of Southern Nevada and its director, Sylvia Campbell," alleging unfair and bias ratings practice. Incorp is a Nevada-based service that advertises over 75,000 worldwide clients. Despite excellent business practice, Incorp refused Bureau membership and consequently received variable ratings "on a daily basis" ranging from "C+" to "F". Its lawsuit claimed, "Defendants' advertisements are false, as their ratings of businesses are intentionally biased and inconsistent, and in particular, heavily favor businesses that have chosen to pay money to and participate in the defendants' accreditation program." Incorp also alleged that "the BBB system can easily be manipulated by a third party in a matter of seconds."

In September 2010, TicketNetwork Inc. and its subsidiary, Ticket Software LLC, represented by Edward J. Heath of Robinson & Cole LLP, sued the Connecticut Bureau for deceptive trade practice. Plaintiffs alleged the Bureau employed "misleading practices" by engaging a "'pay to play" ratings system, in which the bureau routinely assigns higher ratings – on a scale of A+ to F – to businesses that pay it fees." TicketNetwork's CEO, Don Vaccaro, commended Connecticut Attorney General Richard Blumenthal for nationally highlighting the issue. Blumenthal stated, "Beyond the pay-to-play element is a more fundamental defect. The present rating system which grades businesses from F to A-plus may be deceptive, unhelpful to consumers and unfair to businesses."

In November 2010, the ABC *20/20* documentary "Terror Group Gets 'A' Rating From Better Business Bureau," lambasted the Los Angeles Bureau for bias rating scores that favored members and referred to what I earlier coined as "pay-for-play" in my 2008 and 2009 complaints to state and federal authorities. It was the closest that the Bureau came to being sued by a state attorney general for awards and ratings fraud. Thereafter, CBBB continued the same specious programs, scapegoated the LA Bureau's president/CEO, and closed the LA office in 2013. The ABC *20/20* exposé revealed CBBB's ugly underbelly and confirmed that the national headquarters orchestrated all rules, regulations, and decisions.

In 2012, the lawsuit, *Kaufman, Englett & Lynd, PLLC, Plaintiff, v. Better Business Bureau of Central Florida, Inc., Council of Better Business Bureaus, Inc. and Judy Pepper, Defendants*, United States District Court, Middle District of Florida, Orlando Division, Case No. 6:12-cv-31-Orl-28KRS, filed February 13, 2013, alleged the Bureau's rating system was "flawed, erroneous, misleading, and, in short, anything but the unbiased process the BBB claims in its promotional material." Kaufman, Englett & Lynd, PLLC (KEL) alleged defamation when issued an "F" rating score for failure "to resolve a pattern of (client) complaints"; the law firm argued that the Bureau misunderstood the nature of its business. The Bureau retaliated with additional disparagement resulting in KEL's forfeiture of membership akin to a dishonorable discharge and stigmatized operations as the first law firm to be expelled in the Bureau's history.

KEL brought charges under the Lanham Act. Presiding U.S. District Judge John Antoon II described the act: "(1) Any person who, on or in connection with any goods or services, or any container for goods, uses in commerce any word, term, name, symbol, or device, or any combination thereof, or any false designation of origin, false or misleading description of fact, for false or misleading representation of fact, which – (B) in *commercial advertising or promotion*, misrepresent the nature, characteristics, qualities, or geographic origin of his or her or another person's goods, services, or commercial activities, shall be liable in a civil action by any person who believes that he or she is or is likely to be damaged by such act." Plaintiffs argued that the Bureau disparaged the law firm's good name resulting in loss of clients and revenue whereby creating "commercial competition with KEL." Judge Antoon dismissed the case in favor of the Bureau "for lack of personal jurisdiction" citing KEL did not prove "prudential standing" of its claims brought under the Lanham Act because the law firm "did not compete with the Defendants." As a result, the ruling simultaneously empowered the Bureau's rating system as an opinion protected by First Amendment rights while marginalizing consumers as unwitting victims. Truth in advertising was overlooked, and the Bureau was allowed to continue deceptive status quo under a newly ensconced shroud of impunity. Thereafter, the Bureau shadow-boxed nonmembers with lower rating scores to induce memberships and control the marketplace.

My worries worried that the Bureau would exploit the KEL ruling to also embrace its bogus awards program by obfuscating superficial merit as a bastard child of free speech without regard to defrauding victimized consumers. The Bureau has never advised consumers that its awards program is unevaluated and based on an honor code. Instead, consumers are force-fed exaggeration, confusing disclaimers, and misrepresentation to stoke a mask of authority and exceptional quality. In one fell swoop, a judge's discretion empowered the Bureau's disparaging monopolistic initiatives and overturned fundamental protections implemented by the 1890 Sherman Antitrust Act.

The lawsuit also highlighted the legal relationship between CBBB and the Bureau franchise. Accordingly, court ruling mimicked a globalist playbook that acknowledged the national CBBB as a separate Delaware Corporation operating in Arlington, Virginia, that "preserved its identity" while the Bureaus are governed by their own respective "board of directors."

I found contention with the judge's parsed logic that the CBBB "exercises no control over the daily operation of BBB." It is my opinion, based on first-hand experience, research, and knowledge from dealing with the Houston Bureau and CBBB, that CBBB controls the Bureau franchise because it creates all organizational rules and regulations. In fact, the CBBB's annual reports document financial support from Bureau dues.

A centurial review of lawsuits emphasized a disparity in justice between twentieth-century lawsuits that invoked stern adherence to business law and twenty-first-century lawsuits that accommodated globalist sleight of hand. Offenses that were previously deemed antitrust and deceptive trade violations have evolved into elements of free speech. Judicial discretion slants according to wealth and influence. Anyone having participated in a modern lawsuit is aware of the prevailing threat of deep pockets and dirty judges; that the court system kowtows to the privileged. Discretion-for-sell encourages wealthy defendants to seek out the most prestigious law firms because of their judicial clout and ability to grease robed palms. As a result, black-market justice facilitates a malfeasant court system and disparity of justice that underscores the lawyer's creed, "innocent until proven broke."

I remind the Bureau of a befitting warning issued in 1908 by eighth U.S. Supreme Court Chief Justice Melville Westin Fuller (1833-1910) in the Danbury Hatters' Case: "You shall not organize men to destroy other men's business; they have a right to conduct their own business in their own way, so long as it is legal business, and you have no right to destroy or attempt to destroy it."

CHAPTER **36**

UNFORGIVABLE OMISSIONS

The star-struck jury was mesmerized by the employer's celebrity and the Better Business Bureau's presence, but unaware that they were witnessing a courtroom folie à deux. Jurors did not question the Bureau's involvement and blindly assumed that the employer was waving his "A+" rating score to support his acclaimed credibility instead of underworld cover-up. Irony reminded that I transformed him from a window hack to a sparkling star by winning him the Bureau's interstellar Pinnacle. I encouraged him to drop long-time endorsers and self-promote his products. He was 50-deep, feared age, and his thuggish ageism subconsciously controlled his hair-trigger temper, twitchy eyes, and Mafioso mystique, but he had deep pockets that television loved. My convincing clincher compared him to an admired furniture personality his age and Pinnacle recipient. Ultimately, I stood 10 feet across from him as he filmed his debut television commercial inside his warehouse showroom. In coordination with TV ads, I orchestrated an advertorial centerfold spread with the *Houston Business Journal* whereby Wayne and I provided corporate interviews alongside the employer's pitch and pictures; consequently, the employer enjoyed widespread business acclaim. I also promoted highway billboard ads, which he ignored until I left the company and then placed signage at every major Houston spaghetti-bowl. The Bureau welcomed the employer's rising star that magnified the Hollywood pomp and pageantry of its Elysian *Awards for Excellence*. Accordingly, I was responsible for pairing two birds of a "foul" feather that exploited superficial fame and advertising. Jurors noticed my evil-eye exchanges with the employer, but significance was lost because of the Bureau's malfeasance and our attorney's unforgivable omissions.

I believe that our attorney committed malpractice and gutted our cases with inexcusable omissions. Chart-toppers included ignoring opposing counsel's opening presentation whose video screen grabs evidenced the employer's illicit eavesdropping; omitting a psychiatric expert to professionally diagnose the employer's psychopathy, sexual harassment, and age and gender discrimination; omitting critical witnesses due to abandonment; omitting pre-trial media marketing to ally a prospective jury pool; and, most egregiously, omitting our individual backgrounds leaving us no sympathetic inroads with the jury to offset the employer's stardom and the Bureau's gravitas. Additionally, I battled our attorney's prejudice along with the employer's misogyny that catered to Wayne's larger purse prize because the employer's gender discrimination underpaid me.

Opposing counsel's introduction featured our villainized mug shots disgracing the court room walls edited from Peeping Tom company video to seed subliminal criminal implication. Our attorney should have questioned provenance of the screen grabs that undoubtedly originated from the employer's office cameras. We could have won the case by connecting incriminating dots between the screen grabs and employer's depraved sexual harassment since I accused him of eavesdropping and voyeurism. The employer previously bragged about his stash of company-spawned audio cassettes and surveillance tapes featuring his favorite trash-talking employee-banging porno that he admittedly hoarded in his office for personal gratification. His mind was so warped that his wife attempted psychological intervention by encouraging him to watch yesteryear classic movies like *Amos and Andy*, *Three Little Rascals*, and *Laurel and Hardy*. But his sexual deviations became a liability when Wayne and I sued him, so he concocted our "affair" and "extortion" scenario.

Psychiatric testimony would have slam-dunked our favorable verdict because of the employer's violent misogynistic psychopathy that was centerpiece to my discrimination complaint. Expert testimony was critical to deflect jurors' inherent skepticism questioning credibility of a television star versus an assault victim who remained in a hostile work environment. Failure to explore the employer's depravity labeled me a glutton for punishment. Additionally, there was no mention of the worst economic depression since the Great Depression of 1929. Dare I ask them "to walk a mile in my shoes and then we talk." I was victimized and blacklisted by the employer during a morphing jobless workscape that clamored for a youth culture and stigmatized over-50 employees. Furthermore, I was going to leave the employer, but needed time to facilitate my escape; it was not like I could just leave without suffering serious legal and employment repercussions. I was dealing with the employer's awards fraud and was in the midst of starting an MBA degree to accommodate a spiraling job market, but the creep found out on day one, went berserk, and forced me to cancel school. In fact, I lost everything when I did finally leave, which underscored why I stayed. Unfortunately, jurors did not hear any of this and consequently blamed me not the employer.

Witnesses must be nurtured and protected from adversarial threats and bribery. Our attorney lost and/or abandoned several prime witnesses including

UNFORGIVABLE OMISSIONS

Anna, Merit H., Michelle R., Dawn P., Jennie S., Joe B., Robert G., and Charlie C. They each witnessed or experienced the employer's age and gender discrimination. After leaving our attorney's office and stepping into the elevator, Wayne and I confronted Anna, a young Hispanic woman who immediately recognized Wayne as a former co-worker. Her greeting emphatically exclaimed, "[Employer] hated women!" We stared at each other in fortuitous lawsuit-enabling disbelief. Needless to say, we asked and she agreed to testify, but our derelict attorney ignored her for several months and lost her. Merit was a young crack-head installer supporting a growing family. He profusely complained about the employer, approached me on numerous occasions for extra work, and begged me to recoup a "penciled" (debited) installer payment. One occasion involved his $1500 contractor's invoice refused by the employer. Merit was desperate and begged my assistance. I recovered Merit's money under personal threat of abuse and loss of employment. After I filed a lawsuit, Merit agreed to testify, but our attorney left him dangling. Then the employer bribed Merit who proceeded to hang the phone up on me when I re-approached him for his testimony. Michelle was an administrative assistant who hated the employer and wrote me respective notes. One day she rolled her car into a ditch and I was the first person she called for assistance and money; she also borrowed several hundred dollars from Wayne. Our attorney ignored Michelle and she later refused my request for witness testimony stating that the employer patronized the steak restaurant where she worked in Memorial City and gave her $500 tips; she never repaid me or Wayne. Dawn offered critical testimony as the financial manager who replaced me. As usual, our attorney abandoned her witness testimony and the employer bribed her back into his fold, but her temporary alliance exposed the employer's ongoing deceit including his company advertising as a "Toys for Tots" collection center and then discarding the toys. Jennie was the most disappointing of all, she was my personal secretary. I suffered with her through a miscarriage, was prayerful for her subsequent pregnancy, and visited her first birth. The employer harassed her on lesser levels, but abuse was still impactful. Jennie was eight months pregnant when he called her into his office and lambasted her for something that never happened; she left in tears. Her husband appeared the following Saturday morning poised for confrontation. I sent him home before the employer arrived. Disappointingly, Jennie refused to testify and could have singlehandedly swayed trial. And, Joe owed me. I saved his rotten hide on numerous occasions as a wily salesman who was always conniving customers. Over the years, we became friends. He met with Wayne, me, and our attorney at a restaurant and divulged pivotal testimony for our cases. Once again, our attorney left Joe dangling. In the interim, the employer bribed Joe and financed his $30,000 wedding and Philippine fiancé's airline ticket. Then there was Robert who was an installer whom the employer was always shooing from my office.

THE APO$TATE

After leaving the employer, I joined Wayne to work for a competitive window company and managed their installers. Robert appeared looking for work and begged my confidentiality to prevent the employer's knowledge underscoring our trial complaint that the employer controlled "contractors" like "employees." Our attorney never pursued Robert and we lost his testimony after the employer hired him as his service manager. Lastly, Charlie was the boyfriend of the employer's oldest employee, Beth Cecilia Songe, who departed this world and could not speak for herself. Beth would have profoundly impacted my age and gender discrimination complaints. Charlie held intimate knowledge of and witnessed the employer's vicious discrimination against Beth, but our attorney abandoned Charlie. Ultimately, the Bureau's judge forbade mention of Beth in trial.

Our attorney discriminated against me worse than the employer. I sued the employer because of terrorizing age and gender discrimination, but my attorney second-fiddled me in favor of Wayne's $1.5 million punitive damages opposed to my nominal $100,000 damages. Disparity of damage compensation was inherently prejudicial because payment was scaled according to salaries. My discrimination complaint included unequal pay; I was paid a fraction of my male colleagues' salaries despite performing more than comparable work with same corporate status. Unfortunately, unequal pay was not mentioned to jurors.

Pre-trial media marketing is an undervalued counter-corruption trial tactic and one of the last vestiges for fair representation to overcome the three-tiered court system of the poor, wealthy, and filthy rich. I remind readers that in 1909, Coca-Cola discreetly deployed pre-trial marketing when dispatching its illustrious sales manager Samuel Candler Dobbs to pursue the presidency of the prestigious Associated Advertising Clubs of America to influence local jurors prior to the infamous 1911 *Barrels and Kegs Case* trial for violation of the Pure Food and Drug Act; handsome Sam's public relations' histrionics rode the wings of the prestigious AACA and saved Coca Cola. Our case offered similar dynamics and historic weight, but our dense discriminating attorney failed to realize advertising profundities. The employer's 2013 deposition promised the Bureau's trial incursion, but our attorney dismissed my repeated warnings to limit collateral damage by pre-trial marketing. In fact, when we first contracted him, he had a partner who was a litigator and marketer. Although masterful with legal briefs, our attorney scoffed at the influential power of advertising, public relations, and media. He was blind to history's significant lessons that pertained to and would have assisted our lawsuits. Consequently, our malfeasant judge manipulated trial, evidence, and testimony; an illicit jury charge, defaulted by statute of limitation, was presented to an unaware jury to assure the employer's favorable verdict.

Detailing personal history and establishing credibility is imperative to win a trial particularly involving a skeptical employment discrimination case against a local celebrity endorsed by an icon. Plaintiffs must establish a connection with the jury and complaints must personify grievances, but our attorney converted us into hollow stick figures and alienated the jury by ignoring our existence. He did not react to trip-wire antics until after shattering impact had lost to deer-in-the-headlight stupor. A gladiator opposing counsel conquered while our starchy attorney surrendered. As a result, 12 hostile jurists sprung from our attorney's subjugated wake. The employer's shrewd dapper quick-witted amoral ruthless self-proclaimed Renaissance attorney profiled the jury, pursued a juvenile happy-hour angle, and respectively showcased his client in a series of staged theatrics. Our attorney wasted our opening trial advantage and enabled opposing counsel's cheesy convincing prologue that pursued a footprint of smoke and mirrors and established palpable rapport.

Trial closed and we were still strangers. The jury was confused about our business titles, did not know our backgrounds, and was unaware of our moral caliber. Our attorney allowed opposing counsel to transform us into gypster gold diggers despite our valid complaints and noble motives. Jurors were never told that I refused several pricey settlements comparable to trial's potential compensation; that I was defending my name and reputation against a vindictive charlatan; that consumers were being defrauded; that our cases represented senior employees across the nation suffering a plethora of age discrimination; that the legal system is unfair, archaic, and draconian towards older workers enabling corporations to prematurely age-out baby boomers into sunset poverty; and that the courts are corrupt with judicial discretion manipulated by globalist law firms. A worthy attorney would have conjured ways to inform the jury.

My life story, in particular, needed to be told to substantiate me as a person of exceptional integrity especially since my reputation was on the line and the employer convoluted trial to incorporate the "Better Business Bureau" and its revered brand image. I worked extremely hard to establish employment bona fides, which I deserved to benefit from, but was prematurely cut from the workforce by the Deep State Bureau and miscreant employer. I believe that failure to pre-market our biographies guaranteed the Bureau's nefarious participation. Court proceedings are not about telling the truth, but suppression of truth. Consequently, successful attorneys involved in high-profile cases often leak client stories to offset power plays and counter empowered adversaries' courtroom redactions. Information reaching a potential jury pool cannot be unheard and embeds a common consensus. Our omitted plaintiffs' backgrounds would have legitimized our complex employment claims. Otherwise, jurors naturally identified with the employer whom they "knew" from a television screen, particularly when he increased advertising during trial. Henceforth, I will present my life story to readers the same as trial should have, to some degree, informed the

THE APO$TATE

jury to establish rapport and favorable verdict.

I grew up in a big city raised by small town values. God, country, and family were sacred. My maternal German grandmother, Anna Bell, nicknamed "Ginny," bested the fairy godmother as Heaven's gift to children. In times of despair, I think of her. She left me with inspirational memories embraced with love and laughter at the Hamburger Bar, Shipley's Donut, Dairy Queen, Texas Theater, Five and Dime, Piggly Wiggly, Elkhart Lake, Sacred Heart Catholic Church, and Missouri Pacific's *The Texas Eagle* in Palestine. Ginny taught me to pray for the pope and the conversion of Russia, which reflected the extent of my politics at the time. She taught me humor, compassion, and self-worth to deal with the insanity and adversity that found me. Growing older and wiser, my childhood's fairytale evaporated into a pipe dream. The latest pope became a raging Marxist. Russia remained incorrigible. Politics grew apocalyptic. And my seasoned years digressed to fisticuff and fantod.

A typical daddy's girl, I was an only daughter and grew up the middle child of an all-American Catholic Irish-German family of five children. Dad graduated from Texas A&M College (A&M), Class of 1943, whose yearbook cover emblazoned the courageous words, "ABOVE AND BEYOND THE CALL OF DUTY * EXTRAORDINARY HEROISM * GALLANTRY IN ACTION * EXCEPTIONALLY MERITORIOUS SERVICE * GALLANTRY AND INTREPIDITY AT THE RISK OF HIS LIFE." (His senior picture is missing because he sent all extra income to his mother and younger siblings.) The Texas Legislature established the "Agricultural and Mechanical College" in 1871 as the first college institution in Texas; classes started on October 4, 1876. Men were accepted for enrollment only if they joined the Corps of Cadets for military training. A&M was originally an extension of Texas University that had not been built and the Texas Legislature formally separated the schools in 1875.

The Texas Aggie Corps of Cadets supplied America's fighting troops during the Progressive Reformation Era that launched the Bureau's forerunner Sphinx Club in 1896, the far-reaching Pure Food and Drug Act of 1906, the Truth in Advertising Movement in 1911, and the first regulatory Vigilance Committee in 1912 that begat the Better Business Bureau in 1916. Aggies participated in early military battles that facilitated organized advertising, including the Spanish-American War of 1898, WWI (July 28, 1914 to November 11, 1918), WWII (1939-1945), and the Korean War (June 25, 1950 to July 27, 1953) whereby I honor our veterans' insistence that respective military action be called the "Korean War" and not "Korean Conflict" even though war was never declared by Congress.

My family's lineage participated in all of the early U.S. historical wars, including the American Revolutionary War, the American Civil War, both World Wars, and the Korean War. Descendants lived in and/or migrated from the original Thirteen Colonies of the United States, including New Hampshire, New York, Pennsylvania, Massachusetts, Rhode Island, Connecticut, New Jersey, Delaware, Maryland, Virginia, North Carolina, South Carolina, and Georgia. The United States added the Republic of Texas on December 29, 1845.

The following brave soldiers defended the United States of America despite peril, injury, and ultimate blood sacrifice:

Private James Cain Sr. (1748-1826); distant cousin; North Carolina; Bladen County Militia; Patriot in the American Revolutionary War (1775-1783); wounded during the decisive Battle of Elizabethtown in 1781 with Whigs (Patriots) claiming victory over Tories (supported Britain); the battle turned the tide in favor of Patriots; milites requiescentes in North Carolina.

Second Lieutenant James Michael Cain Sr. (1834-1886); my great-great-grandfather; Georgia; the American Civil War (1861-1865); Co. B, 8th Cav. Reg.; Confederate States Army; horse detail with General Robert E. Lee in September 1864; a Freemason; milites requiescentes in Texas.

Several cousins fought and died during WWI. Private Frank Cain (1887-1918); Virginia; CO E 317th INF; killed in action; milites requiescentes in Virginia. Sergeant Olna Young Cain (1887-1918); Illinois; CO D, 5th Regiment Marine Corps; killed in action; milites requiescentes in France. And Private Leroy Cain (1896-1918); Virginia; 153 Depot Brigade; killed in action; milites requiescentes in Virginia.

Sergeant Joseph Chap Cain (1917-1988); my father's older brother; Texas; WWII; TEC 4 U.S. Army; graduate A&M Class of 1941; attended the 1946 "Tokyo Muster" along with 76 Texas Aggies at the Imperial Hotel in Tokyo; milites requiescentes in Texas.

Sergeant Patrick Henry Cain (1920-2003); my father; Texas; U.S. Air Force; post-WWII, January 1946 to July 1947; stationed at Eglin Air Force Base, Florida; information was procured from the F.B.I. pertaining to a "B" registry file ("Burned File") due to a fire on July 12, 1973, at the National Personnel Records Center in St. Louis that destroyed "16-18 million official military files"; milites requiescentes in Texas.

First Lieutenant Mabry ("Mabe") Elder Cain (1926-1950); my father's youngest brother; Texas; Korean War; U.S. Army; Company E, 8th Cavalry Regiment, 1st Cavalry Division; A&M Class of 1950; killed in action; milites requiescentes at Fort Sam Houston National Cemetery, San Antonio, Texas. Mabe was "the first recipient of the Silver Star in the Korean War" for "gallantry in action" against the enemy near Yongdong, Korea, on July 25, 1950. The Silver Star is "the third-highest award for bravery in combat given by the United States military." Mabe's name and place in history were previously omitted; *The Apostate* reminds his honorable mention.

Fate recently brought me to Master Sergeant Joseph Elias Ramirez Sr. (Ret.)

whom I nicknamed "Sniper Joe" because he was a Scout Ranger and sniper. Sniper Joe celebrated his 80s but spoke as though he was 18 again with best friend Mabe being 24. He and Mabe were greenhorn kids fresh out of boot camp at Camp Zama, Japan, 25 miles outside of Tokyo. On the pitch-black morning, 3 a.m, September 3, 1950, Sniper Joe heard Mabe calling "Medic" from his foxhole at advance position; he had been shot. Sniper Joe was eight feet away and belly-crawled towards his voice. But Mabe was bait. As soon as Sniper Joe reached Mabe, North Korean troops opened fire on both of them with Burp Guns (7.62x25mm Soviet PPSh-41, *"Pistolet-Pulemyot Shpagina,"* Russian for "Shpagin machine pistol"), shooting 900 rounds per minute. When smoke cleared, Mabe laid dead in Sniper Joe's blood-soaked arms. I asked Sniper Joe why he wasn't killed and he emphatically answered, "By the grace of God." He told me that the North Koreans wore canvas shoes to sneak up to American foxholes and ambush soldiers. Whereas Mabe's life story tragically ended that night, Sniper Joe's had just begun. Several weeks later, Sniper Joe was shot five times, captured by North Korean soldiers, tortured, and almost starved to death in a P.O.W. camp for three years until war's end. Sniper Joe told me that he met my father after Mabe's funeral in September 1950; that my father was inconsolable and kept questioning if Sniper Joe was sure Mabe was dead before leaving him for pickup by grave patrol. Sniper Joe's eyes-wide-open reaction implied that Mabe had been almost cut in half by enemy fire and his death was irrefutable. Dad had been a father to Mabe and was tormented by the thought of his baby brother dying alone. Consequently, our family spent a lifetime mourning his death, for an uncle whom I never met. Meeting Sniper Joe bridged time, brought closure to my father's death, and introduced me to Mabe.

In 1956, our family transferred overseas to Bogota, Columbia. My father was employed by International Petroleum Company, an affiliate of Standard Oil Company (NJ), founded by John D. Rockefeller in 1870. We hiked the foothills of the Andes Mountains and visited the Columbian Ambassador to the United States at his lavish hacienda. On May 11, 1958, Vice President Richard Nixon's Latin tour visited Bogota. I sat on my father's shoulders looking like a blond-haired pigtailed neon flagpole amid a cheering crowd. We stood directly on the street curb inches away from the vice president's slow-moving motorcade. As he passed by, Nixon rolled his window down, smiled and waved, rendering us special acknowledgment as Americans. Thereafter, Nixon's entourage continued to Venezuela where he was attacked by communist rebels. Mounting political strife in Columbia encouraged Dad to consider a prestigious offer in Australia as president of an oil exploration company. Unfortunately, my mother refused his Australian encore, and we returned to Houston. I kept our South American adventure alive through show-and-tell presentations that became gruesomely popular when presenting human blood-stained Andes Indian spears and arrows as primitive relics from Dad's oil field jungle excursions. Life-altering overseas excitement embedded my interest in history and journalism.

My childhood emphasized integrity, competition, and sportsmanship when moral compass still mattered. Fortunately, I was an athlete, which my father encouraged. After my state champion older brother, I was always chosen second for makeshift teams of kickball, baseball, and football. Dad taught me confidence during an era when feminist rights were practically nonexistent and athletic opportunities were limited. He trained me as a pitcher in girls' softball while realizing my skill as a home-run hitter. With every batter's turn, I would pull a Babe Ruth and glance at Dad sitting above the dugout and nod to the outfield. It was our special signal. Even the outfielders noticed and began backing up, but never far enough. At the end of every season, Dad and I attended the Softball League's banquet that bestowed me an honor trophy. Volleyball was next and I lettered four years at Memorial High School; Dad attended every game no matter in-town or out-of-town destinations. Thereafter, I was among the first women to enroll at Texas A&M University and played softball for the Milner Hall Misses. I was a geology major and nominated treasurer of the Geology Club, which first drew my attention to business. At the time, I was not interested in an "MRS" degree and found it increasingly challenging to study with half of the Aggie Corps of Cadets parked outside my door. Three semesters later, I transferred to Southwest Texas State University (Texas State) in San Marcos and shared a car with a younger brother. I graduated in December 1975 as an honor-roll student with a Bachelor of Science degree in commercial art and minor in industrial art, analogous to present day degrees in advertising and journalism. And I swore an oath to truth in advertising.

I earned my bona fides as an accomplished writer, art director, designer, and businesswoman. Having worked for a tabloid magazine, I published many special-interest articles. One of my favorite memories was interviewing and photographing the incomparable Muhammad Ali (1942-2016) at his Rice Hotel suite when he was in Houston filming *The Greatest*. I first met him in latter June 1976 while he was in-between scenes and chilling on the movie set. I also met and photographed esteemed actor Ernest Borgnine (1917-2012) who portrayed his trainer Angelo Dundee. The film was a classic and documented Ali's victory as a heavy weight champion and conversion to Islam.

Caryn Suzann Cain
Author of *The Apostate*; community theatre publicity photo, 1976; photographer: Caryn Cain.

Muhammad Ali
Between scenes on *The Greatest* movie set, Houston, June 1976; photographer: Caryn Cain.

UNFORGIVABLE OMISSIONS

Muhammad Ali
Mugging for author's camera at Rice Hotel during filming of
The Greatest, June 1976; photographer: Caryn Cain.

Ernest Borgnine
The Greatest movie set, June 1976; photographer: Caryn Cain.

THE APO$TATE

Everyone thought I was a movie extra, but I was really covering the film for a story. I snapped pictures of Ali as he waited for the film crew to stage a classic ring-side scene. Later that afternoon, he passed me in the hotel foyer and recognized me from the movie set. I asked him for an interview and he warmly welcomed me into his entourage mostly comprised of bodyguards. I was the only journalist. We stood side-by-side in a packed elevator that opened steps away from his "Golden Suite." He was approachable, low-key, giving, and strikingly humble despite his celebrity. After everyone settled, Ali's wife Veronica appeared holding their newborn daughter, Hanna. Ali expressed how proud he was to be a father; his face beamed as he spoke.

Also, in 1976, I was a film extra in *Bad News Bears in Breaking Training* and mixed with the late Clifton James who, in 1973, played Sheriff J.W. Pepper in *Live and Let Die*. He usually played a cantankerous character, but he was really a quiet sweet-natured soul.

A whirlwind of community theatre, modeling, and odd jobs brought me to my husband. In-between the birth of our two children, I traveled the world making design samples. I jostled in the back of open-bed trucks while six to eight months pregnant and visiting leather factories in the outlying jungles around Bangkok, Thailand. Soaking monsoon rains poured from every conceivable direction as machine-gun toting soldiers stopped us at ad hoc checkpoints during a government coup d'état. One last jaunt to a Philippine factory forced the indignity of several invasive custom searches canceled when my moving belly proved pregnancy rather than drug smuggling. I had been overseas almost two months and obsessed about going home. The 16-hour return flight agitated my unborn resulting in heavy contractions that threatened a mid-flight birth, which contributed to his early hospital debut a week later. My two-year-old confirmed that I had been gone too long when treating me like a stranger at the airport. There was no Internet at the time, and he could not place my face with my nightly phone calls compounded by a 24-hour time differential. Then, with a newborn and toddler in tow, we traveled to Miami, so I could finish upscale designs for an upcoming New York fashion show.

My creations were magical and attracted orders from large stores, couture boutiques, and major apparel marts located in New York, Atlanta, Dallas, Miami, and Los Angeles. But a greedy Hong Kong factory decided an overriding fate. As orders piled in, the factory demanded a prohibitive lion's share of profit, which forced me out of business. Consequently, thugs stole several-hundred-thousand-dollars' worth of samples and sold my original designs to designer firms. My life catastrophically unraveled while fashion vultures made fortunes from my talent. I cringed finding my products labeled and spotlighted under famous designers on counters at Macy's in Atlanta, Georgia. And my handbags and blouse designs have continued to be replicated until present date.

UNFORGIVABLE OMISSIONS

Others were kingmakers, I was a fortunemaker.

We returned to Houston. I designed art and packaging for my husband's food company in addition to performing marketing, sales, and route services. A glint of hope reappeared when Ciro introduced *Gringo Beer* that aggressively competed against national brews. But bottling issues eventually tanked our enterprise. Years later, I was told that business demise was consequent to Ciro demanding a long-necked bottle instead of a short neck that the factory did not stock. All we seemed to do was make other entrepreneurs wealthy from his ideas and my designs. In fact, I take credit for introducing the first turquoise beer can that another famous brewer copied and continues marketing today. Eventually our business journey ended, and our marriage dissolved in divorce. Otherwise, I thank him for opening my eyes to a world beyond the mundane and for my two exceptional children while reminding that we must cherish all that living life to the fullest brings. On January 8, 2010, death took Ciro.

Thereafter, I shelved my fashion dreams for another day and re-entered the job market working for various industries learning dirt that I did not want to know and meeting insidious scumbags that I wished I had never met. One memorable assignment changed my life forever and redirected my future. I confronted up-close-and-personal terrorism when Radical Islam was first raising its demonic head in America. After that "job" nothing surprised me, and the experience ultimately prepared me to battle the Bureau.

In July 2001, a temporary agency assigned me to a property management group located on the top floor of the tallest 53-story building in the Houston Galleria. I learned, after the fact, that the company was a branch of a Muslim charity organization headquartered in London, England, and was in the process of building mosques around Houston. The bearded Muslim employer, Masaud, managed the Houston-based management company for a wealthy Muslim businessman, Omar, who lived in London and whose Islamic charity network financed the construction of mosques in Britain and the United States. In late August 2001, Masaud scheduled a last-minute blitzkrieg through Germany, Switzerland, and England. About two weeks later, the normally reserved Masaud, who mimicked an imam speaking in Islamic tongue, called the office from overseas and urgently demanded that I procure him return tickets to Houston. After his arrival he hid behind closed doors. On the fateful morning of September 11, 2001, I stepped off the elevator and walked into the office to find Masaud and his Muslim colleagues triumphantly shouting and cheering the televised fall of the Twin Towers. He then issued directives to another Muslim-owned company located on a lower floor to communicate only by fax, which confirmed my horrified suspicion that he was a terrorist enabler and involved in the World Trade Center attacks.

That evening I spoke with a retired Air Force colonel whom I had worked with regarding property that Omar owned in Florida. The colonel's home was located on a small airport in the area and he witnessed alarming events relative to flight-training exercises. He agreed with my concerns that an extensive Islamic underground network assisted the 9/11 attacks. Thereafter, I contacted the FBI and provided overseas bank account numbers and information that exposed a U.S.-European connection financing global terrorism. Revenue was being collected at U.S.-based Islamic charities and mosques and funneled to accounts in Liechtenstein, Europe, and the U.K. As a result, the FBI exposed several Islamic charities and mosques as funding networks and terrorist breeding grounds. I warned authorities that terrorist sleeper cells were embedded throughout the U.S. and exploiting porous Texas borders.

A few days later, the FBI appeared at Masaud's office to question me. I had taken the day off and upon my return found an FBI agent's card positioned in the center of my desk. The agent carelessly exposed me as an informant. Consequently, my job was terminated, and I was dumped by the temporary employment agency whose management was unconcerned that they were doing business with the enemy. It was a turning point in my life when I realized the extent that politics ruled the world.

Within the year, I turned my attention to the West Coast. I had established a competitive design and advertising resume and maintained connections with several California boutiques. But I never left Houston. One last glance at the classifieds noticed Wayne's advertisement for an office manager.

Wayne was charming and offered easy conversation; he was by far the nicest person I had ever interviewed. For a white collar he was endearingly blue collar. He was a smooth talker using what he called the "puppy dog" approach for a sales hook, which he later attributed to survival skills and growing up in dethroned Detroit. Unfortunately, he withheld full disclosure on the owner.

He had already chosen a new manager when I called, but still accepted my interview request. Wayne was in a hurry to train because work was piling up. The job was described as "fast-paced," which proved to be a colossal understatement. The interview was more like a conversation with an old friend. He joked about my lengthy contractor resume featuring numerous temporary employment agencies but was intrigued with my travels and fashion background. I downplayed my over-qualified business experience not wanting to lose a promising entry position. By the end of our interview, he offered me the job.

Within a month, my father suffered an aortic aneurysm and was taken unconscious by ambulance to the hospital. He was 82 years old, suffered untreated diabetes, and had been caregiver to my mother the past 10 years after she suffered a catastrophic stroke that left her incapacitated and wheelchair bound. The Veterans Administration had previously refused to help him despite his sacrifice and duty to country. Nevertheless, years of drilling dry oil wells and my mother's illness took a physical and financial toll on him. I placed my home for sale to raise cash, but too little too late.

Dad lay dying. I felt guilty and regretted approving open-heart surgery suggested by doctors to avoid certain death otherwise. Unfortunately, diabetes complications severely affected his surgery and recovery. Doctors said he suffered complete organ failure and was brain dead. I considered their "failure to thrive" diagnosis equivalent to a doctor's prescription for euthanasia. A date was set to pull the plug on his life as if his execution was nothing more than a casual business transaction.

With distraught frame of mind, I approached the employer for time off and was ruthlessly denied. Instead of a sympathetic response, he treated me like a liar and related instances of employee fraud that fabricated family crisis as an excuse for time off. Yet he heard the phone calls with family and saw me crying at my desk. He was a bitter maladjusted orphan and did not understand parental bond. If anything, he was jealous and enjoyed my wretched pain better than twisting a knife in my gut. The employer made me beg him at the worst time of my life and embedded cruelty for the rest of my employment.

The drive to Austin was traumatic. My brothers were waiting at the hospital. Dad was splayed out on the bed yellowed and swollen from infection. His upper body was riveted with bloody gaping needle holes. And his chest emblazoned a cavernous wound carved from sternum to belly that was crudely stitched as though expecting the worst. His arms lay limp and his eyes were closed. I could do nothing to help him other than pull the sheet over his stark nakedness. Nurses created a mausoleum and disconnected all life-sustaining machines except ventilator and morphine tubes. The air conditioning was turned off while a nearby fan oscillated back and forth as though a reminder that he was still alive.

I was expecting a peaceful transition and was not forewarned or prepared for reality. Medical staff witness end-of-life events every day and forget that families are unaware of the cause and effect of medical procedures. As soon as we gathered, the nurse removed Dad's ventilator tube. He immediately struggled for air and reflexively attempted three ... short ... desperate ... gasps. I was holding his hand and felt his tightened clasp. He suddenly jolted while yanking me towards him in a death grip. I felt an intense electrical shock as his spirit lifted. My inner child desperately screamed "Daddy" while drowning in death's denial. Thoughts of Bogota returned reminding of the many days that he took me with him to work; I wanted to follow. His death settled peacefully, and he looked as though asleep. Yet the word "traumatized" hardly described my subsequent despair. I memorized every feature of his face to carry my remaining days offset by endless nightmares from watching him die.

One hell traded another. The employer refused bereavement leave and I had to return to work to keep my job. Insult to injury compounded when I received

THE APO$TATE

my weekly paycheck. Despite working two extra days over the prior weekend, the employer deducted the day I took off, May 1, 2003; the day my father died. The employer perpetrated a litany of offenses, including an assault, but the pay cut was the worst. He insulted me, my father, and my family.

Beth's backstory is painful for me to write. She was my friend and suffered horribly at the hands of the employer because she was a senior citizen. We both suffered the quintessence of age discrimination by the employer on levels that shock the conscience and break bounds of human decency. She was the only other co-worker who truly understood the employer's pathological misogyny, but trial refused her story.

When I first met Beth, she had just turned 60. She was a feisty Cajun Queen who did not know how to lie. A quiet bookkeeper turned service coordinator. She finagled hundreds of thousands of dollars in vendor credits, but unaware that she was complicit in the employer's respective money laundering. Yet the employer spent the last years of her life threatening to fire her because she was reaching retirement age; her getting older scared the hell out of him.

Along with her proud swamp roots, Beth secreted a heart of gold. After my father died, I could not afford flowers for his funeral. Growing up dirt poor, Beth understood. As I delivered my father's eulogy, I noticed an exquisite wreath of flowers showering love around his casket. It was undersigned by the employer's company, but I knew it was from Beth because it included Baby's Breath, her favorite flowers. She later confided that she ignored the employer's refusal to send flowers. Wayne, Beth, and I became the Three Musketeers.

The employer was vicious to Beth over the four years that I knew her. Beth tried to conceal how much he affected her, but she could not hide how he caused her to uncontrollably tremble. She was 64 years old, and the company's oldest employee, when she died from colon cancer that metastasized in her liver. The employer ignored my pleas to help her when our company's insurance carrier illicitly cut off her benefits, which denied life-saving chemotherapy treatment. And he refused to pay Beth her earned vacation time when she desperately needed money. He was filthy rich. She was desperately poor. He let her die a horrible death without lifting a finger and enjoyed every second of her agony.

Whenever witnessing the employer's condescending behavior towards me, Beth would turn the occasion into a film-noir comedy. After he walked out of range, she appeared at my doorway hunched over, dragging her feet, and acting as though she was being beaten with a whip while flailing her arms and pleading, "Don't beat me masta, don't beat me!" She referred to the employer's vile hatred towards African Americans and treating employees like "plantation slaves." In fact, out of almost six years of employment, we had only one Black employee because Wayne hired her without telling the employer. She quit several weeks later citing issues with the employer.

The employer never appreciated Beth's expert bookkeeping and service skills despite profiting handsomely from her efforts. In the replacement window industry, vendors often produced incorrectly measured windows referred to as "mismeasures." Sometimes, the installers mismeasured windows and vendors were blamed to retrieve credits. And Beth knew how to bird-dog vendors. The employer's contract repeatedly referenced the term "custom-made" that implied "custom-measured." But he substituted fully credited similar-sized mismeasured windows without advising customers and pocketed 100% profit after selling new full-priced windows. Furthermore, additional installation procedures required for mismeasured windows were charged to customers. Sometimes, phantom "buildout" costs were also added. Wayne sold other mismeasures directly from the warehouse as cash sales. Over the years, I watched the employer stash hundreds-of-thousands-of-dollars in his wallet, with undeclared cash transferred to overseas accounts. Additionally, nobody was better than Beth at handling installers and scheduling installations, which produced excellent customer service reviews. Yet the employer treated her viciously and lobbed discriminatory insults that she could not get another job at her age and salary. Afterwards she would despondently retreat to her beat-up red truck for privacy with windows rolled and interior cabin fogged. She was alternately cryin', cussin', and smokin'. I would always follow and lightly knock her window to acknowledge my support. God knows, I understood.

On January 19, 2007, Beth informed me that she had a large lump below her right breast. Her stomach was bloated and hard, her clothes too tight. We discussed her need to seek emergency medical treatment; that she should file for immediate medical leave of absence. But, instead of worrying about herself, she asked me if I would be okay while she was away. She was referring to the employer's physical assault against me a year earlier. I told her that I would call "911" if he ever attacked me again. Ten minutes later, a burly Black policeman came barreling down the hallway asking, "Who called 911?" Beth and I looked at each other in disbelief realizing that the employer had been rat-snooping our conversation. He prank-called 911 and filed a false police report to intimidate us. I have often reflected upon that incident because Beth was confronting a life-and-death medical crisis that proved fatal four months later. I tried to retrieve a copy of the 911 call but was told it had been deleted. Furthermore, when I left the employer a year later, he stalked me and perpetrated a remix of the 911 incident while I was working for the Texas Workforce Commission.

The hospital took two critical weeks to return Beth's diagnosis of colon cancer. Then she had to wait another week for surgery that successfully removed her colon cancer, but doctors discovered cancer had spread to her liver. Consequently, our insurance carrier cut her benefits and denied her life-saving chemotherapy. I begged the employer to help her emphasizing that the doctor said she would die without treatment. The employer still refused. Yet he was mesmerized and wanted to hear every horrible detail of her spiraling health. I suggested she seek treatment at the county hospital and helped her get a "Gold Card" for indigent patients, which took another three weeks to process. I begged the nurse to expedite Beth's enrollment, but was told that she had to wait "in line."

In the meantime, Charlie and I placed Beth in whatever charity hospital would accept her for the night. Her health worsened every passing day. Beth and I spent late night hours talking about her family. She was nervous and memories calmed her cruel reality. I marveled how she maintained entertaining humor. Her mother had seven children and baptized each one in a different religion. I asked her why and she told me that her mother wanted to make sure she covered all the spiritual bases. Out of the lot, Beth was the Baptist, but could pray the Rosary better than any Catholic. She was married three times and trying "to compete with Elizabeth Taylor." Beth considered herself a scarlet woman because she was "shackin' up" with Charlie, who was her boyfriend and a country western musician. But when she spoke of her two sons, she became uncharacteristically silent. Her children meant everything to her, and the thought of leaving them behind was daunting.

I worked every night until about 8:30 p.m. and then drove to Beth's latest hospital. Nurses understood the situation and overlooked closing hours. I usually left between 1:30 a.m. and 3:00 a.m. and was back at work the next morning at 8:30 a.m. Her health drastically deteriorated over the last month. By the time she received her Gold Card, it was too late. Charlie had her transported by ambulance to Ben Taub Hospital. I met him in the crowded emergency room and took over the night watch, standing beside her gurney. Beth writhed in agony and was unable to speak. She was terrified. Her eyes were gaunt, and her stomach was grossly swollen; she had difficulty breathing and had not eaten in days. I hid panic attacks knowing that she was counting on me. She always said that I "was the strong one." Her pain was unbearable. Medication was withheld until she was assigned a room, and it took hours for a bed to come available. I left for the night wondering if she would still be alive the next morning.

By the time I returned the following evening, Beth had been moved ... to the terminal ward. The doctor appeared and solemnly advised Beth that the cancer had spread; that she was dying. Beth did not flinch. She was so accepting; so brave; so dignified. But I felt blind rage. She was sentenced to death because she was poor; because an insurance death panel decided that she was not worth saving; and because a ruthless employer refused to help.

Charlie arranged hospice at his home. He was so good to Beth. I stood by her bed looking around the room at her cherished collection of antique dolls;

my eyes settled on the life-sized porcelain doll that I gave her for Christmas. She was heavily medicated with morphine and anti-anxiety pills and unable to speak; she used her eyebrows to communicate. Her stomach was bloated from the cancer making it impossible to eat and slowed her breathing. She was emaciated and almost unrecognizable. Charlie said she only had a day or so left. I sat with her for hours holding her hand and reminiscing past glories. As I watched Beth drifting away, I tried to think of happier times. She got so tickled whenever I called her "Lounge Lizard." And she cherished the simplest gifts, telling me after Christmas parties that she "made out like a bandit." But time had come to bid farewell to my dear friend; the Big Sleep was embracing her, and the Big Cheat was expecting me; the employer showed no mercy even for the dying. I kissed her forehead as I cupped her hands in both of mine and bid eternal adieu, "Beth, I'm going to miss you so much. You will always be my best friend. I love you."

Looking back, I wanted to say more, but did not want to burden her final journey. Walking towards the door, I felt Beth's concern about her boys. My glancing reminder softly confided, "Your boys are on their way." It was heart-wrenching saying goodbye to the Cajun Queen.

Charlie's woeful call came two days later at work. Beth passed away sometime that Monday morning, between 4 a.m. and 6 a.m., April 23, 2007. She got to see her boys. I told Wayne first. He bowed his head in sorrow and could not talk. They had been close friends. I was going to return to my desk but stopped by the employer's office to make a formal announcement, which I quickly regretted. He and his guilt immediately jumped up from his desk, "It's your fault that I didn't pay for Beth's chemotherapy!" I was already traumatized, and his words added insult to injury. Choosing my words carefully, I told him that it was "your decision to make"; that "you were aware of everything"; and that I asked you "to help Beth." I was flabbergasted when he accusatorily responded, "Then, you should have told [wife] to make me pay for Beth!" That dog did not hunt either; his wife already knew about Beth and she had complimented me for helping her.

The employer tried to transfer his nagging guilt to me. He asked how much Beth's chemotherapy treatments cost, as if it mattered at that point. I told him 10 treatments at $10,000 each. He waved off my answer of $100,000 like it was nothing. In reality, he was symbolically waving off his guilt for refusing to help Beth when she was alive. But Beth saved his miserable life. He was a heavy smoker and quit smoking cold turkey that day and still was not smoking seven years later during trial.

While I assisted Beth's fight for life, the employer was advertising my job. On February 7, 2007, I intercepted the employer's ad in the Houston Chronicle, recruiting for my job as office manager. He wanted to make me a "floater."

THE APO$TATE

Circumstances suggested that after he assaulted me a year earlier, on February 11, 2006, his attorney advised him to wait a year and gradually faze me out of the company over the second year while I trained a replacement; at that point, the two-year statute of limitation for assault would have expired. But I turned the tables on him. I questioned my demotion to floater, which inherently questioned his earlier assault. He panicked and promoted me to chief financial officer, without raise or benefits.

Omission of facts was our Achilles heel. Our attorney failed to introduce us to jurors, explain our cases, and deflect diabolical defense histrionics. To the contrary, opposing counsel converted the employer into a victim, bloated the case, and turned facts into fiction. The Better Business Bureau reined as a "force majeure" plying its gilded reputation like an archangel's shield to deflect our claims. And the employer's distinguished "A+" rated membership was wielded as a testament to irrefutable integrity and disputed the nefarious deeds we alleged he committed. I was not allowed to tell the jury about the employer's complete history of abuse and fraud; that he enjoyed belittling and humiliating older and disabled people; that he perversely hated women; and that he acted with impunity using his wealth to shun the law. Court allowed the Bureau to endorse the employer, but I was prevented from detailing the Bureau's checkered past and bogus programs. I referenced the awards to the jury but could not tell them that the awards were a sham and suffocating monopoly. Nowhere was consumer fraud mentioned and/or the millions of dollars pilfered by the Bureau every year. Trial proved everything that O'Sullivan warned.

Our Swiss-cheesed trial was riddled with omissions and begged consumer reform and accountability. Furthermore, the FTC threw consumers under the bus; the federal watchdog ignored my awards-fraud complaints against the Bureau and allowed B-men to harass me, violate my civil rights, and deny my due process and equal protection of law. The public must understand legal gravity and consequences when the Better Business Bureau summoned Deep State powers to target and destroy me as a private citizen. Each of us is susceptible, and our freedoms are in jeopardy.

Mahatma Gandhi inspired worldwide civil rights and independence that freed India from oppressive British rule. On January 30, 1948, an assassin's bullets killed Gandhi for facilitating Muslim Pakistan's splinter from Hindu India. But his life's message promoted stalwart perseverance that I empirically sympathize, appreciate, and remind myself everyday: "First they ignore you; then they laugh at you; then they fight you; then you win."

CHAPTER **37**

TRIAL

Everyone is entitled to a fair trial except when the Better Business Bureau decides otherwise. Court docket scheduled my private civil employment trial against the employer, but the Bureau intervened and convoluted proceedings into a criminal-theft vendetta to feloniously indict and silence me. I am alleging that the Bureau hijacked my lawsuit, bribed the judge, compromised my attorney, steered jury intake, corrupted evidence, and fabricated the employer's counterclaims in order to hide its specious awards, money laundering, racketeering, and restraint of trade.

Trial began on Monday, January 5, 2015, 8:00 a.m., at the Harris County Courthouse in Houston, Texas. Court's commencement adjudicated gangsta nods between the enforcer judge and Italian employer dredging déjà vu of his wrapped-fish contract with the office manager that deep-sixed my employment. The judge belabored the French pronunciation of "voir dire" conjuring my opinion of her as a "fille de joie"; a high-priced harlot working Court Street's fashionable black judicial robe.

Voir dire interviews and "jury of your peers" proved foreboding. A young jury pool nuanced ageist viewpoints against our age and gender discrimination complaints. How could twenty-something-year-old kids understand discriminatory bias against older workers, corporate issues, and punitive damages? Furthermore, questioning revealed their disturbing cartel-minded respect for a violent employer.

We voted to continue trial realizing Houston's precarious jury pools and our diminishing witness availability. Evasive victory retreated when "coup fatal" struck the only three Black candidates who may have identified with the employer's racial discrimination. As a result, the unusually small jury pool extrapolated exactly 12 court hostages after plaintiff, defendant, and judicial exclusions. Our mature conservative White-raj lawsuits required seasoned professionals, but seated novice millennials (born 1980-2000). A young liberal digital bandwidth promised high frequency opposition because expected Bureau incursion would crystallize virtual comradery. But the stacked deck offered a wild card drawn by a middle-aged White male and former police sergeant and customer of the employer. Sarge was older than the rest and my instinct trusted that he would diffuse trial's complicated legal conundrum.

A dyspepsia lunch followed distasteful voir dire when our attorney questionably changed witness lineup confirming fifth-column treachery. I was supposed to testify last to prevent the employer from exploiting my evidence and testimony, but our attorney feigned unpreparedness and switched my end-of-trial testimony to beginning; akin to handing our case to the Bureau on a silver platter. Despite our heated argument, he insisted upon tightening the Bureau-knotted noose around my neck. His musical chair epiphany was the latest red flag in a series of malpractice alerts sired by the Bureau/employer's 2013 deposition. I realized atomic war with the Deep State Better Business Bureau when learning that its undercover awards director was a scheduled witness for the employer. Accordingly, I redirected our attorney's inbound sortie to mount a rogue witness-stand counterattack against all of them.

Trial opened with the bailiff's bellowing order to "please rise." Jurors solemnly filed into court. Their seated apprehension acknowledged my deep-seated dread anticipating a showdown with the locked-and-loaded Bureau. I was overcome with emotion considering years of rancorous legal proceedings, ruinous losses, and heartache and hell suffered while dealing with the venomous employer and reptilian Bureau.

The difference between combative attorneys subliminally tagged us as underdogs. Opposing counsel was adorned in a custom-made thousand-dollar suit and his evangelistic opening serpent-hissed glossolalia that eloquently dished our condemnation and "short-fused" doom. Contrarily, our dumbfounded attorney impersonated a nervous-nerdy absent-minded professor swaddled in a drab wrinkled lint-covered dime store knockoff whose potholed stuttering synopsis of our cases bored our jury into narcolepsy.

The employer's attorney dazzled jurors with a geeky PowerPoint presentation aimed at a young, hip-hop Internet generation. Heat-seeking illusion targeted cyber-cloned jurors mirroring the Bureau's subliminal brainwashing technique that award-baited compliant spellbound consumers. His web of deceit effortlessly ensnared rapport between the white-collar employer and blue-collar jury. He masterfully spun pettifoggery in a cheesy incriminating slide show to convict me and Wayne as gold digging extortionists blackmailing the rich celebrity employer. In a red herring second, we flipped from victims to victimizers. Our felonious mug shots graced courtroom walls next to a litany of contrived accusations reminiscing "wanted" posters. Desecrated screen grabs were overlaid with what

I coined as "bubblespeak" to subliminally denounce our discrimination allegations. My bubblespeak emblazoned, "Never Mentioned Discrimination," despite my numerous discrimination complaint letters. In glaring contrast, all-American apple pie snapshots canonized the employer and his wife promoting Houston's emblematic rodeo while musically accompanied by imagination's heavenly chorus of tweeting angelical birds. Opposing counsel's plebian angle pitched a milepost photograph of the employer's first Houston office located in a low-income single-story home while omitting tycoon tribute to his two multimillion-dollar gated-community homes. (Two years later, in July 2017, the employer bought a home in Palm Beach, Florida, for $8.9 million.) The attorney closed with the employer's orphaned youth overcome by his Horatio Alger success.

Our attorney befuddled jurors emphasizing loser's disparity. His archaic awkward overhead projector defied all-embracing digital wizardry. Whereas opposing counsel bonded, he bombed. We were fighting a well-known celebrity and jurists knew nothing about us. His opening presentation repelled jurors and forfeited a critical introductory opportunity to embed our respective backgrounds and complaint evidence. Thereafter, our alienation and star-crossed court proceedings bored the jury into Attention Deficit Syndrome.

The revised lineup featured Wayne, two video-taped depositions by Dale and Luis, me, Stephanie, Will, Chris, and Ted. The employer's witnesses included Candace Twyman, representing the Houston Bureau, and David H., who replaced Wayne. Befitting a pre-determined trial, David appeared on the first day and was quickly re-scheduled to appear after the employer at close of trial. Twyman never formally appeared and floated courtroom bandwidth in keeping with the Bureau's secret society. I dealt with Twyman as "Executive Director, The Better Business Bureau Education Foundation" that sponsored the *Awards for Excellence*, but trial documents listed her name on a witness list next to "Corporate Representative, Custodian of Records" as though to downplay her real title and prevent any association with and/or mention of the Bureau's specious awards program. The Bureau was obviously counting on its attorney to prevent me from mentioning the awards. Opposing counsel salivated like the-cat-that-ate-the-canary when handed the entire length of trial to set the stage for the employer's slam-dunk curtain call and David's death knell encore.

Wayne took the stand first and the sanctimonious opposing counsel immediately crucified him by hammering a serious driving offense. Cause was attributed to Wayne's emotional and financial distress after being humiliatingly fired, but masterful browbeating and character assassination embedded reckless irresponsibility. Consequently, Wayne was intimidated into silence, which marginalized both our cases. Opposing counsel's interrogation revealed disturbing modus operandi comprised of ad hominem (abusive arguments), inaccuracies, and hypotheticals, yet our attorney practiced catatonia despite our plaintiffs' hurdle that denied follow-up opportunity to clarify discrepancies; the judge boxed trial to four days and first-round cross exams.

Deposition videotapes of Luis and Dale were altered by opposing counsel to provide misleading testimony. They could not attend trial and pre-taped damning depositions to support my allegations of abuse by the employer, which enabled the tag-teaming judge and opposing counsel to neuter their respective videotapes. Accordingly, I would never recommend videotaped witness statements because they are subject to altered evidence tampering. Luis was our former telemarketing manager and witnessed the employer attacking me. He described hearing the employer screaming at me and seeing his hands outstretched towards my neck. Wayne was across the hall meeting with customers and the employer's caterwauling interrupted his sales pitch. He brushed Luis away not realizing an assault and closed the door leaving me trapped inside with a raging demon. Then Wayne and Luis left the building. Dale was a former salesman whose witness testimony was incriminating. During the Bureau's 2013 depositions, opposing counsel attempted to falsely accuse Dale of crimes committed by another person. Dale described an incriminating account of the employer's abuse and that he was unable to stop the employer from mistreating me. I was sitting next to Dale during his deposition and flashbacks brought silent tears. Opposing counsel sat directly across the conference table staring at me as though mentally bookmarking the moment. Then, during pre-trial proceedings, opposing counsel garnered the judge's approval to edit both videotapes. He first edited Dale's tape; I watched him locate the portion of tape that upset me and gut all of Dale's emotional testimony including my name and description of the employer's abuse. Next, he defanged Luis's video into a docile rendition of a generic company meeting that removed my name and the employer's assault. The jury was not told that witness videos were edited.

My turn came. After Wayne's trouncing, I had a lot of ground to cover. The Bureau was riding dirty and lobbing serious counterclaims that could dress me in prison pinstripes. I planned pointed soliloquies to force linchpin goals of clearing my name and documenting awards fraud.

At the first opportunity, I segued our attorney's questioning into the Houston Bureau's awards and the employer's theft of the coveted Pinnacle. Twyman was floating the courtroom like Forrest Gump's feather with intention to incriminate me, and I had to expose the employer's awards fraud before she testified. First, I explained the Pinnacle and Winner of Distinction awards. Then I angrily pointed at the employer and yelled out into the courtroom, "Mr. (employer) is a liar and a thief! He stole the Bureau's Pinnacle award." I told the jury that I wrote the award-winning application, required to win the Pinnacle, based on the employer's promise to implement my application's procedures; that the employer lied to me and refused to implement procedures after I submitted the application; and that he accepted the Pinnacle anyway under false pretense.

As expected, opposing counsel cut me off, but not before I made my point to the jury. Tricky Lips' subsequent cross examination condemned me for writing a false application. When he failed to prod my recantation, he ludicrously counterclaimed that the employer wrote the application. I firmly reiterated that I wrote the application and the cover letter featured my author's name. At that point, the jury understood that the employer was the thief, not me. The jury was primed and ready.

Next, I slammed the jury with a very graphic description of the employer's sexual assault. You could hear a pin drop. The employer nervously shifted in his chair expecting the worse from knowing the worst. The following narrative paraphrases my actual court testimony in addition to anecdotal details:

It was a Saturday morning. He entered the warehouse angry, slamming doors, and mumbling to himself. Without stopping by his office, he made a B-line for mine. I was working quietly at my desk, which was my typical demeanor and work ethic as verified by several witnesses. He approached, leaned into my face, and with flailing fists screamed, "You're stupid! You don't know anything." It was the only time that I defended myself. I responded in a low-key measured monotone, "I am not stupid, work several positions, make the company millions from awards, and have a college degree." He went berserk.

Blustering out of my office, he yelled, "I want you in my office right now! Get your fat ass in my office right now! You smart ass, I'll teach you a lesson!" He crossed every line and digressed to name calling and insults. My heart was pounding in my throat. I was horrified and thought about calling the police. He was manically out of control and I didn't want to be alone with him in his office. A loaded revolver was stored in his desk drawer and he bragged about using it on anyone that bothered him. He kept screaming at me, so I walked slowly into his office leaving the door open. Wayne was in the showroom with customers. Luis was in the back on the phone. Otherwise, the employer thought everyone had gone home and that he had me all to himself. I entered his office door and he angrily motioned for me to sit down in front of his desk. I said nothing while he talked himself into a blind rage in a matter of split seconds. His anger escalated with every word. I couldn't understand what he was saying. Then he demonized. His face contorted and discolored to a blistering red. He frothed at the mouth. His eyes bulged and his veins enlarged in his neck. He abruptly jumped out of his chair and savagely lunged at me from behind his desk with his arms stretched out towards my neck while sneering, "You ugly bitch," as his spit sprayed my face. I sat paralyzed in my chair, not believing what was happening. Just before making head-on contact, his desk clipped his legs because he was short. He fell mid-air hitting with a loud "thud." Looking shocked and disoriented, he held his shaking hands in front of his face and accusatorily screamed,

"Look what you did to me!" He repeatedly demanded, "Get out!" I heard his words, but I couldn't move. My legs were quivering ... heart was pounding ... chest was throbbing. I could not catch my breath. He tried to kill me. I found myself begging for my life, "Please calm down. Please calm down. Please ..." I kept thinking about the gun in his top drawer.

Wayne was next door closing a sale and shut the employer's door because of his fanatical screaming. Luis later told me he heard everything and came running up to the employer's closed glass door to help me, but Wayne told him to return to his desk thinking the employer was yelling at me as usual. Luis testified that he saw the employer reaching out for my throat. Then, everyone, including shocked customers, left the building while the assault continued.

The employer tried to slut-shame me with taunts of "ugly" while maliciously threatening my livelihood and career and insulting my family. "You're fired! Get your fat ass out of my office! Get out of my building! I'm cutting off your paycheck and throwing your nasty family in the street. I'll decide when you get paid again, if ever! You'll never work again, you ugly bitch." But leaving was not an option as he spewed vomitus hatred to sadistically dehumanize me. He pushed my every feminine button, yet my self-confidence sustained me. I was a former model and could emotionally hold my own having grown up with a family and neighborhood of roughshod boys. In fact, he attacked me wearing my skinny Gloria Vanderbilt jeans worn decades earlier in photo shoots. Malicious name-calling was indicative of his juvenile delinquent past that rapid-fired baseless vulgarity like a Gatling gun. But his *Exorcist* attack was criminal. He abused his power as my employer, trapped me in his office, attempted murder, perpetrated sexual depravity, and threatened me if I reported him.

He laughed hysterically while embracing his psychotic break. My survival instinct urged me to gather composure's steady feet and leave before part two's final kill kicked in. I headed towards my office, but he followed. I passed up my office, detoured into the file room, and rushed to the back while desperately yanking open a top lateral file drawer to step behind. He blocked the doorway. I was totally freaked out and frantically looked around the room for anything to defend myself and eyed a heavy metallic three-holed paper puncher within grabbing distance. As last resort, I planned to use my boots for kick-ass defense. The employer chuckled to himself having relegated me to hunter's quarry. He triumphantly gloated, "Guess I taught you a lesson." Again, he warned me, "Don't even think about getting a lawyer." He left the building acting as though nothing happened, yet I was traumatized, humiliated, and jobless. I do not remember closing the office or driving home. The rest of the weekend was agonizing. I was nauseated and throwing up; suffered chest pain, shortness of breath, numbness; and couldn't sleep. I called Wayne. He told me to come back on Monday.

The courtroom was dead silent. I hit a nerve. My testimony jarred jurors;

they sat in shock trading glances between me and their television avatar. But their horrified reaction also condemned me as though questioning, "Why in the hell didn't you leave?" And their judgmental stares confirmed that they did not understand my underpinning claim of age discrimination in a youth-oriented workforce. They could get another job tomorrow, but I could not at my age. Unfortunately, trial constraints did not allow me to explain my precarious situation to excuse continued employment. The employer was one among thousands of discriminatory employers. Additionally, there were no jobs for anyone, and another Great Depression was setting in. In fact, on October 24, 2008, "Bloody Friday" occurred "with drops of around 10% in most indices." I wanted to quit, but I had a heavy debt load consequent to the employer's quid pro quo hostage deal that shackled me to my job. Furthermore, if I did quit, he would blacklist my employment. In fact, I tried to earn an MBA in order to pursue another job, but he stopped me. Accordingly, I continued employment to buy time for a future escape.

The hostile judge orchestrated malfeasant court proceedings by undermining my testimony against the employer. After I described the assault, she condescendingly warned me not to use any further vulgar language. I reminded her that such vulgarity was recalled verbatim. From then on, the judge censored my every word shouting, "STOP," with cryptic judicial impact to accent opposing counsel's tirades with intent to vilify me. Her actions were meant to portray me as being uncontrollable to discredit my same accusations against the employer. I testified that the employer threatened me "not to talk, smile or laugh." The employer later amplified the judge's setup when telling the jury that he had to "shut me up," and the reason why he issued such directives.

In fact, I rarely spoke at work as several witnesses testified. I was treated like a caged animal and morbidly feared the employer who regularly terrorized me with his ballistic temper. He was a walking grenade with the pin pulled. The employer had already assaulted me once and never acted as such against anyone else. I was also the only one that he warned not to laugh, talk, or smile, except with customers. My office was bugged and videotaped. He threatened employees, salesmen, and installers not to speak to me and would literally come running out of his office to rudely wave them away from my doorway. I have copies of co-worker's notes, not presented in trial, which were passed to me in silence because they needed my input and feared the employer would overhear our conversations. Younger co-workers, half my age, did whatever they pleased while I was threatened into seclusion. Even Wayne had free reign to do as he pleased. After Wayne was fired, the employer instructed me to channel everything through the new chief operations officer despite my duties that included the employer's personal assistant. Additionally, the employer eavesdropped and timed my telephone conversations. Then he would inexplicably yank the telephone receiver out of my hand during high-profile collection calls; I was an outstanding collector with a superb accounts receivable track record and there was no sane reason for his vile behavior. But his favorite vice was to degrade me in front of customers and vendors by accusing me of matters that I had nothing to do with and that he personally handled.

Opposing counsel continued to poke at my victimized jugular and methodically convoluted my personal and work history while dodging any reference to awards. He accused me of slander, distorted an old collection account, revised my quid pro quo deal, contradicted my home's purchase and foreclosure, repurposed the employer's check, and redated my application for unemployment benefits. Accusations incorporated exhibits not previously submitted, which prevented defensive rebuttal.

Staged chaotic photographs of my office were projected onto courtroom walls to seed the employer's counterclaim of breach of fiduciary duties. Files were thrown everywhere. Post-It Notes were haphazardly stuck around my desk. Fax machines and copiers were strewn across the floor. Contrarily, I left a meticulous office and was renowned for being neat and professional because my financial duties demanded order and precision. Yet opposing counsel painstakingly picked apart my office questioning every disheveled inch to discredit me. I continued to respond that the pictures were staged; that I could not work in such shambled mess because "I was borderline OCD" ("Obsessive-Compulsive Disorder"), which surprisingly resonated with jurors.

Then the employer double-downed on his breach of fiduciary counterclaim by accusing me of failure to collect $250,000 dollars in outstanding accounts receivable despite evidence that he refused to allow me to finish collections and refused me discovery access to customer files to prove collections were either made, couldn't be made, or were being collected. Furthermore, it was no coincidence that the collection amount nuanced the felon's amount of theft; the employer previously warned me that "it's easy to set someone up" after he hired the parolee and placed her in my accounting department. Texas Penal Code, Section 32.45, Misapplication of Fiduciary Property, indicts "an officer, manager, employee, or agent carrying on fiduciary functions on behalf of a fiduciary." And respective felony of the second degree includes misapplication of "$150,000 or more but less than $300,000." Accordingly, Texas Penal Code, Section 12.33, Second Degree Felony Punishment, states, "An individual ... shall be punished by imprisonment in the Texas Department of Criminal Justice for any term of not more than 20 years or less than 2 years." Additionally, punishment includes a fine "not to exceed $10,000."

While I was being threatened with prison, our attorney sat unresponsive without pursuing redirect's redemptive rebuttal. He ignored several profound exculpatory facts: that the employer refused our plaintiffs' discovery request demanding access to exonerating customer-account files that were sitting in the courtroom; that I submitted a customer email as a trial exhibit pertaining to one of the largest so-called "uncollected" accounts receivable that confirmed I completed collection and the customer was waiting for David to pick up money; that my resignation letter specifically addressed accounts receivable and requested opportunity to clear outstanding accounts, which the employer refused; and that I inherited all of Wayne's accumulated work in addition to my five jobs and why I had been unable to finish collections. As a side anecdote and warning, I hold the Houston Bureau and Houston Foundation accountable for meddling in my private trial and orchestrating the employer's false breach of fiduciary counterclaims against me. There is a 10-year statute from point of proof relative to "Offenses related to theft by a fiduciary." Accordingly, I believe that the Houston Foundation qualifies as a fiduciary; and that its executive director, Candace Twyman, a listed trial witness, attempted to falsely accuse me of fiduciary fraud to protect the organization's specious *Awards for Excellence* and her $110,172 salary emphasized by her subsequent disappearance after I exposed the employer's respective awards fraud.

Then opposing counsel presented an old collection account that I had paid, but he twisted into evasion of payment. His presentation was confusing, and I did not understand his topic or questioning. Tricky Lips pulled a "Perry Mason" and air-waved a handful of documents above his head without allowing me to see respective paperwork while clumsily explaining provenance from a former attorney of his law firm who subsequently opened his own collection agency. My take was that opposing counsel's ridiculous disclaimer was concocted as a warrant to invade my privacy and steal private settlement documents. He proceeded to accuse me of dodging collectors without giving me opportunity to retrieve paid receipts to counter his false accusations. My every attempt to explain was interrupted. One rebuttal answer would have disproved opposing counsel's accusations by informing jurors that I could not have bought my home if I had an unpaid collection account. But, once again, my attorney said nothing.

Even more incredulous, opposing counsel attempted to connect the collection account with a bonus check that I received the day Wayne was fired; payment was issued as a bribe to facilitate Wayne's pending employment termination later that afternoon. Opposing counsel thoroughly confused jurors by jumbling timeframes and issues as though they occurred in the same timeframe when they were three years apart. I paid the collection account in full prior to receiving a pre-approved mortgage in March 2005 and the employer's check was dated August 7, 2008. Again, my attorney said nothing.

The quid pro quo deal was an open wound for me. I made a deal with the Devil and lost everything that I worked so hard to get and suffered so much trying to keep. The deal gave me a long-belated raise in return for buying a house close to the office and a new car to replace a problematic vehicle. The employer knew that I had already prequalified for a two-story house two miles from the warehouse because he signed respective employment documents. After I became heavily indebted, he turned violent. Degradation, stalking, and assault were not part of the deal.

Age and gender discrimination were never options. He treated me like a whore, tortured my every working second, and forced me to work harder than all others while begging for nominal raises. Male peers received workable relationships, never groveled for jobs or raises, and received additional sales bonuses that were denied to me. I began employment as an accomplished professional but was paid a low-balled $30,000 while men started at $45,000. Later my corporate peers earned over $160,000 plus sales commissions when my last year struggled to earn $65,000 while working my job plus others, seven days a week with no time off. I honored my end of the bargain, but the employer abused his; humiliation, condescension, and submission became the daily grind. He would fire me at moment's notice and savor my horrified reaction intensified by my financial duress. Then he condescendingly threatened, "You'll never find another job like mine at your age." He knew I could not afford to leave and tricked me into "golden shackles."

Opposing counsel deceived jurors by distorting all facts relative to the quid pro quo deal, and I was prevented from presenting evidence to defend myself. The jury was never informed of the following chronology of events: 1) I received mortgage pre-approval on March 29, 2005. 2) About June 2005, I presented an offer on a house near the office. 3) House purchase was funded and ready to close in early September 2005. 4) Employer fired me twice and rehired me on Monday, September 19, 2005. 5) Hurricane Rita blew through Houston on September 24, 2005. 6) Employer offered me a quid pro quo deal on September 25, 2005. 7) I completed home purchase on October 5, 2005. 8) I bought a new car in November 2005. 9) Employer assaulted me on February 11, 2006.

Quid pro quo arose from the employer's wrongful animus derived from a conversation that took place on Monday, September 19, 2005. The previous Friday, Wayne, Jack, and I were talking in my office about the absent employer who had left for the golf course. Jack was a part-time salesman and the employer's best friend. He had seen the employer repeatedly screaming at me and was trying to lighten collateral damage. Jack began making fun of the employer and ended by questioning his mental stability. The following Monday, the employer came charging into my office like a rabid junkyard dog and accusatorily barked, "Did you talk to Wayne?" He prodded me, "Come on, you can tell me the truth!" His line of questioning was strange because my job required speaking to Wayne as his operation's backup. I also wondered why he thought I would lie? He was obviously setting me up for a smackdown. As soon as I answered, "Yes," he retorted, "You're fired!" That was the first time. He obviously snooped our Friday's conversation. But he did not go after the men, only me, despite Jack doing the trash talking.

Being a dutiful fired employee, I began packing my office and placed belongings at the front door. Wayne strolled by, noticed, and apoplectically questioned, "What are you doing?" He panicked when I told him the employer fired me, "Quick, put it back before he shows up!" But it was too late. The employer saw my loot stashed at the door and looked quizzical as though forgetting that he fired me. He got mad again and fired me a second time: "Okay, you're fired! Get your ass out of my building!" The situation was getting confusing; I felt like a yo-yo. Wayne called a meeting. I was rehired after spending 30 minutes begging, groveling, and apologizing for something I did not do. He loved every humiliating second. I was in the throes of closing on my home and had spent several thousand dollars in the process, but that twisted escapade stopped my final signature underscoring why I did not close on my home earlier.

A week later, September 24, 2005, Hurricane Rita hit the Texas coastline. I stayed in Houston and monitored the office and warehouse remaining in contact with the employer who was at his lakeside mansion in Austin. He acknowledged my protective initiative during the storm. The following day, he offered me a quid pro quo deal that included a salary raise to $55,000.

Opposing counsel embedded skepticism by withholding knowledge of my mortgage pre-approval that facilitated the speedy closing of my home. I had copies of respective mortgage approval and closing documents at home; dates would have corroborated my testimony and verified how I was able to close on my home within two weeks of the quid pro quo deal. Part of my lawsuit involved punitive damages for foreclosure. So Tricky Lips ambushed me and distorted facts to discredit me as being financially irresponsible and negligent. He approached the witness stand and shoved foreclosure documents in my face belligerently detailing how I bought my home for $121,000, but foreclosure listed a value of $138,000 leaving a net equity in the amount of $17,000. False insinuation misled jurors. Equity was not obtainable when I realized debauchery by GMAC Home Mortgage; home equity loans required employment for collateral, and I was unemployed. Additionally, jurors were not told that my home was foreclosed in the middle of a loan modification. Otherwise, I would have sold my home! Jurors were young, inexperienced, and gullible; they blindly accepted opposing counsel's lies.

Thereafter, opposing counsel revised the date of Hurricane Rita's landfall to discredit my respective testimony and cut the employer's connection between the quid pro quo deal and purchase of my home. Rita hit Texas in between agreement and mortgage closing. Opposing counsel began dramatically air-waving paperwork again without offering documents to me for review, which meant he was up to no good. He essentially called me liar and changed my stated date of landfall on September 24 to September 26, leaving nine instead of 11 days until closing on October 5, 2005. In fact, Wikipedia stated, "After steadily weakening and beginning to curve to the northwest, Rita gradually weakened and made landfall between Sabine Pass, Texas and Holly Beach, Louisiana with winds of 120 mph (195 km/h) on September 24. It weakened over land and degenerated into a large low-pressure area over the lower Mississippi Valley on September 26." Then, while hiding my pre-approved mortgage, Tricky Lips made fun of me to the jury asking, "How anyone could close a home so quickly?"

That night I pulled a copy of opposing counsel's "quoted" Wikipedia article as well as others to prove he lied. I contacted our attorney and emailed him copies. During the next day's opening court session, our attorney presented the articles to correct court record, but damage was done. The judge casually shrugged, and jurors aimlessly stared.

Next, opposing counsel argued the date that I submitted unemployment benefits. He claimed that I filed for unemployment a week before I left the employer implying that I did not wait for the employer's final answer to my submitted contingency resignation as claimed. A printout of my unemployment application was posted on the large screen. Opposing counsel highlighted the initiation date that was a prior Sunday and a week before my actual resignation date. My response was that I used to work for TWC and they always listed the date of an event in context with the week it was involved; that Sunday started each new week and why it was listed as such. Opposing counsel vehemently argued down my response. He insisted that I filed employment benefits on the Sunday prior to the Friday because I had already planned to leave the employer ahead of his final actions, which underscored his gold digger innuendos. I had my unemployment application at home that verified my statements and date of submittal, but he knew I would not have another opportunity to defend myself. When our attorney finally decided to speak up, he made matters worse and undermined everything I said. He blurted out that the record date may have reflected my entering the TWC system at some earlier point, which supported opposing counsel. I was stunned! My testimony was true; Tricky Lips lied; and our attorney enabled him.

I felt raped. My First and 14th Amendment rights of free speech, due process, and equal protection of law were violated. If nothing else, we did prove the employer's federal status of 15+ employees that was a prerequisite hurdle for our discrimination lawsuits. Furthermore, I discredited the employer's felonious counterclaims of breach of fiduciary duties and theft, red-flagged the employer's assault, and introduced the employer's awards fraud. The conversion verdict was guaranteed because of judicial malfeasance. Tricky Lips omitted the subject of conversion during cross exam to prevent me from telling the jury that statute of limitation expired. And, of course, my attorney did not intervene.

Trial tricks compounded along with witness testimony. On one occasion, opposing counsel and the employer bushwhacked our witnesses while they waited outside the courtroom. Opposing counsel planted himself at the courtroom entrance while the employer walked from the restroom and intentionally veered out of his way to run into two of our witnesses, who were his former installers. The employer knocked Ted into Chris standing next to him. Ted quickly backed away from the employer realizing a set-up. Stephanie and her husband were nearby and witnessed the event. Then the plot thickened. Opposing counsel melodramatically burst into the courtroom and accused Ted of attacking the employer! Ted was easily six-foot five-inches tall while the employer stretched to reach five-feet five. When trial resumed, Tricky Lips methodically questioned each witness regarding the incident. When Ted reached the witness stand, he was told to stand for the jury. The objective was to show jurors that the short employer attacked a tall man undermining one of my linchpin complaints that the employer only assaulted women.

Stephanie was my prime witness as the employer's former office manager whom I replaced. When initially solidifying potential witness testimony, I discovered that the employer had also attacked and mistreated her. We were both tall and fit his victim's profile of being financially vulnerable. Thanks to Stephanie and Wayne, I won a year-long battle pursuing unemployment benefits. The employer went berserk after the TWC ruled against him. He called Stephanie and her family members demanding that she recant her testimony, or he would sue. She offered tape recordings of the employer's threats that proved his misogynistic vitriol towards women. Unfortunately, TWC's verdict was not allowed in court. And opposing counsel had the judge throw out Stephanie's tape recordings that proved the employer's ballistic temper and vile-sounding voice. Consequently, our cases were compromised. The judge only allowed Stephanie to describe tape recordings, which diluted impact and circumstances. Accordingly, at trial's end, the employer gave an Oscar-winning performance using a disguised voice that spoke barely above a whisper accompanied by monkish behavior to counter both our testimonies of assault.

Opposing counsel then attempted to discredit Stephanie. He delved into her past employment and questioned a fire at the employer's previous office building. Stephanie was accused of causing the fire when illegally smoking in the storeroom as a result of throwing a lit cigarette butt into a garbage can. But she expertly rebuffed Tricky Lips' convoluted allegation by referencing the fire marshal's arson report that confirmed the employer's cigarette butts were also found in the garbage can when the fire occurred. She defiantly accused the employer of being ultimately responsible; that he did not give employees time for breaks; and that he routinely smoked in the storeroom setting a bad example for his employees. Another incident occurred whereby the employer physically assaulted Stephanie by repeatedly pressing his finger into her chest. He outrageously accused Stephanie of child abuse; she appeared with her baby to pick up her paycheck; the baby had red swollen eyes due to "pink eye" and she had just returned from the pediatrician to get a prescription. Opposing counsel concluded his tirade of character assassination by taking a feeble swipe at Stephanie's honorable discharge from the Army. She proudly stood her ground and made him look like an ogre for attacking a dedicated veteran who was commended for her patriotic military service.

Will took the witness stand next. He was a former installer whose short stature inherently triggered the employer's "Napoleon Complex." I was present when the employer viciously fired Will using the excuse that he wrongly stacked merchandise in the company truck. Rough roads had jostled windows forcing Will to adjust packing to avoid breakage. Will was left in tears and begging for his job during a jobless economy. His first-born child was only a week old. The employer then refused Will's request to retrieve his toolbox and handyman's livelihood. Will agreed to testify and appeared in court wearing a ski cap. The judge expelled him for improper attire, which prompted one of trial's most notable testimonies. Will gallantly returned and defensively explained that he meant no disrespect; that he was ill and suffering a 101-degree temperature; and that he was trying to stay warm because it was cold outside. He proceeded to hilariously describe the difference between the judge's alleged "robber mask" and the "ski cap" that he wore. Will pulled his cap out of his pocket, held it up to the jury, and, while figuratively outlining two circles, explained that a robber mask had two holes cut into the face panel versus his ski cap with no holes. The jury was visibly amused. The judge was not.

Chris and Ted followed. Their respective witness testimony told the jury how badly the employer treated me and confirmed my orderly and efficient work ethic. They also detailed the extent of the employer's sovereign control over contractors. In fact, he had cheated them out of a $3,000-dollar contest award. Before I left the employer, I had already confirmed that they had won first prize in the company's 2008 "Happy Note" contest. Opposing counsel tried and failed to character assassinate them with petty accusations. Ted brilliantly ended testimony by reminding jurors of the employer's issue with his short height, which offset their earlier courtroom theatrics. Jurors were noticeably entertained and genuinely disappointed at their departure.

And, finally, the employer's turn came. I waited seven years to get that psycho on the witness stand. The courtroom fell deathly silent. Jurors watched his every well-rehearsed move. They were already teetering in his celebrity's favor and had continued star-struck stares throughout trial after decades of hearing his radio commercials and seeing his face on television, highway billboards, and newspaper advertising. In fact, the employer played his fame card and increased advertising during trial. A couple of the jurymen, who were salesmen and/or contractors, displayed special partiality towards the employer after he testified that he paid the most money for sales staff in the window and door industry. They were also among the same jurymen breaking protocol outside the courtroom. Moreover, the juror, who laughed along with the employer during his testimony, previously snooped my private conversation with my attorney and visited the men's room with the employer during court breaks.

My first impression was that the employer was heavily drugged. He channeled a medieval monk and delivered a jaw-dropping performance worthy of critical acclaim; I expected an encore of self-flagellation with a cat-of-nine-tails for special effect. Wayne and I were rendered speechless. But, then again, he was an accomplished con artist having honed his exemplary skills in chicanery since childhood while living off the seedy backstreets of New York City. It was obvious that the employer's ulterior motive was to invoke a calm demeanor to unravel our plaintiff's collective testimony depicting him as an uncontrollable pervert. The employer's farcical theatrics would not have been possible had the judge allowed Stephanie's tape recordings, which exposed his true nature.

Opposing counsel first sought to discredit our age discrimination allegations that the employer was "cleaning house" of older employees and forbid hiring anyone over the age of 45. Opposing counsel soft-pedaled the employer to explain his employment of several older sales staff during the timeframe of our employment, but he did not show respective employment documents to the jury. The employer built on opposing counsel's histrionics and bragged about his chivalrous employment of older workers.

Tricky Lips owned the jury after the employer's interrogation accented by the fifth-column juryman's coordinated antics; I had no doubt that he had been bribed. The employer used the juryman's supportive laughter to entertain jurists with trivial trade stories. And our inert attorney allowed the employer's free-for-all soliloquy that triumphantly grandstanded, joked, and conquered. All the while, the judge kept her nose buried in her computer; she did not threaten the employer to "STOP" or limit his rambling BBB factoid advertorial.

The employer invoked Bureau cronyism when reminding jurors of his influential membership and "A+" rating score. And Opposing counsel introduced the "Better Business Bureau" in a manner that implied the organization was participating in our trial as a co-defendant, which empowered the employer's counterclaims. My witness stand testimony was not given the opportunity to clarify the Bureau's involvement as a sponsor of a phony awards program and collusion with the employer. Furthermore, jurors were denied full disclosure by opposing counsel who did not describe my complaint letters sent to the Texas Attorney General and FTC that incriminated the Bureau as the employer's co-conspirator in awards fraud. Additionally, I was not able to divulge the John Moore Services' defamation lawsuit against the Bureau that directly impacted our lawsuit and delayed our trial for several years. I could only tell the jury that the employer was a "liar and a thief" and stole the Bureau's Pinnacle award. As a result, the Bureau retained its tidy-whitey public image.

Our attorney's closing interrogation of the employer was akin to baptismal rebirth. I think he realized Tricky Lips welched on whatever backdoor deal they made and went after the employer with a vengeance to offset betrayal. He shot down two major inaccuracies; that the employer lied about the date and reason he gave me a $7,500 bonus check on the same day he fired Wayne, and that the employer staged employment of older sales staff to discredit our discrimination claims.

The employer could not answer why the date of the bonus check matched the date Wayne was fired. After awkward silence, he lamely admitted, "I made a mistake." He was busted! The employer lied in a previous deposition claiming that he gave me the check because I begged him for money for groceries, past-due mortgage, and car payments, contrary to my bank statements proving he lied. The date of the check proved my allegation of a premeditated bribe. For years, our attorney ignored the significance of the check as our saving grace. Fortunately, he came to his senses and used the check to impugn the employer's insubordination claim as the reason for Wayne's employment termination. The employer gave me the check the morning of the day that he fired Wayne, which proved that he planned Wayne's termination because his payroll company required two days' notice to process the check.

Our attorney highlighted the employer's deception that he hired older staff after Wayne and I left to offset our discrimination claims. He presented exhibits of employment contracts and hire dates that proved the employer hired older employees in 2010, two years after Wayne and I filed lawsuits, and after being schooled by several sets of employment attorneys. In fact, I was replaced by a 32-year-old male office manager, but the employer hired an employment attorney after my lawsuit and the male office manager was replaced by a 45-year-old female.

The employer was caught red-handed and his testimony was embarrassingly undermined. He demon-glanced opposing counsel's assistant attorney as she sat demurely on the sideline. She dutifully compiled the dirt used against us during depositions and trial, but she made serious mistakes that undermined the employer's lies. Fabricating fraud will do that. Her reaction to the employer was entertainingly telling. I saw fear in her eyes that brought me a strange sense of atonement. In a previous deposition, I sat across from her and noticed her hands nervously trembling while using her laptop. The employer was known for yelling at his attorneys.

TRIAL

I relished every moment of the employer's witness stand comeuppance after years of immeasurable suffering from his drooling psychopathy, vitriol, and depravity. Watching him squirm like a worm in front of a jury was incredibly liberating, vindicating, and therapeutic. And he knew it! He avoided eye contact. Tables had turned and he was not in control. I made him answer my lawsuit and come to court. It was an intense moment when our eyes finally locked in mortal combat. His searing stare, criminal intention, and deranged soul spewed vomitus hatred and cloistered insanity. We mind-melded perverse flashbacks of his deception, condescension, voyeurism, discrimination, and masochism that irreparably scarred my life; when he cornered, demeaned, assaulted, tortured, and entrapped me; when he forced debt and desperation on me; when he cast me into the bowels of his consumer fraud; when he blacklisted my employment; when he caused me to lose my home, career, and credit that broke up my family; and when he conspired with the Houston Bureau to frame and imprison me with felony charges for reporting massive consumer fraud by the *Awards for Excellence*. No, I did not blink. Not once. I forced him to look away. And, in that instant, I won! I restored my honor, dignity, and integrity.

It was also the assistant defense attorney's duty to trudge the employer's sealed customer files back and forth into court. As I politely held the courtroom door open for her, cruel irony reminded that I created those files now weaponized against me. Files that I initiated, managed, and protected for years; that bore my handwriting; that secreted chronology of collections; and that would have exonerated me had our discovery requests been honored.

The employer accused Wayne of stealing over $250,000 dollars of mismeasured windows out of his warehouse. The same number kept reverberating and emphasized the employer's fixation on the felon. I was not concerned about the employer's testimony involving Wayne because our attorney usually did well relative to his $1.5 million discrimination damage claim. Accordingly, our attorney proved the employer knew mismeasures were not missing; that the employer sold or reused mismeasures in new installations; and that the employer had pocketed the cash. "Mismeasures" were windows or doors not made according to custom-ordered specifications and the employer was refunded cost. Wayne alleged that he was accused of theft to cover the employer's money laundering scheme that washed dirty cash in overseas accounts.

Wayne and I managed mismeasures. Sales were handled by Wayne and payment was processed by me. We alleged the employer cheated vendors, customers, installers, and salesmen in the process of double-dipping profit from mismeasures. Vendors refunded money for bogus mismeasures that the employer resold for 100% profit. Customers contracted custom-made items, but were sold mismeasures that were force-fit on their homes at additional cost. As a result, wily salesmen raised prices to ensure a commission while vulnerable

THE APO$TATE

installers were penciled extraneous installation expenses.

Of course, the employer denied our allegation of cooked books. But Wayne and I hand-delivered hundreds-of-thousands-of-dollars in undeclared cash to the employer over a period of several years, which he registered in personal ledgers. And we were required to witness his respective receipt, counting, and recording. Furthermore, I alleged that the employer's pocketed revenue landed in offshore accounts. Some of the material I copied included a document that placed the employer on a chartered boat trip to the Caribbean and proved occasion and opportunity to transfer revenue outside the United States. I also copied the employer's respective handwritten notes as evidence in order to eliminate any doubt as to provenance.

David's deceptive testimony decimated our discrimination cases. He obviously participated in opposing counsel's scheme that switched him from opening trial to closing trial to coordinate with the employer's testimony. Our attorney exposed some of the employer's indiscretions, but his overall interrogation failed to prove age and gender discrimination, which also emphasized damning impact of David's lies. The employer hired David a couple of months prior to firing Wayne. During the interim, David circled our offices like a vulture. Our attorney made little if any mention that David was given the new office previously promised to Wayne as vice president. When reappearing a week later under subpoena, David met with opposing counsel for over 30 minutes to synchronize testimony; they spoke behind closed conference room doors and feet from where we sat in court waiting on them. If not for David, the case would not have gone to trial. He provided false testimony in affidavits that were used against Wayne during his breach of contract lawsuit and against both of us in our employment lawsuits. Interestingly, when our discrimination cases were remanded back to court after a favorable appeals decision, David was fired. Apparently, the employer maintained his employment and six-figure income to buy his favorable testimony.

After David was sworn in "to tell the truth the whole truth and nothing but the truth," he lied. Our attorney revisited inaccuracies starting with staged photographs of my office per the employer's counterclaim for breach of fiduciary duties. I was fired September 5, 2008, and Hurricane Ike blew through Houston on September 13, 2008, creating massive service issues; my former office was used as a catch-all for respective files and equipment. After dodging pointed questions, David reluctantly confirmed taking pictures of my office in such chaotic state *after* the hurricane and not *before* as he originally claimed. He also acknowledged meeting with opposing counsel before testifying and that he was "coached." As a result, David and the employer looked like two gutter thugs trying to frame me.

David's admittance that he was coached countered opposing counsel's earlier accusation that my attorney coached me because I answered his cross-examination questions too well. The sheer thought of our attorney instructing me on anything was ludicrous and far from reality. Our attorney ignored me throughout my lawsuit. We constantly butted heads because he focused on Wayne's pricey $1.5 million payout that excluded the Better Business Bureau's crocodile baggage. Our attorney tried to force me to settle, never set a clear path, showed no interest, lost several of my critical witnesses, refused expert witnesses, ignored explanations, and dismissed the bulk of my hard-won evidence, which is why he couldn't respond to opposing counsel's cross-examination during my testimony.

In fact, I had not communicated with our attorney since the Houston Bureau's forced deposition and the employer's mediation in 2013. An impromptu in-your-face come-to-Jesus meeting after the deposition left us on fractured terms. Wayne literally pulled me away from a heated exchange with our attorney to prevent me from firing him, which I am sure was our attorney's underhanded objective! Years of being terrorized by the employer surfaced with repercussions amplified by our attorney's suspicious behavior. He allowed the Bureau's deposition that ignored felonious consequences of breach of fiduciary duties and conversion/theft. I had no communication with our attorney after mediation and thought that he dropped my case. He refused to meet and review our cases until just three days prior to trial and then half-heartedly focused on Wayne's case. I believed that he made a deal with opposing counsel after I refused the employer's settlement offer at mediation; previous offers ranged up to $100,000. Our attorney salivated at the thought of dumping me and appeared distraught when I declined the employer's offer, but settlement would have silenced me and impeded my ability to expose the Better Business Bureau. Additionally, I would have been left susceptible to the employer's black mail and consumer fraud and unable to clear my name. So I forced trial to document court record, defend my reputation, and report awards fraud via publication.

I felt our attorney misled me regarding the deposition in 2013, which I vehemently objected to, considering he was allowing opposing counsel to add new and statute-expired conversion charges late in the lawsuit. Even a moron would have realized the deposition was a prelude to a rigged trial. I was mystified and alarmed that our self-proclaimed "experienced" attorney could be so idealistic and ignorant to assume opposing counsel was playing by the rules. Additionally, he became unusually cozy with the associate attorney to such disturbing point that I questioned his loyalty to our case. In fact, he began defending his relationship with her by outrageously proclaiming that he was "mentoring" her as a junior attorney despite the fact that she was working against us and was representing the most exclusive law firm in Houston that had two major streets named after it.

THE APO$TATE

One trial reset, five months before the Bureau's conversion deposition, was exceptionally suspect and indicated our attorney was colluding with defense's associate attorney. I could not decipher if the associate attorney was intentionally channeling Mati Hari and twisting our bachelor attorney around her finger, or if he was just embracing self-interests. Nevertheless, he repeatedly acquiesced to her demands. Two days before a previous court docket was scheduled for trial, in May 2013, she cancelled. I was sitting in his office late in the afternoon, just before the court closed at 4:30 p.m., when the receptionist transferred her call. He anxiously answered. While profusely sweating and staring at me as I sat at his conference table, he intently listened and in a low guarded voice mumbled, "She's here." They sounded like two conniving secret agents caught in a tangled web of deceit. I expected a lethal warning voiceover that his phone would self-destruct in 30 seconds. Their shifty behavior triggered a flashback. I was walking in the warehouse door the day I left the employer. David was lying in wait for me like a poisonous snake hiding in the grass. In a hushed tone, he tipped-off the employer, "She's here." Once again, I felt sickening dread.

After the May trial cancellation, our attorney lied to Wayne and me about resetting the case for the next court docket in September 2013. Weeks dragged on with no word of rescheduling. So I called the court clerk who advised that "nobody from either side called him." I confronted our red-faced, side-winding attorney for lying and insisted that he set trial for October, but instead of setting trial he notified us of the Bureau's deposition in September.

I believed that the cleaner backstabbed our attorney during court proceedings, which forced our attorney's last-minute scramble to avoid blatant legal malpractice. As a result, he earnestly interrogated the employer at the end of trial, but brownie points were made too late. The jury was tired and already decided verdict. Had he listened to me and brought in an expert witness to analyze the employer's depravity, we would have clinched our discrimination cases and ended trial with a bang. Instead, we fizzled like a wet fuse.

Time came to draft final jury charges. Jurors were sent out and attorneys and judge huddled at the bench. Opposing counsel and judge laughed, giggled, and connived while our attorney helplessly waved his hands in the air invoking the universal gesture for "screwed." They obviously double-crossed him, and he was left hanging on a sawed limb. If our attorney reported judicial malfeasance, he would have incriminated himself. I warned him many times that the Bureau and employer were dangerous and not to be trusted. Accordingly, the judge submitted all counterclaims including conversion/theft. She left jurors no option; they had to charge me with "converting" copied material because I admitted such activity. The judge did not forewarn the jury that conversion charges were invalid due to an expired statute of limitations.

The verdict was rendered about 4:30 p.m., Monday afternoon, January 12,

2015. The jury deliberated almost five hours. Anxiety overkill reached medication level; I felt stroke symptoms. Jurors filed back into the courtroom with a bounce in their step knowing freedom was at hand. The judge personally read the jury's verdict decree while darting a gratified smile at the employer. Plaintiffs' discrimination cases were denied. The worst of the Defendant's counterclaims were also denied including slander, breach of fiduciary duties, and theft. But Defendant's counterclaim of conversion was upheld. Jurors set Plaintiffs' individual penalties at $500 and lowered Defendant's damages to $2,500. Opposing counsel had requested $5,000 in damages while whining like a drama queen that he had "to come to court and retrieve his client's property." Total judgment was $3,000 each plus court costs. The grapevine express whispered that the employer bragged far and wide that he won a $130,000 judgment. Winning a paltry $3,000 dollar award was too embarrassing when he spent seven years and over $300,000 dollars fighting our lawsuits. Lying emphasized the depth of his defeat.

Accordingly, the employer and Houston Bureau failed to imprison me with felonious counterclaims of breach of fiduciary duties and theft for reporting their awards fraud to regulatory agencies. As previously mentioned, Texas Penal Code, Section 32.45, Misapplication of Fiduciary Property, is punishable by Texas Penal Code, Section 12.33, second degree felony, two to 20 years in prison, and $10,000 fine. And Texas Penal Code, Section 31.05, Theft of Trade, is punishable by Texas Penal Code, Section 12.34, third degree felony, two to 10 years in prison, and $10,000 fine.

Consequently, I charge the Bureau with grand theft, tampering with evidence, bribing court jurists, misapplication of fiduciary property, violation of constitutional rights, and racketeering. I allege that accomplices included the judge and employer. Silver linings cleared my name and documented the employer's awards fraud and the Bureau's participation on court record.

Additionally, verdict established the employer's federal status (15+ employees) when the jury ruled on our discrimination cases. Our lawsuit only referred to salesmen. But the employer was also rendered accountability outside the realm of our lawsuit for his other group of contractors who were installers, e.g., Chris and Ted. Contractors bore the same footprint as salesmen. We set legal precedence by myopically defining specific federal identifiers and qualifiers for sales and service personnel, which was previously ambiguous and hard to prove. We cleared a major hurdle that would have automatically voided our discrimination cases had the jury refused to hear our claims. As a result, we earmarked the employer for an IRS investigation.

While the judge jubilantly read the verdict, the employer wildly jumped up and down. His entire countenance dramatically changed as he derisively pointed and laughed at me, not Wayne. The jury ruled 10 to 2 against our discrimination cases. The complicit juryman pulled an "O. J. Simpson" brandishing a fist pump while cheering along with the euphoric employer. Jurists anxiously filed out of the courtroom oblivious to the employer's schizophrenic personality switch that contradicted his witness stand apparition of a Trappist monk obeying monastic silence by the Rule of St. Benedict's "Conversion of Manners." Sarge was the last to leave. He watched the employer make a fool of himself and glanced back at us as though acknowledging our bum rap.

Wayne was shell-shocked. I was relieved. Verdict could have been much worse; like a complementary trip to the nearest prison. And Wayne expected legal retaliation. But I feared being whacked; I knew too much. Trial ended, and I still had the Bureau in hot pursuit. I was dealing with evil global governance. Accordingly, documenting the *Awards for Excellence* in court record was not only consumer-oriented, but self-preservation.

We hurriedly gathered our belongings and left the courtroom. The employer noticeably winched at our abrupt departure. His warped mind confused the courtroom for his dungeon, and he desperately needed to complete our ultimate humiliation and indignation. Parting company snapped him into harsh reality. He not only lost control of us, but trial exposed his fraud.

Awkward silence overwhelmed our walk from the courthouse to the parking garage. Wayne and Leticia, his wife, were parked down the street and we sentimentally bid farewells. The elevator was crowded, but I felt alone standing beside our attorney. He morphed into a stranger, maintained isolation, stared absently, and avoided eye contact. He fumbled a robotic "good-bye" behind closing elevator doors as I disembarked on my parking level.

I retraced every misstep that always backtracked to the complicit juryman. Voire dire indicated he was a contractor vulnerable to bribery and his trial antics confirmed witness tampering by the employer. The jury pool was not cloistered, and I witnessed him visiting the men's room followed by the miscreant employer who had already bribed several of our witnesses. The juryman aggressively laughed along with the employer during his testimony and noticeably prodded other jurors to do the same. His malfeasant behavior reminded, "One bad apple spoils the bunch." No doubt, he corrupted our jury panel.

As fate would have it, I parked by the juryman. I had recognized him walking in front of me. His white SUV was parked on an inclined level overlooking my car. While he unlocked his vehicle, I asked him, "Why did you vote in favor of the employer? (The judge invited questioning jurors after verdict.) He haughtily replied, "The verdict was unanimous." I waited for him to leave. During the interim, the employer's depraved vitriolic influence overcame him; he grabbed my happenstance glance to condescendingly laugh at and victim shame me!

Humiliation only compounded. Driving through the parking garage, I confronted the employer and his wife. She casually leaned against their Cayenne

TRIAL

Porsche while he jumped into my pathway maniacally laughing, pointing, and sneering. He was finishing his victory lap that I abruptly cut off in court. His psychopathy desperately needed me to react, but, once again, I cut him off. As I drove around him, his wife returned an empty stare. I held her just as guilty. She was a special education teacher and knew he was violent yet taught him to transfer aggression to me. As a result, he tried to kill me! Her reaction was priceless when I emphatically told the jury that I witnessed the employer repeatedly insult her by asking, "Are you STUPID?" She side-glanced the employer acknowledging I drew blood. I fantasized that my testimony headlined their divorce proceedings. At the last company Christmas party, she confided in me that "if he ever yells at me again, I will divorce him and take every penny he owns."

His abuse of employees was mutually beneficial for her and alternated as a marriage counselor. In fact, the employer often referred to "transferal of aggression," which he learned from her because terminology was far beyond his fifth-grader's grasp. He took his misplaced anger out on me as a result of domestic issues with her. She ignored his dangerous proclivities and never sought respective remedial psychiatric treatment. Their $100,000-plus Porsche was a reminder of everything they cost me; the fraud they gainfully perpetrated against me; and the nightmare they forced upon me. I parked next to that car for years. My stomach knotted every time he drove into the parking lot. Whereas they were filthy rich and lived a life of luxury, they lived in a metastasizing hell on earth because of his insidious depravity. But I was free! I drove away laughing to myself that the pathetic losers could not win even when they cheated. Their brokered judgment was worthless; I had nothing left to take. He was laughing at me, but court documents now listed him as a liar and thief. I left them and their folie à deux in my rear-view mirror.

After passing the employer, I confronted the associate attorney as she stood attentively at the back of her SUV watching the employer taunting me. I defiantly drove by her without any acknowledgment. She participated in judicial fraud at our plaintiffs' expense. I had no sympathy for a corrupt officer of the court.

I was disturbed by our attorney's silent treatment after the verdict. There was no consolation, only abandonment. He seemed preoccupied with planning his escape. Unfortunately, the jury also charged Wayne with conversion because he supposedly enjoyed the benefit of my copied material. We needed to file an appeal and pursue retrial, but our attorney was incommunicado. I commenced researching adverse effects of our judgment and essentially determined that our district court IOU was engineered to extend indefinitely. Speaking for myself, Texas law recognized exemptions to judgment that benefited me. I owned no house, property, or investments. It was ironic that the employer caused me to lose assets whose lack thereof prevented his judgment.

THE APO$TATE

A week after verdict, Wayne emailed me that the employer called our attorney bragging that he "made more money in one month than Caryn, Wayne, and you make all year!" Above all, I was impressed that he named me first, which signified newfound respect. Otherwise, his braggadocio suggested their "Plan A" fell apart and they resorted to "Plan B." Accordingly, two weeks later, our attorney notified us that the employer offered a dismissal of judgment in exchange for dropping all claims against him. I questioned our attorney's refusal to seek an appeal and retrial; judicial malfeasance could be proved, and we knew their tricks and game plan. He indicated that efforts were hopeless (meaning "rigged") and dropped our cases, which empowered the crooked judge, employer, and Bureau.

The judgment was engineered to provide the employer leverage including an option for dismissal regardless of the jury's decision. The employer and Houston Bureau failed their primary joint objective to win felonious counterclaims against me. So when judgment was not feasible, a dismissal was imperative to release the employer from our discrimination claims. Nevertheless, we established new case law relative to the employer's misclassification of sales staff that enabled the IRS to pursue him for installers' similar footprints.

The extent of the employer's violence and his physical assault against me was never questioned during trial, but I was blamed for staying. After hearing my detailed description of his demonic attack, the jury's scrutinizing reaction silently convicted me for tolerating a hostile work environment, which was typical for a young transient generation who effortlessly floated jobs. I did not have their options and was fifty-something at the time with substantial overhead while facing history's second Great Depression. I proved my point when I lost everything after leaving the abusive employer.

The TWC Appeal Tribunal's hearing officer astutely outlined the legal points of my case when approving unemployment benefits. Unfortunately, trial did not allow incorporation of her decision and/or mention thereof. The hearing officer was probably an attorney due to her commanding knowledge, articulation, and expertise. I wished that she had represented me against the employer and take this opportunity to thank her for listening to my desperate plea. She held the employer accountable when trial did not, but our attorney refused her expertise. He also chased Wayne's higher purse prize, which was discriminatory and reeked of legal malpractice. Most of my complaints were overlooked, and he ignored my warning to plan a counterattack against the Bureau at trial. Consequently, we "snatched defeat from the jaws of victory."

I close the trial chapter in honor of TWC's appellate hearing officer with the initials "M. I." and, in part, quote the "Findings of Fact" clause of her final decision rendered in my favor: "The claimant has been working for the employer for several years under stressful circumstances. The claimant and the ex-vice president worked closely together, and the ex-vice president would, on many occasions, diffuse any problems that the claimant would have with management. The claimant was assaulted on one occasion by another member of management, but the claimant did not file charges against that individual, as the claimant needed her job. The ex-vice president was terminated from employment, and the claimant's job became even more stressful and more demanding, and the claimant was more afraid of the individual that had attacked her before, as the ex-vice president was no longer there to step in and protect her and diffuse the situation. The claimant provided a resignation letter as a contingent attempt to correct problems at the work place, but the employer accepted the claimant's resignation letter when the employer requested that the claimant train another individual who knew part of her work. The claimant resigned her position due to the hostile work environment."

CHAPTER 38

POST-TRIAL

Our attorney allowed opposing counsel to fixate on fabricated lies. Wayne and I approached trial expecting aegis of truth only to confront a bulwark of crony malfeasance while compensating for our attorney's septic representation.

I would have fired our attorney had I been alone, but Wayne was a Co-Plaintiff and our cases were inextricably co-mingled. Wayne was entitled to his side of representation, which underscored interlinked vulnerabilities. Never again, though, would I participate in a multiple plaintiff lawsuit because individual cases are subject to colleague betrayal, blindsiding misbehavior, personal grievances, case ignorance, and/or legal bias. I forewarned Wayne that our attorney would likely engage divide and conquer tactics, which occurred and upset our friendship and case dynamics. Our attorney was an unfit litigator and his prejudice against me waylaid my 1st and 14th Amendment rights to free speech, due process, and equal protection of law. He exploited my testimony and advice to successfully settle Wayne's breach of contract case for the full amount of $126,000 (they were going to settle for much less). Two years later, I was relegated to third wheel status when proceeding with our employment cases. I sought malpractice action against our attorney after trial, but representation was declined because the Better Business Bureau was involved.

I refused to allow the employer and Houston Bureau ruin my name and imprison me. Déjà vu flashbacks reminded that the employer planted the felon in my accounting department as a setup; consequent counterclaims and trial tricks manifested his diabolical plan. Accordingly, I commandeered my case as an en garde "pro se" from the witness stand. Consequently, I invalidated damaging counterclaims of slander, breach of fiduciary duties, and criminal theft. Aside from a very graphic description of the employer's assault, my second most pivotal soliloquy introduced Bureau awards and the employer's awards theft to emphasize to the jury that he was the thief, not me. I solemnly admitted writing a false awards application that won the highest Pinnacle award, but blamed culpability on the deceptive employer. Jurors accepted my contrite confession and dismissed fabricated theft charges. Conversion judgment stuck because jurists were unaware of statute expiration.

The *Awards for Excellence* was the elephant in the courtroom. When I accused the employer of awards fraud, opposing counsel reflexively backpedaled resorting to improvised damage control and reverse psychology. His line of accusatory questions schemed to make me recant my admission of writing a false application. If I had waivered, I would have lost all credibility and the jury. I realized opposing counsel's desperation when he shifted gears to claim that the employer wrote the awards application, which was an eye-rolling mistake because the jury believed me. As a result, opposing counsel inadvertently decimated his theft charge against me, validated my awards fraud claims, registered the Houston Bureau's incursion into my trial, and enabled this book.

We waited seven rotten-stinking years for trial only to discover that Lady Justice dispensed injustice. The complicit judge engaged banana republic antics that restricted our plaintiffs' testimony, corrupted plaintiffs' witness testimony, gutted plaintiffs' evidence, violated plaintiffs' rebuttal rights, enabled false counterclaims, conspired with opposing counsel to defraud us, violated statute of limitations, and tampered with trial proceedings. Particular court indiscretions cannot be denied: (1) The Judicial Conference of the United States in charge of supervising district courts decreed, "Plaintiff may call rebuttal witnesses to disprove what was said by the defendant's witnesses," yet we were refused rebuttal. (2) TCPR, Section 16.003, confirmed conversion of personal property statute of limitations at two years. (3) TCPR, Section 16.010(a), confirmed misappropriation of trade secrets at three years even though trade secrets were not involved. (4) I never signed a legitimate nondisclosure agreement binding me to respective Texas laws and penalties, which was an egregious oversight and never mentioned.

Early critics vehemently complained about the 1920's Bureau manipulating the court system. My trial reenacted a 1940's "Kate Whelan." Bureau successors unleased the weight of a globalist war chest against me same as predecessors perpetrated against O'Sullivan's loyal secretary to prevent my damning exposure of its multimillion-dollar awards scam. The Bureau attempted to brand me a lifetime felon with bogus charges of felonious theft and breach of fiduciary duties for threatening to report its equally bogus *Awards for Excellence*. I was ultimately indicted for conversion, despite expired statute, by a corrupt judge. According to TCPR, Chapter 16, the employer's counterclaim statutes were as follows: (1) Slander, 1-year statute, TCPR § 16.002(a). (2) Breach of Fiduciary Duty, 4-year statute, TCPR § 16.003(a)(5). (3) Conversion, two-year statute, TCPR § 16.003(a). Furthermore, the Texas Code of Criminal Procedure, Chapter 12, Art.

12.01(4)(A), listed theft as a five-year statute.

David tampered with evidence, filed a fraudulent affidavit, conned the jury, and committed perjury. He continued lying on the witness stand until caught, but not before opposing counsel promoted David's false affidavit to win brownie points throughout trial. I was grilled and incriminated on the witness stand for breach of fiduciary duties based on David's fake pictures that were projected onto the courtroom wall. He was the last witness on the last day of trial and his recantation made little difference. By the time he admitted that the employer made him stage and photograph my office to fabricate negligence, irreversible damage was done. The jury had already decided. Consequently, double standards prevailed, liars succeeded, and justice failed. David walked free of charges.

The judge ignored David's lawlessness and perjury. Yet Texas Penal Code indicted him. SECTION 37.02, PERJURY, states: "(a) A person commits an offense if, with intent to deceive and with knowledge of the statement's meaning: (1) he makes a false statement under oath or swears to the truth of a false statement previously made and the statement is required or authorized by law to be made under oath; or (2) he makes a false unsworn declaration under Chapter 132, Civil Practice and Remedies Code. (b) An offense under this section is a Class A misdemeanor." SECTION 37.03, AGGRAVATED PERJURY, states, "(a) A person commits an offense if he commits perjury as defined in Section 37.02, and the false statement: (1) is made during or in connection with an official proceeding; and (2) is material. (b) An offense under this section is a felony of the third degree." SECTION 37.04, MATERIALITY, states, "(a) A statement is material, regardless of the admissibility of the statement under the rules of evidence, if it could have affected the course or outcome of the official proceeding. (b) It is no defense to prosecution under Section 37.03 (Aggravated Perjury) that the declarant mistakenly believed the statement to be immaterial. (c) Whether a statement is material in a given factual situation is a question of law." And, SECTION 37.09, TAMPERING WITH OR FABRICATING PHYSICAL EVIDENCE, states, "(a) A person commits an offense if, knowing that an investigation or official proceeding is pending or in progress, he: (1) alters, destroys, or conceals any record, document, or thing with intent to impair its verity, legibility, or availability as evidence in the investigation or official proceeding; or (2) makes, presents, or uses any record, document, or thing with knowledge of its falsity and with intent to affect the course or outcome of the investigation or official proceeding. (c) An offense under Subsection (a) or Subsection (d)(1) is a felony of the third degree ... (d) A person commits an offense if the person: (1) knowing that an offense has been committed, alters, destroys, or conceals any record, document, or thing with intent to impair its verity, legibility, or availability as evidence in any subsequent investigation of or official proceeding related to the offense."

The Bureau cannot deny participating in my lawsuit because opposing counsel invoked its name and awards director to defend the employer. The Houston Foundation's Candace Twyman was listed as the employer's trial witness. I dealt with Twyman for several years while participating in the awards contest. Her inclusion as the foundation's highest-ranking officer proved that the Bureau micromanaged trial. Exhibit A represented the "Defendant's Trial Witness List" and the "Better Business Bureau" was listed as witness number 23; the Witness List's preamble stated, "To the Honorable Court: The following represents the names, addresses and telephone numbers of any person that could be expected to testify at trial in connection with the above-entitled and numbered cause." Opposing counsel deviously crafted the Witness List in a manner to misrepresent a Bureau officer as a lowly clerk: "23. Better Business Bureau[,] Corporate Representative, Custodian of Records and Candace Twyman, 1333 West Loop South, Suite 1200, Houston, Texas 77027[,] Tel: 713.341.6141 *Knowledge of the false statements made by Caryn Cain about* [Employer Redacted] *and* [Company Redacted] *to the Better Business Bureau*"(Italics included). Twyman's name was strategically placed after "Corporate Representative, Custodian of Records" to disingenuously imply that the description was her title when her real title was "Executive Director" of "The Better Business Bureau Education Foundation," which sponsors the *Awards for Excellence* program for the Houston Bureau. Furthermore, I have Twyman's letter, dated March 13, 2006, drafted on "The Better Business Bureau Education Foundation" letterhead and addressed to my attention that she undersigned as "Executive Director"; the letter's opening greeting stated, "Congratulations! Your application was reviewed and your company has been selected as a finalist for the 2006 Awards For Excellence." In fact, Twyman has run the awards program since I first participated and until present date. The Bureau's attorney obviously attempted to avoid mention of the *Awards for Excellence* program, which highlighted the Bureau's centurial expertise in humbuggery, evasion, implication, and obfuscation. The Witness List proved that Twyman was the employer's prime witness and brought into our private trial to discredit me and tighten a felonious noose around my neck. But when I exposed the employer's awards fraud, twinkled-toed Twyman faded into thin air and never testified.

The Witness List was a court document and all information was considered the same as a sworn deposition and trial testimony. Accordingly, I offer my opinion of Twyman's "intended" testimony: 1) She committed perjury. The Bureau distorted my awards fraud complaints in accordance with the employer's fabricated counterclaims with intent to incriminate me. Everything I reported about the employer was true and supported by evidence and witnesses. And I wrote the award application so Twyman could not question source, circumstances, and/or authenticity. 2) I never spoke to Twyman after submittal of the 2008 awards application and only dealt with Parsons and his investigator, so her testimony was hearsay. 3) The disingenuous way that opposing counsel listed Twyman's job title intentionally masked her high-profile status with the foundation and awards program and her involvement with the Bureau and employer. 4) Twyman claimed, "Knowledge of the false statements made by Caryn Cain," which evidenced obstruction, slander, collusion, and fraud against me. Furthermore, if Twyman's claims were legitimate she would not have been eliminated as a witness after I exposed the employer's awards fraud and called him "a liar and a thief." And 5) Twyman's false statement on the Witness List inadvertently and irrefutably attached the *Awards for Excellence* to our trial.

Twyman knew me as an upstanding honest professional after years of handling awards and processing consumer complaints through the Houston Bureau. It would have been duplicitous for her to vilify me considering she was complicit in the awards fraud that I reported. In fact, the last correspondence that I received from her was on February 15, 2008, attached below, which acknowledged her receipt of my 2008 awards application and confirmed her involvement and position as "Executive Director" of the *Awards for Excellence*.

From: Candy . Twyman [Email Redacted]
Sent: Friday, February 15, 2008 4:24 PM
To: Caryn Cain
Subject: 2008 BBB Awards for Excellence

Your application to the 2008 Awards for Excellence has been received. The judging process by the Silver Foxes will begin February 18 and conclude at the end of March. If the judges have any questions or need clarification on any issue they will contact you directly. You will be notified of the results of your application in April. The Awards for Excellence luncheon will be held on Wednesday, May 7th at the InterContinental Hotel.

Good luck!

Candice Twyman, LMSW-AP | *Executive Director*

Tel: 713-341-6141
Fax: 713-341-6192

[Email Redacted]
www.bbbhou.org

POST-TRIAL

The Better Business Bureau Education Foundation
1333 West Loop South, Suite 1200
Houston, Texas 77027

Trial was rigged; evidence was distorted; jurists were deceived; the employer walked free; and the Better Business Bureau's dark secrets remained buried. But when the dust settled, I accomplished two linchpin goals; my name was cleared, and trial authorized me to publish *The Apostate* to expose the Bureau's pay-for-play awards racket. I also proved to the Houston Bureau's president that he did handle employer/employee civil matters despite his earlier denial.

Outrageous judicial malfeasance highlighted privilege of perverse wealth. Grave injustice was shoved down my throat because I walked among the poor, disadvantaged, and vulnerable Americans routinely cheated and saddled with unfair verdicts. I consider the U.S. court system the most corrupt, politically bias, and bribery-charged in the world.

Napoleon Hill (1883 -1970), world-renowned attorney, journalist, "founder of the science of success," and advisor to Andrew Carnegie, coined our trial's mindset, "money without brains is always dangerous."

CHAPTER **39**

EPILOGUE

Our attorney promoted his board-certified employment specialty, but district court demoted him to an idealistic fool unable to recognize a forked-tongued snake until poisonously bitten. He imitated the employer's humiliating condescension, telling me I was "full of words," which collaterally besmirched an incredible bygone era and evidence that would have bagged the serpentine Bureau in its slithering tracks. My "words" came from years of exhaustive research that would have exonerated me by describing a century of Bureau scandals; and "words" that would have educated jurors about an unscrupulous consumer advocate manipulating the marketplace and constitutional and statutory laws with bogus awards, bias ratings scores, and paper tiger recipients. He cold-shouldered my ancillary peril despite trial's folie à deux that attempted to imprison me and otherwise embedded blacklisted employment retaliation, whistleblower's vilification, and life-threatening harassment. His flawed logic choked our plaintiffs' offense and championed our adversaries' robber-baron defense. As a result, the Bureau continued expanding globalist operations; the miscreant employer kept cheating consumers with his Pinnacle and "A+" rating score; and I was relegated to streetfighter's cyberhacked transient trenches worrying that tyranny mixed with crazy motivated a bloodthirsty bullet with my name on it.

I was deprived of civil rights by the Bureau's despotic autocracy capable of victimizing anyone … anytime … anywhere. The Bureau connects to a conniving ruthless seditious tyrannical infinite unfettered intelligence community that wields nation-state sovereignty. Warrantless surveillance powers, granted by Obama's expanded Section 2.3 of Reagan's EO 12333, defy laws and control every citizen.

The Deep State Better Business Bureau acted with federal and state impunity to hijack my trial, rig a U.S. district court, tamper with evidence, deny my due process and equal protection of law, retaliate with malicious prosecution, and absolve the psychopathic misogynist employer. The Bureau acted above state and federal laws. Yet the U.S. Constitution's Preamble to the Bill of Rights (first 10 Amendments) declared, "We the people of the United States, in order to form a more perfect union, establish justice, insure domestic tranquility, provide for the common defense, promote the general welfare, and secure the blessings of liberty to ourselves and our posterity, do ordain and establish this Constitution for the United States of America." Respectively, the Texas Constitution, Section 19, decreed, "No citizen of this State shall be deprived of life, liberty, property, privileges or immunities, or in any manner disfranchised, except by the due course of the law of the land."

Accordingly, America's multiculturism, liberties, and privileges are being abused and threatened. As previously asserted, I believe that the EU intended to annex the United States Republic to form a one-government United States of Europe as chronological events suggested; and that Obama imposed American-style Schengen open borders with intent to exploit illegal alien votes to expand a Democratic political base while seeding a sovereign Muslim citizenry. But President Trump temporarily impeded diabolical globalist plans that begat the Democratic Party's unparalleled unrelenting vitriolic hatred towards him and his followers. In the meantime, U.S. laws have been marginalized and the Left's radical insurgents continue to infiltrate media, education, entertainment, law, politics, and government.

On November 6, 2018, two Muslim women made American history. Somali-born Ilhan Omar (Minnesota District 5) and Palestinian-American attorney Rashida Harbi Tlaib (Michigan District 13) were elected to the U.S. Congress. Both women brought troublemakers' contention with issues continuing to mount.

Rep. Omar's election proved traumatic. She was accused of "campaign" and "immigration" violations, changed the U.S. House of Representatives' "181 year old dress code" to incorporate the oppressive hijab, engaged pro-Palestinian anti-Israeli rhetoric, incited violence by encouraging "American Muslims to "raise Hell"," rabble-roused at a Council on American Islamic Relations (CAIR) event, fundraised for Islamic Relief with alleged "ties to terrorism," and wants to dismantle America's government. In fact, Rep. Omar's disparaging rhetoric was so offensive that the House of Representatives passed a resolution on "March 7, 2019," denouncing bigotry.

CAIR has been roundly denounced and was recently forced out of the San Diego Unified School District by a lawsuit brought by Freedom of Conscience Defense Fund (FCDF) for running a "discriminatory, unconstitutional propaganda program … [that] violated the First Amendment's Establishment Clause by favoring one religious group over another and mixing government with religion." The CAIR plan began in "April 2017" in response to President-elect Donald Trump's inauguration on January 20, 2017. FCDF advised, "CAIR intended this plan to be a pilot program for a nationwide rollout." Accordingly, Rep. Omar's questionable actions and affiliations suggest Trojan horse jihadism with ulterior motive to coerce America's path to Islam while disparaging adversaries as being racist, Islamophobes, and/or xenophobes, which has become a standard Muslim intimidation tactic. According to Voltaire, "To learn who rules over you, simply find out who you are not allowed to criticize."

And Rep. Tlaib has acted in tandem with Rep. Omar. She is infamously considered by conservatives as a meritless Muslimah mouthpiece maniacally robo-calling for President Trump's impeachment and Israel's boycott. Trashy Tlaib has also lobbed crude divisive threats against President Trump warning that ""we're gonna go in and impeach the motherf——," referring to the president," according to *Time*.

Women, especially, have been historically suppressed, defiled, humiliated, and denigrated by Islam as chattel slaves. Rep. Omar and Rep. Tlaib continue Islam's medieval practice under false pretense of pursuing democracy and women's rights with ulterior motive to spread creeping Sharia law into American government, education, and politics. Patriots must enforce allegiance to the U.S. Constitution. As matters stand, America gave an inch and anarchists took the country. I would not be complaining if laws of the land were followed, but the rules are that there are no rules.

Accordingly, Illuminati are bankrolling a Muslim-based NWO whose compliant copious procreation is fueled by Radical Islamic Terrorism. Islam's battle cry proclaims, "The mosques are our barracks, the domes our helmets, the minarets our bayonets, and the faithful our soldiers." There was no excuse other than globalism that transported jihad across the world onto American soil forcing homeland Islamification. Middle East conflict should have been kept in-country, but our Democratic and Republican globalist politicians imported their anti-West counterculture. Furthermore, terrorists warned that they would kill us, but we brought them anyway and deadly consequences now spring eternal.

The modern Bureau continues its historic proclivity for stolen thunder by sidesaddling empowered limelight. Respectively, B-men seem to have aligned with a Deep State/EU alliance whose NWO initiatives undermine the U.S. Constitution, facilitate global censorship, mastermind socialist conversion, and seek one-government rule. Puritan predecessors assisted Hoover's Mexican Repatriation program and segued clout into successors' WWII Deep State induction that monitored FDR's internment of Nisei/Japanese Americans. Decades of schmoozing with the executive branch forged an empire.

States are incrementally converting to globalist-infused socialism with the largest about to fall. As a Texan, I am witnessing the conservative "Lone Star State" transform into a swing state. Like the Alamo, first attacks were deflected, but sheer numbers overpowered. History forewarned and is sadly repeating!

I believe that 1800's immigration made America the greatest nation, but today's radical hordes guarantee its cataclysmic destruction. European-bred inventors and scientists contributed nation-building technological innovation and expertise. Contrarily, modern globalist initiatives sponsor domestic terrorism with intent to destroy American laws, culture, and borders by converting the U.S. into an EU-ruled Schengen-style northern hemisphere. In fact, Obama already transformed America by maintaining open borders and dispersing illegal immigrants throughout the United States. Presidential election year 2020 threatens a communist reboot.

America's sabotage was years in the making. In my opinion, Illuminati engineered the election of Barack Hussein Obama Soetoro as America's first Black POTUS, first Muslim POTUS, and first fifth-column POTUS; there would probably be more "firsts," but his records are sealed and a hardcore death list shadows anyone investigating Clinton-Family connections. Obama's presidency was meant to be a pivotal political capstone to the EU's annexation of America emphasized by several exemplars including Obama's affiliation with EU leadership, concession of the Internet to pro-EU ICANN, the EU-US Privacy Shield program, E.O. 12333/Section 2.3, and destructive sanctuary-city and open-border policies.

Obama's re-energized political machinations suggest he never left the presidency. Recently divulged evidence implicated Obama and his supercharged Deep State for sabotaging Trump's campaign and presidency. The former president rented a home less than 15 minutes from the White House, in the "exclusive Kalorama neighborhood," questioning hands-on proximity to IC surveillance since crony lapdogs insinuated that he had dirt on a planetary populace including world leaders. And I was among those reprehensibly hacked daily until completing *The Apostate*. On November 21, 2018, Obama delivered a speech in Chicago accusing President Trump of having "mommy issues," which seemed oddly out of place and duplicated my same description written years earlier about the employer; circumstances seemed "too coincidental to be a coincidence." Accordingly, anti-Christian/Judeo/American forces are coalescing, and Obama re-emerged to lead the globalist charge in the 2020 election questioning if Trump will be the last Republican president? The Bureau's strength grows daily with every empowering globalist court decision fortifying its nation-state invincibility. A judge's black robe supposedly symbolizes objective judicial rendering, but globalist activist judges are marginalizing the U.S. Constitution and embedding socialist servitude.

As previously mentioned, and worth repeating, karma rounded full circle when the Houston Bureau's former chairman sued the Bureau for defamation consequent to a failing rating score. In my opinion, the chairman was ethical, but not the Bureau; the Bureau won because it owned the courts. Chronology of events proved that the Bureau coordinated the former chairman's trial with ours to rig our trial with his verdict. Consequently, the Bureau convoluted defamation into free speech and the right to commit consumer fraud as an opinion under the First Amendment. And the state of Texas was complicit with no excuse otherwise. I notified the Texas Attorney General of the Bureau's awards fraud and nothing was done, which reiterated my belief that the nonprofit finagled immunity from compromised state and federal regulatory agencies.

Mercifully, the U.S. Supreme Court reinforced the Fourth Amendment: "The right of the people to be secure in their persons, houses, papers, and effects, against unreasonable searches and seizures." SCOTUS addressed cell phones and respective time-stamped records called cell-site location information ("CSLI"). On June 22, 2018, the High Court overturned a lower court decision in *Carpenter v. United States* and ruled cell phones were "entitled to Fourth Amendment protection" and required a warrant. Justices ruled against "arbitrary invasions by government officials" declaring, "When an individual "seeks to preserve something as private," and his expectation of privacy is "one that society is prepared to recognize as reasonable," we have held that official intrusion into that private sphere generally qualifies as a search and requires a warrant supported by probable cause."

Internet privacy and piracy regulations and penalties must also be legislated. I hold the Obama administration culpable for instigating a rogue indomitable Deep State culture empowered by an amended EO 12333. The IC alphabet soup, including the FBI, IRS, DOC, FTC, and BBB, forged a globalist cybernation of interactive agencies whose cyberespionage attacked any opposition to their ideology, operations and sweeping powers; agencies must be dethroned and disarmed while alternately managed and monitored. I was cyberbullied and cybersabotaged by "a snooping rat" representing "ghoulish gentry," both coined by Kenner, who stared back at me while remotely controlling my cell phone. Thereafter, my laptop computer digressed to snail's pace; the cursor self-maneuvered; screen grabs repeatedly flashed; typed words simultaneously untyped; email attachments were corrupted; and the computer would not shut off. On March 12, 2018, a respective article announced an insidious "router malware" named "Slingshot" that similarly described my cyber affliction. Spyware could "basically steal any kind of data it wants, from network traffic, keystrokes and passwords to screenshots and even data from a connected USB device," which meant my flash drive was also hacked. Consequently, my intellectual property was stolen and incrementally dispersed prior to publication.

The Bureau's partnership in the EU-US Privacy Shield program seemed to coordinate with Obama's handoff of the Internet to pro-EU ICANN. Centurial inclination predicted the Bureau's placement of brick-and-mortar branch offices

EPILOGUE

throughout the EU. On November 22, 2016, a press release announced that the U.S. and EU were planning a "hybrid threat center in Finland to combat a growing number of cyberattacks and hybrid warfare." Accordingly, the Finland project's cyber dynamics questioned inclusion of the Deep State Better Business Bureau's digital dynasty.

Once again, HISTORY MATTERS! Remarkably, the 1916 and 2016 elections were linked by the same New York Bureau. Pundits declared, "FDR won because of radio, JFK won because of television, and DJT won because of social media." But I believe that Theodore Woodrow Wilson pre-empted all of them when he won re-election in 1916 because of the newspaper that was America's first means of communication and where advertising began, consumer fraud embedded, and fake news currently reigns. All aforementioned presidents spanned the breadth between two exceptional presidential elections that were a century apart and sandwiched the capitalist evolution of the Better Business Bureau.

Today's news pits citizen journalism against MSM. Yesteryear relied upon the media's rigid morality embedded by patriots' underground American Revolutionary newspapers that spied on British soldiers. Thereafter, the newspaper industry begat the advertising industry that created the Vigilance Committee to enforce the *Printers' Ink* Model Statute false advertising law. The Vigilance Committee became the Better Business Bureau and promoted Rowell's ethical advertising and journalism standards until corrupted by the 1920's NYSE. I believe the year 2010 marked a turning point when MSM began transforming into "fake news" and the Bureau began dishing awards to all award applicants.

Current Bureaunomics exploit an iconic reputation and sponsor an awards racket to buy a seat at the NWO's potentate Round Table. The Bureau has transcended "too big to fail" as a free-wheeling autocratic minion representing a planetary cabal. I experienced the brutal brunt of the Bureau's nation-state powers that control the U.S. court system and manipulate national commerce through specious awards and rating scores, which replicate throwback Mafioso muscle tactics. Predecessors' eternal flame was meant to symbolize perpetual truth in advertising, but capitalist successors doused its ethical glow.

Besides the 2008 Pinnacle, I won another Pinnacle in 2009. I acted as a ghost writer and wrote a pre-qualified awards application for the employer's foremost competitor. It was a whistleblower's temptation that I could not resist; one last chance to prove that I could win the Bureau's highest award with gilded words at any time, for any member. After awards' allocation, the competitor called and thanked me for his Pinnacle. He amusingly described the employer's sore-loser implosion at an adjoining table. The employer pitched a childish hissy fit, angrily kicked chairs out of the way, and stormed out of the jam-packed ballroom followed by his entourage of shame-faced salesmen. He knew I wrote the application. Payback's a bitch!

As I forewarned the employer, his customer complaints skyrocketed, and business nose-dived after he refused to implement my awards application's procedures that won him the Pinnacle. I handed him an operational blueprint for unparalleled success, but he had to lie, cheat, and steal. Customers' complainant comments replicated my predictions almost verbatim. By comparison, during my employment customers rarely complained and, if so, issues were immediately resolved.

Unfortunately, trial criminally mentored, empowered, and incentivized the employer. His television advertising began to mirror the Bureau's flim-flam flair that exploited honesty, innocence, and goodness. He shaved his mustache and carnival-barked his wares while standing behind his young grandchildren whereby repeating the grandfather strategy that worked so well during trial. But even humbuggery had pitfalls; in March 2018, his Houston company's job vacancies advertised openings for an entire office staff. Earlier, after trial ended in January 2015, his family moved to Palm Beach; they bought a mansion for $8.9 million dollars and a Bentley for $425,000 dollars. He opened a window business. She opened a design company. Then COVID-19 hit. They reportedly sold the Bentley for $110,000 dollars. And, on July 31, 2020, they asked for $10.38 million but sold their mansion for $8.75 million, which did not include hundreds of thousands of dollars in renovations costs.

I sued the employer but fought the Bureau. The *Roaring Twenties* returned with a vengeance spawning an organized-crime culture. Winning the prestigious Pinnacle award exposed the Bureau's plenary power, widespread deceptive trade practice, crony government corruption, and globalist conspiracy. After our trial ended, CBBB's annual report implied globalist expansion: "In the spring of 2015, CBBB embarked on two corporate engagement campaigns to proactively reach out to top companies in major city markets to build and renew connections with our National Partners and introduce new BBB CEOs and have a conversation on emerging business developments."

Additionally, I call attention to the Texas counties represented by the "BBB of Greater Houston and South Texas," including "Austin, Brazoria, Brooks, Cameron, Colorado, Fort Bend, Galveston, Harris, Hidalgo, Jim Hogg, Kenedy, Matagorda, Montgomery, Starr, Waller, Wharton, Willacy & Zapata." Beneath the listing of counties, the Houston Bureau boasted, "The Houston and South Texas BBB see trust as a function of two primary factors – integrity and performance"; three are known for cartel-related activity. According to WayneDupree.com, "Starr, Hidalgo, and Cameron ... have seen numerous law officials sent to jail for working with cartels."

Henceforth, I believe that the NWO's bait-and-switch shell game sought to

EPILOGUE

convert the United States to a cartel economy followed by an Islamist override forcing native-son displacement, underemployment, and overthrow. The White population is being oppressed under onus of privilege, and the Black population is being suppressed under placation of victim mentality. Meanwhile, the Chinese Communist Party emerged as a biblical threat by dispensing germ warfare, assisting theft of POTUS, and bribing U.S. leaders to conquer the world's most powerful nation.

During high school and college, I was fortunate to travel to Europe and visited many of the EU countries now fallen into rack and ruin. EU initiatives have since embedded open migration, refugees, and Radical Islamic Terrorism in Europe to perpetuate a worldwide Islamist culture and civilization. The beautiful historic streets of France, Italy, Germany, Sweden, and England have been ransacked by savage marauding migrants who have raped and murdered indigenous inhabitants. Respective infestation has spread to American shores and is seditiously transforming the fabric of society including government, religion, and education. Yet lunatic liberals ignore respective menace, preach open borders, denounce the U.S. Constitution, and welcome the oppression of barbaric Sharia law.

The Apostate is my appellate rebuttal to the employer, Deep State Better Business Bureau, Texas Attorney General, and FTC for denying my rights of due process and equal protection of law and facilitating consumer fraud. As a result, the Bureau perpetrated malicious prosecution, tampered with evidence, rigged trial, and attempted my imprisonment to hide its globalist awards racket. I sought legal recourse for valid age and employment discrimination complaints approved by the EEOC, but the Houston Bureau decimated my case, relegating me to an inferior existence enforced by the employer's relentless stalking and employment blacklisting.

Age and employment discrimination are real, rampant, and repulsive with grave consequences accelerated by illegal immigration. Yet ivory-towered politicians proselytize, plunder, and penalize those suffering limited defensive and financial means. Then useless idiots have the audacity to question community repercussions that spawn trench-warfare atrocities of homelessness, desperation, drugs, suicide, murder, domestic violence, mental illness, and sunset poverty.

In July 2019, I re-entered the workforce and submitted over 200 corporate and/or administrative job applications. Two grocery stores hired me. A third grocer advised that my application was declined with no reason given. And Sam's Club/Walmart presented an online application that phished ethnicity, age, and health. Thereafter, Sam's Club sent me on a wild goose chase and scheduled four interviews with three millennial supervisors who had no emotional intelligence and essentially played games, wasted my time, and humiliated me; none of the

THE APO$TATE

trigger fingers hired me. Then I applied at Burnett Staffing, which is a member of the Houston BBB, a former 2016 Pinnacle winner, and a consistent Winner of Distinction recipient. Upon review of my resume, the employment counselor recognized my former employer and confirmed my query that she would contact him for my employment verification. The jig was up, so I explained that my departure from the employer included reporting him for defrauding the Houston Bureau's *Awards For Excellence*. But truth did not set me free. I was politely led to the door and forebodingly warned, "I cannot help some people." I offered more than 25 years of administrative experience, 15 years of food and beverage experience, and excellent references. But I have also been stalked for the past 12 years by my former employer and subjected to substandard living. I blamed the EEOC and Department of Aging for failure to respectively prosecute abusive employers and protect senior citizens.

Accordingly, I propose new legislation to establish a centralized employment verification database and to prohibit age/medical-phishing employment applications, e.g., asking high school graduation date and questioning disability. A third-party centralized employment verification system within the EEOC would prohibit direct-employer contact and monitor discriminatory practice. The database would offer an individual's resume that only includes name of employer, date of employment, and job title with information updated by respective state workforce agencies that already store similar information; and no resume indicates no work history. Additionally, all searches/inquiries must be logged and accessible for applicant's review. Unauthorized tampering would invoke constitutional charges and damages.

Furthermore, I will respond to a denial for information and photographs from a surviving family member of one of my book's foremost characters whose colorful background and entangled efforts resulted in historical Wall Street reform and congressional denouncement of the Better Business Bureau. Locating yesteryear's living relatives was near impossible and I spent years researching leads. I previously described one unfortunate opportunity whereby my elderly contact was unable to speak. Then, miraculously, with hyper-euphoric bated breath, I found the living blood relative of another profound historical trailblazer. But elation succumbed to despair when family assistance and incredible photographic evidence was refused because I was an indie author and *The Apostate* was my debut novel and politically oriented. By denying assistance, though, he cheated his family and perpetuity. I want him to know that my research vindicated his father and proved inaccuracies by a renowned journalist whose book received his permission and photographs, but whose storyline favored the Bureau. Otherwise, my book provided unbiased documented genealogical accounts that defended his father for the hero he was, the times he lived, and the achievements he contributed.

EPILOGUE

The AACA's 1911 Truth in Advertising Movement inspired the Advertising Club of New York's conversion into the first Vigilance Committee; its motto was "work against dishonesty in advertising." Puritan predecessors participated in America's incredible evolution contrary to subversive successors' national exploitation that equates honesty to a court jester. Accordingly, Arthur Sheldon named the Better Business Bureau, but my trial produced a rebranded Cosmic Comic Cyborg.

Peculiar centurial destiny bridged the patriotic 1916 New York Vigilance Committee with the globalist 2016 New York Better Business Bureau to discredit an anti-globalist member who stunningly became the 45th president of the United States. Consequently, globalist conquest was temporarily deflected although relentless counterattacks predict inevitable triumph.

Socialist author Upton Sinclair wrote *The Jungle* to expose immigrant abuse, but, instead, inspired the Pure Food and Drug Act of 1906 that sparked the Truth in Advertising Movement, which created the Better Business Bureau. Over a century later, socialism has escalated, immigration threatens overthrow, and *The Jungle* is more relevant than ever before.

The Bureau quoted Cicero to aggrandize its Wizard of Oz propaganda. Henceforth, I defer to his antiquarian predecessor, Hammurabi, who established civilization's judicial standards dating to "about 1754 BC." The "sixth Babylonian king" created "282 laws, with scaled punishments." My favorite and most appropriate Code of Hammurabi addressed judicial malfeasance and decreed "that a judge who reaches an incorrect decision is to be fined and removed from the bench permanently."

My great-great-grandfather, 2nd Lt. James Michael Cain, was a Freemason and descendant of the Knights Templar. Iconic irony knighted me to pick up his sword and expose the BBB's Templar apostasy to enforce truth in advertising.

Writing *The Apostate* was incredibly enlightening and miraculous because I found dusty evidence to corroborate my combative claims. I located first-edition books written by characters living during the timeframe of the Bureau's genesis; two such luminaries were O'Sullivan and Kenner, representing bitter arch enemies. Their books opened windows to the past; opposing viewpoints excavated buried history and uncovered the Bureau's yesteryear scandals and scams. Both authors began their careers as newspaper reporters, but O'Sullivan became a renowned Bureau critic while Kenner became the Bureau. Nevertheless, fate chose them as the Bureau's quintessential spokesmen.

Hurnard Jay Kenner was a loyal Vigilance man embroiled in historic Wall Street corruption that contributed to the Crash. His book unwittingly documented the Bureau's globalist transformation. And Kenner's entertaining twentieth-century figures of speech subliminally earmarked the Bureau's trail of humbuggery; descriptions included "professional plunderers," "land pirates," "dice-loading fraternity," and "shell-game instincts." He also inadvertently paraphrased modern awards fraud with his vintage swindler's motto, "Never give a sucker a break." Additionally, to my knowledge, *The Apostate* is the first publication to reveal his full birth name opposed to history's renowned "H. J." acronymic anonymity. Kenner rose through Bureau ranks as an honored Templar but exited an obscure liability. His name was swept under the rug to preserve the Bureau's whitewashed image emphasized by the AAF Hall of Fame's snub. Ultimately, H. J. Kenner's initial encouragement to report Bureau indiscretions was superseded by the secret society's scurrilous operations.

Frank Dalton O'Sullivan was a writer, publisher, detective, criminologist, consumer advocate, and patriot who secured history's moral compass. We lived generations apart, but our eerily similar experiences drew us together. We were both hurt by the Bureau for supporting honesty and free trade in the marketplace. And we each exposed the Better Business Bureau as "part of the greatest racket ever known in its history." O'Sullivan's parting immortal words traveled tempestuous time to warn, "The power of the Bureaus was built up by publicity, which they secured free from the local newspapers; and it will be publicity that will prove their undoing in the end. When the public realizes that the Bureau system does not "better business," but reacts in a contrary direction, and when business men generally greet Bureau "investigators" with the boot, as someone has said, then all the powerful support they receive from selfish interests will avail them nothing, and they will go the way of all flesh."

CHAPTER 40

EMAILS AND EVIDENCE

Opposing counsel disingenuously presented author's state and federal awards fraud complaints to the jury as evidence of slander. Front pages of complaints were telescoped onto courtroom walls and jurors were not told content or that complaints involved the Houston Bureau's *Awards for Excellence* program. Accordingly, the author herein presents omitted trial-related documents that include the Houston Bureau, Council of Better Business Bureaus, Texas Attorney General, and FTC.

Subject: Revocation of Pinnacle Award / [Employer's Company Redacted]
From: Caryn Cain (email address redacted)
To: [Parsons' email redacted]
Date: Friday, October 10, 2008 11:39 PM

Mr. Dan Parsons
President
Better Business Bureau of Metropolitan Houston

Mr. Parsons,

My name is Caryn Cain, former Chief Financial Officer of [Company Redacted], and I am herein requesting a revocation of its 2008 Pinnacle award because of fraud with intent to favorably influence public trust based on winning such coveted award. I am alleging such award was accepted fraudulently by [Employer Redacted], owner of [Company Redacted], for his own celebrity and gain while knowing he had not implemented specific procedures listed in such award application and which were the basis for [Company Redacted] Pinnacle award selection.

In retrospect, I authored and submitted [Company Redacted] 2008 application for the Awards For Excellence by which [Company Redacted] was awarded the Pinnacle; [Employer Redacted], owner, accepted the award on May 5, 2008. Such application focused on training video tapes being utilized by all departments upon entry orientation to standardize operations in respective departments, eliminate problems, and optimize customer service. Furthermore, I emphasized background report usage for protection of [Company Redacted] customers and, as CFO, emphasized ultimate confidentiality of credit card information and personal financial data. Before I submitted the awards' application, I approached Mr. (Employer Redacted) to seek his approval and agreement to produce and implement my training tape ideas to prevent massive customer service problems that were reoccurring and counterproductive. I was also going to engage Mr. (Vice President Operations) to participate as well by carrying a video camera on his service calls to include interactive participation with our customers. After I submitted the application on February 15, 2008, Mr. (Employer Redacted) refused to implement such training tapes and called off Mr. (Vice President of Operations) from his participation as well with (Company Redacted) customers. Mr. (Employer Redacted) statement to me was, "Oh, they ain't gonna listen to a tape, forget it! It's a waste of time!"

And, this was AFTER Mr. (Employer Redacted) promised me that he would produce such tapes and I had ALREADY submitted the application. Then (Company Redacted) was chosen to win the Pinnacle on May 5, 2008 and Mr. (Employer Redacted) personally accepted the award even though he was still refusing to implement training tapes or any training for that matter... By May 5, 2008, (Company Redacted) was having massive customer service issues and complaints ... Then, on the day (May 5, 2008) Mr. (Employer Redacted) stood up in front of the BBB and accepted the Pinnacle, he knowingly hired an employee convicted of 1st Degree Felony Theft +<$200K as my (accounting) assistant, directly handling confidential customer file information such as credit cards and [Employer Redacted] (finance) applications containing Social Security numbers and birth dates ... compromising my position as CFO... another section of my application stated [Employer Redacted] guarantee for customer confidentiality and Mr. [Employer Redacted] unethically breached this promise to his customers as well. Then, in later August 2008, Mr. [Employer Redacted] ordered me to cease further background checks on installers and administrative personnel. Customers were calling in angry and asking how we could have won the Pinnacle, because that's why they bought from us ... Mr. [Employer Redacted] fired Mr. (Vice President Operations), on 8/5/08 and I am no longer with [Employer Redacted] as of 9/5/08. Mr. [Employer Redacted] refused to remove Mr. (Vice President of Operation) and my names from the BBB management listing until I expressly requested such again today, 10/10/08, and Mr. [Employer Redacted] continues to feature a group picture on the web home page under "corporate" which features myself and Mr. (Vice President of Operations) and many other personnel no longer at [Employer Redacted]. Furthermore, Mr. [Employer Redacted] is telling customers calling in for me that I am "unavailable," as though I am still there, but ignoring them ...

I met with Monica [Last Name Redacted], Investigations/Trade Practices Coordinator, on 10/3/08 and fully described my complaint and request for a revocation hearing directly with Mr. [Employer Redacted]; I presented evidence to her accordingly. I tried to contact Ms. [Last Name Redacted] earlier this week to seek status of my complaint and was unable to speak with her until this afternoon. I left a phone message for you after my conversation with Ms. [Last Name Redacted] this afternoon because I was extremely disappointed that my complaint was apparently taken so lightly and, essentially, placed on a back burner. Mr. [Employer Redacted] made a mockery of the Pinnacle ... Yet Mr. [Employer Redacted] is flashing the Pinnacle award for his own celebrity and profit, a false inducement for the public to buy from him rather than others. Mr. [Employer Redacted] web home page, radio spots, TV spots, advertising, literature, etc., etc., all feature his Pinnacle status. Again, customers have repeatedly told me they bought from [Employer Redacted] because of the Pinnacle award status.

In summary, as the author of the winning Pinnacle award application, I am requesting a hearing with Mr. Parsons at the BBB, as soon as possible; I have multiple witnesses to prove my case. I cannot allow this situation to be ignored or continue any further. This is not fair to the public. This is fraud. Mr. [Employer Redacted] does NOT deserve this honor. Mr. [Employer Redacted]) did not earn the Pinnacle award.

Sincerely,
Caryn Cain

THE APO$TATE

From: Monica (investigator's email redacted)
To: (Caryn Cain's email)
Date: Wednesday, October 15, 2008 9:39:06 AM
Subject: [Employer's Company Redacted]

Caryn,

I wanted to let you know that Dan did receive your email. We are still looking into this matter. I am aware that you are under time constraints; however, I cannot guarantee you a specific date for a resolution. With that being said, I will make sure that you are contacted once the bureau comes to decision or has any further questions.

Regards,
Monica [Last Name Redacted]| Investigations & Trade Practices Coordinator
Tel: 713-341-6149
Fax: 713-341-6142
(Investigator's email redacted)
www.bbbhou.org

The Better Business Bureau of Metropolitan Houston & South Texas
1333 West Loop South, Suite 1200
Houston, Texas 77027

From: Caryn Cain (email redacted)
Sent: Thursday, October 16, 2008 12:40 PM
To: (Parsons' email redacted)
Cc: (Monica's email redacted)
Subject: Fw: [Employer's Company Redacted]

October 16, 2008

Dan Parsons
President
Better Business Bureau of Metropolitan Houston

Mr. Parsons,

I have been in communications with Monica [Last Name Redacted], Senior Investigator, regarding my request for a hearing concerning bad faith misrepresentation by [Company Redacted] and such relationship to fraudulently accepting the 2008 Pinnacle award. After my meeting with Monica on 10/3/08, to file my fraud complaint against [Company Redacted] matters stalled, and I commenced communication with you whereby leaving a phone message and sending an email request for your intervention on 10/10/08, accordingly. Monica's email herein, on 10/15/08, informs me you received my messages, but you referred me back to Monica with Monica continuing to issue indefinites, and the matter remains essentially in limbo. This is not acceptable considering the circumstances.

I am questioning why [Company Redacted] is being allowed to continue operating without the BBB's reprimand or approach for such a serious breach of public trust. I am trying to right a very wrong situation that is blatant consumer fraud. Mr. [Employer Redacted] cheated the public and lied to the BBB. By ignoring this issue, the BBB is condoning [Company Redacted] actions.

I remind you that I am more than qualified to report this matter as the former Chief Financial Officer who wrote and submitted the original application responsible for (Company Redacted) selection as 2008 Pinnacle winner. I wrote such award based on Mr. (Employer Redacted) promise that he would create and implement the procedures listed, but never were! I spent the entire time from February 2008 to September 5, 2008, when I left (Company Redacted) trying to convince Mr. (Employer Redacted) to do what he won the award for, as I watched (Company Redacted) sinking into the toilet because of Mr. (Employer Redacted) failure to instate the procedures the company desperately needed to get back on track. In the interim, Mr. (Employer Redacted) continued waving the Pinnacle banner to influence more consumers to buy his product over competitors because of his BBB' quality of excellence and Pinnacle credential.

This will be my final transmission to you and I will seek other BBB authorities for reporting such an injustice.

Sincerely,
Caryn Cain

(telephone redacted)
Email: (redacted)

THE APO$TATE

From: Dan . Parsons [email redacted]
To: Caryn Cain [email redacted]
Cc: [Investigator redacted]; [*Awards for Excellence* coordinator redacted/witness at trial] [email redacted]
Sent: Thursday, October 16, 2008 1:07:11 PM
Subject: RE: [Employer's Company Redacted]

Ms. Cain....OK...enough. I have been in the loop through all of this. Monica, the head of our education foundation (who hosts the BBB Awards) and I met with Mr. & Mrs. (Employer Redacted) this morning to hear what they had to say.

From my standpoint, suffice to say that the BBB is taking no further role. This is an employer-employee issue out of the purview of any action we could or would take. If you wish to seek out other "BBB authorities," do so. They will tell you the same thing.

That said, the Foundation is still seeking some information and they will contact you, in writing, with their findings.

Dan Parsons | President

Tel: 713-868-9500
Fax: 713-867-4947
[email redacted]
www.bbbhou.org

The Better Business Bureau of Metropolitan Houston & South Texas
1333 West Loop South, Suite 1200
Houston, Texas 77027

From: Caryn Cain (email redacted)
To: (Investigator email redacted)
Date: Thursday, October 16, 2008 6:59:45 PM
Subject: Fw: [Employer's Company Redacted]

Monica,

This is my last transmission to you. But, since Mr. Parsons, President Houston BBB, wrote me the below response, I deserve a rebuttal to his uncalled for rude comment, "enough." If Mr. Parsons would have answered me the first time I tried to reach him via phone and email, I would not have been forced to continue to seek his response. Please pass my email to him.

In retrospect, I approached the BBB under confidential, private channels to quietly handle this consumer fraud matter and I do not appreciate the manner in which I have been treated and relegated to being "a disgruntled employee" when I previously warned you that [Company Redacted] would claim such in my meeting with you on 10/3/08. I remind you that this is about consumer fraud, not me! I requested a BBB group hearing with Mr. [Employer Redacted], owner of [Company Redacted], to validate my allegations of Mr. [Employer Redacted] fraudulently accepting the 2008 Pinnacle award despite never having implemented award procedures, i.e. training video tapes. Yet, Mr. Parsons "met" with Mr. & Mrs. [Employer Redacted] this morning, Thursday, 10/16/08; never requested copies of the video tapes; and, if tapes were issued, I wasn't given the opportunity to verify creation date and authenticity; then, Mr. Parsons dismissed the case as "employer-employee" related. Such action is ludicrous and tantamount to a blatant cover-up to hide [Company Redacted] actions and the BBB's ultimate responsibility of having never verified application content before final award' selection. Mr. [Employer Redacted] is a long time BBB member and I'm sure he carries influence at the BBB. But, the public is being sold a fake bill of goods by [Company Redacted]. And, the BBB is sweeping the issue under the rug. The BBB is condoning bad faith behavior contradicting its brand image of trust.

Furthermore, Mr. Parsons only responded to me after I exerted pressure to seek other BBB authorities on this consumer fraud issue. I'm very disappointed with BBB behavior. I will seek assistance with the U.S. Council of Better Business Bureaus and, if necessary, the Texas Attorney General's office because the Houston BBB has failed to perform fairly in this investigation.

Sincerely,
Caryn Cain
(phone number redacted)
email : (redacted)

THE APO$TATE

October 29, 2008

The Council of Better Business Bureaus
4200 Wilson Blvd., Ste. 800
Arlington, Virginia 22203-1838

Re: Better Business Bureau of Houston, Texas
       BBB Unfair Investigation/Dismissal of my Complaint that
       Employer Fraudulently Accepted 2008 Pinnacle Award

To Whom It May Concern:

As referenced, I approached the BBB of Houston in early September 2008 to file a complaint against [Company Redacted] for fraudulently accepting the 2008 Pinnacle Award. I requested a revocation of [Company Redacted] Pinnacle award. And, I requested a hearing with [Employer Redacted] owner, [Company Redacted], to fairly voice and prove my complaint in front of the BBB. After I met with the BBB senior investigator, Monica (Redacted), on 10/3/08, and provided detailed information, I was virtually ignored until I repeatedly dogged the BBB President, Dan Parsons, for an answer. Thereafter, Mr. Parsons personally met with Mr. and Mrs. [Employer Redacted] on 10/16/08 and immediately dismissed my complaint as "employer-employee" related. Mr. [Employer Redacted] is a long time BBB member, has invested in BBB co-op advertising, is currently on BBB homepage rotation, and enjoys considerable influence with the BBB board. My complaint was not an "employer-employee" issue, but is "employer-employee" related due to the nature of the award subject matter. If Mr. Parsons had read my award application he would have realized the extent of my complaint.

I am the former Chief Financial Officer who authored the application for said 2008 Pinnacle award ("application"). The application, submitted on 2/15/08, outlined the production and implementation of employee, service and installer video training tapes ("tapes") to optimize customer service excellence. Prior to my authoring and submitting the application, Mr. [Employer Redacted] promised me that he would personally create the tapes with the coordination of the Vice President of Operations, Wayne [Redacted], who would also create field service training tapes while visiting customer complaints. But, after submittal of the application, Mr. [Employer Redacted] refused to create and implement such tapes and still proceeded to accept the Pinnacle award.

Page 2
The Council of Better Business Bureaus
October 29, 2008

Furthermore, I am contending that Ms. [Bureau investigator redacted] improperly handled the evidentiary information that she requested of me to prove examples of [Company Redacted] bad faith in accepting the award. Accordingly, "employer-employee" issues overlapped because my application material was written to eliminate such "employer-employee-consumer" issues; also, [Company Redacted] encouraged consumer fraud issues that directly contradicted application procedures, i.e. discontinuing background checks and hiring 1st Degree Theft (>=200K) Felons to handle customer's credit card information and personal financial information such as Social Security numbers and birthdates. It should be noted that one particular example involved proof of Mr. and Mrs. [Employer Redacted] intentionally defrauding a customer. Ms. [Bureau Investigator redacted] confused the proper dissemination of my complaint and/or Mr. Parsons is attempting to sweep the Houston BBB's ultimate culpability under the rug for not having originally verified [Company Redacted] application or any other applications, for actual implementation and authenticity; the BBB's negligence offers resounding implications.

Before I left on 9/5/08, [Company Redacted] infrastructure was catastrophically disintegrating as a result of lack of training. If [Company Redacted] had implemented tape procedures, such massive problems would not be occurring. I received numerous customer complaints questioning "how [Company Redacted] could have possibly won such a great award with such pitiful service." It is my duty to continue seeking attention to this matter until [Company Redacted] is held accountable for misrepresenting his company's quality of excellence to the public and cheating an alternate, worthy competitor out of fairly winning the 2008 Pinnacle. I am seeking the Council's intervention and review of this matter. I am seeking a revocation of [Company Redacted] Pinnacle award. Again, I wrote the application and Mr. [Employer Redacted] refused to implement such application procedures whereby defrauding the public. I have multiple witnesses. It is my contention that Mr. Parsons is protecting Mr. [Employer Redacted] by vilifying me as a "disgruntled employee" whereby throwing the scent off of Mr. [Employer Redacted] guilty trail. Mr. Parsons did not offer me a fair investigation or a fair rebuttal. Mr. Parsons is condoning Mr. [Employer Redacted] bad faith behavior and undermining the BBB's brand image of truth, honesty, and integrity. Mr. Parsons and Mr. [Employer Redacted] should both be held accountable. Consumers rely on the BBB award system for final vendor selection and invest great sums of

THE APO$TATE

money in the process. This is fraud if the system to determine such awards is knowingly broken. And, fraud is wholesale theft!

Sincerely,
Caryn Cain

Subject: Letter of Complaint
From: Wuest, Shirley (email redacted)
To: carynsuzann (email redacted)
Date: Thursday, November 13, 2008 3:46 PM

Ms. Cain:

We received your letter of October 29, 2008 and reviewed it with our Operations Department.

We have attached our response hereto.

Sincerely,
Shirley Wuest | *Consultant, BBB Resource Center*

Tel: 703-247-3664
Fax: 703-276-0634
Email: (redacted) | *Start With Trust*

Council of Better Business Bureaus, Inc.
4200 Wilson Boulevard, Suite 800
Arlington, VA 22203

EMAIL ATTACHMENT:

November 13, 2008

Ms. Caryn Cain
[Address Redacted]

Dear Ms. Cain:

Thank you for contacting the Council of Better Business Bureaus and allowing us to review your concerns regarding the BBB of Metropolitan Houston.

EMAILS AND EVIDENCE

Local Better Business Bureaus assist in the resolution of marketplace issues, disputes between consumers and businesses, and provide reliability reports on local businesses in their community. There was no marketplace issue in this instance. BBBs do not process complaints regarding employee/employer issues. We are therefore unable to respond to your questions,

Please contact your local, county or state board of labor or your office of employment services regarding this matter. You should find the telephone number in your local telephone directory.

Sincerely,
Shirley Wuest
Consultant, BBB Resource Center

Cc: Mr. Dan Parsons
BBB of Metropolitan Houston

Subject: Re: Letter of Complaint
From: Caryn Cain (email redacted)
To: (Wuest email redacted)
Date: Thursday, November 13, 2008 5:53 PM

Ms. Wuest,

You have missed the point! The Houston BBB issued awards without checking qualification and procedures of the applications; and, then, when the BBB was notified of such fraud, they condoned the winner's actions by declaring me as a problematic employee. I was Chief Financial Officer of the company and I wrote the award application based on my employer's promises to fulfill listed procedures; nothing was done; the award was given to a fraud. I have many witnesses to back me up on my allegations. You are just reiterating what the Houston BBB professed as an excuse for their negligence. The thought pattern is to keep patting the offender on the back to throw the scent off several guilty trails. The BBB thinks they are sacrosanct, but they are not. The Council is condoning consumer fraud and lying to the public about award winning companies whom the public invests great sums of money accordingly. The Council and the Houston BBB are making a mockery of the term "trust." I will continue my complaint with the Texas

THE APO$TATE

Attorney General's office with a copy of this email and your letter response, as well as all communications with the Houston BBB.

Sincerely,
Caryn Cain

December 8, 2008

Office of the Attorney General
P.O. Box 122548
Austin, Texas 78711-2548

Re: Twofold complaints against [Employer's Company Redacted] and
 Houston Better Business Bureau ("BBB"); Alleging Collusion:
 Public Fraud – [Employer's Company Redacted] Fraudulent Advertising Campaign – "Pinnacle" "Trust" "Reputation"
 Public Fraud – BBB Fraudulent Advertising Campaign – [Employer's Company Redacted] Cover-up/Web Rotation

----

 [Employer's Company Redacted] Fraudulently Accepted 2008 BBB Pinnacle Award
 BBB Ultimately Responsible – No Verification of Award Applications
 BBB Performed Unfair Investigation; Dismissed Complaint; Continued Award Benefits
 BBB Cover-up to Protect Against Widespread Repercussions; Scam Implications
 Public Being Sold False Bill of Goods and Suffering Consequences

To Whom It May Concern:

As referenced, and per my attached complaint form, I am alleging fraud concerning [Employer's Company Redacted] acceptance of the 2008 BBB Pinnacle award and that the BBB is fully aware of such transgression and is attempting to cover-up such issue because of the BBB's ultimate culpability in not pre-confirming the 2008 award applications, essentially scamming the public; such charges carry extraordinary repercussions and undermine the entire infrastructure of the Better Business Bureaus around the country. After the Houston BBB dismissed my complaint filed on October 3, 2008, I wrote the Council of Better Business Bureaus ("Council") and found them supportive of the Houston BBB and non-cooperative to me as well. As promised to the Council, I am now forwarding my complaint to the Office of the Attorney General and beg your review and intervention. All rebuttal letters and communicative emails are attached herein along with the required "Consumer Complaint Form."

In retrospect, I am the former Chief Financial Officer of [Employer's Company Redacted] from March 2003 to September 2008. I wrote three award winning BBB applications for [Employer's Company Redacted] for 2006, 2007, and 2008; [Employer's Company Redacted] won the highest and most prestigious Pinnacle Award for best in its class of home improvement for 2008. Prior to writing and submitting the 2008 application, [Employer Redacted], owner of [Employer's Company Redacted], promised me that he would create and implement interdepartmental training video tapes and also allow Wayne [Last Name Redacted], Vice President of Operations, to participate by recording and creating field service training video tapes with customers (please refer to Mr. [Wayne's Last Name Redacted] attached verification email dated November 14, 2008), but the training tapes were never created nor implemented per

Page 2
Office of the Attorney General
December 8, 2008

Mr. [Employer's Last Name Redacted] direct instructions before and after he accepted the Pinnacle award on May 7, 2008; other witnesses are also available to confirm application circumstances and fraud. As a result of no training being implemented, massive customer service issues erupted.

Accordingly, I am filing a consumer fraud complaint against Mr. [Employer's Last Name Redacted] for accepting the 2008 BBB Pinnacle award and I am filing a consumer fraud complaint against the BBB for refusing to properly investigate my complaint and protect the public against fraud as the BBB advertises. I repeatedly confronted Mr. [Employer's Last Name Redacted] to initiate and implement award winning procedures as Mr. [Employer's Last Name Redacted] has always held tight, personal control of his company operations but, Mr. [Employer's Last Name Redacted] refused and threatened "don't bother me anymore about the BBB!" When I approached the BBB to reprimand Mr. [Employer's Last Name Redacted], I was vilified and treated disrespectfully by Dan Parson, BBB President. Mr. [Employer's Last Name Redacted] had lied to me and used my high ethics and excellent writing skills to scam the public and the BBB has condoned his actions. For his own intent and purpose as well as celebrity satisfaction and gain, Mr. [Employer's Last Name Redacted] has continued to advertise and boast his Pinnacle and "trust" award status across radio, television, [Employer's Company Redacted] and BBB web homepages (see attachments dated December 8, 2008), and newspaper advertising (see Houston Chronicle ad attachment dated November 27, 2008). In turn, the BBB has ignored fraudulent behavior and honored Mr. [Employer's Last Name Redacted] by granting him the Pinnacle award benefit of purchasing advertisement that currently features his picture and [Employer's Company Redacted] advertising on the BBB homepage rotation next to the words "Start Your Search With Trust"; whereby directly associating trust with Mr. [Employer's Last Name Redacted].

[Employer's Company Redacted] accepted an award they didn't earn with the BBB's blessings. Winning the Pinnacle award is monumentally prestigious and always tantamount to the BBB's approval for public investment in services of such recipients. The public invests tremendous sums of money every year based on BBB ratings and award allocations; the public counts on the BBB for its brand image of truth and trust, but the BBB has let the public down; the BBB has lied about the quality of a major winner. [Employer's Company Redacted] and the BBB have engaged in fraud and collusion to cover such fraud. [Employer's Company Redacted], a major, renown Houston-based company, fraudulently accepted a very prestigious award under extremely false pretenses and was allowed to continue all benefits and gain in order to cover-up the BBB's indiscretions. [Employer's Company Redacted] and the BBB have perpetrated unconscionable and outrageous fraud against a trusting public. Thank you for your consideration and I look forward to your reply.

Sincerely,
Caryn Cain

January 12, 2009

Certified Mail Receipt (xxxx5047)
Return Receipt Requested

Office of the Attorney General
Consumer Protection Division
P. O. Box 12548
Austin, Texas 78711-2548

Re: Twofold Fraud complaints against [Company Redacted], Houston, TX and Better Business Bureau ("BBB") of Houston, TX; Alleging Fraud, Collusion, and Cover-up:
Public Fraud – [Company Redacted] Fraudulent Advertising Campaign – "Pinnacle" "Trust" "Reputation"
Public Fraud – BBB Fraudulent Advertising Campaign – [Company Redacted] Cover-up/Web Rotation

---

[Company Redacted] Fraudulently Accepted 2008 BBB Pinnacle Award
BBB Ultimately Responsible – No Verification of Award Applications; Defective Honor System
BBB Performed Unfair Investigation; Dismissed Complaint; Continued Award Benefits
BBB Cover-up to Protect Against Widespread Repercussions; Scam Implications
Public Being Sold False Bill of Goods and Suffering Consequences

To Whom It May Concern:

I have not received any acknowledgment of receipt or interest in pursuing investigation of the referenced matter as mailed to the Office of the Attorney General on December 8, 2008. I respectfully request a status if possible so that I may proceed accordingly for due process.

I am alleging improprieties against the BBB and [Redacted], Houston, Texas; that the BBB is ignoring and condoning [Company Redacted] fraudulent acceptance of the 2008 BBB Pinnacle award of excellence to cover its own negligence. I filed a complaint with the BBB at earliest availability in September 2008, resulting in an unfair, biased investigation as [Company Redacted] is a longtime, influential BBB member. I am further alleging a BBB cover up due to the ramifications and repercussions of the BBB depending upon a defective honor system to evaluate applications for award allocations without ever actually verifying onsite operations and award application content. After the BBB was informed of [Company Redacted] indiscretions, the BBB engaged in pay-for-play activities and promoted [Company Redacted] on its radio ads and its website as a valued Pinnacle winner as though condoning [Company Redacted] fraudulent activities. I created and authored the application and can prove my claims as well as provide witnesses. The BBB has abused its brand image of "truth, honesty, and integrity" which the consumer relies for investment and quality of service.

THE APO$TATE

Thank you for your considerations and I look forward to your reply.

Sincerely,
Caryn Cain

February 11, 2009
Certified Mail Receipt (xxxx4903)
Return Receipt Requested

Office of the Attorney General
Consumer Protection Division
Attn: Charlene [Last Name Redacted]
P. O. Box 12548
Austin, Texas 78711-2548

Re: **Complaint remains unanswered regarding Better Business Bureau of Houston, Texas [Previous letter, Dated December 8, 2008, Detailed Twofold Fraud complaints against [Company Redacted] and Better Business Bureau ("BBB") of Houston, TX; Alleging Fraud, Collusion, and Cover-up]

Dear Ms. [Last Name Redacted]:

As referenced, I am in receipt of your letter, dated January 12, 2009, which only addresses one of two complaints submitted. Your answer does not address the second party complaint against the Better Business Bureau of Houston, Texas. I believe your January 12, 2009 letter crossed in the mail with a second letter I sent certified on January 12, 2009 requesting status on my December 8, 2008 letter and included complaint forms for both [Company Redacted] and the BBB. Accordingly, please advise the position of the Office of Attorney General on the matter regarding the BBB. This matter is not an employer-employee issue as the BBB states. My complaint relates to the BBB scamming the public by falsely implying that allocated excellence awards have been justly earned and award applications have been pre-verified while knowing billions of dollars every year are spent based on BBB affiliation and award recognition. I am alleging that the BBB has abused its brand image of "truth, honesty, and integrity."

Additionally, I question your suggestion to seek legal representation to remedy a blatant public fraud issue and why such responsibility is mine rather than the state of Texas? I don't believe you understand the ramifications and magnitude of my complaint nor the extent of effort I have already exerted on behalf of correcting such consumer fraud. Your letter states "it is through the efforts of citizens like yourself that we are able to continually monitor the businesses across the State and bring appropriate enforcement action when necessary." Accordingly, I am requesting the state of Texas intervene and investigate the BBB for ongoing massive consumer fraud. The current awards program should be suspended until fair and ethical award procedures are implemented. Thank you for your considerations and I look forward to your earliest reply.

Sincerely,
Caryn Cain

January 23, 2009
Certified Mail Receipt (xxxx5030)
Return Receipt Requested

Federal Trade Commission
Consumer Response Center
600 Pennsylvania Avenue, NW
Washington, DC 20580

Re: Better Business Bureau of Houston, Texas
     Massive Consumer Bad Faith Misrepresentation/Fraud/Collusion/
     Cover-up

To Whom It May Concern:

I am seeking your investigation of the annual Better Business Bureau award program and the manner with which award recipients are chosen. I am alleging that such award program is corrupt and dependent upon a defective honor system for selection of winner recipients. Award Recipients are not prequalified yet win awards from the BBB implying otherwise. The ramifications are mindboggling and affect consumers worldwide involving billions of dollars annually. The repercussions are that consumers suffer quality of service and are sold a fake bill of goods under the BBB brand image of "truth, honesty and integrity." I have approached the BBB of Houston, Texas and was refused involvement for investigation. I have approached the U.S. Council of BBB's and was refused involvement for investigation. I have then approached the Office of the Attorney General of Texas and, again, was refused involvement for investigation. I am obviously fighting the BBB's ingrained image, power and influence despite its negligence in protecting consumers from fraud and corruption, and, in fact, collusion with businesses to cover-up the BBB's negligence.

I realized the extent of the BBB's negligence after my employer won the BBB's 2008 Pinnacle award. The BBB offers participating businesses two awards every year – distinguished excellence and the Pinnacle as the highest award. The Pinnacle winners obviously gain the most attraction from consumers and its image automatically escalates such winner's public rating. The awards are won through submitted applications to the BBB in February and winners are announced in May. My position of Chief Financial Officer required me to draft and submit the BBB application for 2008 for my employer [Company Redacted]. The application was regarding interdepartmental training tapes to alleviate and pre-empt reoccurring customer service problems. I approached the owner with my ideas and he agreed to comply and implement the training tapes. Consequently, I drafted and submitted the application and won the Pinnacle. Only, the owner never created nor implemented the training tapes and later approached me to stop bothering him about the matter accordingly. Yet, the owner still accepted the Pinnacle and now enjoys featured BBB website rotation and waves the Pinnacle award on all advertising and radio spots. In the meantime, his quality of service has fallen into the toilet and customers are complaining and valued employees are leaving a badly run company. The owner features an outdated corporate group picture on his website where a

Page 2
Certified Mail Receipt (xxx5030)
January 23, 2009

majority of the employees are no longer at the company including the Vice President of Operations and myself.

The point is the BBB has never checked application submittals. Awards are based on the honor system that what was written in the applications had been done. My former employer is a perfect example that such honor system is defective and subjects the consumer to fraud. The BBB was notified of such fraudulent activity by me and yet still refused to properly investigate claiming it was an "employer-employee" issue despite the fact that the award application was about employer-employee training tapes. The BBB purposefully bloated and confused the issue, vilified me, and chose to sweep the issue under the rug to cover-up its negligence in pre-qualifying applications because of the enormous public repercussions. The consumer is falsely assuming the BBB has checked winners thoroughly and this is bad faith misrepresentation. And, wholesale theft! I don't know how widespread the practice is and can only verify the BBB of Houston's negligence. Please consider, though, that this matter is not contained within Texas. My former employer utilizes the web for local, national and international business as well; his website [Company Redacted] BBB awards for its celebrity and gain. Such matter carries national concern. I am begging the Federal Trade Commission to step in and investigate. I have witnesses and would appreciate your review.

Sincerely,
Caryn Cain
Attachments

February 10, 2009

Caryn Cain
[Address Redacted]

RE: FTC Ref. No. 1633992

Dear Caryn Cain:

Thank you for recent correspondence. The Federal Trade Commission acts in the public interest to stop business practices that violate the laws it enforces. Letters from consumers and businesses are very important to the work of the Commission. They are often the first indication of a problem in the marketplace and may provide the initial evidence to begin an investigation. The Commission does not resolve individual complaints. The Commission can, however, act when it sees a pattern of possible violations developing.

The information you have provided will be recorded in our complaint retention system. This computerized system enables us to identify questionable business practices that are generating numerous complaints and may be in violation of the law.

Thank you for providing information that may be used to develop or support Commission enforcement initiatives.

Sincerely Yours,
Consumer Response Center

REFERENCES

PRIMARY CITATIONS PER QUOTED CHRONOLOGICAL ORDER:

Frank Dalton O'Sullivan, *Rackets: Including the Practices of the Better Business Bureau System* (Chicago, Illinois, O'Sullivan Publishing House), 1933.

H. J. Kenner, *The Fight For Truth in Advertising* (New York, N.Y., Round Table Press, Inc.), 1936.

Frank W. Dressler, *The Better Business Bureau Murders* (New York, Writers Club Press), 2000.

E. C. Riegel, *Barnum and Bunk* (New York, N.Y., The Riegel Corporation of New York), 1928.

B. Charles Wansley, *History and Traditions*, address for Institutes for Organization Management, Washington University, St. Louis, Missouri, 1971; original link removed at: https://boston.bbb.org/history-and-traditions (Author has copy of original article printed on 11/14/13 pursuant to book's references); ancillary link found at: https://www.bbb.org/oklahomacity/get-to-know-us/history-and-traditions.

Advertising Federation of America, *Truth in Advertising* (New York, H. Wolff), 1936.

2009 Form 990; http://990s.foundationcenter.org/990_pdf_archive/237/237079691/237079691_20 0912_990O.pdf.

2011 Annual Report; http://www.bbb.org/us/storage/113/documents/annual-reports/CBBB2011Annual-Report.pdf.

2012 Annual Report; http://www.bbb.org/us/storage/113/documents/CBBB_AR_2012.pdf.

2013 Annual Report; http://www.bbb.org/globalassets/local-bbbs/council-113/media/annual-reports/cbbb_annual_report_2013-final.pdf.

2015 Annual Report; https://www.bbb.org/globalassets/local-bbbs/council-113/media/annual-reports/cbbb-2015annual-report.pdf.

Printers' Ink, Printers' Ink 50 Years (New York, N.Y., Printers' Ink Pub. Co.), 1938.

Joseph H. Appel, *Growing Up With Advertising* (New York, NY, The Business Bourse, Publishers), 1940.

Mark Pendergrast, *For God, Country & Coca-Cola* [Second Edition: Revised and Expanded] (New York, NY, Basic Books), 2000.

Stephen Fox, *The Mirror Makers* (New York, William Morrow and Company, Inc.), 1984.

The Sphinx Club, *The Sphinx Club, New York* (1904) (Boston, Massachusetts, The Barta Press), 1904.

Jerome R. Corsi, PH.D., *The Obama Nation* (New York, Threshold Editions), 2008.

David E. Kyvig, *Daily Life In The United States, 1920 – 1940* (Chicago, Ivan R. Dee, Publisher), 2004.

William Seale, *The President's House* (Washington, D.C., White House Historical Association), 1987.

Joseph H. Appel, *Business Biography of John Wanamaker* (New York, The Macmillan Company), 1930.

Theodore Roosevelt, *The Rough Riders* (New York, Fall River Press, Reprint of 1899 Edition), 2014.

H. W. Brands, *The Reckless Decade: America in the 1890s* (Chicago, The University of Chicago Press), 1995.

Upton Sinclair, *The Jungle* (First Edition: Double Day, Page, New York, 1906) (Reprint: The Heritage Press, New York, 1965).

James C. Auchincloss, *The Better Business Bureau: Its Growth and Work*, Chicago Assoc. of Commerce, (November 2, 1927).

Michael Perino, *The Hellhound of Wall Street* (New York, The Penguin Press), 2010.

S.L.A. Marshall, *World War I* (New York, Mariner Books), 2001.

REFERENCES

Ralph Blumenthal, *Stork Club* (New York, Little, Brown and Company), 2000.
Charles R. Geisst, *Wall Street: A History* (New York, Oxford University Press), 1997.
Charles R. Geisst, *100 Years of Wall Street* (New York, McGraw-Hill), 2000.
Frank Dalton O"Sullivan, *Crime Detection* (Chicago, Illinois, The O'Sullivan Publishing House), 1928.
Frank Dalton O'Sullivan, *Enemies of Industry* (Chicago, Illinois, The O'Sullivan Publishing House), 1933.
Frank Dalton O'Sullivan, *The Poison Pen of Jersey* (Chicago, Illinois, The O'Sullivan Publishing House), 1936.
James Ballowe, *A Man of Salt and Trees* (DeKalb, Illinois, Northern Illinois University Press), 2009.

PREFACE

Page
ii "unfair trade practices…   O'Sullivan, (1933), p. 33.

INTRODUCTION

Page
viii "August 1, 2016," Ec.europa.eu/info/law/law-topic/data-protection/international-dimension-data-protection/eu-us-data-transfers_en.
viii "BBB EU Privacy Shield" Bbb.org/EU-privacy-shield/about-program; bbbprograms.org/programs/bbb-privacy-shield; privacyshield.gov/NewsEvents.
ix "The world can… Http://www.presidency.ucsb.edu/ws/?pid=19253.
ix "1,000" The guardian.com/usnews/2016/sep/11/9-11-illnesses-death-toll.
ix "20,874" Abcnews.go.com/us/911- toll-growsl-16000-ground-responders-sickfound/story?id=57669657.
ix "Islam is peace." Https://georgewbush-whitehouse.archives.gov/ news/releases/2001/09/20010917-11.html
x "Vigilance Committee… Kenner, (1936), p. 34.
x "From advertising review… Https://www.bbb.org/globalassets/local-bbbs/ council-113/media/annual-reports/cbbb2015annual-report.pdf.
x "HomeAdvisor uses… Ibid.
xii "Muslim, Socialist Puppet" Www.thenationalpatriot. com/2014/01/the-real-obama-an-indonesian-muslim-socialist-puppet.
xii "information superhighway." Dressler, (2000), p. 111.
xii "global assets" Https://www.bbb.org/globalassets/local-bbbs/ council-113/media/annual-reports/cbbb2015annual-report.pdf.
xiii "swells," Https://en.wikipedia.org/wiki/Eleanor_ Roosevelt.
xvii "To be humbugged… Riegel, (1928), p. 9.
xvii "agency of assistance" Wansley, *History and Traditions,* 1971.
xvii "No honestly intentional… O'Sullivan, (1933), p. 62.
xviii "1,500 Newspapers; 1,100… Https://onsizzle.com/i/illusion-of-choice-there-are-1-500- newspapers-1- 100-magazines-9-000-3990416.
xviii "media" Https://www.dictionary.com/browse/media.
xviii "The hook-up between… O'Sullivan, (1933), p. 34
xix "the greatest racket… Ibid.
xix "These Wikileaks emails… Https://www.dailymail. co.uk/news/article-3835460/Now-Podestas-Twitter-account-gets-hacked-day-Clinton-campaign-chair-accuses-Russia-hacking-emails.html#ixzz5EM24ifYY.

PART ONE
CHAPTER ONE: WHISTLEBLOWER

Page
3 "My master, the… Https://en.wikipedia.org/wiki/I_Dream_of_ Jeannie.
4 "kink scene." Https://www.newstatesman. com/politics/2015/01/if-we-liberate-men-ssexuality-war-against-women-can-end.

5	"Lucy's psychiatry…	Https://peanuts.wikia.com/wiki/Lucy%27s_ psychiatry_booth.
11	"Start Your Search…	Https://Houston.bbb.org/WWWRoot/SitePage. aspx?site=148&id=e53c622a-5a6f-4629-bc19.
11	"BBB is in the top…	Https://www.bbb.org/Detroit/for-businesses/ about-bbb-accreditation.
15	"the recession of 2007-2009…	Https://finance.yahoo.com/ news/where-missing-american-workers-gone-090641178.html.
18	"number of people…	Https://www.alexa.com/siteinfor/bbb.org.
18	"1,048,614." Ibid.	
20	"Almighty Latin Kings"	Blabber.buzz/ conservativenews/686764-latin-kings-gang-leader-freed-by-first-step-act-arrested-for-murder-after.
20	"less than a year… Ibid.	
22	"If through error…	Kenner, (1936), p. 266.

CHAPTER TWO: AWARDS FOR EXCELLENCE

Page

24	"a former chairman…	Https://casetext.com/case/ better-bus-bureau-of-metro-hous-inc-v-john-moore-servs-inc-4.
24	"2007 to 2008"	Https://caselaw.findlaw.com/tx-court-of-appeals/1639061.html
24	"John Moore Services, Inc. and…	Ibid.
24	"Chief Executive Officer…	Https://casetext.com/case/ better-bus-bureau-of-metro-hous-inc-v-john-moore-servs-inc-4.
25	"Terror Group Gets…	Https://abcnews.go.com/Blotter/business-bureau-best-ratings-money-buy/ story?id=12123843.
25	"to "NR" for…	Https://caselaw.findlaw.com/tx-court-ofappeals/1639061.html.
25	"two state court…	Https://casetext.com/case/ better-bus-bureau-of-metro-hous-inc-v-john-moore-servs-inc-4.
25	"over a business quality…	Https://caselaw.findlaw.com/tx-court-ofappeals/1639061.html.
25	"[C]laims for fraud, tortious…	Https://casetext.com/case/ better-bus-bureau-of-metro-hous-inc-v-john-moore-servs-inc-4.
25	"[C]laims for fraud, state… Ibid.	
26	"The Supreme Court of Texas… Ibid.	
27	"any enterprise which…	O'Sullivan, (1933), p. 59.
27	"the BBBest"	Https://www.bbb.org/Houston/migration/othernews/2008/11/ bbb-awards-for-excellence-app.
27	"Barnum and Bunk"	Riegel, (1928).
27	"hokum and make-believe"	Ibid., 9.
28	"Better Business Bureau warns…	Https://nbcmontana.com/news/local/ betterbusiness-bureau-warns-that-award-scams-are-going-around.
28	"vanity awards" Ibid.	
28	"money grabs" Ibid.	
28	"Most legitimate awards… Ibid.	
29	"$353,033"	Form 990, BBB of Metropolitan Houston Educational Foundation, p. 9.
29	"IRC Section 6103…	IRS letter to Caryn Cain from Director of Compliance.
30	"to organize financial…	Foundation Group; https://www.501c3.org/wpcontent/uploads/ Resources/Successfully-Starting-aNew-Nonprofit.pdf?utm_term=You%20can%20 click%20 here%20to%20view%20the%20 eBook%20%22Successfully%20Starting%20 a%20New%20 Nonprofit.%22&&utm_ content=landing+page&utm_source=ActOn+Software&utm_ medium=landing+page; p. 6.
30	"to clog up the courts…"	O'Sullivan, (1933), pp. 28-29.
31	"In franchising, franchisors…	Https://www.franchise.org/what-is-a-franchise.
31	"Bureau dues"	Https://www.bbb.org/us/storage/113/documents/ CBBB_AR_2012.pdf; https:// www.bbb.org/ globalassets/local-bbbs/council-113/media/ annual-reports/cbbb_annual_report_2013-final. pdf.

REFERENCES

31	"report sources of income…	Https://bizfluent.com/about-5579857-history501-c--3--non-profit.html.
31	"August 17, 2006,"	Https://www.irs.gov/charities-non-profits/ public-disclosure-and-availability-of-exempt-organizations-returns-and-applications-documents-subject-to-public-disclosure.
31	"open to public inspection."	Https://www.irs.gov/pub/irs-pdf/f990.pdf.
31	"$4,884,226."	Https://990s.foundation.center.org/990_pdf_ar chi ve/237/237079691/237079691_200912_99 0O.pdf.
31	"$2,117,000"	Https://www.bbb.org/us/storage/113/ documents/annual-reports/CBBB-2011AnnualReport.pdf.
31	"$4,349,530"	Ibid.
31	"$4,951,068"	Https://www.bbb.org/us/storage/113/ documents/CBBB_AR_2012.pdf.
31	"$5,225,003"	Https://www.bbb.org/globalassets/local-bbbs/council-113/media/annual-reports/cbbb_annual_ report_2013-final.pdf.
31	"$9,662,715"	Https://www.bbb.org/globalassets/local-bbbs/council-113/media/annual-reports/cbbb2015annual-report.pdf.
31	"$13,735,934"	Ibid.
31	"…passage was the result…	Https://www.irs.gov/pub/irs-tege/eotopick03.pdf.
31	"to permit…	Ibid.
31	"Section 501c6 recognizes…	Https://budgeting.thenest.com/501-c-6- organization-27618.html.
31	"Reg. 1.501(c)(6)-l defines…	Https://www.irs.gov/pub/irs-tege/eotopick03.pdf.
32	"Reg. 1.501(c)(6)-l speaks…	Ibid.
32	"all donations, contributions,…	Https://www.jesus-is-savior.com/Evils%20in%20 Government/Police%20State/501c3_unbiblical. htm.
32	"supplemental income tax"	Https://en.wikipedia.org/wiki/Alternative_ minimum_tax.
32	"Organizations described…	Https://www.irs.gov/charities-non-profits/privatefoundations/private-operating-foundations.
32	"a private operating foundation…	Ibid.
32	"Each year, private…	Cof.org/public-policy/private-foundation-excise-tax.
32	"charitable expenditures"	Ibid.
32	"the private foundation…	Cof.org/sites/default/files/documents/files/ PF%20Excise%20Tax--Issue%20Paper.pdf.
32	"calculating the tax rate…	Cof.org/public-policy/private-foundation-excise-tax.
32	"To be tax-exempt under…	Https://www.irs.gov/charities-non-profits/ charitable-organizations/inurement-private-benefit-charitable-organizations.
33	"to be of use, benefit…	Legal-dictionary.thefreedictionary.com/inure.
33	"organized or operated for…	Https://www.irs.gov/charities-non-profits/ charitable-organizations/inurement-private-benefit-charitable-organizations.
33	"gifts, grants, contributions…	Better Business Bureau of Metropolitan Houston, TX 77027, Form 990, EIN 74-1662104, For Year 2016.
33	"In 2010, public charities…	Https://www.urban.org/sites/default/files/ publication/25901/412674-The-NonprofitSector-in-Brief-Public-Charities-Giving-andVolunteering-.PDF.
33	"mobilized resources"	Https://www.discoverthenetworks.org/ printgroupProfile.asp?grpid=7150.
34	"web-based, not-for-profit…	Ibid.
34	"notable friendly ties…	Ibid.
34	"had "regular contact…	Ibid.
34	"George Soros announced…	Https://www.politico.com/blogs/onmedia/1010/ Soros_gives_1_million_to_Media_Matters. html] also[http://www.discoverthenetworks.org/ printgroupProfile.asp?grpid=7150.
34	"Benefiting the Better…	Https://www.bbb.org/Houston/for-businesses/ programs-services/bbb-awards-for-excellence.
34	"The Better Business Bureau…	Https://www.bbb.org/houston/for-businesses/ programs-services/bbb-awards-for-excellence.

35 "Exempt Organizations Business…   Https://www.irs.gov/charities-non-profits/exempt-organizations-business-master-fileextract-eo-bmf.
35 "record count"   Ibid.
35 "1,669,731."   Ibid.
35 "Federal ID Tax…   Https://www.bbb.org/houston/public/Form/ Form.aspx?f=293&e=5-c3-9e-c3-9c.
36 "Form 990, Part III…   Better Business Bureau of Metropolitan Houston, TX 77027, Form 990, EIN 74-1662104, For Year 2016.
36 "the wrongful taking…   Https://www.dictionary.com/browse/larceny.
36 "creating or confirming…   Https://www.statutes.legis.state.tx.us/Docs/PE/ htm/PE.31.htm.
37 "the process by which…   Https://www.int-comp.org/careers/a-career-inaml/what-is-money-laundering.
37 "placement,"   Ibid.
37 "layering,"   Ibid.
37 "integration."   Ibid.
37 "crimes committed…   Investopedia.com/terms/r/racketeering.asp.
37 "a criminal entity [that]…   Ibid.
37 "committing multiple violations…   Https://en.wikipedia.org/wiki/Racket_(crime).
37 "RICO Act" Ibid. "the elimination of…   Https://www.justice.gov/usam/file/870856/ download. 37 "Section 1962(a)…   Ibid., 2
37 "Section 1962(b)…   Ibid.
37 "Section 1962(c)…   Ibid.
37 "Section 1962(d)…   Ibid., 3
39 "the BBB system seeks…   Https://www.ftc.gov/sites/default/files/ documents/advisory_opinions/council-better-business-bureaus-inc./100815cbbbletter.pdf.
43 "misuses of advertising"   Kenner, (1936), Preface xvii.
44 "Truth Trophy"   Ibid., 39.
44 "The pyramid is a symbol…   Https://timeforchange.org/human_development.
44 "While the all-seeing eye…   Https://scottishrite.org/scottish-rite-myths-and-facts/eye-in-the-pyramid.
44 "Accreditation Seal"   Https://www.bbb.org/globalassets/local-bbbs/council-113/media/annual-reports/cbbb2015annual-report.pdf.
44 "Whether or not the new…   Kenner, (1936), p. 44.
44 "for a fee"   Ibid.
45 "The opponents of the…   Ibid., 45.
45 "Advocates thought that…   Ibid.
45 "controversial"   Ibid.
45 "Experience through the years…   Ibid.
45 "Today, the certification of…   Ibid.
45 "The experiment went…   Ibid., 44.
45 "does not endorse any…   Dressler, (2000), p. 68.
46 "2008 BBB Torch Award…   Https://abcnews.go.com/Blotter/ page?id=12132519.
46 "Specifically, my investigation…   Ibid.
46 "were false and/or …   Https://www.fraudwhistleblowersblog.com/ federal-false-claims-act/sanofi-aventis-cant-invoke-the-first-amendment-to-escape-fca-liability.
46 "The Relator alleges…   Ibid.
46 "that Aventis had engaged…   Ibid.
48 "All applicants must be…   Https://www.bbb.org/globalassets/local-bbbs/ houston-tx-148/media/awards/bbb-awardsbusiness-app-2016.pdf.
48 "You can use the Logo ONLY…   Https://www.bbb.org/Houston/for-businesses/ programs-services/bbb-awards-for-excellence.
50 "The first BBB site…   Https://clevelandbbb100.org/wp/about-us/funfacts.
50 "no decision had been made…   Dressler, (2000), p. 110.

REFERENCES

51 "I understand that... Https://www.bbb.org/Houston/migration/othernews/2008/11/bbb-awards-for-excellence-app...; Houston Better Business Bureau's 2009 awards application.
52 "70% of consumers... Https://www.ripoffreport.com/r/BetterBusiness-Bureau-BBB-CBBB/Arlington-SelectStateProvince/Better-Business-Bureau-or-Buyer-Better-Beware-BBB-Nationwide-Alert-THE-FOX-GUARDIN-1343.
53 "BBBs' websites... Ibid.
53 "132,385,251 BBB... Https://www.bbb.org/globalassets/local-bbbs/ council-113/media/annual-reports/cbbb_annual_ report_2013-final.pdf.
53 "Better Business Bureaus... Ibid.
54 "This coveted award... Https://bbb.org/Houston/for-businesses/ programs-services/bbb-awards-for-excellence.
54 "Standards for Charity... Https://www.bbb.org/us/standards-for-charity-accountability.
54 "truthfulness of... Ibid.
54 "Out of the 122,517... Http://www.bizjournals.com/houston/ news/2012/07/23/houston-has-more-than-100000-small.html.
54 "is roughly the same size... Http://www.texasmonthly.com/daily-post/if-you-needed-it-further-proof-houston-so-much-bigger-most-cities.
54 "In 2010 the Houston... Http://www.reactionsearch.com/construction_ executive_search/houston-construction-executive-search-firm.htm.
54 "Houston is second only... Ibid.
55 "NEW guidelines... Http://www.bbb.org/Houston/for-businesses/ programs-services/bbb-awards-for-excellence.
55 "1) Anytime you advertise... Ibid.
55 "national initiatives... Http://www.bbb.org/council/about/council-of-better-business-bureaus.
55 "BBB Code of... Https://www.bbb.org/council/for-businesses/about-bbb-accreditation/bbb-accreditation-standards.
55 "Standards of Trust." Ibid.
55 "CBBB is the network... Http://www.bbb.org/council/about/council-of-better-business-bureaus
55 "recognizes excellence... Https://en.wikipedia.org/wiki/Academy_Awards.
55 "the creative spirit... Http://www.americanadvertisingawards.com.
55 "secondary design check" Https://ricochet.com/502890/political-correctness-kills-4-more-in-florida-another-deadly-obama-initiative.
55 "first of its kind" Https://news.fiu.edu/2018/03/first-of-its-kind-pedestrian-bridge-swings-into-place/120385.
55 "Accelerated Bridge... Ibid.
55 "Funding for the $14.2... Ibid.
56 "The TIGER program... Https://ricochet.com/502890/political-correctness-kills-4-more-in-florida-another-deadly-obama-initiative.
56 "good-business awards" Http://abcnews.go.com/Blotter/ page?id=12132519.
56 "In our mad scramble... Advertising Federation of America, (1936), pp.40-41; Address Title: "The Business Everybody Knows," By Ken R. Dyke, Chairman of the Board, Association of National Advertisers.

CHAPTER THREE: RATING SCORE

Page
57 "Father of Hollywood," Https://en.wikipedia.org/wiki/Hollywood.
57 ""I holly-wood"... Ibid.
57 "already started ... Ibid.
57 "Hollywood, California"." Ibid.
59 "information super-highway." Dressler, (2000), p. 111
59 "defense force." Https://www.rt.com/ news/368564-europe-defense-fund-details.
60 "BBB grades are... Http://www.bbb.org/council/overview-of-bbb-grade.
60 "grading elements" Ibid.

THE APO$TATE

60 "maximum number of…   Ibid.
60 "100 point scale"   Ibid.
60 "Total revenue"   2009 Form 990.
60 "$16,015,721"   Ibid.
60 "$15,154,047"   Ibid.
60 "$18,336,000"   2011 Annual Report.
61 "$18,742,702"   Ibid.
61 "$21,243,431"   2012 Annual Report.
61 "$21,765,742"   2013 Annual Report.
61 "$23,725,023"   2015 Annual Report.
61 "$28,020,198"   Ibid.
61 "Better Business Bureau grades…   Http://articles.latimes. com/2009/jan/21/business/fi-lazarus21.
61 "…a random search….   Ibid.
61 "Why do so many…   Ibid.
61 "I can't explain that…   Ibid.
61 "Better Business Bureau…   Http://abcnews.go.com/ Blotter/business-bureau-best-ratings-money-buy/ story?id=12123843.
61 "Two small-business owners"   Ibid.
61 "Better Business Bureau telemarketers"   Ibid.
61 "that their grades of C…   Ibid.
62 "teamed up with…   Http://www.slate.com/ articles/business/the_customer/2010/12/busted_ watchdog.html.
62 "Aryan Whitney"   Http://abcnews.go.com/ Blotter/business-bureau-best-ratings-money-buy/ story?id=12123843.
62 "an F for…   Http://www.slate.com/ articles/business/the_customer/2010/12/busted_ watchdog.html.
62 "called on the Bureau…   Http://abcnews.go.com/ Blotter/ business-bureau-president-apologizes-errors-grading-system.
62 "I am deeply concerned…   Http://abcnews.go.com/Blotter/business-bureau-best-ratings-money-buy/story?id=12123843; link to Blumenthal letter scrubbed, author's copy avail.
62 "I am also concerned…   Ibid.
62 "I am concerned that the new …   Ibid.
62 "There are clear…   Ibid.
62 "Restitution…   Original link scrubbed; refer to: https://ctwatchdog.com/business/custom-basements-customers-to-get-94000.
63 "The Torch Awards…   Original link scrubbed; refer to: https://www.bbb.org/local-bbb/ bbb-cincinnati.
63 "skews rating results…   Http://abcnews.go.com/Blotter/business-bureau-best-ratings-money-buy/ story?id=12123843; link to Blumenthal letter scrubbed, author's copy avail.
63 "special meeting"   Http://reloroundtable.com/ blog/how-to/moving-tips/consumer-help/ bbb-revises-rating-sys.
63 "By next week, the BBB…   Ibid.
63 "Better Business Bureau To Investigate…   Http://abcnews.go.com/ Blotter/ business-bureau-investigate-los-angeles-chapter/story?id=1.
63 "It is ironic that the BBB…   Http://www.marketwired.com/press-release/ business-consumer-alliance-responds-to-bbb-.
64 "BBB accreditation and…   Http://abcnews.go.com/ Blotter/business-bureau-best-ratings-money-buy/ story?id=12123843.
64 "plain and simple…   Ibid.
64 "While we want to recognize…   Http://abcnews.go.com/ Blotter/ business-bureau-president-apologizes-errors-grading-system/.
64 "Businesses must submit…   Http://www.bbb.org/globalassets/ local-bbbs/hartford-ct-29/media/ events/website-marketing-message-award-2016.pdf.
64 "the winning company…   Ibid.

REFERENCES

64	"In March, we expelled…	Http://www.bbb.org/globalassets/local-bbbs/ council-113/media/annual-reports/cbbb_annual_ report_2013-final.pdf.
65	"virtual BBB"	Http://www.bbb.org/council/newsevents/news-releases/2013/12/better-business-bureau-opens-full-service-office-in-los-angeles.
65	"in an historic building at 448…	Ibid.
65	"the first in downtown…	Http://www.bbb.org/globalassets/local-bbbs/ council-113/media/annual-reports/cbbb_annual_ report_2013-final.pdf.
65	"struck down"	Http://dailycaller. com/2012/06/28/supreme-court-strikes-down-stolen-valor-law.
65	"branding the false claim…	Ibid.
65	"Blumenthal's firewall…	Http://www.dailyructions.com/supreme-court-nixes-stolen-valor-act-relief-for-blumenthal.
67	"useful idiots."	Joseph Stalin.
67	"Trump is raising…	March 19, 2016; Women For Donald Trump, Twitter.
68	"fired"	Https://www.indiewire.com/2018/10/megyn-kelly-fired-nbc-news-69- million-buyout-1202015231.
68	"muzzled by NDA's…	Conservativeinstitute.org/ conservative-news/kelly-feuds-abc-reporter.htm.
68	"Trump Entrepreneur Initiative"	Https://en.wikipedia.org/wiki/Trump_ Entrepreneur_Initiative.
68	"multiple lawsuits alleging…	Http://www.nbcnews.com/ politics/2016-election/better-business-bureau-trump-right-rating-mostly-n527671.
68	""98 percent approval…	Ibid.
68	"We have an A from…	Ibid.
68	"Better Business Bureau: Trump…	Ibid.
68	"We have a 98 percent…	Http://www.cbsnews.com/news/republican-debate-fact-check-how-did-the-better-business-bureau-rate-trump-university.
69	"questions regarding Trump…	Https://www.foxbusiness.com/features/the-better-business-bureau-stays-tight-lipped-about-trump-university.
69	"The document presented…	Ibid.
69	"Megyn Kelly: Claim of 'A'…	Http://www.newsmax.com/Headline/megynkelly-trump-university-claim-a/2016/03/14/ id/719075.
69	"Ever since she tangled…	Www.Breitbart.com, "Megyn's Secret: Star Anchor Kept Trump Meeting From Fox Boss Ailes, NY Mag Reports."
69	"had an 'A-plus' rating but…	Http://www.nbcnews.com/ politics/2016-election/better-business-bureau-trump-right-rating-mostly-n527671.
69	"BBB Serving Metro…	Http://www.nbcnews.com/politics/2016- election/better-business-bureau-trump-right-rating-mostly-n527671.
70	"tight-lipped"	Https://www.foxbusiness.com/features/the-better-business-bureau-stays-tight-lipped-about-trump-university.
70	"Political parties choose…	Http://www.msn.com/en-us/news/politics/rncmember-%e2%80%98political-parties-choos…
71	"We're trying to let voters…	Breitbart.com, "Manafort: GOP Presidential Nominating Process A 'System of the 1920s- Not 2016," April 17, 2016, by Jeff Poor.
71	"In 2015, local BBBs…	Https://www.bbb.org/globalassets/local-bbbs/ council-113/media/annual-reports/2016-annualreports/cbbb-2015annual-report.pdf.
71	"Member businesses' names…	Http://www.slate.com/articles/business/the_ customer/2010/12/busted_watchdog.html.
71	"protecting the integrity…	Dressler, (2000), p.110.
72	"BBB accreditation does not…	Http://www.bbb.org/council/for-businesses/about-bbb-accreditation.
72	"BBB grades are not…	Http://www.bbb.org/council/overview-of-bbb-grade.
72	"Tell the Truth…	Https://www.bbb.org/council/for-businesses/about-bbb-accreditation/bbb-accreditation-standards.

THE APO$TATE

PART TWO
CHAPTER FOUR: BBB HISTORY

Page
75 "Today fifty-six local Bureaus… *Printers' Ink*, (1938), p. 258.
75 "over Madison Square… Https://untappedcities.com/ 2012/12/06/history-of-streets-the-great-white-way.
76 "illuminated" Ibid.
76 "The friends of the Better… O'Sullivan, (1933), pp. 33-34.
77 "Vigilance Committee of the … Kenner, (1936), p. 34.
77 "first" Http://www.bbbis100org/about-us/timeline.
77 "Barrels and Kegs Case" Pendergrast, (2000), p. 120.
78 "National Partner" Http://www.bbb.org/globalassets/local-bbbs/ council-113/media/annual-reports/cbbb2015annual-report.pdf.
78 "2015 Board of Directors… Ibid.
78 "Chair." Ibid.
78 "It is evident that the 1916… *Printers' Ink*, "Help Afforded Advertisers by A.N.P.A. Bureau of Advertising" (Vol. XCIX, No. 4, April 26, 1917), pp. 65-68.
78 "U.S. Post Office Department." Https://en.wikipedia.org/wiki/Postal_Service_Act.
78 "Continental Post" Ibid.
78 "the first postmaster general." Ibid.
79 "American Advertising Federation (AAF)" Http://www.aaf.org; http://www.advertisinghall.org/history/index.html; http://www.bbb. org/houston/business-reviews/professionalorganizations/american-advertising-federation-houston-aaf-houston-in-houston-tx-62040.
79 "National Association of Better… Kenner, (1936), p.140.
79 "were first called… Http://www.u-s-history.com/pages/h1682.html.
80 "Dr. John Coleman: Know… Https://socioecohistory.wordpress. com/2012/04/23/current-membership-list-of-the-illuminati-committee-of-300.
80 "inner circle" Ibid.
80 "Order of the Garter." Ibid.
80 "The Committee of 300… Ibid.
80 "Each is a hierarchy… Ibid
80 "Secret societies exist… Ibid.
80 "to gain world-wide control." Ibid.
80 "a product of the British… Ibid.
80 "chartered by the British… Ibid.
80 "untouchable ruling class." Ibid.
80 "the largest company… Ibid.
80 "wallowing in tainted… Ibid.
80 "British Crown" Ibid.
80 "the United States from top… Ibid.
81 "Haus Wettin" Https://en.wikipedia.org/wiki/House_of_Wettin.
81 "became the rulers… Ibid.
81 "ascended the thrones… Ibid.
81 "Duchy of Saxe-Coburg-Saalfeld" Ibid.
81 "the United Kingdom, Belgium… Https://en.wikipedia.org/wiki/Saxe-Coburg_ and_Gotha.
81 "upper Bavaria, Germany" Https://en.wikipedia.org/wiki/Coburg.
81 "was a rich trading town… Https://en.wikipedia.org/wiki/Gotha.
81 "changed the name… Https://en.wikipedia.org/wiki/Saxe-Coburg_ and_Gotha.
81 "Windsor" Ibid.
81 "the Royal Family's… Ibid.
81 "to *van België*… Https://en.wikipedia.org/wiki/House_of_SaxeCoburg_and_Gotha.
81 "the driving force… Https://socioecohistory.wordpress. com/2012/04/23/dr-john-coleman-know-yourenemy-the-illuminat-committee-of-300.

REFERENCES

81 "Western Illuminati... Ibid.
82 "an annual private... Https://en.wikipedia.org/wiki/Bilderberg_Group.
82 "the Hotel de Bilderberg... Ibid. "one-world government" Ibid.
82 "untouchable" Https://socieoecohistory.wordpress. com/2012/04/23/dr-john-coleman-know-your-enemy-the-illuminat-committee-of-300.
82 "the One World Government... Ibid.
82 "Better Business Bureau: Protecting... Https://danielsethics.mgt.unm.edu/pdf/BBBand-NAD.pdf.
83 "Advertising vigilantes" Kenner, (1936), p. 35.
84 "Prior to 1871, approximately ... Https://www.loc.gov/teachers/ classroommaterials/presentationsandactivities/ presentations/timeline/riseind.
84 "Republican Congressman and steel... Http://www.thetribunepapers.com/2014/01/05/true-causes-of-the-uncivil-war-understanding-the-morrill-tariff.
84 "On February 14, 1861... Https://en.wikipedia.org/wiki/Morrill_Tariff.
84 "first year," Ibid.
84 "increased the effective rate... Ibid.
84 "American tariff rates were... Ibid.
84 "less than $500,000... Ibid.
84 "This act provided Federal... Http://www.loc.gov/rr/program/bib/ourdocs/ PacificRail.html.
84 "Last Spike" Http://www.tcrr.com.
84 "Golden Spike Ceremony" Ibid.
84 "Despite the publicity... Ibid.
84 "[O]n June 4, 1876 a train... Ibid.
84 "Civil War effort" Http://learningabe.info/Transcontinental_ Railroad_Act.html.
84 "would support communities... Ibid.
85 "give settlers safe and... Ibid.
85 "tie new states California... Ibid.
85 "a 1,907-mile contiguous... Ibid.
85 "By 1900, four additional... Http://www.loc.gov/teachers/classroommaterials/ presentationsandactivities/presentations/timeline/ riseind/railroad.
85 "his first steel mill... Https://en.wikipedia.org/wiki/Carnegie_Steel_ Company.
85 "for $480 million in 1901" Https://www.carnegie.org/interactives/ foundersstory/#!.
85 "over 2,500 libraries" Http://historicindianapolis.com/indianapolisthen-and-now-spades-park-library-1801-now-land-avenue.
85 "colleges, schools, nonprofit... Https://www.carnegie.org/interactives/ foundersstory/#!.
85 "Carnegie Corporation... Ibid.
85 "In short, this convention... Https://babel.hathitrust.org/cgilpt?id=umn.3195 1002210587j&view=1up&seq=29.
85 "Educational Course Committee" Https://babel.hathitrust.org/cgilpt?id=umn.3195 1002210587j&view=1up&seq=26.
86 "the first federal income... Http://www.taxhistory.org/thp/readings.nsf/ ArtWeb/C82515A4B6B7 A24C85257D1B0041C86E?OpenDocument.
86 "All things should be... Wansley, (1971).
86 "As a nail sticketh... Appel, (1940), p. 54.
86 "the first organized... Printers' Ink, (1938), p. 76.
87 "$95,000,000." Ibid. 142.
87 "$145,000,000." Ibid.
87 "International Federation... Ibid.
87 "suggesting that a natural... Ibid., 143
87 "was active in the preliminary... Ibid.
87 "at the helm." Ibid., 143, 146.
88 "The Agate Club was formed... Ibid., 78.
88 "lays undisputed claim... Ibid.
88 "imposition" En.wikipedia.org/wiki/Imposition.

497

THE APO$TATE

88 "to ensure that furniture... Https://commons.wikimedia.org/wiki/File:Printers_mallet.jpg.
88 "a locking tool used... Https://letterpresscommons.com/general-tools-and-supplies.
88 "sixteen members" *The Sphinx Club, New York* (1904), p. 7.
89 "develops and administers... Https://www.mapquest.com/us/new-york/advertising-club-of-ny-352417384
89 "the first organized stand... Appel, (1940), p. 133
89 "in a bedroom at the Bellevue-Stratford... Ibid., 136-137.
89 "The voice of the famous ... Ibid., 134.
89 "was famous during two... Ibid., 133.
90 "general advertisers, advertising... *The Sphinx Club, New York* (1904), p. 6.
90 "The first thundering... Appel, (1940), p. 135.
90 "Advertising men, in 1903... Kenner, (1936), p. 12.
90 "It was just about... Appel, (1940), p. 136.
90 "The men in the business... Fox, (1984), p. 38.
90 "In New York this group... Ibid.
90 "What happens in Vegas... Https://blog.illumine8.com/bid/374514/theorigin-of-marketing-vegas-what-happens-in-vegas-stays-in-vegas.
90 "What happens here... Ibid.
91 "R&R Partners" Ibid.
91 "monthly at the Fifth Avenue ... Https://adage.com/article/news/100-years-york-ad-events/74963/.
91 "Thus it will be seen... Appel, (1940), p. 135.
91 "contained a calendar... Https://en.wikipedia.org/wiki/Poor_ Richard%27s_Almanack.
91 "best seller" Ibid.
91 "witty phrases" Ibid.
91 "wordplay" Ibid.
91 "A penny saved... Https://www.brainyquote.com/authors/ benjamin_franklin.
91 "When the wine enters... Ibid.
91 "Honesty is the best policy" Ibid.
91 "It takes many good deeds... Ibid.
91 "Either write something... Ibid.
91 "In this world nothing ... Ibid.
91 "Fish and visitors stink... Ibid.
91 "Poor Richard Club was born... Appel, (1940), p. 137.
92 "When I again faced the Sphinx ... Ibid., 140.
92 "Unlike the postman ... Ibid., 141.
92 "over 7,000,000 copies... *Simmons' Spice Mill*, "EXPLAINING ADVERTISING TO THE PUBLIC," June 1915, p. 662.
92 "likely reach 25,000,000 people." Ibid.
92 *Who's Who* of Advertising." Duff, B. D., Mason, K., "*Who's Who* in Advertising," Detroit Business Service Corporation, 1916.
92 "Periodical Publishers' Association" *Advertising & Selling*, "Periodical Publishers' Association and the Advertiser," by Ralph Bevin Smith (New York, Vol. 29, Number 51, June 12, 1920), p. 16.
92 "The Bureau has been asked ... *Printers' Ink*, "Help Afforded Advertisers by A.N.P.A. Bureau of Advertising," (Vol. XCIX, No. 4, April 26, 1917), p. 67.
93 "postal rates, service and... *Advertising & Selling*, "Periodical Publishers' Association and the Advertiser," by Ralph Bevin Smith (New York, Vol. 29, Number 51, June 12, 1920), p. 16.
93 "The purpose of national... *Simmons' Spice Mill*, "EXPLAINING ADVERTISING TO THE PUBLIC," June 1915, p. 662.
93 "NATIONAL PERIODICAL... *The Outlook*, April 11, 1917, p. 668.
93 "FOR FIFTEEN YEARS ... Ibid.
93 "Ainslee's, American Magazine... Ibid.

REFERENCES

93   "retail sales."   *The Publishers' Weekly*, "AMERICAN PRICES ON PHOTO-ENGRAVINGS TWICE AS HIGH AS ENGLISH," August 19, 1916, p. 551.
93   "Private parties may also…   Http://www.ag.ny.gov/antitrust/antitrustenforcement.
94   "Suit was brought during 1917…   *Editor & Publisher*, "AMEND ANTI-TRUST LAW ON MONOPOLY OF PRODUCTS USED IN TRADE," April 23, 1921, p. 20.
94   "the restriction concerning…   Ibid.
94   "anything in the nature…   Ibid.
94   "emergency message"   Ibid.
94   "thirty-five advertisers…   *Printers' Ink*, (1938), p. 146.
94   "one hundred and thirty-five"   Ibid.
94   "The Louisiana Purchase Exposition,"   Ibid.
94   "a proclamation inviting…   Https://www.loc.gov/rr/news/topics/stlouis.html.
94   "gangrene."   Https://en.wikipedia.org/wiki/William_ McKinley.
95   "executed by electric chair…   Ibid.
95   "banned food and drugs…   Https://en.wikipedia.org/wiki/Theodore_ Roosevelt.
96   "March 13, 1911,"   Pendergrast, (2000), p. 117.
96   "out of court"   Ibid., 121.
96   "November 12, 1917,"   Ibid.
96   "[b]orn in 1869…   Https://adage.com/article/adage-encyclopedia/scott-walter-dill-1869-1955/98871.
96   "earned a Ph.D. in psychology …   Ibid.
96   "consumer suggestibility…   Https://en.wikipedia.org/wiki/Walter_Dill_Scott.
96   "the precursors of what…   *Printers' Ink*, (1938), p. 146.
96   ""There is no force in America…   Kenner, (1936), p. 35.
96   "advertising clubs should organize…   Ibid., 27.
97   "[I]t was here that…   Http://www.yorkcity.org/history.
97   "firsts"   Http://www.history.com/topics/new-york-city.
97   "dark blue uniforms"   Https://conservativetribune.com/reason-police-uniforms-are-blue.
97   "In 1895, residents of Queens…   Http://www.history.com/topics/new-york-city.
97   "In the agreement they agreed…   Http://wallstreetwalks.blogspot.com/2013/05/ the-buttonwood-agreement.html.
98   "on June 14, 1865."   Ibid.
98   "located at the northwest…   Ibid.
98   "April 22, 1903,"   Http://architecture.about.com/od/usa/ss/1903- NYSE-Broad-St-NYC.htm#step3.
98   "8-18 Broad Street"   Https://en.wikipedia.org/wiki/New_York_Stock_ Exchange.
98   "11 Wall Street."   Ibid.
98   "exclusive members-only"   Http://architecture.about.com/od/usa/ss/1903- NYSE-Broad-St-NYC.htm#step2.
98   "In 1891, the first electric…   Robert Rusie, Broadway 101: The History of the Great White Way; https://www.talkinbroadway. com/bway101/1.html.
98   "in 1920"   Https://www.census.gov/population/censusdata/ table-4.pdf.
99   "on the balcony of Federal …   Https://www.whitehouse.gov/1600/presidents/george-washington.
99   "As newspapers and periodicals…   Kenner, (1936), p. 3.
99   "Activities of those…   Http://Boston.bbb.org/history-and-traditions.
99   "any obscene or disloyal…   Http://en.wikipedia.org/wiki/Post_Office_Act_ (1872).
99   "obscene, lewd, or lascivious"   Http://www.thebirthcontrolmovie.com/blogall/2014/5/13/on-this-day-139-years-ago.
99   "Act of the Suppression of Trade…   Http://www.britannica.com/event/Comstock-Act.
99   "immoral use."   Ibid.
99   "language concerning contraception"   Ibid.
100   "The first opium dens…   Diana L. Ahmad, *The Opium Debate and Chinese Exclusion Laws in the Nineteenth-century*, p.25.

100	"commonly morphine…	Https://en.wikipedia.org/wiki/Narcotic.
100	"cure-all"	Http://en.wikipedia.org/wiki/Laudanum.
100	"wide-range uses"	Ibid.
100	"was a laudanum addict"	Http://en.wikipedia.org/wiki/Mary_Todd_Lincoln.
100	"Between 150,000 and…	Http://en.wikipedia.org/wiki/Opium.
101	"being slashed across..	Http://en.wikipedia.org/wiki/John_S_Pemberton.
101	"Amputation was the…	Https://www.factinate.com/cool/bizarre-historical-facts-school3/2?fact=1&utm_source=TBTTRD&utm_medium=BIZARREHIST_D_V2_US.
101	"Dr. Tuggle's Compound…	Http://en.wikipedia.org/wiki/John_S_Pemberton.
101	"Pemberton's French…	Ibid.
102	""habit-forming" and…	Pendergrast, (2000), p.119.
102	"Controlled Substances Act …	Https://en.wikipedia.org/wiki/Controlled_Substances_Act.
102	"about 12,000 chemical tests"	Pendergrast, (2000), p. 21.
102	"Divine Plant."	Ibid.
102	"In 1844, the alkaloid…	Http://www.druglibrary.org/schaffer/history/casey1.htm.
102	"when the syrup…	Pendergrast, (2000), p. 7.
102	"gained complete…	Ibid., 52.
102	"ended in July of 1901…	Ibid., 88.
102	"found old testimony from…	Ibid.
102	"that there was a…	Ibid.
102	"a chemist found four-hundredths…	Ibid.
102	"Schaefer Alkaloid Works…	Ibid.
102	"decocainize the coca leaves."	Ibid.
102	"no contest"	Ibid., 121.
102	"the case was settled…	Ibid.
102	"agreed to reduce the caffeine…	Ibid.
102	"in 1887."	Http://coca-cola.wikia.com/wiki/Frank_Mason_Robinson.
102	"Spencerian script"	Http://en.wikipedia.org/wiki/Frank_Mason_Robinson.
102	"opium user,"	Pendergrast, (2000), p. 51.
102	"for a total investment…	Https://en.wikipedia.org/wiki/Asa_Griggs_Candler.
102	"The two main charge…	Pendergrast, (2000), p. 117.
103	"then advertising manager…	Kenner, (1936), p. 32.
103	"Henry B. Humphrey of the…	Https://babel.hathitrust.org/cgi/pt?id=umn.31951002210587j;view=1up;seq=93.
103	"President Dobbs got the surprise…	Https://babel.hathitrust.org/cgi/pt?id=umn.31951002210587j;view=1up;seq=92.
104	"LAST WORDS OF THE…	Https://babel.hathitrust.org/cgi/pt?id=umn.31951002210587j;view=1up;seq=102.
104	"I am now laying down…	Ibid.
105	"Confederate sympathizer"	Http://www.history.com/topics/abraham-lincoln-assassination.
105	"labor-intensive cash…	Http://www.history.com/news/slavery-profitable-southern-economy.
105	"almost exclusively in the two cities…	*Printers' Ink*, (1938), p. 142.
105	"expanded into many…	Ibid.
105	"By 1906 there was at…	Ibid., 142-143.
106	"George P. Rowell, the Grand…	Https://babel.hathitrust.org/cgi/pt?id=umn.31951002210587j;view=1up;seq=39.
106	"in 1906 the advertising clubs…	Kenner, (1936), p. 18.
106	"score"	Www.phrases.org.uk/meanings/380400.html.
106	"threescore"	Ibid.
106	"threescore and ten"	Ibid.
106	"retiring national president"	Https://babel.hathitrust.org/cgi/pt?id=umn.31951002210587j;view=1up;seq=116.

REFERENCES

106 "President Dobbs read a letter… Https://babel.hathitrust.org/cgi/pt?id=umn.3195 1002210587j;view=1up;seq=22.
106 "educational committee," Https://babel.hathitrust.org/cgi/pt?id=umn.3195 1002210587j;view=1up;seq=26.
107 "Houston Adcraft Club, Houston, Texas" Https://books.google.com/books?id=uXY_AQA AMA AJ&pg=PA37&dq=houston+texas+adcraft+ club,+houston+advertisers+association&hl=en& sa=X& ei=hh2OVYneCMmxggTrrIDQAw&ved =0CD0Q6AEwAg#v=onepage&q=houston%20 texas%20 adcraft%20club%2C%20houston%20 advertisers%20association&f=false; p. 37.
107 "Southwestern Division." Ibid.
107 "Houston Advertising Federation" Https://vimeo.com/aafhouston/about.
107 "Houston-Advertising Club, Inc." Https://www.aaf-houston.net/about.
107 "American Advertising Federation-Houston." Ibid.
107 "Truth." Http://www.aaf-houston.org/aafhouston-history.
107 "An illustration of the manner… *Printers' Ink*, "HOW AD CLUB PROTECTS THE ADVERTISING PUBLIC" (Vol. LXXVII, No. 5, November 2, 1911), p. 38.
107 "When that live organization… Https://books.google.com/books?id= 0HNIAQAAMAAJ&pg=RA1-PA64&lpg=RA1- PA64&dq=Houston+AdCraft+club +in+19 13&source=bl&ots=Z5qUpmPnb8&sig=n eCcNdmHMc1UtZxEKkMhCY-dZz3A& hl=en&sa=X&ei=n56NVaTYEcnZ-QHiJi4Cg&ved=0CDQQ6AEwBA#v= onepage&q=Houston%20AdCraft%20club%20 in%201913&f=false.
107 "first War Advertising Committee" Http://www.aaf-houston.org/aaf-houston-history; https://www.aaf-houston.net/about.
107 "three national awards… Ibid.
107 "The world stamped… Kenner, (1936), p. 34.
107 "circular seal with "Truth"… Ibid.
107 "Vigilance Committee of the… Ibid.
107 "[a] Dallas newspaper… Ibid., 33.
107 "Sixteen noted advertising… Ibid.
108 "Gone to Texas" *Printers' Ink*, (1938), p. 214.
108 "It was first published… Http://en.wikipedia.org/wiki/The_Daily_News_ (Texas).
108 "Its ads, dealing mainly… *Printers' Ink*, (1938), p. 214.
108 "Declaration of Principles" Kenner, (1936), p. 274.
108 "leadership" Ibid., 36.
108 "President George W. Coleman… Ibid.
108 "Fifth Avenue Building." *Printers' Ink*, "New York Delegates Meet" (Vol. LXXXIII, No. 8, May 22, 1913), p. 82.
108 "President: Richard Waldo… Ibid.
108 "The Minneapolis BBB… Https://www.bbb.org/boston/get-to-know-us/ vision-mission-and-values/history-and-traditions.
109 "thousands of advertising… Kenner, (1936), p. 58.
109 "Truth is the holiest name … Ibid.
109 "Bishop Warren A. Candler… Ibid.
109 "Emory College president… Emory University; www.emory history.emory. edu/facts-figures/people/makers-history/profiles/ candler-warren.html.
109 "$1 million" Emory University; www.emoryhistory.edu/factsfigures/dates/timeline.html.
109 "adopted a resolution… Kenner, (1936), p. 50.
109 "Fraudulent or doubtful… Ibid., 50-51.
109 "Big advertisers" Fox, (1984), pp. 68-69.
110 "On June 4, 1917, the New York… Http://adage.com/article/adage-encyclopedia/american-association-advertising-agencies/98313.
110 "Pressure to form an… Ibid.
110 "feckless reform gestures" Fox, (1984), p. 302.
110 "weak leadership." Ibid.

110	"I wish very much that truth…	Kenner, (1936), p. 60.
110	"legal tender."	Http://www.wikiwand.com/en/Federal_Reserve_ Act.
110	"The Great-After-The-War…	Associated Advertising magazine (Vol. X, No.9, September 1919), p. 152.
110	"The Roosevelt"	Http://medianola.org/discover/place/173; http://www.therooseveltneworleans.com/aboutthe-waldorf/history/hotel-history.html.
110	"on June 4, 1919"	Https://en.wikipedia.org/wiki/Nineteenth_ Amendment_to_the_United_States_Constitution.
110	"August 18, 1920."	Ibid.
110	"adopted a resolution for…	Associated Advertising magazine, "Great Men, Great subjects, High Promise of Our Coming Convention"(Vol. X, No. 7, July 1919), p. 7; http://babel.hathitrust.org/cgi/pt?id=iau.318580 34256317;view=1up;seq=245.
111	"copywriter"	Http://adage.com/article/special-report100-most-influential-women-in-advertising/mad-women-made-history-long-time-peggy-olson/237372.
111	"advertising manager for Sperry…	Associated Advertising Magazine, "Miss J. J. Martin Worked for Advertising Women" (Vol. X, No. 10, November 1919), p. 74; https://babel. hathitrust.org/cgi/pt?id=iau.31858034256317;vi ew=1up;seq=604.
111	"largest and oldest trading…	Https://supreme.justia.com/cases/federal/ us/405/233.
111	"in 1896."	Https://en.wikipedia.org/wiki/S%26H_Green_ Stamps.
111	"founding member"	Http://adage.com/article/special-report-100-mostinfluential-women-in-advertising/mad-women-made-history-long-time-peggy-olson/237372.
111	"president of the New York…	Ibid.
111	"Advertising Women of…	Ibid.
111	"Miss Martin did much …	Associated Advertising Magazine, "Miss J. J. Martin Worked for Advertising Women" (Vol. X, No. 10, November 1919), p. 74; https://babel. hathitrust.org/cgi/pt?id=iau.31858034256317;view=1up;seq=604.
111	"The Germans developed a…	Https://en.wikipedia.org/wiki/Military_strategy.
112	"Some of these bureaus became…	Kenner, (1936), p. 72.
112	"Spanish Flu"	Https://virus.stanford.edu/uda.
112	"La Grippe"	Ibid.
112	"pledged, on behalf of the Exchange…	Kenner, (1936), p. 105.
112	"the Associated Advertising Clubs…	Ibid.
112	"June 1922"	Ibid.
112	"July 1, 1922."	Ibid.
112	"Before You Invest, Investigate"	Ibid., 106.
112	"Charles Beadon…planned…	Ibid.
112	"Post Office…	Ibid., 107-108.
113	"Post Office Inspection Service"	Ibid., 114.
113	"Especially in cooperation…	Ibid.
113	"The Thirty Club"	Http://www.hatads.org.uk/catalogue/clubsassociations/40/The-Thirty-Club.
113	"in 1905 or 1906"	Ibid.
113	"dining club for "the betterment…	Ibid.
113	"National Better Business Bureau…	Kenner, (1936), p. 126.
113	"The first step…	Http://www.lib.uiowa.edu/scua/msc/tomsc650/ msc627/herberthoover.html.
114	"California Gold Rush"	Https://en.wikipedia.org/wiki/California_Gold_ Rush.
114	"Babylon on the Bayou"	Https://www.visithoustontexas.com/abouthouston/history.
114	"shortly after the battle…	Https://www.dallasfed.org/-/media/documents/ research/houston/2002/hb0204.pdf.
114	"where 17 railroads…	Ibid.
114	"up the Buffalo Bayou."	Https://www.visithoustontexas.com/abouthouston/history.
114	"36-foot-deep Houston Ship…	Ibid.
114	"Colonneh or the "Raven"."	Https://www.shsu.edu/today@sam/heritageonline/summer-2018/the-raven.

REFERENCES

114	"founded in 1835 by…"	Oakwood Cemetery Walking Tour Brochure, Huntsville, Texas.
114	"Vigilance Committee of …"	Kenner, (1936), p. 34.
115	"U.S. Public Law 85-425…"	Http://uscode.house.gov/statutes/pl/85/425.pdf.
115	"3rd Lieutenant"	Https://tshaonline.org/handbook/online/articles/ fho73.
115	"first and third"	Https://en.wikipedia.org/wiki/Sam_Houston.
115	"he refused to take the oath…"	Https://tshaonline.org/handbook/online/articles/ fho73.
115	"passionate Unionist,"	Ibid.
115	"warned Texans that civil…"	Ibid.
116	"historical preservation"	Richmond.com/news/ virginia/charlottesville-judge-says-confederate-statues-cannot-be-removed-will-award/article_8228a5ca-4.
116	"racial discrimination"	Ibid.
116	"National Association of Better…"	Kenner, (1936), p. 140.
116	"to provide for greater…"	Ibid.
116	"a governor of the New York…"	Ibid., 140-141.
116	"Solicitor of the Post Office…"	Ibid., 267.
116	"The first Canadian BBB…"	Http://clevelandbbb100.org/wp/about-us/funfacts.
116	"the periodical publishers, in a trade…"	Http://boston.bbb.org/history-and-traditions.
117	"Advertising Federation of America"	Kenner, (1936), p. xvi.
117	"advertising organizations in Canada…"	Ibid.
117	"that advertising was…"	Appel, (1940), p. 203.
117	"Such leadership carries…"	Ibid., 205.
117	"Better Business Bureau was…"	O'Sullivan, (1933), p. 94.
117	"Better Business Bureau of New York"	Ibid.
117	"section 70 of the general…"	Ibid.
117	"[c]hairman of the Executive…"	Https://en.wikipedia.org/wiki/Edward_J._Flynn.
117	"Attorney General Hamilton…"	Kenner, (1936), p. 145.
117	"operators."	Ibid.
118	"On occasions which are far…"	Ibid., 154.
118	"The Chief Examiner of the…"	Ibid., 191.
119	"outline a plan for…"	Ibid., 161.
119	"The files of the Securities…"	Ibid.
119	"Probably more than…"	Advertising Federation of America, (1936), pp. 45-46.
119	"The Federation is now publishing…"	Ibid., 56.
119	"Securities Violations Section…"	Kenner, (1936), p. 161.
120	"The Securities and Exchange…"	Ibid., 162.
120	"reprints of previous articles…"	Wansley, (1971).
120	"Miss Whalen, however…"	Ibid.
120	"racket"	O'Sullivan, (1933), p. 34.
121	"Judge Edward J. Jeffries…"	Ibid., 104.
121	"I do not think that anybody…"	Ibid.
121	"Corporate Counsel John H…"	Ibid.
121	"I am in accord with…"	Ibid.
121	"During the war…"	Wansley, (1971).
121	"Office of the Coordinator…"	Https://www.cia.gov/about-cia/history-of-the-cia.
121	"Neighborhood enforcement…"	Http://newapproachtofreedom.info/ffi/editorial. htm.
122	"[I]n 1941…a Senate…"	Wansley, (1971).
122	"In wartime and early…"	Kenner, (1936), p. 78.
122	"Declaration by United…"	Http://www.un.org/en/sections/history/history-united-nations.
122	"United Nations"	Ibid.
122	"United Nations Charter,"	Ibid.
122	"to work for the protection…"	Http://www.ohchr.org/EN/ AboutUs/Pages/MissionStatement.aspx.
122	"that has killed…"	Https://www.cbc.ca/news/world/un-ends-haiti-peacekeeping-mission-october-1.4069356.

122 "the U.N.'s Office of Internal... Https://www.washingtonpost.com/news/morning-mix/wp/2015/06/11/report-u-n-peacekeepers-in-haiti-had-transactional-sex-with-hundreds-of-poor-women/?utm_term=.f34f113927ca.
123 "investigation detailing how... Http://time.com/4739564/un-peacekeeping-haiti-abuse-nikki-haley.
123 "The City of Chicago... Https://www.americasfreedomfighters.com/2017/12/16/chicago-emmanuel-un.
123 "Belgium, the Netherlands... Https://en.wikipedia.org/wiki/NATO.
123 "chief military assistant" Https://en.wikipedia.org/wiki/Hastings_Ismay,_1st_Baron_Ismay.
123 "to keep the Russians... David Reynolds, "The Origins of the Cold War in Europe: International Perspectives" (Yale University Press, 1994).
123 "the Alliance's creation was... Http://www.nato.int/history/natohistory.html.
123 "an armed attack... Https://en.wikisource.org/wiki/North_Atlantic_Treaty#Article_5.
123 "initially based in London... Http://www.nato.int/cps/en/natolive/ topics_49284.htm.
123 "A new €750 million ... Https://en.wikipedia.org/wiki/NATO.
124 "Belgium, Canada... Http://www.nato.int/cps/en/ natolive/topics_52044.htm.
124 "political-economic" Https://en.wikipedia.org/wiki/ European_Union.
124 "near the town... Https://en.wikipedia.org/wiki/Schengen_Area.
124 "internal border... Https://en.wikipedia.org/wiki/NATO.
124 "with other Schengen... Ibid.
124 "Presidency of the Council... En.wikipedia.org/wiki/President_of_the_ European_Union.
124 "Charter of Fundamental... Http://ec.europa.eu/justice/ fundamental-rights/charter/index_en.htm.
124 "developing nuclear energy... Https://en.wikipedia.org/wiki/European_Atomic_Energy_Community.
124 "separate legal... Https://en.wikipedia.org/wiki/Euratom_Treaty.
124 "to produce full-scale... Https://en.wikipedia.org/wiki/ITER.
124 "funded and run... Https://en.wikipedia.org/wiki/NATO.
124 "The facility is expected... Ibid.
125 "Initially, fusion... Https://en.wikipedia.org/wiki/Nuclear_fusion.
125 "On November 13, 2017... Https://www.globalresearch.ca/european-union-building-its-own-army/5624351.
125 "armored vehicles... Https://conservativedailypost.com/social-media-blazes-after-eu-army-stormed-paris-streets.
125 "Frontex" Http://europa.eu/rapid/press-release_SPEECH-16-3043_en.htm.
125 "European Border and ... Ibid.
125 "600 agents on... Ibid.
125 "at least 200 extra... Ibid.
125 "there is not enough Europe... Ibid.
125 "This is why Parliament... Ibid.
125 "Yellow Vests" Https://www.npr.org/2018/12/03/672862353/who-are-frances-yellow-vest-protesters-and-what-do-they-want.
126 "...drivers found without... Https://www.frenchentree.com/living-in-france/driving/safety-vest-regulations.
126 "Mouvement des gilets jaunes" Https://en.wikipedia.org/wiki/Yellow_vests_movement.
126 "lower fuel taxes... Ibid.
126 "Guardian of the... Https://en.wikipedia.org/wiki/European_Union.
126 "an executive cabinet... Ibid.
126 "two-house legislature... Https://www.britannica.com/topic/bicameralsystem.
126 "the mother country" Ibid.
126 "drew the exact design... Https://en.wikipedia.org/wiki/Flag_of_Europe.
127 "Begone Satan," Https://www.lifesitenews.com/news/murdered-french-priests-last-words-begone-satan.

REFERENCES

127 "fake guns and Imitation… Http://www.breitbart.com/ london/2016/07/26/ knifemen-take-several-hostages-french-normandy-church.

127 "The powerful European… Https://www.jihadwatch. org/2016/07/ juncker-no-matter-how-badmigrant-crisis-jihadi-terrorism-get-well-never-give-up-on-open-borders.

128 "Germany will become… Http://beforeitsnews.com/ opinion-conservative/2017/05/germany-will-become-an-islamic-state-says-merkel-theyll-have-to-come-to-terms-with-it-3282685.html.

128 "Code of conduct… Http://europa.eu/rapid/pressrelease_IP-18-261_en.htm.

128 "have committed to… Ibid.

128 "complements legislation… Ibid.

128 "5,000 euros for… Https://voiceofeurope. com/2018/05/paris-court-fines-french-author-for-calling-the-migrant-crisis-a-muslim-invasion-and-warning-of-a-civil-war.

128 "Islamic invasion" Ibid.

128 "religious civil war… Ibid.

128 "targeting online a… Http://www.breitbart.com/ london/2018/05/10/six-years-in-jail-proposed-for-online-hatred-of-religion-or-gender.

129 "Whenever the President… Https://www.gpo.gov/fdsys/granule/USCODE2011-title8/USCODE-2011-title8-chap12- subchapII-partII-sec1182.

129 "entry to the U.S. if… McCarran Walters Act, Chapter 2, Section 212.

129 ""un-American" and… Https://en.wikipedia.org/wiki/immigration_and_Nationality_Act_of_1952.

129 "Little Boy" Https://www.trumanlibrary.org/teacher/abomb. htm.

129 "Fat Man" Ibid.

129 "The consensus of… O'Sullivan, (1933), p. 88.

130 "The Advertising Hall of… Https://adage.com/article/news/100-years-york-ad-events/74963.

130 "Annual Conference… https://www.bbb.org/greater-san-francisco/get-to-know-us/history-and-traditions.

130 "Your Bureaus… Ibid.

130 "I am aware that thousands… Ibid.

130 "It is good sense… Https://www.theguardian.com/ politics/2001/jun/29/comment.

130 "gone into general circulation… Ibid.

130 "The business meritocracy… Ibid.

131 "board of directors." United States District Court, Middle District of Florida, Orlando Division, Case No. 6:12-cv-31- Orl-28KRS, Filed 2/13/13.

131 "Twelve Triple-Three," Https://theintercept. com/2017/01/13/obama-opens-nsas-vast-trove-of-warrantless-data-to-entire-intelligence-community-just-in-time-for-trump.

131 "Timely, accurate, and… Https://www.dni.gov/index.php/ic-legalreference-book/executive-order-12333.

131 "The U.S. intelligence budget… Https://www.dni.gov/index.php/what-we-do/ic-budget.

131 "total budget In 2015… Https://www.latimes.com/ nation/la-na-17-intelligence-agencies-20170112-story.html.

132 "The potential for substantial… Https://www.documentcloud.org/ documents/3283349-Raw-12333-surveillance-sharing-guidelines.html.

132 ""USPI" for "U.S. person… Ibid.

132 "shorthanded" Http://www.reuters. com/article/us-usa-surveillance-watchdogidUSBRE98Q14G20130927.

132 "LOVEINT" Ibid.

132 "spy on the emails… Ibid.

133 "the former commander… Https://www.cnsnews.com/blog/ michael-w-chapman/admiral-lyons-obama-sstrategy-it-s-anti-american-pro-islamic-it-s-pro.

133 "illegal and unconstitutional… Http://themillenniumreport. com/2017/03/explosive-interview-general-thomas-mcinerney-reveals-the-existence-of-thehammer.

133 "The NSA started to… Https://www.zdnet.com/article/prism-heres-how-the-nsa-wiretapped-the-internet.

134 "Year Zero" Https://www.wired.co.uk/article/ cia-files-wikileaks-vault-7.

134 "showed the CIA's iOS... Ibid.
134 "Dark Matter" Ibid.
134 "is said to include details... Ibid.
134 "Marble Framework" Ibid.
134 "is used to hamper... Ibid.
134 "Grasshopper" Ibid.
134 "customized malware... Ibid.
134 "awarded its $10 billion... The hill.com/policy/defense/467545-pentagon-awards-10-billion-cloud-contract-to-microsoft-over-amazon.
134 "soliciting and publishing... The guardian.com/media/2019/ jun/13/julian-assange-sajid-javid-signs-us-extradition-order.
134 "Assange faces an 18-count... Ibid.
134 "developed numerous attacks... Https:/wikileaks.org/ciav7p1.
134 "PROCEDURES FOR... Https://www.documentcloud.org/ documents/3283349-Raw-12333-surveillance-sharing-guidelines.html.
135 "several hundred million... Https:/wikileaks.org/ciav7p1.
135 "appears to have been circulated... Ibid.
135 "the CIA has gained political... Ibid.
135 "hacking division" Ibid.
135 "over 5,000 registered... Ibid.
135 "software development group... Ibid.
135 "is responsible for the development... Ibid.
136 "As of October 2014... Https://www.news.com.au/ finance/business/media/wikileaks-vault-7-dump-reignites-conspiracy-theories-surrounding-death-of-michael-hastings/news.
136 "a contributing editor... Https://en.wikipedia.org/wiki/Michael_ Hastings_(journalist).
136 "critic of the Obama... Ibid.
136 "140 royals, corporate kings... Https://freddonaldson.com/2018/04/16/ bilderberg.
137 "On June 18, 2013, Hastings... Https://en.wikipedia.org/wiki/Michael_ Hastings_(journalist).
137 "CIA Director John... Ibid.
137 "Larry Page and... Https://www.the guardian. com/news/2018/dec/20/googles-earth-how-the-tech-giant-is-helping-the-state-spy-on-us.
137 "19,605,052 shares... Https://en.wikipedia.org/wiki/Google.
137 "Keyhole EarthViewer." Https://en.wikipedia.org/wiki/Google_Earth.
137 "in 2005." Https://ipfs.io/ipfs/QmXoypizj W3WKnFiJnKLwHCnL72vedxj QKDDP1mXWo6uco/wiki/Keyhole_Inc.html.
137 "for $1.65 billion in Google... Https://en.wikipedia.org/wiki/Google.
137 "for $12.5 billion... Ibid.
137 "the most visited... Ibid.
138 "government (taxpayer)... Https://en.wikipedia.org/wiki/In-Q-Tel.
138 "to identify and invest... Ibid.
138 "Virginia-registered... Ibid.
138 "to stream large databases... Https://en.wikipedia.org/wiki/Google_Earth.
138 "As it turns out... Https://www.the guardian.com/news/2018/ dec/20/googles-earth-how-the-tech-giant-is-helping-the-state-spy-on-us.
138 "2003 invasion... Https://en.wikipedia.org/wiki/Google_Earth.
138 "contacted by the CIA's... Ibid.
138 "[Painter] came with deep... Https://www.the guardian.com/news/2018/ dec/20/googles-earth-how-the-tech-giant-is-helping-the-state-spy-on-us.
138 "The typical argument... Https://en.wikipedia.org/wiki/Google_Earth.
139 "Few organizations... Https://www.bbb.org/atlanta/get-to-know-us/history-and-tradition.
139 "Illuminati." Https://socioecohistory.wordpress. com/2012/04/23/current-membership-list-of-the-illuminati-committee-of-300.
139 "One of the greatest... Https://www.bbb.org/atlanta/get-to-know-us/history-and-tradition.

REFERENCES

139 "a decorated naval... Https://www.cia.gov/news-information/featured-story-archive/2018-featured-story-archive/george-h-w-bush2014the-11th-director-of-central-intelligence.html.
139 "came to be known as... Ibid.
139 "What is at stake... Http://www.presidency.ucsb.edu/ws/?pid=19253.
140 "They're taking the jobs... Https://onenewsnow.com/nationalsecurity/2019/07/09/black-leader-illegals-hurt-the-black-community-send-em-back.
140 "On Thursday, [10/24/2019]... Immigrationinfo@ numbersusa.com.
141 "It increased total... Https://en.wikipedia.org/wiki/Immigration_Act_ of_1990.
142 "a large band... Http://www.ontheissues.org/Celeb/George_W_ Bush_Immigration.htm.
142 "Valens has his modern... Ibid.
142 "How do you get out... Dressler, (2000), p. 110.
143 "did not endorse... Ibid., 68.
143 "reliability reports" Ibid., 110, 126.
143 "provided solely to assist... Ibid., 68.
143 "Virtually all of the Bureau's... Ibid., 111.
143 "One way or another... Ibid., 110.
144 "Unlike most other associations... Ibid.
144 "The BBB recognized... Http://www.slate.com/articles/business/the_ customer/2010/12/busted_watchdog.html.
144 "Online Interest-based... Http://www.bbb.org/us/storage/113/documents/ annual-reports/CBBB-2011Annual-Report.pdf.
144 "Online Behavioral... Ibid.
144 "Principles" Ibid.
144 "the collection and use... Ibid.
144 "refers cases of non-participation... Ibid.
145 "Chair, Board of Directors," Ibid.
145 "the umbrella organization... Ibid.
145 "first government affairs... Ibid.
145 "Congress, the Administration... Ibid.
145 "more than six million... Ibid.
145 "regular "Scam Alerts" to... Ibid.
145 "BBB Business Reviews." Http://www.bbb.org/houston/business-reviews/professional-organizations/american-advertising-federation-houston-aaf-houston-in-houstontx-62040.
146 "White House Privacy summit... 2012 Annual Report; http://www.bbb.org/us/storage/113/documents/ CBBB_AR_2012.pdf.
146 "New BBB advertising... Http:// www.bbb.org/upstatenew-york/news-events/news-releases/2014/10/ new-bbb-advertising-standards-reflect-21st-century-advertising-in-traditional-and-new-media.
146 "Comprehensive changes" Ibid.
146 "websites, social media... Ibid.
146 "lighted In a vigilant... Advertising Federation of America, (1936), p. 65.
146 "The key proviso... Http://www.bbb.org/upstatenew-york/news-events/news-releases/2014/10/new-bbb-advertising-standards-reflect-21st-century-advertising-in-traditional-and-new-media.
146 "those gallant... Advertising Federation of America, (1936), p. 65.
146 "National Vigilance Committee is... Http://www.bbb.org/us/storage/113/documents/ CBBB_AR_2012.pdf.
146 "A Quarter Century... Advertising Federation of America, (1936), Foreword, p. 17-18.
146 "held in Boston... Ibid., xi.
146 "Better Business Bureau of Minnesota... Https://www.bbb.org/minnesota/get-to-know-us.
147 "1945 New Ad... Http://www.bbb.org/us/storage/113/documents/ CBBB_AR_2012.pdf.
147 "Better Business Bureau of the Cleveland... Kenner, (1936), p. 99.
147 "getrichquick" Wansley, (1971).
148 "individual worker" Kenner, (1936), p. 100.

507

148 "industrial plants"   Ibid.
148 "service to protect…   Ibid.
148 "War Savings Protection…   Wansley, (1971).
148 "aimed at keeping…   Ibid.
148 "the way that U.S. companies…   https://searchcio.techtarget.com/definition/Safe-Harbor.
148 "Procedure Report"   Https://www.bbb.org/EU-privacy-shield/ procedure-report.
148 "between 1998 and…   Https://en.wikipedia.org/wiki/International_ Safe_Harbor_Privacy_Principles.
148 "Safe Harbor Framework"   Http://safeharbor.export.gov/companyinfo. aspx?id=17227.
148 "the European Court of Justice…   Https://en.wikipedia.org/wiki/International_ Safe_Harbor_Privacy_Principles; https://techcrunch.com/2016/02/03/ euus-data-transfers-wont-be-blocked-while-privacyshield-details-are-hammered-out-says-wp29.
148 "of US government agencies'…   Ibid.
149 "On July 16, 2020…   FTC.gov/tips-advice/business-center/privacy-and-security/privacy-shield.
149 "includes exceptions…   Https://techcrunch. com/2016/02/03/ eu-us-data-transfers-wontbe-blocked-while-privacy-shield-details-arehammered-out-says-wp29.
149 "helping grow…   Ibid.
149 "Third Annual Review"   Trade.gov/press-release/2019/U.S.%20 Secretary%20of%20 Commerce%20Wilbur%20 Ross%20Welcoms%20Release.
149 "more than 5,000…   Ibid.
149 "September 30, 2016,"   Https://www.theregister. co.uk/2016/09/30/internet_handover_is_go_ go_go.
149 "BBB has played a critical…   Https://bbb.org/council/newsevents/news-releases/2016/07/ new-eu-u.s.- privacy-shield-adopted-to-support-trans-atlanticdigital-commerce.
150 "a computer scientist…   Https://www.usatoday. com/story/tech/news/2016/09/29/icanniana-internet-address-book-autonomousdepartment-of-commerce-ip-address-transitioninternet-corporation-for-assigned-names-andnumbers/91281960.
150 "the Domain Name System"   Ibid.
150 "actual computer addresses."   Ibid.
150 "The 18-year-old contract…   Ibid.
150 "a nuclear weapons…   Https://www.nytimes.com/2017/03/06/world/ europe/european-union-nuclear-weapons.html.
150 "recurrent failure to…   Http://www.bbb.org/globalassets/local-bbbs/ council-113/media/annual-reports/cbbb_annual_ report_2013-final.pdf.
151 "An ethical marketplace where…   Ibid.
151 "To be the leader in advancing…   Ibid.
151 "Creating a community…   Ibid.
151 "Encouraging and supporting…   Ibid.
151 "Setting standards…   Ibid.
151 "Celebrating marketplace…   Ibid.
151 "Denouncing substandard…   Ibid.
151 "Buró de Mejores Practicas…   Http://www.bbb.org/us/storage/113/documents/ CBBB_AR_2012.pdf.
152 "Consumer Protection and…   Ibid.
152 "to articulate best…   Http://news.virginia.edu/content/ darden-better-business-bureau-team-examine-self-regulation-dc-conference.
152 "Maureen Ohlhausen…   Ibid.
152 "special assistant/communications…   Https://www.pridepublishinggroup.com/ pride/2018/07/05/peter-woolfork-named-board-chairman-council-better-business-bureaus.
152 "Crazy"   Dr. Corsi, (2008), p. 45.
152 "The *Times* also…   Ibid., 56.
153 "black-liberation…   Ibid., 188.
153 "a calculated decision…   Ibid.

REFERENCES

153 "For the majority… Ibid.
153 "the Blessed" Http://en.wikipedia.org/wiki/Pope_Benedict_ XVI.
153 "at the University of Regensburg… Https://abcnews.go.com/ International/pope-benedict-xvi-resignation-controversy-religious-outreach-mark/ story?id=18462811.
153 "abortion, contraceptive services… Ibid.
154 "told the Italian newspaper… Http://www.m2voice.co.uk/ pope-francis-a-one-world-government-must-rule-u-s-for-their-own-good; January 3, 2019; https:// explainlife.com/pope-francis-world-government-must-rule-u-s-for-their-own-good-6447.
154 "Unholy Alliance: Christian… Https://www.breitbart.com/ politics/2015/11/29/unholy-alliance-christian-charities-profit-1-billion-fed-program-resettle-refugees-40-percent-muslim.
154 "in all 50 states and… Ibid.
154 "hundreds of millions of dollars" Ibid.
154 "a number of entitlements" Ibid.
154 "the Obama administration increased… Https://www.migrationpolicy.org/ article/refugees-and-asylees-united-states.
154 "pursued Obama's extensive… Dr. Corsi, (2008), Preface, p. xv.
154 "used the battle cry… Ibid.
155 "produced by Republicans… Http://www.foxnews.com/ politics/2016/02/08/senate-report-illegalimmigrants-benefited-from-up-to-750m-inobamacare-subsidies.html.
155 "as of June 2015… Ibid.
155 "despite a provision… Http://dailycaller. com/2016/03/25/states-are-ignoring-federal-ban-against-giving-illegals-obamacare-benefits.
155 "Occidental College records… SouthernBelle4Trump@Southern4MAGA; Twitter; 12/27/17.
155 "Six American Islamist… Http://www.investigativeproject. org/3869/egyptian-magazine-muslim-brotherhood-infiltrates#
156 "Arif Alikhan, assistant… Ibid.
156 "members of the Muslim… Http://www.breitbart.com/ big-government/2016/06/30/capt-joseph-john-muslim-brotherhood-fifth-column-infiltrated-us-government.
156 "is riddled with… Http://freedomoutpost.com/obamas-muslim-homeland-security-adviser-demands-national-gun-registry.
156 "Cairo-born," Ibid.
156 "worked at the FBI… Ibid.
156 "FBI veteran Investigators" Ibid.
156 "ongoing terror investigations… Ibid.
156 ""international permission… Http://thetruthnews.info/ US_Military_Is_Now_Officially_ Controlled_ By_The_UN_And_NATO.html.
157 "refurbish mosques" Linkus.com, "Investigation Finds Obama Financing Mosques Worldwide With U.S. Taxpayer Dollars," June 28, 2016.
157 "in western Iraq… Https://en.wikipedia.org/wiki/Islamic_State_of_ Iraq_and_the_Levant.
158 "the Diyanet Center… Https://patch.com/maryland/ bowie/turkeys-president-inaugurate-islamic-campus-lanham-0.
158 "16-acre" Ibid.
158 "This is Erdoğan's dream… Http://freedomoutpost.com/ obama-turkish-president-to-attend-opening-of-largest-mosque-in-the-world-next-week-to-the-sounds-of-allahu-akbar.
158 "had completely rebounded… Breitbart London, "FTSE 100 STILL AT HIGHEST LEVEL IN A WEEK," June 30, 2016.
158 "form "a cabinet… Https://www.foxnews.com/world/boris-johnson-queen-officially-prime-minister-britain-brea.
158 "has already invested E10… Http://www.dailymail.co.uk/ news/article-2113159/Qatar-bought-BritainThey-Shard-They-Olympic-Village-And-don't-care-Lamborghinis-clamped-shop-Harrod.
159 "swathes of the Canary… Ibid.
159 "20 per cent of the London… Ibid.
159 "20 per cent of the Camden… Ibid.

159 "In 2014 about 1.3 million… Http://www.migrationobservatory.ox.ac.uk/ resources/briefings/migrants-in-the-uk-anoverview.
159 "For example, Army Chief… Https://www.heritage.org/defense/ commentary/obamas-cuts-leave-every-military-branch-weaker-911.
159 "Thanks to Pamela… Https://flatoutunconstitutional. com/2015/10/06/alert-u-n-military-invading-america-with-obamas-blessing.
159 "mysterious troop… Http://www.dcclothesline. com/2016/06/26/u-n-vehicles-mysterious-troop-movement-spotted-in-va-nc-wv-ohio.
159 "U.N. vehicles were… Ibid.
159 "Humvees, troop transport… Ibid.
159 "there have been numerous… Ibid.
160 "dhimmitude" Https://en.wikipedia.org/wiki/Dhimmitude.
160 "Lebanon is our homeland… Https://en.wikipedia.org/wiki/Bachir_Gemayel.
160 "BREAKING: Egypt Charges… Http://conservativetribune.com/hillary-obama-charged-terrorists-egypt-muslim-brotherhood.
160 "national registry" Https://pjmedia.com/homelandsecurity/2016/06/20/gamal-wants-your-guns-homeland-security-adviser-demands-national-gun-registry-after-orlando.
160 "gave the National Counterterrorism… Http://thefederalist-gary. blogspot.com/2012/12/obama-keeping-500000- secret-files-on.html.
160 "The President has put in place… Http://theconspolitics.com/maxine-waters-saysobama-has-big-brother-database-on-all-of-us-the-likes-of-which.
160 "database will have information… Ibid.
161 "is a non-governmental… Https://en.wikipedia.org/wiki/Financial_Industry_Regulatory_Authority.
161 "U.S. Commodity Futures… Https://www.cftc.gov/ConsumerProtection/FraudAwarenessPrevention/index.htm.
161 "Institute for Marketplace… Https://www.bbbmarketplacetrust.org/ story/28199823/ask-and-check.
161 "Ask and Check." Https://www.bbbmarketplacetrust.org/ story/28199823/ask-and-check; Http://www. bbb.org/council/smart-investing.
161 "Before You Invest" Https://www.cftc.gov/ConsumerProtection/ FraudAwarenessPrevention/index.htm; Http:// www.bbb.org/council/smart-investing.
161 "the Nasdaq stock market… Http://www.investopedia.com/terms/n/nasd.asp.
161 "The Maloney Act of 1938… Https://www.testopedia.com/definition/1345/ maloney-act-of-1938.
161 "electronic exchange… Ibid.
161 "In 1971, NASD… Https://en.wikipedia.org/wiki/Financial_ Industry_Regulatory_Authority.
161 "consolidated" Ibid.
161 "regulates trading… Ibid.
161 "All firms dealing… Ibid.
161 "US$878.6 million… Ibid.
161 "funded primarily by… Ibid.
162 "professional edifice… Http://www.sec.gov/news/ speech/1938/102338mathews.pdf.
162 "regulation committee" Http://en.wikipedia.org/wiki/Financial_ Industry_Regulatory_Authority.
162 "largest independent regulator" Ibid.
162 "FINRA is not part of… Http://www.finra.org/about.
162 "the greatest racket… O'Sullivan, (1933), p. 34.
162 "short-selling" Ibid., 35.
162 "all ramifications… Ibid.
163 "The voluminous evidence… Ibid., 109.
163 "are the very same Interests… Ibid.

REFERENCES

CHAPTER FIVE: GEORGE PRESBURY ROWELL

Page
- 165 "included estimates…   Http://advertisinghall.org/members/index.php.
- 165 "list system"   Ibid.
- 165 "promoted…to the position…   *Printers' Ink*, "LOOKING BACKWARD AND FORWARD" (Vol. LXIV, No. 3, July 15, 1908), p. 37.
- 165 "he sold ads for a theater…   Fox, (1984), p. 20.
- 165 "he contracted with a number…   *Printers' Ink*, (1938), p.51.
- 165 "wholesale"   *Printers' Ink*, "LOOKING BACKWARD AND FORWARD" (Vol. LXIV, No. 3, July 15, 1908), p. 37.
- 165 "Rowell Advertising Agency"   Ibid.
- 165 "THE GRAND OLD MAN…   *Printers' Ink*, "THE GRAND OLD MAN OF ADVERTISING" (Vol. LXXVI, No. 3, July 20, 1911), pp. 102-107.
- 165 "primarily a house organ…   *Printers' Ink*, (1938), p. 76.
- 165 "first complete list"   *Printers' Ink*, "LOOKING BACKWARD AND FORWARD" (Vol. LXIV, No. 3, July 15, 1908), p. 37.
- 165 "signed statements…   *Printers' Ink*, (1938), p. 59.
- 165 "a standing reward of $100…   Ibid.
- 166 "The American Newspaper Directory…   *Printers' Ink*, "LOOKING BACKWARD AND FORWARD" (Vol. LXIV, No. 3, July 15, 1908), p. 37.
- 166 "The *Telegraph* is the latest…   *Printers' Ink* (Vol. LXIV, No. 10, September 2, 1908), p. 33.
- 166 "Guaranteed Star"   Ibid., 16.
- 166 "affidavit"   Ibid., 5.
- 166 "July 20, 1888."   *Printers' Ink*, "Printers' Ink's Birthday" (Vol. LXXVI, No. 2, July 13, 1911), p. 68.
- 166 "little Printers' Ink"   *Printers' Ink*, "LOOKING BACKWARD AND FORWARD" (Vol. LXIV, No. 3, July 15, 1908), p. 37.
- 166 "the Little Schoolmaster"   Ibid.
- 166 "the Little Schoolmaster In The Art…   *Printers' Ink*, "The Little Schoolmaster In The Art of Advertising Trophy" (Vol. XXVIII, No. 1, July 5, 1899), p. 9.
- 166 "That paper after four months'…   Ibid.
- 166 "his life-long pet."   *Printers' Ink*, "LOOKING BACKWARD AND FORWARD" (Vol. LXIV, No. 3, July 15, 1908), p. 37.
- 166 "By an arcane system…   Fox, (1984), pp. 20- 21.
- 166 "Bull's Eye Gold Marks…   *Printers' Ink* (Vol. XLIII, No. 13, June 24, 1903), pp.3-9.
- 167 "the paper bearing…   *Printers' Ink* (Vol. XLIV, No. 1, July 1, 1903), pp. 34-35.
- 167 "The requirements are…   *Printers' Ink* (Vol. XLIII, No. 13, June 24, 1903), pp.3-9.
- 167 "The *Directory* made Rowell…   Fox, (1984), p. 21.
- 167 "made him untold enemies…   *Printers' Ink*, "THE GRAND OLD MAN OF ADVERTISING" (Vol. LXXVI, No. 3, July 20, 1911), pp. 102-107.
- 167 "no higher tribute…   Ibid.
- 167 "false promises."   George Rowell, *Forty Years an Advertising Agent 1865-1905*.
- 167 "organized fighting for truth…   Kenner, (1936), Introduction, p. xvi.
- 167 "united as the Associated…   Ibid.
- 168 "In your issue of July 1st …   *Printers' Ink*, "LOOKING BACKWARD AND FORWARD" (Vol. LXIV, No. 3, July 15, 1908), p. 37.
- 168 "So, Rowell finds this…   Https://www.nhpr.org/post// you-asked-we-answered-what-percy-summer-club-0#stream/0.
- 168 "old world scenes."   *Printers' Ink*, "Mr. Rowell's Death" (Vol. LXIV, No. 11, September 9, 1908), p. 26.
- 168 "nothing amused him…   Ibid.
- 168 "was originally built in 1893…   Https://polandspringps.org.
- 168 "a life member of…   *New York Times*, https://timesmachine.nytimes.com/ timesmachine/1908/08/29/104753106.pdf.

168 "a member of the Sphinx...   Ibid.
168 "Masonic Fraternity,"   Http://www.msana.com/historyfm.asp.
168 "GEORGE P. ROWELL DEAD...   *New York Times*, 8/29/1908; http://query.nytimes.com/gst/abstract.html?res=9A05E6DC1 33EE233A2575AC2A96E9C946997D6CF.
169 "I complete my three score...   *Printers' Ink*, "Looking Backward and Forward" (Vol. LXIV, No. 3, July 15, 1903), p. 37.
169 "Perhaps with a premonition...   *Printers' Ink*, "Mr. Rowell's Death" (Vol. LXIV, No. 11, September 9, 1908), p. 27.
169 "What Geo. P. Rowell has done...   Ibid., 26.
169 "At a meeting of the Executive...   *Printers' Ink*, "SPHINX CLUB RESOLUTIONS" (Vol. LXIV, No. 11, September 9, 1908), p. 27.

CHAPTER SIX: JOHN IRVING ROMER

Page
171 "German and Swiss...   Http://www.ancestry.com/nameorigin?surname=romer.
171 "ethnic name for a Roman."   Ibid.
171 "STATEMENT OF THE OWNERSHIP...   *Printers' Ink* (Vol. CIII (Vol. 103), No. 2, August 24, 1918), p. 177.
171 "Such a man of practical...   Kenner, (1936), p. 26.
172 "The only criticism of the Boston...   *Printers' Ink*, "LEGAL REPRESSION OF DISHONEST ADVERTISING" (Vol. LXXVII, No. 7, November 16, 1911), pp. 3-4.
172   "the biggest thing ...   *Printers' Ink*, "Utilizing the Convention Impetus" (Vol. LXXVI, No. 6, August 10, 1911), pp. 102- 103.
172 "one general train of thought"   Ibid.
172 "to put advertising on a higher ...   Ibid.
172 "one taper will light...   Ibid.
172 "that could not be shot...   *Printers' Ink*, "LEGAL REPRESSION OF DISHONEST ADVERTISING" (Vol. LXXVII, No. 7, November 16, 1911), p. 3.
172 "We call attention ...   Ibid., 3-4.
172 "Any person, firm, corporation...   Advertising Federation of America, (1936), p. 26.
173 "The only criticism of ...   *Printers' Ink*, "LEGAL REPRESSION OF DISHONEST ADVERTISING" (Vol. LXXVII, No. 7, November 16, 1911), pp. 3-4.
173 "The trouble has been...   Ibid.
173 "board of directors"   Kenner, (1936), p. 29.
173 "first local vigilance committee."   Ibid., 30.
173 "33"   Https://carm.org/how-old-was-jesus-when-hewas-crucified.
173 "Illuminati"   Https://www.scribd.com/document/169050934/ The-Illuminati-Code.
173 "National Vigilance Committee of...   Kenner, (1936), p.31.
174 "The Printers' Ink model statute was...   Ibid,, 34.
174 "backed up by a police power."   John Irving Romer, *Printers' Ink*, "Increasing the Value of Space" (Vol. LXXVII, December 14, 1911), pp. 70-71.
174 "the millionaire publisher...   *Reading Eagle* Newspaper, November 18, 1935.

CHAPTER SEVEN: THE ASSOCIATED PRESS

Page
175 "appeared"   Http://www.nysl.nysed.gov/nysnp/history.htm.
175 "By 1828, about 120 newspapers...   Ibid.
175 "issued by John Peter Zenger...   Ibid.
175 "seditious libel"   Http://en.wikipedia.org/wiki/John_Peter_ Zenger.
175 "oppressive"   Ibid.
175 "making her the first woman...   Http://www.nysl.nysed.gov/nysnp/history.htm.
175 "The Zenger Trial."   Http://en.wikipedia.org/wiki/John_Peter_ Zenger.
175 "that truth is a defense...   Ibid.

REFERENCES

175	"a liberty both of exposing…	Http://en.wikipedia.org/wiki/Andrew_ Hamilton_(lawyer).
175	"May 22, 1946,"	Https://en.wikipedia.org/wiki/ Associated_Press.
175	"six New York newspapers"	Http://www.nysl.nysed.gov/nysnp/history.htm.
175	"David Hale, publisher…	Ibid.
176	"by pigeon, pony express…	Http://www.ap.org/company/ history/ap-history.
176	"expanded to radio…	Https://en.wikipedia.org/wiki/ Associated_Press.
176	"a global video news …	Ibid.
176	"span the years 1848…	Http://www.ap.org/company/ history/ap-history.
176	"joined YouTube"	Https://en.wikipedia.org/wiki/ Associated_Press.
176	"operates AP Network"	Ibid.
176	"more than 5,000…	Ibid.
176	"a not-for-profit cooperative…	Http://www.ap.org/company/ history/ap-history.
176	"comprised of publishers…	Ibid.
176	"280 locations in more…	Ibid.
176	"$183.6 million…	Https://en.wikipedia.org/wiki/ Associated_Press.

CHAPTER EIGHT: SCIENTIFIC DISCOVERIES

Page

177	"electric street lamps"	Http://www.universetoday.com/82402/whodiscovered-electricity.
177	"direct-current system (DC)."	Ibid.
177	"far reaching"	Http://www.pbs.org/tesla/ll/ll_warcur.html.
177	"alternating current…	Ibid.
177	"stepped up"	Science.howstuffworks.com/innovation/famousinventors/nikola-tesla-tesla2.htm.
177	"inventor of railroad….	Https://en.wikipedia.org/wiki/George_ Westinghouse.
177	"filed for seven U.S. patents…	Http://www.pbs.org/tesla/ll/ll_warcur.html.
177	"electrical resonant…	Http://www.pbs.org/tesla/ins/lab_tescoil.html.
177	"all electric."	Http://www.pbs.org/tesla/ll/ll_warcur.html.
178	"The Columbian Exposition…	Ibid.
178	"American lawyer, engineer…	Https://en.wikipedia.org/wiki/John_Stevens_ (inventor,_born_1749.)
178	"served as a delegate…	Ibid.
178	"Founding Father"	Https://en.wikipedia.org/wiki/Robert_R._ Livingston_(chancellor).
178	"a member of the Committee…	Ibid.
178	"constructed the first steam-powered…	Https://en.wikipedia.org/wiki/John_Stevens_ (inventor,_born_1749).
178	"influential in the creation…	Ibid.
178	"was the first common carrier…	Http://en.wikipedia.org/wiki/Timeline_of_ United_States_railway_history.
179	"first stone"	Http://en.wikipedia.org/wiki/Baltimore_and_ Ohio_Railroad.
179	"last surviving signer."	Ibid.
179	"the first President to arrive…	Https://www.loc.gov/rr/program/bib/inaugurations/harrison/index.html.
179	"Pacific Railway Act of 1862"	Http://www.sdrm.org/history/timeline/pac_rr_ act_1862.html.
179	"the construction of a railroad …	Ibid.
179	"Pacific Railway Act, July 1, 1862…	Http://www.nps.gov/home/historyculture/ lincolnandwest.htm.
179	"The Homestead Act opened…	Ibid.
179	"preliminary Emancipation Proclamation"	Http://www.history.com/topics/american-civilwar/emancipation-proclamation.
179	"free land"	Http://www.nps.gov/home/historyculture/ lincolnandwest.htm.
180	"clay pots with sheets…	Http://www.universetoday.com/82402/who-discovered-electricity.
180	"electricus"	Ibid.
180	"electricity."	Ibid.

513

THE APO$TATE

180 "a kite, a key…   Ibid.
180 "lightning and tiny electric …   Ibid.
180 "electric dynamo"   Ibid.
180 "intensity batteries"   Http://edisontechcenter.org/JosephHenry.html.
180 "President Lincoln's science…   Ibid.
180 "scientific unit 'Henry' (H)…   Ibid.
180 "founding father of …   Ibid.
180 "incandescent filament light…   Http://www.universetoday.com/82402/who-discovered-electricity.
180 "filament lamp."   Ibid.
180 "direct-current system (DC)."   Ibid.
180 "the person responsible…   Http://en.wikipedia.org/wiki/Joseph_Swan.
180 "Edison-Lalande primary …   Http://edison.rutgers.edu/list.htm.
180 "The Wizard of Menlo Park"   Http://en.wikipedia.org/wiki/Thomas_Edison.
180 "stock ticker"   Http://en.wikipedia.org/wiki/Stock_ticker.
181 "the engineering department…   Http://en.wikipedia.org/wiki/Daniel_McFarlan_ Moore.
181 "light-producing tubes…   Ibid.
181 "Moore Electric Company"   Ibid.
181 "Moore Light Company."   Ibid.
181 "the Moore Lamp"   Ibid.
181 "absorbed"   Ibid.
181 "glow lamps"   Ibid.
181 "neon"   Http://en.wikipedia.org/wiki/Neon_lamp.
181 "brilliant red color."   Ibid.
181 "Edison of France,"   Https://en.wikipedia.org/wiki/Georges_Claude.
181 "the Claude system…   Ibid.
181 "supplies industrial gases…   Http://en.wikipedia.org/wiki/Air_Liquide.
181 "had applied for the first…   Http://www.referenceforbusiness.com/history2/22/L-AIR-LIQUIDE.html.
181 "appeared on the streets…   Ibid.
181 "covering the design…   Http://en.wikipedia.org/wiki/Neon_lamp.
181 "became the basis for…   Ibid.
181 "was imprisoned in 1945"   Https://en.wikipedia.org/wiki/Georges_Claude.
181 "collaborator"   Ibid.
181 ""The Great White Way" became…   Http://untappedcities.com/2012/12/06/history-of-streets-the-great-white-way.
181 "The world's first electrically lit…   Thomas E. Rinaldi, New York Neon; (New York, W. W. Norton & Company, 2012); http:// untappedcities.com/2012/12/06/history-of-streets-the-great-white-way.
181 "since 1897"   Http://www.artkraft.com.
182 "Thousands upon thousands…   *Printers' Ink*, "THE GREAT WHITE WAY" (Vol. LXIV, No. 9, August 26, 1908), p. 3.
182 "this magnificent illumination"   Ibid.
182 "Tear down every sign…   Ibid.
182 "WATCH THE FORDS…   David L. Lewis, The Public Image of Henry Ford (Detroit, Michigan, Wayne State University Press, 1976), p. 31.
182 "electric spectacular"   Ibid.
182 "MARCH SALES 43,849"   Ibid.
182 "Tin Lizzie,"   Kyvig, (2004), p. 30.
182 "customers could buy a Model T…   Ibid., 29.
182 "bought up numerous auto…   Ibid., 30.
183 "[T]he credit for inventing…   Http://www.history.com/topics/inventions/telegraph.
183 "Morse Code"   Http://en.wikipedia.org/wiki/Samuel_Morse.
183 ""S" is three dots…   Http://www.history.com/topics/inventions/telegraph.
183 "Joseph Henry's 1836…   Http://historywired.si.edu/detail.cfm?ID=324.

REFERENCES

183 "telegraph system between...   Http://www.history.com/topics/inventions/telegraph.
183 "What hath God...   Ibid.
183 "the first major use of radio...   Http://earlyradiohistory.us/sec005.htm.
183 "that electricity can be...   Http://www.famousscientists.org/heinrich-hertz.
183 "Hertz"   Http://transition.fcc.gov/omd/history/radio/ documents/short_history.pdf.
183 "a new and useful Machine...   Http://rmc.library.cornell.edu/Ezra-exhibit/EClife/EC-life-5.html.
183 "telegraph patent rights"   Http://en.wikipedia.org/wiki/Samuel_Morse.
183 "Western Union Telegraph Company"   Http://www.history.com/topics/inventions/telegraph.
184 "installed the first telegraph...   Seale, (1987), p. 426.
184 "Quadruplex System"   Http://www.history.com/topics/inventions/telegraph.
184 "electric light wiring"   Seale, (1987), p. 596.
184 "crude"   Http://www.engineersgarage.com/inventionstories/telephone-history.
184 "Mr. Watson--come here...   Http://www.americaslibrary.gov/jb/recon/ jb_recon_telephone_1.html.
184 "discovered how to transmit...   Kyvig, (2004), p. 72.
184 "advances in vacuum tube...   Ibid., 72-73.
184 "voice message"   Ibid.
184 "electrical resonant...   Https://www.pinterest.com/ pin/123637952240557245.
184 "Italian inventor and...   Http://en.wikipedia.org/wiki/Guglielmo_ Marconi.
184 "for the invention ...   Ibid.
184 "long range radio signals."   Ibid.
185 "amplitude-modulated...   Http://en.wikipedia.org/wiki/History_of_radio.
185 "more than one station"   Ibid.
185 "ships at sea."   Ibid.
185 "regular transatlantic...   Ibid.
185 "Clifden, Ireland ...   Ibid.
185 "ship to shore...   Ibid.
185 "His radio apparatus...   Http://transition.fcc.gov/omd/history/radio/ documents/short_history.pdf.
185 "second radio station"   Http://en.wikipedia.org/wiki/Spark_gap.
185 "spark-gap"   Ibid.
185 "creating the only wireless...   Http://en.wikipedia.org/wiki/History_of_radio.
185 "shipboard radio stations...   Ibid.
185 "into the North Atlantic Ocean...   Http://www.history.com/this-day-in-history/titanic-sinks.
185 "British journalist William...   Ibid.
185 "wireless telegraphy using ...   Http://en.wikipedia.org/wiki/History_of_radio.
185 "In the disaster's aftermath...   Http://www.history.com/this-day-in-history/titanic-sinks.
185 "wireless transmission"   Appel, (1930), p. 414.
185 "the Mayor of Philadelphia...   Ibid.
186 "official stations of the Marconi ...   Ibid.
186 "$2 for...   Ibid.
186 "the winter of 1922...   Ibid.
186 "the first radio broadcasting...   Ibid., 414-415.
186 "one of the first operators...   Ibid., 415.
186 "the first word...   Ibid.
186 "I began to receive...   Ibid.
186 "But the very tragedy...   Ibid.
186 "Radio Corporation of ...   Https://en.wikipedia.org/wiki/RCA.
186 "a national radio...   Ibid.
186 "British-owned"   Ibid.
186 "The result was...   Ibid.
186 "all-electronic"   Ibid.
187 "commercial television...   Ibid.
187 "Comcast,"   Ibid.
187 "government services."   Ibid.

187 "The first radio news… En.wikipedia.org/wiki/History_of_radio.
187 "sponsored a one night… Http://www.oldradio.com/current/bc_spots.htm.
187 "Long Island real estate… Fox, (1984), p. 152.
187 "U.S. Department of Commerce… Https://en.wikipedia.org/wiki/United_States_Department_of_Commerce_and_Labor.
187 "create jobs, promote economic … Ibid.
187 "The Act provided for… Https://www.mtsu.edu/first-amendment/article/1090/radio-act-of-1912.
187 "Federal Radio Commission." Https://en.wikipedia.org/wiki/Federal_Radio_Commission#The_Radio_Act_of_1927.
188 "objectionable advertising." Kenner, (1936), p. 236.
188 "WDZA, WEEI, WHDH… Ibid., 237.
188 "Radio broadcasting stations… Ibid., 236.
188 "telephone and telegraph.." Https://en.wikipedia.org/wiki/Federal_Radio_Commission.
188 "code of standards" Kenner, (1936), p. 237.
188 "conference reports," https://en.wikipedia.org/wiki/Federal_Radio_Commission.
188 "fireside chats" Http://www.history.com/this-day-in-history/fdr-broadcasts-first-fireside-chat.
189 "that was signed into law… Https://en.wikipedia.org/wiki/Federal_Radio_Commission.
189 "[Hoover's] powers were limited… Ibid.
189 "banking, unemployment… Http://www.history.com/topics/fire-side-chats.
189 "During the 1930s… Http://www.history.com/this-day-in-history/fdr-broadcasts-first-fireside-chat.

CHAPTER NINE: SPANISH-AMERICAN WAR 1898

Page
190 "The first armored cruiser… Http://www.globalsecurity.org/military/system/ship/acr.htm. 190 "Remember the *Maine*!… Http://en.wikipedia.org/wiki/USS_Maine_(ACR-1).
190 "splendid little war" Http://historyrfd.net/isern/104/lecture6.htm.
190 "Spain renounced… Http://www.history.com/topics/spanish-american-war.
190 "because of the airfield… Https://en.wikipedia.org/wiki/Guantanamo_Bay_Naval_Base.
190 "land and water" Ibid.
190 "detention" Ibid.
190 "alleging that the base… Ibid.
191 "return the base… Ibid.
191 "occupied" Ibid.
191 "Rough Riders," Roosevelt, (reproduction of 1899), 2014, p. 23.
191 "recruits from Harvard… Ibid., 25.
191 "embalmed" Ibid., 319.
191 "opened their tins… Ibid.
191 "tasted of boric acid… Brands, (1995), p. 320.
191 "injected by… Ibid.
191 "the Union army… Ibid., 317.
191 "more than 2,500… Ibid., 320-22.

CHAPTER TEN: JOHN WANAMAKER

Page
192 "full and frank facts… Kenner, (1936), p. 11.
192 "…tell the truth about goods." Ibid.
192 "John Wanamaker of Philadelphia… Ibid, 10-11.
193 "Postmaster General John … Http://about.usps.com/publications/pub100.pdf.
193 "in 1890, nearly 41 million … Ibid.
193 "populations of from 300… Ibid.
193 "isolation." Ibid.
193 "Grays Ferry neighborhood… Https://en.wikipedia.org/wiki/John_Wanamaker.
193 "Rittershoffen in Alsace… Ibid.

REFERENCES

193 "a penchant for merchandise... Appel, (1930), p. xi.
194 "an apprenticeship as assistant... Ibid., xi-xii.
194 "laying the foundation... Ibid., xii.
194 "the largest Sunday school... Http://www.phillymag.com/news/2016/07/11/john-wanamaker-philadelphia-history.
194 "went to work with a scant... Appel, (1930), p. xvi.
194 "Oak Hall" Appel, (1930), p. xi, 13; https://explorepahistory.com/hmarker.php?markerId=1-A-335.
194 "The Grand Depot" Appel, (1930), p.74; https://explorepahistory.com/hmarker.php?markerId=1-A-335.
194 "Iron Palace" Https://explorepahistory.com/hmarker.php?markerId=1-A-335.
194 "cast-iron front, glass dome... Https://en.wikipedia.org/wiki/John_Wanamaker; https://explorepahistory.com/hmarker.php?markerId=1-A-335 .
194 "Tin Lizzie" Https://media.ford.com/content/fordmedia/fna/ us/en/news/2013/08/05/model-t-facts.html.
194 "horseless carriage." Https://en.wikipedia.org/wiki/Ford_Quadricycle.
194 "Association of Licensed ... Appel, (1930), p. 155.
195 "In taking over the Ford... Ibid.
195 "Remember that John Wanamaker... Ibid.
195 "he was intrenched... Ibid., 158.
195 "it is important to note... Ibid., 158-159.
195 "the greatest merchant... Ibid., xvi.
195 "a model for all other stores... Ibid.
195 "Wanamaker Grand ... Https://en.wikipedia.org/wiki/John_Wanamaker.
195 "2,500-pound bronze... Ibid.
195 "One price and... Ibid.
195 "Wanamaker's money-back... Appel, (1930), p. 53.
195 "established mutual confidence... Ibid., xvi.
196 "White Sale" Https://www.pbs.org/wgbh/theymadeamerica/ whomade/wanamaker_hi.html. 196 "crusading pioneer" Appel, (1930), p. xv.
196 "to call himself a merchant... Ibid., xv.
196 "No marks or labels... Ibid., 144.
196 "the advertising of the store... Ibid.
196 "a merchant who... Ibid., xv.
196 "three of his chief executives... Ibid., 358.
196 "deep cold." Ibid., 359.
196 "Bracken, don't go empty-handed.... Ibid.
196 "Cape May Point, New Jersey... Https://en.wikipedia.org/wiki/John_Wanamaker.
196 "$100 million (USD)... Ibid.
196 "the last surviving member... Ibid.
196 "he was interred ... Ibid.
197 "were sold to the May... Ibid.
197 "To be frank... Appel, (1930), p. 363.

CHAPTER ELEVEN: JOSEPH HERBERT APPEL

Page
198 "first in Philadelphia... Appel, (1940), p. x.
199 "Poor Richardites." Ibid., 140.
199 "as a director of the Advertising... Ibid., xi.
199 "the first *organized* stand... Ibid., 133.
199 "Honesty in Advertising." Ibid.
199 "It was just about at this... Ibid., 136.
199 "Adelbod, Adbold... Ibid., 1
199 "in 1733 from... Ibid.

517

THE APO$TATE

199 "his wife and three... Ibid., 2.
199 "250-acre farm" Ibid.
199 "Bucks county." Ibid.
199 "his famous crossing... Ibid.
199 "Fish him out... Ibid.
199 "zealous church-folk." Ibid., 3.
199 "a strong Lutheran" Ibid.
199 "florid face, fair... Ibid., 2.
199 "a strong Reformed" Ibid., 3.
199 "a miller" Ibid.
199 "to put his boys... Ibid.
199 "if it took the last coat... Ibid.
200 "The age was full... Appel, (1940), p. 3.
200 "the seventh son... Ibid., 4.
200 "the classical school... Ibid.
200 "took charge of ... Ibid.
200 "appointed president ... Ibid., 4-5.
200 "a long time editor... Ibid., 6.
200 "brother's office" Ibid., 17.
201 "sworn in as... Ibid., 19.
201 "first law-case... Ibid.
201 "[W]ant a newspaper job... Ibid., 21.
201 "was to read... Ibid.
201 "city editor, telegraph... Ibid., 23.
201 "I feel confident... Ibid., 27.
201 "the reply came... Ibid.
201 "Come and see me." Ibid.
201 "a writer of advertising" Ibid.
201 "In advertising one must... Ibid., 28.
201 "Better Business Bureaus have ... Ibid., 201.
201 "I am strongly for... Ibid., 214.
202 "The misuse of scientific ... Ibid., 228.
202 "In New York the misuse of... Ibid., 227.
202 "The Federal Trade Commission itself... Ibid., 226.
202 "Advertising Federation of America." Kenner, (1936), p. xvi.
202 "advertising organizations in Canada... Ibid.
202 "disparagement of competitors" Appel, (1940), p. 241.
202 "reference to the merchandise... Ibid.
202 "distributing business cards ... Ibid.
202 "It thus appears that Germany... Appel, (1940), p. 242.
202 "inadequate, against... Ibid.
203 "that makes it ... Ibid.
203 "evangelistic spirit." Kenner, (1936), p. 19.
203 "more than a hundred... Ibid.
203 "truth fires burst... Ibid.
203 "It is always hard... Appel, (1940), p. 147.

CHAPTER TWELVE: DR. HARVEY WASHINGTON WILEY

Page
204 "Father of the FDA" Http://www.fda.gov/aboutfda/whatwedo/history/ centennialoffda/harveyw.wiley/default.htm.
205 "All through the 1880s... Ibid.
205 "the food and patent-medicine... Ibid.

REFERENCES

205 "in a log farmhouse"   Http://www.arlingtoncemetery.net/hwwiley.htm.
205 "antebellum country farm"   Pendergrast, (2000), p. 110.
205 "Preston Prichard Wiley...   Http://www.findagrave.com/cgi-bin/fg.cgi?page=gr &GSln=wiley&GSby=1844&GSbyrel=in&GSdyr el=in&GScntry=4&GSob=n&GSsr=41&GRid=6 619&df=all&.
205 "Lucinda Weir Maxwell ...   Ibid.
205 "strictly observed Sundays"   Pendergrast, (2000), p. 110.
205 "heinous sin"   Ibid.
205 "a lay preacher"   Https://dash.harvard.edu/bitstream/ handle/1/8852144/Gaughan.html?sequence=2.
205 "local schoolteacher."   Http://www.fda.gov/aboutfda/whatwedo/history/ centennialoffda/harveyw.wiley/default.htm.
205 "Be sure you are right...   Pendergrast, (2000), p. 110.
205 "a righteous cause...   Https://dash.harvard.edu/bitstream/ handle/1/8852144/Gaughan.html?sequence=2.
205 "a corporal in Company ...   Https://en.wikipedia.org/wiki/Harvey_ Washington_Wiley.
205 "discharged as ill ...   *The New York Times*, "Dr. H. W. WILEY DIES; PURE FOOD EXPERT," July 1, 1930, p. 29.
205 "hookworm."   Https://dash.harvard.edu/bitstream/ handle/1/8852144/Gaughan.html?sequence=2.
205 "A.M. degree"   Http://library.hanover.edu/pdf/MSS23_Wiley.pdf.
205 "AB"   Http://www.archives.upenn.edu/histy/ features/1800s/1852/curriculum.html.
205 "AM"   Ibid.
205 "Latin and Greek"   *The New York Times*, "Dr. H. W. WILEY DIES; PURE FOOD EXPERT," July 1, 1930, p. 29.
206 "post-graduate studies"   Http://library.hanover.edu/pdf/MSS23_Wiley. pdf.
206 "as a freshman, took ...   *The New York Times*, "Dr. H. W. WILEY DIES; PURE FOOD EXPERT," July 1, 1930, p. 29.
206 "from 1874 to 1883"   Http://library.hanover.edu/pdf/MSS23_Wiley.pdf.
206 "founded on May 6, 1869,"   Https://en.wikipedia.org/wiki/Harvey_ Washington_Wiley.
206 "the post of Chief Chemist...   *The New York Times*, "Dr. H. W. WILEY DIES; PURE FOOD EXPERT," July 1, 1930, p. 29.
206 "as a professor of physics...   Http://library.hanover.edu/pdf/MSS23_Wiley. pdf.
206 "including a Ph.D. from...   Ibid.
206 "the Polariscope"   *The New York Times*, "Dr. H. W. WILEY DIES; PURE FOOD EXPERT," July 1, 1930, p. 29.
206 "the first reports ever made...   Ibid.
206 "domestic"   Https://en.wikipedia.org/wiki/Harvey_ Washington_Wiley.
206 "adulteration of sugar...   Ibid.
206 "by George Loring...   Http://library.hanover.edu/pdf/MSS23_Wiley. pdf.
206 ""too young and too jovial...   Ibid.
206 "Father Wiley"   Pendergrast, (2000), p. 111.
206 "preacher of purity."   Ibid.
206 "a flair for the dramatic."   Http://www.quackwatch.org/13Hx/TM/14. html.
206 "infractions"   Ibid.
206 "at Purdue he had been...   Ibid.
206 "a dozen young men...   *The New York Times*, "Dr. H. W. WILEY DIES; PURE FOOD EXPERT," July 1, 1930, p. 29.
206 "volunteered to eat...   Ibid.
207 "borax, benzoates...   Http://www.digplanet.com/wiki/Pure_Food_ and_Drug_Act.
207 "harmless."   *The New York Times*, "Dr. H. W. WILEY DIES; PURE FOOD EXPERT," July 1, 1930, p. 29.
207 "Squad"   Ibid.
207 "some discovery in the Arts...   Https://en.wikipedia.org/wiki/Elliott_Cresson_ Medal.
207 "Cranford Village Improvement ...   Http://medlibrary.org/medwiki/Alice_Lakey.
207 "over one million"   Ibid.

519

207 "the first woman to be listed... Ibid.
207 "balcony" Http://www.quackwatch.org/13Hx/TM/14.html.
207 "on June 30, 1906." Http://www.fda.gov/aboutfda/whatwedo/history/ centennialoffda/harveyw.wiley/default.htm.
207 "testing all foods and drugs... Http://www.u-s-history.com/pages/h917.html.
207 "prescriptions from licensed... Ibid.
207 "label warnings on... Ibid.
207 "largely written" Http://www.fda.gov/aboutfda/whatwedo/history/ centennialoffda/harveyw.wiley/default.htm.
208 "chemical fundamentalist" Pendergrast, (2000), p. 111.
208 "poisonous substance." Ibid.
208 ""guaranteed" under... Ibid.
208 "serial number." Ibid.
208 "I have heard many... Ibid.
208 "On February 27, 1911," *The New York Times*, "Dr. H. W. WILEY DIES; PURE FOOD EXPERT," July 1, 1930, p. 29.
208 "March 15, 1912" Https://en.wikipedia.org/wiki/Harvey_Washington_Wiley.
209 "Injurious Food Adjuncts: The Part... Https://dash.harvard.edu/bitstream/ handle/1/8889492/Diamond.pdf?sequence=1; p. 21.
209 "Injurious Food Adjuncts: Formaldehyde... Ibid.
209 "launching a national ... Ibid., 18.
209 "the Good Housekeeping ... Ibid., 24.
209 "rarely addressed the problem... Ibid., 33.
209 "mobilizing the women's... Ibid., 51-52.
209 "the coveted symbol... Http://www.fda.gov/AboutFDA/WhatWeDo/ History/CentennialofFDA/HarveyW.Wiley/ default.htm.
209 "Swindled Getting Slim" Ibid.
209 "improved infant care." Ibid.
209 "mounting evidence" Ibid.
209 "the Kendal Scholarship... Http://www.nytimes.com/1964/01/07/mrs-h-w-wiley-suffragette-dies.html?
210 "secretary to Dr. Wiley" Ibid.
210 "on a streetcar." Ibid.
210 "obstructing traffic." Ibid.
210 "served six terms as chairman... Ibid.
210 "with unfailing interest... *The New York Times*, "DR. H.W. WILEY DIES: PURE FOOD EXPERT," July 1, 1930, P. 29.
210 "director-emeritus." Ibid.
210 "Congressional committee at... Ibid.
210 "patriot's funeral" Http://www.fda.gov/aboutfda/whatwedo/history/ centennialoffda/harveyw.wiley/default.htm.
210 "Find A Grave" Http://www.findagrave.com.
210 "WOMEN WEEP... Http://www.fda.gov/aboutfda/whatwedo/history/ centennialoffda/harveyw.wiley/default.htm.

CHAPTER THIRTEEN: UPTON SINCLAIR, THE JUNGLE

Page
212 "jokes, dime novels... Https://en.wikipedia.org/wiki/Upton_Sinclair.
212 "hack writing." Http://www.nytimes.com/ref/timestopics/topics_ uptonsinclair.html.
212 "Spanish, German... Https://en.wikipedia.org/wiki/Upton_Sinclair.
212 "serious novelist" Http://www.nytimes.com/ref/timestopics/topics_ uptonsinclair.html.
212 "King Midas (1901)... Https://en.wikipedia.org/wiki/Upton_Sinclair.
212 "twenty thousand workers... Sinclair, (1965), p. v.

REFERENCES

212 "paralyzed"   Ibid.
212 "weekly four-page…   Ibid.
212 "hard-fighting organ…   Ibid.
212 "a little money for…   Ibid.
212 "source of information"   Ibid.
212 "the strike leaders…   Ibid.
213 "I had everything but…   Ibid., vi.
213 "blood and guts"   Ibid.
213 "three or four"   Ibid.
213 "that he had been receiving…   Ibid., vii.
213 "kitchen cabinet."   Ibid.
213 "Mr. Sinclair, you don't have…   Ibid.
213 "the United States Senate over …   Ibid., viii.
213 "luncheon table,"   Ibid.
213 "their political and financial…   Ibid.
213 "Neill and McReynolds"   Ibid.
213 "They had only one uncertainty…   Ibid.
213 "[Roosevelt's] representatives now…   Ibid.
214 "desperately-needed reforms"   Ibid.
214 "English specialist on…   Ibid, ix.
214 "newly elected member…   Ibid.
214 "a two-part review…   Ibid.
214 "Let me say at once…   Ibid.
214 "The Jungle became…   Ibid., ix-x.
214 "Their leaders have paid…   Ibid., x.
214 "a list of the cases…   Ibid., xi.
214 "staunch communist"   Https://en.wikipedia.org/wiki/Upton_Sinclair.
214 "founded the state's…   Ibid..
214 "Red"   Https://www.ssa.gov/history/sinclair.html.
214 "crackpot."   Ibid.
214 "wrote and produced… ."   Https://en.wikipedia.org/wiki/Upton_Sinclair.
214 "the Pulitzer Prize…   Https://www.cliffsnotes.com/literature/j/thejungle/upton-sinclair-biography.
215 "I have the experience of writing…   Sinclair, (1965), p. v.

CHAPTER FOURTEEN: DR. HERBERT SHERMAN HOUSTON

Page
216 "in organized advertising …   Http://www.zoominfo.com/s/#!search/profile/ person?personId=8480 51076&targetid=profile.
216 "first board of directors"   Kenner, (1936), p. 105-106.
216 "Because many advertisers…   Ibid., 46.
217 "International Motion Picture …   Http://www.mocavo.com/ International-Motion-Picture-Almanac-1937-38-Volume-1937-38/705462/470.
217 "Dr. Herbert S. Houston."   Ibid.
217 "Doctor of Laws"   Http://prabook.com/web/person-view. html?profileId=1083351.
217 "The Diamond of PSI…   "The Diamond of PSI Upsilon" (Volume XXIV, Number Two, January 1938), pp. 82-83.
217 "Herbert S. Houston's Recent…   Ibid.
217 "stories from all…   *Publishers' Weekly*, "Periodical Note" (Volume 101, April 8, 1922), p. 1047. 217 "Printers' Ink plan."   *Printers' Ink*, "HOUSTON ADDRESSES AD LEAGUE ON DISHONEST ADVERTISING," Vol. LXXVII, No. 1, October 5, 1911.
218 "the League to Enforce…   Https://commons.wikimedia.org/wiki/ Category:Herbert_Sherman_Houston.

218	"headed the department of ethics… Http://www.zoominfo.com/s/#!search/profile/person?personId=848051076&targetid=profile.

CHAPTER FIFTEEN: SAMUEL CANDLER DOBBS

Page
219	"Women's Christian Temperance… Https://en.wikipedia.org/wiki/Woman%27s_Christian_Temperance_Union.
220	"Resolved by the Executive… *Associated Advertising* (Vol X, No. 9, September 1919), p. 92; https://babel.hathitrust.org/cgi/pt?i d=iau.31858034256317;view=1up;seq=462.
220	"unsound loans to investors… Https://scholarship.law.gwu.edu/cgi/viewcontent. cgi?referer=&http sredir=1&article=2477&contex t=faculty_publications, p. 1289.
220	"an illiterate farm boy" Http://advertisinghall.org/members/member_ bio.php?memid=602 &uflag=d&uyear=;Retri eved.10/3/2015].[http://home.lagrange.edu/ library/hilltop_news_digi-tized/1927-06.pdf.
220	"assumed charge" *Who's Who* In Advertising (Volume 1, Detroit Business Service Corporation, 1916), p. 21.
221	"first salesman on… Ibid.
221	"curly-headed… Http://archive.org/stream/ lagrangecollegeb1928lagr/ lagrangecollegeb1928lagr_djvu.txt.
221	"beautiful north Georgia… Http://rabuncounty.ga.gov.
221	"60% of the land is… Ibid.
221	"originally was a horse… Http://www.lakerabun.com/Lake_Rabun/Amenities.html.
221	"barn was converted… Ibid.
221	"In 1920 Samuel Candler Dobbs… Http://www.barninn.com/About.htm.
221	"railroad" Http://query.nytimes.com/gst/fullpage.html?res= 9A01E6DC1F3FF937A3575BC0A9639C8B63.
221	"Annie's at Alley's… Https://anniesatalleys.wordpress. com/2012/02/06/and-along-came-annie.
221	"black porter, a former… Pendergrast, (2000), p. 52.
221	"drummed up trade" Ibid.
221	"gained complete legal… Ibid.
221	"the end of 1899," Ibid., 104.
221	"general office man, road… *Who's Who* In Advertising (Volume 1, Detroit Business Service Corporation, 1916), p. 21.
221	"Whenever you see an arrow… Ibid.
221	"the brains and beauty… Pendergrast, (2000), p. 104.
222	"medicinal image" Ibid., 62.
222	"Drink Coca-Cola… Ibid., 63.
222	"Coca-Cola girls" Ibid.
222	"flash advertising." Ibid., 105.
222	"special Yiddish signs… Ibid.
222	"Cuba, Hawaii, and… Ibid.
222	"forty-five million people" Ibid.
222	"repeated entreaties from… Ibid.
222	"Department of Agriculture's chief… Http://www.arlingtoncemetery.net/hwwiley.htm.
222	"Dr. Wiley's Law." Pendergrast, (2000), p. 109.
222	"referred" Ibid.
222	"pure food cranks." Ibid.
222	"complained of 'misguided … Ibid.
222	"virtuous" Ibid.
222	"'bad' patent medicines." Ibid.
222	"*pure* and wholesome" Ibid.
222	"the Great National Temperance… Ibid.
222	"Refreshing as a Summer Breeze" Ibid.

REFERENCES

222 "it aids digestion and is genuinely…   Ibid.
223 "Coca-Cola was a habit-forming…   Ibid., 114.
223 "Dr. Wiley Will Take Up Soda…   Ibid., 110.
223 "These famous "poison squad"…   Http://www.arlingtoncemetery.net/hwwiley.htm.
223 "cocaine, caffeine, choral hydrates…   Pendergrast, (2000), p. 114.
223 "screaming"   Ibid., 113.
223 "ordered the jury to return…   Ibid., 119.
223 "coca and kola."   Ibid.
223 "not an added ingredient"   Ibid.
223 "to the list of "habit-forming"…   Ibid.
223 "unwritten rule"   Ibid.
224 "Coca-Cola was not…   Ibid., 121.
224 "added ingredient."   Ibid.
224 "no contest."   Ibid.
224 "by half."   Ibid.
224 "sanctioned the secret sale…   Ibid., 133.
224 "all but seven shares…   Ibid., 127.
224 "all of his real estate…   Ibid.
224 "$15 million in cash…"   Ibid., 130.
224 "500,000 shares of…   Ibid.
224 "$40 a share."   Ibid., 131.
225 "bottling rights in perpetuity"   Ibid., 136.
225 "right to cancel"   Ibid., 137.
225 "as of May 1, 1920."   Ibid.
225 "invested over $20 million…   Ibid., 138.
225 "Fulton County"   Ibid., 139.
225 "Delaware federal court"   Ibid.
225 "the Sword of Damocles"   Ibid.
225 "Coca-Cola's legal rights…   Http://earlycoke.com/the-1920s.html.
225 "Woodruff is as busy…   Pendergrast, (2000), p. 140.
226 "Woodruff's personal chauffeur…   Https://en.wikipedia.org/wiki/Robert_W._ Woodruff.
226 "Godfather's Pizza."   Http://www.makemyfamilytree.com/articles/ herman_cain_family_tree_and_biography.html.
226 "The early pages of the truth…   Kenner, (1936), pp. 18-19.
226 "The truth fires burst…   Ibid., 19.
227 "The challenge of creating…   Wansley, (1971).
228 "S. C. Dobbs, vice-president…   *Associated Advertising* magazine, "August Assemblage Honors Associated Clubs Leaders" (Vol. X, No. 7, July 1919), p. 3.
228 "Festus J. Wade, president …   Ibid.
228 "The National Vigilance Committee…   Http://www.zoominfo.com/p/SamuelDobbs/8632427.
228 "After speaking with other…   Ibid.
229 "tenth president and…   Http://www.georgiaencyclopedia.org/articles/arts-culture/warren-akin-candler-1857-1941.
229 "Shorty,"   Ibid.
229 "Methodist Episcopal Church…   Ibid.
229 "spiritual advisor" Ibid. "Asa Candler wrote a check…   Ibid.
229 "In 1913, the top tax bracket…   Http://bradfordtaxinstitute.com/Free_Resources/Federal-Income-Tax-Rates.aspx.
229 "In effect, the law forced…   Pendergrast, (2000), p. 121.
229 "The Lamar Dodd Art…   Http://www.georgiaencyclopedia.org/articles/education/la-grange-college.
230 "banker."   Advertising Federation of America, (1936), pp. 17-18.
230 "SAMUEL CANDLER DOBBS…   Ibid., 18.
230 "Samuel Candler Dobbs, LL.D."   Ibid., 17.

523

230 "LaGrange Alumnae Association." Http://home.lagrange.edu/library/hilltop_news_ digi-tized/1928-01.pdf.
230 "The Board of Trustees Minutes... Patricia Barrett, LaGrange College, 10/5/2015.
230 "Samuel Candler Dobbs to Deliver... LaGrange College, The Scroll (Volume VI, Number 8), June 1927.
230 "a prominent capitalist" Ibid.
230 "well-known throughout... Ibid.
230 "as an authority on business ... Ibid.
230 "he is also a member of the Board... Ibid.
230 "Samuel C. Dobbs Accepts ... LaGrange College, The Scroll (Volume VII, Number 3), January 1928; http://home.lagrange. edu/library/hilltop_news_digitized/1928-01.pdf.
231 "an outstanding figure... Ibid.
231 "When Georgia Methodism... Ibid.
231 "Atlanta Chapter of the L.C... Ibid.
231 "The Atlanta auxiliary... Ibid.
231 "Mrs. Samuel C. Dobbs" Http://home.lagrange.edu/library/hilltop_news_ digitized/1928-01.pdf.
231 "national president" Ibid.
231 "received" Ibid.
231 "Mrs. Candler poured tea... Ibid.
231 "LaGrange College Bulletin... LaGrange College Bulletin (Volume LXXXIV, Number 1), August 1928; http://archive. org/stream/lagrangecollegeb1928lagr/ lagrangecollegeb1928lagr_djvu.txt.
231 "more than 56,000 of our boys... Http://archive.org/stream/lagrangecollegeb1928lagr/ lagrangecollegeb1928lagr_djvu.txt.
231 "I can pick up my phone... Ibid.
232 "SAMUEL CANDLER DOBBS Newest... LaGrange College, The Scroll (Volume IX, Number VI), April 1930; http://home.lagrange.edu/library/hilltop_news_digitized/1930-04-sp-ed.pdf.
232 "Returning Alumnae see... Ibid.
232 "Whatever sum of money... Ibid.
232 "before it was remodeled... LaGrange College Alumnae Bulletin, (Volume 1, Number 2), November 20, 1951; LaGrange College, Email dated 10/5/2015.
232 "This building was named... Ibid.
232 "chartered" Http://www.georgiaencyclopedia.org/articles/education/lagrange-college.
232 "Joseph, Telemachus... Ibid.
232 "the Georgia Conference... Ibid.
232 "The LaGrange College... LaGrange College Bulletin (Catalogue 28-29, Announcements 1930-1931, Annual Catalogue, Volume LXXXV, Number 2).
232 "first dormitory" Http://provost.emory.edu/faculty/SVP_ Academic_Affairs/SCDobbs.html.
232 "to honor some of the University's... Ibid.
233 "We are assembled here... Advertising Federation of America, (1936), p. 17.
233 "educational and welfare work... *Atlanta Journal Constitution*, "Mrs. Ruth Mixon Dobbs, 72, Wife of Capitalist, Is Dead," December 18, 1941, p. 10.
233 "Mrs. Dobbs was active... *Atlanta Journal Constitution*, "Mrs. Dobbs, Rites To Be Held Today" (December 11, 1941), p. 3.
233 "in his business" Http://www.legacy.com/obituaries/atlanta/obituary.aspx?pid=14277708.
234 "extended illness" *Atlanta Journal Constitution*, (December 10, 1941), p. 10.
234 "on the high seas... *Atlanta Journal Constitution*, (December 7, 1941), p. 9.
234 "F.D.R. TO TALK ... *Atlanta Journal Constitution*, (December 8, 1941), p. 9.
234 "a private sanitarium" *Atlanta Journal Constitution*, (December 10, 1941), p. 10.
234 "Emory hospital." Ibid.
234 "JAPANESE ATTACK... Ibid., 1.
234 "Hospitals Here Set... Ibid., 2.
234 "Funeral service" *Atlanta Journal Constitution*, (December 11, 1941), p. 3 (Mrs.), p.9 (Judge).

REFERENCES

CHAPTER SIXTEEN: VIGILANCE COMMITTEE

Page
236 "organize vigilance committees for... Kenner, (1936), p. 27.
236 "In November, 1911, Printers'... Advertising Federation of America, (1936), p. 26.
236 "Three dynamic speakers... Kenner, (1936), p. 29.
237 "Vigilance Committee" Ibid., 30.
237 "nearly 100 cases of... Ibid., 31.
237 "fifteen states in 1913... Ibid., 34.

CHAPTER SEVENTEEN: NATIONAL VIGILANCE COMMITTEE

Page
238 "National Vigilance Committee" Kenner, (1936), p. 31.
238 "national investment banking... Ibid.
238 "Vigilance Committee of the Advertising... Ibid., 34.
238 "following the convention." Ibid., 31.
238 "dissatisfied purchasers." *Associated Advertising*, "Vigilance Committee Arbitrates A Difficulty" (Vol. 10, No. 8, August 1919), p. 29.
238 "members" Kenner, (1936), p. 31.
239 "Manager" Auchincloss, (1927), p. 8.
239 "September, 1914." Ibid., 7.
239 "the advertising capital... Kenner, (1936), p. 79.
239 "July 1, 1919." *Associated Advertising* (Vol. 10, No. 7, July 1919), p. 37.
239 "father of United States Senator... *Associated Advertising*, "Olwin Leaves Vigilance Secretaryship" (Vol. 10, No. 7, July 1919), p. 48.
240 "This is a big business... Kenner, (1936), p. 80.
240 "sixteen local Better Business... *Associated Advertising*, "Better Advertising Means More Advertising" (Vol. 10, No. 7, July 1919), p. 57; http://babel.hathitrust.org/cgi/pt?id=iau.31858034256317;view=1up;seq=295.
240 "Canada, England, France... Ibid.
240 "national advertisers" *Associated Advertising*, "Better Advertising Means More Advertising" (Vol. 10, No. 7, July 1919), p. 57; http://babel.hathitrust.org/cgi/pt?id=iau.31858034256317;view=1up;seq=295.
240 "as a member of the Board... Auchincloss, (1927), p. 8.
240 "to provide for greater specialization... Kenner, (1936), p. 140.
240 "the umbrella organization... Http://www.bbb.org/council/news-events/news-releases/2016/07/new-eu-u.s.-privacyshield-adopted-to-support-trans-atlantic-digital-commerce (link removed); refer to: https://bbbprograms.org/programs/all-programs/bbb-privacy-shield/about-bbb-eu-privacy-shield.
240 "governor of the NYSE... Https://en.wikipedia.org/wiki/James_C._Auchincloss.
240 "founder, treasurer, president... Ibid.
241 "The National Bureau has over... Auchincloss, (1927), p. 11.
241 "well established as a... Kenner, (1936), p. 64.
241 "National Association of Piano... Ibid.
242 "Then the National Better Business... O'Sullivan, (1933), p. 16.
242 "literally hundreds of millions... Kenner, (1936), p. 78.
243 "voted to alter its charter... Auchincloss, (1927), p. 10.
243 "It is proposed that business... Kenner, (1936), pp. 286-287.
243 "Fair Practice Code" Ibid., 287.
244 "Those of us who are responsible... Auchincloss, (1927), p. 13.

CHAPTER EIGHTEEN: MERLE SIDENER

Page
246 "Committee on Relation" http://advertisinghall.org/members/member_bio.

php?memid=800&uflag=s&uyear=; http://advertisinghall.org/members/index.php.
246 "a representative... Ibid.
246 "charter member... Ibid.
246 "Council of Departmental... Ibid.
246 "agency-client relations" Ibid.
246 "he helped prepare three... Ibid.
246 "U.S. National Register ... Https://en.wikipedia.org/wiki/Shortridge_High_ School. The Shortridge Daily Echo Http://www.webcitation.org/query?url=http:// www.geocities.com/hollywood/4953/kv_bio. html&date=2009-10-26+00:08:26.
246 "recognized as one of the... Http://indianagenweb.com/inmontgomery/ bios/c/coons-wallace-e.htm.
246 "part owner" Ibid.
247 "Room 607 Majestic Building... Ibid.
247 "The National Paving Brick... Ibid.
247 "Publicity Counsel" Ibid.
247 "Sidener was responsible... Ibid.
247 "policy" Ibid.
247 "accept only employment... Ibid.
247 "Kokomo Rubber Company" Ibid.
247 "The Howard Caldwell... Ibid.
247 "published its first color... Ibid.
247 "promoted the sale of war... Ibid.
247 "He not only launched... Http://www.advertisinghall.org/members/ member_bio.php?memid=800&uflag=s&uyear=; http://advertisinghall.org/members/index.php.
247 "guinea pig" Kenner, (1936), p. 29.
248 "Merle Sidener of Indianapolis... *Editor and Publisher*, "Ad Vigilantes Meet In Chicago July 10-11" (Volume 52, Part 1, June 26, 1919), p. 11.
248 "Cleveland merchant," Kenner, (1936), p. 99.
248 "Cleveland plan" Ibid.
248 "The purchasing power... Ibid., 98.
249 "foreign securities" O'Sullivan, (1933), p. 34.
249 "American banking houses." Ibid.
249 "The unsavory testimony... Ibid.
249 "founded the Santa Claus... Sidener Academy for High Ability Students website; http://www.sideneracademy.com/?page_ id=32.
249 "he served as a member... Ibid.
249 "active in the Chamber... Ibid.
249 "a director of the Citizens... Ibid.
249 "member of the Columbia... Ibid.
249 "founder of the Christian... Ibid.
249 "received the Junior Chamber... Http://www.advertisinghall.org/members/ member_bio.php?memid=800&uflag=s&uyear=.
249 "There is no twilight zone... Advertising Federation of America, (1936), p. 23.
250 "Caldwell, Larkin &... Http://www.indianahistory.org/our-collections/ collection-guides/caldwell-vanriper-collection. pdf.
250 "for his contributions to... Ibid.
250 "Ed Van Riper" Ibid.
250 "By 1981" Ibid.
250 "one of the Midwest's largest... Ibid.
250 "demonstrated academic excellence... Http://www.donnelly.senate.gov/newsroom/ press/donnelly-congratulates-indianas-2014- national-blue-ribbon-schools.
250 "He had some new ideas... Kenner, (1936), pp. 48-49.
250 "late" *Greensburg Daily News*; May 11, 1948.

REFERENCES

250 "declining health"   Ibid.
250 "bedfast"   Ibid.

CHAPTER NINETEEN: ARTHUR FREDERICK SHELDON

Page
251 "He Profits Most ...   Http://www.kingstonnyrotary.org/ArthurFrederickSheldon.cfm.
251 "author, lawyer...   Ibid.
251 "scientific method...   Http://libertyvillespast.blogspot.com/2014/08/arthur-sheldon.html.
252 "emphasized that a salesman...   Http://www.nlis.net/freedomi/rotary/caulder/ArthurFrederickSheldon.htm.
252 "over 10,000 students...   Http://libertyvillespast.blogspot.com/2014/08/arthur-sheldon.html. 252 "persuaded villagers...   Http://www.encyclopedia.chicagohistory.org/ pages/855.html.
252 "advertising and the allied...   Terrence H. Witkowski, "The Art of Commerce According to American Norms," California State University, Long Beach, USA; p. 314.
252 "Silvester Schiele, a coal...   Http://www.rotarypavia.org/en/the-rotary/rotary-international.
252 "in turn at the office...   Ibid.
253 "Rotary International."   Ibid.
253 "He Profits Most....   Http://www.rotaryfirst100.org/leaders/Sheldon.
253 "London and Manchester,"   Http://www.rotarypavia.org/en/the-rotary/rotary-international. 253 "friendships, promote equality...   www.ask.com.
253 "the gifted apostle...   Http://www.kingstonnyrotary.org/AuthurFrederickSheldon.cfm.
253 "night-riders and tar...   Kenner, (1936), p. 61.
253 "Sidener, Van Riper...   Advertising Federation of America, (1936), p. 24.
253 "Mr. Sheldon walked to...   Kenner, (1936), p. 61.
253 "Mission, Texas"   Http://libertyvillespast.blogspot.com/2014/08/ arthur-sheldon.html.
253 "BUSINESS. SCIENTIST...   Https://www.findagrave.com/ memorial/47846826/arthur-fredericksheldon#view-photo=25512876.

CHAPTER TWENTY: FEDERAL TRADE COMMISSION

Page
255 "Ref. No. 1633992"   FTC letter to Caryn Cain; Dated February 10, 2009.
255 "The Commission does not...   Ibid.
255 "opinion letter,"   Https://www.ftc.gov/sites/default/files/ documents/advisory_opinions/council-better-business-bureaus-inc./100815cbbbletter.pdf; https://www.ftc.gov/policy/advisory-opinions/council-better-business-bureaus-inc.
255 "accountability program"   Ibid.
255 "ethics."   Ibid.
255 "Under this program...   Ibid.
255 "was formed through funding...   Ibid.
255 "Statement of Pertinent Facts"   Ibid.
256 "the BBB system...   Ibid.
256 "subsequent telephone...   Ibid.
256 "For the reasons stated...   Ibid.
256 "agency of assistance"   Wansley, (1971).
257 "No honestly intentional...   O'Sullivan, (1933), p. 62.
258 "Individual Recourse"   Https://www.bbb.org/EU-privacy-shield/privacyshield-principles.
258 "conciliation and/or arbitration...   Ibid.
258 "Data Processing Addendum"   Https://www.cisco.com/c/dam/en_us/about/ doing_business/legal/docs/cloud-services-EUdpa-2.pdf.
258 "Main Agreement"   Ibid.
258 "Data Protection Laws...   Ibid.
258 "plain arrangements among ...   Https://www.ftc.gov/tips-advice/competitionguidance/guide-antitrust-laws/antitrust-laws.

258 "Any combination …   Https://www.ourdocuments.gov/doc. php?flash=true&doc=51.
258 "By 1899, the Supreme Court…   Https://www.ftc.gov/sites/default/files/attachments/federal-trade-commission-history/ origins.pdf.
259 "progressive legislative policies"   Https://en.wikipedia.org/wiki/Woodrow_ Wilson.
259 "Rule of Reason"   Https://www.ftc.gov/sites/default/files/attachments/ftc-90-symposium/90thanniv_ program.pdf; p. 6.
259 "Standard Oil Co. v United States…   Ibid.
259 "trusts and antitrust"   Ibid.
259 "Like the Bureau of Corporations…   Ibid.
259 "unfair methods of competition"   Https://www.ftc.gov/tips-advice/competitionguidance/guide-antitrust-laws/antitrust-laws.
259 "unfair or deceptive acts…   Ibid.
259 "Its "blue sky" cases…   Https://www.ftc.gov/sites/default/files/attachments/ftc-90-symposium/90thanniv_ program.pdf; p. 8.
260 "May this permanent home…   Http://www.ftc.gov/about-ftc/our-history.
260 "prohibits mergers and …   Https://www.ftc.gov/tips-advice/competitionguidance/guide-antitrust-laws/antitrust-laws.
260 "bans certain discriminatory…   Ibid.
260 "companies planning large…   Https://www.ftc.gov/tips-advice/competitionguidance/guide-antitrust-laws/antitrust-laws.
260 "prevent unfair methods…   Https://www.ftc.gov/enforcement/statutes/federal-trade-commission-act.
260 "The 1938 Wheeler-Lea Act…   Https://www.ftc.gov/sites/default/files/attachments/ftc-90-symposium/90thanniv_ program.pdf.
260 "abuses of advertising…   Https://www.ftc.gov/system/files/documents/ public_statements/676351/19380517_freer_ whe_wheeler-lea_act.pdf.
260 "administer a variety of laws…   www.answers.com.
260 "when challenging deception…   Https://www.ftc.gov/sites/default/files/attachments/ftc-90-symposium/90thanniv_ program.pdf, p. 8.
260 "a series of provisions…   Ibid.
261 "The Cabinet includes the Vice…   Https://www.whitehouse.gov/administration/cabinet.
261 "Perhaps the earliest large…   Wansley, (1971).
261 "the Investment Bankers…   Https://en.wikipedia.org/wiki/U.S._Securities_ and_Exchange_ Commission; Joel Seligman, The Transformation of Wall Street (Aspen), 2003, pp. 45, 51-52.
262 "the greatest racket…   O'Sullivan, (1933), p. 34.
262 "set a thief to catch…   Perino, (2010), p. 300.
263 "No government agency will…   Wansley, (1971).
263 "member of the Federal Trade…   Kenner, (1936), p. 190.
263 "The Chief Examiner of…   Ibid., 191.
263 "[a]ttorney in the Solicitor's…   Ibid.
263 "To your organization, the Better…   Ibid.
263 "It began conferences with…   Ibid., 253.
263 "The records of the Federal…   Ibid., 158.
264 "the actual organization and…   Ibid., 161.
264 "We look forward to the continuance…   Ibid., 162.
264 "C. Lee Peeler, deputy…   Adage.com/article/news/ftc-official-head-national-advertising-review-council/110707.
264 "C. Lee Peeler, Esq.,…   Bbb.org/council/about/council-of-better-business-bureaus/cbbb-management-team/c-leepeeler-cbbb-evp-and-pre.
264 "The FTC regards the council…   Ftc.gov/system/files/documents/ public_statements/1262563/pahl_-_nad_ keynote_10-3-17.pdf.
264 "the body that establishes…   Http://www.bbb.org/council/migration/bbbnews-releases/010/10/lee-peeler-named-narc-.

REFERENCES

264 "NAD/NARC/NARB's sole… Ibid.
265 "Bureau dues," 2013 annual report.
265 "National partner dues," Ibid.
265 "BBB programs" Ibid.
265 "CHANGE IN NET ASSETS" Ibid.
265 "the U.S. Secretary of Commerce… Https://www.commerce.gov/news/secretaryspeeches/2016/07/remarks-us-secretary-commerce-penny-pritzker-eu-us-privacy-shield.
265 "ensure access to the latest… Http://safeharbor.export.gov/companyinfo. aspx?id=17227.
265 "accepting certifications" Ibid.
265 "The decision by a U.S.-based… Https://www.commerce.gov/sites/commerce. gov/files/media/files/2016/how_to_join_privacy_ shield_sc_cmts.pdf.
265 "enhance privacy protections… Http://www.bbb.org/council/news-events/news-releases/2016/07/new-eu-u.s.-privacy-shield-adopted-to-support-trans-atlantic-digital-commerce.
265 "the agency could be used… Http://www.washingtonexaminer.com/america-to-hand-off-internet-in-under-two-months/ article/2599521.
266 "Clinton has promised… Http://thefederalist.com/2016/08/22/the-coming-free-speech-apocalypse.
266 "Rip-off Report supports… Http://www.ripoffreport.com/r/BetterBusiness-Bureau-BBB-CBBB/Arlington-SelectStateProvince/Better-Business-Bureau-or-Buyer-Better-Beware-BBB-Nationwide-Alert-THE-FOX-GUARDIN-1343.
266 "Why is the BBB listed… Ibid.
266 "The BBB is a Franchise… Http://www.ripoffreport.com/r/BetterBusiness-Bureau-BBB-CBBB/Arlington-SelectStateProvince/Better-Business-Bureau-or-Buyer-Better-Beware-BBB-Nationwide-Alert-THE-FOX-GUARDIN-1343.
266 "the Commission now enforces… Https://www.ftc.gov/sites/default/files/ attachments/ftc-90-symposium/90thanniv_ program.pdf; p. 9.
267 "The FTC encourages… Https://www.ftc.gov/news-events/mediaresources/identity-theft-and-data-security/filingcomplaint.
267 "Thank you for recent… Caryn Cain, FTC Letter Ref. No. 21633992, 2009.
268 "a staunch supporter… Https://en.wikipedia.org/wiki/Hugo_Black.

CHAPTER TWENTY-ONE: WORLD WAR I

Page
269 "Two rounds from one pistol… Marshall, (2001), p. vii.
269 "Young Bosnia" Https://en.wikipedia.org/wiki/Gavrilo_Princip.
269 "Austro-Hungarian rule… Ibid.
269 "creation of Yugoslavia… Https://en.wikipedia.org/wiki/World_War_I.
269 "be freed from Austria." Https://en.wikipedia.org/wiki/Gavrilo_Princip.
270 "in the prison of the court… *Duluth News Tribune*, "Executed for Crimes Causing World War," February 4, 1915, Front Page.
270 "a series of ten demands… Https://en.wikipedia.org/wiki/World_War_I; H. P. Willmott, World War I (New York, Dorling Kindersley), 2003, p. 27.
270 "partial mobilization… Https://en.wikipedia.org/wiki/World_War_I.
270 "to expand its sphere… Ibid.
270 "by United Kingdom of… Https://en.wikipedia.org/wiki/Treaty_of_ London_(1915).
270 "I order that unrestricted… Marshall, (2001), p. 275.
270 "an internal diplomatic … Ibid.
271 "U.S. Senate voted 82 to 6… Http://www.history.com/this-day-in-history/us-enters-world-war-I.
271 "by a vote of 373… Ibid.
271 "Committee on Public … Http://www.firstworldwar.com/bio/creel.htm.
271 "In only two years… Fox, (1984), p. 75.
271 "bulletins" *Printers' Ink*, (Vol. CV, No. 1, October 3, 1918), p. 86; https://books.google.com/books?id=rP-hG 4QanK0C&printsec=frontcover#v=onepage&q &f=false.
271 "Sergeant Jim Says… Ibid.

529

THE APO$TATE

271 "newspaper of the American... *Printers' Ink*, (1938), p. 290.
271 "was edited by Guy... Ibid.
271 "The Official Publication... *Stars and Stripes* ad, *Printers' Ink* (Vol. CV, No. 2, October 10, 1918), p. 13.
271 "Advertising Space Sold ... *Printers' Ink*, "Advertising Space Sold by the Inch," 1918.
271 "was delivered on the day... Ibid.
272 "agency of assistance in... Wansley, (1971).
272 "I Want YOU..." Https://en.wikipedia.org/wiki/James_ Montgomery_Flagg.
272 "a model" Ibid.
272 "U.S." Ibid.
272 "Uncle Sam." Ibid.
272 "gained him the moniker... Http://www.findagrave.com/cgi-bin/fg.cgi?page= gr&GSln=Wilson&G Sfn=Samuel&GSbyrel =in&GSdyrel=in&GSob=n&GRid=1114&]. [Findagravemarker1114.
272 "Most of the vigilance staff... Kenner, (1936), pp. 72, 79.
272 "labor-saving appliances" *Printers' Ink*, (1938), p. 303.
272 "power farming equipment." Ibid.
272 "the Government insisted... Ibid.
273 "national daylight saving... Ibid.
273 "as a means of providing... Ibid.
273 ""eleventh hour... Https://en.wikipedia.org/wiki/Armistice_Day.
273 "national commander of... Http://www.usmemorialday.org/?page_id=2.
273 "The 30th of May, 1868... Ibid.
273 "was intended to ensure... Http://www.va.gov/opa/vetsday/vetdayhistory. asp.
273 "sold the war to... *Printers' Ink*, (1938), p. 290.
273 "Both the Government and... Ibid.

CHAPTER TWENTY-TWO: PROHIBITION

Page
274 "to ban...whiskey." Ibid.
274 "Temperance Theater" Ibid.
274 "144 shows" Ibid.
274 "dead, wounded... Https://en.wikipedia.org/wiki/Battle_of_ Antietam.
275 "manufacture, sale... Http://www.archives.gov/exhibits/charters/ constitution_amendments_11-27.html#18.
275 "conceived and drafted" Https://en.wikipedia.org/wiki/Volstead_Act.
275 "to provide the government... Http://www.history.com/topics/18th-and-21st-amendments.
275 "TITLE II. PROHIBITION... Http://www.historycentral.com/documents/Volstead.html.
275 "Any person who manufactures... Ibid.
276 "No one but a physician... Ibid.
276 "Prescription Forms for... Https://www.atlasobscura.com/articles/doctorsbooze-notes-prohibition.
276 "medicinal alcohol... Https://www.smithsonianmag.com/history/during-prohibition-your-doctor-could-write-youprescription-booze-180947940.
276 "patient" Ibid.
276 "After February 1, 1920... Http://www.historycentral.com/documents/Volstead.html.
276 "Jones-Stalker Act" Https://en.wikipedia.org/wiki/Increased_ Penalties_Act.
276 "Jones Act," Ibid.
276 "CHAP. 473. An Act... Http://legisworks.org/sal/45/stats/STATUTE-45- Pg1446b.pdf.
277 "Coolidge Signs Bills... *New York Times*, "Coolidge Signs Bills for Stiff Dry Penalties; Two Are Arrested at Capital Under New Law," March 3, 1929, p. 3.
277 "liquor raids" Ibid.
277 "Eugene Liverpool and... Ibid.
277 "$3,000,000.00 additional... Ibid.
277 "drastic" *St. Louis Globe Democrat*, "Fifteen Dry Law Violators Sentenced," March 8, 1929, p. 3.

REFERENCES

277 "fifteen bartenders…   Ibid.
277 "illegal sale and possession…   Ibid.
278 "working-class poor"   Https://en.wikipedia.org/wiki/Prohibition_in_the_ United_States.
278 "President Harding kept…   Http://www.1920-30.com/prohibition.
278 "liquor runners."   *St. Louis Post Dispatch*, "Prohibition Agent Killed, Aid Shot, Two Others Hurt," June 17, 1930, Front Page.
278 "Fay Likens Higherups…   *Denver Post*, "Fay Likens Higherups and 'Pullmen' to Gangsters and His Clan," March 2, 1932.
278 "Underworld"   Ibid.
278 "Upperworld."   Ibid.
278 "When a racketeer's territory …   Ibid.
278 "'DEATH CAR' IN CHICAGO…   *St. Louis Globe-Democrat*, "'DEATH CAR' IN CHICAGO GANG MASSACRE FOUND," VOL 54, NO 279, February 22, 1929, Front Page.
279 "Business Bureau Explains…   Ibid.
279 "declared invalid any chattel…   Http://scholarship.law,.mikssouri.edu/mlr/vol16/iss3/3.
279 "salary buyers."   Ibid.
279 "Answering criticism…   *St. Louis Globe-Democrat*, "'DEATH CAR' IN CHICAGO GANG MASSACRE FOUND," VOL 54, NO 279, February 22, 1929, Front Page.
279 "The Bureau does have…   Ibid.
279 "moral decline"   Http://www.ohiohistorycentral.org/w/Anti-Saloon_ League_of_America?rec=845.
279 "Anti-Saloon League…   Ibid.
280 "The Anti-Saloon League's primary…   Http://www.ohiohistorycentral.org/w/Anti-Saloon_ League_of_America?rec=845.
280 "Carry-A-Nation."   Https://en.wikipedia.org/wiki/Carrie_Nation.
280 "hatchetations" Ibid.
280 "breaking saloon windows…   Http://www.history.com/topics/18th-and-21stamendments.
280 "by 1925 in New York City…   Http://www.archives.gov/education/lessons/ volstead-act.
280 "6000 speakeasies…   *St. Louis Post Dispatch*, "Police Shakeup Demanded Due To Murder Of Lingle," June 14, 1930, p. 4B.
280 "beer, whiskey…   Ibid.
280 "$5,785,000 is paid weekly…   Ibid.
280 "Including the speakeasies…   Ibid.
280 "an alliance between crime…   Ibid.
280 "liquor law violation…   *St. Louis Globe Democrat*, "6 Months, $1000 Fine for Ex-Police Chief," March 5, 1929, Front Page.
280 "the Boswell trial"   Ibid.
280 "six months in the Franklin…   Ibid.
280 "sent to the penitentiary."   Ibid.
280 "running pistol fight"   *St. Louis Post Dispatch*, "Prohibition Agent Killed, Aid Shot, Two Others Hurt," June 17, 1930, Front Page.
280 "an automobile they suspected…   Ibid.
280 "liquor runners"   Ibid.
280 "rear window."   Ibid.
280 "two small children."   Ibid.
281 "90 per cent of liquor…   The *Denver Post*, "Doctor Assails Bootlegging In Prescriptions," February 3, 1932, p. 3.
281 "bootlegging prescriptions…   Ibid.
281 "about $1,200…   Ibid.
281 "the lower half…   Ibid.
281 "were arrested by deputy…   The *Denver Post*, "Mayor And Police Chief Are Arrested," March 5, 1932, p. 2.
281 "in a conspiracy to violate…   Ibid.
281 "Prohibition's toll was grim…   Blumenthal, (2000), p. 121.

531

THE APO$TATE

281 "fifteen hundred Episcopal… *St. Louis Globe Democrat*, "Temperance Body Seeks to Modify Prohibition Law," February 18, 1929.
281 "more practical legislation… Ibid.
281 "all but a few… Ibid.
281 "Blue Laws" Http://www.history.com/topics/18th-and-21stamendments/videos/blue-laws.
281 "restrict alcohol sales… Ibid.

CHAPTER TWENTY-THREE: "BEFORE YOU INVEST, INVESTIGATE"

Page
283 "It was in 1919 that a change… O'Sullivan, (1933), p. 18.
283 "While legislation is being… Kenner, (1936), pp. 100-101.
284 "presidents of the leading… Ibid., 101.
284 "I am genuinely glad… Ibid.
284 "Cleveland plan" Kenner, (1936), p. 99.
284 "This phrase was suggested… Ibid.
284 "wage-earners through… Ibid.
284 "to protect wage-earning… Ibid., 100.
284 "in cooperation with the investors'… Ibid., 106.
284 "draw a state law which… Ibid., 97.
284 "The Act was not a licensing… Ibid.
285 "worthless certificates." Ibid., 98.
285 "The actual line-up existing… O'Sullivan, (1933), pp. 34-35.
286 "lent more than tacit support… Ibid., 20.
286 "The nation was about to… Ibid., 18.
286 "So the Better Business Bureaus… Ibid., 19.
286 "…the public was enabled… Ibid., 60.
286 "By the mid-1920s one of… Kyvig, (2004), p. 28.

CHAPTER TWENTY-FOUR: STOCK MARKET CRASH

Page
287 "16,410,030 shares." Frederick Lewis Allen, *Only Yesterday* (New York, Harper Perennial Modern Classics), 2010, p. 290.
287 "$14 billion" Http://www.blacktuesday.org.
287 "$30 billion in… Ibid.
287 "It was a record… Https://www.senate.gov/artandhistory/history/ common/investigations/Pecora.htm.
287 "On July 8, 1932… Http://www.blacktuesday.org.
287 "nearly 10,000 banks… Https://www.federalreserveeducation.org/aboutthe-fed/history.
287 "Wall Street and the banking… Geisst, (1997), p. 182.
287 "the Regius Poem… Masonic Service Association of North America; www.msana.com/historyfm.asp.
288 "Jolly Roger," Https://www.ancient-origins.net./history/ultimate-pirate-branding-symbol-origin-jolly-roger-002696.
288 "By August 1929, brokers… Https://en.wikipedia.org/wiki/Wall_Street_ Crash_of_1929; Richard Lambert (July 19, 2008).
288 "by selling agricultural … Geisst, (1997), p. 200.
289 "The Wall Street interests… O'Sullivan, (1933), p. 26.
289 "authorizing the Committee… Https://www.senate.gov/artandhistory/history/ common/investigations/Pecora.htm.
289 "Senate Democrats scored… Https://www.senate.gov/history/1921.htm.
289 "Seventy-third Congress" Https://www.senate.gov/artandhistory/history/ common/investigations/pdf/Pecora_FinalReport. pdf.
289 "INVESTIGATION OF BANKING… Https://www.senate.gov/artandhistory/history/ common/investigations/pdf/Pecora_SenRes56. pdf.

REFERENCES

290 "to investigate the matter… Ibid.
290 "Such legislation shall… Https://www.senate.gov/artandhistory/history/ common/investigations/pdf/Pecora_FinalReport. pdf.
290 "It should be noted… Ibid.
290 "because of "its recognized… Https://www.senate.gov/artandhistory/history/ common/investigations/Pecora.htm.
290 "abusive securities practices… Https://scholarship.law.gwu.edu/cgi/viewcontent. cgi?referer=&https redir=1&article=2477&context =faculty_publications,p. 1289.
290 "unsound and deceptive… Ibid.
290 "high-risk securities," Ibid.
290 "ill-advised loans" Ibid.
290 "speculative securities." Ibid.
290 "Investment Bankers Association… Kenner, (1936), p. 64.
290 "well established" Ibid.
290 "close cooperation" Ibid.
290 "then advertising director… Ibid., 31.
291 "George W. Hodges, former… Ibid., 104.
291 "a series of conferences… Ibid.
291 "the leading trade association… Https://www.sifma.org/about.
291 "more than $185 trillion… Https://www.investopedia.com/terms/s/sifma. asp.
291 "an investment banking… Https://www.sifma.org/wp-content/uploads/2016/12/sifma-history-2017.pdf.
291 "separated commercial… Http://www.federalreservehistory.org/Events/ DetailView/25.
292 "created the Federal Deposit… Ibid.
292 "This Committee, actuated… Stock Exchange Practices Report Of The Committee On Banking And Currency; Submitted by Chairman Duncan Upshaw Fletcher; June 16, 1934, p. 394.
292 "The merchant banks lent… Http://economics.emory.edu/home/documents/ workingpapers/fohlin_14_16_paper.pdf; p. 3.
292 "Although a few traders… Geisst, (2000), p. 36.
292 "Bank Closes After Suicide," *St. Louis Post-Dispatch*, "Bank Closes After Suicide," June 30, 1930.
292 "Brooklyn business man, fell… *St. Louis Globe Democrat*, "Man Leaps Twenty Stories to Death," Associated Press, July 23, 1930.
292 "an official of the Commonwealth … Ibid.
293 "had offices as an "employment… *The New York American*, "Work 'Counsel' Ends Own Life," October 1, 1931.
293 "recent business losses." Ibid.
293 "from a window in his office… *The New York American*, "15-Story Fall Kills Broker," October 1, 1931.
293 "extricate the body." Ibid.
293 "Mexican Repatriation" Https://en.wikipedia.org/wiki/Herbert_Hoover; https://hoover.blogs.archives.gov/2016/08/04/ hoover-on-immigration.
293 "forced migration…" Ibid.
293 "until 1936" Ibid.
293 "in South Korea in 1951… Https://en.wikipedia.org/wiki/Shir%C5%8D_ Ishii.
293 "shacktowns and homeless… Http://depts.washington.edu/depress/hooverville. shtml.
294 "Hooverville[s]" Ibid.
294 "Hoover blankets." Geisst, (1997), p. 200.
294 "1931 to 1941" Http://depts.washington.edu/depress/hooverville. shtml.
294 "nine acres of… Ibid.
294 "state level anti-fraud statutes… Http://www.investopedia.com/exam-guide/ series-7/securities-markets/blue-sky-laws.asp.
294 "observed that certain fraudulent… Https://en.wikipedia.org/wiki/Blue_sky_law.
294 "addressed the constitutionality" Ibid.

533

THE APO$TATE

294 "issued a bulletin to...   *Associated Advertising*, "Newspapers Shut Out Unsanctioned Promotions"(Vol. 10, No. 8, August 1919), p. 46.
294 "The Better Business Bureaus...   O'Sullivan, (1933), p. 20.
294 "Thus the Better Business Bureaus...   Ibid., 60.
295 "It was 1919...   Ibid., 18-19.
295 "on special posters in industrial...   Kenner, (1936), p. 100.
295 "This gave him time...   Ibid.
295 "Then the National Better Business...   O'Sullivan, (1933), p. 16.
295 "This was the situation when...   Kenner, (1936), pp. 109-110.
296 "Where a Better Business Bureau has...   Ibid., 267.
296 "Since the collapse of...   O'Sullivan, (1933), p. 28.
297 "president of the National...   Kenner, (1936), p. 140.
297 "a governor"   Ibid., 141.
297 "also president of the New...   Ibid.
297 "Trowbridge Callaway...   Ibid., 262.
297 "defend the law."   Ibid., 53.
297 "the Better Business Bureau, as a tool...   O'Sullivan, (1933), p. 124.
297 "The year 1930 saw...   Ibid., 105.
297 "He stole funds...   Http://en.wikipedia.org/wiki/Richard_Whitney_ (financier).

CHAPTER TWENTY-FIVE: LOGAN BILLINGSLEY

Page
298 "president of the Bronx...   Http://www.nycgovparks.org/parks/beanstalkplayground/history.
299 "December 5, 1933,"   Http://constitution.laws.com/21st-amendment.
299 "Section 70 Business Law"   O'Sullivan, (1933), p. 94.
299 "intimate connection of...   Ibid., 34.
299 "the crooked banker...   Ibid., 35.
300 "Senate Congressional Record...   Ibid.
300 "In addition to the federal...   Http://www.sec.gov/answers/bluesky.htm.
300 "December 20, 1882[,]"   Http://www.findagrave.com/cgi-bin/fg.cgi?page= gsr&GSfn=Logan&GSmn=&GSln=Billingsley& GSbyrel=in&GSby=1882&GSdyrel=in&GSdy=1 963&GScntry=4&GSst=38&GScnty=0&GSgrid =&df=all&GSob=n.
300 "Claiborne County, Tennessee"   Blumenthal, (2000), p. 66.
300 "six feet tall, straight as...   Ibid.
301 "several defendants"   *St Louis Globe Democrat*, "Gets 18 Months and $1500 Fine for Liquor Making," June 10, 1930, Front Page.
301 "to the manufacture...   Ibid.
301 "it was better to make...   Ibid., 8.
301 "bootlegging was the only ...   Ibid.
301 "June 1904,"   Blumenthal, (2000), p. 70.
301 "Chloe Wheatley"   Ibid.
301 "Andrew,"   Ibid.
301 "two large knives"   Ibid.
301 ".45 double-barrel pistol"   Ibid.
301 "through the heart."   Ibid.
301 "self-defense."   Ibid., 71.
301 "a little red wagon"   Ibid., 65.
302 "forbidden alcohol."   Ibid.
302 "fifty cents a bottle"   Ibid.
302 "saloons."   Ibid.
302 "the University of Oklahoma"   Ibid., 73.
302 "in the Indian service."   Ibid.
302 "a gallon a month,"   Ibid.

REFERENCES

302 "by the pint or...   Ibid.
302 "operating a gambling...   Ibid.
302 "city's largest bootlegging...   Ibid., 76.
303 "by a streetcar"   Ibid., 77.
303 "descendent of Francis...   Ibid., 91.
303 "many apartment houses"   Http://forgotten-ny.com/2008/03/universityheights-bronx.
303 "Prohibition agents"   Https://untappedcities.com/2014/07/10/vintage-nyc-photography-the-swanky-stork-club-where-hemingway-the-vanderbilts-and-the-kennedys-hobnobbed.
303 "was the place where actors...   Ibid.
303 "Walter Winchell on...   *Denver Post*, March 4, 1932, p. 19.
303 "New York's New Yorkiest...   Http://lostpastremembered.blogspot.com/2014/12/new-years-stork-club-and-chicken-la.html.
303 "October 4, 1965."   Https://untappedcities.com/2014/07/10/vintage-nyc-photography-the-swanky-stork-club-where-hemingway-the-vanderbilts-and-the-kennedys-hobnobbed.
304 "built Columbia Broadcasting...   Https://en.wikipedia.org/wiki/William_S._Paley.
304 "over 100,000"   O'Sullivan, (1933), p. 109.
304 "served on Mayor James...   Http://forgotten-ny.com/2008/03/university-heights-bronx.
304 "In 1927, [Logan] spearheaded...   Ibid.
304 "We have 246 publications...   O'Sullivan, (1933), pp. 62-63.
304 "April 1930,"   Blumenthal, (2000), p. 129.
305 "racket."   Ibid.
305 "January 1931,"   Ibid.
305 "the Better Business Bureau was...   O'Sullivan, (1933), p. 93.
305 "dirty judge"   *St. Louis Post Dispatch*, "Judge, Indicted, Resigns," June 9, 1930, p.2.
305 "grand larceny, mail fraud ...   Ibid.
305 "Vause is charged ...   *St. Louis Post Dispatch*, "Ex-Judge On Trial For Mail Fraud Weeps In Court," June 17, 1930, p. 2A.
305 "attempted to bribe...   Ibid.
305 "attempted to have an operation...   Ibid.
305 "The public paid approximately ...   *St. Louis Globe Democrat*, June 1, 1930, front page.
305 "muleted from the public....   Ibid.
306 "[T]hat during the five months'...   Ibid.
306 "The Billingsley letter"   O'Sullivan, (1933), pp. 31-32.
306 "challenged"   Ibid., 30.
306 "We are endeavoring to bring...   Ibid., 30-31.
306 "As the Senatorial committee...   Ibid., 35.
307 "1. When the Stock Exchange...   Ibid., 28-29.
308 "formal charges...   Ibid., 33.
308 "Mr. Billingsley's prediction...   Ibid., 31.
308 "over the years"   Blumenthal, (2000), p. 129.
308 "file"   Ibid.
308 "disappeared,"   Ibid.
308 "racket"   O'Sullivan, (1933), p. 34.
308 "Fiorello."   Http://en.wikipedia.org/wiki/Fiorello_H._La_Guardia.
308 "Little Flower,"   Ibid.
308 "a coalition opposed...   Http://www.virtualny.cuny.edu/EncyNYC/tammany_hall.html.
308 "block"   Ibid.
308 "Roosevelt heavily funded...   Http://en.wikipedia.org/wiki/Fiorello_H._La_Guardia.
309 "milk bottle thieves,"   O'Sullivan, (1933), p. 45.
309 "proficient liar,"   Ibid., 38.
309 "racket."   Ibid., 34.
310 "National Hall of Fame...   Http://www.bizapedia.com/people/NEW-YORK/NEW-YORK/LOGAN-BILLINGSLEY.html.

THE APO$TATE

310 "132 ½ W Bdwy...   Ibid.
310 "executive director."   Http://forgotten-ny.com/2008/03/universityheights-bronx; http:// www.findagrave.com/cgi-bin/fg.cgi?page=pv&G Rid=64037881&PIpi=71649374.
310 "the Association of American Indian...   Ibid.
310 "Southern Plains Indian...   *Anadarko Tribune*, Billingsley Obituary, AUGUST1963.

CHAPTER TWENTY-SIX: EDWIN CLARENCE RIEGEL

Page
312 "Free exchange"   Http://newapproachtofreedom.info/ffi/editorial. htm.
312 "He traced the massive...   Ibid.
312 "Zuckriegel."   Ibid.
312 "non-academic student....   Ibid.
312 "libertarian"   Ibid.
312 "distinguished personal...   Ibid.
312 "Edwin Controversy Riegel"   Ibid.
312 "Uncle Ned"   Ibid.
313 "individualism,"   Ibid.
313 "separation of money...   Ibid.
313 "The Camorra is a responsibly...   Ibid.
313 "Neighborhood Enforcement...   Ibid.
313 "that jobs and charity...   Https://hoover.blogs.archives.gov/2016/08/04/hoover-on-immigration.
313 "In the late 1920s, about 60,000...   Ibid.
314 "The purpose of the Consumers...   Http://newapproachtofreedom.info/ffi/editorial. html.
314 "a phamplet"   O'Sullivan, (1933), p. 23.
314 ""operating program" presented...   Ibid.
314 "From our experience," – said...   Ibid.
314 "exempted from the....   Http://newapproachtofreedom.info/ffi/editorial. html.
314 "During World War I, some western...   Geisst, (1997), p. 163.
315 "The Stock Exchange is interested....   O'Sullivan, (1933), pp. 26-27.

CHAPTER TWENTY-SEVEN: SENATOR DUNCAN UPSHAW FLETCHER

Page
317 "State house of representatives"   Http://www.everglades.fiu.edu/reclaim/bios/ fletcher.htm.
317 "as chairman of the board of public...   Ibid.
317 "chairman, Committee on Printing...   Http://bioguide.congress.gov/scripts/biodisplay. pl?index=f000200. "as chairman of the United States...   Http://www.everglades.fiu.edu/reclaim/bios/ fletcher.htm.
317 "a delegate to the International...   Ibid.
317 "before five departments...   O'Sullivan, (1933), pp. 37-38.
317 "Better Business Bureau system"   Ibid., 37.
318 "Charges of unlawful...   Ibid., 33.
318 "We shall file briefs and evidence...   Ibid., 38.
318 "Chairman of the Board...   Ibid., 30.
318 "to a debate before the Syracuse...   Ibid.
318 "We are endeavoring...   Ibid., 30-31.
319 "would interfere with...   Ibid., 31.
319 "Representative A. J. Sabath...   Ibid.
319 "Mr. Logan Billingsley, Chairman...   Ibid.
319 "My dear Mr. Billingsley...   Ibid., 31-32.
320 "From the nature of the charges...   Ibid., 63.
320 "The unsavory testimony coming ...   Ibid., 34-35.
320 "The remarks of Senator Fletcher...   Ibid., 35.
320 "The daily press shows...   Ibid., 34.

REFERENCES

320 "millions of dollars... Ibid.,34.
320 "hired a new chief counsel... Http://www.senate.gov/artandhistory/history/common/investigations/Pecora.htm.
321 "Standards of Practice of... Kenner, (1936), p. 288.
321 "Stock Exchange Practices... Http://www.senate.gov/artandhistory/history/ common/investigations/pdf/Pecora_FinalReport. pdf.
321 "Fletcher Report." Geisst, (1997), p. 205.
321 "concentration of control... Stock Exchange Practices Report, Chairman Duncan U. Fletcher, June 16, 1934, p. 333.
321 "Attempts have been made... Ibid., 32.
321 "The testimony before... Ibid.
321 "truth in securities law," Https://www.sec.gov/about/laws.shtml.
322 "During the year 1920... Stock Exchange Practices Report, Chairman Duncan U. Fletcher, June 16, 1934, p. 33.
322 "Alleghany Corporation; Allegheny... Ibid.
323 "In 1932, two issues... Ibid.
323 "Coca-Cola Co., S.S. Kreage... Ibid.
323 "Richard Whitney, president... Https://en.wikipedia.org/wiki/Ferdinand_Pecora.
323 "Mitchell more than any... *Time* Magazine, "Damnation of Mitchell," March 6, 1933; http://content.time.com/time/ magazine/article/0,9171,745272-1,00.html.
323 "was arrested and indicted... Https://en.wikipedia.org/wiki/Charles_E._ Mitchell.
323 "but the government won ... Ibid.
324 "The "preferred list"... Stock Exchange Practices Report, Chairman Duncan U. Fletcher, June 16, 1934, p. 103.
324 "that National City sold off ... Https://en.wikipedia.org/wiki/Ferdinand_Pecora.
324 "the banking committee... O'Sullivan, (1933), p. 88.
324 "We are trying to find... Ibid.
325 "These Individuals are... Ibid.
325 "Capitol" Https://www.encyclopedia-titanica.org/community/threads/senator-duncanfletcher.29541.
325 "was the longest serving... Https://en.wikipedia.org/wiki/Duncan_U._ Fletcher.

CHAPTER TWENTY-EIGHT: FRANK DALTON O'SULLIVAN

Page
326 "You're an iconoclast... O'Sullivan, (1933), p. 51.
327 "the greatest racket... Ibid., 34.
327 "I have sold over... Ibid., 51.
327 "earmarks of which a racket ... Ibid., 63.
327 "1. A secret membership... Ibid., 63-64.
327 "Membership in the Bureau... Ibid., 27.
327 "...alleged news...gave... Ibid., 106.
328 "he refused to be scared... Ibid., 48-52.
328 "Thus we find that the New ... Ibid., 27.
329 "What facilities had the average... Ibid., 18-19.
329 "predominantly Republican" Http://en.wikipedia.org/wiki/History_of_ Wisconsin.
329 "As I write this sketch... O'Sullivan, (1928), p. 416.
330 "In 1908 I had an idea... Ibid., vii.
330 "second metropolis" Ibid., viii.
330 "crime capital..." Ibid.
330 "twenty years." Ibid.
330 "The detective profession... Ibid., 1.
330 "Hoodlum – Gangster... O'Sullivan, Enemies (1933), p. 48.
330 "Gangsters should be shot... Ibid., 19.

537

330 "working newspaperman"   O'Sullivan, (1928), p. 415.
330 "For more than twenty years...   Ibid., viii.
331 "Today, as I glance...   Ibid., ix.
331 "decreased by one third"   Http://en.wikipedia.org/wiki/New_Deal.
331 "Within ten days after...   O'Sullivan, Enemies (1933), pp. 102-103.
332 "The American economy ...   Http://en.wikipedia.org/wiki/Recession_ of_1937%E2%80%9338.
333 "When a band of storm-tossed...   O'Sullivan, (1936), Prologue vii.
333 "This country is overrun...   O'Sullivan, (1928), p. 275.
333 "Reform organizations may...   Ibid., 278.
334 "Wonder when this ...   Ibid., 279.
334 "the most unsuccessful...   Ibid., vii.
334 "In my opinion this...   Ibid., 527.
334 "[T]he proper way to cope...   Ibid.
334 "In Chicago, New York...   Ibid.
335 "Arbor Day"   Http://en.wikipedia.org/wiki/Joy_Morton.
335 "literary workshop"   Ballowe, (2009), p. 254.
335 "the Santa Fe Building"   Http://en.wikipedia.org/wiki/Santa_Fe_ Building_(Chicago).
335 "Chicago style"   Ibid.
335 "biographer."   Ballowe, (2009), p. 254.
335 "private edition,"   Ibid.
335 "If too many cooks...   Ibid.
336 "The Stock Exchange Reform...   *Brooklyn Daily Eagle*, "Asks Senate Probe Probers," February 9, 1933.
336 "prominent Democrats...   Http://en.wikipedia.org/wiki/Anti-Saloon_League.
336 "Beer should be sold...   O'Sullivan, Enemies (1933), p. 94.
336 "Racketeering has become...   Ibid., 96.
336 "Capone gang's "board...   Ibid., 97.
336 "The hoodlums foresee...   Ibid., 98.
336 "I am just a businessman...   Http://en.wikipedia.org/wiki/Al_Capone.
336 "All I do is satisfy...   Ibid.
336 "Century of Progress Exposition,"   Http://www.cityclicker.net/chicfair.
337 "World's Columbian Exposition."   Http://muse.jhu.edu/journals/tech/summary/ v051/51.1.houltz.html.
337 "technological innovation"   Https://en.wikipedia.org/wiki/Century_of_ Progress.
337 "Science Finds, Industry Applies...   Http://muse.jhu.edu/journals/tech/summary/ v051/51.1.houltz.html.
337 "Fountain of Progress"   Ibid.
337 "two humans, male and female...   Ibid.
337 "Secret Six"   O'Sullivan, (1933), p. 67.
337 "resembles the Better...   Ibid., 67-68.
337 "The director of the "Secret Six,"...   Ibid., 69.
337 "group of crime-fighting...   Http://en.wikipedia.org/wiki/Timeline_of_ organized_crime_in_Chicago.
337 "Corrupt Chicago Mayor Anton...   Ibid.
337 "100,000,000 Guinea Pigs...   Arthur Kallet and F. J. Schlink,100,000,000 Guinea Pigs: Dangers in Everyday foods, Drugs, and Cosmetics, The Vanguard Press, 1933.
338 "100 Most Influential...   Http://100greatestamericans.org/?page_id=208.
338 "bachelor's degree in mechanical...   Dennis Dimond, "Research Pioneer Awakened Consumers," *Journal Star*, Peoria, Illinois, October 27, 1981.
338 "worked as an associate...   Ibid.
338 "a consumer product-testing...   Gregory L. Williams, "Records of Consumers' Research, Inc., Special Collections and University Archives, Rutgers University Libraries, January 1995.
338 "scurrilous publication."   O'Sullivan, (1936), back dust cover.
338 "Communist"   Ibid., 92.

REFERENCES

338 "always had an eye...   Ibid., 90.
338 "American City Has Ordinance...   Ibid.
338 "self-appointed critics...   Ibid., back cover.
338 "Note: It is somewhat...   Ibid.
339 "Probably the most notorious...   Wansley, (1971).
339 "long-time assistant,"   Ibid.
339 "In 1917, America entered...   Http://www.history.com/this-day-inhistory/19th-amendment-adopted.
339 "Deaths and Stillbirths Index...   Http://en.wikipedia.org/wiki/Proviso_Township_Cook_County_Illinois.
340 "by the issuance of...   O'Sullivan, (1933), p. 123.
340 "The Better Business Bureau system...   Ibid., 124.
340 "we must invoke the Lord...   Ibid., 128.
340 "We have other information...   Ibid.

CHAPTER TWENTY-NINE: HURNARD JAY KENNER

Page
342 "Probably no one single...   Wansley, (1971).
343 "muckraker."   Kenner, (1936), p. 262.
343 "detractors,"   Ibid., 264.
343 "destructionists,"   Ibid.
343 "fanatics,"   Ibid.
343 "cynics,"   Ibid., 264.
343 "business-baiters"   Ibid.
343 "scurrilous slander in...   Ibid.
344 "newspaper man and advertising...   The_Political_Economy_of_Truth_in_Advert. pdf.
344 "BBB annual convention"   Http://www.tiki-toki.com/timeline/entry/10778/Better-Business-ureau/#vars!panel=132840!.
344 "In the years prior to 1914...   Http://alphahistory.com/weimarrepublic/worldwar-i.
344 "educated in the Chicago...   Auchincloss, (1927), p. 7.
345 "German and Jewish...   Http://www.ancestry.com/nameorigin?surname=kenner.
345 "German: habitational name...   Ibid.
345 "UK Incoming...   Http://search.ancestry.com/cgi-bin/sse.dll?rank=1&new=1&MSAV=0&msT=1&gss=angs-c&gsln=Hurnard&uidh=000&gl=40&gst=&ghc=20&fh=20&bsk=BEFq368IgAALtQCcsRw-61-.
345 "Vigilance Committee of the Minneapolis...   Wansley, (1971).
345 "Secretary H. J. Kenner"   *Aberdeen Weekly American*, "Boosters Rule at Devils Lake," Friday, March 21, 1913, p. 4.
345 "boosters" group holding...   Ibid.
345 "spent his early career...   *The Business History Review*, Vol. 83, No. 1, "Private Cops on the Fraud Beat," Edward J. Balleisen, 2009, p. 122.
345 "to make investigations...   Kenner, (1936), pp. 55-56.
345 "A prominent retail clothier...   Ibid., 53.
346 "first chairman"   Ibid., 65.
346 "untrue and misleading...   Ibid.
346 "the Vigilance Committees merged...   Advertising Federation of America, (1936), p. 20.
346 "a great gathering of advertising...   Kenner, (1936), p. 60.
346 "The only thing that...   Ibid.
346 "On Sale - $9.98"   Ibid., 63.
346 "the skit depicted...   Ibid.
346 "This playlet, with changes...   Ibid., 64.
347 "Will Everwork, Bureau...   Ibid., 63.
347 "two years"   *Duluth News Tribune*, "Kenner Acts As A Watchman," February 8, 1920, p. 9.

THE APO$TATE

347 "retail advertising"   Kenner, (1936), p. 70.
347 "Northwestern Knitting Co.,"   *Associated Advertising* Magazine (Vol. 10, No. 7, July 1919), p. 36.
347 "St. Louis in May…   Kenner, (1936), p. 71.
347 "a broad national campaign…   Kenner, (1936), pp. 100-101.
347 "Business Men's Anti-Stock…   Ibid., 101.
347 "July 1, 1919,"   *Associated Advertising* Magazine, "H. J. Kenner Returns to Vigilance Department Work" (Vol. 10, No. 7, July 1919), p. 37.
347 "Mr. Kenner's coming…   Ibid.
348 ""blue sky" commissioners"   *Editor and Publisher*, "Ad Vigilantes Meet In Chicago July 10-11" (Volume 52, Part 1, June 26, 1919), p. 11.
348 "Bricks That Build Walls…   *Associated Advertising* Magazine (Vol. 10, No. 7, July 1919), p. 14.
348 "The Danger Line in…   Kenner, (1936), p. 138.
348 "security gyps"   Ibid.
348 "announced an agreement…   Ibid.
348 "a code of practice…   Ibid.
349 "also known as…   Http://en.wikipedia.org/wiki/1924_Democratic_ National_Convention.
349 "Madison Square Garden…   Ibid.
349 "over 50 votes from…   Http://www.rootsweb.ancestry.com/~sclancas/ bios/lenasprings.htm. 349 "beautiful,"   Ibid.
349 "level-headed,"   Ibid.
349 "as the hit…   Ibid.
349 "Oh, You Beautiful Doll"   Ibid.
349 "The message from…   Advertising Federation of America, (1936), "Message From His Excellency."
349 "almost a department of…   O'Sullivan, (1933), p. 28.
349 "since the collapse of…   Ibid.
350 "against the Better Business Bureau"   Ibid., 38.
350 ""undesirable" publicity"   Ibid., 105.
350 "Better Business Bureau Head…   Ibid.
350 "for alleged damages…   *New York Herald-Tribune*, "Better Business Bureau Head Under Bail in Suit – Kenner Freed on $5,000 Bail," January 12, 1928.
350 "was based on the claiming…   Ibid.
350 "it was libeled in a…   Ibid.
351 "obtained a temporary injunction…   Ibid.
351 "Thief Caught - He Charges…   O'Sullivan, (1933), p. 104.
351 "known criminal"   *New York Evening World*, "Thief Caught – He Charges Better Business Bureau Ordered Burglary…," January 26, 1929.
351 "denied that they knew…   Ibid.
351 "boosting certain stocks"   Ibid.
351 "arrested by postal authorities…   Ibid.
351 "employing high-pressure…   Kenner, (1936), p. 106.
351 "head of the promotion"…   Ibid.
352 "planned to unload…   Ibid.
352 "Beadon and his colleagues…   Ibid.
352 "the corporation was forced…   Ibid.
352 "The promotion was nipped…   Ibid., 106-107.
352 "This law exempts securities…   O'Sullivan, (1933), p. 35.
352 "to investigate suspected…   Kenner, (1936), p. 97.
353 "Business Bureau Criticized –…   O'Sullivan, (1933), p. 105.
353 "that there is "no mechanism…   *New York World*, "Better Business Bureau Criticized – General system Opposed – Report Attacks Activities of Paid Managers," September 15, 1930, p. 8.
353 "The New York bureau, the report…   Ibid.
353 "The Better Business Bureau system…   *New York World*, "Better Business Bureau Criticized – General system Opposed – Report Attacks Activities of Paid Managers," September 15, 1930, p. 8.

REFERENCES

353 "The year 1930 saw... O'Sullivan, (1933), p. 105.
354 "Unfairness Charged – ... Ibid.
354 "Sale of Blue-Sky... Ibid.
355 "The Denver Better Business... Ibid.
355 "Better Business Bureau Bunk... Ibid.
355 "as an institution pretending... *Pittsburgh National Labor Tribune*, "Better Business Bureau Bunk and False Pretenses," March 31, 1932.
355 "charity racketeers took... Ibid.
355 "A large department store"... Ibid.
355 "for 800 girls" Ibid.
355 "shoppers" Ibid.
355 "racketeers or fake... Ibid.
355 "It was just an advertising... Ibid.
355 "an opportunity to break... O'Sullivan, (1933), p. 106.
355 "attempted to plant... Ibid., 45.
356 "the probe by the Senatorial... Ibid., 31.
356 "First New Deal" Millercenter.org/president/fdroosevelt/domesticaffairs.
356 "original issues" En.wikipedia.org/wiki/Securities_Exchange_Act_of_1934.
356 "primary market." Ibid.
356 "An act To provide for the regulation... Ibid.
356 "secondary trading... Ibid.
356 "aftermarket" En.wikipedia.org/wiki/Secondary_market.
356 "stocks, bonds, options... Ibid.
356 "power to approve stock... Http://www.sechistorical.org/museum/timeline.
357 "the Texas oil industry." Http://spartacus-educational.com/JFKcorcoran.htm.
357 "built on his wartime... Https://en.wikipedia.org/wiki/Joseph_P._Kennedy,_Sr.
357 "Haig & Haig Scotch... Ibid.
357 "Early in 1929, the National... Kenner, (1936), p. 159.
357 "National Fraud Conference" Ibid., 160
358 "These groups had long ... Ibid., 160.
358 "to develop further... Ibid., 159.
359 "accepted" Ibid., 161.
359 "The Commission accepted... Ibid.
359 "Securities Violations Section... Ibid.
359 "Bulletins" Ibid.
359 "law-enforcement agencies... Ibid.
359 "engaged in the sale... Ibid.
359 "The Securities and Exchange... Ibid., 162.
359 "the greatest racket... O'Sullivan, (1933), p. 34.
360 "The affair was largely... *Aberdeen Weekly American*, "Boosters Rule at Devil's Lake," March 21, 1913, p. 4.
360 "H. J. Kenner, secretary... *Duluth News Tribune*, "Would Discard 'Caveat Emptor': H. J. Kenner of Minneapolis Speaks to Duluth Ad Men and Retail Merchants," February 3, 1915.
360 "We believe that untruth... Ibid.
360 "Seeking to Protect the Public... *Kansas City Times*, "Truth Is The Rule In Ads: Advertising Fakers Are Passing H. J. Kenner says," November 10, 1915.
360 "the better advertising... Ibid.
360 "secretary of the National... Ibid.
360 "Honest advertisers and... Ibid.
360 "Mr. Kenner left the... *Associated Advertising* Magazine, "H. J. Kenner Returns to Vigilance Department Work" (Vol. 10, No. 7, July 1919), pp. 36-37.
361 "His brilliant record... *Duluth News Tribune*, "Kenner Acts As A Watchman, Vigilance Official Re-Enlists With Associated Advertising Clubs of World," February 8, 1920.

THE APO$TATE

361 "H. J. Kenner, in his excellent...   Advertising Federation of America, (1936), p. 26.
361 "The Committee on "History...   Kenner, (1936), Acknowledgments, p. vii.
361 "H. J. Kenner, New York...   Ibid., Acknowledgments, p. viii.
361 "the Cradle of Liberty."   Http://en.wikipedia.org/wiki/Faneuil_Hall.
361 "fænəl"   Ibid.
361 "bounded by Congress Street...   Http://en.wikipedia.org/wiki/Dock_Square_ (Boston).
361 "Declaring renewed...   Kenner, (1936), p. 269.
362 "BBB Standards For Trust"   Https://www.bbb.org/standards-for-trust.
362 "In their long history...   Wansley, (1971); https://www.bbb.org/oklahomacity/get-to-know-us/history-and-traditions.
362 "manufacturing magnificence,"   Kenner, (1936), p. 73.
362 "oil pirates,"   Ibid., 89.
362 "wolf packs,"   Ibid., 113.
362 "financial parasites,"   Ibid.
362 "security gyps,"   Ibid., 137.
362 "minions of Wall Street,"   Ibid., 132.
362 "snooping rats,"   Ibid.
362 "sucker-money,"   Ibid., 131.
362 "land sharks,"   Ibid., 123
362 "white-collar bandits,"   Ibid., 148.
362 "ghoulish gentry,"   Ibid., 151.
362 "tipster-sheet and boiler-room...   Ibid., 153.
362 "In their long history...   Wansley, (1971).
363 "spreading scurrilous slander...   Kenner, (1936), p. 264.
363 "racketeer"   Wansley, (1971).
363 "war chest"   Ibid.
363 "This writer has had...   Kenner, (1936), p. 261.
363 "muck-rakers"   Ibid., 262.
363 "propagandists"   Ibid.
363 "probably the most...   Wansley, (1971).
363 "This volume relates...   Kenner, (1936), p. 262.
364 "The Better Business Bureaus are not...   Ibid., 265.
364 "The so-called Better Business...   O'Sullivan, (1933), pp. 61-62.
364 "Années folles"...   Http://en.wikipedia.org/wiki/Années_folles.
365 "[I]t has benefited by...   Kenner, (1936), p. 272.
365 "Even though it seems...   Ibid., 261.
366 "masqueraders,"   Ibid., x.
366 "wolves in sheep's...   Ibid.
366 "security gyps,"   Ibid., 137.
366 "fakers,"   Ibid., 142.
366 "tricky trading."   Ibid., 179.
366 "at the end of 1947."   *The New York Times*, "H.J. Kenner, Ex-Head Here of Better Business Bureau," January 9, 1973, p. 42.
366 "1955...Minneapolis hosts...   Http://www.tiki-toki.com/timeline/entry/10778/Better-Business-Bureau/#vars!panel=132840!.

CHAPTER THIRTY: JOHN JAMES BENNETT JR.

Page
368 "September 4, 1923,"   *The American Catholic, Who's Who* 1946-1947, Volume 7 (Seventh Biennial Edition), Walter Romig, Publisher, Michigan, 1931, p. 19.
368 "Elks Knights of Columbus...   Ibid.
369 "chair of the Kings County...   Https://en.wikipedia.org/wiki/John_H._McCooey.
369 "joined Tammany Hall...   Ibid.

542

REFERENCES

369 "BENNETT REPORTED M'COOEY... *The New York Times*, "Bennett Reported M'Cooey Candidate," September 19, 1930.
369 "Commander-in-Chief of... Https://en.wikipedia.org/wiki/Hamilton_Ward_ Jr.
370 "An attempt was made... O'Sullivan, (1933), p. 93.
370 "My conclusion is... Ibid., 94.
370 "This brings up a grave... Ibid.
370 "The legal point thus... Ibid., 94-95.
370 "If it is your intention.... Ibid., 94.
370 "no license was taken out... Ibid.
371 "But a new Attorney General... Ibid.
371 "large contributor" Ibid.
371 "Democratic Corporate Counsel ... *The American Catholic, Who's Who* 1946-1947, Volume 7 (Seventh Biennial Edition), Walter Romig, Publisher, Michigan, 1931, P. 19.
371 "Could they measure up... O'Sullivan, (1933), p. 95.
371 "Could damages be collected... Ibid., 95-96.
371 "a delegate to the New York... Http://politicalgraveyard.com/bio/bennett5.html.
371 "in Chicago, Illinois from July 15... Https://en.wikipedia.org/wiki/1940_Democratic_National_Convention.
371 "American Bar Association; American... Http://politicalgraveyard.com/bio/bennett5. html.
371 "served as Deputy Mayor ... Ibid.
372 "October 4, 1967," *TheNew York Times*, October 5, 1967; http://query. nytimes.com/gst/abstract.html?res=9C06EFD6 1238E53BBC4D53DFB667838C679EDE.

CHAPTER THIRTY-ONE: THOMAS EDMUND DEWEY

Page
374 ""Dapplemere" which was... Https://en.wikipedia.org/wiki/Thomas_E._ Dewey.
374 "news agency" Http://www.sdl.lib.mi.us/history/dewey.html.
374 "hired nine other boys... Ibid.
374 "editor-in-chief" Ibid.
374 "Central High School... Ibid.
374 "From 1931 to 1933... Ibid.
374 "72 of the 73 people... Https://en.wikipedia.org/wiki/Dutch_Schultz.
374 "30 to 50 years" Https://en.wikipedia.org/wiki/Lucky_Luciano.
374 "62 counts of compulsory... Ibid.
374 "gang buster." Http://www.history.com/topics/al-capone.
374 "the former president... Https://en.wikipedia.org/wiki/Thomas_E._ Dewey.
374 "District Attorney of... Ibid.
375 "for revers[ing] the decision... O'Sullivan, (1933), p. 94.
375 "racial and religious... Http://www.wnyc.org/story/117609-freedomsladder.
375 "New York became... Ibid.
375 "rebellious southern states" Http://www.civilwar.org/education/history/ emancipation-150/10-facts.html.
375 "Five months after... Ibid.
375 "perhaps the greatest... Http://hallofgovernors.ny.gov/ThomasDewey.
375 "DEWEY DEFEATS... Http://www.chicagotribune.com/news/ nationworld/politics/chi-chicago-daysdeweydefeats-story-story.html.
375 "became Dewey, Ballantine... Https://en.wikipedia.org/wiki/Dewey_Ballantine.
375 "On October 1, 2007, Dewey... Ibid.
375 "Midtown Manhattan." Ibid.
375 "one of the biggest collapses... Http://www.nytimes.com/2015/10/20/business/ dealbook/mistrial-is-declared-indewey-leboeuf-case. html?&moduleDetail=section-news-0&action=click&contentCollection=Business%20Day&regi on=Footer&module=MoreInSection&version=WhatsNext&contentID=WhatsNext&pgtype=article.

543

THE APO$TATE

375 "Root, Clark & Bird," Https://en.wikipedia.org/wiki/Dewey_Ballantine.
376 "massive heart attack" Https://en.wikipedia.org/wiki/Thomas_E._Dewey.

CHAPTER THIRTY-TWO: EUNICE ROBERTA HUNTON CARTER

Page
377 "mob buster." Http://www.philasun.com/diaspora/eunice-hunton-carter-womens-rights-activist-mob-buster.
378 "Ku Klux Klan" Https://en.wikipedia.org/wiki/Ku_Klux_Klan.
378 "William Alphaeus, Sr. and… Http://www.blackpast.org/aah/eunice-hunton-carter-1899-1970.
378 "founder of the black… Https://en.wikipedia.org/wiki/Eunice_Carter.
378 "graduated cum laude… Http://articles.chicagotribune.com/2012-02-23/news/ct-met-kass-0223-20120223_1_blackhistory-month-table-manners-special-prosecutor.
378 "nominated by the Republican … Http://www.blackpast.org/aah/eunice-hunton-carter-1899-1970.
378 "secretary on the Committee… Ibid.
378 "Women's Court." *Chicago Tribune*, "A Black History Month story that shouldn't be forgotten," By John Kass, February 23, 2012.
378 "largest prosecution… Http://www.blackpast.org/aah/eunice-hunton-carter-1899-1970.
378 "Racketeer Influenced… Https://en.wikipedia.org/wiki/Racketeer_Influenced_and_Corrupt_Organizations_Act.
378 "Mafia Commission Trial" Ibid.
379 "U.S. Attorney for the Southern… Https://en.wikipedia.org/wiki/Rudy_Giuliani.
379 "Women's Court" *Chicago Tribune*, "A Black History Month story that shouldn't be forgotten," By John Kass, February 23, 2012.
379 "lawyers, bondsmen… *Time* Magazine, ""Unsung Heroes, Eunice Hunton Carter, Mob Buster," By Madison Gray, January 12, 2007.
379 "As it turns out, the … Ibid.
379 "Twenty Against … Http://content.time.com/time/specials/packages/article/0,28804,1963424_1963480_1963450,00.html.
379 "200 brothels" Http://www.blackpast.org/aah/eunice-hunton-carter-1899-1970.
379 "125 prostitutes… Https://www.history.com/news/major-mob-busts-in-u-s-history.
379 "compulsory prostitution" Https://en.wikipedia.org/wiki/Eunice_Carter.
379 "organize cathouses… Http://www.history.com/news/major-mob-busts-in-u-s-history.
379 "head of the D.A.'s… Http://content.time.com/time/specials/packages/article/0,28804,1963424_1963480_1963450,00.html.
379 "the Abandonment Bureau… Http://www.blackpast.org/aah/eunice-hunton-carter-1899-1970.
379 "served as Assistant District… Http://www.philasun.com/diaspora/eunice-hunton-carter-womens-rights-activist-mob-buster.
379 "the first International… Http://www.blackpast.org/aah/eunice-hunton-carter-1899-1970.
379 "a consultant to the Economic… Ibid.
379 "elected to chair… Ibid.
379 "Commission On… Ibid.
379 "elected 'Chairman' of… Ibid.
380 "served as legal advisor… Ibid.
380 "Nana in New York." Http://law.fordham.edu/25399.htm.
380 "She had shelves… Ibid.

CHAPTER THIRTY-THREE: DUTCH SCHULTZ

Page
381 "Italian lottery" Https://en.wikipedia.org/wiki/Dutch_Schultz.
382 "as a feeder and pressman… Ibid.
382 "Dutch" Ibid.

REFERENCES

382 "Dutch Schultz"   Https://vault.fbi.gov/Arthur%20Flegenheimer%20%28Dutch%20Schultz%29.
382 "Hub Social Club"   Https://en.wikipedia.org/wiki/Dutch_Schultz.
382 "tributes"   Ibid.
382 "fees"   Ibid.
382 "600 to 1."   Http://www.history.com/topics/al-capone.
382 "ganglord"   Ibid.
382 "arrested on sight"   Https://en.wikipedia.org/wiki/Dutch_Schultz.
383 "associates"   Ibid.
383 "The Commission,"   Ibid.
383 "ricocheted"   Ibid.
383 "rust-covered"   Ibid.
383 "Sing Sing Correctional…   Https://en.wikipedia.org/wiki/Sing_Sing.
383 "Last Rites"   Https://en.wikipedia.org/wiki/Dutch_Schultz.
383 "Gate of Heaven"   Https://en.wikipedia.org/wiki/Gate_of_Heaven_Cemetery_(Hawthorne,_New_York).

CHAPTER THIRTY-FOUR: WORLD WAR II

Page
387 "secret protocols"   Https://www.britannica.com/event/World-War-II.
387 "in the presence of…   Https://www.britannica.com/event/GermanSoviet-Nonaggression-Pact. 387 "western third…   Https://www.britannica.com/event/World-War-II.
387 "eastern two-thirds."   Ibid.
387 "Great Britain and France…   Ibid.
387 "Operation Fritz,"   Ibid.
387 "Operation Barbarossa"   Ibid.
387 "Holy Roman emperor…   Ibid.
387 "from August 1942…   Https://www.history.com/topics/russia/ joseph-stalin.
387 "40,000,000 and 50,000,000…   Https://www.britannica.com/event/World-War-II.
387 "the bloodiest conflict…   Ibid.
388 "forgotten"   Https://rationalwiki.org/wiki/Depression_of_1920#:~:text=The%20Depression%20of%201920%20was%20a%20brief%20economic,the%20beginning%20of%20the%20Warren%20G.%20Harding%20administration.
388 "No government agency…   Wansley, (1971).
388 "cash and carry"   Http://en.wikipedia.org/wiki/Neutrality_Acts_ of_1930s.
388 "Fireside Chat"   David M. Kennedy, *Freedom From Fear* (New York, Oxford University Press), 1999, pp. 468-469.
388 "If Great Britain goes down…   Ibid.
388 "the Lend-Lease Act"   David M. Kennedy, *Freedom From Fear* (New York, Oxford University Press), 1999, p. 474.
388 "[P]ermitted the lending…   Http://www.history.co.uk/study-topics/historyof-ww2/us-entry-and-alliance.
388 "was the result of the greatest…   Joseph E. Persico, *Roosevelt's Secret War* (New York, Random House, Inc.), 2001, photos section (after p. 264).
388 "Office of Naval…   Https://en.wikipedia.org/wiki/Office_of_Naval_ Intelligence.
388 "Federal Bureau…   Https://en.wikipedia.org/wiki/Federal_Bureau_ of_Investigation.
388 "Military Intelligence…   Https://en.wikipedia.org/wiki/Military_Intelligence_Division_(United_States).
389 "Coordinator of Information …   Https://www.cia.gov/library/center-for-the-studyof-intelligence/kent-csi/vol37no3/pdf/v37i3a10p. pdf.
389 "First War Powers Act"   Https://en.wikipedia.org/wiki/War_Powers_Act_ of_1941.
389 "Second War …"   Ibid.
389 "Office of Strategic …   Https://www.cia.gov/library/center-for-the-study-of-intelligence/kent-csi/vol37no3/pdf/v37i3a10p. pdf.

THE APO$TATE

389 "Executive Order 9621"   Ibid.
389 "Strategic Services...   Https://en.wikipedia.org/wiki/Strategic_ Services_Unit.
389 "Central Intelligence...   Https://www.cia.gov/library/center-for-the-study-of-intelligence/kent-csi/vol37no3/pdf/ v37i3a10p.pdf.
389 "Central Intelligence...   Ibid.
389 "wartime economy."   Wansley, (1971).
389 "After hearing testimony...   Ibid.
389 "awarding $20,000 each...   History.com/topics/world-war-ii/Japanese-american-relocation.
390 "Executive Order 9066"   Ibid.
390 "facilities in Montana...   Ibid.
390 "of land for military...   Https://en.wikipedia.org/wiki/War_Powers_Act_ of_1941.
390 "Government-financed capital...   Http://www.bloombergview.com/ articles/2011-12-16/how-did-world-war-ii-end-the-great-depression-echoes.
390 "According to Inger Stole...   Http://news.nationalgeographic.com/news/2014/12/141207-world-war-advertising-consumptionanniversary-people-photography-culture.
390 "War Advertising Council"   Https://en.wikipedia.org/wiki/Ad_Council.
390 "Loose Lips Sink Ships"   Ibid.
390 "Only You Can...   Ibid.
391 "Ultimately, the industry...   Fox, (1984), pp. 169-170.
391 "The Ad Council marshals...   Https://www.scribd.com/adcouncil#.

CHAPTER THIRTY-FIVE: LAWSUITS

Page
392 "Did Mr. Kenner further...   O'Sullivan, (1933), pp. 28-29.
395 "Better Business Bureau...   *New York Herald Tribune*, "Better Business Bureau Head Under Bail in Suit," January 12, 1928.
395 "it was libeled...   Ibid.
395 "from 1925...   Https://en.wikipedia.org/wiki/Albert_Ottinger.
395 "obtained a temporary injunction...   *New York Herald Tribune*, "Better Business Bureau Head Under Bail in Suit," January 12, 1928.
395 "salary buyers."   O'Sullivan, (1933), p. 107.
395 "declared invalid any...   Http://scholarship.law.missouri.edu/mlr/vol16/ iss3/3, Vol. 16, p. 208.
395 "the existence of a racket...   Ibid., 208-209.
395 "straw parties"   Ibid.
395 "The defendant paid $50...   Ibid., 209.
396 "made it a crime to charge...   Ibid., 208.
396 "wage assignments"   Ibid., 210.
396 "pay day loans."   Ibid.
396 "to charge more...   Ibid.
396 "42 Per Cent Lenders."   *St. Louis Globe-Democrat*, "Business Bureau Explains Its Stand on Small Loan Act," February 22, 1929, Front Page.
396 "May 1928,"   O'Sullivan, (1933), p. 47.
396 "money-lending institutions"   Ibid., 46.
396 "salary-buyers."   Ibid.
396 "Senate Committee hearings."   *St. Louis Globe-Democrat*, "42 Per Cent Lenders Hold Memberships in Business Bureau," February 22, 1929.
396 "promised"   O'Sullivan, (1933), p. 46.
396 "who were hauled into court...   Ibid.
397 "42 percent Lenders Hold...   *St. Louis Globe-Democrat*, "42 Per Cent Lenders Hold Memberships in Business Bureau," February 22, 1929.
397 "Attorney of Lenders Defends...   Ibid.
397 "$20,000.00"   O'Sullivan, (1933), p. 46.
397 "more than one-third"   Ibid., 46-47.

REFERENCES

397 "I charge that you did... Ibid., 47.
397 "A total of fifty-eight... Ibid., 82
397 "estimated to amount... Ibid.
397 "$240,000.00." Ibid., 83.
397 "many of the members... Ibid.
397 "on February 3, 1908" Http://www.jud.ct.gov/lawlib/History/Hatters. htm.
397 "on January 5, 1915" Https://supreme.justia.com/cases/federal/ us/235/522.
397 "Every contract, combination... Http://teachers.dadeschools.net/jzoeller/APGovt/ APGovt/01_A_Landmark_Supreme_Court_ Cases_Summaries_files/6ec83e589db019befc169 aa05916358b-237. html.
397 "of a verdict for damages... Https://supreme.justia.com/cases/federal/us/235/522.
397 "men joining organizations... O'Sullivan, (1933), p. 83.
397 "open shop" Https://en.wikipedia.org/wiki/Open_shop.
397 "closed shop." Ibid.
397 "striking workers," Http://www.jud.ct.gov/lawlib/History/Hatters. htm.
398 "retailers, wholesalers... Https://en.wikipedia.org/wiki/Loewe_v._Lawlor; William H. Holley and Kenneth M. Jennings. The Labor Relations Process. South-Western, Division of Thomson Learning, 2008, p. 78.
398 "for slightly over $234,000... Https://en.wikipedia.org/wiki/Loewe_v._Lawlor; Gould, William B. A Primer on American Labor Law. MIT Press, 2004. p. 14.
398 "$216,000 in voluntary... Ibid.
398 "Hatters' Day" Http://www.jud.ct.gov/lawlib/History/Hatters.htm.
398 "an hour's pay." Ibid.
398 "price-fixing" O'Sullivan, (1933), p. 81.
398 "local dyers and... Ibid., 80-81.
398 "drive a competitor... Ibid.
398 "throw the Gigantic Cleaners... Ibid., 81.
398 "There is very little difference ... Ibid., 48.
398 "We find that the Bureau... Ibid., 81.
398 "upwards of $3,000... Ibid.
398 "commissions for their work ... Ibid., 82.
399 "Hence Bureau managers... Ibid., 86.
399 "advertising methods" Ibid., 84.
399 "R. H. Macy & Co.... Ibid., 84-85.
399 "The investigators did find... Ibid., 85.
399 "Paf Manufacturing Company... Ibid.
399 "categorically" Ibid., 86.
399 "that they have authorized... Ibid.
399 "printed reports" Ibid., 41.
399 "damaging and libelous ... Ibid.
399 "business in perfect shape." Ibid., 42.
399 "interfering with legitimate... Ibid.
399 "the Superintendent of Police... Ibid.
399 "racketeers or fake stock... *Pittsburgh National Labor Tribune*, "Better Business Bureau Bunk and False Pretense," March 31, 1932.
400 "It was just an advertising... Ibid.
400 "charity racketeers took... Ibid.
400 "an institution pretending... Ibid.
400 "in Central Police Court" Ibid.
400 "800 girls" Ibid.
400 "crowding the store." Ibid.; O'Sullivan, (1933), p. 43.
400 "dastardly trick" Ibid.

400 "Denniston, head of…   *Pittsburgh National Labor Tribune*, "Better Business Bureau Bunk and False Pretense," March 31, 1932.
400 "Bulletins"   O'Sullivan, (1933), p. 86.
400 "containing reports…   Ibid.
400 "the medium used for…   Ibid.
400 "a case"   Ibid.
400 "charged that several of …   Ibid.
400 "justified"   Ibid., 87.
401 "blackened"   Ibid.
401 "A system of numbers…   Ibid.
401 "No. 17750"   Ibid.
401 "three numbers, 17444…   Ibid.
401 "No. 17622"   Ibid.
401 "No. 17185"   Ibid.
401 "Case No. 17191"   Ibid.
401 "No. 17548"   Ibid.
401 "No. 17219"   Ibid.
401 "No. 17916."   Ibid.
401 "offenders"   Ibid.
401 "other than that of possibly…   Ibid.
401 "Thus "birds of a feather…   Ibid.
401 "Chicago newspaper"   Ibid., 106.
401 "Chicagoan"   Ibid.
401 "head of a national…   Ibid.
401 "There was certainly nothing…   Ibid.
401 "simply an expert…   Ibid.
401 "an opportunity to break…   Ibid.
401 "real estate investment …   Ibid., 107.
401 "five executives…   Ibid.
401 "the membership list…   Ibid.
401 "was one of the presumably…   Ibid.
401 "asleep or winking…   Ibid., 108.
402 "At Boston, in 1931…   Kenner, (1936), p. 237.
402 "Excerpts From Code…   Ibid., 295.
402 "the professional managers…   O'Sullivan, (1933), p. 109.
402 "free of charge"   Ibid.
402 "if there were no other…   Ibid., 110.
403 "not to purchase frivolous…   *San Francisco Examiner* , "Sellers of Wooden Nutmegs Are Not All Vanished," December 30, 1932.
403 "the public to beware…   *New York American*, "Stock Tipster Racket Again Being Worked," January 3, 1933.
403 "the endless-chain…   O'Sullivan, (1933), p. 111.
403 "bill-folds, fountain pens…   Ibid.
403 "The defendant, Better…   Http://www.leagle.com/decision/19391015107F 2d908_1775.
403 "an editorial in Printers' Ink…   Ibid.
403 "several and grave"   Ibid.
403 "no person or firm…   Ibid.
404 "eighteen and twenty-four…   Ibid.
404 "letters and leaflets…   Ibid.
404 "palliate"   Ibid.
404 "the Better Business Bureau of Southern…   Http://www.lasvegassun.com/news/2010/ may/10/ company-sues-over-better-business-bureau.
404 "on a daily basis"   Ibid.

548

REFERENCES

- 404 "Defendants' advertisements... Ibid.
- 404 "the BBB system can easily... Ibid.
- 404 "misleading practices" Http://articles.courant.com/2010-09- 08/business/ hc-ticket-network-suesbbb-20100908_1.
- 404 ""pay to play" ratings... Ibid.
- 404 "Beyond the pay-to-play... Http://articles.courant.com/2010-11-23/business/ hc-bbb-changes-policy-20101123_1_conn.
- 404 "Terror Group Gets 'A'... Https://abcnews.go.com/ Blotter/business-bureau-best-ratings-money-buy/ story?id=12123843.
- 405 "flawed, erroneous, misleading... Http://articles. orlandosentinel.com/2012-02-21/business/ oskel-firm-sues-better-business-2.
- 405 "to resolve a pattern... Ibid.
- 405 "(1) Any person who, on ... United States District Court, Middle District of Florida, Orlando Division, Case No. 6:12-cv-31- Orl-28KRS; Filed February 13, 2013.
- 405 "commercial competition... Ibid.
- 405 "for lack of personal... Ibid.
- 405 "prudential standing" Ibid.
- 405 "did not compete..." Ibid.
- 406 "preserved its identity" Ibid.
- 406 "board of directors." Ibid.
- 406 "exercises no control... Ibid.
- 406 "You shall not organize... O'Sullivan, (1933), p. 83.

CHAPTER THIRTY-SIX: UNFORGIVEABLE OMISSIONS

Page
- 413 "Tokyo Muster" Henry C. Dethloff, Texas Aggies Go To War (College Station, Texas, Texas A&M University Press), 2006, pp. 215-218.
- 413 "the first recipient of... Army Silver Star Citation, Mabry Elder Cain.
- 413 "gallantry in action" Ibid.
- 413 "the third-highest award... Http://usmilitary.about.com/od/ medalsanddecs/a/silverstar.htm.
- 414 "*Pistolet-Pulemyot*... Https://simple.wikipedia.org/wiki/PPSh-41.
- 414 "Shpagin machine... Ibid.

CHAPTER THIRTY-SEVEN: TRIAL

Page
- 429 "Executive Director... 2008 BBB *Awards for Excellence*; Candace Twyman email to Caryn Cain.
- 429 "Corporate Representative... Defendant's Trial Witness List, #23.
- 433 "with drops of around... Onthisday.com/date/2008/october/24.
- 434 "an officer, manager, employee... Statutes.capitol.texas.gov/Docs/PE/html/PE.32. htm.
- 434 "$150,000 or more... Ibid.
- 434 "An individual ... shall... Statutes.capitol.texas.gov/Docs/PE/htm/PE.12. htm.
- 434 "not to exceed $10,000." Ibid.
- 435 "Offenses related to theft... Https://www.samfugatelaw.com/criminal-statutes-of-limitation.
- 448 "Conversion of Manners." Http://trappists.org/newcomers/monasticdiscipline/lifestyle.

CHAPTER THIRTY-EIGHT: POST-TRIAL

Page
- 453 "Plaintiff may call rebuttal... Http://www.scd.uscourts.gov/Jury/trialjuror.asp.
- 454 "(a) A person commits... Sec. 37.02. PERJURY; http://www.statutes.legis.state.tx.us/Docs/PE/ htm/PE.37.htm.
- 454 "(a) A person commits... Sec. 37.03. AGGRAVATED PERJURY; http://www.statutes.legis.state. tx.us/Docs/PE/ htm/PE.37.htm.

549

THE APO$TATE

454 "(a) A statement is material… Sec 37.04. MATERIALITY; http://www.statutes.legis.state.tx.us/Docs/PE/ htm/PE.37.htm.
454 "(a) A person commits… Sec. 37.09. TAMPERING WITH OR FABRICATING PHYSICAL EVIDENCE; http://www.statutes.legis.state.tx.us/Docs/PE/ htm/PE.37.htm.
457 "founder of the science… Http://napoleonhill.wwwhubs.com.
457 "money without brains… Http://izquotes.com/quote/85219.

CHAPTER THIRTY-NINE: EPILOGUE

Page
459 "No citizen of this… Https://statutes.capitol.texas.gov/Docs/SDocs/THETEXASCONSTITUTION.pdf.
459 "campaign" Https://100percentfedup. com/newly-elected-muslim-congresswomanilhan-omar-under-investigation-for-campaignfinance-violationagain-representative-omar-is-aserial-violator-of-our-laws.
459 "immigration" Ibid.
459 "181 year old… Https://rwnofficial.com/u-shouse-changes-181-year-dress-code-rule.
459 "American Muslims… Https://clarionproject.org/ilhan-omar-stokesmuslims-to-raise-hell.
459 "ties to terrorism," Https://rightwingtribune.com/2019/03/23/ secret-fundraisers.
459 "March 7, 2019" Https://www.washingtontimes. com/news/2019/mar/7/ilhan-omar-anti-semiticcomments-condemned-house-r/.
459 "discriminatory, unconstitutional… Https://clarionproject.org/court-kicks-cair-outof-san-diego-school-district.
459 "April 2017" Ibid.
459 "CAIR intended this plan… Ibid.
460 ""we're gonna go in… Http://time.com/5494817/ ocasio-cortez-defends-tlaib-profanity.
460 "The mosques are our… Unknown.source/Recep.Tayyip.Erdogan.read. poem.
461 "exclusive Kalorama… Southernliving.com/home/barack-obama-homehouse-washington-dc-obamas.
461 "mommy issues" Http://insider.foxnews. com/2018/11/21/mommy-issues-barack-obamajabs-donald-trump-chicago-speech.
461 "too coincidental… Lawrence.Peter."Yogi".Berra.
462 "The right of the people… Http://www.uscourts.gov/about-federal-courts/ educational-resources/about-educationaloutreach/activity-resources/what-does-0, p. 4.
462 "entitled to Fourth … Https://www.supremecourt.gov/ opinions/17pdf/16-402_h315.pdf, p. 8.
462 "arbitrary invasions… Ibid., 4.
462 "When an individual "seeks… Ibid., 5.
462 "router malware" Www.idropnews.com/news/fasttech/newly-discovered-slingshot-router-malwarelikely-created-by-govt-agency/65760.
462 "Slingshot" Ibid.
462 "basically steal any… Ibid.
463 "hybrid threat center… Http://www.cbsnews.com/ news/the-eus-plans-to-fight-cyber-warfare/?utm_ source=dlvr.it&utm_medium=twitter.
463 "FDR won because… Unknown.source.
464 "In the spring of 2015, CBBB… Hhttp://www.bbb.org/globalassets/local-bbbs/ council-113/media/annual-reports/cbbb2015annual-report.pdf.
464 "Austin, Brazoria, Brooks… Https://www.bbb.org/local-bbb/bbb-of-greaterhouston-and-south-texas.
464 "The Houston and South Texas … Ibid.
464 "Starr, Hidalgo, and Cameron… Https://www.waynedupree. com/spending-bills-mexican-cartel-texas-counties.
467 "work against dishonesty… Kenner, (1936), p. 28.
467 "about 1754 BC." Https://en.wikipedia.org/wiki/Code_of_ Hammurabi.
467 "sixth Babylonian king" Ibid.

REFERENCES

467 "282 laws, with…   Ibid.
467 "that a judge who reaches…   Ibid.
468 "never give a sucker…   Kenner, (1936), p. 82.
468 "part of the greatest racket…   O'Sullivan, (1933), p. 34.
468 "The power of the Bureaus…   Ibid., 39.

www.ingramcontent.com/pod-product-compliance
Lightning Source LLC
Chambersburg PA
CBHW031937290426
44108CB00011B/591